GLBAL POLITICS

the essentials of...

GL🌍BAL POLITICS

Richard Langhorne

Hodder Arnold

A MEMBER OF THE HODDER HEADLINE GROUP

First published in Great Britain in 2006 by Hodder Education, a member of the Hodder Headline Group, 338 Euston Road, London NW1 3BH

www.hoddereducation.com

Distributed in the United States of America by
Oxford University Press Inc.
198 Madison Avenue, New York, NY10016

Hodder Headline's policy is to use papers that are natural, renewable and recyclable products and made from wood grown in sustainable forests. The logging and manufacturing processes are expected to conform to the environmental regulations of the country of origin.

The advice and information in this book are believed to be true and accurate at the date of going to press, but neither the authors nor the publisher can accept any legal responsibility or liability for any errors or omissions.

Every effort has been made to trace and acknowledge ownership of copyright. The publishers will be glad to make suitable arrangements with any copyright holders whom it has not been possible to contact.

British Library Cataloguing in Publication Data
A catalogue record for this book is available from the British Library

Library of Congress Cataloging-in-Publication Data
A catalog record for this book is available from the Library of Congress

ISBN-10 0340816910
ISBN-13 9780340816912

1 2 3 4 5 6 7 8 9 10

Typeset in 8/10pt New Baskerville by Dorchester Typesetting Group Ltd
Printed and bound in Spain

What do you think about this book? Or any other Hodder Education title?
Please send your comments to the feedback section on www.hoddereducation.com

Contents

Acknowledgements	vii
Foreword	viii
Introduction	xi

PART A: General Context: Globalisation and its Consequences — 1

PART B: The Theatre: Given Conditions — 11
1: Context — 13
2: Maps — 14
3: Lists and tables — 24

PART C: The Cast: Users of Power — 69
1: Context — 71
2: Associations of states — 79
3: Global capitalism and markets — 105
4: Global civil society — 112
5: States — 123
6: Transnational corporations — 138

PART D: The Play: Sources of Crisis and Conflict — 151
1: Context — 153
2: Access to and management of the Internet — 158
3: Transnational organised crime and the drug industry — 164
4: Economic inequality and welfare — 176
5: Environmental degradation and climate change — 188
6: Politics and instability in the global markets — 200
7: Religion — 212

PART E: The Performance: The Machinery of Interaction — 223
1: Context — 225
2: Communications systems — 233

3: Diplomacy   244
4: Foreign aid and debt relief   257
5: Humanitarian action   271
6: Media   287
7: International migration and diasporas   298
8: Trade and investment   318
9: War and conflict   334
10: Terrorism   346

Appendix: Timelines   355
1: Humanitarian action   355
2: Politics and instability in global markets   357
3: Transnational organised crime and the drug industry   359
4: Terrorism   361
5: Foreign aid and debt relief   362
6: World trade and investment   363
7: Diplomacy   364
8: Environment   365

Index   367

This book is for my friends and colleagues, Yale Ferguson and Harvey Feder, to mark a decade of close collaboration

Acknowledgements

This book could not have been produced without the generous support of the Carnegie Corporation of New York to whom the author expresses most grateful thanks.

Grateful thanks are also due to Deborah Edwards of Hodder Arnold for her most sympathetic and helpful editing during the preparation of this book.

The following contributed drafts and assisted in many other ways:

Pablo Castillo Diaz
William Tricot Laventhal
Candace Halo
Robert Saunders
Alison Sherley
Edward LeRoy Long
Srinivas Vaitla
Jonathan Bach
Nevena Yakova
Giselle Datz
Steven Zaki
Maurice Cohen and Anne Egelston
Katalin Dancsi
John Fousek

Foreword

Every now and then a book comes along which is a 'must' read for anyone interested in its subject matter. This is one such book. It is a *tour de force* of everything and anything the layman might wish to know about the political economy of globalisation – and more besides! It embraces a medley of perspectives on the burgeoning cross-border interconnectivity of people and organisations, and its impact on economic prosperity, political autonomy, traditional cultures and treasured traditions. It pulls no punches as it describes some of the downsides (or possible downsides) of globalisation, as carefully and critically as it identifies its benefits. Above all, this is an eminently readable book. Professor Langhorne has an enviable and elegant writing style, which should appeal to even the most discerning purist.

Let me walk the reader through some of the book's main contents; and do so by using the allegory which the author himself uses, viz. viewing the story of globalisation as a drama played out on the world's stage of events. I liked this analogy. It nicely narrates how, over the last two centuries, the interest and actions of the peoples, organisations and institutions of this planet have become more closely entwined and integrated; and how communication advances, changing values, political priorities and social mores have affected this growing interdependence. If there is a plot to the play it is how these events have shaped the desires and aspirations of men and women, particularly in respect of increasing their economic wellbeing, while protecting their human dignity and social traditions. The play sometimes takes on the form of a mystery, of 'who has done what to whom and why!' Sometimes, however, it borders on a romance as the achievement and sustenance of responsible global capitalism demands an intricate network of constructive and empathetic partnerships both among and between the wealth creating entities.

After setting his figurative framework, Professor Langhorne then goes on to describe the scenery for his play. In Part B of his volume he constructs a powerful edifice of facts and figures, not only about the economics of globalisation, but of many of its political, social and cultural aspects. The scenery he uses – in the form of maps, charts, drawings and tables – are also viewer friendly. They depict data ranging from those on foreign trade and global competitiveness, to the identification of some of the leading environmental and human rights non-government organisations, and the military and defence expenditures of various countries.

The next part of the book describes the roles played by the main actors (or users of power as Professor Langhorne prefers to call them) in the evolving drama of global politics. Essentially these are markets (made up of buyers and sellers of goods and services traded across national borders), states (or national governments), civil society (mainly NGOs) and supranational entities (which include a range of associations of states). The role of each of these performers, or constituents of contemporary global capitalism, has varied a great deal over time. Thus in the last fifty or more years that of large international companies – better known as multinational enterprises (MNEs) or transnational corporations (TNCs) – has become increasingly powerful in fashioning both the extent, content and geography of globalisation, and its effects on the lives of the world's citizens. So, indeed, have the advocacy and actions of a wide variety of special interest groups in influencing the values and attitudes of the other main actors – particularly those of national governments. On the other hand, the role played by national governments in affecting or being affected by the advent of globalisation has probably become relatively less important as several of their traditional tasks and responsibilities have been assumed by other actors. At the same time, I believe, those that remain – and their ability to affect the institutions and competitive environment underpinning the creation of wealth – are critically affecting the 'national' story line of globalisation, and how it is played out.

In his description of the role of the actors, it seems clear that at any given moment of time, most take on the role of either 'villains' and 'heroes'. In the 1970s, the TNCs were cast as the villains, and governments the heroes of the international economic and political scenario. In the 1980s and 1990s the reverse seemed to be the case. In the 2000s it is clear that each of the actors in the drama of global politics can (and do) perform dual (or multiple) roles. But, as Professor Langhorne is at pains to point out, there *are* genuine villains of our contemporary global village which threaten its peace, wellbeing, stability and security. These are the villains of international terrorism, organised crime, corporate malfeasance and social dysfunction – not to mention the presence of abject poverty and blatant social injustice.

In Part D of the book, Professor Langhorne identifies the sources of crisis and conflict arising from, or associated with, twenty-first-century globalisation. This, perhaps, is the most original and insightful part of the monograph. While the author is fully aware of the economic benefits of cross-border interconnectivity, the focus of his attention is directed to the interaction between these and some of its possible social and environmental downsides; of how these affect the various constituents of globalisation; and of how these can be mitigated or reconciled. This indeed is the sheer drama of the Langhorne play. Above all, the twenty-first century is an age of paradox and of anxiety. *Inter alia* these characteristics comprise the volatility, complexity and uncertainty endemic in globalisation and rapid technological change, and the response of the economic and political actors to them. It is here the greatest challenges to the cast of actors arise. What part can TNCs play in coping with climatic change or international drug trafficking? What is the role of supranational agencies in helping to make more stable global financial markets? What part might religious belief play in promoting a more moral and socially just global society? Is indeed religion the problem or the solution to advancing such a goal? In what ways may the advocacy and action of civil society affect the attitude of governments and supranational agencies to reducing environmental pollution? How might individual consumers, workers and investors use their collective power to help make poverty history?

These are all inputs into the drama of global politics. What about the actual performance of the actors? Here in Part E of his volume, Professor Langhorne focuses on the dynamic and changing dialogue between the cast, and the various mechanisms by which they might affect the contents and outcomes of their performance. Such mechanisms revolve around the institutions affecting the motivation and belief systems of individuals and organisations, and how these are translated into courses of action. Professor Langhorne describes how the media provide the tools by which both diplomacy and direct action, for example debt relief and humanitarian action, may be exercised and implemented. Issues to do with the larger economic picture viz. trade, technology and capital flows, and people movement are then discussed. Here, once again, the drama turns on the need for concord and cooperation, along with healthy entrepreneurship and competition, if global capitalism is to produce economically efficient, socially acceptable results. It also underlines the importance of strong governance and clear rules of the game and enforcement mechanisms, if the players are to do the jobs asked of them.

So what of the ending of the play? I sense that Professor Langhorne's message is that the drama is continually unfolding; and that next year's ending might not be that of today. And that is one of the fascinating things about contemporary globalisation. We live in a dynamic, volatile and complex world; its scenery, people and events are changing all the time. The task of the director of the play,

– Professor Langhorne's proxy for the governors of globalisation – is surely to capture the key themes and ensure that the actors interpret these in the way it best pleases the audience – in this case the peoples of the world.

In this volume, and within the allegory he sets his thoughts, Professor Langhorne gives his readers a brisk run through a wide range of issues. Though inevitably, at times, he only briefly touches upon important topics, this is more than compensated by his presentation of a holistic and integrated view of globalisation. In describing his drama, the reader is not only given a glimpse of the plot, and how it is being played out, but on how the actions of the players fit together and indeed how the performance of each is enhanced by that of the others. As I said at the beginning of the foreword, this is a 'must' read.

John H. Dunning
Reading and Rutgers Universities
May 2006

Introduction

This book is intended to provide a straightforward account of the principal components of contemporary global politics. It runs the risk of over simplifying a highly complicated subject, and particularly avoids theorising about it. At the end of each chapter is a list of further work that would be useful for thickening the texture of discussion and adding more information where the reader needs it. The benchmark reader is taken to be an intelligent and curious person who would like to be able to make sense of the daily diet of news and commentary but who needs a source which will provide the basic context within which to place and comprehend the natural flow of events as well as the mass of rapid-fire and insistent information which these events evoke. It is useful and sometimes essential for people in many kinds of employment, as well as for students studying many different subjects, to have a background of this kind.

The material in this book attempts to mirror actuality. Many people have a pre-developed sense of how the world is arranged which has been derived from accumulated attitudes and experiences inherited from the recent history and sometimes the deeper past of different countries, societies and regions across the world. This is inevitable and cannot be abolished; nor are all its effects damaging. But confusion and unreality can also result in damaging mis-assessments of both events and policies and, in a rapidly globalising world, it is worth trying to reduce that effect.

The organisation of the book is simple. First comes some essential information, expressed as far as possible in cartographic form. This information forms the theatre within which global society performs. Next come descriptions of the different characters who exercise power and influence and play a role in the ebb and flow of global politics. In the contemporary world, for example, this means that it is as important to note the newly powerful role of global civil society as it is to describe familiar entities like nation-states. If the given conditions create a theatre, then these are the actors. The following section describes the subject matter of the play they are performing: these are the sources of the world's daily business, its arguments and conflicts. In this section, the contemporary world situation indicates, for example, that global economic inequality requires more attention than the traditional anxiety concerning disputes between states. The techniques the actors have available to create their performance – the means of communication they use to connect with each other and between themselves and the global population – are then set out in Part E. Here, for example, it is clearly as important to explain the function of the Internet as it is to discuss the more traditional role of diplomacy, and both are there. Finally, at the end there are time-lines of significant global events since 1945.

At the start of each section there is a general introductory discussion of its main themes. The reader who needs to establish a general context or just wants a more rapid account of global politics can read through these essays as if they were a continuous account, turning to the more detailed chapters when convenient or necessary.

The current crises in global politics are not dealt with as separate entities because they spring from the deeper factors discussed in this book and because like all crises they are essentially temporary and will be replaced by others. The preoccupations with the Middle East, civil conflict in Africa and elsewhere, nuclear proliferation in Iran and North Korea are likely to be displaced by crises over the global water supplies, the consequences of climate change, particularly for food supply and the physical viability of some states, and the dispute between China and Taiwan. Over both the present and the future hangs the greatest political question facing the global community: how are the irreversible consequences of the process of globalisation to be made broadly beneficial and accepted as fair, and how are such measures to be carried out with the consent of the global population? At present, the problem is coming to be understood, but there are no plausible answers to the governance question in sight. The chief beneficiary of the confusion and anger that result is terrorism. Terrorists' methods are not new in principle and their existence is age old. But the modern world has delivered them the means to magnify their effect just because it is so completely interconnected that it risks rapid economic destabilisation, and because its reliance on easily disrupted technologies provides obvious targets to attack.

Part A

General Context: Globalisation and its Consequences

Contemporary global politics are haunted by an ever-present ghost at the feast. The apparition is inescapable yet evanescent. It can inspire wonder, fear and loathing: it is the phenomenon widely called globalisation. Its elements are not new, but its magnitude and pace give it a special importance in the early twenty-first century. Its universal significance means that in one sense it is impossible to exaggerate its role; yet it is not a replacement for the international politics of an earlier era but has joined them in a highly pluralistic and complicated world. Failing to remember this, it can be all too easy to give globalisation an exaggerated interpretation. Care is needed; old maps once placed warnings at the outer edges of a known world with the words: 'Here be Dragons.'

Why should a special effort be made to understand globalisation? There are two important reasons. The process and the results of globalisation are changing the way we live our lives on a personal basis and they are changing the institutions which we collectively use to give form and predictability to our economic, social and political relationships. The second reason is that the word has become so widely used that it has taken on all sorts of levels of meaning which confuse rather than enlighten, and constrain logical thinking about the exceedingly difficult problems that globalisation has brought. To give an example: views about globalisation have moved within a few years from seeing it as an irresistible lava flow, to assessing it as only one among many features of the contemporary world, to dismissing it as 'globaloney', yet still being capable of fearing it as 'globaphobia'. Plainly some straightening out is required, or we shall begin to feel like Russell Mearns' nonsense poem:

> As I was going up the stair
> I met a man who wasn't there.
> He wasn't there again today;
> I wish, I wish, he'd stay away.

Technology advances

To begin at the beginning: what is globalisation and why has it happened? Globalisation is the latest stage in a long accumulation of technological advance which has given human beings the ability to conduct their affairs across the world without reference to nationality, government authority, time of day or physical environment. These activities may be commercial, financial, religious, cultural, social or political; nothing is barred. Technological advances in global communications have made global-isation possible, while the fact of globalisation itself is to be seen in the contemporary surge in human activities conducted globally. The effects of these activities on the whole range of humanity's expectations, systems and structures have been and are a heady mixture: they have come and keep coming at different paces in different places; sometimes they create entirely new significant activities, sometimes they share them with older systems and structures; sometimes they induce adaptation but sometimes they erode and destroy. They represent both opportunities and threats.

Globalisation has happened because technological advances have broken down many physical bar-riers to worldwide communication which used to limit how much connected or cooperative activity of any kind could happen over long distances. Think what has happened to a book, which, in its printed form, was the product of a previous cutting-edge technology. In addition to being a collec-tion of atoms, a physical object usable only by individuals possessing copies, it can now become a col-lection of bytes, having no physical existence but usable by everyone connected to cyberspace. The limitations of the past show how much has changed. American Indian smoke signals, Inca relay run-ners, French semaphores, English hilltop beacons and slow sailing ships in general all tell their sto-ries of labourious and cumbrous communications over distance. Compare that with the almost instant effect of contemporary faxes, e-mail and the Internet. This communications revolution is the cause of globalisation. The result of these technological advances has been a huge increase in human activities carried on without hindrance across the world; and these consequences are also often described as globalisation, very obviously when politicians wish to find a useful explanation for action or inaction at particular moments.

Thus globalisation has come to mean both an ongoing process and a contemporary condition, the result of that process. Plainly the two things are intertwined, but it can be important to remember that the word has these two meanings. It particularly helps to understand this when objections to globalisation lead to public protests and demands that globalisation be stopped. At such times there has usually been confusion about the difference between process and effect. The process of globali-sation is not optional and certainly cannot be stopped. But the protests arise because the necessary political and economic mechanisms for mediating the effects of globalisation have not yet evolved. The incomplete state of this evolution provides the context for many of the sources of conflict in the contemporary world and is discussed in Part E. Here the processes of globalisation will come first.

Developments

Technological advances in communications have accelerated steadily since the early nineteenth cen-tury. There were earlier and important improvements such as the invention and development of the printing press in Western Europe – the Chinese made the same discovery, but did not develop it – which enabled a far faster dissemination of ideas and information and had a crucial effect during the Renaissance and Reformation periods. And there were improvements to sailing ships and the tech-niques of navigation which enabled long-distance, but epically slow, sea journeys to begin. So tech-nological improvements have always been important. However, the age of continuous and rapid development in communications did not start until the industrial revolution had accomplished its first stage in Great Britain and the age of steam had truly begun. Thereafter, three stages of devel-opment followed. The first was the longest and flowed from the combined effects of applying the steam engine to land and sea transport and the invention and installation worldwide of the electric telegraph. The second, which began during the Second World War, was also a combination. The per-fecting of rocket propulsion led to the ability to launch orbiting satellites. This, when there were enough of them and when combined with the previous invention of the telephone, gave a global and reliable communications coverage. The telephone, hitherto somewhat restricted to short- or at best medium-distance use, was thus transformed into the major communications channel. The third stage, following rapidly in the 1970s, applied the computer, itself transformed in speed, volume and efficiency by the evolution of the microchip, as both manager and transmitter of the system. The Internet was the result.

The first stage began with the application of the steam engine to land transport. The first attempts to fit it into a road-running machine failed, often explosively. But in the 1820s, Robert Stephenson succeeded in fitting an engine into a vehicle that ran on rails. The notion that railways made moving heavy goods easier, whether by human energy as used in mines, or horse power as applied to lines between mines and wharves, had already become familiar, so the marriage of steam with rail was not in principle difficult to arrange. It was instantly effective, raising the speed of transport by a factor of five even in its earliest development and spreading rapidly in Europe, North America and India. It began to have revolutionary effects at once.

There were three principal consequences. The first was industrial. The railway created an infrastructure industry of its own and it greatly accelerated and expanded the scope of other industrial activities. Second, the railway hugely increased the amount, the speed and the conceivable geographical range of transporting goods and people. Third, the railway carried news, technical information, questions and replies far faster than had hitherto been imaginable. At around the same time, another technological breakthrough accelerated written communication even more dramatically than the railway had done: the electric telegraph. Pretty primitive short-distance telegraphing by means of flags was already in use, particularly for military signalling and messages of the simplest kind – 'danger', for example, was alerted through the use of bonfires on top of lighthouses placed strategically along the coast. Transmitting electrically by wire and using symbols for encoding and decoding the message divorced the technique from any relationship to the speed of land transport. At its most dramatic, it could, provided it worked well and was not interrupted by ignorant handling or civil strife en route, cut the time it took to send a message from London to Peking from three months to three minutes. The combination was potent. At its most blatant, the possession of both railways and the telegraph enabled government to learn quickly what was happening at the edges of its territory, and put into its hands the ability to despatch by train troops and/or officials in response to that information. They could then be told what to do by telegraph when they reached their destination, a command which could be adjusted in the light of the latest news both from the distant point and at the administrative centre.

Communications

The kind of society over which newly empowered governments presided was also changed by speeded-up internal communications. The railway, the telegraph, eventually the car and the telephone created both national markets satisfied by national suppliers and nationally shared news provided by national newspapers. This had the effect of 'branding' a society both informally and formally with shared cultural and commercial symbols which marked it clearly and distinguished it from others. The coming of the railways even required the imposition of an agreed national time, or time zones, depending on size, a fact which explains why British national time was for a long time called 'railway time'. The development of much larger areas of coherent social and political polities which the railways made possible was a primary cause of the emergence of fully national politics in the later nineteenth century, accompanied by the emergence of mass political parties, using the national press to promote a highly simplified and sloganised form of political debate. The result was to promote even further the sense of national differences. The vertical divisions between state structures were emphasised and created an alignment between what technology had enabled governments to do and what their peoples therefore wished from them, thus further cementing the political bond between government and governed.

The most striking, and eventually violently destructive, effect of these developments was that they increased the potential size of a state in a dramatic way. Since the seventeenth century, a pattern had developed which showed that the power and authority of rulers and governments were steadily increasing. This was first driven by the fact that governments which ruled as efficiently as the contemporary situation made possible were more secure both internally and externally. During the eighteenth century in Europe, the connection between reasonable efficiency and the power of a state settled into an observable optimum size and what determined that size was the ease with which the total territory of a ruler could be coherently governed. That ease was in turn related to a contemporary speed of communication which linked the centre to the periphery in not more than about five days' travel. States that were bigger could not be efficiently ruled and those that were smaller suffered from insufficient basic resources. The contemporary optimum thus arrived at turned out to be roughly the size of France. Over time, as the speed of communications increased, what was optimum also increased. Much of international politics and warfare was fundamentally the result of changes in this condition from the late seventeenth century until the last part of the nineteenth.

So also was much of the domestic political turmoil of the period, though here the question was related but different. Basically the more significant the activity of government became, the more significant a role those who conducted it played in the lives of those they ruled. Populations understandably began to want to be sure that so much power and influence was subject to perceptible controls, sufficient to check potential abuses. This meant that intense struggles, both philosophical and real, developed about how to arrive at an acceptable framework for government, which on the one hand allowed that it had to exist in an effective way but on the other set limits to its power. The outcome of these internal struggles will be assessed later.

The expansion of the territorial area over which government and administration could be effective benefited two states in particular: the United States and the Russian Empire, subsequently the Soviet Union. They already possessed great land mass and once they had installed the new mechanisms of communication could expect to enjoy the advantages in resources, demography and strategy that great size conferred. The United States moved much more rapidly than Russia, but both were visibly becoming actually or potentially globally dominant by the turn of the twentieth century. In the case of Imperial Russia, even facing the 1905 revolution, it was the potentiality that mattered: Germany for example was not lulled into any sense of security by Russian internal instability and never took her eyes off Russia's industrial and armaments capacity.

For states overtaken by these changes, new problems of security, both economic and strategic, began to intrude. Two states, Germany in Europe and Japan in Asia, which had benefited from late and therefore relatively advanced industrial revolutions, became very powerful in their regions, but could not advance further unless they added to their restricted land mass. Plainly the temptation to capitalise on short-term regional predominance to make sufficient territorial gains to even up the balance with the USA and Russia would be very strong – and in fact it proved irresistible. From the late nineteenth century onwards this factor began to overtake in importance the more familiar patterns of inter-state competition, which Lenin had identified as capitalism and imperialism. For almost 100 years, from 1895 to 1990, the optimum size which contemporary communications systems had imposed dominated the direction world politics took. Attempts by Japan and Germany to expand their territory were successfully resisted by the USA and Russia until, after 1955, the year of the Geneva Conference which both President Eisenhower and General Secretary Krushchev attended, the two great land mass states achieved a kind of balance between them which expressed itself in the sterile stability of the Cold War years.

The next phase

This outcome in international politics became the chief propellant of the next phase in the advancing technology of global communications. It was to rejoin in a crucial way the two paths of development which had become separated since the invention of the electric telegraph. The telegraph had made the transmission of messages and information independent of the techniques of land, sea and eventually air transport. Improved railways, improved ships, the invention of the car and the achievement of human flight in its ever-increasing speed and efficiency pushed along human and commercial mobility, both in speed and quantity, and is still doing so. The effects of the sheer numbers of people who move about the planet by plane can already be seen, for this is a world in which the ecology itself is troubled by eco-tourism. The separate and independent path taken by communications added cables to telegraph lines, then the telephone was joined to cables and the radio telephone to the telephone. The technique of communication advanced from coding messages to the transmission of voice conversation. As it turned out, the two tracks were to be reunited by military technology: the development of the jet engine during the Second World War, followed by the first successful production and use of a rocket weapon – the V2 – by Germany towards the end of the war, furthered the pace and distance of travel by people and goods, and the refinement of the computer in the second half of the twentieth century sharply advanced communications efficiency. In the 1970s a conjunction of the two was to occur.

When the USA and the USSR began their military competition after the defeat of Germany and Japan, they picked up the developments achieved during the Second World War and refined them. They were soon able to improve the delivery of nuclear weapons by using rockets, and by doing so greatly improved the power and range of missiles until they had created the Intercontinental Ballistic Missile. The technological advances thus gained became available for launching satellites and orbiting them within the earth's immediate inner space. Soviet Man orbited the earth, American Man went to the moon and both types of men learnt how to inspect and spy on each other by using satellites of ever-increasing sophistication. The communications that could be made from and to satellites turned out to have even more significance than their intelligence capabilities, and ended, among other things, by transforming the role of the telephone.

The telephone

The telephone was invented by Alexander Graham Bell in 1876 and much improved by Thomas Edison in the 1890s. It solved some of the problems of carrying voice messages which the telegraph had not been able to do. It remained, however, linked to a land line for nearly 100 years and no effective under-sea cable relay telephone link – for example, between the USA and Europe – was installed until the 1950s. The result was that the telephone remained an essentially local convenience, particularly in urban areas. Long-distance or international calling remained rare, with connections often difficult to establish, and then it could be hard to hear the other caller distinctly or reliably. What rapidly increased the usefulness of the telephone was the divorce from land or under-sea lines, which radio had not been able to achieve satisfactorily, but which the combination of the computer and the orbiting satellite made possible.

Once there were enough satellites continuously orbiting the earth, a global telephone relay service could be created. The first such service began in 1969 and, using microwaves rather than radio waves, provided the opportunity for the development of global communications using telephone conversations, TV programmes, high-speed digital data and facsimile pictures. At the same time, the old limitations on the quantity of traffic which land lines had imposed were almost dissolved.

The line of evolution which led from the jet engine to the launching of satellites met and joined up with another line of technological advance. This, too, owed much for its rapid development to the strategic imperatives of the Cold War. There were two major considerations. Developing computers, particularly through the introduction of the microchip and the ending of the use and storage of inefficient and cumbrous tapes, was an important adjunct to the management and control of technologically advanced weapons and equipment. Second was the need to develop a means of maintaining information stores and communications systems in the event and aftermath of a nuclear war. Having been given accelerated development under these pressures, the commercial and administrative application of the modern computer was naturally rapid and, like the steam engine, its effect both on manufacturing industry generally and in creating a whole new industry in itself has had profound consequences. Nor has its effect been confined to industry. It has also revolutionised the conduct of financial and investment business as well as ordinary daily domestic life.

Going digital

From the point of view of global communications, the development of digital information transfers was the technological advance that mattered most. This emerged from the need to safeguard information and systems in the event of nuclear attack and followed from the realisation that in order to send data, which are more sensitive to circuitry distortion than the human voice, transmission should be digital if it is to be both quick and reliable. It also became clear that whereas in the early days of computer involvement its principal use was as a tool to keep increasingly complicated systems up and running, the future required that the computer should act as the actual transmitting device itself. In 1962, at Massachusetts Institute of Technology, the first steps were taken to bring together these developments and the idea of sending data digitally in packets was born. In 1966, at the Defence

Advanced Research Projects Agency, the mechanism for putting this principle to work on computer networks was designed, and the first form of the contemporary Internet, ARPANET (Advanced Research Projects Agency Network), was planned and published in 1967. While this was going on, the Rand Corporation had been working on something very similar for military purposes, while in the UK the National Physical Laboratory had also come up with and named the idea of 'packets'.

All three originators contributed to the actual construction of ARPANET. The new network was a combination of computer hardware and software used to compress messages into packets and send them over the telephone line. To make the system more broadly available, further simplifications had to be made, but with the worldwide web and the emergence of search engines, the Internet as we know it became possible. It represented the completion of the junction between the telephone facilities offered by the orbiting satellite, as well as existing ground-based networks, and the computer networked system developed by ARPANET.

The intersection of these paths, which was so significant for the development of a totally globalised telecommunications system, came in the 1970s and the result was the heady mixture available to us today: faxes, e-mail and the full panoply of Internet activity involving the provision and exchange of information and views, electronic commercial transactions and entertainment. There can be no doubt that this was a revolution, but it was still a revolution with limitations – not of scale but of quantity. The telephone/satellite link was not adequate to carry the traffic that developed: put in more contemporary terms there was not enough band width. The solution to this problem has come in very recent times with the invention and installation of the fibre optic cable: it is being laid under the world's oceans and will soon be available to every household in highly developed societies. There is as yet no sign where its limits may be and the traffic it can carry will ensure the continuation of the modern communications revolution into the foreseeable future.

Communications revolution

These systems have produced a communications revolution at least the equal of that yielded by the train/telegraph combination and with equally momentous consequences. The first phase, playing out during the nineteenth century, altered the scope of human economic and political activity and created a global distribution of power among states: in doing so, it significantly increased the power and security of the USA and Russia and eventually relatively reduced the power of others. It did not, however, change the name of the game: the scope of government of every size and description was increased and governments maintained supervision or control over all the instruments of communication. This remained true during the essentially military-driven second phase, serving the needs of the Cold War. The third and most recent phase, however, dominated by modern computer technology, has put the instruments of communication above and beyond the control of governments since the system was, after all, designed to withstand a nuclear war which governments themselves were deemed unlikely to do, and created a network which serves individual human beings and their activities rather than specific societies and their authorities. In a nutshell, activities rather than traditional governmental authorities have been the beneficiaries. Many previously important, even formerly vital, systems of administration – political, economic and social – have been rendered increasingly redundant as a result. It may well also turn out that future historians will attribute the end of the Cold War, at least in part, to the emergence of a self-propelling and universal communications system.

All governments, whether large or small, have been to some extent bypassed by these events, and the international consequences have also been momentous. The advantages that the first phase gave to the great land mass states have been withdrawn but this time there have been no successors. The second phase has not transferred power and security to a different optimum size of state so much as moved them away from existing states of any sort. It may lead to the complete reconstruction of the institutions of human society. If it does so, then the likely pattern will be one of large-scale, global activities, generating their own styles of management and authority, accompanied by small-scale, geographically described local mechanisms, as small or smaller than existing provincial structures, designed to accomplish the basic minimum of local government.

These are the circumstances which importantly help to explain both the collapse of the Soviet Union and the puzzling inconsistencies which seem to affect the USA in its lonely role as only remaining superpower. What had once propelled their rise to global dominance and then sustained them both no longer does so: the USSR, which was inherently more divided, internally fell to pieces; the USA, which was essentially a unitary structure, survived but sits uncomfortably in such a changed environment, uncertain how to behave or how others will react. This is chiefly because such predominance arrived suddenly and unexpectedly, after a period of considerable self-doubt and, even more difficult to interpret, because predominance itself has lost a clear meaning: predominant over what, exactly, or whom? The attack on the World Trade Center in New York City in 2001 and its various aftermaths clearly demonstrate the difficulty of dealing with a globalised enemy that feels no need to negotiate and does not share the ambitions or fears of traditional states and governments. Such an enemy is thus not subject to the pressures of reciprocity which have usually set limits to violent behaviour and created an agreed framework for the conduct of business. Its presence changes the meaning of global power and renders the highly developed rule book for exercising such power largely irrelevant.

Structure

The best way of thinking about these changes is to imagine the organisational structures of the past, whether commercial and economic or political, as functioning vertically. They operated up and down and narrowed at the top like a pyramid. They related to each other from the top and regarded each other as separate systems, having individual characteristics, particularly for example in economic policies and political organisation, and generally expected that their relationships would be competitive and adversarial, sinking from time to time into actual conflict. Advantages were sometimes anticipated to flow from cooperative arrangements, particularly where convenience for all would come from generally accepted administrative norms; for example, in matters of disease control or the regulation of international commercial traffic. This led to the appearance of inter-government organisations, which gave a more complicated texture to their relationships from the end of the nineteenth century. But however much the texture was complicated either by international organisations or by the emergence of multinational companies, there was a complete expectation that, at the end of the day, final authority lay with governments and the decisions that they took at the apex of their particular structure.

This vertically structured and territorially arranged system of government has been pushed over by the advent of the most recent communications revolution. Some of the most important human activities and exchanges now cross these vertical divisions with complete ease. They do not achieve this by some kind of victorious push but by using technological changes in communications systems to ignore them. They are thus happening across the globe on a horizontal basis, without reference to territorial location, time of day or local political and legal authority. They are able to do so because the use of the fax, e-mail and the Internet takes place without either the permission of governments or the need to pay dues to them. Relationships can be global or local in scope entirely at will: question, answer, information and command can pass instantly across the globe. Financial exchanges and stock market trading have become continuous activities operating like a global horizontal plate, interacting with other plates similarly arranged – for example, industrial and manufacturing businesses. These now locate themselves where it is most advantageous to undertake any particular part of their operation and create alliances with other firms as is most appropriate.

This process, which has many other ramifications, has fundamentally impaired the ability of governments to run independent macro-economic policies and reduced most of them to micro-management designed to ensure that they create the optimum conditions for attracting global investment to their own area. This is not sovereignty in any recognisable sense, it is a form of servanthood – serving the needs of one of the most important horizontal plates of global activity but, nonetheless, it also represents a new and significant role for the state to play. These effects will be examined further in the next section.

Cultural consequences

The effects are not confined to political, economic and commercial operations. There have been notable cultural consequences as well. In this field, as in others, the communications revolution has worked at both the broadest and the narrowest level, tending to squeeze the familiar middle. The ubiquity of the Internet has the effect of confirming and extending an existing tendency towards the spread of the English language in its North American form and with it the culture of the United States and to a much lesser extent of the United Kingdom, the latter derived to some extent from the extraordinary global use that is made of the radio and now television services of the BBC. What had been spread as the language of two successive economic and political hegemonies has become the language of global communication operating horizontally and independently of the views and intentions of its progenitors. This is one reason why attempts by both the French and the Chinese to limit its spread have failed and will continue to fail. The predominance of English is not a political projection, but a matter of convenience. It is extremely fortunate that the language itself is so welcoming to neologism and grammatically plastic and that its literary tradition is so rich and powerful.

Nonetheless, other cultural features of the English-speaking world have not proved to be universally welcome. Its association with moral degradation, as liberal attitudes may seem to some, with Christianity in various forms and with the propagation of the ideas associated with democracy are all offensive in some degree and in different places. The combination of rapid change accompanied by a comprehensible sense of unfamiliarity, rootlessness and dismay, emphasised by the decline of traditional political structures, with a sense of aggressive and implacable 'westernisation' at the hands of a dominant global culture, contributes to the rise of religious fundamentalisms and other forms of suspicious backlash, sometimes terrorist in form. Conspiracies of every kind, religious oddities, many predicting the end of the world, and various versions of violently extreme political views all populate the Internet and gain global exposure thereby. And the fundamentalist response seems particularly ungrateful and even dangerous to those who deeply believe that they are only purveying things that are good in an equally fundamental sense.

Away from the global stresses of an unfolding convergent culture, the contemporary communications network encourages the pursuit of highly local and particularist activities. The steady improvement in the ability of the Internet to accommodate additional languages and alphabets encourages this. Small societies can propagate their individual approaches to all cultural media and thus provide reliable focuses for daily life. Sometimes these represent a revival of older provincial feelings, submerged in the process of forming larger states. Particular skills and activities, always a focus for loyalty and association on a small geographical scale, can now achieve a wider participation, and enthusiasms of every sort have received a kind of shot in the arm from the ease of global contact with the like minded. So have less satisfactory activities: transnational crime has become a growth industry, particularly in the field of financial fraud and money laundering, as has the provision of undesirable information – on pornographic networks, for example, and how to make terrorist weapons, including chemical and biological ones. In all, we have to note the fact that the Internet has empowered smaller groups following sometimes micro-enthusiasms and skills as much as it has furthered a macro-predominance of English and English-based culture on a global basis, but that both these effects weaken rather than enhance the older forms of loyalties and expectation based on medium-sized societies organised in the more traditional state form.

It is gradually becoming possible to discern through the mist what this is leading to as well as what it is caused by. The shift to horizontally arranged areas of activity rather than vertically constructed centres of power is evoking a response in much the same way as the emergence of states did two-and-a-half centuries ago. States, their internal structure and their external associations, have been the principal losers and human activities of every sort – good and bad – have been the beneficiaries. Long before the processes underlying globalisation made it a reality, Shakespeare put a striking description of the condition into Hamlet's mouth: 'O God! I could be bounded in a nutshell, and count myself a king of infinite space...' (Hamlet, II, ii, 263). In some of these activities, pressure can be detected in rising anxieties about management and control – even demands for it – without yet having yielded any hard consequences: the easy availability of potentially damaging information and techniques via the Internet is an example of this. Some organisations, generally not connected with or originating from national governments, have also been beneficiaries. Global companies, quickly modifying themselves to take advantage of new opportunities, are one example. The emergence of globally operating private humanitarian organisations is another. Here, the consequences of their vastly enhanced role in international crises caused by the collapse of states – such as Bosnia or Rwanda – are already taking administrative and representative form such that they exist side by side with the older forms of state-based entities, for example, the United Nations. The result of this is a steadily unfolding shift of emphasis in the most traditional stronghold of state-centred relationships – the sole ownership and use of the machinery of international diplomacy by governments or bodies certified by governments.

Shaping the future

The heady mixture of entities all having some kind of role at one level or another in the process of global relations makes up the global political environment in which we live: some are rising, some declining. Old rules and familiar practices are decaying, while new ones are being tested. Nor is this merely the result of a sharp rise in the number of entities involved in the global system, however powerful a factor that is. The presence of a strikingly larger number of states operating at very different levels of power and sophistication undoubtedly creates complications. The rising number and importance of private organisations does the same. The transnational global economy brings larger numbers of transnational companies both creating a larger global commerce and increasing their share of it. All this would create a new global economic and political context and many anxieties and uncertainties on its own. But it is not on its own. The increasing quantity has not just produced new kids on the block: the block itself has changed shape. The present period is, more than most, markedly pluralistic in the structures and mechanisms by which its affairs are conducted. Important activities of government remain, with systems arranged vertically within states that used to do more, but which still do enough, in some cases actually acquiring different responsibilities, to avoid actual extinction.

Remaining also from the past web of relationships between states and their governments is a range of international organisations created by states which share in the decline of their members, but which, like their members, still do enough to justify survival or are capable of adequate adaptation. Even if these justifications were not so, the sheer weight of historical expectations and the force of inertia would keep their motors at least idling for some time yet. So the landscape has important, if somewhat run-down, structures in it which play a part and have to be made to work alongside newer modes of organising human activities. These occur globally and have the expectable horizontal rather than vertical shape. They seep like a gently rising inundation across and around those physical facts, structures and ideas which are territorially located – like night and day – or carry out territorially based administration and jurisdiction. That is why, just to take one example, it is proving so hard to find the right mix of horizontal and vertical detection, jurisdiction and penalty with which to cope with the rising and dangerous effects of transnational crime on individual human beings as well as on their local systems of governance. It is a good example for another reason: more clearly than in other areas of activity which are similarly affected, it is impossible to describe any part of the activity in any place or country as 'foreign'; everywhere it is in fact domestic in its consequences. Transnational crime has penetrated the foundations of the familiar structures of administration and control and it erodes them as seepage will always do. In this it is a particularly comprehensible example of a general condition: the mounting significance of the Internet and all the related elements of the global information system, as well as electronic commerce, global markets and global companies – in short, the whole panoply of global capitalism.

Conclusion

Some conclusions at least are very clear. Human global society is having to develop a new way of accommodating both upright and flattened mechanisms of economic and political management. At the same time both the global and the local dimensions of human activities and loyalties have to be meshed into a balanced set of interconnected responsibilities. The two together have to be helped to generate acceptable means by which human beings can give their consent to power being exercised in new ways and arrive at a common understanding in broad terms of what the moral basis is from which economic, administrative and political decisions will have their starting point.

Perhaps there is a useful analogy in the fate of the great rail stations of the United States. The grand union stations constructed in many cities at the apex of the economic and political power of the big railroads were a representation of their status as much as they were a convenience for travellers. Time passed and so did the railroad passengers. In most cases, though not all, as the destruction of the old Pennsylvania Station in New York City demonstrated, the structures remained unused and semi-ruined. But their old single use has now been supplanted by a wholly different multi-use. Restored to grandeur, the rail operation either abandoned or confined to a small role, they have become flagship malls, monuments to global consumerism. They demonstrate that it is possible to adapt structures, to put new wine into old bottles, and that they need not be broken. A similar process has turned the great Christian cathedrals of Western Europe into religious museums, temples for the modern global tourist. None of this adjustment is going to be easy. It was a prolonged, difficult and occasionally violent process when the last great evolution produced sovereign states and the states system.

Thus there can be no immediately reassuring things to say about the general situation that we have been exploring. Attempts by politicians to develop them are one of the reasons why electorates believe them less and less. The contemporary world confronts not just the onset but the secondary stages of a general change of direction, equal to and perhaps even more compelling than those that accompanied the fall of the Roman Empire, successive collapses of Chinese dynasties or the Renaissance and Reformation periods in Europe. It is certain that new accommodations to new circumstances will be arrived at; they always are. It is at least likely that these accommodations will arise in an evolutionary way in response to needs and events and that attempts either to redirect the flow of events or to resist them are likely to fail, and fail in violent circumstances. There are already signs – welcome signs – that new areas of power and activity are beginning to self-generate initial systems of management and control. However, there are no signs yet that these new structures are inheriting traditional methods of ensuring that their operations have democratic consent or are acquiring new constitutional arrangements of their own.

This gap is likely to be the stuff of political conflict and dispute in the immediate future and it contains within it a serious risk of mounting violence. It is quite certainly the most urgent item on the global political agenda.

Part B

The Theatre:
Given Conditions

CHAPTER 1: Context

This section contains maps and other sources of information which indicate the basic facts and materials lying behind the conduct of global politics. They form the building in which the actors perform the play. First comes the fundamental global political geography, followed by other maps showing religions, language groups and connectivity.

After the maps come tables, organized in groups, including directions to other sources of information, particularly tables and maps. Lists of global organisations both private and public and a comparative table of military expenditure by governments follow.

CHAPTER 2: Maps

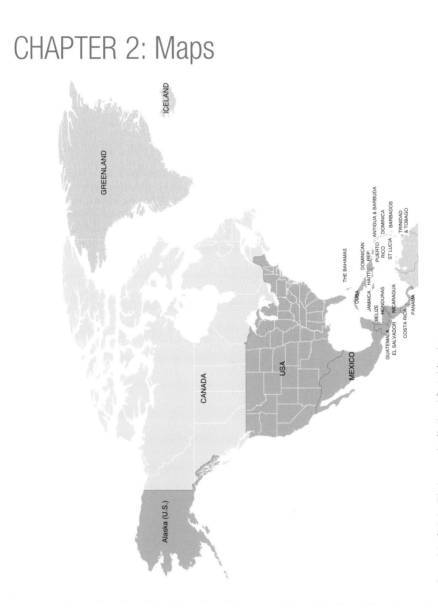

Figure 2.1a Global political geography: North and Central America

Figure 2.1b Global political geography: South America

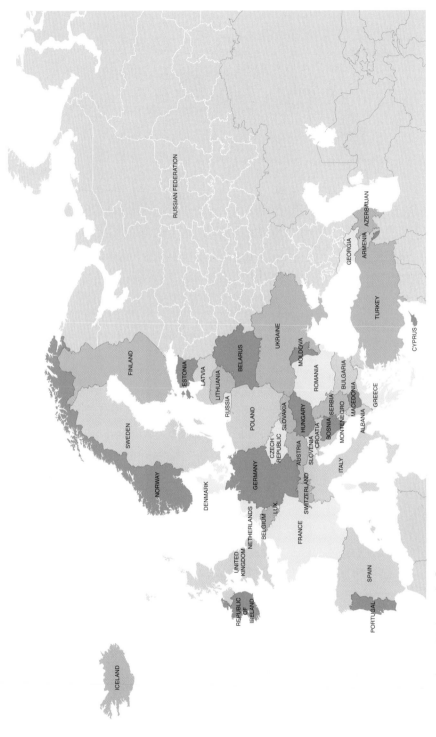

Figure 2.1c Global political geography: Europe

Figure 2.1d Global political geography: Africa and the Middle East

Figure 2.1e Global political geography: Asia

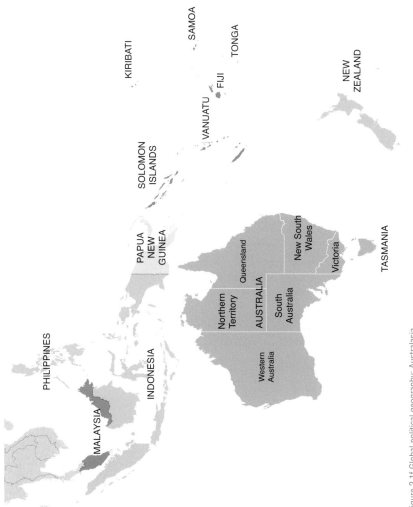

Figure 2.1f Global political geography: Australasia

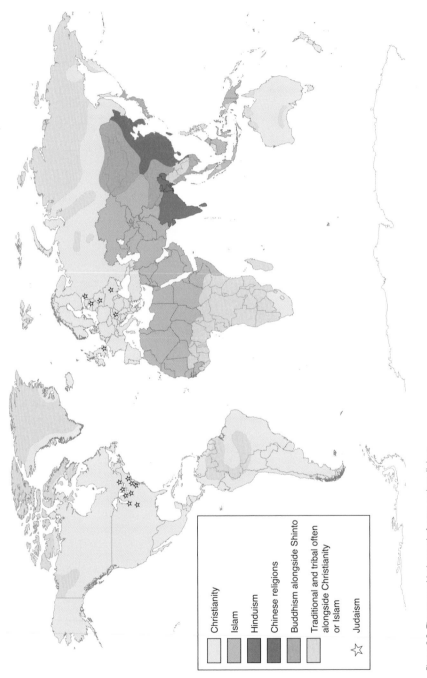

Figure 2.2 The geographical spread of some major religions

Legend:
- Christianity
- Islam
- Hinduism
- Chinese religions
- Buddhism alongside Shinto
- Traditional and tribal often alongside Christianity or Islam
- ☆ Judaism

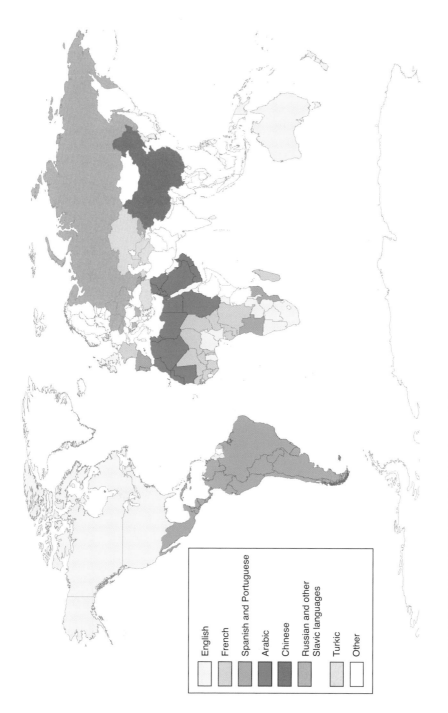

Figure 2.3 The geographical spread of some major languages and language families

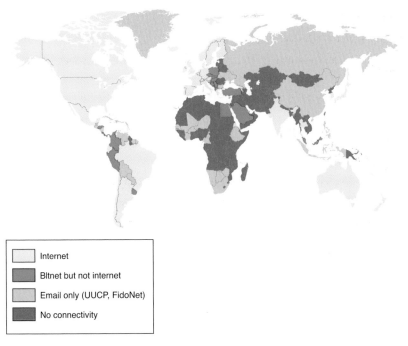

Figure 2.4a Global connectivity in 1991

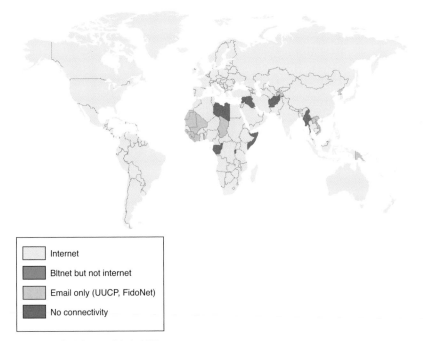

Figure 2.4b Global connectivity in 1997

Source: Copyright 1991, 1997, Lawrence H. Landweber and the Internet Society

Further Reading

For further data on religious populations, see:

www.mapsofworld.com/world-top-ten/world-top-ten-countries-with-largest-buddhist-populations-map.html

www.mapsofworld.com/world-top-ten/world-top-ten-countries-with-largest-hindu-populations-map.html

www.mapsofworld.com/world-top-ten/world-top-ten-countries-with-largest-muslim-populations-map.html

For further data on computer and Internet use, see:

www.mapsofworld.com/world-top-ten/world-top-ten-internet-using-countries-map.html

www.mapsofworld.com/world-top-ten/world-top-ten-personal-computers-users-map.html

www.mapsofworld.com/world-top-ten/countries-with-highest-proportion-of-computer-users.html

CHAPTER 3: Lists and tables

Population

Largest populations, 2003

		(Millions)				(Millions)
1	China	1304.2		24	Myanmar	49.5
2	India	1065.5		25	Ukraine	48.5
3	United States	294.0		26	South Korea	47.7
4	Indonesia	219.9		27	South Africa	45.0
5	Brazil	178.5		28	Colombia	44.2
6	Pakistan	153.6		29	Spain	41.1
7	Bangladesh	146.7		30	Poland	38.6
8	Russia	143.2		31	Argentina	38.4
9	Japan	127.7		32	Tanzania	37.0
10	Nigeria	124.0		33	Sudan	33.6
11	Mexico	103.5		34	Kenya	32.0
12	Germany	82.5		35	Algeria	31.8
13	Vietnam	81.4		36	Canada	31.5
14	Philippines	80.0		37	Morocco	30.6
15	Egypt	71.9		38	Peru	27.2
16	Turkey	71.3		39	Uzbekistan	26.1
17	Ethiopia	70.7		40	Uganda	25.8
18	Iran	68.9		41	Venezuela	25.7
19	Thailand	62.8		42	Iraq	25.2
20	France	60.1			Nepal	25.2
21	United Kingdom	59.3		44	Malaysia	24.4
22	Italy	57.4		45	Saudi Arabia	24.2
23	Congo	52.8		46	Afghanistan	23.9

(continued)

	(Millions)			(Millions)
47	North Korea	22.7	57	Côte d'Ivoire	16.6
48	Taiwan	22.6	58	Netherlands	16.1
49	Romania	22.3	59	Cameroon	16.0
50	Ghana	20.9	60	Chile	15.8
51	Yemen	20.0	61	Kazakhstan	15.4
52	Australia	19.7	62	Cambodia	14.1
53	Sri Lanka	19.1	63	Angola	13.6
54	Mozambique	18.9	64	Burkina Faso	13.0
55	Syria	17.8		Ecuador	13.0
56	Madagascar	17.4		Mali	13.0

Source: *The Economist, Pocket World in Figures, 2006 edition* (Profile Books, 2005)

Further Reading

For size, rate of growth, labour force and unemployment, death and disease, life expectancy, education expenditure, see:

The Economist, Pocket World in Figures, 2006 edition (Profile Books, 2005)

For age structure, see:

The Economist, Pocket World in Figures, 2005 edition (Profile Books, 2004)

See also:

www.mapsofworld.com/world-top-ten/world-top-ten-most-populated-countries-map.html

www.mapsofworld.com/world-top-ten/world-top-ten-least-populated-countries-map.html

www.mapsofworld.com/world-top-ten/highest-per-school-leavers-in-fur-edu-map.html

www.mapsofworld.com/world-top-ten/world-top-ten-countries-with-largest-urban-population-map.html

www.mapsofworld.com/world-top-ten/world-top-ten-countries-by-spending-on-healthcare-map.html

World economy

Biggest economies by purchasing power

		(GDP PPP, $bn)			(GDP PPP, $bn)
1	United States	10,923	8	Italy	1563
2	China	6446	9	Brazil	1376
3	Japan	3568	10	Russia	1324
4	India	3078	11	Canada	970
5	Germany	2291	12	Mexico	938
6	France	1654	13	Spain	920
7	United Kingdom	1611	14	South Korea	861

(continued)

	(GDP PPP, $bn)			(GDP PPP, $bn)
15	Indonesia	722	28	Saudi Arabia	298
16	Australia	589	29	Belgium	294
17	Taiwan	556	30	Egypt	267
18	Turkey	479	31	Ukraine	266
19	Netherlands	476	32	Bangladesh	244
20	South Africa	474	33	Austria	243
21	Thailand	471	34	Sweden	240
22	Iran	464	35	Malaysia	236
23	Argentina	445	36	Switzerland	225
24	Poland	435	37	Greece	220
25	Philippines	352	38	Vietnam	203
26	Pakistan	311	39	Algeria	194
27	Colombia	299	40	Portugal	189

Source: *The Economist, Pocket World in Figures, 2006 edition* (Profile Books, 2005)

Highest GDP per head

		$			$
1	Luxembourg	52,990	17	Belgium	29,170
2	Norway	49,080	18	Germany	29,130
3	Switzerland	44,460	19	Qatar[b]	27,990
4	Denmark	39,330	20	Canada	27,190
5	Ireland	38,430	21	Australia	26,520
6	United States	37,240	22	Italy	25,580
7	Iceland	36,960	23	United Arab Emirates[b]	23,650
8	Bermuda	35,940	24	Hong Kong	22,380
9	Sweden	33,890	25	Virgin Islands	22,320
10	Japan	33,680	26	Faroe Islands[ac]	21,600
11	Netherlands	31,770	27	Singapore	21,490
12	Austria	31,410	28	New Zealand	20,400
13	Finland	31,070		Spain	20,400
14	Cayman Islands[ab]	30,950	30	Guam[ad]	19,750
15	United Kingdom	30,280	31	Greenland[ac]	19,640
16	France	29,240	32	Aruba[b]	18,940

(continued)

		$				$
33	Andorra[a]	18,790		52	Barbados	9690
34	Brunei[d]	18,260		53	Saudi Arabia	8870
35	Macau	17,790		54	Czech Republic	8790
36	Puerto Rico[b]	17,420		55	Hungary	8360
37	Israel	17,220		56	Trinidad and Tobago	8010
38	Kuwait	16,700		57	Guadeloupe[a]	7950
39	Bahamas	16,590		58	Oman	7480
40	Greece	15,650		59	Estonia	6990
41	Martinique[a]	15,560		60	Croatia	6540
42	Cyprus	14,790		61	Mexico	6050
43	Portugal	14,640		62	Slovakia	6040
44	French Polynesia[d]	14,190		63	Equatorial Guinea	5900
45	Slovenia	14,130		64	Réunion[a]	5750
46	South Korea	12,690		65	Poland	5430
47	Taiwan	12,670		66	Lithuania	5360
48	Malta	12,160		67	Lebanon	5040
49	New Caledonia[d]	11,920		68	Latvia	4770
50	Netherlands Antilles	11,140		69	Chile	4590
51	Bahrain[b]	10,790		70	Gabon	4510

a Estimate b 2002 c 2001 d 2000

Source: *The Economist, Pocket World in Figures, 2006 edition* (Profile Books, 2005)

Biggest exporters

	% of total world exports (visible and invisible)			% of total world exports (visible and invisible)	
1	Euro area	17.48	10	Netherlands	3.54
2	United States	12.72	11	Belgium	2.77
3	Germany	9.55	12	Spain	2.53
4	United Kingdom	6.42	13	South Korea	2.30
5	Japan	6.02	14	Switzerland	2.07
6	France	5.32	15	Mexico	1.75
7	China	4.85	16	Taiwan	1.74
8	Italy	4.04	17	Russia	1.58
9	Canada	3.67	18	Ireland	1.55

(continued)

% of total world exports (visible and invisible)				% of total world exports (visible and invisible)	
19	Sweden	1.51	32	Poland	0.72
20	Austria	1.44	33	Turkey	0.70
21	Singapore	1.19	34	Finland	0.68
22	Malaysia	1.18	35	Indonesia	0.67
23	Hong Kong	1.06	36	United Arab Emirates	0.64
24	Denmark	1.04	37	Czech Republic	0.57
25	Saudi Arabia	0.99	38	Hungary	0.51
26	Australia	0.98	39	Portugal	0.49
	Norway	0.98	40	South Africa	0.46
28	Thailand	0.94	41	Philippines	0.45
29	Luxembourg	0.85	42	Israel	0.43
30	Brazil	0.84	43	Greece	0.37
31	India	0.80		Iran	0.37

The figures are drawn from balance of payment statistics and, therefore, differing technical definitions from trade statistics taken from customs or similar sources. The invisible trade figures do not show some countries due to unavailable data. For Hong Kong and Singapore, domestic exports and retained imports only are used.

Source: *The Economist, Pocket World in Figures, 2006 edition* (Profile Books, 2005)

Global competitiveness

	Overall	Government	Infrastructure
1	United States	Hong Kong	United States
2	Hong Kong	Singapore	Switzerland
3	Singapore	Finland	Japan
4	Iceland	Denmark	Finland
5	Canada	Australia	Denmark
6	Finland	Iceland	Singapore
7	Denmark	Switzerland	Sweden
8	Switzerland	New Zealand	Canada
9	Australia	Canada	Norway
10	Luxembourg	Ireland	Germany
11	Taiwan	Chile	Iceland
12	Ireland	Luxembourg	Netherlands
13	Netherlands	Estonia	Australia
14	Sweden	Thailand	Belgium

(continued)

	Overall	Government	Infrastructure
15	Norway	Norway	France
16	New Zealand	United States	Taiwan
17	Austria	Slovakia	Israel
18	Chile	Taiwan	Hong Kong
19	Japan	Austria	Austria
20	United Kingdom	China	South Korea
21	Germany	Sweden	Luxembourg
22	Belgium	Netherlands	United Kingdom
23	Israel	Malaysia	New Zealand
24	Estonia	United Kingdom	Hungary
25	Thailand	Jordan	Czech Republic
26	Malaysia	Israel	Ireland
27	South Korea	Spain	Spain
28	France	South Korea	Malaysia
29	China	South Africa	Portugal
30	Czech Republic	Germany	Italy
31	Hungary	Hungary	Greece
32	Spain	India	Slovenia
33	India	Japan	Estonia
34	Slovakia	Portugal	Jordan
35	Jordan	Belgium	Slovakia
36	Portugal	Colombia	China
37	South Africa	Czech Republic	Chile
38	Colombia	France	Russia
39	Turkey	Russia	Thailand
40	Philippines	Philippines	Argentina
41	Greece	Mexico	Colombia
42	Brazil	Slovenia	Poland
43	Slovenia	Turkey	Turkey
44	Italy	Greece	Brazil

Rankings reflect assessments for the ability of a country to achieve sustained high rates of GDP growth per head. Column 1 is based on 259 criteria covering: the openness of an economy; the role of the government; the development of financial markets; the quality of infrastructure; technology; business management; judicial and political institutions; and labour-market flexibility. Column 2 looks at the extent to which government policies are conducive to competitiveness. Column 3 is based on the extent to which a country is integrated into regional trade blocks.

Source: *The Economist, Pocket World in Figures, 2006 edition* (Profile Books, 2005)

Largest market capitalisation

		$m, end 2003				$m, end 2003
1	United States	14,266,266		27	Mexico	122,532
2	Japan	3,040,665		28	Thailand	118,705
3	United Kingdom	2,412,434		29	Greece	106,845
4	France	1,355,643		30	Norway	94,679
5	Germany	1,079,026		31	Chile	86,291
6	Canada	893,950		32	Ireland	85,070
7	Spain	726,243		33	Israel	75,719
8	Switzerland	725,659		34	Turkey	68,379
9	Hong Kong	714,597		35	Portugal	58,285
10	China	681,204		36	Indonesia	54,659
11	Italy	614,842		37	Austria	54,528
12	Australia	585,475		38	Argentina	38,927
13	Netherlands	488,647		39	Luxembourg	37,333
14	Taiwan	379,023		40	Poland	37,165
15	South Korea	329,616		41	Iran	34,444
16	Sweden	287,500		42	New Zealand	33,052
17	India	279,093		43	Egypt	27,073
18	South Africa	267,745		44	Philippines	23,565
19	Brazil	234,560		45	Kuwait[a]	20,772
20	Russia	230,786		46	Czech Republic	17,663
21	Belgium	173,612		47	Hungary	16,729
22	Finland	170,283		48	Pakistan	16,579
23	Malaysia	168,376		49	Peru	16,055
24	Saudi Arabia	157,302		50	Colombia	14,258
25	Singapore	145,117		51	Morocco	13,152
26	Denmark	127,997		52	Jordan	10,963

a 2000

Source: *The Economist, Pocket World in Figures, 2006 edition* (Profile Books, 2005)

Biggest agricultural producers

		'000 tonnes				'000 tonnes
	Cereals				**Fruit**	
1	China	376,123		1	China	76,893
2	United States	348,897		2	India	46,911
3	India	232,785		3	Brazil	34,298
4	Brazil	66,895		4	United States	28,953
5	Russia	65,464		5	Spain	17,497
6	Indonesia	62,989		6	Italy	15,727
7	France	54,914		7	Mexico	14,743
8	Canada	50,168		8	Iran	12,697
9	Bangladesh	40,667		9	Indonesia	12,277
10	Germany	39,358		10	Philippines	11,804
	Meat				**Vegetables**	
1	China	70,899		1	China	401,538
2	United States	38,911		2	India	79,671
3	Brazil	18,388		3	United States	37,043
4	Germany	6601		4	Turkey	25,672
5	France	6394		5	Russia	15,250
6	India	5941		6	Italy	15,155
7	Spain	5474		7	Egypt	14,873
8	Russia	4934		8	Spain	12,052
9	Mexico	4908				
10	Canada	4248				

Source: *The Economist, Pocket World in Figures, 2006 edition* (Profile Books, 2005)

Further Reading

For purchasing power; human development; economic growth rates; traders; businesses and banks; innovation; information and communications technology; research and development; largest industrial output; highest and lowest growth in industrial output; largest manufacturing output; largest services output; and agricultural and commodity production, see:

The Economist, Pocket World in Figures, 2006 edition (Profile Books, 2005)

See also:

www.mapsofworld.com/world-top-ten/world-top-ten-fastest-growing-economies-map.html

www.mapsofworld.com/world-top-ten/world-top-ten-fastest-growing-economies-map.html

www.mapsofworld.com/world-top-ten/world-top-ten-biggest-exporters.html

www.mapsofworld.com/world-top-ten/world-top-ten-countries-by-competitiveness-map.html

Foreign aid

For statistics on debt and aid (donors and recipients) see:

The Economist, Pocket World in Figures, 2006 edition (Profile Books, 2005)

See also:

www.mapsofworld.com/world-top-ten/countries-most-in-debt-map.html

www.mapsofworld.com/world-top-ten/world-top-ten-doners-of-foreigner-aid-map.html (sic)

Energy

Largest producers of energy

		Million tonnes oil equivalent, 2002			Million tonnes oil equivalent, 2002
1	United States	1666.1	16	Algeria	150.3
2	China	1220.8	17	South Africa	146.5
3	Russia	1034.5	18	United Arab Emirates	142.1
4	Saudi Arabia	462.8	19	Germany	134.8
5	India	438.8	20	France	134.4
6	Canada	385.4	21	Kuwait	106.0
7	United Kingdom	257.5	22	Iraq	105.4
8	Australia	255.2	23	Japan	98.1
9	Indonesia	240.9	24	Kazakhstan	95.8
10	Iran	240.5	25	Argentina	81.7
11	Norway	232.2	26	Malaysia	80.2
12	Mexico	229.9	27	Poland	79.6
13	Venezuela	210.2	28	Colombia	72.3
14	Nigeria	192.7	29	Ukraine	71.5
15	Brazil	161.7	30	Libya	69.5

Source: *The Economist, Pocket World in Figures, 2006 edition* (Profile Books, 2005)

Largest consumers of energy

		Million tonnes oil equivalent, 2002			Million tonnes oil equivalent, 2002
1	United States	2290.4	5	Japan	516.9
2	China	1228.6	6	Germany	346.4
3	Russia	617.8	7	France	265.9
4	India	538.3	8	Canada	250.0

(continued)

		Million tonnes oil equivalent, 2002				Million tonnes oil equivalent, 2002
9	United Kingdom	226.5		20	Australia	112.7
10	South Korea	203.5		21	Nigeria	95.7
11	Brazil	190.7		22	Poland	89.2
12	Italy	172.7		23	Thailand	83.3
13	Mexico	157.3		24	Netherlands	77.9
14	Indonesia	156.1		25	Turkey	75.4
15	Iran	134.0		26	Pakistan	65.8
16	Spain	131.6		27	Belgium	56.9
17	Ukraine	130.7		28	Argentina	56.3
18	Saudi Arabia	126.4		29	Venezuela	54.0
19	South Africa	113.5		30	Egypt	52.4

Source: *The Economist, Pocket World in Figures, 2006 edition* (Profile Books, 2005)

Further Reading

For energy consumption per head, net energy importers and energy efficiency see *The Economist,* Pocket World in Figures, 2006

See also:

www.mapsofworld.com/world-top-ten/world-top-ten-oil-reserves-countries-map.html

www.mapsofworld.com/world-top-ten/countries-with-most-reliance-on-nuclear-power.html

Environment

Environmental sustainability index

Highest				Highest		
1	Finland	75.0		11	Gabon	61.7
2	Norway	73.4		12	Australia	61.0
3	Uruguay	71.8		13	New Zealand	60.9
4	Sweden	71.7		14	Latvia	60.4
5	Iceland	70.8			Peru	60.4
6	Canada	64.4		16	Paraguay	59.7
7	Switzerland	63.7		17	Costa Rica	59.6
8	Argentina	62.7		18	Bolivia	59.5
	Austria	62.7			Croatia	59.5
10	Brazil	62.2		20	Ireland	59.2

(continued)

Highest			Highest		
21	Colombia	58.9	27	Slovenia	57.5
	Lithuania	58.9	28	Japan	57.3
23	Albania	58.8	29	Germany	56.9
24	Central African Rep	58.7	30	Namibia	56.7
25	Denmark	58.2	31	Russia	56.1
	Estonia	58.2	32	Botswana	55.9
Lowest			**Lowest**		
1	North Korea	29.2	17	Lebanon	40.5
2	Taiwan	32.7	18	Zimbabwe	41.2
3	Turkmenistan	33.1	19	Libya	42.3
4	Iraq	33.6		Philippines	42.3
5	Uzbekistan	34.4		Vietnam	42.3
6	Haiti	34.8	22	Mauritania	42.6
7	Sudan	35.9	23	Angola	42.9
8	Trinidad & Tobago	36.3	24	South Korea	43.0
9	Kuwait	36.6	25	Liberia	43.4
10	Yemen	37.3		Sierra Leone	43.4
11	Saudi Arabia	37.8	27	Dominican Republic	43.7
12	Ethiopia	37.9	28	El Salvador	43.8
13	China	38.6		Syria	43.8
	Tajikistan	38.6	30	Belgium	44.0
15	Iran	39.8		Egypt	44.0
16	Burundi	40.0		Guatemala	44.0

Based on 20 key indicators, including: environmental systems and stresses; human vulnerability to environmental risks; institutional capacities on environmental issues; shared resources.

Source: *The Economist, Pocket World in Figures, 2006 edition* (Profile Books, 2005)

Further Reading

See also:

www.mapsofworld.com/world-top-ten/countries-with-highest-deforestation-map.html

www.mapsofworld.com/world-top-ten/countries-with-most-largest-area-of-forest.html

www.mapsofworld.com/world-top-ten/world-top-ten-environmental-treaties-map.html

www.mapsofworld.com/world-top-ten/world-top-ten-fresh-water-supply-map.html

Private organisations (non-governmental organisations)

Environmental non-governmental organisations (NGOs)

NGO	Country	IGO affiliation
Consultative Group on International Agricultural Research www.cgiar.org	Transnational	UN
Friends of the Earth www.foe.co.uk	Transnational	
Greenpeace www.greenpeace.org	Transnational	
International Centre for Research in Agroforestry www.icraf.cgiar.org	Transnational	
National Councils for Sustainable Development www.ncsdnetwork.org	Transnational	UNCSD
Nature Conservancy www.nature.org	Transnational	
Public Services International www.world-psi.org	Transnational	ILO/UN
Taiga Rescue Network www.taigarescue.org	Transnational	
World Conservation Union www.iucn.org	Transnational	
World Wide Fund for Nature www.panda.org	Transnational	
Desert Research Foundation of Namibia www.drfn.org.na	Namibia	
Empowerment for African Sustainable Development www.easd.org.za	South Africa	
Environment Liaison Center International www.elci.org	Kenya	UNEP
Green Earth Organization www.greenearth.org.gh	Ghana	UNEP, UN ECOSOC, UN CSD
Technical Centre for Agricultural and Rural Cooperation (CTA) www.agricta.org	Netherlands	EU
Wildlife and Environment Society of South Africa www.wildlifesociety.org.za	South Africa	
World Commission on Dams www.dams.org	South Africa	
Yonge Nawe Environmental Action Group www.yongenawe.com	Swaziland	
Centre for Science and Environment www.cseindia.org	India	
Greenpeace: Hong Kong www.greenpeace-china.org.hk	Hong Kong	
Tata Energy Research Institute www.teriin.org	India	
Conservation Council of South Australia www.ccsa.asn.au	Australia	

(continued)

NGO	Country	IGO affiliation
Conservation Council of Western Australia www.conservationwa.asn.au	Australia	
A Rocha International www.arocha.org	United Kingdom	
Advisory Committee on Protection of the Sea www.acops.org	United Kingdom	
Amigos de la Tierra www.tierra.org	Spain	Several
Association for the Defense of the Nature and the Resources of Extremadura www.adenex.org	Spain	
Clubul Ecologic UNESCO www.pronatura.ro	Romania	UNESCO
Consejo Iberico para la Defensa de la Naturaleza www.bme.es/cidn/	Spain	
Earth Action www.earthaction.org	United Kingdom	
Earthscan www.earthscan.co.uk	United Kingdom	
EUROPARC Federation www.europarc.org	Germany	UNEP
European Center for Nature Conservation www.ecnc.nl	Netherlands	UNEP, EUCC
Fauna and Flora International www.fauna-flora.org	United Kingdom	
Federation of American Women's Clubs Overseas www.fawco.org	France	
Global Witness www.globalwitness.org	United Kingdom	
Green Alliance www.greenalliance.org.uk	United Kingdom	
International Association on Water Quality www.iwahq.org.uk	United Kingdom	UNEP, UNDP, UNESCO
International Institute for Environment & Development www.iied.org	United Kingdom	
International Office for Water www.iowater.org	France	
International Petroleum Industry Environmental Conservation www.ipieca.org	United Kingdom	UNEP
IRC International Water and Sanitation Centre www.irc.nl	Netherlands	
Mediterranean Information Office for Environment, Culture, and Sustainable Development www.mio-ecsde.org	Greece	
NEREO – Preservador del Medi Ambiente www.nereo.org	Spain	
People and Planet www.peopleandplanet.net	United Kingdom	
Pronatura – Swiss League for the protection of nature www.pronatura.ch	Switzerland	

(continued)

NGO	Country	IGO affiliation
Societatea Ecologica BIOTICA www.scils.rutgers.edu/~olejka/biotica/en/home.html	Moldova	UNDP
Stiftung Europaisches Naturerbe www.euronatur.org	Germany	
UNED Forum www.unedforum.org	United Kingdom	UNEP/UNDP
Water Supply and Sanitation Collaborative Council www.wsscc.org	Switzerland	
World Water Council www.worldwatercouncil.org	France	UN
Center for Environment and Development for the Arab Region and Europe www.cedare.org.eg	Egypt	UNDP
Center for International Climate and Environmental Research www.cicero.uio.no	Norway	
Corporate Watch www.corpwatch.org	United States	UN
Agua Bolivia www.aguabolivia.org	Bolivia	
Centro de Derecho Ambiental y de los Recursos Naturales www.cedarena.org	Costa Rica	
Centro de Estudios Agrarios & Ambientales www.ceacorporacion.cl	Chile	
Centro Ecuatoriano de Derecho Ambiental www.ceda.org.ec	Ecuador	
Centro Mexicano de Derecho Ambiental www.cemda.org.mx	Mexico	
Fondo de las Americas www.fdla.cl	Chile	
Iwokrama International Centre for Rain Forest Conservation and Development www.iwokrama.org	Guyana	
Liga de Defensa del Medio Ambiente www.lidema.org	Bolivia	
Amazon Watch www.amazonwatch.org	United States	
Cloud Forest Alive www.cloudforestalive.org	Costa Rica	
ITeM-The Third World Institute www.item.org.uy	Uruguay	
Panos Institute www.panosinst.org	United States /Haiti	
Rios Vivos www.riosvivos.org.br	Brazil	
World Rainforest Movement www.wrm.org.uy	Uruguay	
Green Front of Iran www.greenfront.org	Iran	
Green Line www.greenline.org.lb	Lebanon	
Center for International Environmental Law www.ciel.org	United States	

(continued)

NGO	Country	IGO affiliation
CIESIN (Center for International Earth Science Information Network) www.ciesin.org	United States	
Conservation International www.conservation.org	United States	
Earth Council, The www.ecouncil.ac.cr	United States	
Earth Island Institute www.earthisland.org	United States	
Earth Summit Watch earthsummitwatch.org	United States	
Earth Times Foundation www.earthtimes.org	United States	
Forests and Communities www.forestsandcommunities.org	United States	
Interhemispheric Resource Center www.irc-online.org	United States	
International Institute for Sustainable Development iisd1.iisd.ca	Canada	UN
International Rivers Network www.irn.org	United States	
Natural Resources Defense Council www.nrdc.org	United States	
Physicians for Social Responsibility www.psr.org	United States	
Rainforest Action Network www.ran.org	United States	
Wildlife Trust www.wpti.org	United States	
Women's Environment and Development Organization www.wedo.org	United States	
World Business Council for Sustainable Development www.wbcsd.ch	United States	
Canadian Institute for Environmental Law and Policy www.cielap.org	Canada	
Canadian Nature Federation www.cnf.ca	Canada	
Caribbean Conservation Association www.caribbeanconservation.org	Barbados	
Cousteau Society, Inc. www.cousteau.org	United States	
Earth Rights International www.earthrights.org	United States	
Earth Society Foundation www.earthsocietyfoundation.org	United States	UN
Earth Trust www.earthtrust.org	United States	
Earth Watch Institute www.earthwatch.org	United States	UNEP
Environmental Defense www.environmentaldefense.org	United States	
International Wildlife Coalition www.iwc.org	United States	

(continued)

NGO	Country	IGO affiliation
National Ground Water Association www.ngwa.org	United States	
National Wildlife Federation www.nwf.org	United States	
Rainforest Alliance www.rainforest-alliance.org	United States	
Rene Dubos Center for Human Environments, Inc. www.dubos.org	United States	
Unit for Sustainable Development and Environment www.oas.org/usde/	United States	
United Earth www.unitedearthonline.org	United States	
Water Environment Federation www.wef.org	United States	
World Resources Institute www.wri.org	United States	UNEP

Source: docs.lib.duke.edu/igo/guides/ngo/

Human rights NGOs

NGO	Country	IGO affiliation
Amnesty International www.amnesty.org	Transnational	
Centre on Housing Rights and Evictions www.cohre.org	Transnational	
Derechos Human Rights www.derechos.org	Transnational	
FoodFirst Information & Action Network www.fian.org	Transnational	UN
Freedom House www.freedomhouse.org	Transnational	
Human Rights in China www.iso.hrichina.org	China	
Human Rights Watch www.hrw.org	Transnational	
International Commission of Jurists www.icj.org	Transnational	
Oxfam www.oxfaminternational.org	Transnational	
Action for Southern Africa www.actsa.org	United Kingdom	
Equality Now www.equalitynow.org	Kenya	
Zimbabwe Human Rights NGO Forum www.hrforumzim.com	Zimbabwe	
Aliran www.malaysia.net/aliran/	Malaysia	UN ECOSOC
Asian Human Rights Commission www.ahrchk.net	Hong Kong	UNHCR
People's Union for Civil Liberties www.pucl.org	India	
Revolutionary Association of the Women of Afghanistan (RAWA) www.rawa.false.net	Afghanistan	

(continued)

NGO	Country	IGO affiliation
Tapol tapol.gn.apc.org	Indonesia/ United Kingdom	
Tibetan Center for Human Rights and Democracy www.tchrd.org	Tibet	
Watch Indonesia home.snafu.de/watchin/	Indonesia	
ConGo www.congo-online.com	Australia	
Anti-Slavery International www.antislavery.org	United Kingdom	
Global Witness www.globalwitness.org	United Kingdom	
International Federation of University Women www.ifuw.org	Switzerland	
International Helsinki Federation for Human Rights www.ihf-hr.org	Austria	
International Society for Human Rights www.ishr.org	Germany	
International Work Group for Indigenous Affairs www.iwgia.org	Denmark	
Marie Stopes International www.mariestopes.org.uk	United Kingdom	
Minority Rights Group www.minorityrights.org	United Kingdom	UN ECOSOC
Survival International www.survival-international.org	United Kingdom	
World Organization Against Torture (OMCT) www.omct.org	Switzerland	UN
World Population Fund www.wpf.org	United Kingdom	
Corporate Watch www.corpwatch.org	United States	UN
International Alert www.international-alert.org	United Kingdom	
Nuevos Derechos del Hombre www.ndh.org.ar	Argentina	
Al-Haq www.alhaq.org	Palestine	
B'Tselem--The Information Center for Human Rights in the Occupied Territories www.btselem.org	Israel	
Egyptian Organization for Human Rights www.eohr.org.eg	Egypt	UN ECOSOC
Human Rights Foundation of Turkey www.tihv.org.tr	Turkey	
Kurdish Human Rights Project www.khrp.org	United Kingdom	
Organization for Defending Victims of Violence www.odvv.org	Iran	UN ECOSOC
Center for Economic & Social Rights www.cesr.org	United States	

(continued)

NGO	Country	IGO affiliation
Global Lawyers and Physicians www.glphr.org	United States	
Human Rights Internet www.hri.ca	Canada	UNICEF
International Human Rights Law Group www.hrlawgroup.org	United States	
International League for Human Rights www.ilhr.org	United States	UN, COE, ILO
Lawyers Committee for Human Rights www.lchr.org	United States	
Physicians for Human Rights www.phrusa.org	United States	
Sisterhood is Global Institute www.sigi.org	Canada	
American Civil Liberties Union www.aclu.org	United States	
Athletes United for Peace www.athletesunitedforpeace.org	United States	UN UNICEF and UN UNESCO
Cultural Survival, Inc. www.cs.org	United States	
Earth Rights International www.earthrights.org	United States	
Eleanor Roosevelt Centre at Val-Kill www.ervk.org	United States	
Global Fund for Women www.globalfundforwomen.org	United States	
Human Rights Advocates, Inc. www.humanrightsadvocates.org	United States	UNHCR
International Council of Jewish Women www.ncjw.org	Canada	
International Human Rights Association of American Minorities www.ihraam.org	Canada	UNESCO
International League of Human Rights www.ilhr.org	United States	UN
International Women's Health Coalition www.iwhc.org	United States	
RAINBOW www.rainbo.org	United States	
United States Committee for UNIFEM www.uscommitteeforunifem.org	United States	UNIFEM
Women, Law, and Development International www.wld.org	United States	UN ECOSOC
Women's Peace Network (MADRE/W.P.N) www.madre.org	United States	

Source: docs.lib.duke.edu/igo/guides/ngo/

Women in development NGOs

NGO	Country	IGO affiliation
Development Alternatives with Women for a New Era (DAWN) www.dawn.org.fj	Transnational	UNDP
Family Health International www.fhi.org	Transnational	UN/USAID
International Planned Parenthood Federation www.ippf.org	Transnational	
Public Services International www.world-psi.org	Transnational	ILO/UN
WomenAction www.womenaction.org	Transnational	UN
Women's Learning Partnership www.learningpartnership.org	Transnational	
African Gender Institute www.uct.ac.za/org/agi/	South Africa	
African Medical and Research Foundation (AMREF) www.amref.org	Kenya	UNESCO
Akina Mama wa Afrika www.akinamama.org	United Kingdom	
Equality Now www.equalitynow.org	Kenya	
Pan Pacific and Southeast Asia Women's Association International www.ppseawa.org	Mali	UN ECOSOC
Women in Law and Development in Africa www.wildaf.org.zw	Zimbabwe	
Family Care International www.familycareintl.org	United States	
Isis International Manila www.isiswomen.org	Philippines	
Arab Women's Solidarity Association www.awsa.net	United States	UN ECOSOC
BRAC (Bangladesh Rural Advancement Committee) www.brac.net	Bangladesh	
Center for Sustainable Development Actions interconnection.org/csda/	Pakistan	
EC/UNFPA Initiative for Reproductive Health in Asia www.asia-initiative.org	Transnational	EU/UNFPA
Institute of Social Studies Trust www.indev.org/isst/	India	UN ECOSOC
Revolutionary Association of the Women of Afghanistan (RAWA) rawa.false.net	Afghanistan	
Women in Security, Conflict Management and Peace www.furhhdl.org/wiscompindex.htm	India	
Associated Country Women of the World www.acww.org.uk	United Kingdom	UN ECOSOC

(continued)

NGO	Country	IGO affiliation
Committee for International Cooperation in National Research in Demography www.cicred.org	France	UN
EuroNGOs www.eurongos.org		
Face to Face www.facecampaign.org	United Kingdom	UNFPA
Federation of American Women's Clubs Overseas www.fawco.org	France	
International Community of Women Living with HIV/Aids www.icw.org	United Kingdom	UNAids
International Federation of University Women www.ifuw.org	Switzerland	
Reproductive and Family Health (Centre for) www.rafh-vie.org	United Kingdom	UN
Safe Motherhood www.safemotherhood.org	United Kingdom	UNFPA
Vaestoliitto www.vaestoliitto.fi	Finland	EU/UNFPA
WIDE (Network Women in Development Europe) www.eurosur.org/wide/porteng.htm	Belgium	
Womankind Worldwide www.womankind.org.uk	United Kingdom	
Women's International Democratic Federation www.fdif.eu.org	France	
Women's World Summit Foundation www.woman.ch	Switzerland	ECOSOC, UNFPA, DPI
World Young Women's Christian Association www.worldywca.org	Switzerland	UN ECOSOC, UNESCO
Instituto Social y Politico de la Mujer www.ispm.org.ar	Argentina	
Social Watch www.socwatch.org.uy	Uruguay	
Union Nationale de la Femme Tunisienne www.unft.org.tn	Tunisia	UN ECOSOC
Women's International Zionist Organization www.wizo.org	Israel	UN ECOSOC, UNICEF
Action Canada for Population and Development www.acpd.ca	Canada	EU/UN
Alan Guttmacher Institute www.agi-usa.org	United States	
Association for Progressive Communications www.apc.org	Canada	UN ECOSOC
Center for International Health Information www.tfgi.com/cihi.asp	United States	USAID

(continued)

NGO	Country	IGO affiliation
Center for Reproductive Law and Policy www.crlp.org	United States	
Centre for Development and Population Activities www.cedpa.org	United States	
Demographic and Health Surveys www.measuredhs.com	United States	
Engenderhealth www.engenderhealth.org	United States	
International Center for Research on Women www.icrw.org	United States	UN/USAID
International Human Rights Law Group www.hrlawgroup.org	United States	
International Women's Tribune Centre www.iwtc.org	United States	
Pacific Institute For Women's Health (PIWH) www.piwh.org	United States	
Population Action International www.populationaction.org	United States	
Sisterhood is Global Institute www.sigi.org	Canada	
Women's Environment and Development Organization www.wedo.org	United States	
Women's International Coalition for Economic Justice www.wicej.addr.org	United States	
World March of Women www.ffq.qc.ca/marche2000/en/index.htm	Canada	
American Association of University Women www.aauw.org	United States	
Armenian International Women's Association www.aiwa-net.org	United States	
Association for Women in Development www.awid.org	Canada	UN ECOSOC
Association for Women in Science www.awis.org	United States	
Association of Junior Leagues International, Inc. www.ajli.org	United States	
Captive Daughters www.captivedaughters.org	United States	
Eleanor Roosevelt Centre at Val-Kill www.ervk.org	United States	
General Federation of Women's Clubs www.gfwc.org	United States	
Global Alliance for Women's Health www.gawh.org	United States	UNICEF, UNDCP, UNIDO

(continued)

NGO	Country	IGO affiliation
Global Fund for Women www.globalfundforwomen.org	United States	
Hunger Project www.thp.org	United States	
International Council of Jewish Women www.ncjw.org	Canada	
International Women's Health Coalition www.iwhc.org	United States	
National Council of Women of Canada www.ncwc.ca	Canada	UN ECOSOC
RAINBOW www.rainbo.org	United States	
United States Committee for UNIFEM www.uscommitteeforunifem.org	United States	UNIFEM
Women's Federation for World Peace International www.wfwp.org	United States	UN ECOSOC
Women, Law, and Development International www.wld.org	United States	UN ECOSOC
Women's Peace Network (MADRE/W.P.N) www.madre.org	United States	
World Federation of Ukranian Women's Organizations www.wfuwo.org	Canada	UN ECOSOC, UNICEF
Zonta International www.zonta.org	United States	UN ECOSOC, DPI

Source: docs.lib.duke.edu/igo/guides/ngo/

Development NGOs

NGO	Country	IGO affiliation
CARE International www.careinternational.org	Transnational	
Forest, Trees and People Program www.cof.orst.edu/org/istf/ftpp.htm	Transnational	
Global Vision www.global-vision.org	Transnational	UNCSD
International South Group Network www.isgnweb.org	Transnational	
MAP International www.map.org	Transnational	
oneworld.net www.oneworld.net	Transnational	
Oxfam www.oxfaminternational.org	Transnational	
PROUT www.prout.org	Transnational	
Solidaridad Internacional www.solidaridad.org	Transnational	UN
Third World Network www.twnside.org.sg	Transnational	
Africa Action www.africaaction.org	United States	

(continued)

NGO	Country	IGO affiliation
Africa Confidential www.africa-confidential.com	United Kingdom	
Africa Research Bulletin www.africa-research-bulletin.com	United States	
African Academy of Sciences www.oneworld.org/aas/org.htm	Transnational	
African Affairs www3.oup.co.uk/afrafj/	United Kingdom	
African Community Publishing and Development Trust www.mweb.co.zw/acpdt/	Zimbabwe	
African Economic Research Consortium www.aercafrica.org	Kenya	
African Medical and Research Foundation (AMREF) www.amref.org	Kenya	UNESCO
Alternative Information and Development Centre (AIDC) aidc.org.za	South Africa	
Centre for Development and Enterprise www.cde.org.za	South Africa	
Green Earth Organization www.greenearth.org.gh	Ghana	UNEP, UN ECOSOC, UN CSD
Human Sciences Research Council www.hsrc.ac.za	South Africa	
Jeune Afrique www.lintelligent.com	Algeria	
MSNepal www.msnepal.org	Nepal	
Namibia Nature Foundation www.nnf.org.na	Namibia	
Namibian Economic Policy Research Unit www.nepru.org.na	Namibia	
Olive (Organisation Development and Training) www.oliveodt.co.za	South Africa	
ResourceAfrica www.resourceafrica.org	United Kingdom	
TROPENBOS International www.tropenbos.org	Netherlands	
Association for Stimulating Know How www.askindia.org	India	
Association of Social Engineering, Research and Training www.indev.nic.in/assert/	India	
BRAC (Bangladesh Rural Advancement Committee) www.brac.net	Bangladesh	
Center for Sustainable Development Actions interconnection.org/csda/	Pakistan	

(continued)

NGO	Country	IGO affiliation
China Youth Development Foundation www.cydf.org	China	
Indev www.indev.org	India	
Institute of Southeast Asian Studies www.iseas.edu.sg	Singapore	ASEAN
International Centre for Integrated Mountain Development www.icimod.org.sg	Nepal	
Propoor www.propoor.org	South Asia	
Korean International Volunteer Organization www.kvo.or.kr	Korea	
International Water Management Institute www.cgiar.org/iwmi/	Sri Lanka	
Demography and Population Studies demography.anu.edu.au/VirtualLibrary/	Australia	
A Rocha International www.arocha.org	United Kingdom	
Advisory Committee on Protection of the Sea www.acops.org	United Kingdom	
Amigos de la Tierra www.tierra.org	Spain	several
Bretton Woods Project www.brettonwoodsproject.org	United Kingdom	
British Overseas NGOs for Development www.bond.org.uk	United Kingdom	
Clubul Ecologic UNESCO www.pronatura.ro	Romania	UNESCO
Committee for International Cooperation in National Research in Demography www.cicred.org	France	UN
Ecologistas www.nodo50.org/ecologistas/	Spain	
EUROPARC Federation www.europarc.org	Germany	UNEP
European Environmental Bureau www.eeb.org	Belgium	EU, UN ECOSOC, UN CSD, OECD
Forum for the Future www.forumforthefuture.org.uk	United Kingdom	
Fundacion Desarrollo Sostenido www.fundeso.org	Spain	
Institute of Development Studies www.ids.ac.uk	United Kingdom	
Intermediate Techology Development Group www.itdg.org	United Kingdom	
Netherlands Interdisciplinary Demographic Institute www.nidi.nl	Netherlands	
Overseas Development Institute www.odi.org.uk	United Kingdom	

(continued)

NGO	Country	IGO affiliation
SUNS-South-North Development Monitor www.sunsonline.org	Switzerland	
Center for Environment and Development for the Arab Region and Europe www.cedare.org.eg	Egypt	UNDP
INTERCOOPERATION www.intercooperation.ch	Switzerland	
Asociacion ANAI www.anaicr.org	Costa Rica	
Asociacion Guatemalteca para la Conservacion Natural www.rds.org.gt	Guatemala	
Consejo Latinoamericano de Ciencias Sociales www.clacso.org	Argentina	UNESCO
Instituto de Derecho y Economia Ambiental www.idea.org.py	Paraguay	
Instituto de Desarrollo y Medio Ambiente www.geocities.com/RainForest/vines/6274/	Peru	UNPD, PNUMA
Sociedad Peruana de Derecho Ambiental www.spda.org.pe	Peru	
Haitian Movement for Rural Development (MHDR) www.panosinst.org/MHDR/defaulte.shtml	Haiti	FAO
ITeM-The Third World Institute www.item.org.uy	Uruguay	
Social Watch www.socwatch.org.uy	Uruguay	
Center for Sustainable Development www.cenesta.org	Iran	UNDP, FAO, UNICEF
Jamaica Conservation and Development Trust http://64.45.40.146/	Jamaica	
Academy for Educational Development www.aed.org	United States	
Bank Information Center www.bicusa.org	United States	
Environmental Defense Fund www.environmentaldefense.org	United States	
Futures Group, The www.tfgi.org	United States	
Global Development Network www.gdnet.org	United States	
Grassroots International www.grassrootsonline.org	United States	
Institute for Development Research www.jsi.com/idr/	United States	
InterAction www.interaction.org	United States	
International Development Research Centre www.idrc.ca	Canada	

(continued)

NGO	Country	IGO affiliation
NetAid app.netaid.org	United States	UNDP
Peace Corps www.rpcv.org	United States	
Popnet www.popnet.org	United States	
Population Action International www.populationaction.org	United States	
Population Reference Bureau www.prb.org	United States	
Population Services International (PSI) www.psi.org	United States	
RAND's Labor and Population Program www.rand.org/labor/	United States	
World Neighbors www.wn.org	United States	
World Watch www.worldwatch.org	United States	
Association for Women in Development www.awid.org	Canada	UN ECOSOC
Association of Junior Leagues International, Inc. www.ajli.org	United States	
Athletes United for Peace www.athletesunitedforpeace.org	United States	UN UNICEF and UN UNESCO
Caribbean Conservation Association www.caribbeanconservation.org	Barbados	
Earth Watch Institute www.earthwatch.org	United States	UNEP
Unit for Sustainable Development and Environment www.oas.org/usde/	United States	
Women's Federation for World Peace International www.wfwp.org	United States	UN ECOSOC

Source: docs.lib.duke.edu/igo/guides/ngo/

Prominent inter-governmental organisations (IGOs)

World Trade Organisation (WTO)

Origin

The WTO was established in January 1995. It was created by the Uruguay Round negotiations (1986–1994) as a substitute for the General Agreement on Tariffs and Trade (GATT).

Organisation

Headquarters: Geneva, Switzerland.
Membership: 148 countries, which account for 97 per cent of world trade.

Management: Current Director-General: Supachai Panitchpakdi.

Decisions are made by the entire membership. This is typically by consensus. A majority vote is also possible but it has never been used in the WTO and was extremely rare under the WTO's predecessor, GATT. The WTO's agreements have been ratified in all members' parliaments.

The WTO's top-level decision-making body is the Ministerial Conference which meets at least once every two years. The Fifth WTO Ministerial Conference was held in Cancún, Mexico from 10 to 14 September 2003.

Below this is the General Council (normally ambassadors and heads of delegation in Geneva, but sometimes officials sent from members' capitals) which meets several times a year in the Geneva headquarters. The General Council also meets as the Trade Policy Review Body and the Dispute Settlement Body.

At the next level, the Goods Council, Services Council and Intellectual Property (TRIPS) Council report to the General Council.

Numerous specialised committees, working groups and working parties deal with the individual agreements and other areas such as the environment, development, membership applications and regional trade agreements.

Functions

The WRO functions can be summarised as:

- Administering WTO trade agreements
- Forum for trade negotiations
- Handling trade disputes
- Monitoring national trade policies
- Technical assistance and training for developing countries
- Cooperation with other international organisations

World Bank

Origin

The World Bank was established on 1 July 1944 by a conference of 44 governments in Bretton Woods, New Hampshire.

Organisation

Headquarters: Washington, DC, USA and more than 100 country offices.
Membership: 184 countries.
President: James D. Wolfensohn (ninth president of the World Bank Group since 1 June 1995).

Functions

The World Bank is the name that has come to be used for the International Bank for Reconstruction and Development (IBRD) and the International Development Association (IDA). Together these organisations provide low-interest loans, interest-free credit and grants to developing countries. They also sponsor or coordinate several projects ranging from anti-corruption initiatives to infrastructure development.

In addition to IBRD and IDA, three other organisations make up the World Bank Group. The International Finance Corporation (IFC) promotes private-sector investment by support-

ing high-risk sectors and countries.

The Multilateral Investment Guarantee Agency (MIGA) provides political risk insurance (guarantees) to investors in and lenders to developing countries. The International Centre for Settlement of Investment Disputes (ICSID) settles investment disputes between foreign investors and their host countries.

International Monetary Fund (IMF)

Origin

The Fund was conceived at a United Nations conference convened in Bretton Woods, New Hampshire, in July 1944. The 44 governments represented at that conference sought to build a framework for economic cooperation that would avoid a repetition of the disastrous economic policies that had contributed to the Great Depression of the 1930s.

Organisation

Headquarters: Washington, DC, USA
Membership: 184 countries.
Managing Director: Rodrigo Rato (from Spain).

The IMF is accountable to the governments of its member countries. At the apex of its organisational structure is its board of governors, which consists of one governor from each of the IMF's 184 member countries. All governors meet once each year at the IMF-World Bank Annual Meetings; 24 of the governors sit on the International Monetary and Finance Committee (IMFC) and meet twice each year. The day-to-day work of the IMF is conducted at its Washington DC headquarters by its 24-member executive board; this work is guided by the IMFC and supported by the IMF's professional staff. The managing director is head of IMF staff and chairman of the executive board, and is assisted by three deputy managing directors.

The IMF's resources are provided by its member countries, primarily through payment of quotas, which broadly reflect each country's economic size. The total amount of quotas is the most important factor determining the IMF's lending capacity. The annual expenses of running the Fund are met mainly by the difference between interest receipts (on outstanding loans) and interest payments (on quota 'deposits').

Functions

The IMF was established to promote international monetary cooperation, exchange stability and orderly exchange arrangements; to foster economic growth and high levels of employment; and to provide temporary financial assistance to countries to help ease balance of payments adjustment.

United Nations (UN)

Origin

In 1945, representatives of 50 countries met in San Francisco at the United Nations Conference on International Organisation to draw up the United Nations Charter. The Organisation officially came into existence on 24 October 1945, when the Charter had been ratified by China, France, the Soviet Union, the United Kingdom, the United States and a majority of other signatories. United Nations Day is celebrated on 24 October.

Organisation

Headquarters: New York, US (See box 'United Nations Systems and Organisations' for specific headquarters locations).

Secretary General: Kofi Annan of Ghana is the seventh secretary-general of the United Nations.

Staff: The secretariat has a staff of about 8,900 people under the regular budget drawn from 170 countries. As international civil servants, staff members and the secretary-general answer to the United Nations alone for their activities, and take an oath not to seek or receive instructions from any government or outside authority.

Organs: The six principal organs of the United Nations are the General Assembly, Security Council, Economic and Social Council, Trusteeship Council, International Court of Justice and Secretariat. The United Nations family, however, is much larger, encompassing 15 agencies and several programmes and bodies. (See 'United Nations System of Organisations'.)

Functions

The purposes of the United Nations, as set forth in the Charter, are to maintain international peace and security; to develop friendly relations among nations; to cooperate in solving international economic, social, cultural and humanitarian problems and in promoting respect for human rights and fundamental freedoms; and to be a centre for harmonising the actions of nations in attaining these ends.

Organisation of American States (OAS)

Origin

On 30 April 1948, 21 nations of the western hemisphere met in Bogota, Colombia, to adopt the Charter of the Organisation of American States (OAS), which affirmed their commitment to common goals and respect for each nation's sovereignty. Since then, the OAS has expanded to include the nations of the Caribbean, as well as Canada.

Organisation

Headquarters: Washington, DC, USA.

Membership: 35 independent countries in the Americas. They are: Antigua and Barbuda, Argentina, The Bahamas, Barbados, Belize, Bolivia, Brazil, Canada, Chile, Colombia, Costa Rica, Cuba[1], Dominica, Dominican Republic, Ecuador, El Salvador, Grenada, Guatemala, Guyana, Haiti, Honduras, Jamaica, Mexico, Nicaragua, Panama, Paraguay, Peru, Saint Kitts and Nevis, Saint Lucia, Saint Vincent and the Grenadines, Suriname, Trinidad and Tobago, United States of America, Uruguay, and Venezuela.

Secretary General: Luigi R. Einaudi (from United States), acting Secretary-General.

Functions

The organisation's stated goals include: strengthening democracy, advancing human rights, promoting peace and security, expanding trade and tackling complex problems caused by poverty, drugs and corruption. More recently, through the Summit of the Americas[2] process, the OAS has focused on:

■ Strengthening freedom of speech and thought as a basic human right;
■ Promoting greater participation by civil society in decision-making at all levels of government;

---

1. Despite being a member, by resolution of the Eight Meeting of Consultation of Ministers of Foreign Affairs (1962) the current government of Cuba is excluded from participation in the OAS.
2. The latest Summit of the Americas was the Third Summit, which occurred in Quebec City, Canada, on 20–22 April 2001.

- Improving cooperation to address the problem of illegal drugs; and
- Supporting the process to create a Free Trade Area of the Americas.

Organisation of the Petroleum Exporting Countries (OPEC)

Origin

The Organisation was created at the Baghdad Conference on 10–14 September 1960 by Iran, Iraq, Kuwait, Saudi Arabia and Venezuela. The five founding members were later joined by eight others: Qatar (1961); Indonesia (1962); Socialist Peoples Libyan Arab Jamahiriya (1962); United Arab Emirates (1967); Algeria (1969); Nigeria (1971); Ecuador (1973–1992) and Gabon (1975–1994).

Organisation

Headquarters: Vienna, Austria.
Membership: Algeria, Indonesia, Iran, Iraq, Kuwait, Libya, Nigeria, Qatar, Saudi Arabia, the United Arab Emirates and Venezuela. These eleven members of the OPEC collectively supply about 40 per cent of the world's oil output, and possess more than three-quarters of the world's total proven crude oil reserves.
Secretary General: Currently assuming this position is Purnomo Yusgiantoro, Minister of Energy and Mineral Resources of Indonesia.

Decisions about matching oil production to expected demand are taken at the Meeting of the OPEC Conference. Details of such decisions are communicated in the form of OPEC press releases.

Functions

The members of the organisation aim to bring stability to the oil market by adjusting their oil output to help ensure a balance between supply and demand. Twice a year, or more frequently if required, the oil and energy ministers of the OPEC members meet to decide on the organisation's output level and consider whether any action to adjust output is necessary in the light of recent and anticipated oil market developments.

Asia-Pacific Economic Cooperation (APEC)

Origin

APEC was established in 1989.

Organisation

Headquarters: Singapore.
Membership: APEC's 21 Member economies are Australia; Brunei Darussalam; Canada; Chile; People's Republic of China; Hong Kong, China; Indonesia; Japan; Republic of Korea; Malaysia; Mexico; New Zealand; Papua New Guinea; Peru; The Republic of the Philippines; The Russian Federation; Singapore; Chinese Taipei; Thailand; United States of America; Vietnam.
Management: Choi Seok Young (from South Korea) is the Executive Director of the Secretariat for 2005. It rotates annually.

Functions

The goal of the organisation is to further enhance economic growth and prosperity for the region and to strengthen the Asia-Pacific community. Since its inception, APEC has worked to reduce tariffs and other trade barriers across the Asia-Pacific region, creating efficient domestic economies and dramatically increasing exports. Key to achieving APEC's vision are what are referred to as the 'Bogor Goals' of free and open trade and investment in the Asia-Pacific by 2010 for industrialised economies and 2020 for developing economies. These goals were adopted by leaders at their 1994 meeting in Bogor, Indonesia.

Association of South-East Asian States (ASEAN)

Origin

ASEAN was established on 8 August 1967 in Bangkok by the five original member countries, namely, Indonesia, Malaysia, Philippines, Singapore and Thailand. Brunei Darussalam joined on 8 January 1984, Vietnam on 28 July 1995, Laos and Myanmar on 23 July 1997 and Cambodia on 30 April 1999.

Organisation

Headquarters: Jakarta, Indonesia.
To support the conduct of ASEAN's external relations, ASEAN has established committees composed of heads of diplomatic missions in the following capitals: Brussels, London, Paris, Washington DC, Tokyo, Canberra, Ottawa, Wellington, Geneva, Seoul, New Delhi, New York, Beijing, Moscow, and Islamabad.
Membership: Brunei Darussalam, Cambodia, Indonesia, Laos, Malaysia, Myanmar, Philippines, Singapore, Thailand and Vietnam.

Secretary General: Ong Keng Yong from Singapore (since January 2003).

The highest decision-making organ of ASEAN is the Meeting of the ASEAN Heads of State and Government. The ASEAN Summit is convened every year. The ASEAN Ministerial Meeting (Foreign Ministers) is held on an annual basis. Ministerial meetings on several other sectors are also held: agriculture and forestry, economics, energy, environment, finance, information, investment, labour, law, regional haze, rural development and poverty alleviation, science and technology, social welfare, transnational crime, transportation, tourism, youth, the AIA Council and the AFTA Council. Supporting these ministerial bodies are 29 committees of senior officials and 122 technical working groups.

Functions

The ASEAN Declaration states that the aims and purposes of the Association are: (i) to accelerate the economic growth, social progress and cultural development in the region through joint endeavours in the spirit of equality and partnership in order to strengthen the foundation for a prosperous and peaceful community of South-East Asian nations, and (ii) to promote regional peace and stability through abiding respect for justice and the rule of law in the relationship among countries in the region and adherence to the principles of the United Nations Charter.

African Union (formerly Organisation of African Unity)

Origin

In 1999, the heads of state and government of the Organisation of African Unity issued a Declaration (the Sirte Declaration) calling for the establishment of an African Union, with the goal of accelerating the process of integration in the continent.

Organisation

Headquarters: Addis Ababa, Ethiopia.
Membership: 53 Member States: Algeria, Angola, Benin, Botswana, Burkina Faso, Burundi, Cameroon, Cape Verde, Central African Republic, Chad, Cameron, Congo, Côte d'Ivoire, Democratic Republic of Congo, Djibouti, Egypt, Eritrea, Ethiopia, Equatorial Guinea, Gabon, Gambia, Ghana, Guinea, Guinea Bissau, Republic of Kenya, Lesotho, Liberia, Libya, Madagascar, Malawi, Mali, Mauritania, Mauritius, Mozambique, Namibia, Niger, Nigeria, Rwanda, Sahrawi Republic, Sao Tome and Principe, Senegal, Seychelles, Sierra Leone, Somalia, South Africa, Sudan, Swaziland, Tanzania, Togo, Tunisia, Uganda, Zambia and Zimbabwe.
Chairperson: Olusegun Obasanjo, President of Nigeria.

Functions

The main objectives of the OAU were to rid the continent of the remaining vestiges of colonisation and apartheid; to promote unity and solidarity among African states; to coordinate and intensify cooperation for development; to safeguard the sovereignty and territorial integrity of Member States and to promote international cooperation within the framework of the United Nations.

As a continental organisation the OAU provided a forum that enabled all Member States to adopt coordinated positions on matters of common concern to the continent in international fora and defend the interests of Africa effectively.

Caribbean Community (CARICOM)

Origins

The establishment of the Caribbean Community and Common Market (CARICOM)[1] was the result of a 15-year effort to fulfil the hope of regional integration which was born with the establishment of the British West Indies Federation in 1958. The West Indies Federation came to an end in 1962. The end of the Federation meant the beginning of more serious efforts on the part of the political leaders in the Caribbean to strengthen the ties between the islands and mainland by providing for the continuance and strengthening of the areas of cooperation that existed during the Federation.

Organisation

Headquarters: Georgetown, Guyana
Membership: Antigua and Barbuda, The Bahamas, Barbados, Belize, Dominica, Grenada, Guyana, Haiti, Jamaica, Montserrat, Saint Lucia, St Kitts and Nevis, St Vincent and the Grenadines, Suriname, and Trinidad and Tobago.
Secretary-General: Edwin Carrington.

---

1. The Caribbean Court of Justice is part of CARICOM.

Functions

From its inception, the Community has concentrated on the promotion of functional cooperation, especially in relation to human and social development, and in integrating the economies of Member States.

The independent Member States however, have also been pursuing a coordinated foreign policy.

All these initiatives are being supported by structural developments and adjustments to bridge gaps, eliminate barriers and forge a unified response among the stakeholders of the region in response to the challenging circumstances to secure a viable and sustainable community.

The establishment in 1994 of the Association of Caribbean States (ACS), the brainchild of CARICOM, and the Caribbean Forum of African, Caribbean and Pacific States (CARIFORUM) which convened its first session in 1993, are major hemispheric links of the Community.

European Union (EU)

Origin

The historical roots of the European Union lie in the Second World War. The idea of European integration was conceived to prevent such killing and destruction from ever happening again. It was first proposed by the French Foreign Minister Robert Schuman in a speech on 9 May 1950. This date, the 'birthday' of what is now the EU, is celebrated annually as Europe Day. It stems from the European Steel and Coal Community, created in 1951 and the European Atomic Energy Community (EURATOM) and the European Economic Community (EEC), created in 1957.

Organisation

Headquarters: The European Parliament works in France, Belgium and Luxembourg.

Membership: Austria, Belgium, Denmark, Finland, France, Germany, Greece, Ireland, Italy, Luxembourg, Portugal, Spain, Sweden, The Netherlands and United Kingdom. Also, new members include: Cyprus, Czech Republic, Estonia, Hungary, Latvia, Lithuania, Malta, Poland, Slovakia and Slovenia. Applicant countries for accession are: Bulgaria, Romania and Turkey.

There are five EU institutions, each playing a specific role:

- European Parliament (elected by the peoples of the Member States)
- Council of the European Union (representing the governments of the Member States)
- European Commission (driving force and executive body)
- Court of Justice (ensuring compliance with the law)
- Court of Auditors (controlling sound and lawful management of the EU budget).

These are flanked by five other important bodies:

- European Economic and Social Committee (expresses the opinions of organised civil society on economic and social issues)
- Committee of the Regions (expresses the opinions of regional and local authorities)
- European Central Bank (responsible for monetary policy and managing the euro)
- European Ombudsman (deals with citizens' complaints about maladministration by any EU institution or body)
- European Investment Bank (helps achieve EU objectives by financing investment projects).

A number of agencies and other bodies complete the system.

Functions

The European Union (EU) is a family of democratic European countries, committed to working together for peace and prosperity. It is not a state intended to replace existing states, but it is more than any other international organisation. The EU is, in fact, unique. Its Member States have set up common institutions to which they delegate some of their sovereignty so that decisions on specific matters of joint interest can be made democratically at European level.

European Bank for Reconstruction and Development (EBRD)

Origin

Established in 1991, when communism was crumbling in central and eastern Europe, to help countries in the region nurture a new private sector in a democratic environment.

Organisation

Headquarters: London, United Kingdom.

Membership: Albania, Armenia, Australia, Austria, Azerbaijan, Belarus, Belgium, Bosnia and Herzegovina, Bulgaria, Canada, Croatia, Cyprus, Czech Republic, Denmark, Egypt, Estonia, Finland, France, Georgia, Germany, Greece, Hungary, Iceland, Ireland, Israel, Italy, Japan, Kazakhstan, Korea, Republic of Kyrgyz, Latvia, Liechtenstein, Lithuania, Luxembourg, Former Yugoslav Republic of Macedonia, Malta, Mexico, Moldova, Mongolia, Morocco, Netherlands, New Zealand, Norway, Poland, Portugal, Romania, Russia, Serbia and Montenegro, Slovak Republic, Slovenia, Spain, Sweden, Switzerland, Tajikistan, Turkey, Turkmenistan, Ukraine, United Kingdom, United States of America, Uzbekistan, European Community and European Investment Bank.

President: Jean Lemierre (from France) took office as the fourth President of the Bank on 3 July 2000.

Functions

The EBRD is the largest single investor in the region and mobilises significant foreign direct investment beyond its own financing. It is owned by 60 countries and two intergovernmental institutions. But despite its public sector shareholders, it invests mainly in private enterprises, usually together with commercial partners.

It provides project financing for banks, industries and businesses, both new ventures and investments in existing companies. It also works with publicly owned companies to support privatisation, restructuring state-owned firms and improvement of municipal services. The Bank uses its close relationship with governments in the region to promote policies that will bolster the business environment.

The mandate of the EBRD stipulates that it must work only in countries that are committed to democratic principles. Respect for the environment is part of the strong corporate governance attached to all EBRD investments.

Through its investments, the EBRD attempts to promote:

- structural and sectoral reforms
- competition, privatisation and entrepreneurship
- stronger financial institutions and legal systems

- infrastructure development needed to support the private sector
- adoption of strong corporate governance, including environmental sensitivity.

Inter-American Development Bank (IADB)

Origin

Founded in 1959 as an initiative of the Latin American countries themselves, the IDB is the world's oldest and largest regional development institution. The Bank was the first regional institution with its own policies and instruments ever created to support economic and social development.

Organisation

Headquarters: Washington, DC, USA. The Bank also has offices in all its borrowing member countries, as well as in Paris and Tokyo that facilitate contacts in those regions.

Membership: 26 borrowing member countries in Latin America and the Caribbean, and 20 non-borrowing countries, including the United States, Japan, Canada, 16 European countries, and Israel. The 46 member countries are Argentina, Austria, Bahamas, Barbados, Belgium, Belize, Bolivia, Brazil, Canada, Chile, Colombia, Costa Rica, Croatia, Denmark, Dominican Republic, Ecuador, El Salvador, Finland, France, Germany, Guatemala, Guyana, Haiti, Honduras, Israel, Italy, Jamaica, Japan, Mexico, Netherlands, Nicaragua, Norway, Panama, Paraguay, Peru, Portugal, Slovenia, Spain, Suriname, Sweden, Switzerland, Trinidad and Tobago, United Kingdom, United States, Uruguay and Venezuela.

President: Enrique V. Iglesias (from Uruguay), who was re-elected president of the Inter-American Development Bank on 8 November 2002. He began his fourth five-year term on 1 April 2003.

Functions

Principal source of multilateral financing for economic, social and institutional development projects in Latin America and the Caribbean. These include policy and sector reform programmes and support for public and private investment. The Bank provides loans and technical assistance using capital provided by its member countries, as well as resources obtained in world capital markets through bond issues. The Bank also promotes and participates in a significant number of projects, co-financing arrangements with other multilateral, bilateral and private organisations. In its four decades of operations, the Bank has helped to transform Latin America and the Caribbean. Although much remains to be done, the region's social and economic indicators have improved significantly in such areas as literacy, nutrition and life expectancy.

North Atlantic Treaty Organisation (NATO)

Origin

NATO was established through the North Atlantic Treaty signed on 4 April 1949.

Organisation

Headquarters: Brussels, Belgium.
Membership: 19 countries: Belgium, Canada, Czech Republic, Denmark, France, Germany, Greece, Hungary, Iceland, Italy, Luxembourg, Netherlands, Norway, Poland, Portugal, Spain, Turkey, United Kingdom and United States.
Secretary-General: Jakob Gijsbert (Jaap) de Hoop Scheffer from the Netherlands, since 2004.

Functions

In accordance with the North Atlantic Treaty, the fundamental role of NATO is to safeguard the freedom and security of its member countries by political and military means. During the last fifteen years, NATO has also played an increasingly important role in crisis management and peacekeeping.

All member countries that participate in the military aspect of the Alliance contribute forces and equipment, which together constitute the integrated military structure of the Alliance. These forces and assets remain under national command and control until a time when they are required by NATO for a specific purpose (i.e. conflict or crisis, peacekeeping). NATO, however, does possess some common capabilities owned and operated by the Alliance, such as the AWACS early warning radar aircraft.

Member nations allocate the resources needed to enable NATO to function on a day-to-day basis. There are three budgets: one civil and two military. Each NATO member country pays an amount into the budgets based on an agreed cost-sharing formula. Taken together, these budgets represent less than half of 1 per cent of the total defence budget expenditures of NATO countries.

Organisation for Economic Cooperation and Development (OECD)

Origin

The OECD grew out of the Organisation for European Economic Co-operation (OEEC), which was formed to administer American and Canadian aid under the Marshall Plan for the reconstruction of Europe after the Second World War. Since it took over from the OEEC in 1961, the OECD's vocation has been to build strong economies in its member countries, improve efficiency, hone market systems, expand free trade and contribute to development in industrialised as well as developing countries. In recent years the OECD has moved beyond a focus on its member countries to offer its analytical expertise and accumulated experience to developing and emerging market economies.

Organisation

Headquarters: Paris, France.
Membership: 30 countries: Australia, Austria, Belgium, Canada, Czech Republic, Denmark, Finland, France, Germany, Greece, Hungary, Iceland, Ireland, Italy, Japan, Korea, Luxembourg, Mexico, Netherlands, New Zealand, Norway, Poland, Portugal, Slovak Republic, Spain, Sweden, Switzerland, Turkey, United Kingdom, United States.
Secretary-General: Donald J. Johnston from Canada, since 1 June 1996.

Functions

The OECD groups 30 member countries in a forum to discuss, develop and refine economic and social policies. They compare experiences, seek answers to common problems and work to coordinate domestic and international policies to help members and non-members deal with an increasingly globalised world. Their exchanges may lead to agreements to act in a formal way – for example by establishing legally binding agreements to crack down on bribery, or codes for free flow of capital and services. The OECD is also known for 'soft law' – non-binding instruments on difficult issues such as its guidelines for multinational enterprises. Beyond agreements, the discussions at the OECD make for better-informed work within member countries' own governments across the broad spectrum of public policy and help clarify the impact of national policies on the international community.

Exchanges between OECD governments flow from information and analysis provided by a Secretariat in Paris. Parts of the Secretariat collect data, monitor trends, analyse and forecast economic developments, while others research social changes or evolving patterns in trade, environment, agriculture, technology, taxation and more.

Bank of International Settlements (BIS)

Origin

BIS is the world's oldest financial organisation. It was established in the context of the Young Plan (1930), which dealt with the issue of the reparation payments imposed on Germany by the Treaty of Versailles following the First World War. The new bank was to take over the functions previously performed by the Agent General for Reparations in Berlin: collection, administration and distribution of the annuities payable as reparations. The Bank's name is derived from this original role. The BIS was also created to act as a trustee for the Dawes and Young Loans (international loans issued to finance reparations) and to promote central bank cooperation in general. The reparations issue quickly faded, focusing the Bank's activities entirely on cooperation among central banks and, increasingly, other agencies in pursuit of monetary and financial stability.

Organisation

Headquarters: Basel, Switzerland. The BIS also has two representative offices: in the Hong Kong Special Administrative Region of the People's Republic of China and in Mexico City.
Membership: Members are the central banks or monetary authorities of 55 countries: Algeria, Argentina, Australia, Austria, Belgium, Bosnia and Herzegovina, Brazil, Bulgaria, Canada, Chile, China, Croatia, the Czech Republic, Denmark, Estonia, Finland, France, Germany, Greece, Hong Kong SAR, Hungary, Iceland, India, Indonesia, Ireland, Israel, Italy, Japan, Korea, Latvia, Lithuania, the Republic of Macedonia, Malaysia, Mexico, the Netherlands, New Zealand, Norway, the Philippines, Poland, Portugal, Romania, Russia, Saudi Arabia, Singapore, Slovakia, Slovenia, South Africa, Spain, Sweden, Switzerland, Thailand, Turkey, the United Kingdom and the United States, plus the European Central Bank.
Management: The General Manager of the BIS is

Malcolm D Knight and the Deputy General Manager is André Icard.

The BIS currently has 55 member central banks, all of which are entitled to be represented and vote in the General Meetings. Voting power is proportionate to the number of BIS shares issued in the country of each member represented at the meeting.

Functions

The Bank for International Settlements is an international organisation which fosters international monetary and financial cooperation and serves as a bank for central banks.

The BIS fulfils this mandate by acting as:

- a forum to promote discussion and facilitate decision-making processes among central banks and within the international financial community
- a centre for economic and monetary research
- a prime counterparty for central banks in their financial transactions
- agent or trustee in connection with international financial operations.

North Atlantic Free Trade Agreement (NAFTA)

Origin

NAFTA was preceded by an agreement between the United States and Canada entitled the US-Canada Free Trade Agreement, which was enacted on 1 January 1989, but has been superseded by the NAFTA since 1 January 1994.

Organisation

Membership: United States, Canada, Mexico.
Headquarters: Caratina L. Alston, Secretary, NAFTA Secretariat US Section
14th Suite 2061, Constitution, Ave. Washington DC
Secretary: Françoy Raynauld, NAFTA Secretariat Canada Section
90 Sparks Street, Suite 705, Ottawa ON, K1P 5B4
Secretariado del TLCAN Seccion Mexicana
Blvd. Adolfo López Mateos 3025, 2° Piso, Col. Héroes de Padierna. C.P. 10700, Mexico, D

The cabinet-level Ministerial Council is the highest level of authority of the Commission and comprises the three labour Ministers of each country. It acts as the governing body of the Commission and directs the actions of the Secretariat. It meets at least once a year in regular session and can meet more times by request of any country.

NAFTA requires each Member State to set up three National Administrative Offices in the Labor Ministry of each country. A Secretary, designated by each government, is responsible for the administration and management. This is the NAFTA Secretariat and its primary function is to assist the Free Trade Commission in its work and to administer the dispute settlement procedures. The NAFTA Secretariat is comprised of a Canadian section located in Ottawa, a Mexican section, located in Mexico City and a USA section located in Washington, DC.

Functions

The objectives of this Agreement, including national treatment, most-favoured-nation treatment and transparency are to: (a) eliminate barriers to trade in, and facilitate the cross border movement of, goods and services between the territories of the Parties; (b) promote conditions of fair competition in the free trade area; (c) increase substantially investment opportunities in their territories; (d) provide adequate and effective protection and enforcement of intellectual property rights in each Party's territory; (e) create effective procedures for the implementation and application of this Agreement, and for its joint administration and the resolution of disputes; and (f) establish a framework for further trilateral, regional and multilateral cooperation to expand and enhance the benefits of this Agreement.

Western European Union (WEU)

Origin

WEU was created by the Treaty on Economic, Social and Cultural Collaboration and Collective Self-Defense signed at Brussels on 17 March 1948 (the Brussels Treaty), as amended by the Protocol signed at Paris on 23 October 1954, which modified and completed it. The Brussels Treaty was signed by Belgium, France, Luxembourg, the Netherlands and the United Kingdom. Conceived largely as a response to Soviet moves to impose control over the countries of Central Europe, the Treaty represented the first attempt to translate into practical arrangements some of the ideals of the European movement. Its main feature was the commitment to mutual defence should any of the signatories be the victim of an armed attack in Europe.

In 1999 the EU voted to absorb all the functions of the WEU in preparation for making the EU a defensive and peacekeeping military organisation as well as a social and economic one.

Organisation

Membership: 10 Member States (Brussels, 1954). Belgium France, Luxembourg, Netherlands, Germany, Portugal, Greece, Spain, United Kingdom, Italy; 6 Associate members (Rome, 1992) Poland, Hungary, Iceland, Turkey, Czech Republic, Norway; 5 Observers (Rome, 1992) Austria, Ireland, Denmark, Sweden, Finland; 7 Associate Partners (Kirchberg , 1994); Bulgaria Estonia, Slovenia, Latvia, Slovakia, Lithuania, Romania.

Headquarters: Brussels, Belgium.

Management (key officers): Dr Javier Solana (WEU Secretary-General) He simultaneously serves as the High Representative for the CFSP (Common Force and Security Policy) and Secretary-General of the Council of the EU. Jacomet Arnaud (Head of Secretariat). Roland Wegener (Deputy Secretary General).

Functions

The Western European Union (WEU) was designated as the defence arm of the European Community (not the European Union, or EU) at the Maastricht Conference in 1991. The WEU has a nascent command staff, and modest forces at its disposal. The European Union at its Intergovernmental Conference held in 1996 addressed the next stage of EU integration and discussed plans for a common foreign and security policy. In 1999, consequently, the EU voted to absorb all the functions of the WEU in preparation for making the EU a defensive and peacekeeping military organisation, as well as, a social and economic one.

Southern Common Market (MERCOSUR)

Origin

Mercosur, the Southern Common Market, was formed by the Treaty of Asunción signed on 26 March 1991, involving Argentina, Brazil, Paraguay and Uruguay, and came into effect on 31 November 1991. The Southern Cone Common Market was established as a Latin American trade organisation to increase economic cooperation among the countries of

South America. Mercosur was significantly weakened by the collapse of the Argentine economy in 2002.

Mercosur is one of South America's two main trade blocs (the other one being the Andean Community, of Bolivia, Colombia, Ecuador, Peru and Venezuela). Mercosur and the Andean Community began negotiations in 1999 towards a merger of the two groupings, with the potential of creating a South American Free Trade Area (SAFTA). At the Third South American Summit on 8 December 2004 presidents or representatives from twelve S. American states signed the *Cuzco Declaration*, a two-page statement of intent, announcing the foundation and the merger of the two trading blocs of the South American states. It will be a continent-wide free trade zone that will unite two existing free trade organisations. Complete integration between these two trade blocs is expected by 2007. Leaders announced their intention to model the new community after the European Union including a common currency, parliament, and passport.

Organisation

Headquarters: Montevideo, Uruguay.

Membership: Brazil, Argentina, Paraguay and Uruguay.

Management: The presidency, or chair, of MERCOSUR rotates every six months among the member countries. The Presidents of the member countries have a great impact on the direction of the organisation.

■ Council of the Common Market (CMC): This is the highest body, responsible for the political aspects of the integration process. Composed of the foreign and economic ministers of the members, the CMC is a decision-making body

■ Common Market Group (GMC): the executive body of MERCOSUR, and is coordinated by the Ministries of Foreign Affairs of the Member States.

■ Administrative Secretariat of MERCOSUR: The Secretariat is responsible for providing services to the various MERCOSUR institutions, such as keeping an official archive of documents and adopted decisions.

Functions

Mercosur also has the role of helping each member country to attract foreign investors as well as to develop joint projects in energy, especially in relation to natural gas and transmission lines, as well as in transport and telecommunications. Following the trend set by the European Union, Mercosur's role is not restricted to trade. It has also a mandate to facilitate the cooperation in many cultural and political aspects. Another role of Mercosur is to help member countries to overcome their internal problems such as those linked with public administration and the control of inflation.

Organisation for Security and Cooperation in Europe (OSCE)

Origin

The OSCE was established as the Conference on Security and Cooperation in Europe (CSCE) in 1973, during the cold war, to promote East-West cooperation. The CSCE's 1975 meeting in Helsinki, Finland, ratified the acts commonly known as the Helsinki Accords, which were signed by every European nation (except Albania, which did so later) and the United States and Canada. The OSCE is responsible for reviewing the implementation of those accords. Since the end of the cold war, it has also aimed to foster peace, prosperity, and justice in Europe.

Organisation

Membership: Albania, Germany, Andorra, Armenia, Austria, Azerbaijan, Belgium, Belarus, Bosnia and Herzegovina, Bulgaria, Canada, Cyprus, Croatia, Denmark, Spain, Estonia, USA, Finland, France, Georgia, Hungary, Ireland, Iceland, Italy, Kazakstan, Latvia, Liechtenstein, Lithuania, Luxembourg, Macedonia, Malta, Moldavia, Monaco, Norway, Uzbekistan, Netherlands, Poland, Portugal, Czech Republic, Romania, United Kingdom, Russia, Saint Marin, Holy See, Slovakia, Slovenia, Sweden, Switzerland, Tajikistan, Turkey, Ukraine, Yugoslavia.

Headquarters: Vienna, Austria.

Management: The Secretary General acts as the OSCE Chief Administrative Officer. Ambassador Ján Kubis, of Slovakia, is the present Secretary General of the OSCE. The Secretariat encompasses the following structures: Office of the Secretary General, Conflict Prevention Centre, Strategic Police Matters Unit, Department of Management and Finance, Department of Human Resources,

Coordinator of OSCE Economic and Environmental Activities, Prague Office of the Secretariat, Anti-Trafficking Assistance Unit.

Name of Current Head: Dr Dimitrij Rupel, Minister of Foreign Affairs of Slovenia

Slovenia holds the OSCE Chairmanship in 2005.The Chairmanship rotates annually, and the post of the Chairman-in-Office (CiO) is held by the Foreign Minister of an OSCE participating State.

Functions

OSCE is the largest regional security organisation in the world with 55 participating states from Europe, Central Asia and North America. It is active in early warning, conflict prevention, crisis management and post-conflict rehabilitation.

The OSCE approach to security is comprehensive and cooperative: comprehensive in dealing with a wide range of security-related issues including arms control, preventive diplomacy, confidence- and security-building measures, human rights, democratisation, election monitoring and economic and environmental security; cooperative in the sense that all OSCE participating States have equal status, and decisions are based on consensus.

Economic Community of West African States (ECOWAS)

Origin

The Economic Community of West African States (ECOWAS) was created on May 28, 1975 in Lagos, Nigeria. At the Abuja Summit in 1999, the ECOWAS Mechanism for Conflict Prevention, Management, Resolution and Security was signed, and it significantly organized the peace-keeping capabilities of ECOWAS.

Organisation

Membership: Benin, Burkina Faso, Cape Verde, Côte d'Ivoire, Gambia, Ghana, Guinea, Guinea-Bissau, Liberia, Mali, Niger, Nigeria, Senegal, Sierra Leone, and Togo.

Headquarters: Lome, Republic of Togo. The Secretariat is in Abuja, Nigeria.

Management: President Mamadou Tandja of Niger is the current ECOWAS Chairman.

Its bodies are the Authority of Heads of State and Government; the Council of Ministers; the Community Parliament (120 seats); the Economic and Social Council; the Community Court of Justice; the Executive Secretariat; the Mediation and Security Council [established by the Mechanism] and the fund for Cooperation, Compensation and Development.

Functions

ECOWAS was established to promote cooperation and integration in order to create an economic and monetary union for promoting economic growth and development in West Africa. Although originally formed as a regional trade bloc, its functions are primarily security, having intervened mainly in Liberia and Côte d'Ivoire.

League of Arab Nations

Origin

The Arab League was founded in Cairo in 1945 by Egypt, Iraq, Lebanon, Saudi Arabia, Syria, Transjordan (Jordan, as of 1950), and Yemen. Countries that later joined are: Algeria (1962), Bahrain (1971), Comoros (1993), Djibouti (1977), Kuwait (1961), Libya (1953), Mauritania (1973), Morocco (1958), Oman (1971), Qatar (1971), Somalia (1974), Southern Yemen (1967), Sudan (1956), Tunisia (1958), and the United Arab Emirates (1971). The Palestine Liberation Organisation was admitted in 1976. Egypt's membership was suspended in 1979 after it signed a peace treaty with Israel; the league's headquarters was moved from Cairo, Egypt, to Tunis, Tunisia. In 1987 Arab leaders decided to renew diplomatic ties with Egypt. Egypt was readmitted to the league in 1989 and the league's headquarters was moved back to Cairo.

Organisation

Membership: Jordan, United Arab Emirates, Bahrain, Tunisia, Algeria, Djibouti, Saudi Arabia, Sudan, Syria, Somalia, Iraq, Oman, Palestine, Qatar, Comoros, Kuwait, Lebanon, Libya, Egypt, Morocco.

Management: The Egyptian Amre M. Moussa is the Secretary-General. The Council of the Arab League is the supreme authority within the League system.

Headquarters: Cairo, Egypt.

Functions

The Arab League is an organisation of mostly Arabic-speaking countries whose main stated purposes are to strengthen ties among the Member States, coordinate their policies, and promote their common interests. The Arab League is involved in political, economic, cultural, and social programs designed to promote the interests of Member States. The Arab League has served as a forum for Member States to coordinate their policy positions and deliberate on matters of common concern, settling some Arab disputes and limiting conflicts such as the Lebanese civil wars of 1958. The Arab League has served as a platform for the drafting and conclusion of almost all landmark documents promoting economic integration among Member States, such as the creation of the Joint Arab Economic Action Charter, which set out the principles for economic activities of the league. It has played an important role in shaping school curricula, and preserving manuscripts and Arab cultural heritage. The Arab League has launched literacy campaigns, and reproduced intellectual works, and translated modern technical terminology for the use of Member States. The Arab League has also fostered cultural exchanges between Member States, encouraged youth and sports programmes, helped to advance the role of women in Arab societies, and promoted child welfare activities.

Council of Europe[1]

Origin

The Council of Europe is the continent's oldest political organisation, founded in 1949 by the Treaty of London.

Organisation

Headquarters: Strasbourg, France.
Membership: 46 countries, including 21 countries from Central and Eastern Europe. Five more countries: the United States, Canada, Japan, Mexico and the Holy See have observer status. Belarus' application is under consideration.
Management: Secretary-General Terry Davis, from the United Kingdom (since September 2004).

The main component parts of the Council of Europe are:

- the Committee of Ministers, composed of the 46 Foreign ministers or their Strasbourg-based deputies (ambassadors/permanent representatives), which is the Organisation's decision-making body
- the Parliamentary Assembly, grouping 630 members (315 representatives and 315 substitutes) from the 46 national parliaments. The current President is René van der Linden (the Netherlands, EPP/CD)
- the Congress of Local and Regional Authorities, composed of a Chamber of Local Authorities and a Chamber of Regions. Its current President is Giovanni Di Stasi (SOC, Italy).

Functions

The Council was set up to:

- defend human rights, parliamentary democracy and the rule of law
- develop continent-wide agreements to standardise member countries' social and legal practices
- promote awareness of a European identity based on shared values and cutting across different cultures.

Since 1989, its main job has become:

- acting as a political anchor and human rights watchdog for Europe's post-communist democracies
- assisting the countries of central and eastern Europe in carrying out and consolidating political, legal and constitutional reform in parallel with economic reform
- providing know-how in areas such as human rights, local democracy, education, culture and the environment.

International Criminal Court (ICC)

Origin

The International Criminal Court was created in July 1998 when 120 countries signed its foundational treaty in Rome, Italy. The Rome Statute entered into force in 2002, upon ratification of 60 countries. After the election of judges and the chief prosecutor, the Court was officially inaugurated as a functioning body in 2003, and is already conducting investigations

---

1. The European Court of Human Rights is connected to the Council of Europe.

in Uganda and the Democratic Republic of Congo.

Organisation

Headquarters: The Hague, Netherlands.
Membership: Currently the Rome Statute of the ICC has 139 signatories and 97 ratifications.
Management: Argentinean Luis Moreno Ocampo is the first Chief Prosecutor.

The Court is composed of the following organs: the Presidency; the Chambers (Appeals Chamber, Trial Chamber, Pre-Trial Chamber); the Office of the Prosecutor; the Registry.

Functions

The ICC is the first permanent international tribunal with jurisdiction over individuals accused of committing genocide, crimes against humanity or massive war crimes. An investigation can be initiated by the chief prosecutor, the United Nations Security Council, or any Member State as long as the accused is a national of that country or has committed the crime in the country's territory.

Cooperation Council for the Arab States of the Persian Gulf (formerly Persian Gulf Cooperation Council, GCC)

Origin

Created on 25 May 1981 in Abu Dhabi, Kuwait, with the general purpose of addressing economic and security challenges in the area and promote Arab regional unity.

Organisation

Membership: Kuwait, Qatar, Oman, Saudi Arabia, Bahrain, United Arab Emirates.
Headquarters: Riyadh, Saudi Arabia.
Management: The Supreme Council is the highest authority of the GCC, and it is formed by the Heads of Member States. Its presidency rotates according to the Arabic alphabetical order of the names of Member States. Resolutions on substantive matters are issued by unanimous approval of the members present, while a majority is enough to approve those of procedural nature.

Functions

The GCC Charter states that the basic objectives are to effect coordination, integration and interconnection between Member States in all fields, strengthening ties between their peoples, formulating similar regulations in various fields such as economy, finance, trade, customs, tourism, legislation, administration, as well as fostering scientific and technical progress in industry, mining, agriculture, water and animal resources, establishing scientific research centres, setting up joint ventures, and encouraging cooperation of the private sector.

Common Market for Eastern and Southern Africa (COMESA)

Origin

The history of COMESA began in December 1994 when it was formed to replace the former Preferential Trade Area (PTA) which had existed from the earlier days of 1981. COMESA (as defined by its Treaty) was established 'as an organisation of free independent sovereign states which have agreed to co-operate in developing their natural and human resources for the good of all their people' and as such it has a wide-ranging series of objectives which necessarily include in its priorities the promotion of peace and security in the region. However, due to COMESA's economic history and background its main focus is on the formation of a large economic and trading unit that is capable of overcoming some of the barriers that are faced by individual states.

Organisation

Membership: 21 countries. Angola, Burundi, Comoros, Democratic Republic of Congo, Djibouti, Egypt, Eritrea, Ethiopia, Kenya, Madagascar, Malawi, Mauritius, Namibia, Rwanda, Seychelles, Sudan, Swaziland, Uganda, Zambia, Zimbabwe.
Headquarters: The Secretariat is located in Lusaka, Zambia.

Several institutions have been created to promote sub-regional cooperation and development. These include:

- The COMESA Trade and Development Bank in Nairobi, Kenya
- The COMESA Clearing House in Harare, Zimbabwe
- The COMESA Association of Commercial Banks in Harare, Zimbabwe
- The COMESA Leather Institute in Ethiopia
- The COMESA Re-Insurance Company (ZEP-RE) in Nairobi, Kenya.

In addition a Court of Justice was also established under the COMESA Treaty and became formally operational in 1998.

Management: COMESA has evolved a comprehensive decision making structure at the top of which are the heads of state of the 21 member countries. There is then a Council of Ministers responsible for policy making, 12 technical committees and a series of other advisory bodies (including specific relations with partner countries and the business community).

Currently, the Secretary General is Erastus J. O. Mwencha, and the Chairperson of Authority of Heads of State and Government is Ugandan Yoweri Museveni.

Functions

COMESA's stated goals are the implementation of a free trade through removal of all internal trade tariffs and barriers; introduction of a common external tariff structure to deal with all third party trade; trade promotion through trade liberalization, customs cooperation, harmonization of macro-economic and monetary policies throughout the region.

The United Nations System of Organisations (in alphabetical order)

- United Nations System Chief Executives Board for Coordination (CEB) – New York, USA.
- Comprehensive Nuclear-Test-Ban Treaty Organisation (CTBTO) (Preparatory Commission) – Vienna, Austria.
- United Nations CyberSchoolBus – New York, USA.
- Administrative Committee on Coordination (ACC) (now CEB) and its former Subcommittees
- Economic Commission for Africa (ECA) – Addis Ababa, Ethiopia
- Economic Commission for Europe (ECE) – Geneva, Switzerland
- Economic Commission for Latin America and the Caribbean (ECLAC) – Santiago, Chile
- Economic and Social Commission for Asia and the Pacific (ESCAP) – Bangkok, Thailand
- Economic and Social Commission for Western Asia (ESCWA) – Beirut, Lebanon
- Food and Agriculture Organisation of the United Nations (FAO) – Rome, Italy
- Global Programme on Globalization, Liberalization and Sustainable Human Development – Geneva, Switzerland [UNCTAD-UNDP]
- High Level Comittee on Management (HLCM) – Geneva, Switzerland
- High Level Comittee on Programmes (HLCP) – Geneva, Switzerland
- Integrated Regional Information Networks (IRIN) – Nairobi, Kenya [OCHA]
- Inter-Agency Meeting on Sustainable Development (IAMSD) (former IACSD) – New York, USA
- Inter-Agency Network on Women and Gender Equality (IANWGE) (former IACWGE) – New York, USA
- Inter-Agency Procurement Services Office (IAPSO) – Copenhagen, Denmark
- Inter-Agency Working Group on Evaluation (IAWG) – New York, USA
- International Atomic Energy Agency (IAEA) – Vienna, Austria
- International Bank for Reconstruction and Development (IBRD) – Washington, USA [World Bank Group]
- International Bureau of Education (IBE) – Geneva, Switzerland [UNESCO]
- International Centre for Genetic Engineering and Biotechnology (ICGEB) – Trieste, Italy [UNIDO]
- International Centre for Science and High Technology (ICS) – Trieste, Italy [UNIDO]
- International Centre for Settlement of Investment Disputes (ICSID) – Washington, USA [World Bank Group]
- Abdus Salam International Centre for Theoretical Physics (ICTP) – Trieste, Italy [UNESCO/IAEA]
- International Civil Aviation Organisation (ICAO) – Montreal, Canada
- International Civil Service Commission (ICSC) – New York, USA
- International Computing Centre (ICC) – Geneva, Switzerland
- International Court of Justice (ICJ) – The Hague, The Netherlands
- International Criminal Tribunal for the Former Yugoslavia (ICTY) – The Hague, The Netherlands
- International Criminal Tribunal for Rwanda (ICTR) – Arusha, Tanzania
- International Fund for Agricultural Development (IFAD) – Rome, Italy
- International Institute for Educational Planning (IIEP) – Paris, France [UNESCO]
- International Institute on Ageing (INIA) –

Valetta, Malta

- International Labour Organisation (ILO) – Geneva, Switzerland
- International Maritime Organisation (IMO) – London, UK
- International Monetary Fund (IMF) – Washington, USA
- International Research and Training Institute for the Advancement of Women (INSTRAW) – Santo Domingo, Dominican Republic
- International Seabed Authority (ISA) – Kingston, Jamaica
- International Strategy for Disaster Reduction (ISDR) – Geneva, Switzerland
- International Telecommunication Union (ITU) – Geneva, Switzerland
- International Trade Centre (ITC) – Geneva, Switzerland [UNCTAD/WTO]
- International Training Centre of the ILO (ITC/ILO) – Turin, Italy
- Joint Inspection Unit (JIU) – Geneva, Switzerland
- Joint Inter-Agency Meeting on Computer-Assisted Translation and Terminology (JIAMCATT) – Geneva, Switzerland
- Joint United Nations Programme on HIV/AIDS (UNAIDS) – Geneva, Switzerland
- Media and Peace Institute (University for peace) – Paris, France
- Multilateral Investment Guarantee Agency (MIGA) – Washington, USA [World Bank Group]
- United Nations Non-Governmental Liaison Service (NGLS) – Geneva, Switzerland and New York, USA
- Office for the Coordination of Humanitarian Affairs (OCHA) – Geneva, Switzerland
- Office for Outer Space Affairs (OOSA) – Vienna, Austria
- Organisation for the Prohibition of Chemical Weapons (OPCW) – The Hague, The Netherlands
- Panel of External Auditors of the United Nations, the Specialized Agencies and the International Atomic Energy Agency – New York, USA
- ReliefWeb – Geneva, Switzerland [OCHA]
- United Nations System Standing Committee on Nutrition (SCN) (formerly ACC Subcommittee on Nutrition) – Geneva, Switzerland
- United Nations (UN) – New York, USA
- United Nations Atlas of the Oceans –

Washington, USA

- United Nations Board of Auditors – New York, USA
- United Nations Children's Fund (UNICEF) – New York, USA
- United Nations Commission on International Trade Law (UNCITRAL) – Vienna, Austria
- United Nations Common Supplier Database (UNCSD) – Oslo, Norway
- United Nations Communications Group (former JUNIC) – New York, USA
- United Nations Compensation Commission (UNCC) – Geneva, Switzerland
- United Nations Conference on Trade and Development (UNCTAD) – Geneva, Switzerland
- United Nations Convention to Combat Desertification (UNCCD) – Bonn, Germany
- United Nations International Drug Control Programme (UNDCP) (now UNODC)- Vienna, Austria
- United Nations Development Fund for Women (UNIFEM) – New York, USA
- United Nations Development Group (UNDG) – New York, USA
- United Nations Development Programme (UNDP) – New York, USA
- United Nations Educational, Scientific and Cultural Organisation (UNESCO) – Paris, France
- United Nations Environment Programme (UNEP) – Nairobi, Kenya
- United Nations Framework Convention on Climate Change (UNFCCC) – Bonn, Germany
- United Nations Fund for International Partnerships (UNFIP) – New York, USA
- United Nations Geographic Information Working Group (UNGIWG) – New York, USA
- United Nations High Commissioner for Human Rights, Office of the (OHCHR) – Geneva, Switzerland
- United Nations High Commissioner for Refugees, Office of the (UNHCR) – Geneva, Switzerland
- United Nations Human Settlements Programme (UN-Habitat)- Nairobi, Kenya
- United Nations Industrial Development Organisation (UNIDO) – Vienna, Austria
- United Nations Information and Communication Technologies Task Force (UNICT TF) – New York, USA
- United Nations Institute for Disarmament Research (UNIDIR) – Geneva, Switzerland

- United Nations Institute for Training and Research (UNITAR) – Geneva, Switzerland
- United Nations International School (UNIS) – New York, USA
- United Nations Interregional Crime and Justice Research Institute (UNICRI) – Rome, Italy
- United Nations Joint Staff Pension Fund (UNJSPF) – New York, USA
- United Nations Mine Action Service – New York, USA
- United Nations Office on Drugs and Crime (UNODC) (formely UNDCP) – Vienna, Austria
- United Nations Office at Geneva (UNOG) – Geneva, Switzerland
- United Nations Office at Nairobi (UNON) – Nairobi, Kenya
- United Nations Office at Vienna (UNOV) – Vienna, Austria
- United Nations Office for Project Services (UNOPS) – New York, USA
- United Nations Population Fund (UNFPA) – New York, USA
- United Nations Postal Administration (UNPA) – Vienna, Austria
- United Nations Relief and Works Agency for Palestine Refugees in the Near East (UNRWA) – Gaza, Gaza Strip and Amman, Jordan
- United Nations Research Institute for Social Development (UNRISD) – Geneva, Switzerland
- United Nations Resident Coordinators Network (RCNet) – New York, USA
- UN System Network on Rural Development and Food Security – Rome, Italy [FAO/IFAD]
- United Nations System Staff College (UNSSC) – Turin, Italy
- United Nations University (UNU) – Tokyo, Japan
- United Nations Volunteers (UNV) – Bonn, Germany
- Universal Postal Union (UPU) – Bern, Switzerland
- University for Peace (UPEACE) – San Jose, Costa Rica
- WomenWatch – New York, USA
- World Bank Group – Washington, USA
- World Food Programme (WFP) – Rome, Italy
- World Health Organisation (WHO) – Geneva, Switzerland
- World Intellectual Property Organisation (WIPO) – Geneva, Switzerland
- World Meteorological Organisation (WMO) – Geneva, Switzerland
- World Tourism Organisation – Madrid, Spain
- World Trade Organisation (WTO) – Geneva, Switzerland
- World Volunteer Web – Bonn, Germany [UNV]

Source: http://www.unsystem.org.

Sources

The information on IGOs in this chapter was derived from the following sources:

www.wto.org
www.worldbank.org
www.imf.org
www.un.org
www.oas.org
www.opec.org
www.aseansec.org
www.apecsec.org.sg
www.ecowas-fund.org
www.bis.org
www.oecd.org
www.nato.int
www.iadb.org
www.caricom.org
www.europa.eu.int
www.african-uinon.org
www.icc-cpi.int
www.coe.int
www.comesa.int
www.arableagueonline.org
www.gcc-sg.org

International comparisons of defence expenditure and military manpower, 2001–2003

Country	Ranking	Defence expenditures (2003 data)	% GDP	Country	Ranking	Defence expenditures (2003 data)	% GDP
United States	1	404,920	3.7	Kuwait	30	3794	9.4
Russia	2	65,200	4.9	Switzerland	31	3486	1.1
China – Mainland	3	55,948	3.9	Denmark	32	3334	1.6
France	4	45,695	2.6	Colombia	33	3234	4.2
Japan	5	42,835	1.0	Portugal	34	3173	2.1
United Kingdom	6	42,782	2.4	Pakistan	35	3129	4.5
Germany	7	35,145	1.5	Iran	36	3051	2.4
Italy	8	27,751	1.9	Mexico	37	2938	0.5
Saudi Arabia	9	18,747	8.9	Vietnam	38	2901	7.4
India	10	15,508	2.6	Egypt	39	2732	4.0
South Korea	11	14,632	2.8	South Africa	40	2633	1.6
Australia	12	11,758	2.3	Chile	41	2537	3.9
Turkey	13	11,649	4.9	Austria	42	2488	1.0
Israel	14	10,325	9.5	Oman	43	2468	11.6
Canada	15	10,118	1.2	Malaysia	44	2412	2.3
Spain	16	9944	1.2	Belarus	45	2400	4.0
Brazil	17	9274	1.8	Finland	46	2300	1.4
Netherlands	18	8256	1.6	Algeria	47	2206	3.4
Greece	19	7169	4.1	Uzbekistan	48	2200	5.0
Indonesia	20	6443	3.0	Argentina	49	2030	1.5
China – Taiwan	21	6632	2.4	Thailand	50	1931	1.3
Myanmar	22	6260	9.6	Qatar	51	1923	10.0
Sweden	23	5532	1.8	Czech Republic	52	1871	2.2
North Korea	24	5500	25.0	Morocco	53	1826	4.2
Ukraine	25	5500	2.1	United Arab Emirates	54	1642	2.1
Singapore	26	4741	5.2	Hungary	55	1589	1.9
Norway	27	4387	2.0	Syria	56	1522	7.0
Poland	28	4095	2.0	Kazakhstan	57	1500	1.5
Belgium	29	3923	1.3	Romania	58	1313	2.3

(continued)

Country	Ranking	Defence expenditures (2003 data)	% GDP	Country	Ranking	Defence expenditures (2003 data)	% GDP
Venezuela	59	1283	1.5	Luxembourg	91	233	0.9
Cuba	60	1200	4.0	Kyrgyzstan	92	220	2.6
New Zealand	61	1171	1.5	Latvia	93	194	1.9
Azerbaijan	62	950	3.2	Estonia	94	172	2.0
Peru	63	893	1.4	Cameroon	95	172	1.4
Jordan	64	886	8.7	Ivory Coast	96	172	1.2
Nigeria	65	835	1.8	Dominican Republic	97	162	1.0
Ireland	66	803	0.5	Bosnia-Herzegovina	98	152	2.2
Yemen	67	798	7.0	Moldova	99	150	2.4
Philippines	68	783	1,0	Tajikistan	100	150	2.1
Angola	69	750	5.7	Macedonia	101	137	3.1
Libya	70	742	4.2	Bolivia	102	131	1.7
Armenia	71	700	6.4	Congo	103	112	3.1
Bangladesh	72	645	1.2	Nepal	104	110	1.9
Ecuador	73	640	2.4	El Salvador	105	106	0.7
Slovakia	74	627	1.9	Namibia	106	105	2.3
Croatia	75	596	2.1	Zimbabwe	107	105	1.7
Sri Lanka	76	515	2.8	Uruguay	108	103	0.9
Lebanon	77	512	2.8	Guatemala	109	102	0.4
Tunisia	78	494	2.3	Costa Rica	110	101	0.6
Bulgaria	79	471	2.4	Panama	111	100	0.9
Sudan	80	426	2.7	Malta	112	95	2.1
Slovenia	81	378	1.4	Mozambique	113	93	2.2
Georgia	82	350	2.7	Senegal	114	86	1.4
Turkmenistan	83	350	1.2	Mali	115	81	1.8
Lithuania	84	342	1.8	Madagascar	116	81	1.5
Ethiopia	85	326	4.9	Albania	117	76	1.2
Botswana	86	304	3.8	Eritrea	118	73	9.2
Tanzania	87	301	3.1	Guinea	119	71	1.9
Cyprus	88	294	2.3	Rwanda	120	69	4.1
Brunei	89	259	5.1	Cambodia	121	68	1.7
Kenya	90	237	1.8	Bahrain	122	61	5.6

(continued)

Country	Ranking	Defence expenditures (2003 data)	% GDP	Country	Ranking	Defence expenditures (2003 data)	% GDP
Benin	123	60	1.6	Belize	146	19	2.4
Zambia	124	60	1.6	Mauritania	147	19	1.7
Burkina Faso	125	55	1.3	Papua New Guinea	148	19	0.5
Honduras	126	53	0.8	Sierra Leone	149	17	2.2
Jamaica	127	52	0.7	Mongolia	150	15	1.4
Liberia	128	45	11.4	Gabon	151	15	0.2
Burundi	129	42	7.2	Barbados	152	13	0.5
Maldives	130	40	6.4	Mauritius	153	13	0.2
Laos	131	38	2.0	Seychelles	154	12	1.6
Chad	132	34	1.3	Malawi	155	11	0.7
Fiji	133	33	1.5	Guinea Bissau	156	9	4.0
Togo	134	31	1.7	Suriname	157	8	0.7
Nicaragua	135	31	1.2	Equatorial Guinea	158	6	0.2
Central African Republic	136	29	2.3	Cape Verde	159	5	1.5
Bahamas	137	29	0.6	Guyana	160	5	0.7
Trinidad and Tobago	138	29	0.3	Antigua	161	4	0.6
Zambia	139	27	0.6	The Gambia	162	2	0.6
Lesotho	140	26	2.3	Iceland	163	0	0
Niger	141	25	1.0	Afghanistan		N.A.	N.A.
Djibouti	142	24	3.9	Democratic Republic of Congo		N.A.	N.A.
Ghana	143	23	0.3	Iraq		N.A.	N.A.
Bhutan	144	22	3.3	Sao Tome & Principe		N.A.	N.A.
Haiti	145	22	0.8	Serbia and Montenegro		N.A.	N.A.
				Swaziland		N.A.	N.A.

Source: International Institute for Strategic Studies, *The Military Balance: 2004–2005*, Oxford University Press, pp. 353–358

Part C

The Cast: Users of Power

CHAPTER 1: Context

The physical and geographical make-up of the world, its climates, its peoples, its resources, its production, create the theatre in which the great drama of global politics is played out. Inside the theatre, as with any play, the programme contains a list of the characters; these characters speak from a script which relates them to the topics of the play and there is a production which determines how they interact. This section introduces the characters chiefly involved in conducting global politics.

The order of the following chapters is alphabetical and thus makes no attempt to list the cast in an order of relative importance. This is chiefly because that order has sharply changed in recent times and because it is always on the move to some degree. However, we will begin now with states, the most difficult of contemporary characters to assess. They were once, not long ago, effectively the only characters on stage and had been for the 350 years since they chased all others away in early seventeenth-century Europe. This has given time for deeply ingrained attitudes to develop about them.

The very different backgrounds of the world's populations produce naturally different underlying assumptions about the likely nature of the conduct of politics. They exhibit this characteristic more in their own territory and in relationship to the government and administration of their own state than in considering the politics of the globe. This is partly because considering the politics of the world as such is a relatively new activity which followed soon after the emergence of global politics as we know them. It is also because global politics are the successors of international politics and international politics had been a part of everyone's world for a substantial slice of history – long enough to have acquired techniques, assumptions, machinery, staff and, above all, ingrained expectations and attitudes which were so deep-seated that they might not always be expressed. Moreover, international politics had also become part of academic studies, giving rise to a filigree of theoretical argument, creating a minor publishing industry and some vested interests in maintaining the subject beyond its natural shelf life. The result of this is that the attitudes derived from the conduct of international politics still form the natural reference point when most people consider global politics, however aware they may be that something has happened in recent years that has put intolerable stresses on traditional assumptions and mechanisms. Hence the continuing predominance of the assumption that states remain the principal participants in global politics.

States

Where and how did a world of states emerge? The answer is in Europe about 350 years ago. The refinement of its development was accompanied by the steady spread of European power across the globe and thus the institution spread with it until, by the early twentieth century, the state form had become the global norm. The most complex forms of political relationship and commercial and cultural exchange so far seen have developed over the past 300 years and have been the product of an era when most societies turned themselves into or aspired to become nation-states. Such evolutionary changes usually produced episodes of conflict and warfare. The study of these relationships, and particularly their occasional descent into violence, has become an intellectual discipline, rising to greater and greater sophistication as it has sought to understand more about the shifting sands of inter-state activities, economic, political and strategic. It is useful to remember this pattern because it lasted for so long that it came to be regarded as a given condition, an unchanging basis for discussion, an inalienable template by which to explain the affairs of states and their external relations. This in turn helps to throw light on why much muddle and anxiety has developed in the face of recent fundamental evolutionary shifts which have invalidated the template: these are the shifts in both power and the distribution of power which have come to be called globalisation.

Both the machinery of international relations and the fixed assumptions which societies have come to make about the likely consequences of their own or their government's actions have been shaped by the effects which technological change has had on the nature and distribution of power – economic and political. On the whole, the period from the middle of the nineteenth century to the later part of the twentieth can be seen as a single evolution, itself emerging from earlier and more geographically restricted versions of a similar structure, first in Northern Italy in the fifteenth century and then in Europe as a whole. In both these situations the principal propelling agent in the equations of power was the unfolding development of the state, both internally and externally. After about 300 years of continuous, expansionary activity, it is not surprising that the central role of the state itself, never mind what whirligigs of changing fortune might occur between them, became a fixed expectation, a given condition of the political life of humanity.

State functions

During the twentieth century, in addition to retaining its role as the only broadly accepted idea about how human societies should be organised, the state acquired the full panoply of administrative and political powers. Technological advances, particularly in communications, following the industrial revolution gave governments the ability to intervene effectively in the generation and implementation of social policy and populations the desire that they should do so. The degree and the manner of these interventions became the stuff of political dispute, both directly and indirectly, in the sense that state intervention is expensive and carries a second argument about levels and incidence of taxation. These developments led to an increase in popular participation in politics, fuelled in part by growing literacy and a burgeoning if sensationalist press. Suffrage was made largely universal and its significance was such that when non-democratic regimes developed in the 1920s and 1930s, they felt obliged to rig elections rather than forbid them. Their emergence was a response to the intensity of the problems inherent in governing industrialised societies, made worse by the consequences and experience of the 1914 war. So also was the extreme stress that came to the surface in liberal democracies at the time of the Great Depression and led to governments of national unity and the policies of The New Deal.

The rapid evolution of the functions of the state whether in the Soviet Union or elsewhere was further advanced by the extreme emergency of the Second World War. At its end, various questions that had troubled the first half of the century had been answered. It was clear that fascism had proved an unviable way of handling either the internal or external operations of a state and that communism and liberal democracy were left to fight it out. The result of the match emerged with dramatic suddenness in the 1990s, when communism withdrew from the ring. The competition was more than ideological because the war had also answered a question about the distribution of global power and the future management of international politics. The USA and the USSR had defeated any potential competitors for equal power within what had become a global system, and faced each other in an uncomfortable but stable stalemate for 50 years. Maintaining the viability of this arrangement became the focus of national security policies, the object of vast expenditure, the goal of immense quantities of scientific research and the basis of political rhetoric and electoral campaigning.

The result was the most complete dominance of the state form and, at the same time, the beginning of its end, as has been discussed in Part A. There was another consequence too: although there were gaps, quite large ones, between the size and efficiency of different states, the gaps were less significant than the similarities. This was only possible because until the 1960s and 1970s, the parts of the world which could not have joined the club of developed states were being administered by colonial or other proprietors. As empires were being dissolved into independent states, it did not occur to the successful leaders of independence movements that they would not create states of their own. The result, as has become clear in the last quarter century, was a contrast between spread and depth.

The idea of the state in a variety of forms was universal, but its roots varied greatly in their depth and stability. Under the stresses of the contemporary world, examples of states which tottered and sometimes collapsed have accumulated. A perceptible and growing weakness in the power and authority of states, ranging in degree from discomfort to failure, is not, however, the only significant fact affecting the relative roles of the actors in global politics. Equally important is the ending of the fact and expectation that states and their creations were the only actors on the stage. For reasons that will be further discussed, the stage now hosts other actors, different in style, appearance and experience. States may remain the most completely organised and familiar purveyors of administration and channels for the exercise of political power, but they now have to share authority in a plural global political and economic system.

The new or newer arrivals fall into three groups: associations of states or inter-governmental organisations (IGOs) – this group has the longest history and several sub-groups of which one, global economic organisations, is undergoing such significant contemporary evolution that it is becoming a separate group; global civil society, which consists of private entities often called non-governmental organisations (NGOs), though simply to name them for what they are not seems perverse given their importance; and transnational corporations.

Associations of states

The first associations of states were military alliances and they continue to exist, but not in the numbers or significance that they had up to and including the Cold War years. This is an unsurprising consequence of the decline in actual or anticipated inter-state war. One survivor has been the North Atlantic Treaty Organisation (NATO). Its original purpose of containing the Soviet Union has disappeared, leaving it with the strategic attitudes, the equipment and the structure to fight the kind of inter-alliance, high-tech war that is no longer going to happen. The alliance has scrambled to add to its membership and change its primary objectives so that they match the very different needs of Euro-Atlantic security in the age of collapsing states and the rising threat of terrorist attacks. It may or may not succeed, but its survival through the intense disagreements among its members about the 2004 war in Iraq suggests that it may.

Two other kinds of inter-governmental association developed during the nineteenth century: one attempted to manage what were then international politics so as to prevent war, and its contemporary manifestation is the United Nations (UN) and its accompanying system. These associations asserted the continuation of the full sovereign rights of member states because without doing so there would have been no members. But the inherent contradiction between maintaining those rights and the effectiveness of the organisation has remained a continuous difficulty and it affects the UN today. In the case of the UN, the situation is complicated by the increasingly plural nature of the global system. The UN strictly represents states and because of that represents only a part of the cast of global actors. It may represent the actors with leading roles, because states remain the most significant element in the system, but it does suffer from the twin disadvantages of being constitutionally bound to deal only with governments, even when they have become too weak to function, and of having few formal ways of including other, newer members of the troupe. It has made great efforts to improve the latter aspect and while its role in high politics has atrophied, as the events of 2003 and 2004 in Iraq showed, its relationship with NGOs has become more productive. There is no doubt that the UN in early 2005 was facing a fully acknowledged crisis over its future design and role, but it is equally clear that there are no obvious or agreed ways in which to remodel it.

The second type of inter-governmental arrangement which emerged during the nineteenth century dealt with shared administrative responsibilities on the part of governments whose interventionist role was increasing. To give an example: attempts to limit diseases, both human and animal, began to increase quite sharply, but, particularly in states with land borders, such efforts had to be backed by cooperative agreements with neighbours in order to be effective. The spread of railways had the same effect, as did the establishment of telegraphic communications. They all needed international regulation and they got it. These kinds of arrangements have increased over the years and form an unsung but essential backdrop to the world's daily business. Some have been incorporated into the UN system. There have been times when the relative ease with which these agreements have been made and maintained has led to the idea that they could and should be extended from the administrative to the political sphere, but universally without success.

Global economic organisations

A type of inter-governmental organisation that has gained in importance in recent years has been economic and financial. The three concerned are the World Bank, the International Monetary Fund (IMF) and the World Trade Organisation (WTO). The Bank of International Settlements has also become more significant because of the enormous power of the global currency market. The WTO is the successor to the General Agreement on Tariffs and Trade (GATT). The GATT, the World Bank, though under a different name, and the IMF were established at the end of the Second World War in order to try to make certain that the disastrous economic conditions of the 1930s, which many thought had caused the war, would never be repeated. As such they were very much the creatures of their member governments and designed to smooth the flow of the world economy seen to be controllable by and through governments. When the world divided into the Cold War blocs, these institutions were confined to the Western bloc. With the collapse of communism, their intended global scope became fully operational.

But it was a very different world from that of 1945. A rapid process of economic globalisation was under way and some states and their governments were encountering overwhelming problems for reasons which are discussed elsewhere. Confusion and disagreement arose about both appropriate policies and the appropriate roles for these institutions, particularly after the Asian currency crisis in the 1990s. So acute has this disagreement become that there have been public demonstrations in places where they have held meetings and the hitherto entirely neutral figure of the President of the World Bank has had to be given 24-hour security cover. The result is beginning to appear in changing policies and perhaps even more significantly in a clear tendency for these institutions to take on independent roles in global economic policy, making them something more than the collective representation of the wishes of their chief members. They are thus both moulded by and are moulding the processes of globalisation and are very clear examples of the changing nature of global politics.

Regional organisations

The second half of the twentieth century spawned many regional inter-governmental organisations, usually primarily economic in motivation. Not all, particularly in Africa, have been long lived. Some, however, have become well established. The Association of South East Asian Nations (ASEAN), Asia Pacific Eonomic Cooperation group (APEC), the North American Free Trade Association (NAFTA), Mercosur in South America, the Economic Community of West African States (ECOWAS) and the African Union (AU) are all examples. The range of activity and scope among them is quite wide, but none has developed in the way that the European Union (EU) has. There have been occasional examples in Africa and the Middle East – the United Arab Republic – where attempts to create new and larger federal states have been made and failed. In the case of the EU the attempt is still being made and has reached a point where it seems inevitable that, even if a fully constructed federation does not occur in the end, a highly complex political and economic structure will remain.

The EU began as a response to the conditions in Europe immediately after the Second World War. It was an economic association first and foremost, based on the European Coal and Steel Community which was expanded first to become the Common Market and then the European Economic Community. Because it had been originally intended to bind the old foes Germany and France into a single unbreakable economic system, its first members were those two states and their immediate neighbours, or at least those of them which were willing to pool a significant degree of economic sovereignty. In the 1970s it expanded, though solely within Western Europe, and then again after the demise of the Soviet bloc when it gradually expanded further to include states on the Baltic coast and in central Europe. The eventual accession of Turkey, which would take the EU into Asia, was in 2005 under active discussion.

This expansion has emphasised the fact that the EU has always had a dual intention, set out in treaties, beginning with the first, the Treaty of Rome of 1957. The first intention was to create a large and prosperous free trade area within Europe. The second was to proceed more slowly and build a new federal European state on the foundation of the steadily deepening economic and administrative integration. This ambition was reaffirmed particularly in the Treaty of Amsterdam in 1998. The first objective has been remarkably successful, although the crowning achievement of creating a single currency for all the members has not yet happened and may never do so. The second objective may, however, turn out to be anachronistic. In the later 1950s it was reasonable to suppose that political and economic well-being was likely to spring from belonging to a state or federation of substantial size. All the immediate evidence suggested that this was so. To seek to replicate that condition in Europe, an area with a common cultural heritage and a very large quantity of shared historical experience, mainly unpleasant, seemed to be a reasonable ambition – difficult to bring off, but reasonable.

By the early twenty-first century, not only was the EU much bigger and more diverse than was initially anticipated, but the general premise was also in question. The surrounding world was no longer the sole preserve of states, nor was it more or less solely affected by the balance of power between them. It was a much more complex assemblage of entities exercising different kinds of power at different levels within the global system. Nor was it clear that any serious advantage was derived from sheer size. Indeed, the sole remaining superpower seemed to indicate that apart from economic weight – and even that has become problematic – being a superpower no longer had the consequences, still less the rewards, that once it did. Thus not only has it become more difficult for the EU to implement the treaty obligations calling for ever-deepening integration, the motive for doing so has become much less clear.

In 2005, this formerly rather shadowy sense of things acquired a gritty political reality when referenda in both France and the Netherlands rejected a draft European constitution. The reasons were not solely to do with the text of the constitution or the principle of having one at all, but they were primarily so and strongly suggested that popular opinion would not support any further attempts to create a new European state. It is most probable that the EU is in fact going to settle into a kind of midway position between being a state and being an association of states. If so, it will contribute to the contemporary fact that the meaning of being a state has changed substantially and at the same time will contribute to a new definition of it.

Global civil society

The newest arrivals on the stage as star performers rather than as a mildly disapproving chorus have been private organisations, chiefly those involved with humanitarian action, human rights, the global environment and economic development. However much governments try to adjust to new conditions, the effort is limited by the effective absence of 'the other side'. The conduct of relations between states may well be transformed, but it is only part of a picture. In more recent times, further factors of great force have emerged. The need to face and try to resolve the great questions surrounding the fate of the global environment has created mixtures of the highly political with the professionally scientific which require profoundly different authors of international exchanges from those of the past. If previous pressure had served to blur the familiar lines of responsibility for international negotiation between and within states, these new areas of activity look set to erase them altogether. More than that, they involve establishing new relationships between state governments and the private entities which have created highly significant roles for themselves on environmental issues, seeking and obtaining political support for their activities transnationally. Little about these developments is entirely clear and there could be no successful attempt yet to describe them definitively; nor are these episodes of diplomacy involving both states and non-state entities completely effective. It is an inevitably muddled, if fascinating, area.

The relationship, however, between the UN and UN agencies and private actors in the humanitarian field generally has changed in a quite clear way. The effect of the series of world conferences on economic and social issues which occurred during the 1990s made insiders of private actors who used to think of themselves as outsiders. Both in planning agendas and in forming delegations, private actors came to take leading roles, and the UN found ways of by-passing bureaucratic restrictions on the process. In effect, flowing from the accreditation of 1,400 private organisations for the Rio Conference on Environment and Development, a new layer of recognised participants in the global political order has been created. A new world of global diplomatic activity has thus been created for both old and new actors.

This has occurred, too, in an even more striking way over crises involving humanitarian and human rights issues, and the major question that arises is, where the internal administration of a state to all intents and purposes disappears, who will provide it, either while reconstruction proceeds or while something completely different evolves? Plainly one answer often supplied to these questions is: the UN system. It has, however, become perfectly evident that the system is not capable of dealing with these problems. The reasons are not entirely straightforward, and emotional rhetoric sometimes serves to conceal natural limitations on what can be done by referring only to the need for rooting out corruption and adopting administrative reforms. Achieving either of these will not change the fact that the UN is an association of states and, as such, shares in the disadvantages that the contemporary world has dealt out to its members. This makes many expectations of what could be achieved wildly over optimistic, and returns us to the questions asked above.

The answer, as events have unfolded, has been that the only practical source of help – however woefully inadequate the circumstances often make it – has come from private organisations, most often from the great charities such as Oxfam and Médécins Sans Frontières (Doctors Without Borders), both of which have graduated from local to global status, and also from a wide variety of other private actors, specific in origin by country and by activity, and large in numbers. The reasons go beyond the nature of the problems on the ground. State collapse renders the traditional way in which other states have responded irrelevant: a bilateral approach and the consequent use of bilateral diplomatic and other machinery become useless. The same, even more awkwardly, applies to the UN. Dealing with the government of a state is the only proper manner for the UN to operate and if there is no government in effective existence, the mechanisms of the UN run into formal difficulties. The most likely solution can be to put the UN into a coordinating role, with all the weaknesses that that implies, so that it can arrange to operate through deliberately established or pre-existing local and international private actors.

For governments, there is another motive over and beyond evading the problems caused by the failure of bilateral relationships. In a post-collectivist atmosphere, the direct use of tax revenue to relieve external humanitarian disasters can be politically infeasible: the 'privatisation' of humanitarian efforts relieves this problem. The free market in humanitarian feeling – and the contributions which flow from it – allows private charitable actors to multiply. They then become available to governments as the recipients of funds delivered in a competitive environment and influencing their activities thus makes it possible to evade the objections that an even partly effective domestic government would have raised. For both intervening governments and the UN, this is particularly true of human rights issues but is not confined to them.

The result has been an impressive shift in the route by which resources reach crisis areas, as private actors have increased their share of the financial action. In 1970, 1.5 per cent of the income of private actors was derived from public grants; in 1996, it was probably over 40 per cent. In 1992, some 13 per cent of overseas development assistance from the industrialised world was being channelled through private actors and the amount has risen since. Such flows have inevitably caused a change in expectations as to how much private actors must contribute from their own resources before being entitled to matching funds. In some cases, deliberately created organisations are being 100 per cent funded from public sources. Such inflows give influence to the donors, and particularly where the intention is to find substitutes for direct intervention, the donors expect performance and behaviour consistent with developed models. This contributes to the tendency of private organisations not only to supply the administrative functions of dead states but to conform their own organisational structures to the patterns of 'Western' state institutions.

Problems of provision

At a basic level, organisations founded and funded on the basis of a transcendent, sometimes essentially religious, desire to give aid and comfort to individual human beings in distress find themselves involved in something almost infinitely more complicated. The simple river of both intention and intended actions runs out into a complex delta of slow-moving muddy channels, difficult both to map and to navigate. The principal problem is deciding how to apply the practical help to individual sufferers when no infrastructure – even a primitive one – exists any longer. Thus it has to be decided to what extent it is the proper function of private actors to provide the prior conditions in which help can be effectively given. There is always then a further problem in a seemingly never-ending chain of difficulties: providing anything other than direct assistance to individuals carries a political message of some kind or another to one group – usually armed – or another, and therefore creates the risk that the best of intentions may be being used for less good purposes either acciden-tally or deliberately. And this complication may go further than the local political and administrative morass. It may involve the wishes and policies of state governments, most likely neighbours, but also possibly others hoping to have influence from further afield. In such circumstances, the private actors concerned may find themselves divorced from the kind of neutral status maintained by the Red Cross, whether justly or not, and thus put themselves and their staff at risk of attack and assassi-nation. People who have volunteered to serve in such circumstances have always accepted a degree of risk, but becoming potential participants in warfare has not generally been seen as that kind of risk.

The thickening texture of communication between private actors and the pre-existing machinery of the international system is a mark of the breaking down of the hierarchy of international signifi-cance. The role of private actors is more nearly equal with that of states and institutional groupings of states, like the UN. The role of their staff has followed suit. The importance of the private organ-isation's perspective in political forums has been demonstrated by its increasing relevance in official delegations or in the emergence of humanitarian units attached to government departments. Revolv-ing-door assignments are widespread between private-sector and UN positions, particularly in oper-ational programmes such as those of UNHCR, UNICEF and the World Food Programme (WFP), where there is a tradition of picking talent from private organisations. In many ways these links between non-governmental and governmental spheres of activity are a novel feature of the UN scene, impossible to imagine a decade ago.

There can be no doubt that all this represents the development of a new layer in the global polit-ical system, evolving from major changes in the machinery of global politics. It is more than a quan-titative change. However easy it may be to point to the presence of private actors with influence on international politics in the past, their role in the present has altered in a qualitative way, both in its frequency and in its direction. The balance of power among the entities involved has shifted – away from state governments and associations of states and towards private actors. To set against this, it is to be remembered that some of this change has occurred because the new entrants are acting as sur-rogates for governments. They do so in circumstances where traditional bilateral relationships can-not survive a state collapse or the objections of domestic public opinion to interventionist policies.

Global capitalism and markets

The fact that both states and a wide variety of private organisations are prime movers in global poli-tics is clear in a reasonably precise way. The same cannot be said of the involvement of the global economy. There is a wide consciousness that global economic pressures have become independent actors in global politics, but such a consciousness is plainly derived from an inchoate sense that there are unstoppable economic movements taking place which may be beneficial but are more usually regarded as both uncontrolled and unfair. This perception may arise just because it is so difficult to get a clear conception of the global economy which then seems to be a plot rather than an activity. The result has been public displays of unhappiness in the form of street demonstrations where meetings and conferences of the major global economic institutions are taking place.

Globalised markets in labour, capital and currencies have been made possible by the communica-tions revolution which has created a globalised economy. They can be the subject of local regulation in highly organised and well-established states, but in their capacity to operate globally, their activi-ties both occur in less developed administrations unable to regulate successfully or even at all, and escape beyond those that are more effective. In the absence of any central global economic political structure, this gives the global markets a striking freedom of movement and, perhaps even more important, the ability to act without the need to win acceptance for their intentions in advance or justify them retrospectively. This becomes power without responsibility, once famously described as being the prerogative of the harlot throughout the ages. Or put another way, it is the exercise of power which has not been legitimised by any of the methods which human societies have developed over centuries in the context of government conducted through and by the state. The sole mitigating factor is the sanction that can be exercised by shareholders in transnational firms whose interest is not necessarily that of the general good, but who may become conscious of their company's growing undesirable and economically damaging unpopularity among the global public and demand changes of policy.

There are two particular points of friction between societies and the markets: the first is that freedom to locate manufacturing where labour is cheapest, or at least cheap and effective, draws employment away from the richer economies. The second is that the effects of inward investment on poorer economies, though they can be dramatically enriching, can put unbearable strains on local facilities and local environments. Moreover, the greater ability of highly developed states to influence the flow of trade by protective mechanisms can produce, particularly over agriculture, a very strong sense that the global economy is an unfair economy.

The combination of a globalising economy powered by global markets and transnational firms with a growing weakness in the authority and scope of state government has tended to break the familiar connection between relative public security and effective local administration and achieving successful economic performance. To achieve the optimum workforce or physical conditions or propinquity to raw materials, firms may go to places where the political and the physical environment may be a great deal less than optimum. When this happens, the firm may well begin to supply on its own behalf what is lacking locally. Security is the clearest example and leads to the once unimaginable spectacle of a company providing security for largely foreign staff by employing mercenary forces to protect the immediate area of the company's operation – but doing so in somebody else's country. It is this kind of evolution in both states and the global economy that makes it necessary to include both the markets and transnational firms as actors in global politics. Global policies cannot be disentangled from national policies, global interests from national interests, and national interests may indeed have become impossible to define any more. Global activity will have local consequences and local consequences will in turn influence the next stage of global activity.

CHAPTER 2: Associations of states

Associations of states, sometimes called inter-governmental organisations (IGOs), form a very important part of the fabric of global politics. With some exceptions they once were the only examples of cooperative action in what was an international system dominated by states, and the phrase 'international organisation' still often carries that meaning. In the contemporary world there are many different kinds of transnational organisations and it is necessary to distinguish between those that originate with states and those that do not. The latter are discussed in the previous chapter.

International organisations, under that description, have become familiar entities and became topics of research and intense discussion during the twentieth century. They have, however, a much longer history: some institutions of the ancient Greek city states have been so described, as has the universal church of the Middle Ages. The continuous history of international organisations which are part of the fabric of global politics in the early twenty-first century began in the nineteenth century.

They fall essentially into three categories: first, supervisory systems for administering non-political international treaty regulation, such as transport, commerce, disease control, postal and telegraphic communications; second, global and regional organisations, either economic or military; and third, organisations designed to prevent political disputes from leading to war. It is these last which attracted most attention during the twentieth century, because of the scale and destructiveness of its warfare and weaponry, and the term 'international' organisation has at times seemed only to refer to them.

Supervision of international activity

International activity of all sorts expanded both rapidly and extensively in the nineteenth century, chiefly as a result of industrialisation and technological improvement. People and goods were travelling across oceans and continents in ever greater numbers and in ever shorter timeframes, while international communications expanded exponentially. Postal reforms that started in Great Britain in 1840 were soon copied by other European states and the successful laying of a telegraph cable in 1851 between England and France began an extraordinary period of expansion in the reach of electric telegraphic systems. As the connections between countries increased, the need to coordinate and regulate the interaction became apparent and inevitable.

As the industrial revolution transformed assumptions about how things were or could be done, political leaders soon grasped the clear linkage between industrial advance and power and security. International commerce and trade filled the coffers of the state, while the foundries that churned out tons of steel, more powerful engines and new weapons of greater destructiveness added to the firepower and mobility of national armies. But as a matter of policy, states largely left business alone to pursue profits, following the classic laissez-faire approach to commerce.

The relationship between the state and the fledgling industrial economy was indeed intimate – state funds did finance, partly or fully, certain industries (railway construction, steelworks, telegraphs) and protected many industries and commercial enterprises from foreign competition through tariffs and customs duties. But economic growth could not be achieved in isolation. In order to realise greater national wealth and increase their power, states found it necessary to cooperate; however, cooperation was confined to specific technical or administrative activities such as coordination of postal services or telegraphic communications. This type of cooperation was the first to be institutionalised in formal international governmental organisations.

First international organisations

The first international organisations were established to supervise, administer or regulate the rising tide of international activity (i.e. the Central Commission for the Navigation of the Rhine (1815), Conseil Superieur de Santé (1838), the European Commission for Control of the Danube (1856), International Telegraph Union (1865), International Meteorological Organisation (1873), Universal Postal Union (1874), International Office of Weight and Measures (1875), Union for the Protection of Industrial Property (1883), the Intergovernmental Organisation for International Carriage by Rail (1890), Comité Maritime International (1897)).

They are commonly known as 'public international unions' and were the products of international treaties or agreements. For example, in 1865 a comprehensive international convention for regulating and establishing uniformity of telegraph services was reached, creating the International Telegraph Union (now called the International Telecommunications Union) and less than ten years later, in 1874, the Conference of Berne reached an international agreement on regulating postal services, establishing the Universal Postal Union to administer this accord. This pattern was repeated in other areas – transportation (railroads and sea shipping), health (sanitation and disease control), science and industry (intellectual property, weights and measures, agriculture) and economics (finance and trade) – that increasingly fell within the expanding jurisdiction and/or administrative competence of central governments.

The initial impetus for establishing administrative and regulatory agencies on the international level was the obvious need to ease or eliminate constraints on commercial transactions between sovereign jurisdictions. For states, all of which jealously guarded their sovereign prerogatives, creating these international organisations was a pragmatic response to the challenges posed by technological developments and economic change. But states were also careful not to vest international bodies with too much authority, limiting their scope, function and tasks to specific purposes and/or technical matters. States have preferred to establish international institutions to collect and exchange information, to coordinate national policy and practices, and/or to formulate and promulgate uniform or minimum standards in a particular field rather than any duties which might involve high politics. Some, like the Central Commission for the Navigation of the Rhine and other river commissions, were given responsibilities and the authority to regulate, adjudicate, supervise and administer.

Contributing to the proliferation of public international unions was a parallel development of private international organisations for professionals (e.g. lawyers and physicians), industrialists and business leaders (e.g. bankers, railway owners and publishers) and scientists (e.g. physicists, chemists and biologists). These organisations, such as the International Union for Conservation of Nature and Natural Resources, the World Conservation Union, the International Council of Scientific Unions, International Chamber of Commerce, International Broadcasting Union and the Association of German Railroads, have often led the way in calling for the creation of international regulatory agencies, and it is usually these which provide the experts and technical personnel of the international secretariat or bureaucracy.

The early success of this approach to easing constraints on cross-border transactions and overcoming conflicting jurisdictions and customs encouraged organisational growth across the spectrum of international human activity. This trend accelerated during the twentieth century, particularly after each world war, as governments steadily broadened their role in economic affairs, reflecting the impact of the Great Depression in the 1930s and a shift towards Keynesian economics, and turned to international organisations as the method for managing the expanding dimensions and difficulties of international collaboration in the economic field. This process has resulted in a more thickly textured international system as the number of international organisations has increased. To this day, the majority of the nearly 2,000 international governmental organisations listed in the Union of International Associations' annual *Yearbook of International Organisations* (37th edition) are technical or functional agencies in the economic field and many are regional or limited membership organisations (e.g. the European Union, Organisation of Economic Cooperation and Development, and the Multilateral Development Banks).

Technological innovation and international regulation

Technological innovation in manufacturing, medicine, transportation and communications is the driving force in the internationalisation and more recently globalisation of the world and, therefore, the expansion of the international regulatory system.

Since the Second World War, the most developed international regulatory frameworks (and perhaps the most complex) are in the areas of international trade through the General Agreement on Tariffs and Trade, after 1995 the World Trade Organisation, and international finance and banking, which is managed by the Bretton Woods Institutions of the International Monetary Fund and the World Bank. Furthermore, the post-Second World War period has created additional international organisations to manage or regulate new technological developments, such as the International Civil Aviation Organisation, International Atomic Energy Agency, the Food and Agricultural Organisation, the International Seabed Authority and the World Health Organisation. All these organisations, as well as those established earlier, have been pulled together into the decentralised United Nations system as autonomous 'specialised agencies'.

In general, the international regulatory infrastructure as it has developed since 1945 has proved to be surprisingly adaptable to the impact of technology and the increasing pace of change. One of the key reasons for its success seems to be the built-in capacity of the organisations to keep up with and, in some ways, facilitate the technological innovations that constantly alter the environment by applying or adapting regulations already established and revised at periodic administrative conferences of member states. However, this capacity is proving more difficult under the more recent conditions of economic and cultural globalisation. The transformation from an international to a global economy is stretching the limits of existing international organisations and specialised agencies as they struggle to manage the immense changes of this global transition. At the same time, new and novel approaches based on the corporate model of the private sector are appearing, such as the Internet Corporation for Assigned Names and Numbers (ICANN), indicating the start of a shift away from traditional inter-governmental organisations and towards independent private global entities for regulating the emerging global economic order.

Global organisations

United Nations Organisation and its predecessors

The UN is the only comprehensive, global organisation set up with the object of preserving peace. As such it has always been an object of profound hopes, often hopes beyond practical fulfilment, and because of that the UN also attracts sharp criticism. Like all human constructions, the UN bears in its constitution – the Charter – and in its physical structure the marks of its historical origin, and it is impossible to understand its contemporary role or its limitations without knowledge of its past.

The Charter of the UN was agreed in 1945 in San Francisco and the organisation was subsequently established in New York City. Two particular factors affected its shape and direction: the first was contemporary opinion about why its predecessor, the League of Nations, had failed to stop the course of events which had led to the wars of 1937/41–1945 in Asia and 1939/41–1945 in Europe. The second was contemporary opinion about what had been the causes of the Second World War. The first had an important effect on the physical structure of the organisation and the second powerfully determined its objectives.

The Concert of Europe 1815–1914

The first attempt to create an organisation for the maintenance of peace was made in Europe after the end of the Napoleonic Wars in 1815. The length and relative severity of the wars motivated the attempt and three particular contemporary conditions gave it the practical possibility of success. The first of these three conditions was that the distribution of power among the greater states was more or less equal and had been proved to be so by the outcome of the war. This meant that constructing a system for maintaining peace did not have to be, or seem to be, a defence against any particular state or ruler; it could be common property. Second, it was widely believed that the prime cause of the war had been the effects of the ideology unleashed by the French Revolution. Preventing revolutions from happening, or if they did from causing wars, could therefore become a primary and universally agreed objective. The third condition was that the course of the war in its latter stages had required the development of a diplomatic means for keeping together the alliance against Napoleon and in so doing had created the idea of holding conferences of the great powers and refined it to the point where it could be added to the permanent stock of diplomatic techniques. In fact it became the piece of machinery by which it was expected that crises would be resolved, and flourished through much of the period between 1815 and 1914.

Compared with the League of Nations and the UN, this system, which became known as the Concert of Europe (because governments concerted together), lacked definition. Its constitution was extremely brief, it had no geographical base and thus no physical structure or permanent staff. But its fundamental purpose – to regulate international affairs and to do so by consensual agreements achieved at conferences or by rapid telegraphic exchanges after 1850 – was basically the same as that of its successors. It lasted longer and had greater success than either of them, despite their much greater elaboration. This suggests that the success or failure of international organisations depends on contemporary conditions and the consequent behaviour of their members rather than the contents of their constitutions.

The League of Nations 1920–1945

The immediate predecessor of the UN was the League of Nations, created in 1919 and established in 1920. Its makers were, like the delegates of 1815, powerfully moved by the horrors of the preceding war, in this case the deeply shocking First World War (1914–18). Unlike the situation of 1815, however, they had a previous system to think about and they came to the conclusion that it had been too weak and unstructured to prevent war in 1914. They particularly thought that the Concert's reliance on voluntary attendance at conferences had allowed the German government to refuse one in late July of 1914 and that this refusal had been a major immediate cause of the war. They were thus interested in finding ways of making the League stronger than the Concert and to make it impossible to evade a discussion about a crisis.

Their chosen method was to give the League a physical existence – at Geneva in Switzerland – a

small permanent staff and a well-defined constitution, the Covenant of the League. The organisation would thus never have to be called into existence when a crisis arose – it would always be there and someone would always be in the office when the League's attention was required. The Covenant was also equipped with various alternative ways of resolving disputes, particularly imposing moratoria and providing for in-depth reporting on difficult issues and events.

Having given the League broad duties and its members serious obligations, the makers also tried to give it some coercive power. The state of public opinion after 1918 would not have allowed the League to be given any military force, indeed general disarmament had been supposed to follow the war. But the interconnected nature of the world economy brought about the belief that the right to impose economic sanctions – exclusion from the world economy – would give the League adequate teeth to make certain that its decisions were obeyed. Economic sanctions have subsequently turned out to be an uncertain weapon by their very nature, but in the case of the League, such sanctions shared with all the other provisions in the Covenant the absolute need that the members of the organisation should be agreed about what should be done and then actually do what they had agreed upon. There was no executive power to speak of and no majority voting.

Even in stable international conditions, complete success for the League would have been a tall order. In the conditions that existed after 1920, where acute instability rapidly led to international disorder, its failure was rapid and certain, made the more so by the refusal of the United States to join and the initial absence of both Russia, which was in the process of becoming the USSR, and Germany, which was excluded until proved to be of good behaviour. The League was wound up on the formation of the UN in 1945, but had been moribund for some years. Famously, its last Secretary complained that when the war in Europe began in 1939, nobody bothered even to inform the League of Nations.

The United Nations

The Charter of the United Nations reflects the same mixture of intentions as emerged in both 1815 and 1919. The new organisation was designed to prevent what contemporaries believed caused wars and to do so by improving the machinery which had failed to prevent the previous conflict. What the makers of the UN had come to fear was not so much diplomatic failure, aided by secrecy, or disputes and crises slipping out of control, and certainly not revolutions as such, but episodes of naked aggression. They therefore did not share the belief that the very existence of a permanent international council or techniques such as cooling-off periods and the provision of opportunities for the legal resolution of disputes were adequate to control warfare.

So they designed something that would respond immediately to any aggression and they intended it to have military force at its disposal, something deliberately denied to the League. They believed the League to have been in general too weak, not just in its lack of force but also in the powers assigned to the Council of the League. They also wished, however, to maintain the principle of the sovereign equality of member states. This circle had to be squared and the device used was to put the five great powers of the period in charge of the sanctions available to the UN Security Council, but to release them, alone among member states, from the obligation of obedience to them. This was done by giving them permanent membership and a unique veto. Only on such terms could Marshal Stalin and the US Congress be persuaded to accept the proposed constitution.

It cannot be known whether the Charter would have been an improvement on the Covenant of the League, because the Cold War developed rapidly after 1945 and a consequential stalemate kept the Security Council in a vegetative state. The UN began to evolve other uses, chiefly on behalf of newer and less economically advanced states and particularly after the later 1960s; but the exigencies of the bi-polar period (1955–1985) had the paradoxical effect of allowing the UN to continue to exist and carry a huge burden of propaganda, but forbade it from playing the central role that had been designed for it in the international system. The disastrous fate of a briefly possible intervention in the former Belgian Congo in the early 1960s confirmed this general situation.

The end of bi-polarity in the later 1980s initially seemed to give new opportunities for the UN to come into its own. However, the causes of conflict at the beginning of the twenty-first century have changed markedly from those expected by those who framed the Charter, and a constitution designed to prevent sudden inter-state acts of aggression has seemed relevant only in the circumstance of the invasion of Kuwait by Iraq which, chiefly using the forces of the USA, the Security Council was able to reverse.

Despite much talk of reform, usually meaning rooting out corruption, real evolutionary development at the UN has arisen out of its unfolding relationships with private organisations which help to deal with the crises that evolve from internal conflicts. These have become the most common contemporary type, but because in theory the UN is prevented from acting directly in such cases, it has had to develop indirect, cooperative methods in order to become involved. Events in former Yugoslavia, and perhaps particularly in Iraq in 2003–2004, make it seem likely that the more state-centred and straightforwardly political role that the UN is supposed to play will continue to atrophy, despite the end of the bi-polar stasis, while future internal conflicts and state failures will continue to swell the significance and relevance of its participation in humanitarian, human rights and environmental issues.

Institutions of the United Nations

The institutions of the United Nations Organisation can be divided into three categories: the central institution, the specialised agencies and the residual category of other related organisations established under the 'aegis' of the UN. As for the central organisation, the United Nations, its Charter established six principal organs: the General Assembly, the Security Council, the Secretariat, the International Court of Justice, the Economic and Social Council and the Trusteeship Council.

Of these six, the Security Council is the most important. It is the only organ whose decisions are binding on all UN members. The Council consists of fifteen members, five of which are permanent (Britain, China, France, Russia and the United States) and ten which are elected to two-year terms by the General Assembly. Because the five permanent members all maintain veto power over any Security Council decision, their approval is needed before the UN can pursue a given course of action. The remaining UN organs all lack the power to issue binding decisions and are dependent on the willingness of member state governments to comply with their directives.

UN specialised agencies are inter-governmental institutions separate from the main organs of the UN. Each has an autonomous existence and operates in conjunction with the UN by special agreements. The most important specialised agencies, some of which pre-date the establishment of the UN, include the World Bank, the International Monetary Fund, United Nations Scientific and Cultural Organisation (UNESCO), the International Atomic Energy Agency (IAEA), the International Labour Organisation (ILO), the Food and Agricultural Organisation (FAO) and the World Health Organisation (WHO). For a complete list of the UN system, see Part B, Chapter 3.

The International Criminal Court

One of the newest inter-governmental organisations is the International Criminal Court (ICC). It is specifically designed to deal with the most serious crimes, particularly war crimes. Although the idea of creating a permanent international criminal court had been mooted for a long time, it has only quite recently become a reality. The delay was due particularly to concerns over the sovereign rights of the states, which made them reluctant to discuss the issue until 1998. In July of that year, at a conference in Rome held to establish an International Criminal Court, the Rome Statute establishing such a Court was adopted and opened for signature.

The treaty provided that it would enter into force after 60 ratifications had been reached. The Court was thus not automatically created by the conference. Although the vast majority of the participant states at the conference signed the treaty, showing their willingness and commitment to abide by the treaty content, the number of states that have signed the treaty but are not party to the ICC is 'significant'. There are now 139 signatories, of which 97 have ratified the treaty. Nevertheless, it is worth noting that the threshold for the treaty coming into force was reached in an impressively short time. After the required number of ratifications had been reached, the Rome Statute, along with the ICC, officially entered into force in July 2002. Its seat is at The Hague in the Netherlands, sometimes thought of as the 'capital of international law'.

Although the Court has not yet decided any case, first referrals by Uganda and the Congo Democratic Republic have officially involved it in international criminal matters.

The Court will be dealing with the gravest crimes, that is, genocide, crimes against humanity, war crimes and crimes of aggression. At first sight, it might seem that the list is narrow. However, there are many 'sub-crimes' that could be justly termed crimes against humanity, such as systematically committed rape, forced prostitution and so on. Furthermore, the inclusion of aggression is an important step in preventing future conflicts. Although aggression is yet to be defined, there is an agreement that the definition would be consistent with the UN Charter.

The Court's involvement with a criminal matter can be initiated in three ways. First, the United Nations Security Council is given the authority to refer cases to the ICC. Second, as stated in the Statute, any State Party to the ICC may bring a case to the Court. And finally, the independent prosecutor has the power, although subject to certain conditions and limitations, to initiate an investigation into events to which the prosecutor believes national authorities have not paid adequate attention.

As one of the most recently established inter-governmental organisations, the ICC has the potential to influence global politics deeply. However, at the same time, its creation triggered a major controversy between the EU and the United States, which, if not eventually resolved, may cause the court to have less impact and to be used less than was first expected.

The ICC can be seen as a 'small' revolution in international law and global politics. Traditionally, international law has created responsibilities for states only. However, with the creation of the ICC, individuals become responsible in international law. Although there was individual criminal responsibility before the creation of the ICC, it was either temporary, or the individual concerned, while being responsible under the principles and rules of international law, was brought to justice by the state authorities.

International legal arrangements dealing with piracy, and the Genocide Convention and the Geneva Conventions dealing with war crimes, recognise individual responsibility. However, none of them specifies an international authority to punish the individuals. That is to say, national authorities are expected to proceed against those who have committed the crimes covered by the above. However, there is no clearly and solidly defined sanction against a state that shows reluctance to deal with the matter concerned.

The Rome Statute, at least to some extent, replaces the national authorities with the ICC in the matter of proceeding against individuals accused of the relevant crimes. The States Parties have vested in the ICC the power to formally ask for a criminal suspect to be handed over to the Court. The Court is thus expected to act as if it is a national court, where the national court concerned has failed to handle the matter properly.

It is also worth noting that the *ad hoc* Tribunals established to deal with the crimes in Rwanda and former Yugoslavia are temporary and responsible to the UN Security Council. Their predecessors, the Nuremberg and Tokyo Tribunals, were established by a few states and might be seen as the tools of the victorious powers after the Second World War. Moreover, all had limited power in terms of both time and scope.

However, unlike these early examples, the ICC has a permanent seat and a much more comprehensive authority. But most importantly, it is not controlled by the UN Security Council, where major powers have the right to veto. Although the Security Council is given prominent roles in the functioning of the ICC, it is the Assembly of States Parties to which the ICC is responsible.

Although seriously and eagerly involved in the preparatory work for establishing an international criminal court, the USA hesitated to sign the Rome Statute at the conference, being one of the seven participant but non-signatory states, instead insisting on retaining the state's discretion over criminal matters. In addition, it wanted the Court to act under the control and authority of the Security Council. However, other participants rejected some of the US proposals, while a compromise was reached on others. For example, it was agreed that the Court would be 'complementary' to the national authorities and act only if the state party concerned could not deal with the matter.

Under the Clinton administration the USA signed the Rome Statute on 31 December 2000, the virtual deadline for signing as, under the Statute, a state willing to accede the ICC after that date would also have to ratify it. However, the treaty was never introduced in the Senate for ratification. Indeed, the Bush administration launched a campaign against the ICC. First, sending a letter to the UN Secretary-General, the USA formally withdrew the undertakings and commitments which originated from its signature. This came to be known as 'unsigning', a popular term, which may or may not have a legal effect. The US

Congress then adopted the American Servicemembers' Protection Act (ASPA), which gives the US President extensive authority to deal with the ICC. Under ASPA, the President is authorised to take 'any' measure to free US personnel from the ICC's jurisdiction. Since the Act contains a hypothetical military intervention option, it caused serious anger in Europe and came to be known as 'The Hague Invasion Act'.

Global economic institutions

A particular importance attaches to the organisations which emerged from the Bretton Woods conference in 1944, where 44 states met at a hotel in New Hampshire, USA to establish the post-Second World War economic system. A major goal was an open international trading system based on the argument that protectionist trade blocks had crippled the global economy in the 1930s, leading to the rise of dictatorships and world war.

The United States was the dominant state in the talks due to its economic and military might. The size of the US economy allowed it to provide aid in the form of loans, grants and trade to help rebuild Western Europe. Its military power offered protection from the Soviet Union, which gave it considerable leverage over the form of the post-war economic system. However, the United States offered benefits in return for states following its lead, offering, for example, to reduce its tariff barriers on a reciprocal basis.

The United States' liberal view of an international trade system was the basis for the post-war, free trade system. Non-discrimination was another aspect of the post-war system, although the USA, and other states, used selective trade discrimination for foreign policy purposes.

The Bretton Woods system

The Bretton Woods conference led to the establishment, in December 1945, of the International Monetary Fund. The IMF was designed to stabilise exchange rates and alleviate balance of payments problems by supplying credit resources, while imposing corrective practices and policies on borrowers.

The Bretton Woods conference also led to the creation of the World Bank. It started operations in June 1946 and, at first, provided assistance to states rebuilding after the war, although its focus shifted to the third world in the 1950s. An attempt to establish an International Trade

Organisation (ITO), which was designed to be the counterpart of the IMF in the area of trade, was stillborn when the US Congress failed to ratify the charter and other states were unwilling to join without the United States. The ITO charter, however, later formed the basis of the General Agreement on Tariffs and Trade and at the end of the twentieth century the GATT was given a new form and greater responsibilities as the World Trade Organisation.

Collapse of the Bretton Woods system

In the late 1960s and early 1970s the Bretton Woods system collapsed, largely due to trends in the US economy. So long as the United States was economically dominant, the dollar served as an international currency and was accepted all over the world. Technically, the dollar was on the gold standard and could be exchanged for gold. With confidence in the US economy very high, Americans could spend freely. US military and economic aid, military bases and the war in Vietnam were financed, in part, by the strength of the dollar. Other states accepted dollars because they could use them to purchase goods and services anywhere.

However, by the late 1960s the costs of the Vietnam War and a growing US budget deficit had eroded the strength of the dollar. In a sense, the United States was exporting inflation. It also faced a growing trade deficit from 1971. US governments considered devaluing the dollar to reverse the unfavourable trade deficits. However, devaluation would also reduce the value of dollars held overseas. Therefore, foreign governments and bankers put pressure on the United States to remedy its economic problems without devaluing the dollar, but to no avail. In 1971 President Richard Nixon announced that the dollar would no longer be convertible into gold and let the dollar float against other currencies, effectively ending the Bretton Woods system. This act led to the devaluation of the dollar in December 1971 and again in February 1973.

The demise of the Bretton Woods system left a hole in the non-communist sector of the global economy. Regional groups tried to stabilise their exchange rates and economic policies, most significantly the EU, first with the European Monetary System and subsequently with the introduction of a European currency. The spread of deregulated liberalised economies in the 1980s and 1990s and the subsequent extension of such economic policies into the former communist bloc after the collapse of the Soviet Union introduced new problems into the management of the global economy. The globalising effects of the communications revolution of the last quarter of the twentieth century, combined with weakening individual government control over economic policies generally, produced a succession of major crises caused by currency speculation, particularly the Mexican peso crisis (1995), the Russian rouble crisis (1996) and the even broader crisis in Asia in the later 1990s which began in Indonesia.

After Bretton Woods: the IMF and the World Bank

Such crises put great pressure on the IMF in particular but also on the World Bank. These institutions had been established to deal with a very different set of economic conditions and were primarily designed to reflect the views of their members on what contemporary policies of development and relief should be. The late twentieth-century situation seemed to call for more directly global initiatives.

The advent of a more globalised economy, with serious problems of stability and clear needs for development, led to powerful feelings of increasing global economic injustice, partly because the beneficial effects of globalisation were generally strong and thus the sense of unfairness became very marked in areas where they did not occur, or operated only feebly. To add to the difficulties of the global economic institutions, there came to be a public belief – sometimes violently expressed – that their policies were adding to a global environmental crisis as well as prolonging social injustices. During the currency crisis in Asia, the IMF's attempt to help Indonesia through the application of traditional belt-tightening remedies created large-scale unemployment and imposed a serious burden of debt which in turn caused the collapse of the government and thus removed the only authority capable of maintaining the IMF's prescriptions. These effects coincided with an environmental crisis throughout the region caused by huge forest fires, the result of uncontrolled logging and a consequence of attempts to make quick economic gains at a time of acute economic distress.

The IMF response was perhaps somewhat slow, but nonetheless striking. Its efforts to reduce the likelihood that its attempts to restore the international credibility of a crisis-struck country would, at least temporarily, yield internal impoverishment can be seen in a series of decisions taken since 1996. Against a background of much greater openness in its discussion of policies and in reporting the results, the series began with its September 1996 decision to establish the Heavily Indebted Poor Countries Initiative (HIPC). In December 1997 a new Supplemental Reserve Facility was introduced to deal with sudden losses of market confidence and was immediately applied to South Korea.

In October 1998, the Fund announced five tenets which it believed should lie behind the construction of a new global financial architecture. Their general effect was to allow a more gradual approach to the solution of political and structural problems in countries going through an economic crisis. A September 1999 decision of the Fund established the International Monetary and Financial Committee and gave it an explicit provision to hold preparatory meetings with representatives and agreed to a sale of gold in order to fund its share of the HIPC Initiative.

In December 1999 off-market gold sales were used to assist Mexico and Brazil and to obtain further funding for debt relief and financial support for the poorest countries. During 2001, the IMF agreed both to monitor the international capital markets more closely and to reconsider the conditions attached to the use of IMF resources.

Although in the first years of the twenty-first century the IMF remained an object of some suspicion, particularly as a device for maintaining the economic superiority of only one part of the global economy, it had undergone great changes of attitude, operation and policy, as it had also to make the transition from being a broadly non-political international agency to becoming a global institution in a highly charged political atmosphere.

A remarkably similar progression can be seen at the World Bank, though with more concentration on issues of development, particularly education, than on economic management and currency. After almost 50 years, the World Bank began to respond to new conditions and criticisms and in 1993, following allegations of corruption and inefficiency, established a panel to check that the implementation of its development projects was following the Bank's own policies and procedures. In 1996, the World Bank decided to play an enthusiastic role in the HIPC

Initiative and in 1997 introduced the Strategic Compact to encourage fundamental reform and reduce poverty. Then 1998 saw the beginning of the Human Resources Reform and the Comprehensive Development Framework.

By 2000, the World Bank's new-found political significance led to the President, James Wolfensohn, being invited to address the UN Security Council. However, it also led to a highly critical report of its activities being given to the US Congress, and to criticism of a different kind expressed in riots in Washington, DC during the April meeting of the Bank's Development Committee. During the summer of 2001, the World Bank took new initiatives in environmental and poverty issues, both of which represented sources of great public hostility.

Like the IMF, there was no question that by the end of the twentieth century the World Bank had been propelled into high-profile political engagement with the developmental problems emphasised by the onset of globalisation, among other things, and which brought about serious change in the structure and attitudes of the institution. Both of them had moved away from acting as the guardians of the interests and general political stance of their members and begun to act as global authorities in their own right – a change of striking importance.

Through the Cold War years and until the early twenty-first century, these IGOs acted in accord with the wishes of their members and tended not to be any more than the sum of their parts. But associations of governments dealing only with governments, particularly in the case of the IMF, came to seem inadequate when governments under review or in need of assistance, or both, might quite easily collapse when expected to implement decisions from outside. Moreover, the importance of non-state actors, both commercial and private, began to increase to the point where they needed to be drawn into the process of global economic management – as evidenced by the mixture of state, private and business representatives at the Davos meetings of the World Economic Forum (WEF).

The result has been a change in the role of all three institutions by which they have begun to act in the interests of a stable global community and not necessarily in accordance with the preferences of their members. This gradual sea change makes them independent actors on the world stage for at least some of the time, and it seems likely to continue. The extent of the change can be sensed from the public interest and protests that have accompanied meetings compared with the lack of public knowledge or concern that characterised their proceedings until just a decade ago.

Organisation of Petroleum Exporting Countries

The Organisation of Petroleum Exporting Countries (OPEC) was created in Baghdad on 14 September 1960 by Iran, Iraq, Kuwait, Saudi Arabia and Venezuela. These were later joined by Qatar in 1961, Indonesia and Libya in 1962, Abu Dhabi (now part of the United Arab Emirates) in 1967, Algeria in 1969 and Ecuador and Gabon in 1973. This oil-producer cartel was initially formed to counter oil-price cuts by US and European oil companies, but during the 1970s it actively pursued rate increases in the price of oil.

In the post-Second World War period until 1970 there was an oil surplus on the world market relative to demand, which resulted in the low posted price of oil. The firms which dominated the international oil market – Exxon, Texaco, Mobil, Standard, Gulf, Shell and British Petroleum – determined both the level of production and the price of crude oil in virtually all oil-producing states. In 1959 they imposed a reduction of 10 per cent in the posted price of oil. In 1960, as a result of US import control legislation which reduced demand, prices dropped even further. In response to this plummeting of prices, the primary oil-producing states formed OPEC and adopted resolutions to prevent price fluctuations and to unify petroleum policies. The OPEC members vowed to oppose any future attempts to lower the posted price of oil. In order to oppose the major oil companies, however, OPEC members had to form an oil-producing cartel; joint action was a prerequisite to success.

During the 1960s the oil-producing states were in a weak position vis à vis the oil companies; because of the glut of oil on the world market, OPEC's activities were of little consequence. In the 1970s, however, several factors led to increased demand for oil and to the rise in OPEC's power. Industrialised states were operating at the peak of their business cycles and were enjoying economic prosperity. This extraordinary level of aggregate economic activity placed immense pressure on existing global oil production, resulting in a tight international oil market. During this period US consumption of oil also began to exceed domestic production and the United States entered the world market

for oil purchases. This was beneficial to the oil-producing states of the Middle East in particular, whose production costs could not be matched by other producers. Furthermore, there was a significant change in the structure of the international oil industry. The number of oil firms had been expanding in the 1950s and 1960s; as new independent firms sought to develop access to their own supplies of crude oil, the major firms began to lose control of the oligopolistic international oil market that they had long dominated.

Libya's oil

The event that finally served as a catalyst to OPEC's assertion of control over pricing and production of oil, however, was the attempt by Libya's Mu'ammar al-Qadhafi to renegotiate terms regarding Libya's oil concessions. Libyan oil was attractive to buyers because it had a very low sulphur content and was more economical to deliver to the United States and Europe than oil from the Persian Gulf. In addition, because the independent oil firms did not have other sources, they had to acquiesce in Qadhafi's demands. The major firms were forced to raise their prices as well. These factors allowed Qadhafi to demand higher prices for Libyan oil.

Libya's success triggered similar attempts by the Middle East oil-producing states to demand higher prices. Although in 1971 an agreement was reached at Teheran and Algiers to establish a price structure for oil that was mutually acceptable to the oil-producing states, global demand continued to push the actual market prices higher than the posted price negotiated in 1971 of $1.80 to $2.50 a gallon, with 2.5 per cent increases each year through to 1975. In addition, the devaluation of the dollar in 1971 and 1973, and the Arab-Israeli war in October 1973, continued to drive prices upwards, such that by the end of the year the price of oil had reached $11.67 a barrel. The rest of the decade was a success for OPEC. It exploited its position and Japanese and US dependence on oil from the Middle East and North Africa by raising the price of oil fifteen fold between 1973 and 1980. By 1982 OPEC states had accumulated $339 billion in current account surpluses.

Decline

By 1984, however, OPEC's oil revenues were less than half those of 1980 and by 1985 oil production had dropped to less than 17 million barrels a day in comparison with the 31 million barrels a day produced in 1979. The decline in OPEC's production, revenues and power was the result of several events in the 1980s: a global recession that led to decreased demand, conservation efforts in industrialised states and increased production of non-OPEC oil encouraged by the price hikes of the 1970s. These led to an increased supply of oil relative to demand that resulted in lower world market prices and created competition and rifts between the members of OPEC. OPEC's cohesion as a price setter eventually broke down. Unified action had been key to OPEC's success, but the individual incentive to each of the member states during the latter 1980s was to negotiate price unilaterally. Furthermore, the production quotas that OPEC had established broke down as members increased production to sustain earnings in the face of falling prices. OPEC's power had withered by the mid 1980s.

OPEC's worldwide political and economic impact, however, was significant. Its gains were realised at a tremendous economic cost to the rest of the world, it introduced severe strains among the Western allies over energy policies and diplomacy in the Middle East, and it sparked third world demands and hopes for a New International Economic Order (NIEO).

OPEC's economic success led it to initiate economic assistance programmes for less developed countries and encouraged citizens of its member states to place their money in Western banks and make investments. Much of the money was loaned by the banks for industrialisation programmes to developing nations, some of which were oil producers themselves (Venezuela). With the slowing of the world economy in the latter 1970s and early 1980s, together with the failure of many of the industrialisation programmes, the borrowers of OPEC money found themselves unable to pay their debts. OPEC, therefore, had a direct connection to the debt crisis of the 1980s.

The oil crisis also served to prove to the United States and other developed states that they were vulnerable, that they needed to explore alternative energy sources and strengthen conservation efforts, and that the Persian Gulf could be a.significant security concern. The crisis sparked by OPEC led the Western states, with the exception of France, to create the International Energy Agency in order to coordinate their response to OPEC's actions. The oil embargo imposed by the Arab oil-producing states on the United States for its support of Israel during the Arab–Israeli war had a significant impact on US foreign policy. In particular it led President Nixon to seek closer ties with the Shah of Iran, culminating in a virtual alliance between the United States and Iran. Nixon promised arms shipments in exchange for oil. Finally, the oil crisis was also partially responsible for undermining detente. The United States believed that, in the spirit of detente, the Soviet Union should have warned them of the Egyptian attack on Israel in 1973.

During the 1980s, a dramatic decline in oil prices followed high levels in the early years of the decade. Collective action by OPEC averted a crisis at the beginning of the 1990s on the outbreak of hostilities in the Middle East and helped the recovery from the collapse that accompanied the economic downturn in South-East Asia in 1998. Ecuador and Gabon withdrew their membership in 1992 and 1995 respectively, and Iraq has not been a part of OPEC quota agreements since 1998. Lately, Indonesia has been reconsidering its membership, having become a net importer and being unable to meet its production quota.

Due to skyrocketing barrel prices in 2004, OPEC's 11 members received $338 billion in revenue from oil exports, a 42 per cent increase from the previous year, and a more significant amount when compared with the $23 billion they received in 1972. However, OPEC has been communicating lately that its members have little excess pumping capacity, indicating that the cartel is losing influence over crude oil prices, thereby undermining its capacity to have an effect on the world economy and global politics.

Regional organisations

The other important area occupied by associations of states is that of regional organisations. They are generally economic in their purposes and vary greatly in size and complexity. Small groups of Pacific island states create cooperative organisations. Africa has generated a steady flow of generally economic regional institutions, although in recent years these have sometimes been security based. Their survival rate has been poor as they have become the victims of the continent's political instabilities, but the African Union, which succeeded the Organisation of African States, has become a long-running feature of African politics. Asia has generated both ASEAN and APEC and they have become important elements in Asian economic cooperation, so much so that membership in them carries with it political significance.

The Commonwealth

Two rather different organisations have resulted from the end of particular empires. The Commonwealth has a membership which is global rather than regional and consists of states which were formerly British overseas territories, plus others which joined later on. The role of the Commonwealth is particularly difficult to define, chiefly because the attitudes and ambitions of the independent dominions – Canada, Australia and New Zealand, together with the UK itself – frequently differ greatly from those of the African members, and the South Asian members as frequently find themselves holding a middle ground. Without a security function or any very deliberate economic purpose, the Commonwealth nonetheless seems to be valuable enough to its members as a source of some shared traditions buttressed by substantial educational programmes.

The Commonwealth of Independent States brings together former republics of the USSR and is designed to serve a residual security purpose, though it, too, principally runs on much the same basis as the (formerly British) Commonwealth. There are many others and, expectably, the more functional they are, the more securely they exist, and the more purely political, such as the Arab League, the more their membership tends to be divided and their effective influence curtailed.

The European Union

Of all the regional organisations, the most complicated is the European Union. The reason is that the EU, successor to the European Community and before that the Common Market, has always had two purposes: one to bring about a European free trade area with its own rules, practices and controls and the other to create a European con-federal, perhaps eventually federal, state, the first being the chosen route by which to reach the second. The result of these hybrid intentions has been to create an entity which is partly an economic association of states and partly an incipient federal government. This has produced an institution with some of the traditional characteristics of an international organisation run by a council of member governments and at the same time some of the familiar administrative and, more recently, political characteristics of a single state.

Both purposes and their associated characteristics have been rendered more difficult by the steady enlargement of the EU which has taken place since 1972. It is currently facing its greatest challenge so far with the entry of 10 new members from central and eastern Europe, raising the number of members to 25. Apart from the inherent difficulty of an enterprise which includes so many divergent levels of development, administrative traditions and languages, the fundamental problem is of a different order. The economic objectives of the EU have been generally in tune with the contemporary economic policy consensus and have proved to be malleable. By contrast, the project to create a close European political union has been overtaken by events. It had its origins in the international situation of the 1940s and 1950s when it seemed entirely rational to try to base European security on the creation of a great state, since all contemporary evidence suggested that economic and political security was most clearly present in large-scale, land-mass states – the USA, the USSR. Moreover, the experience of the two wars of 1914 and 1939 strongly suggested that combining Germany and France in a single entity would be the best guarantee of future peace.

The unfolding of the processes of globalisation have removed the premise: it is no longer true that large size conveys such benefits and the spirit of the times celebrates individual activities and beliefs rather than political authorities and prefers smaller, sometimes very small, focuses of loyalty to the grandeurs of the traditional state. It is not surprising therefore that the second objective of the EU has consistently run into difficulties and that further progress in the direction of a federal state seems uncertain. Certainly the original idea that the consequences of creating a European economic entity would lead via a single currency inexorably to a unitary state is plainly no longer sustainable. Nonetheless, there is no doubt that the EU is a giant among regional IGOs and, more than any other, plays a role as a serious independent actor on the global stage.

Details of other significant regional associations of states follow and basic information and a longer list of them can be found in Part B, Chapter 3.

ASEAN

The Association of South East Asian Nations was founded on 8 August 1967. The foreign ministers of five nations (Indonesia, Malaysia, Singapore,

Thailand and the Philippines) represented their governments at the founding meeting.

ASEAN was born at a time when the fear of North Vietnam and China's regional political and military ambitions was a primary concern to the five member states. They were motivated by both a search for collective regional security and a mutual need for reducing the threat of domestic guerilla movements. Initially the containment of Vietnam was a major focus, but with the end of the Cold War, and in the new international environment, Vietnam was admitted as a member in 1995. In 1999 Cambodia also joined ASEAN, which now comprised all South East Asian states.

ASEAN members had a number of initial primary goals. They were deeply concerned in the late 1960s with the need to accelerate economic growth in their countries and to create mechanisms of cooperation between their economies. Growth was one avenue to reducing the perceived danger of domestic communist insurgencies. Plans for ASEAN activities included such collaborative areas as transportation, communication and agriculture.

ASEAN possesses a permanent secretariat, based in Jakarta, and is governed by a Standing Committee that acts between the annual conference of foreign ministers. The Standing Committee oversees nine programme committees that act in such areas as grain reserves, tariffs and the ASEAN Petroleum Sharing Plan. While these committees have achieved some successes, the individual nations of ASEAN have gone their own ways in terms of economic development and growth. One difficulty for implementing the association's cooperative programmes has come from the growing economic differences between member states. While all the ASEAN members would have been considered 'developing' when the organisation was founded, their economic success has been highly mixed.

The countries within the ASEAN community have enjoyed significant economic growth, with the notable exception of the Philippines. Compared with the late 1960s, countries such as Indonesia, Malaysia and Thailand have made enormous strides in terms of economic development and the creation of significant internal industries. Singapore has advanced even more rapidly as an international finance, trade and processing centre. Brunei, which joined in 1984, is an exceptionally wealthy oil-exporting country. The increasing gap between those countries that might be classified as newly industrialising and the Philippines has made economic cooperation difficult at some levels.

North American Free Trade Agreement

In 1989 Canada and the United States concluded the Canada–US Free Trade Agreement (FTA). Each is the other's largest single trading partner and both expected to benefit from the agreement. The agreement provided for a much-needed dispute resolution mechanism, and in 1992 Canada's exports to the United States reached Can. $122.3 billion, a 13.6 per cent increase over 1991. Eighty per cent of Canadian exports are destined for the United States and the United States provides 65 per cent of foreign direct investment in Canada. The FTA laid the groundwork for NAFTA. Expanding the trade agreement to include Mexico was a logical step, opening up a hitherto protected market for goods and services of 85 million people to US and Canadian exports and investment.

The tripartite negotiations began in June 1991. In 1992 Canada's merchandise trade with the United States had a value of Can. $125.5 billion, and with Mexico Can. $771 million. Mexico's merchandise trade with Canada stood at Can. $2.8 billion and with the United States at Can. $42.6 billion. The value of US merchandise trade with Canada was Can. $96.6 billion and with Mexico Can. $48.6 billion. In 1993 the flow of trade and investment between the three countries had reached around Can. $500 billion.

NAFTA came into effect on 1 January 1994 and created the world's largest free trade area. It removed the majority of tariffs and import licences on all manufactured goods (immediately or over a ten-year phase-in period), provided greater market access for service industries, permitted greater mobility for professional and business travellers, and generally allowed freer entry into an integrated North American market of 360 million consumers. More precise North American rules of origin, to determine which products qualified for duty-free treatment in North America, were established. Government procurement contracts were opened up to foreign bidders; equal access to bid processes was to be made available in several sectors. Trade dispute resolution procedures were created. Each signatory, however, continued to protect key domestic industries, culture (film, publishing, recording and broadcasting), education, water, health care, labour standards and social services, natural resources, the environment and telecommunications.

NAFTA was not without its critics, who were concerned, for example, about the environmental impact, loss of US jobs to Mexico, trade imbalances, investment diversion rather than growth and the political and economic stability of Mexico. Despite that, political leaders in all three countries continued to speak optimistically of NAFTA's long-term beneficial effects and look to expand its relations with, and even extend membership to, countries in Central and South America.

Mercosur

As a key piece in a sweeping effort towards trade liberalisation in a previously protectionism-prone Latin America region, Mercosur emerged in 1991 as a commercial treaty, establishing a common market among Argentina, Brazil, Uruguay and Paraguay. As an economic entity, Mercosur ranks fourth with the world's largest, after the European Union, the United States and Japan. It has more than 200 million consumers and boasts a combined gross domestic product (GDP) of more than US$1 trillion. The four countries' intra-regional trade grew by 300 per cent between 1990 and 1998, up to approximately $21 billion. Despite the impressive intra-regional figures, trade with non-member countries has also risen considerably since the treaty's implementation. From 1990 to 1996, for example, Mercosur imports from the European Union and the United States increased by 246 per cent and 195 per cent, respectively.

The intent of those who are part of Mercosur is that it should play an increasingly prominent role at the international level, with a dynamic external agenda covering processes of negotiation and consultation across and beyond the Western hemisphere. As of 1 January 1995, Mercosur became both a free trade area and a customs union at the same time. A customs union represents a deeper stage in integration compared with a free trade area. In other words, a customs union is a free trade area which adopts a common trade policy in relation to other countries. The basic element of a customs union is the Common External Tariff (CET), which establishes the level of tariff protection imposed on produce from other countries when entering the integrated market. Aside from the CET, there are other elements of common trade policy, such as unified rules of origin, common

competition policies and common trade remedies against disruptive imports.

Internally, Mercosur also has a broad agenda, which extends beyond economic and trade issues. In its institutional structure, there are several working groups dealing with the so-called 'social dimension', which covers areas such as education, labour, culture, environment, justice and consumer protection. Mercosur has adopted a flexible approach, whereby every advance is made in incremental steps, after consolidation of previous developments. For example, even though the Treaty of Asunción, which established Mercosur, foresaw that the Common Market would be implemented by the end of 1994, member states decided to revise the timetable and concentrate on the completion of a customs union in the light of the complexities faced during the course of negotiations. Mercosur does not have quantitative restrictions between its members, with the exception of the automotive sector, where Brazil has about 60 per cent share of the Argentine auto market, while Argentina commands less than 3 per cent of the Brazilian market. Other non-tariff barriers are being gradually eliminated.

However, Mercosur endured tough times with the Argentine crisis of 2001 which spilled over to Uruguay, which also had to reschedule its foreign debt in 2003 – a successful negotiation that has not, however, freed the country from debt sustainability concerns. Also, trade relations between Brazil and Argentina have proved problematic since Brazil devalued its currency considerably in January 1999, while Argentina pursued what is now known to have been an inherently unsustainable policy of exchange rate parity with the dollar. The trade deficit Argentina developed with Brazil, and the Argentine decrease in competitiveness, are two of many factors at the root of the Argentine collapse of 2001. The dispute between Brazil and Argentina that erupted in July 2004 concerned the production of 'white goods', such as refrigerators and other electrical appliances. At that time, Argentina withdrew automatic licensing for imports of large household appliances from Brazil and started to charge a 21 per cent tax on television sets made in the Brazilian duty-free zone of Manaus in the state of Amazonas. The dispute became known as 'the refrigerator war'. Later in 2004, the problem was slightly smoothed over when the two countries agreed on a system of quotas for some of the Brazilian goods. But Brazilian manufacturers remain dissatisfied with the remaining restrictions, which they say should not exist under the framework of Mercosur. Yet Argentina maintains that the measures are included under a series of 'safeguard' mechanisms permitted under Mercosur rules.

Nevertheless, despite sectoral disagreements, with the remarkable turnaround of the Argentine economy – which grew by 8 per cent between 2001 and 2003 – there might be reason for optimism regarding trade relations between these two key partners. This may be helped by the fact that there remains some room for manoeuvre to help local industries struggling to remain productive, particularly in Argentina.

Organisation for Economic Cooperation and Development

On 30 September 1961, the Organisation for Economic Cooperation and Development (OECD) was founded to coordinate the economic and social policies of Western industrialised countries. The OECD became the successor to the Organisation for European Economic Cooperation (OEEC), an organisation created by participants of the Marshall Plan. The OECD included the United States and Canada in an Atlantic alliance that was originally viewed by supporters as an economic counterpart to NATO. One of its key creators, Jean Monnet, hoped to link Europe and the Atlantic powers and thereby permanently ensure US support for the European Economic Community .

The OECD was guided by broad mandates to contribute to overall economic growth and employment in its member countries, and to coordinate economic policies, trade and aid to lesser developed nations. Today, in addition to these functions, it facilitates discussion and monitors international monetary policy, and sets guidelines for multinational corporations and development aid. The organisation's resolutions are voluntary and designed to establish agreement on global economic matters. Probably the OECD's greatest service has been that of an international forum.

The organisation has its headquarters in Paris and includes an appointed secretary-general, a council and chairman, and an executive committee (with Canada, France, Germany, Italy, Japan, the United Kingdom and the United States as permanent members and with seven other rotating seats). The Commission of the European Communities participates in the council meetings. There are 14 OECD standing committees of varying degrees of importance. The Economic Policy Committee played a significant role in reforming the international monetary system in the 1960s and 1970s and is represented at the IMF and in other economic bodies. The Development Assistance Committee, established in 1960, manages $50 billion in aid and reviews member contributions to various aid programmes, encouraging each member to contribute 0.7 per cent of its gross national product (GNP) to aid. The Trade, Financial and Fiscal Affairs Committee considers trade and commerce between members and with non-industrialised regions. The Economic Development and Review Committee evaluates each country's economic situation and at the end of each year publishes a report on economic conditions, employment and the environment in member states. The objectivity of these reports has been called into question, particularly since each government must approve the report on its own country. Nevertheless, the reports shape the discussion at annual OECD conferences where economic ministers consider current and projected trends and the progress of economic talks, such as those held by the General Agreement on Tariffs and Trade.

In the late 1970s the OECD attempted to make recommendations to the Group of Seven (G7) industrial nations regarding the drastic altering of monetary and fiscal policy as the only way to stem inflation and reduce unemployment spurred by the OPEC oil price increases. President Carter and other Western nations rejected what they called an attempt by the OECD to dictate policy to its members. Subsequently, the OECD refrained from overtly trying to influence international economic policy.

The OECD boasts that it does not conceal disagreements but encourages participants to learn from a so-called confrontational approach not typically welcomed in international politics, but which the organisation claims to have inherited from the OEEC. Thus it argues that US–German differences in the 1970s and early 1980s over Germany's tight monetary policy were an example of the system at work. Again in the early 1990s confrontation appeared rampant, with the United States questioning Japanese trade surpluses and Japan in turn protesting the US demand for so-called 'managed trade'.

What effect, if any, the OECD has on global

economic advancement is unclear. It does not consider or enforce concrete regulations like the GATT. In fact, it was with the intention of keeping the GATT as the leading economic institution that the Eisenhower administration refused to grant the OECD much freedom. The OECD has also been criticised as a form of economic collaboration against the lesser developed nations and the newly independent East European and Eurasian states. While several individual agencies may serve a valuable purpose for member nations, the organisation as a whole lacks strong leadership and is pushed and pulled along by competing national interests.

Organisation for Security and Cooperation in Europe

The OSCE was previously the Conference on Security and Cooperation in Europe (CSCE), which began on 3 July 1973 and lasted until the signing of the Helsinki Final Act on 1 August 1975. While the CSCE began and ended in Helsinki, the majority of the meetings took place in Geneva. It was attended by all 33 European countries (with the sole exception of Albania), the United States and Canada.

The idea of a security conference goes back to the 1950s, stimulated by both the absence of a peace treaty ending the Second World War and the tensions and temporary respites of the Cold War. The initiative was taken up by Poland and other Warsaw Pact members in 1964 but was not received enthusiastically by governments in the West, particularly after the Soviet invasion of Czechoslovakia in 1968. The West also insisted that there could be no possibility of a conference until the issue of Germany's borders and status had been settled. West Germany's policy of *Ostpolitik* thereby created the basis for a conference, since the policy had resulted in agreements with the Soviet Union and Poland, the Basic Agreement with East Germany, and allowed for the Quadripartite Rights Agreement on Berlin between the United States, Britain, France and the Soviet Union. At the same time, a general relaxation of tension, or detente, became apparent with the US–Soviet dialogue on strategic arms (SALT I and II) and agreement to begin negotiations on mutual and balanced force reductions in Europe. Detente, particularly the policies of President Richard Nixon, laid the foundation for the CSCE and the CSCE, in turn, came to embody the spirit of detente.

However, the aims of the 35 participating states were invariably different. The overriding aim of the Soviet Union and its Warsaw Pact allies was to gain recognition of and legitimacy for the geo-political post-Second World War settlement, especially a Western commitment to territorial changes that had taken place. A secondary aim was to try to bring about closer economic cooperation, including improved trade access to the West and more significant technology transfers to the East. The link between security and detente was recognised by the West and was developed beyond a mere code for safer inter-state behaviour to encompass a means of bringing about a wider reduction of risk in Europe. It also included not only state-to-state relations but much more complex linkages between states and individual human rights and fundamental freedoms. To European neutrals and non-aligned countries, the CSCE offered the opportunity of going beyond bloc-to-bloc confrontation to develop a new security relationship in Europe. Overall, the conference not only reflected a relaxation of tension but aimed to make a further contribution to the process of detente between East and West.

The result of two years of negotiation, the Helsinki Final Act, was signed on 1 August 1975, thus making the CSCE a permanent institution. The Act included four 'baskets' or categories. The first three baskets linked security issues, economic cooperation and humanitarian cooperation in a variety of general principles designed to guide behaviour combined with specific commitments that each participating state undertook to carry out. Since the Act was not a treaty and no legal enforcement was possible, the fourth basket included the provision of follow-up meetings at which implementation could be discussed along with ways of improving East–West relations.

The first follow-up meeting took place in Belgrade between October 1977 and March 1978. However, it was dominated by the deterioration in relations between the United States and the Soviet Union. The United States was concerned with the plight of many human rights activists in the East and saw the meeting as a tribunal in which to arraign the Soviet Union and its allies. The Soviet Union, for its part, tended to regard the CSCE and the Final Act as achievement enough in securing recognition of Soviet domination of Eastern Europe, although Soviet leader Leonid Brezhnev had suggested a number of pan-European conferences on energy, transport and the environment. The 1977–1978 meeting ended with no substantive results beyond a reaffirmation of commitments already entered into and agreement to meet again. The next meeting included three additional expert discussions – on the peaceful settlement of disputes, the Mediterranean and a scientific forum –presaging the wider development of the CSCE or Helsinki process.

The second follow-up meeting took place between November 1980 and September 1983 at a time of particularly tense East–West relations caused by the Soviet invasion of Afghanistan, the deployment of new Soviet missiles in Eastern Europe and increasingly repressive measures against human rights groups in the East. The imposition of martial law in Poland in December 1981 and the suppression of the Polish trade union movement, Solidarity, caused the meeting to be suspended for seven months. Despite these problems, there was enough of a consensus, led by West Germany and France together with the neutrals and nonaligned, to press for a substantive concluding document that sought to build on the Helsinki Final Act.

While there were limited advances against Soviet and East European intransigence on the human rights side, a mandate for a Conference on Confidence and Security-Building Measures and Disarmament (CDE) was agreed to, despite US reluctance. The CDE opened in Stockholm in September 1983. In addition, further expert meetings on human rights issues were arranged in Ottawa and Bern, a second meeting on the peaceful settlement of disputes in Athens, a cultural forum in Budapest and a seminar on the Mediterranean in Venice.

The third follow-up meeting in Vienna between November 1986 and January 1989 occurred against a backdrop of increasing change in the Soviet Union and Eastern Europe. The meeting therefore provided a useful forum for discussions on those changes as well as offering the opportunity of harnessing those changes to new international commitments. The earlier trade-off between the West's desire for an improvement in human rights and the East's emphasis on military security became much more complicated. Among the issues covered in the concluding document and related statements was the opening of negotiations on Conventional Armed Forces in Europe (CFE) within the CSCE process, which were to take place alongside further negotiations on confidence

and security-building measures. But the reforming ideas of *glasnost* and *perestroika* introduced by Soviet leader Mikhail Gorbachev profoundly changed the debate on human rights and other humanitarian issues, not least by allowing for the recognition of the legitimacy of international discussion and by recognising the right of individuals and groups to monitor implementation. Other elements in the concluding document covered religious freedom, the rule of law and freedom, and of movement for individuals both within their own countries and outside them. Moreover, in addition to the security negotiations agreed to at Vienna, further meetings were scheduled on information (in London), human rights (in Paris, Copenhagen and Moscow, the last in autumn 1991), the environment (Sofia), economic cooperation (Bonn), the Mediterranean (Majorca) and culture (Cracow).

A summit meeting to be held in Paris in November 1990 was also arranged to mark the fifteenth anniversary of the Final Act and to discuss the profundity of the changes in Eastern Europe. This itself broke new ground through the establishment of permanent bodies: a small secretariat in Prague, a Conflict Prevention Centre in Vienna, and an Office for Free Elections in Warsaw. In addition, foreign ministers were to meet at least annually. The meeting in effect marked the end of the Cold War and sought in very broad terms to set the framework for a new security system in Europe. It was decided to institutionalise the work of the CSCE as an organisation and as a result it was renamed the OSCE (effective from 1 January 1995), with a small secretariat in Prague. The OSCE currently consists of 55 members – the European and Central Asian states plus the United States and Canada. Its current remit covers a wide range of security-related issues including arms control, preventive diplomacy, confidence- and security-building measures, human rights, election monitoring and economic and environmental security.

Organisation of American States

Founded in 1948 at a conference in Bogota, the OAS includes most of the states of the Western Hemisphere, with Canada the principal exception. The Bogota conference followed a series of pan-American conferences.

The OAS holds regular ministerial meetings and, via the 1947 Rio Pact, which is also called the Pact of Petropolis, all of the OAS member states are obligated to provide mutual aid if any of them is attacked. The OAS is dominated by the United States, which used the organisation to condemn communism, most notably at the 1954 Caracas Conference, and to ostracise Fidel Castro's Cuba, especially at the Punta del Este Conference in 1961. It facilitates debate and an exchange of views, but lacks influence and authority.

African Union

Formerly the Organisation of African Unity (OAU), the African Union is the most influential pan-African regional organisation. Ethiopian Emperor Haile Selassie called African leaders to a conference in Addis Ababa (now the organisation's home) on 25 May 1963 to found the OAU. The new organisation pledged to work towards improving political and economic cooperation in Africa. The OAU generally preferred the moderate Monrovia or Brazzaville group (led by Julius Nyerere of Tanzania) plan to gradually increase such ties rather than follow the Casablanca group's (led by Kwame Nkrumah of Ghana) call for Africans to take revolutionary steps towards total political unification. The OAU did not ignore the issue of unification, but success has been limited to support for regional attempts such as the Joint African Madagascar Association, the East African Common Market, the West African Economic Union and the Central African Economic Union, all formed between 1965 and 1970. Attention to African unity was renewed with the 1980 Lagos Plan of action that led to the establishment of an African Economic Community in June 1991, but so far only a few states have agreed to adhere to the treaty.

A secretary-general oversees the AU secretariat and its specialised socio-economic commissions. Each year a different chairman hosts the AU Heads of State meeting and opens the AU Assembly. A Council of Ministers meets semi-annually. The lack of a clear division of responsibilities between the chairman and the secretary-general has led to some leadership confusion. While the secretary-general was originally intended to oversee administrative duties, he took on a political role, especially regarding the settlement of disputes. The OAU founders also created an Arbitration Commission, which can rule on petitions regarding human rights abuses, and a Liberation Committee to work for the independence of all African states. The declaration of liberation led to extreme action at its second (1964) meeting, supporting rebels against Moise Tshombe's pro-European regime during the Congo crisis. The states favouring less drastic action protested by forming the short-lived African Madagascar Organisation. Moreover, the OAU's inability to settle the Congo crisis represented its first failure and thus began the disillusionment with the OAU.

The AU comprises all 70 African states with the exception of Morocco (which initially chose not to join because of territorial claims to Mauritania, then withdrew in 1984 to protest the membership of Western Sahara over which it claimed sovereignty), South Africa (until the Mandela regime officially brought an end to apartheid) and Namibia (while under South African rule until 1990). The OAU agreed to isolate South Africa economically and diplomatically in a resolution of 1970 and did not surrender its opposition to apartheid until the 1994 elections brought Nelson Mandela to power.

Objectives

The original OAU Charter stated its objectives as the promotion of unity, cooperation with the United Nations, economic improvement, the elimination of colonialism and support for self-determination. In 1964 the Cairo resolution added a respect for the boundaries of members' states and suggested that changes should be brought about only by peaceful means. This stipulation was justified by the general feeling that to open up colonial boundaries for negotiation would bring chaos to the continent. Somalia in particular has emphasised the contradictory nature of these principles.

The OAU has been criticised for shying away from internal political disputes. It watched on the sidelines in the late 1960s as civil war tore apart Nigeria and a five-year crisis raged in the Congo, and witnessed repression in Uganda under Idi Amin and the Central African Republic under Jean Bedel Bokassa. Continued conflict between Libya and Chad (where the OAU's peacekeeping expedition attempt failed), Ethiopia and Somalia, Ethiopia and the Eritrean Liberation Movement, the Biafra secessionist movement from Nigeria, and the civil wars in Angola and Mozambique were met with little action by the OAU.

The organisation, however, is involved in finding a settlement to roughly one third of the inter-state African disputes in which it is involved. It successively helped end, for example, disputes between Algeria and Morocco, Congo and Nigeria, Uganda and Tanzania, Rwanda and Burundi, and Guinea and Ivory Coast. The OAU has paid particular attention to the problem of refugees and in 1967 established a commission to assist refugees. Its creation in 1986 of a council of 'wise men' recognised political means and a case-by-case approach as the best way to ameliorate the plight of refugees. OAU activism increased in the early 1990s with attempts to find peace for the Horn of Africa, negotiate between the Sudanese government and the southern-based liberation movement, and its oversight of elections in South Africa.

The OAU remains limited to facilitating negotiations since it has no peacekeeping force at its disposal. Although currently studying the prospects of such a force, limited resources have prevented much headway. The OAU is more likely to continue its close cooperation with the United Nations. The staggering crises across Africa continuously present the OAU with formidable tasks. It struggles with its momentous debt problem as unpaid bills each year equal total annual expenditure. However, internal differences over the best solutions and spending practices have delayed financial reform. The OAU's problems go beyond the financial, however, to include ethnic differences, ideology, population pressures, development and different regional affiliations.

In 2002 the OAU reformed itself as the African Union (AU) and has tried, though much handicapped by the inherent problems in the continent, to play a greater role in matters of good governance and the resolution of long-standing feuds. The global recognition of the crisis and possible genocide taking place in the Dharfur region of southern Sudan in 2004 has drawn the AU into a small military intervention and given it a highly exposed role to play. In early 2006, however, the AU announced that it had run out of funds to continue the operation in Sudan.

Western European Union

Western European Union was a term often used during the 1940s and 1950s to denote the growing number of links among Western European governments. It took on a formal definition in May 1955 with the ratification of protocols agreed to in London in September and signed in Paris in October 1954. These protocols extended and developed the Treaty of Economic, Social and Cultural Collaboration and Collective Self-Defence signed in Brussels on 17 March 1948. The signatories of the Brussels Treaty were Belgium, France, Luxembourg, the Netherlands and Great Britain; the signatories of the protocols on 23 October 1954 included, in addition to these, the Federal Republic of Germany and Italy. Spain and Portugal became members of the Western European Union (WEU) in November 1988.

The 1954 protocols established a council made up of the member governments and a consultative assembly comprised of national parliamentarians who were representatives to the consultative assembly of the Council of Europe. The headquarters of the WEU are in London and in Paris; however, there have been discussions about moving them to a single location, Brussels.

The aim of the WEU was to allow for the rearmament of West Germany and the entry of Germany and Italy into NATO. There was a certain irony in the use of the Brussels Treaty to bring this about since that treaty had originally been designed to safeguard France and the Benelux countries from a resurgent, aggressive and remilitarised Germany. However, it became clear with the communist coup in Czechoslovakia, pressure over Berlin and other threats from the Soviet Union that Germany was no longer the primary enemy and that it needed to take part both in its own and in the West's defence against communism. Efforts to bring this about began in 1950 with the proposals from French Premier René Pleven for a European Defence Community. This followed closely on the heels of proposals from his foreign minister, Robert Schuman, in May 1950 for a common European Coal and Steel Community. For the defence community, the general aim was to develop the idea of a supra-national authority which would command a European army containing German troops along with those from France and the Benelux countries. The plan was signed in 1952 but, after considerable debate in France, was defeated in the French National Assembly in August 1954.

It was in these circumstances that Sir Anthony Eden, the British Foreign Secretary, took up the idea of modifying the Brussels Treaty which had largely been overtaken by the North Atlantic Treaty that brought the United States and Canada into a European defensive alliance against the communist threat. The advantages of a modified Brussels Treaty stemmed from the fact that it did not create a new supra-national authority but retained a more traditional inter-governmental structure. It allowed German troops to become a part of NATO forces and, therefore, an unlikely threat to security within Western Europe. It also provided for the station-ing of British troops in Germany to safeguard further against any German breach of its obliga-tions (an important factor in that it was the first time that Britain had stationed forces on the continent of Europe in peacetime). Germany also undertook not to manufacture nuclear, bio-logical or chemical weapons, to abide by the Charter of the United Nations and not to seek the reunification of Germany, or any changes in its boundaries, by force. An agency for the con-trol of armaments in Europe was set up in Paris. In a separate protocol, France, Britain and the United States agreed to end the occupation regime in Germany.

The immediate importance of the WEU lay in allowing Germany and Italy to become members of NATO, to which the military responsibilities of the WEU were immediately transferred. Dur-ing the 1960s, the WEU was generally ignored. It proved useful in allowing Britain to remain in touch with the six members of the European Community, especially after the two vetoes on British membership in the Community by French President Charles de Gaulle, but was used for little else.

Revival

During the 1980s, however, there was increasing talk about reviving the WEU as an organisation expressing the defence and security identity of the European Community (EC). This came about largely as a result of efforts within Euro-pean Political Cooperation (EPC) to establish a greater security identity. These efforts, however, were quashed, largely through the opposition of Denmark, Greece and Ireland. Closer coopera-tion between France and Germany, which led to the establishment of a joint brigade and a defence council, was seen as potentially divisive by other European members of NATO and also contributed to increased talk of reviving the WEU. Since the WEU included France and Ger-many but excluded those reluctant to move further towards a European security system, it became the logical organisation to develop. That development, however, has been far from smooth. Increased efforts have been made to coordinate ideas on security and to coordinate force policies (particularly out of the NATO area and especially in the Middle East), but not by all members in every crisis. Moreover, there have been doubts about the precise relationship between WEU activities and those of NATO and the impact of WEU discussions and actions on relations with the United States.

With the end of the Cold War the role of the WEU once again evolved. The European Union (EU), led by France and Germany, began to attempt the development of a Common Foreign and Security Policy (CFSP). In 1992 the WEU defined its operational role in the 'Petersburg Tasks' (named after the place near Bonn where they were agreed) as humanitarian and rescue tasks, peacekeeping tasks and tasks of combat forces in crisis management, including peace-making. The 1997 EU Amsterdam Treaty incor-porated the Petersburg Tasks. In 1994 NATO leaders lent their support to a European Security and Defence Identity (ESDI) and agreed to pro-vide NATO support for WEU operations. As the EU sought to establish a security capacity autonomous of NATO, the possibility of in effect absorbing the WEU's functions as the EU's 'third pillar' finally occurred at the turn of the twentieth century. Currently the WEU consists of EU states that are also NATO members.

Council of Europe

The Statute of the Council of Europe was signed in London on 5 May 1949 by Belgium, Denmark, France, Ireland, Italy, Luxembourg, the Nether-lands, Norway, Sweden and the United King-dom. Other countries have since acceded, beginning with Greece and Turkey in 1949. With the end of the Cold War the former Soviet-dom-inated states began to seek membership after the revolutionary changes of 1989. Czechoslovakia became the 25th member of the Council in February 1991. Russia has associate status.

Membership is open to any European state which accepts 'the principles of the rule of law and of the enjoyment by all persons within its jurisdiction of human rights and fundamental freedoms...' (Article 3). The Statute provides for both withdrawal and suspension, the threat of the latter leading Greece and Turkey to with-draw during their periods of military dictator-ship. The aim of the Council is 'to achieve a greater unity between its Members for the pur-pose of safeguarding and realising the ideals and principles which are their common heritage and facilitating their economic and social progress' (Article 1). The official languages of the Council are English and French. Its headquarters are in Strasbourg, France.

The Council consists of two main bodies, the Consultative or Parliamentary Assembly, composed of 170 representatives, and the Committee of Ministers. Under the Statute, the Committee of (Foreign) Ministers was set up to represent each member state. The committee meets twice a year to make decisions, on the basis of unanimity, regarding a wide range of issues excluding national defence.

The Consultative Assembly can make recommendations on any matter which falls within the aim and scope of the Council. The Assembly has determined that, unlike the Committee of Ministers, it can discuss defence matters. A joint or liaison committee was set up in 1950 to try to harmonise the views of the two bodies, but it has not always proven successful. The Assembly usually meets three times a year for approximately a week. Since 1951 its membership has been determined by national parliaments. Much of the work of the Assembly is carried out in parliamentary committees. The output of the Council, meanwhile, is generally the result of discussions within Council-sponsored conferences, such as those of local and regional authorities, ministers of education and justice ministers.

The idea of bringing European states together into some form of union was far from new, but the Second World War created a strong body of opinion in most countries of Western Europe that extreme nationalism had been the cause of war and, therefore, a new regional structure was necessary. Winston Churchill, in a speech at Zurich University in 1946, called for such a structure, suggesting the possibility of some form of a 'United States of Europe'. Many others were also inspired by the idea of a federal Europe which would ensure peace between traditional enemies, especially France and Germany. A variety of groups to pursue European unity was formed. A meeting of federalists from 16 European democracies in the Congress of Europe at The Hague in May 1948 provided further stimulus for governmental action. Many looked to Britain for leadership. Although the British government was drawn into the study of a European Assembly, and the statute establishing the Council was signed in London, Britain, together with the Scandinavian countries, favoured only limited inter-governmental cooperation as opposed to the more extensive cooperation envisioned by the rest of the Council.

Conventions

Despite the British and Scandinavian reservations, the Council has agreed on a considerable number of conventions concerning social issues, culture, patents, broadcasting and television, public health, travel, youth and human rights. Advances on the last issue have been most significant, both for individuals seeking redress and for governments in gaining international recognition of their democratic systems.

The European Convention on Human Rights and Fundamental Freedoms was signed in November 1950. It set up two institutions, the Commission and the Court of Human Rights, to examine and adjudicate on possible breaches of human rights. One of its most important provisions is the right, once all domestic procedures have been exhausted, of individuals to appeal to the Commission and the Court against the actions of their own governments. Signatories to the Convention have pledged to accept the decisions of the Court. Thus, although the Council was designed to be an inter-governmental body with only a consultative assembly, it has introduced, at least in terms of respect for human rights, an element of supra-nationality to its proceedings.

Since 1989, Europe has sustained both integrating trends of cooperation and fragmenting shifts of conflict and division. Member states now number 46 and at the time of writing there is one pending application from Belarus. The United States, Canada, Japan and Mexico hold Observer Status from outside the region. The organisation's role is now more complex as the Council of Europe's members straddle more geography. The first Council Summit held in Vienna in 1993 reassessed its political goals for the organisation, focusing on 'democratic security' via human rights, democracy and the rule of law.

To accomplish its ambitions, the Council is adapting in many ways. In 2000, the Committee of Ministers realised the need to make additional reforms within the organisation in order to manage its institutions more efficiently. The Council continues to assist integration with new member states of the European Union. In 1990, the Council initiated the Cooperation and Assistance Programmes with Central and Eastern European Countries which organise expert missions, training, workshops, dissemination of information and legal assistance. During its own transition, the Council has maintained itself as a forum for transnational dialogue in the region as well as providing an international legal resource.

The Council is also increasing its standard-setting role. It has concluded almost 200 legally binding treaties or conventions within Europe and is an asset to the European Union in this regard. Membership of the Council is also an unofficial precedent for EU membership as all 25 members first acceded to the Council before becoming party to the EU. It provides advisory opinions to states on policies and has elaborated human rights charters extensively, including the European Convention on Human Rights, resulting in longer-term initiatives. In 1998, the European Court of Human Rights became a permanent court, the only judiciary body on human rights in Europe, replacing the temporary court system that had been in place since the establishment of the organisation. In 1999, the institution of a Commissioner for Human Rights was established to advance human rights awareness and education as well as to promote effective human rights compliance among the Council's member states.

Most state members assume a strong political will to absorb the Council's conventions into their national legislation. This has given the Council more influence to help with this process, enforce its standards, settle disputes and provide other requested services. This aspect of the Council's work is expanding as membership increases. The European Convention on Human Rights, the European Social Charter and the European Convention for the Prevention of Torture and Inhumane or Degrading Treatment or Punishment are some of the important ways in which Council activities are setting standards on human rights across Europe (signing the Convention on Human Rights is now a requisite for Council membership). The Council has also drafted frameworks for the protection of minorities within nation-states, trans-border migration issues such as trafficking in persons and guidelines on the fight against terrorism.

The monitoring aspect of the Council has been increasing due to the expanded number of members. States that sign treaties or conventions voluntarily accept the responsibility to report to the Council (in the first year and then at three-year intervals) on measures they have taken to align their policies and legal systems with those treaties. Commissions are usually established to assist states in reviewing their internal policies to make certain that treaty provisions are implemented from the regional level all the way to the local level. The Council's activities in the monitoring sphere include issuing opinions and recommendations, collecting information, discussing matters with the Assembly and any other activities that fall within its realm of given power.

New focus

In recent years the Council is continuing to develop the strategy of a participatory democracy through cooperating with and supporting civil society. This strategy has resulted in increased coordination with local entities. In 1994, the Congress of Local and Regional Authorities of the Council of Europe was established as a consultative body to give a larger voice to local entities in policymaking and provide a forum for dialogue on shared problems and experiences crossing multi-levels.

The new focus on civil society also resulted in a resolution of the Council on the status of partnership between the Council and national NGOs (NNGOs), which indicates a deepening partnership between NNGOs and international NGOs (INGOs), particularly those that focus on the Council's aim of democratic reform. Since 2000, four interrelated civil society programmes have been put into place in which INGO activity is a major part: Civil Society Initiatives, the Democratic Leadership Programme, the Schools of Political Studies, and Confidence-building Measures in Civil Society. However, I/NNGOs are now being accessed across the entire spectrum of Council activities. In 2003, all INGOs that had previously achieved consultative status with the Council and some NNGOs were elevated to Participatory Status (374 organisations as of January 2005) and given greater responsibility and sometimes full-scale cooperation with individual projects carried out in the various states. Consultative NNGOs are now being grouped by themes and continue increased dialogue with the Council. The Council also helps in defining the legal personality of NGOs, which is beneficial to other intergovernmental organisations such as the United Nations, in this period of burgeoning NGOs and the importance of creating consistent standards for establishing credible, legitimate and legal NGOs to be recognised on an international scale.

Finally, the Council has most recently taken the initiative to increase collaboration with other inter-governmental organisations, having begun to see the benefits of combining resources and efforts with other entities. For instance, new cooperative trends have emerged between the European Union and the Council. Both the EU and the Council have realised opportunities to network for shared goals based on the same values of democracy, human rights and the rule of law. Since 1993, their joint programmes have been initiated mostly in newly acceded states to complement country-specific multi-lateral thematic activities such as training, workshops and seminars that support legal and institutional reform. However, this is only the beginning. The Council pledged, on 18 February 2005, alongside the OSCE and the UN, to work together to promote the rule of law as a means of promoting and sustaining peace, democracy and development. They look to the future as partners in working towards those principles in post-conflict societies, societies affected by natural disasters, and building a common framework for dealing with terrorism, racism, xenophobia, intolerance and all forms of discrimination.

Economic Community of West African States

ECOWAS was created on 28 May 1975 in Lagos, Nigeria to promote cooperation and integration in order to create an economic and monetary union for encouraging economic growth and development in West Africa. ECOWAS has encountered many problems in the process of regionally integrating West Africa, including political instability and lack of good governance that has plagued many member countries; the insufficient diversification of national economies; the absence of reliable infrastructure; and the multiplicity of organisations for regional integration with the same objectives.

ECOWAS leaders adopted two important defence protocols in 1978 and 1981. These provisions have facilitated regional conflict resolution efforts initiated by ECOWAS. The ECOWAS Monitoring Group (ECOMOG) was established initially on an ad hoc basis as a multinational peacekeeping/peace enforcement force and was the first such group to be established by a regional body. ECOMOG teams are normally comprised of military units or technical experts from ECOWAS member states.

At the Abuja Summit in 1999, the ECOWAS Mechanism for Conflict Prevention, Manage-

ment, Resolution and Security was signed, and it significantly organised the peacekeeping capabilities of ECOWAS. Along with ECOMOG, the Security Council, a Defence and Security Commission and the Early Warning and Monitoring System were officially launched and in operation by May 2000. The Security Council has the authority to make final decisions on the appropriate measures to be taken with regard to situations under consideration. It can authorise all forms of intervention, including the decision to deploy military missions. The Defence Commission's role is to examine all technical and administrative issues and assess logistical requirements for peacekeeping operations. It examines reports from the Observation and Monitoring Centres and makes recommendations to the Security Council. The Observation and Monitoring Centre is the hub of the ECOWAS Early Warning System that has four observation and monitoring zones within the sub-region.

During May 2001 ECOWAS signed a headquarters agreement with Benin to establish an observation zone in Cotonou whose role would be to signal the potential of conflicts in Benin, Nigeria and Togo, collecting data on potential disputes for transmission to the central ECOWAS observatory in Abuja. This would be the fourth zone. The others are in Banjul (The Gambia), Monrovia (Liberia) and Ouagadougou (Burkina Faso).

ECOWAS was originally formed as a regional trade bloc but its functions are primarily concerned with security. ECOWAS Monitoring Group operations started in Liberia to prevent the overthrow of the unpopular government of President Samuel Doe by the National Patriotic Front of Liberia (NPFL) led by Charles Taylor. The intervention force that landed in Liberia on 24 August 1990 consisted of troops contributed by Nigeria, Ghana, Guinea, Sierra Leone and The Gambia. Successive fighting, looting and killing were temporarily halted by a number of short-lived peace accords until the fourteenth peace accord was signed in Abuja in August 1996. ECOMOG oversaw the subsequent elections on 19 July 1997 and was principally responsible for the restoration of peace in Liberia in that year. Renewed crisis in Liberia during 2003 led to ECOWAS deploying a second peacekeeping operation in the region, after a Comprehensive Peace Agreement was reached on 18 August 2003. The ECOWAS Mission in Liberia

(ECOMIL) began deploying outside Monrovia from 9 September 2003, with 3,563 troops from Nigeria, Mali and Senegal. The UNSC approved conversion of ECOMIL into a UN International Stabilisation Force from 1 October 2003.

Since September 2002, a military rebellion in Ivory Coast has drawn ECOWAS into peacekeeping duties in that country. The ECOWAS Security Council met on 26 October and agreed to the deployment of West African troops to monitor a ceasefire signed on 17 October. The ECOWAS Mission in Côte d'Ivoire (ECOMICI) deployed approximately 1,400 troops from Ghana, Togo, Benin, Niger and Senegal. On 28 February 2004, the UN Security Council voted in favour of integrating these West African peacekeepers into a UN Operation in Côte d'Ivoire (UNOCI), from 4 April 2004 for an initial period of 12 months. On 21 February 2005 the chairman of ECOWAS, President Mamadou Tandja of Niger, announced a number of sanctions against the new government in Togo headed by Faure Gnassingbe, who had succeeded his father without an election. He subsequently resigned.

NATO

After the Second World War, Western European states were left economically and militarily exhausted. The Soviet Union was showing signs of strengthening its military and was perceived as a threat among Western European countries. The United Kingdom, France, the Netherlands and Belgium struck a military alliance through the Brussels Treaty in 1948. However, without assistance from allies abroad, the Treaty was not seen as capable of withstanding an aggressive force such as the Soviet Union. Therefore, the United States and Canada were brought into the negotiations. These two countries entered into a new treaty alongside the Brussels Treaty signatories as well as Denmark, Iceland, Italy, Luxembourg, Norway and Portugal as a sound means of providing collective security for all parties. Hence, the North Atlantic Treaty Organisation, an intergovernmental organisation, was established in 1949.

The transatlantic alliance of NATO became a foothold for defence against the Soviet Union particularly, but declared that the possibility of any armed attack against any party was an attack on all parties of the Treaty. The commitment of each state was specifically to 'assist the Party or Parties so attacked by taking forthwith, individually and in concert with the other Parties, such action as it deems necessary, including the use of armed force, to restore and maintain security in the North Atlantic area', as stated in keystone Article 5 of the Treaty.

In the early years of NATO, its efforts were mainly focused on developing its military forces and establishing a presence in the region. New parties signed up to the Treaty, including Greece, Turkey, the Federal Republic of Germany and finally Spain in 1982. The Soviet Union countered with the Warsaw Pact soon after West Germany joined NATO. It aligned itself with the German Democratic Republic, Poland, Hungary, Czechoslovakia, Romania, Bulgaria and Albania.

NATO's ground troops brought in nuclear weapons in 1957 via the USA to counter strong ground forces of the Warsaw Pact allies. The Cold War now posed a more massive threat of total destruction but for that reason may have maintained a stalemate for 40 years until the collapse of the Berlin Wall and the dissolution of the Soviet Union. When the threat disintegrated along with the Warsaw Pact allies, NATO's agenda needed to be reassessed. The changes brought about by the end of the Cold War, including increased globalisation processes and inter-state interactions, also brought increased intra-state security challenges due to ethnic and minority conflicts. NATO's members, meeting at the Rome Summit in 1991, seemed to understand that the very nature of security was in flux and outlined a mission of security in a larger sense than was traditionally viewed.

New collaborations were initiated, including the establishment of the North Atlantic Cooperation Council (NACC, now currently the Euro-Atlantic Partnership Council or EAPC). The role of the NACC was to assist with Central and Eastern European states in their transition towards reform in predominantly political and military matters. The EAPC has become a forum for cooperation and dialogue between NATO and non-member countries. At the Brussels Summit in 1994, NATO began another programme to bring stability to Europe called Partnership for Peace (PfP). PfP was designed to encourage states from NACC to enlist in a variety of cooperative activities of their own choosing to deepen relations with NATO and to prepare states to undertake multilateral peacekeeping and rescue activities in the region.

Joint Council

In 1996, NATO began talks with Russia on building a new relationship, which resulted in the NATO–Russia Permanent Joint Council in 1997. This Council provides a forum for consultation on political and security issues and a structure for military cooperation between NATO and Russia. The same year NATO began cooperative activities with the Ukraine, recognising its key strategic position.

As the period of expansion continued in Europe, NATO looked for partnerships from a wider geopolitical sphere. In 1999, the Czech Republic, Poland and Hungary joined the alliance. NATO also established dialogue, known as 'the Mediterranean Dialogue', with Egypt, Israel, Jordan, Mauritania, Morocco, Tunisia and Algeria to promote relationships and security in the region.

Not only have NATO activities included a softer security preventative agenda of dialogue, cooperation and increased partnerships over the past decade but it has flexed its muscles in the military interventions in Bosnia (1995), Kosovo (1999) and the former Republic of Macedonia (2001). These have been followed up by active peacekeeping missions in the former two intervention areas to follow through with security issues.

NATO membership has now reached 26. The last seven accessions came through a programme called the Membership Action Plan that was designed to assist states in their application for membership and help them to meet certain political goals that are required of NATO members, including the rule of law and democratic control of their militaries.

NATO has taken on a broad range of activities to accommodate the changes taking place across Europe and the world. NATO, like other IGOs, has evolved and adapted in many ways, but most recently it was the events of September 11 2001 that most changed the alliance's agenda. NATO reassessed its activities and started an extensive reform package, outlined at the Prague Summit in 2002. NATO leaders addressed the changing nature of security challenges, recognising that they cannot be defined in terms of geographical location but may arise anywhere, and especially outside the parameters of the European–Atlantic region.

The current global security challenges such as terrorism and weapons of mass destruction are areas where NATO sees itself as being in a prime position to respond. Interventions of force have not disappeared from the agenda, as the last decade of military campaigns in the region has shown, but have been expanded to address the new security challenges outside the region.

Strategically, NATO has begun to increase its military capacities and cooperation with not only NATO countries but partner/non-member countries and other IGOs such as the OSCE, the UN and the EU through the Defence Capabilities Initiative. A Partnership Action Plan was implemented against terrorism and a Weapons of Mass Destruction Centre was established where information is shared and responses to terrorism are coordinated. These plans have already been acted on through the Afghanistan intervention by NATO allied forces and the International Security Assistance Force. A European Security and Defence Identity has been developed in order to increase the duties of NATO members with regard to security matters. Other plans made at the Prague Summit include increasing military aircraft, equipment and munitions four-fold in Europe, creating a NATO Response Force to mobilise quickly and efficiently, and adding command bases in Belgium and the USA to oversee NATO's military reforms.

Expansion

Scientific research projects also mark the expansion of NATO initiatives. The organisation is bringing its influence to bear in coordinating humanitarian relief at the Euro-Atlantic Disaster Relief Coordination Centre. It was also active in relief during and after its military campaign in Kosovo in 1999, has provided assistance to states affected by earthquakes and floods, and aided Turkey with prevention measures against a possible attack with weapons of mass destruction from Iraq in 2003.

NATO continues to try to make changes within the organisation in order to act swiftly in the face of many diverse challenges. The institution has gone through such drastic expansion that often the bureaucratic aspects of large institutions hold up progress. To reduce this effect, NATO has diminished its working committees by one-third in order to achieve the flexibility of a smaller organisation without compromising the effectiveness of its activities by relying on the Council for determining strategic issues.

The Prague Summit in 2002 was the latest turning point among a series of milestones for the organisation. There was a large expansionary step with the accession of seven states (fully acceded as of March 2004) and an intensive call for reform has been the focus of NATO's new agenda. NATO's capacities, however, do not exist within a vacuum and the trend for increased collaboration with other IGOs, including the EU and the European security defence organisation or WEU, has been instituted to consolidate resources and make feasible plans for a stable European region.

Whether NATO can continue to adapt and make progress in its large, multi-layered approach to security is seen as a challenge that its members are willing to embrace. Nonetheless, there has been an air of desperation about the vigorous efforts NATO has made to redefine its role in the post-Cold War world and the strong disagreements among its members over the 2004 Iraq war put the organisation under great stress. Yet it has survived and may become a unique example of an alliance that remains valuable to its members after the original reason for its creation has disappeared.

Further Reading

Bennett, A. LeRoy and Oliver, James K. (2002) *International Organisations: principles and issues*, Upper Saddle River, NJ: Prentice Hall.

Karns, Margaret P. and Mingst, Karen A. (2004) *International Organisations: the politics and processes of global governance*, Boulder, CO: Lynne Rienner Publishers.

Taylor, Paul (2003) *International Organisation in the Age of Globalisation*, New York, London: Continuum.

CHAPTER 3: Global capitalism and markets

At the beginning of the twenty-first century, it looks to be clear that there has been a kind of triumph of global capitalism. The emergence of a larger number of states almost universally pursuing market-oriented policies, accompanied by liberalisation and deregulation, has produced a remarkable platform of shared attitudes and policies.

This is not to say that different societies and geographical areas do not pursue different forms of capitalism: they plainly do. Malaysia's is not the same as Argentina's, to take two widely separated examples. In Latin America, new leaders are emerging who intend to give the market economy a human face. Nor has every society embraced the market with full-hearted assent. The Russian Federation is an outstanding example of pervasive doubt about the benefits of global capitalism, as it is equally an example of the apparent impossibility of a government escaping from it. But the sense that the global economic system shares more than just an instant and ever-ready connectivity is strong.

It is possible to list the most significant features of global capitalism. Cross-border transactions have become deeper, more extensive and more interconnected than ever before. Resources, capabilities, goods and services have become more mobile than ever. Multinational enterprises create and disseminate more wealth and they originate and produce in more countries. One result is increasing real and financial volatility in cross-border markets – particularly obvious in capital and currency markets. The character of cross-border transactions, especially in services, has been permanently changed by the digital environment and the onset of e-commerce. This last is plainly on the brink of a major expansion, beginning with intra-business transactions. Private personal use has been slower to

take off. In addition to these consequences of the spatial widening which the technological basis of globalisation has brought, global capitalism has other distinctive features.

The technological advances in communications have vastly increased the significance of the economic asset represented by knowledge and downgraded the importance of 'things' in the global economy. This shift has been the chief motor of contemporary development. A computing skill may be more valuable than auto engines or knives and forks. This is partly because of the needs of the system itself: to use it, operate it, administer it and improve it has evoked both a new area of highly technical knowledge and a new manufacturing industry to support it. But it is also, importantly, because the very existence of the system makes the dissemination of all forms of knowledge more or less immediate. Knowledge no longer has a territorial location in terms of access or use. It still does, however, in respect of training and education, with highly advantageous effects – if most likely quite temporary, since equalisation is already beginning to occur – on those areas where they are available. In all cases and in all places, it puts a revolutionary pressure on the character, purpose and timing of education, giving it for the first time fully global norms to meet.

A further notable feature is that although the production of many enterprises, particularly multinationals, spreads across the globe, a greater concentration of some kinds of economic activity has appeared both between and within some countries than has occurred before. Finally, all forms of alliances and cooperative ventures, within and between firms, between governments and between firms and non-market institutions, have become more important elements in the global economic system than before.

The result of this has been to complete the emergence of a global economy. In addition to the empowerment of individuals, the spatial change is significant and different from the fully interdependent global economy which became familiar in the twentieth century. The comparison is interesting. At the end of the twentieth century, both the similarities and differences in circumstances were striking compared with those experienced 100 years previously. Both periods show common characteristics: widespread and dramatic technological change; a new generation of telecommunications advances shrinking the boundaries of economic activity; a state of flux in the organisational structures and managerial strategies of firms; a realignment of the geography of economic and political power. Then, as now, the jurisdiction of nation-states was entering a new era and civic responsibilities were being redefined and new relationships were being forged between, and within, private and public institutions and among different religious and ethnic groups.

Differences

Nonetheless, the differences are more marked than these similarities. Most obvious is that while the globalising economic tendencies of the early twentieth century were taking place within a well-established and widely accepted social, economic and political order, today's revolution challenges long-established ideologies and values and, indeed, the very institutional fabric of society, more as the creation of great manufacturing conurbations did during the industrial revolution. And there is no clear guide to the pattern of future developments. Contemporary developments may divide individuals and institutions as much as unify them and the hierarchical capitalism which created wealth for 100 years looks vulnerable.

Transnational flows of capital, goods, services, technology and information have now acquired a speed, intensity, comprehensive and self-reinforcing relevance and fully global reach that make them qualitatively different from their precursors of even recent decades. Figures for foreign direct investment, foreign trade and foreign portfolio investment make the point perfectly clear. Foreign direct investment, as a proportion of world gross product, rose from 7.8 per cent in 1967 to 14 per cent in 1988 and to 21.4 per cent in 1996. The value of cross-border mergers and acquisitions rose dramatically from $25 billion in 1980 to $350 billion in 1996. The annual average per centage growth of world trade rose by 4 per cent between 1853 and 1913 and by 6 per cent between 1950 and 1985 and then by 7.5 per cent between 1985 and 1996. After dipping in the early 2000s, world trade rose by 6.8 per cent in 2004 alone and was expected to repeat that performance in 2005. Trade between firms rose from 10 per cent to 40 per cent between 1960 and 1996. Foreign portfolio investment rose 14 times between 1970 and 1996.

In earlier conditions, different economic units or blocs or states could not completely evade the effects of what was going on in the others and were inextricably linked in a financial system based on the 'single currency' of the gold standard. During the Great Depression of the 1930s, it was discovered that attempting a controlled economic isolation failed to work and during the post-war period the capitalist world moved gradually but with increasing speed towards the general deregulation of the 1980s. The implosion of the communist bloc after 1989 globalised the pursuit of basically capitalist economic policy, though causing some parallel economic collapses while doing so: in Ukraine, for example. The effect has been called the triumph of global capitalism.

The triumph of global capitalism has not, however, been solely the result of the collapse of communism, nor, looking at it from another angle, was the collapse of communism solely caused by the advance of global capitalism. Fully global capitalism has also needed the effects of the contemporary communications revolution to come into existence.

Global markets

This can clearly be seen in the emergence of the global markets – in stocks, in currencies, in banking – and in the changing structures of multinational entities. Stock markets, as the events of 1929–1930 showed vividly enough, have been both interconnected and only unreliably amenable to government policies or decisions for some time. But at that time, they remained territorial and separate, vertical structures communicating with each other across global space with reasonable but not perfect ease. The number of individuals involved in their operations both as investors and operators was comparatively small.

The de-territorialised global stock market created by total global communications is a different beast. The number of individuals involved, particularly as investors, has risen sharply and neither the time of day nor the physical location of an investor matters much at all. Access to cyberspace from anywhere on the globe will allow personal and instantaneous participation in the global stock market. The fate of single-state economies is affected by the movements of the markets, but the fate of individual investors can be affected even more. And that in turn de-territorialises the influence of stock holders on companies, their policies, investment decisions and ultimate fate. In short, the market in which companies generate capital has become global – that does not mean that all parts of the globe take part, but it does mean that all parts of the globe are potential sources of investment. It also means that all parts of the globe are potential objects of investment – a development which we will return to shortly. The single most important short-term effect of this is that the global stock market has become highly volatile; the umbilical cord that connected it to 'real' economic activity has been broken and the extent that governments could, either by domestic policy measures or by combined action, attempt to control it has been reduced to almost nothing. The global stock market now presents itself as a leviathan, yet an unexpectedly capricious and nimble one.

Capriciousness is also a compelling character-istic of another important global marketplace. Currency speculation has long been a difficult area for governments. They have from time to time been able to bring off temporary, but always welcome, victories against attacks upon particular currencies. But they have generally lacked success and their failure has been largely to do with the fact that currency speculation was related to some basic changes in the real economic situation in the currency area in question. What has now emerged is a 'virtual' market unamenable to government activity – coopera-tive or singular – and to a large degree unre-lated to real economic conditions. There is no doubting the size of the shift. Since 1979, the turnover in the foreign exchange markets has risen to $1.9 trillion each day, up by 36 per cent since April 2001, 12 times the level of 1979 and over 50 times that of world trade. The effects on societies and individuals can be either cata-strophic or enriching, but the circumstances are equally volatile.

The global flows of capital moving round the world at more than $1 trillion a day are routed through the global banking system. Here, too, a formerly cooperative and understood set of arrangements between effective banks operating vertically in relation both to each other and to particular economic areas has been undermined by the emergence of a global economy. The size of the world banking market as a per centage of world gross output rose from 1.2 per cent in 1964 to 45 per cent in 1994. This quantity of cap-ital flooding round the globe looking for the most advantageous temporary destination has become a frequently quixotic economic activity, an end in itself, not necessarily the servant of physically located real economic action expressed as factories, goods and services lead-ing to employment and commerce.

Volatility

Global banking operates increasingly as a single unit, not as an interdependent system. It thus functions without familiar landmarks and includes areas without any tradition of free domestic, let alone international, banking, and the result has been chaotic mixtures of some-times little understood and recently installed domestic arrangements coming under pressure from a global system, itself at sea in uncharted waters. The result is further volatility, to match that arising in the stock markets and the cur-rency markets. So serious has this problem become that in 1999 the first proper efforts to gain control began to emerge from within the market through a mechanism derived from the Bank of International Settlements. It will be interesting to see how this interacts with the market on the one hand and with national governments on the other.

It seems unlikely that the emergence of this situation is a temporary phenomenon, to be endured before we all return to normal condi-tions. Normal has now become global and while, as we have seen, the development of the new is proving hard, the adjustments required of the old are perhaps even harder. Even in the older economically interdependent world, familiar since the end of the nineteenth century, it was a reasonable expectation that governments would and could fulfil an obligation to manage both the macro- and micro-economic policies of their state. That there were some limitations on what might be achievable against a cyclical economic movement was accepted; but that governments had the greatest role to play was simply assumed. The electoral rhetoric of parties assumed it, the propaganda of dictators equally assumed it and the actual policies of governments of every type acted upon it. The growth of multinational companies seemed in the 1960s particularly to dent it, but contrary to some expectations never went further than that. How different the situation is now. Not only have national governments found themselves having to adjust to a serious loss of economic power, multinational companies have found themselves as subject to the effects of globalisation as states have, in one sense, almost equally victims.

What has produced this effect has chiefly been a substantial de-territorialisation of the labour market. The basic change is simple: the global communications system is now so complete and so immediate that there is no necessary connection between the point of ownership of a company, the point of manufacture of its goods – in whole or in part – and the point of their sale. Indeed it is quite possible, even likely, that all these activities will in fact be globally spread and physically widely separated – ownership, manufacture and sale. With the onset of electronic consumer purchasing – still in its infancy – it will shortly be true that even the point of acquisition will be globalised. You may manufacture where it is cheapest and/or most convenient to do so, administer in the same way, buy and pay the bill similarly. The current obvious examples of the emergence of a global labour market are the almost wholesale departure of clothing manufacture to Asian sites, attracted by less regulated conditions and cheap labour, and second, the ability of Indian-educated computer programmers to deal with the Y2K problem. This effectively transfers most of the work from the highly developed economies that most require it to India which in practice needs it somewhat less, but nonetheless profits greatly. Other forms of manufacture show similar signs and the trend towards highly subsidiarised operations in which quite small parts of a mechanism will be made on the opposite side of the world, and then assembled in a different place under the management of a company physically based in yet another location, is significant in this regard. TVs, VCRs, fax machines and microwave ovens are all examples of this.

Paradox

This is an example of a commonly observed contemporary phenomenon: the pressures are coming globally, but the response is often paradoxically local or regional. In economic terms this means that the conditions which an investing company regards as most attractive are likely to be set by factors which are highly localised: wage levels, environmental conditions, taxation, the educational level of the workforce, building standards. The smaller the state, the more these will be centrally controlled, but in larger states they are generally part of the remit of regional government. A national government is seldom the best proprietor of a business park or a development area: subsidiarity, that is to say decisions taken at the lowest appropriate level, is generally applied. And since one region may see itself in competition with another for attracting external investment and thus employment, it may be powerfully motivated into supplying the desired conditions. Squeezed between the demands of the global economy and the response of its regions, the space in which national governments operate diminishes and even traditionally strongly unitary states find themselves devolving authority, willingly or unwillingly. They do so to units small enough to make the most effective and successful decisions in respect of attracting foreign direct investment to the region.

In very general terms the effects of all this have been favourable. For less developed societies particularly, globalisation brings tremendous opportunities. It can bring employment and investment in hitherto unimaginable quantities and, perhaps in the longer term more significantly, it brings some levelling in comparative knowledge. What is globally accessible can be available to all and enables some remarkably rapid catching-up to take place. Easily available capital and electronic information can be a kind of leveller and in less developed countries they can level up. The effect can be seen in the following IMF figures: in 2004 the world economy grew by 4.6 per cent, the advanced economies grew by 3.5 per cent, while the emerging and developing economies grew by 6 per cent. Africa grew by 5.4 per cent, though it was the developing economies of Asia which stole the show with 7 per cent growth.

Yet rapid expansion puts great strains on underdeveloped   infrastructures,   under-developed financial systems and inefficient domestic administration. The cumulative effect of this and concomitant often endemic corruption can lead to crises, as recently observed in Asia. For more developed societies, these factors may not apply, but the short-term effect, chiefly on employment, can be more damaging.

Global private companies

If the consequences of globalisation for markets and for national governments are volatility as the first and deeply puzzling for the second, the same is true for organisations, whether commercial or public. A tendency, paralleling that occurring in the experience of national governments, has developed for formerly vertically arranged business structures to be flattened into more horizontal shapes. This has arisen partly out of the need to respond to the global/local paradox that we have already noted.

The telecommunications revolution has removed the need for multinational firms to have a single international presence and thus to see each other as ranged against, or at least different from, other firms – almost as if they were commercial versions of states. Nor do they need to support their core activity, whatever it might be, by running a variety of other related activities so as to keep the whole operation 'in house'. Being a globally functioning entity has become even more desirable than being a multinational corporation once was. The multinational company was generally a nationally based concern, having distinctively national characteristics but a multinational operation. They walked upright in the economic landscape and dealt with each other and national governments from that posture. A change of posture is now very evident: look, for example, at the tendency for formerly national airlines to go global in their cooperative partnerships and to compete by putting emphasis on the global reach which those associations give them. Even their symbols tend to drop the resonance with a national tradition and substitute motifs which are either global in significance or have none at all. The late 1990s redesign of the tailplanes on British Airways aircraft is a particularly good illustration of this: the distinctively British national marking gave way to a wide range of colourful but entirely abstract designs, and even a 1999 modification left the national motif somewhat vague.

The global company has subsumed the multinational both in its style and operationally because of the arrival of fully global markets, the availability of a global labour force, the emergence of global electronic commerce and, with some commodities, the existence of a global culture creating global fashions. These can work both positively and negatively: Coca-Cola is an example of the first and the late 1990s decline in the fashion for Levis jeans is an example of the second. Yet there is no longer any need for a solidly hierarchical structure of administration, since links are best created horizontally rather than vertically, which tends to flatten out the systems and greatly reduce the size of the central offices of major corporations. Similarly, there is a conjunction between the development of regionalism and the desire of global companies to base manufacture in the most advantageous place – anywhere in the world.

Flexibilities

Flexibility of communication and administration now means that it is better to create global coalitions of regionally based firms, whose local existence is socially desirable and politically acceptable and can be the object of locally decided advantages – for example in tax breaks or favourable variations in zoning regulations. Here it is possible to make a marriage between the needs of the global company and the rising significance of regional and local activities, cultural, economic and political. The ability to 'think global and act local' also affects what is produced as well as where and how it is produced. The emergence of a global culture is balanced by a reaction to it, and to global economic and political power, which emphasises local particularities: of tradition, of taste, of expectation. The flexibilities of the contemporary global firm allow it to produce goods and services that are tailored to local preferences, and gain competitive advantage thereby, while also serving global markets with other products. It is another example of the contemporary economic paradoxes at work.

Yet another is that one effect of this has been to create a renaissance of the small to medium-sized firm, in a world that also sees a procession of major global mergers, by which the giant becomes even more dominant in the market for high technology and branded goods and services.

Nor does the process stop here. The emergence of the new-style global firm, with its concentration on core activities, has changed the essentially adversarial nature of the previous competition between international companies. One result has been the emergence of inter-firm alliances. The increase has been startlingly brisk and the intention is to improve penetration of new markets, share costs and speed up the process of innovation. The same feature is to be seen in research and development. At a time of vastly accelerated technological obsolescence, leading to closer interdependence between cutting-edge technologies and more immediate effects of research and development on manufacturing processes, both the importance and the costs of the exercise have risen. The result has been hitherto unimaginable cooperation in the field of research and development between firms, despite the fact that their ultimate fate is to be commercial rivals. Of course, these developments pose difficult problems, not least when to cooperate and when to compete, but the contemporary plasticity in these notions is creating a new kind of alliance capitalism in which there is no mutual exclusivity between them but a synergy of competition and cooperation. In this respect the adjustments which multinational firms are making to new global conditions are more sensitive and successful than the more stumbling responses from national governments.

A good example of this tendency arises out of the problem of corruption. Some degree of corruption has been endemic in both government and commerce throughout history. The more economically and politically developed societies became, the more damaging and inconvenient extensive and pervasive corruption appeared to be, and it became a part of the modern state's duty to legislate against it and enforce that legislation. Traditional and deep-seated corruption continues in less developed areas where, as globalisation brings rapid development opportunities, it becomes less and less acceptable and a perceptible hindrance both to a genuine free market and to the rule of law in a Western sense, which itself is a crucial contribution to the context for successful economic development. For the national governments concerned, weakened by other aspects of globalisation which we will discuss further on, the reform of corruption has proved too difficult to achieve in any full enough sense. Into the gap have moved multinational companies, which, via their own internal policies and behaviour and by remarkable displays of cooperative solidarity in individual countries, have gone some way towards taking over the functions of the state in this respect and in these places.

Moreover, they have done so in other ways as well. The tendency for governments to collapse where either they have been subject to great pressures or where the institutions of the modern state were never deeply rooted in any case, has created administrative crises of a kind so serious that they make economic activity impossible. They also lead to political disruption and bitter conflict which has the same effect except for those who trade in armies and armaments. We shall later see that private organisations of many kinds, rather than other states or their associations, are tending to supply the deficiencies in governance that inevitably occur, but it is also worth noting that in some cases, private companies are doing so, too.

It is a practice well known in history. Both the Dutch and the British created East India Companies which preceded their own direct rule in Indonesia and India respectively and there were also examples in the Ottoman Empire. But the practice had largely ceased and what was expected was the indirect influence rather than the direct involvement of public companies with foreign governments. At the beginning of the twenty-first century, it is notable that what is 'foreign', certainly in economic terms, can be quite obscure; and that direct involvement in and assistance to administrative infrastructures by commercial enterprises is now part of the extraordinarily complex weave of the global political economy. Examples of this kind of behaviour are most common in Africa, particularly in the eastern Congo and in the relationship between a whole district of Nigeria and the Chevron oil company. A newer and rather different version of the same idea is emerging in discussions in developed countries where it is being suggested that the best interests of companies will be served, when times are hard and specifically when employment moves out of an area, by the introduction of company-run and financed schemes of social welfare.

It can no longer be assumed that governments can or will undertake the burden of avoiding the social dislocation that unrelieved downsizing will cause, or subsequently will control the public disorder that may follow.

Further Reading

Baker, Andrew, Hudson, David and Woodward, Richard (eds) (2005) *Governing Financial Globalisation: International Political Economy and Multi-Level Governance*, London and New York: Routledge.

Bhagwati, Jagdish (2004) *In Defence of Globalisation*, Oxford University Press.

Dunning, John (ed) (2003) *Making Globalisation Good: The Moral Challenges of Global Capitalism*, Oxford University Press.

Germain, Randall (1997) *The International Organisation of Credit: States and Global Finance in the World Economy*, Cambridge: Cambridge University Press.

Porter, Tony (2005) *Globalisation and Finance*, Cambridge: Polity Press.

Strange, Susan (1998) *Mad Money: When Markets Outgrow Governments*, Manchester: Manchester University Press and Ann Arbor: University of Michigan Press.

CHAPTER 4: Global civil society

What is global civil society?

In the early decades of the 1800s anti-slavery societies became a major force in the UK and the United States, helping turn a moral issue into a political one that fundamentally reshaped the internal structures and economies of the Great Powers and their colonial relations. Abolitionism, temperance, workers' rights, women's suffrage and anti-foot-binding – to name only a few of the most popular causes – became transnational issues.

Their proponents realised that only solidarity and cooperation across borders could create sufficient pressure to address the ills of the brave, new modern world being disgorged from the holds of ships in the form of raw materials, slaves, immigrants, commodities, opium, liquor and soldiers. During this period of rapid change the mechanisms of civil society expanded beyond domestic issues to embrace causes across the globe. This was not yet what we today call global civil society, but just as we can trace the roots of our global economy to the dynamics of comparative advantage in the eighteenth and nineteenth centuries, we can trace global activism on the most pressing issues of today – among them genocide, global warming, landmines, AIDS/HIV, corruption, and socio-economic inequality – to the dynamics of transnational networks of the previous centuries.

Global civil society is not merely a new name for transnational activities; rather it refers to the increasing institutionalisation of citizen and non-governmental networks in the governance of our complex world. The idea of world government has long disappeared from serious discussion, but almost all current observers of the international order recognise the existence of what has been called governance without government. States, associations of states, supranational organisations, transnational organisations and non-state actors weave an intricate tapestry of rules, norms and laws which govern actions from trade to military intervention to legal jurisdiction. It is unthinkable that citizens would not want to have a voice in the emerging structures of our world, just as citizens seek to raise their voice when confronted with problems that government seems incapable of solving. Global civil society emerges from networks of organisations that make citizens' voices and actions commensurate with the realities of an interconnected world.

The idea of a global civil society is closely related to widespread desires for a more democratic global political architecture. On the level of democratic nation-states, civil society itself has a rich history in democratic states as the engine for the marketplace of ideas. This 'marketplace' exists in institutionalised spaces where citizens can discuss, argue, lobby and above all influence each other's ideas and ultimately – through elections and citizen pressure – the direction of government as a whole. As a space for the diverse

Historical trajectory of global civil society	
1775–1918:	Emergence around issues of abolition, suffragism and labour.
1918–1945:	Increasing interaction between early NGOs and national governments on trade and humanitarian issues.
1945–1960s:	Formalisation of an international NGO presence in the UN system.
1960s–1980s:	Growth of development and humanitarian aid networks.
1990s–present:	Significant increase in international civil society organisations in response to complex emergencies and decreasing national government capacity to respond to crises effectively.

and dissenting voices of citizens, civil society is the necessary condition for the informed and dynamic political participation central to democracy. The state-level institutions of civil society include all manner of organisations, from Rotary clubs to church and volunteer groups, professional associations, unions, animal rights, abstinence, anti-genetically modified food, pro-gun rights and any of a host of causes organised into a group with a name, address and presence in the public realm.

The competing voices of civil society ideally keep in check the cold logic of the market on the one hand, and the bureaucratic and totalising tendencies of government on the other. Without civic organisations of various stripes that exist outside of formal government control there would be little institutionalised room for influencing policy outside the formal mechanisms of elections and individual action. Civil society also implies the rule of law, since after all the word 'civil' signifies a measure of good faith and respect for the law, even among the most passionate proponents of a cause. Extremist organisations that seek extra-legal means such as violence or fraud to pursue their agenda are beyond the pale.

At the global level, civil society organisations (CSOs) have emerged ranging from workers' societies such as the International Metalworkers' Federation and the International Conference of Trade Unions to environmental organisations such as Greenpeace to religious organisations such as Catholic Relief Services. Two of the most famous civil society organisations today are Médécins Sans Frontières (Doctors Without Borders) and the International Campaign to Ban Landmines, both of which have won the Nobel Peace Prize. Like at the national level, global civil society organisations do not fall under one definition and include social movements, religious and labour groups, and associations and societies of all sorts. Of all the organisations that make up global civil society, however, the most common and increasingly most important type is non-governmental organisations.

The NGO phenomenon

In an increasingly globalised world non-governmental organisations have become the standard bearers of global civil society, analogous to civic organisations within domestic civil society. Global civil society cannot be reduced to NGOs,

but neither can it be understood without them. While transnational networks took hold in the nineteenth and early twentieth centuries, there was little institutionalisation into organisations with status recognisable by states or early intergovernmental bodies. What we today call NGOs – incorporated not-for-profit organisations formally independent from government – numbered a few hundred by the beginning of the last century, and grew to a modest presence only by the 1970s. It was during the 1980s – the decade when globalisation became ensconced in our vernacular – that NGOs experienced exponential growth, expanding from several hundred to tens of thousands or even, depending on how strict one's criteria are, hundreds of thousands.

Today NGOs are engaged, directly or at the margins, in the transformation of national, international and transnational political space. In their engagement they appear in various, often conflicting, guises: as building blocks for a global civic culture, incubators for new international institutions, barefoot revolutionaries carrying out globalisation from below, or new missionaries imposing Western ideals from above. They are lauded as pioneers in forging a global civil society, disparaged as tools of the ruling class, and championed as the vanguard for globalisation from below. Regardless of ideological perspective, however, there is no doubt that NGOs are fundamentally altering patterns of international interaction.

Today's international NGOs often began as organisations based squarely in a home country with a humanitarian mandate. Coming into their own mainly in the mid twentieth century, NGOs tended to be Western in origin, focused on welfare issues such as homelessness or poverty, service provision to under-served populations, or advocacy in support of under-represented groups. Others identified with social movements such as pro-ecology or anti-nuclear weapons. To increase their influence many NGOs developed professional staffs and sought long-term funding from philanthropists or, increasingly, from the government itself. As NGOs extended their services such as famine relief or medical assistance to other countries, their operations grew and they entered into alliances with other NGOs or set up branch offices or chapters overseas. Many NGOs ultimately evolved into global organisations such as Amnesty International, Human Rights Watch, CARE, Oxfam and Médécins Sans Frontières.

Grassroots organisations are a major alternative organisational form within global civil society, emerging parallel with more professional NGOs. They often start as church-based organisations focusing on local issues, relying on volunteers more than professional staff, emphasising self-help and drawing on membership contributions rather than large external grants for funding. But as with more conventional NGOs, grassroots organisations face similar problems of professionalism as they begin to operate in multiple countries and with ever larger numbers of people.

The **International Campaign to Ban Landmines** (ICBL) is a prime example of the network-based growth of global civil society. As the Cold War was ending, six different NGOs came together to coordinate their work on banning anti-personnel landmines. From this grew a flexible network that shares the common goal of a global ban on the use, production, stockpiling and transfer of anti-personnel landmines. They also advocate for humanitarian mine clearance and mine victim assistance. The Campaign was formalised in 1993 and burgeoned into dozens of national campaigns joined by hundreds of organisations, representing by the early twenty-first century over 1,100 human rights, demining, humanitarian, children's, veterans', medical, development, arms control, religious, environmental and women's groups in over 60 countries. In 1997 the ICBL and its coordinator, Jody Williams, received the highest recognition – the Nobel Peace Prize.

The number of NGOs active in two or more countries – what many call international NGOs or INGOs – experienced their most rapid historical growth in the twentieth century, and of this most in the 1990s. In 1914 there were 1,083 registered international NGOs, and their growth was modest but steady until it leapt by almost 30 per cent in the 1990s to a total of over 37,000 NGOs active in 2000. What can explain such rapid growth, from a handful of such formally registered organisations by the turn of the nineteenth century to around 1,000 by the end of the First World War, to many thousands today? There are three categories of factors to consider: geopolitical, economic/ideological and technological.

Geopolitics and the rise of NGOs

The single most important historical event that defined the 1990s was, of course, the end of the Cold War. The term 'civil society' had experienced a renaissance in East Central Europe as it emerged from the dour hopelessness of the late socialist era to the promise of joining the European Union as free, democratic states. The civic organisations of East Central Europe, such as the Czechoslovak group Charter 77, showed the importance of a vibrant civil society for the legitimacy of a democratic government. These organisations demanded transparency and accountability rather than secrecy and deception. As civil society became increasingly identified as a prerequisite for democracy (often, at times, to the exclusion of other vital factors), money began to flow from Western philanthropic foundations and government agencies to support civil society in East Central Europe and beyond. The philanthropist George Soros' Open Society Institute was instrumental in this process, as were Western foundations such as Ford and MacArthur, but major money came from Western government agencies. The ensuing 'NGO rage' sometimes approached the point of absurdity: one account from Central Asia has a visitor receiving a business card with the person's name and 'NGO'. When asked what type of NGO, the response was simple yet direct – he would figure it out after he got money.

While hucksters exist everywhere, the need for more civil society know-how was real and directly related to the increasing number of democratic regimes. The end of the Cold War caused a massive wave of democratisation, building on an already growing trend under way in Latin America. Since 1980, 33 military regimes have been replaced by civilian governments, and 81 countries have moved towards democracy. Though the UN considers only 47 of these to be full democracies today, that is still a huge increase from the 17 regimes considered democratic a mere four decades earlier, in 1973. And the more fragile the new democracy, the more important the institutionalisation of a civil society. Research showed that democracy was key for higher growth rates, better economic performance, and peace and stability. Based on such findings, Western governments began to devote more resources to supporting civic participation and what the lingo calls 'democracy building'. NGOs sprang up around the world to assist in this process, to channel funds, and to train a new generation of democratic citizens.

Yet if the end of the Cold War unleashed democratic impulses around the globe, it also ushered in an era of much turmoil and catastrophe, from the Balkans to the killing fields of Rwanda, from political vacuums caused by collapsing regimes to humanitarian crises caused by war and chaos. The most common covering term for the disasters that beset our world today is 'complex humanitarian emergencies' – situations caused by war or natural disaster where a civilian population is displaced, thrown into precarious living conditions and faces disease and death. Today there are more than 14 million refugees in the world and 15–20 million internally displaced persons, the majority in Africa. This is a refugee crisis of unprecedented proportions, exacerbated by the AIDS/HIV pandemic, continued political instability across much of the developing world, and equally unprecedented movement of people from rural areas to cities with the attendant problems of adequate and safe water, food, housing and employment.

The system of sovereign nation-states has never been efficient or elegant in its response to humanitarian crises. With the rise of complex humanitarian emergencies, NGOs have become increasingly the vehicle of choice for addressing urgent and delicate tasks, from reconstruction of villages to providing food aid and medicine to refugees. Trained in community issues, non-partisan, privately funded, NGOs quickly moved to the front of most major crises in the world. NGOs also increased their presence behind the scenes, staying on after others had left for more urgent problems, engaging in community development, seeking reconciliation and justice, training civil servants, educators and care givers, monitoring human rights situations, helping build infrastructure, providing medical services, micro-credit financing, disaster relief, and functioning as the eyes and ears of the international community.

Economics, ideology and volunteerism

It was not lost on governments that NGOs were not only politically more palatable than official missions in certain circumstances but could be convenient and potentially efficient conduits for government aid. In the 1980s most foreign development aid was given government to government, and NGOs were at best tolerated and at worst viewed as antagonists (and the feeling

was often mutual). By the 1990s, however, the neoliberal (in economic terms) regimes of Margaret Thatcher and Ronald Reagan created an environment where markets replaced governments as the motors of growth, and development aid began to be more donor- rather than government-driven. NGOs began an unprecedented cooperation with official aid agencies such as the United States Agency for International Development (USAID), the UK Department for International Development (DFID) and the World Bank.

There is an irony in this development, since many of the problems that NGOs were called upon to address by aid agencies were exacerbated directly by neoliberal policies of structural adjustment and privatisation. As developing nations were forced to reduce budgets from sanitation to education and to cut social services in the name of deficit reduction, NGOs were moving in to help countries pick up the pieces, often with the support and money of the very same governments back home that were pushing for the socially disastrous policies.

NGO partnerships

NGOs are changing their form and function as their role increases in humanitarian response, poverty alleviation and socio-economic development. The most significant changes are taking place through partnerships:

- NGO–NGO partnerships, especially North–South and South–South partnerships
- NGO–private sector partnerships
- NGO–international organisation partnerships
- NGO–government partnerships.

These forms of collaboration are both opportunities and challenges, as NGOs must navigate a delicate terrain between the dangers of co-optation and manipulation and the goals of genuine collaboration and systemic transformation.

This irony, however, fits well with the overall neoliberal emphasis on privatisation as the cure for society's ills. Distributing aid money through private organisations such as development NGOs became an increasingly standard method; by the first year of the new millennium, the World Bank was estimating that over 15 per cent of total overseas development aid was being channelled through NGOs. NGOs began to form partnerships with governments and financial institutions, out of necessity, frustration or convenience. Parallel to this trend was a rise in volunteerism. While often a response to the shrinking of government services, this trend was also supported by conservative Western governments, whose ideology sought to reduce the role of government, emphasise the logic of the market, and rely on volunteerism rather than government policies to address ills within society. Concepts such as social entrepreneurship became popular along with 'faith-based initiatives' and a significant increase in philanthropic activity. One major result of all of this was an increase in careers in non-profit management, the professionalisation of NGOs, and NGO–government and NGO–business partnerships. Social and business ventures began to be combined, separating revenue generation from the NGOs' social mission and evaluating it according to business standards. Some NGOs turned to income generation alternatives that mimic commercial enterprises, with side products, large staffs and public relations teams.

Information technology

Besides the geopolitical factors following the end of the Cold War and the impact of neoliberal economics and the rise in volunteerism, NGOs and CSOs in general would not have gained such global prominence without the advent of information technology. The Internet, email and the worldwide web suddenly made it possible for many NGOs to radically increase their capacities at relatively low cost. Suddenly the basic tasks of getting information to constituents changed immeasurably: web pages and electronic attachments replaced the printing and distributing of newsletters and announcements; phone lists became email lists; membership and contributions were solicited online; archives and resources were suddenly available to constituents around the world; communication between offices could happen in real time. The very tasks of the NGO – mobilising, organising, collecting and disseminating information – all changed with the advent of the Internet.

One emerging powerful use of the Internet is 'blogging' (short for 'weblogs'), where millions of online diarists around the world share and advocate views. While most 'bloggers' engage in exaggerated comments about trivial events in daily life, many have emerged as agenda-setters who influence local and global politics. Some,

like the 'Baghdad Blogger' or the hundreds of pictures streaming out of South Asia during the tsunami disaster in December 2004, provide uncensored real-time information that is often used as a source by mainstream media outlets. Activism in political blogging ranges from simply amplifying certain news stories to expressing dissent and advocating specific policies. It is an easy way to become published, with the most popular rising to the top and becoming widely read and influential. From creating a buzz around certain news, issues and events to providing information from remote or repressed areas of the world, blogging places important power at the fingertips of civil society (Drezner and Farrell, 2004).

Of course only those organisations with computers and Internet access can take full advantage of these changes, but many NGOs have emerged to help others – both in less developed countries and in the West – acquire the equipment, training and funding to get online, and tens of thousands of NGOs are actively represented on the Internet.

For all this expansion of its role, the Internet is only part of the way information technology profoundly affects the forces of global civil society, such as NGOs, grassroots campaigns and protest movements. Mobile telephones were central to anti-globalisation demonstrators who used them to transmit information and coordinate tactics during protests. Digital cameras provide instant images of protests, documents and human rights violations. With the right equipment, sensitive documents and pictures can be uploaded via satellite and need not be kept by local offices or individuals who might be subject to persecution for their human rights activities. By the same token information campaigns can alert people, governments and news organisations to issues within hours.

The organisation Witness is an excellent example of the convergence of information technology and new forms of NGOs. It is the brainchild of the artist Peter Gabriel, the legal advocacy group Human Rights First (formerly known as the Lawyers' Committee for Human Rights) and the philanthropic arm of a major corporation, Reebok. In its own words, the nonprofit, non-governmental Witness 'unleashes an arsenal of computers, imaging and editing software, satellite phones and email in the struggle for justice', mostly through giving local activists video cameras and training so they can document conditions and abuses around the world.

By working in partnership with a network of 150 NGOs in 50 countries, Witness not only provides video technology and training but helps the videos of otherwise unreported human rights violations to become part of court records, tribunals, UN documentation, classrooms and the global news media such as the BBC, CNN, CBS, ABC, PBS, Canal +, Telemundo and Worldlink Satellite Television. Its website (www.witness.org) receives over 1.5 million hits per month.

In Witness we see the development of a true global civil society organisation: embedded in a network of partner NGOs, influencing policies and legal proceedings, giving a voice to sweatshop workers, displaced persons, abused women and victims of torture and degradation, using information technology to accomplish its mission, distributing equipment and training local activists to be technically proficient, media savvy and connected to the international community.

Thus, well into the first decade of the twenty-first century, not only are more NGOs more active around the world in more areas than ever before, but they are more intricately connected to government and business than ever before, more essential for the implementation of government policies at home and abroad, and more an important part of any global governance mechanism. This development is far too complex to be seen as intrinsically positive or negative – it is, as this book argues, part of the new playing field of global politics with which we all have to contend.

Changing roles for global civil society

The organisations of global civil society are paradoxical creatures. On the one hand, by working closely together with governments and international institutions, they legitimise official practices and policies. On the other hand, they challenge these very same practices, policies and partners. Global civil society is part of the democratisation of global politics, and like democracy itself it is an inherently messy business. Global civil society organisations are rooted in a normative commitment to transforming the international system to make it more responsive to the diverse and changing needs of citizens of all countries. It is no secret that the bureaucratic machinery of the state and

entrenched commercial interests rarely welcome criticism, yet it is also true that civil society organisations increasingly achieve change by partnerships with government and the private sector. The tension at the heart of global civil society is the simultaneous legitimation and challenge of the international system. This tension is driven by a broad array of amicable and hostile forces to which civil society organisations respond and to which they are accountable.

Protest

The most time-honoured expression of citizens' voices is the protest, and as the millennium approached the world saw an upsurge of protest against international organisations that few laypersons had ever bothered to notice before. Since the late 1990s nearly every major meeting of international note, especially those of international financial institutions such as the WTO, IMF and World Bank, and the summits of the leading industrial nations known as the G8, has been accompanied by protests.

The most well known perhaps was the protest against the WTO's meeting in Seattle from 27 November to 3 December 1999 when 50,000 protestors, representing nearly every conceivable interest, from trade unions to animal rights activists, briefly united against the forces of the global economy and the lack of transparency of global governance organisations. Anarchists in the group vandalised storefronts and engaged in skirmishes with the police, and the protests effectively prevented the meeting from carrying on business as usual. It was a wake-up call that citizens around the world were now taking note of how global economic policy was being made and wanting a voice in it. As one activist put it: 'Anti-globalisation activists understand that sympathetic and mutually beneficial global ties are good. But we want social and global ties to advance universal equity, solidarity, diversity, and self-management, not to subjugate ever-wider populations to an elite minority. We want to globalise equity not poverty, solidarity not anti-sociality, diversity not conformity, democracy not subordination, and ecological balance not suicidal rapaciousness' (Albert, 2001).

The 'battle in Seattle' was followed by massive protests against the World Bank, the IMF and the G8 in Prague, Washington and Genoa, the latter resulting in pitched battles with police leaving 600 injured and one protestor dead. While the violence of Genoa was sobering and the patience of most participants with the violent anarchist contingent was wearing thin, a new alliance had been forged among groups that had never previously shared a common agenda. The idea was indeed radical: major trade agreements and international summits were no longer to be the exclusive provenance of states (and business interests) but must also include the voices of people represented in ways other than through formal diplomatic and ministerial channels.

Recent major globalisation protests

Seattle 1999 (World Trade Organisation)
Washington DC 2000 and 2002 (IMF and World Bank)
Prague 2000 (IMF and World Bank)
Genoa 2001 (G8 Summit)
New York 2002 (World Economic Forum)
Cancun 2003 (World Trade Organisation)
Protests have also taken place in Argentina, Brazil, Ecuador, India, Indonesia, South Korea and dozens of other countries. While colloquially labelled 'anti-globalisation', most protestors seek a more humane globalisation less dominated by corporate interests.

The results of this first wave of anti-elitist globalisation were striking and are only now becoming clear. While recent protests have shifted their focus to issues of war and peace, the legacy of the watershed demonstrations of 1999–2001 can be seen in two developments: the creation of a parallel machinery of civil society summits alongside the established meetings of heads of state and international institutions, and the acceleration of civil society inclusion into international decision making, especially at the UN level.

Global civil society summits

In 1992 the United Nations Conference on Environment and Development held in Rio de Janeiro ushered in a new era in civil society–government interaction. Civil society groups held an 'NGO forum' alongside the UN meetings with substantial impact on the policies emerging from the conference. New networks among NGOs were cemented, media visibility was heightened, expertise sought and confrontations between civil society and government

showcased. In short a new creature was born: the idea of 'parallel summitry'.

In short order after the Rio conference, parallel summits became the standard operating procedure for civil society organisations, themselves growing in number and strength. Expanding from the Rio environmental conference to meetings on human rights, population, social development and women, the culmination of this trend was the World Social Forum held for the first time in 2001 in Porto Alegre, Brazil under the slogan 'A different world is possible'. The World Social Forum was civil society's answer to the famous World Economic Forum in Davos, where heads of state rubbed shoulders with business executives and policy elite. In Porto Alegre, 20,000 representatives of landless peasant groups mixed with trade unions and human rights activists with various demands such as a tax on international currency transactions.

World Social Forum

Since 2001, thousands of social movement organisations, NGOs and individuals have gathered in response to the annual meeting of world business and political leaders at the World Economic Forum in Davos, Switzerland. The World Social Forum, which began in Porto Alegre, Brazil, is 'an open meeting place where social movements, networks, NGOs and other civil society organisations opposed to neoliberalism and a world dominated by capital or by any form of imperialism come together to pursue their thinking, to debate ideas democratically, to formulate proposals, share their experiences freely and network for effective action' (www.forumsocial mundial.org.br).

While the World Social Forum is a process and not an institution, it serves as a catalyst and inspiration for networking and empowerment of local civil society groups around the world. Regional and thematic forums have emerged in nearly every part of the world.

Parallel summits seek to propose alternative policies, to enable networking and coalition building among diverse civil society organisations, to lobby official conference representatives, and to raise public awareness and pursue political confrontation. They allow for NGOs to contribute procedurally or substantively to issues before the respective international institution. While at first such summits were always in tandem with formally organised international meetings, the success of the World Social Forum has led to autonomous global civil society events. These meetings are gathering steam, with more than 30 per cent of the 108 recorded parallel summits since 1981 taking place in 2002 and early 2003. Even more interestingly, over 55 per cent of these recent events had more than 10,000 participants, and the majority of the meetings take place in the South.

Parallel and independent summits began as ways to harness the potential of civil society, create ever-wider networks and channel the energy of protests into productive, legitimate settings. In a way these summits have become the global equivalents of the legendary coffee houses of nineteenth-century civil society, where writers, revolutionaries, visionaries and ordinary folk gathered to discuss, debate and plan for a better future. Parallel and independent summits also point to something even more striking: the diplomatic machinery of the nation-state is being supplemented by new fora that promise levels of representation, efficiency and responsiveness that transcend the constraints of the state. The growing number of summits indicates an increasing desire and ability for global civil society groups to identify as such and to articulate their respective roles vis à vis each other and the state in the management of global issues.

Impact on multilateral organisations

If global civil society is asserting itself through summits and protests, its organisations have increasingly become part of the workings of multilateral organisations. One of the key complaints during the protests at the WTO meeting in Seattle in 1999 was the short shrift given to NGOs and other civil society organisations in the deliberations. Today NGOs are laying claim to a central role in the decision-making process of supranational institutions, though many in the field say there is still a long way to go before they are given their due.

While frustrations abound, the enhanced role of civil society has never been clearer. The United Nations Environment Programme (UNEP) puts it clearly: 'Decisions that take into account civil society views early in the policy-making process will have stronger and broader recognition and support by the public when being implemented. In addition, common strategies between UNEP and civil society are necessary as civil society plays a direct role in the formation of policy, and as an advocate for policies and strategies in the global environment' (http://www.unep.org/dpdl/cso/global_csf/about.html). The United Nations General Assembly Special Session on HIV/AIDS (UNGASS) regards partnerships between NGOs and governments as critical for developing effective national HIV/AIDS responses and strategies, and the list goes on. 'Whether through formal contracts, standing agreements, or ad hoc arrangements, UN organisations collaborate with and often rely on NGOs and NGO networks to deliver services, test new ideas, and foster popular participation. By belonging to an NGO network that has systematic relations with UN organs, an NGO has a certain additional legitimacy and also has the opportunity to join in the collective exercise of responsibility and to influence the decision making of that UN body' (Ritchie, 2002). In fact, a recent high-level panel set up by the UN Secretary-General Kofi Annan noted the changing reality of global governance by stating that 'global policy networks' composed of governments, civil society, business and other interested actors are essential to address future global problems. The panel recommended that the UN system take greater account of the potential of civil society actors by incorporating civil society not only in implementing programmes but also in policy-making deliberations such as in the General Assembly (United Nations, 2004).

International financial institutions such as the World Bank have also found NGOs to be not only gadflies but also valued partners. In the quest for sustainable development, the World Bank has cooperated formally with civil society organisations since 1981, but it has been only since the late 1990s that interaction and cooperation have increased markedly. The World Bank lists NGOs, trade unions, faith-based organisations, community-based organisations and foundations as partners to improve the effectiveness and sustainability of its programmes, and the Bank has set up civil society specialists in more than 70 developing countries and created a 'civil society thematic team' at its Washington headquarters.

Not all civil society organisations are convinced by the motives of the World Bank or even the UN. The World Bank is often criticised for co-opting small NGOs to boost its own legiti-

macy, and critics point out that civil society dialogues do not allow for any direct role for NGOs
in the Bank's main mission or decision making.
Other critics emphasise that large international
NGOs are often the main beneficiaries of World
Bank partnerships, leaving local actors out of the
loop. Despite all their progress, civil society
actors still feel marginalised when it comes to
real decision making by governments or the UN
and note how the rhetoric of civil society participation is rarely translated into action, with the
private sector given privileged access over civil
society. Accreditation of NGOs and access to
information remains heavily politicised and
bureaucratic, and NGOs are wary of calls for
increased accountability if they think this means
new ways of disciplining or controlling them.

Impact on peacemaking

Though much of the role of civil society in cooperating with governments and multilateral
organisations involves complementing their
roles in implementation of programmes, some
civil society actors have ventured into areas normally thought of as under the strict competence
of governments – namely diplomacy for peacemaking. Typically called Track II (for unofficial)
diplomacy, some civil society organisations have
made peace between parties in situations government third parties have found intractable.
For example, the non-governmental organisation Moral Re-Armament (now called Initiatives
of Change) assisted the peaceful transition of
power from white-rule Rhodesia to black-rule
Zimbabwe in 1979–1980. England, the United
States, Zambia and Tanzania found themselves
unable to pressure or negotiate a political stand-
off between the white rule of Ian Smith and the
extremist black coalition led by Robert Mugabe.
In an attempt to prevent the impending bloody
conflict, members of Moral Re-Armament brokered secret meetings between Smith and
Mugabe that led to the peaceful transition of
power. Similarly, in 1992 the religious Community of Sant'Egidio successfully eased a peace
process in Mozambique into existence.

More commonly, civil society organisations
contribute to peacemaking through activities
such as encouraging parties to meet with counterparts, facilitating or training parties in negotiation or rallying the public to pressure the
protagonists to reach agreement. For example,
in 2002 the Mano River Women Peace Network
met the heads of state of Liberia, Sierra Leone

and Guinea, and persuaded them to meet President Charles Taylor of Liberia in order to nor-
malise relations in the Mano River Union (West
Africa). Also it was reported locally that some of
these and other Liberian refugee women later
surrounded Charles Taylor in Accra in June
2003, refusing to allow him to leave without concluding negotiations to bring peace to and his
own departure from Liberia.

Groups such as these have been involved in
peacemaking for hundreds of years – with the
Quakers recording their history of peacemaking
back 300 years. However, the local nature of
most civil society activities often means these stories go unnoticed and unpublicised. Nevertheless, civil society organisations continue to
contribute to making and building peace with
and sometimes in spite of governments. A future
peace settlement in the Israeli–Palestinian conflict may indeed draw upon ideas in the civil society generated Geneva Initiative/Accord of 2003.

Challenges for non-governmental organisations

While civil society organisations are seen in the
first instance as improving democracy, accountability and transparency, it is also true that civil
society organisations are rarely democratic,
accountable or transparent themselves. The lack
of standards and governance of NGOs has
allowed the field to burgeon uncontrollably to
the point where anyone can begin an NGO, as
the previous anecdote of the man from Central
Asia shows. The UN, certain international organisations and some governments, like the Australian government, have accreditation
processes for NGOs that assist their bureaucracies in deciphering the meaningful NGOs in the
midst of the millions out there. Despite these
efforts, often there is no way to ensure the competency (expertise), capacity (resources to carry
out programmes) and credibility (accountability
and trustworthiness) of NGOs beyond the personal experience of having worked together.
Some have suggested that the NGO field should
govern itself by creating codes of conduct. The
humanitarian assistance community adopted
such a code in the mid-1990s called the International Red Cross and Red Crescent Movement
and NGOs in Disaster Relief Code.

Civil society organisations are often torn
between the demands of donors, members and

the constituencies they serve. They must balance business-like concerns about efficiency and increasingly meet reporting and accounting requirements while also remaining true to their principles and values. How to manage these different forms of accountability while maintaining independence and flexibility is a difficult task indeed.

Consider the problem of NGOs that have become involved with monitoring labour standards. The principle is straightforward: corporations must be held accountable for their treatment of workers, from wages and hours worked to safety. But as NGOs assume the responsibility for monitoring such activity they must also bear the costs of training and conducting inspections. More problematically, NGOs have to avoid being used by companies as effective public relations ploys, giving a 'politically correct' seal of approval to corporations engaged in questionable practices. Perhaps more troubling is the prospect that NGOs might end up doing what governments should properly do, thereby letting them off the hook and undermining the development of local laws and unions and ultimately hurting rather than helping the regulatory process.

This fear of states devolving core functions onto civil society actors is a double-edged sword. On the one hand, it can only be regarded as a positive indication of the power of civil society when a government, such as that of the Czech Republic, adopts laws for the systematic and transparent distribution of a substantial portion of the state budget (0.3 per cent, or about US$53 million in 2001) to civil organisations (Pajas, 2001). On the other hand, when civil society becomes dependent on government funds for its operation it raises questions not only about their motivations but also about the risks of dependency on the state for putatively independent organisations.

unprecedented numbers. As a recent study showed, the average number of links among civil society actors has increased by 110 per cent in the decade between 1990 and 2000 (Anheier et al., 2003, p. 14). In sheer numbers, recent decades have shown a steady increase in the number and type of organisations and their donors, members, volunteers, summits, protests, consultations, partnerships and media visibility.

Such increasing density suggests that global civil society will play an increasingly important role as the modern state system undergoes evergreater challenges. New waves of complex emergencies, increasing global inequality and future wars will continue to expose the limits of national governments and international institutions to respond in a timely and effective fashion. Global civil society organisations cannot replace these governments or institutions, but they can provide the much-needed expertise, flexibility and indignation necessary for change.

Global civil society is not a unitary actor, or even an actor at all – it is the societal precondition for democratic global governance. As such it will always be contentious, uneven and dynamic. Perhaps it is best to think of global civil society organisations as the spaces where global citizens are forged. With no prospect of an illusory world government, and faced with the need for more accountable and more effective global governance, citizens around the world are transforming existing institutions through consultation, confrontation and compromise. While the nation-state system might not be disappearing any time soon, the forces of global civil society are an important part of the shifting ecology of global politics that is producing deep changes in the way nations and citizens interact. The key to managing and understanding this change is to be open to the transformation of the main actors and to keep a sharp eye out for the emergence of new ones.

A thickening network: the future of global civil society

The last decade and a half has seen the thickening and spreading of structures of global civil society. NGOs are now spread across more of the world, although their headquarters remain concentrated in Europe and the United States. NGOs, INGOs and international governmental organisations are connecting with each other in

Further Reading

Albert, Michael (2001) 'What are we for?', *Znet*, 6 September.

Anheier, Helmut, Glasius, Marlies and Kaldor, Mary (eds) (2003) *Global Civil Society 2003*, Oxford: Oxford University Press.

Boli, John and Thomas, George (1999) *Constructing World Culture: International*

Nongovernmental Organisations Since 1875, Palo Alto, CA: Stanford University Press.

Diamond, Louise and McDonald, John W. (1996) *Multi-Track Diplomacy: A Systems Approach to Peace*, Hartford, CT: Kumarian Press.

Drezner, Daniel W. and Farrell, Henry (2004) 'Web of influence', *Foreign Policy*, November/December.

Edwards, Michael (2004) *Civil Society*, Cambridge: Polity Press.

Fisher, Julie (1998) *Nongovernments: NGOs and the Political Development of the Third World*, Hartford, CT: Kumarian Press.

Keck, Margaret and Sikkink, Kathryn (1998) *Activists Beyond Borders*, Ithaca and London: Cornell University Press.

Pajas, Petr (2001) 'The Czech government and NGOs in 2001', *International Journal of Not-for-Profit Law*, vol. 3 issue 3, March.

Ritchie, Cyril (2002) 'NGO Cooperation and Networking', Centre International de Conférence de Genève (CCIG), Geneva.

United Nations (2004) 'We the peoples: civil society, the United Nations and global governance', UN Document A/58/817, 11 June.

Weiss, Thomas G. and Gordenker, Leon (eds) (1996) *NGOs, the UN & Global Governance*, Boulder, CO: Lynne Rienner.

CHAPTER 5: States

One of the most significant and certainly one of the oldest performers in the theatre of global politics is the state, often since the nineteenth century called the national state. The idea of the state both in the past and the present has encompassed many different versions or editions of the basic object. This was particularly true at the time states first evolved and wide variations are also a marked feature of contemporary global politics. In between the variations have tended to be less and the convergence in institutions, style and expectations rather more. The common denominator has been and is the notion that the state represents the most effective means by which human societies can make the necessary activity of government acceptable to the population.

The fully developed state has certain expected characteristics: it will exercise administrative power within and conduct external relations outside a defined territorial area. It will have advanced institutions for central and local administration. It will be the sole proprietor of military and police forces. It will have a regime or type of government through which it will govern, usually by consent, using democratic systems, or by force, as happens under a military dictatorship. The state has also expected to be something more than the supplier of tolerated governance by acting as the focus of the population's loyalty. Backed up by a shared social and political history, love of a characteristic set of landscapes, often a dominant language and literature, provision and control of education and equipped with symbolic architecture in a capital city suitably arranged for parades, anthems and flying flags on state occasions, the state has been able to call on the devotion of its people to the point of dying for it in battle. The complete centralisation of power within a physical area is what is meant by describing a state as sovereign. Provinces, regions and states which are members of a federation as in the United States, India,

Russia or Germany are not sovereign entities and do not exercise complete power over the governance of their populations.

Not all these characteristics have been acquired by states at any one time. They represent an historical accretion and appeared at somewhat different times in different places. It is particularly true that the idea that a state ought to coincide physically with a single or very dominant nationality – the national state – is relatively new, as has been the evolution of a heavy weight of domestic administration and regulation. The first followed from the French revolutionary period at the turn of the nineteenth century – around 1800 – and the second arose out of the enormous increase in government authority that followed from the technological advances released by the industrial revolution. Many of these made significant social improvements possible, ranging from the provision of effective sewage systems to the transport revolution created by the building of railways. Both these examples had important effects on modern societies, the one dramatically cutting the incidence of disease and the other making suburbs possible together with the social revolution inherent in suburban living. The net effect was to increase the weight of the basic bargain: the obligations of the state steadily expanded and the duties of the citizen followed suit. The combination then in turn put comprehensible pressure on the provision and defence of citizens' rights, to which the onset of globalisation has given added emphasis.

The state and the various forms of government that it has evolved over time have been the mechanism by which most human societies – though not all – have resolved, as far they have been able to, the essential contradiction between achieving the best conditions of life for the majority and what each person might want for themselves. The most acceptable routes for arriving at the compromises which thus have to be made have been tested and re-tested, written down as constitutions and precedents, and enshrined in law. The shorter-term adjustments and modifications which are always required are the stuff of daily political life and inform the ideologies of regimes, sometimes leading to tough dictatorships, more frequently to brands of democracies. Resistance movements in the first case and the urgent vigour of political parties in the second have been the chosen engines for propelling that political life.

Position of the state

Whatever its individual style, the state and the particular government it has extruded at any given moment has been the place where the great political choices on economic and social issues have been made. It possesses the kind of power which makes the governing of societies possible because of a public acceptance that such government is both necessary and effective. It confers political legitimacy and thus political authority. If either of these conditions is weakened or disappears, confusion results and familiar distributions of power come into question and may be operationally challenged in ways that stretch between mild unrest and violent, revolutionary change. It is therefore not surprising that these structures loom so large and it is no more surprising that there is a contemporary tendency to ask increasingly worried questions about their health and effectiveness.

One reason for this anxiety is that the state has occupied this central position for a very long time and it is not easy for people to think that it was ever different and thus might as easily be different again. It is not an area in which change is easy to contemplate. However, looked at with a twenty-first-century eye, it is clearly becoming easier to see that states have not been creatures only of a particular period but that even during their primacy of people's political imaginations, other groupings of authority or activity – polities – have existed concurrently. The seemingly dominant role of the state has always been more apparent than real. The force of the idea, nonetheless, is not to be underestimated, even if the process of demythologising it may turn out to be easier than might have been predicted.

Thus it is important to understand that the state was the product of a particular place and time in human development which took root deeply and naturally in many parts of the world, and was imposed and operated more shallowly elsewhere, until by the end of the nineteenth century it had ceased to be possible for people to imagine an alternative: it might be differently represented, it might be the object of revolutionary attempts to change its immediate political character, but the institution itself had become a given condition – so much so that one of the last great efforts to generalise its functions in a particular way, as proposed by Karl Marx, thought of itself as supplanting and abolishing all other forms.

Erosion of the state

The cause of anxiety about the contemporary role of the state lies in the complex and often contradictory results of the contemporary global communications revolution. The conjunction of microchip computers and the orbiting satellite has brought in its wake a fundamental restructuring of the global economy. The effect has been to abolish state frontiers as far as the traffic of information, particularly technological knowledge, is concerned. This has created a global market in technologically dependent commodities. At the same time, ease of communication and thus control and command has made it possible for globally operating businesses to locate their activities wherever local conditions make it most desirable to do so. This has brought basic manufacturing work to formerly underdeveloped economies and subtracted it from advanced ones.

One paradoxical result of this has stemmed from a marked increase in global migration flows, partly made possible by the ease of contemporary travel. But two motives chiefly fuel it: one is the wish to escape from cruel political or economic conditions and the other is to go in pursuit of better paid work or better state welfare systems. The result in a country like Germany is that migrants may arrive seeking better paid work in a society where unemployment is high and rising because manufacturing has itself migrated to where wages are lower. The problems associated with migration are severe, ranging from housing to health and crime. Governments are not proving capable of controlling it and have not or are politically unable to deliver the resources to deal effectively with its awkward domestic consequences.

Before looking more closely at the problems surrounding the future of the state, the economic context must be remembered. The activities of deeply integrated multinational enterprises, together with the cross-border inter-firm alliances that they engender, have become the principal form of international transactions. Banking and stock market activity has gone in the same direction and has little or no geographical location left: it exists where there are terrestrial monitors connected to cyber space. The picture that emerges is of a global economic system of great complexity. Significant participants in the preceding interdependent global economy, governments, groups of governments, territorially based markets and banks, and multinational companies, dealt with each other as singular, temporally and physically located entities. They thus acted in ways that were analogous with, if not sharing their mechanisms, the kind of essentially vertical relationship which states had established with each other since the seventeenth century. These vertical relationships remain in the new situation, but their roles are different and generally reduced and their physical shapes, formerly pyramidal, have tended to flatten and spread. Global markets, global manufacturers and purveyors of knowledge, and global consumers, already either horizontal in shape or lacking any physical shape at all, have arrived as new participants, stirring like a rising mist on a summer's morning round the soaring trunks of the trees in an old wood. They move inexorably across global space and time without respect for physical geography, political frontiers or night and day.

The traditional state

These economic effects have been joined by others. News, comment and information of all kinds have taken on an independent life of their own, divorced from the control of governments. Defence and the conduct of war have been affected similarly and occupy a transitional position in which national defence mechanisms and attitudes survive but often have to be expressed through cooperative peacemaking or peace-keeping operations. All this vigorous life, intellectual, technological and commercial, is being conducted horizontally, cutting across the old vertical divisions typical of the traditional state. What are the consequences for the state? Can it be remoulded to fit contemporary requirements? If so, it can only be by reducing expectations as to what functions it can best perform and fitting it into a much more pluralistic global system of governance.

This will be very hard. The weight of tradition is against it and the traditional state can come to be seen as a defence against those aspects of economic globalisation which are not popular. Yet what it needs to do for the benefit of its people in the global economy can only be tough and unpopular. Meanwhile, some of its authority trickles away in the face of the instinctive as well as practical realisation on the part of electorates that many of its functions have been eroded by global change. Thus a paradox remains for resolution: there is a job for the state to do, but it is hard to do, and the same events that have produced that job have also reduced the political legitimacy of the state to the point where public support for tough measures is much less easy to assemble and maintain. And if the state tries to resist globalisation, it will be equally if not more difficult and will require privations on the part of the people, which they may not be willing to accept from a weakened system of government.

The best outcome will be uncomfortable evolutionary change, the worst – of which there are already clear warnings – will be public disorder leading to the collapse of the existing institutions of government and the probability of more general disturbances.

Politically legitimate governance of states

There is another side to this coin which complicates the problem further. Because the exercise of public domestic authority came to be associated almost completely with states, the devices which have been developed to make that authority acceptable to populations have also been linked to the machinery of states. These devices consist of constitutional limitations and other conditions that are imposed on the exercise of power. They are part of the expected, necessary structure of the national state and it is their governments and rulers who have, willingly or unwillingly, to accept them.

Democratic systems of government provide further means of mediating power. Both constitutional limitations and democratic systems, when in full working order, supply political legitimacy and therefore public consent for the exercise of power. When power and authority begin to seep away from national governments, they also escape from the controls which have evolved in association with states and from their democratic systems, wherever they exist. Newer sources of globalised power and authority are being exercised without any of the familiar and expected restraints, thus destroying the link between public acceptance that power must be exercised and the maintenance of some controls over it. This produces in global circumstances what in the regional conditions of the European Union has been described as a democratic deficit. In that case, the exercise of power, subtracted from member states, by administrative organs in Brussels has not yet been subjected to the ultimate control of the European Parliament and the actions of individual European Commissioners have only very recently been the object of its scrutiny. Pressure for greater accountability is mounting and some changes are evolving but, like the Parliament's defective control over the European budget, there is a long road to walk yet.

All this raises the issue of the vertical, wherein lies existing legitimacy, and the horizontal, wherein lies power, in an acute form. For there is a direct clash of interest between the evolution of horizontal limitations on the exercise of horizontal power and the vertically arranged structures and controls with which we are familiar, if increasingly disenchanted. In the past, an acceptable exercise of power was achieved through violence as much as or more than through evolutionary change, and the fact is at least a warning if not a prediction. There is an urgent and growing need therefore to begin developing new systems, global in scope, in order to reproduce the controlling effects on horizontally exercised power which were long ago developed within states to restrain the abuse of vertically exercised authority. These will not necessarily be echoes of those devised in the light of the evolution of the state. It is more likely that the shape of successful alternative validations of global sources of power will turn out to be very different if they are to guard against violent rejections of irreversibly established global authorities when people discover how uncontrolled they actually are.

This problem amounts to a contemporary crisis of governance and political legitimacy. It requires that the traditional means of protecting citizens from over-mighty rulership be reduced and redirected while at the same time allowing globally focused controls to evolve, shaped to match the sources of power they are intended to restrain. The vertical and the horizontal have

to be accommodated within a single system. This is clearly such a serious matter that it is worth taking a much closer look at it. The fundamental problem – making the existence and exercise of power acceptable to individuals – has not changed, but its practical expression has; and as the evolution of states has yielded at least one highly significant historical experience of solving it, it would not be sensible to think about the contemporary situation without knowing something about how the existing arrangements came about.

The most complex forms of political relationship and commercial and cultural exchange have developed over the last 300 years and have been the product of an era when most societies turned themselves into or aspired to become nation-states. Such evolutionary changes usually produced episodes of conflict and warfare. The study of these relationships, and particularly their occasional descent into violence, has become an intellectual discipline, rising to greater and greater sophistication as it has sought to understand more about the shifting sands of inter-state activities, economic, political and strategic. It is useful to remember this pattern because it lasted for so long that it came to be regarded as a given condition, an unchanging basis for discussion, an inalienable template by which to explain the affairs of states and their external relations. This in turn helps to throw light on why much muddle and anxiety has developed in the face of recent fundamental evolutionary shifts which have invalidated the template: these are the shifts in both power and the distribution of power which have come to be called globalisation.

Role of communications technology

In order to assess further the contemporary internal impacts of globalisation on states, the consequences of the successive technological revolutions in communications need to be included. Their influence on both internal political stability and external relationships since the early nineteenth century has been profound. Both the machinery of international relations and the fixed assumptions which societies have come to make about the likely consequences of their own or their government's actions have been shaped by the effects which technological change has had on the nature and distribution of power – economic and political.

On the whole, the period from the middle of the nineteenth century to the later part of the twentieth can be seen as a single evolution, itself emerging from an earlier and more geographically restricted version of a similar structure. In both these situations, as we shall see, the principal propelling agent in the equations of power was the unfolding development of the state, both internally and externally. After about 300 years of continuous, expansionary activity, it is not surprising that the central role of the state itself, never mind what whirligigs of changing fortune might affect it, became a fixed expectation, a given condition of the political life of humanity. Nor is it surprising that the world steadily acquired the mechanisms that matched the realities on the ground.

Understanding how and why this situation developed is an essential precondition for appreciating why the contemporary environment can seem so alarmingly strange, where familiar, previously reliable, points of reference no longer provide base lines, as if the lighthouses that make sense of difficult coasts had been switched off. The contemporary world is seeing change on a greater scale and at a deeper level than anything that has happened since the sovereign state began to evolve in Europe towards the end of the sixteenth century: the lighthouses really have been turned out and it is crucial to comprehend where the coastline actually is if we are to make sense of the inevitable, and potentially violent, transitions which must occur.

The overwhelming difficulties of land transport before the machine age affected almost every aspect of human life. Internally it meant that all forms of centralised government were bound to be weak at best or merely amoebic at worst and therefore it was highly localised units which most affected everyday life, even if they were formally part of and subject to a loosely structured larger entity. The difficulty also affected external relationships. During the Roman Empire, for example, ordinary diplomatic exchanges were rendered almost impossible by the length of time it might take for an embassy to find the Emperor, whose court – and therefore the government – had a strong tendency to be peripatetic. In such an immense space, it was easy to miss and difficult to catch up with the constantly moving target that the imperial entourage represented. In general circumstances like these, the advantages lay with seaborne traffic, for commerce, information and strategy. Coasts tended to enjoy higher civilisation and greater wealth, but also to be a focus for conflict. Political entities which enjoyed effective water communication tended to be more sophisticated administratively and any technological improvement in ships extended their commercial and naval reach.

By the sixteenth century, the Chinese had already visited East Africa, though they did not follow up on their seagoing expertise, and in Europe, the Portuguese, the Venetians, the Genoese, the Spanish, the English and the Dutch were demonstrating the importance of waterborne communications and naval power. Those who did not have such access were either restrained – for example the Russians locked into the Eurasian land mass behind ice-bound ports – or showed signs of failing development, as the largely landlocked Holy Roman Empire did in Germany and Central Europe.

At much the same time, other factors, particularly the consequences of the emergence of fully monetarised economies and the secularising effects of the Reformation, caused the gradual evolution of fully independent states in Europe. The decline of formerly pan-European, Roman-originated forms of authority both religious and political allowed individual rulers to assert their own untrammelled legal and political jurisdiction which they were able to establish over the rights of local lords within their territories as well as excluding former external suzerains. The result was a downsizing of the most effective political unit and the further result was that entities emerged which were small enough to be able to ignore the serious problems of communication over long distances. The improved possibilities for their internal administration which followed further reinforced the authority of sovereign or nearly sovereign rulers.

The consequence was a maelstrom of internal and external conflict in Europe, lasting for a century. The movement of power flowed away from highly traditional authorities, to some degree still legitimised by the Roman inheritance, and away from highly localised barons and princes whose position was based upon ancient rights by which they could command services and goods in kind. Authority now flowed towards the rulers of states who based their claim to internal and external sovereignty on their ability to provide coherent and functional administration, essentially paid for out of monetary wealth obtained from taxation, borrowing or seizure. These new-style regimes were providing a stability which populations regarded as necessary in an age when their numbers were rising, recovering after the trauma of the Black Death, and at a time of quickening economic and commercial activity. But they were also the beneficiary of another development.

Distribution of power

Changes in the nature of power did not just affect new users. The fact that there were new users also meant that there were consequential changes in the distribution of power, away from the centres of the past, which created one kind of conflict, and into new hands, among whom the pecking order was as yet uncertain, which created another. The wars which wracked Europe from the beginning of the sixteenth century were the consequence. Their climax came in the period 1618 to 1648, but they did not finally abate until 1713. They began as struggles to defend or reject the older dispensations, religious wars and wars surrounding the position of the Holy Roman Empire and its Hapsburg rulers. After 1648, the new had essentially triumphed over the old and turned to the business of settling a new distribution of power among the beneficiaries. This chiefly turned on the question of whether the French, who came to full statehood first among European societies, would be able to transform their advantage into a European hegemony. The answer was that they could not and that answer was to have significant effects on contemporary international politics. An additional effect of so much conflict over so long a period was to create a basis of loyalty within societies whose citizens had suffered so much together. They came to see themselves as ranged together against others, as communities, political and economic, as well as units of sovereign government.

In one sense this smoothed the path of the sovereign ruler. In another, it created intense problems. The supplanting of loose, traditional forms of authority may have been supported by secularisation and by the need for unity in the face of external conflict, but these alone did not supply legitimacy and thus a secure and well-based regime. There had been substantial restrictions on the practical operation of traditional political and legal controls. The source was likely to be distant and where it was local,

there were obvious practical reasons why local lords would be more effectively served by driving on a comfortable rein rather than using the whip. Their presence was highly personal and their reward was goods and services. The contrast with the incoming system was important. The domestic power of sovereign rulers was significantly greater and their rule more tightly organised, if nowhere near the expectation that a late-twentieth-century citizen might have.

Societies, understandably, turned out to want a substitute for the natural restrictions on the use and abuse of power that would be effective in the new situation and they particularly wanted it in respect of taxation. At different paces and in different places, the combination of the arguments of political philosophers and the often violent objections of populations began to force an entirely new set of restrictions on the power of rulers. The growing authority of the English parliament, followed by the military defence of its role within the English system of government, including as it did the execution of the king, is the classic example of a process where the acquisition of great power was quickly followed by the evolution of important restraints upon the use of that power. Failure to observe those restraints led to the withdrawal of the consent of the governed and the collapse of political legitimacy. Gradually a vastly complicated rule book of acceptable ways of achieving a stable political society developed, malleable but essential in all advanced states. Maintaining this balance between wielding effective power and preserving the rights of citizens has been part of the evolution of states.

Over time, rulers became equally conscious that going to war had destructive effects on the domestic sinews of power and compromised the effort to reform and improve domestic management. Moreover, by the eighteenth century, an age which was apt to produce rationalist rather than religious arguments, the divine right of rulers had ceased to have the force it once did and even inheritance seemed less compelling than competence. The notion that rulers might rule for as long as they patently attempted to do so in the interests of their populations was likely to put a premium on avoiding war and to increase the level of stress that would be required before rulers would resort to it. Thus achieving a delicate balance, in an era of more sophisticated state structures, between the demands of the business of government and maintaining security within an international community became a primary ambition for rulers and their ministers.

Both the internal balance with its resulting political legitimacy and the external balance of power were destroyed by the French Revolution of 1789. Like the English revolution in the 1640s, it was induced by a breakdown of government in the face of the need to deal with bankruptcy. The right to tax on the part of governments and the right to have an influence on the incidence of taxation and the purposes for which the resulting revenue was spent had long been an important issue. Quite recently it had figured among the causes of the American War of Independence and had there led to a new statement of the rights of individuals and the duties of government which reflected both English traditions from the preceding century and the writings of contemporary Enlightenment political philosophers. The result was a new mechanism for expressing the relationship between the individual and governments in a constitutionally defined system.

States and nationalism

The French Revolution pushed this process further and seriously shifted the previous balance in the direction of more popular participation in the processes of government. This had the effect of increasing a people's perception of itself as a nation in the modern sense. The idea of nationalism, however, also had an important origin in the opposition that eventually developed to Napoleonic hegemony.

The Napoleonic Empire was a remarkable combination of old and new. It claimed to be able to realise the best principles of the revolution in terms of good and modern government and to be able to protect and advance the achievements of civilisation. It also sought to return to an older, and to some degree imaginary, Europe, which retained its status as a *maxima civitas*, inherited from the days of Rome. In such a Europe, the quarrels and wars of independent states would not occur, peace would be assured and all the benefits of a unitary rule would accrue. To make the point, Napoleon himself occasionally dressed up as a Roman Emperor and sometimes as Charlemagne, while abolishing the Holy Roman Empire but carefully marrying the daughter of the last Emperor. This attempt to reverse the tide of history and sup-

press a developed community of sovereign states was predictably unsuccessful and by the end the process of defeating it had induced not only the natural hostility of other rulers but also the opposition of ordinary people who came to see the Napoleonic imperium as an affront to their nationalities. They thus became amenable to appeals to nationalism as a ground for supporting the war against the Emperor. Once that genie was out of the bottle, it could not be returned and corked up again.

The state, which had pre-existed the revolution as the normal form of organisation for European societies, acquired a new object of existence: to represent the well-being and aspirations of a particular ethnic group, or at least to contain and be supported by a population of which a majority came from one nationality. This new ingredient in the mix of factors which conferred domestic political legitimacy shifted the distribution of power during the next century. Those states to which history had given a mixed population, and were thus states without nations, began to decline, and those nationalities which were not represented by a state of their own, and were thus nations without states, began to demand that they should acquire statehood and in some cases to achieve that ambition. The Hapsburg Empire and the Ottoman Empires belonged to the first category, Italy (1860), Hungary (1867) and Germany (1871) belonged to the second. These three all emerged at the expense of the Hapsburg Empire and in the latter case, France as well.

The collectivist state

The predominance of the idea of the state itself was increased by these developments: the arguments were all about defending existing states or becoming new states; and while this evolution proceeded, other factors were rapidly accelerating the domestic power of governments and thus the political significance of governing. These factors were the consequence of technological advances flowing from the industrial revolution and they were to push the nation-state into becoming the collectivist state.

In virtually every aspect of human existence, more advanced mechanisms, industrially produced, could improve the quality of life. Health, safety, travel, the availability of goods and services were all examples. What was possible was increasingly and comprehensibly demanded by populations. The result was a huge expansion of activity. New forms of construction, for example, for railway lines, new forms of physical plant, such as sewage treatment plants, electricity- and gas-generating facilities, and their vast delivery networks, either fell directly into the scope of government or provoked the establishment of regulatory systems. The result was an unprecedented expansion in the scope and size of the machinery of government – an administrative revolution.

The effect rapidly became circular: new roles required new monies, new monies required new taxation, both required additional state employees whose salaries required further new monies. Thus taxation also inevitably grew and the significance of the machinery of the state in the daily lives of ordinary people became more compelling. The spread of literacy across far wider sections of populations which followed from improved educational systems created a basis for the growth of a popular press, which, anxious to increase its readership and profits, did not hesitate to cast political and even social life in highly dramatic, and often deeply inaccurate, terms. Moreover, governments, finding it ever harder to obtain and then to keep the support of fickle electorates, jumped onto the bandwagon and began to resort to simplified sloganeering internally and to describe foreign policy either in the rhetoric of aggressive nationalism or by emitting loud cries of foul play and a consequent need to defend the fatherland.

The awkwardnesses of this situation led to the emergence of two alternative, though in many ways similar, modes of political justification for an intensively active role for government in industrialised societies: communism and fascism. After the catastrophe of the 1914 war, which itself put the organs of states under intense pressure and greatly expanded their authority, both joined the more traditional liberal, if increasingly collectivist, state not just as theoretical models but as practical examples. Notwithstanding the Marxist belief in the eventual withering away of the state, both in practice greatly contributed to the sense of vertical division between them. This division now took not only political, economic and ethnic forms but ideological ones as well.

Consequences

The ideological consequences have worked or are still working themselves out in the early twenty-first century. The physical architectural consequences are very much still to be seen. It is somehow easier to comprehend the full weight of the state and its governmental system when we remember to look at its physical expressions as just that, rather than the familiar architectural clothing of capital cities and regional centres.

It is not surprising that there was a temporal connection between the opening of the greatest period of state authority and the rebuilding of capital cities. The habit started in the eighteenth century with St Petersburg, followed by Washington. Both sought to give an air of permanence to a state which was in fact under construction. Older state forms had almost accidentally acquired administrative or royal court centres, usually located in places already important for strategic or commercial reasons. Until the second half of the nineteenth century, however, they remained jumbled and chaotic masses: a mix of official buildings and palaces and slums. The needs of an expanding central government machine, together with the feelings of an emotionally nationalist society, evoked major rebuilding schemes: vast administrative departmental buildings appeared, specifically devoted to named government activities arranged on great avenues, themselves laid out to accommodate the processions by which the national state and/or empire gave expression to their grandeur and individuality. Just how far contemporary activities and needs have changed may be judged from the fact that in the late twentieth century, the Treasury building of the British government, grandly located in Whitehall, the traditional seat of government, was deemed inappropriate for duties which have become principally computerised and can be substantially contracted out. For a time it was actually made available for conversion, most probably as an hotel, though in the end the change of use never happened.

This would have been, of course, an extreme example. But, particularly in developed countries, the property markets have been full of former state civil and military buildings and complexes for sale, not necessarily or even usually very grand, but indicative of a slimming diet in national government machines. It is equally instructive to observe the contemporary tendency to regard great national cities as museums in themselves and to treat them as such. In the past, they were assumed to be the proper place to locate the great national collections of art and artefacts, themselves often the result of past competitive theft from the place of origin, and sometimes now the object of increasingly successful demands for their return. The converse also exists. There has developed a perceptible global similarity in the construction of extremely grand international airports and in their appearance and management. A sleepy traveller might have considerable initial difficulty in deciding where he or she had actually landed and, if the final destination was a commercial or industrial concern, an equal problem in identifying exactly in which country or continent the building or plant was located. Little in the furniture or general design culture, nothing in the computerised systems, and probably not a lot in the language in use would be very helpful, and even climatic difference would be controlled into the background. Of course, there are still many places where that is not true, but there is no doubt of the tendency or of how far it has already gone.

The relative decline of the state

The swan song of the system of national states came after 1945. The superpowers were to be the last of their kind, stately dinosaurs accompanied by their families awaiting the onslaught of the impacting meteorite. In this case, the analogy with an impact catastrophe will not hold. What was coming had been more like a lesion in the earth's crust, invisible at first, then the source of visible cracks and finally quite suddenly the cause of collapse.

As we now know, the agent of this change was the most recent stage in the global communications revolution which had been brewing since the invention of the railway and the electric telegraph. These had remained within the control or, if privately owned, the regulation of states and had enhanced their authority, as well as their potential size. The addition of the oceanic cables in the very early twentieth century globalised international relations in ways which at first emphasised the individual sovereignty of states as well as increasing the potential geographical scope of their activities. The arrival of the telephone had more of a cementing effect within individual societies and only a limited role in inter-state communications until the later twentieth century. The most recent stage has, however, brought a genuine revolution with it. The combination of the microchip computer and the orbiting satellite has created not so much an improved means for states and soci-

eties to communicate with each other, though of course it does that, but a network of communications which exists in its own global environment. The effects have become famous, even notorious, and they have begun to reverse the persistent rise in the role of states and rulers which has been so marked since the seventeenth century.

This shift is most clearly visible in two areas: an absolute reduction in the authority of governments and an increase in the relative differences between states. The first affects the willingness of well-established governments to act decisively and by extension affects the authority of organisations set up by states – often called inter-governmental organisations – in a similar way. A second consequence of this factor has more serious effects. Since 1945, there has been a sharp increase in the number of states in the world. They have appeared in three waves. The first came in the late 1940s and occurred in Asia with the establishment of the modern Chinese state in 1949, the independence of India, Pakistan and Ceylon (Sri Lanka) in 1947, Indonesia in 1948 and the Philippines in 1946. The second wave started in the late 1950s and continued through the 1960s and chiefly involved the establishment of independent states in Africa, the Caribbean and some Pacific islands. The third phase followed the end of the Cold War and resulted from the break-up of Czechoslovakia, Yugoslavia and the Soviet Union.

It has been a tribute to the extraordinary power of the idea of the state as essentially the only conceivable way of organising human societies. This primacy has meant that wherever separation into smaller units has taken place, for example as a result of de-colonisation or the collapse of the Soviet Union, the name and, at least at the outset, the institutions of a state have been applied to the resulting new entities, whether they exhibited the underlying characteristics of a state or not. It has turned out that the ability to understand and operate a state has not been as general as was assumed. Some states have failed, some have become weak simulacra of the original notion, some have adopted it more or less successfully. This wide range of performance is matched by an extraordinarily wide range of power and influence. It is as possible for a tiny and insecure island in, say, Oceania to be called a state and given legal recognition as it is for the United States or India. What it takes to be a plausible state has now been reduced to a very short list of attributes, if, indeed, it is still possible to draw up such a list at all. The result has brought confusion to the global system whose effects are discussed in the section on sources of conflict in the chapter on associations of states and in the section on interactions in global politics.

The result has begun to reverse some if not all of the effects of the verticalisation which the creation of states had involved. Human activities are in a sense reverting to horizontal patterns, identifiable by topic rather than geography, by subject rather than ethnicity, but this time they are fully global in their scope and they portend a major reorganisation of the way in which human beings order their daily lives. These developments are having noticeable effects in two main areas: on the internal government of states because of the erosion of political legitimacy and because of structural changes required in the machinery of government, and on the external relations between states because they are no longer the sole players on the global stage and, by extension, on inter-state entities, because of the weakened position of their sponsoring bodies and because they, too, have to live in a more pluralistic world.

Contemporary political legitimacy

We will discuss first the contemporary problems associated with the idea of political legitimacy. The problem starts with economic changes: manufacturing and commercial activity which was formerly confined to Western Europe, America and Japan can now take place anywhere and is doing so in Asia, Central Europe and China. The result is the emergence of new sources of market outlets and of competition, a growing convergence of living standards among advanced countries and a better appreciation in both developing and developed countries of the part which international business activities can play in improving national competitiveness.

These changes have necessarily complex factors underlying them: wealth-creating assets, chiefly people, money and knowledge, move freely across national boundaries; natural resources have declined in relative significance while physical capital and human knowledge have increased. The kinds of products now being produced require new forms of economic organisation, notably cooperative networks and ventures between firms. Competition between

governments for global resources and markets has grown and they have to take account of and try to improve the way in which their domestic resources are performing relative to those of other countries so as to benefit the performance of nationally based firms. This is because globalisation has produced serious competitive pressure on productivity levels which have to be constantly improved or governments will find domestic living standards falling as economic activity takes itself to more advantageous sites elsewhere.

All of these factors imply that the role of government is changing in two major directions. First, the opportunity of delivering social benefits to their populations, formerly an internal decision, is now crucially dependent on achieving an effective macro-economic global strategy operating in a horizontal relationship with other entities, whether countries, organisations or firms. If such a strategy is either misconceived or mishandled and thus fails in its cooperative aspect, the domestic results are likely to be harrowing. In these circumstances, decisions become much more difficult to arrive at because decision makers have a both internal and external constituency to satisfy, but will probably have to describe their activities in the largely internal terms that electorates can easily comprehend.

Second, achieving this requires not just changing attitudes but changing the functions of government itself, as firms have already done. Increasingly, the functions required to maximise the investment advantages and jobs to be harvested from the global economy are becoming interdependent and administratively interwoven, yet the actual structures have been slow to follow suit. The old physical administrative extrusions of the sovereign state arranged in vertical boxes of responsibilities cannot cope with a world where competition policy, environment policy, tax policy, innovation policy and education policy must be managed as a coherent whole, undivided by the vested interests of administrative systems located in clearly labelled ministries or departments of state.

Decisions about environmental issues are a good example of the problem. The level at which an environmental question needs to be decided can vary sharply. It may be very local, but equally, as in the case of arguments over the disposal of toxic waste, it may be both local, emotionally powerful and yet external because the point of departure or destination of the waste can easily be far away. It may arise from government action or inaction, or from private action or inaction. It refuses to be boxed even at that level. It may, however, involve decisions which affect or threaten global climatic change, in which case there is likely to be a muddled combination of national economic interests, private and/or public, the particular interests of other countries or regions and the need to protect the global climatic system as a whole. In this kind of situation, an internal decision made by allowing the trading-off of interests negotiated by government departments between themselves, as if they were playing on a level field, is unlikely to lead to an acceptable outcome; still less will it do so when the matter is at the least international but most probably global in scope.

To make matters more complex still, environmental issues are an area where the Internet has created a highly vocal and effective global constituency. The pressure comes not so much from organised national groups, or from business interests, against which it is often directed, but from individuals. The most obvious example of this kind of pressure can be found in the USA and seen at the Internet website Scorecard. It contains large quantities of accurate information about industrial pollution and polluters which can be directly accessed by individuals who are thus freed from having to rely on the highly nuanced information generally supplied by both government and business. Scorecard can supply information on a localised basis as well as draft letters of complaint to be faxed directly to the polluter concerned and a copy to be e-mailed to the Environmental Protection Agency in Washington DC. This kind of approach can produce puzzling and delicate situations for lobbyists who may find their favourite legislators bombarded with e-mails taking an entirely contradictory line to that proffered by their corporate clients.

So what are the political consequences of all this for states? The political loyalty of populations is generally given to individuals and institutions that are deemed to be effective agencies in controlling and moderating the effects of a basically hostile environment. This hostility might take the form of a natural disaster such as a major flood; or an economic collapse, threatening prosperity and jobs; foreign affairs, in the form of invasion or attack; social or political dislocation and unrest, requiring immediate protective reactions. By the twentieth century all and more of

these protective attributes were expected of a state and states, in various manifestations, were the object of most forms of loyalty and were generally able to deliver. The fate of the last Tsar of Imperial Russia or the demise of Reichskanzler Hitler indicated what might happen when they did not. These two particular events were made stark by the conditions of overwhelming conflict.

What is happening now is the result of further evolution rather than current conflict, though the technological advance which underlies it is the result of preparation for war and the picture is perhaps fortunately less stark. The Tsar and, eventually, Adolf Hitler were replaced by new versions of what had failed and no one supposed it should be otherwise. But the replacement for the Tsar, the Soviet Union, collapsed, and the replacement for the Nazi regime in reunited Germany has obvious structural and emotional problems, as has the EU of which it is a principal member. What is going on?

Russia, the United States and the European Union

We can best get a picture by considering some examples, one of which comes from a state in continuing crisis: Russia.

The initial collapse of the Soviet Union was itself instructive. The presence of political legitimacy in any state is and has always been the product of a domestic coalition of interests based on the belief that the abandonment of some particular desires, traditions and loyalties by each very local interest was worth it for the sake of the advantages conferred by belonging to the larger group. It was the collapse of this kind of coalition rather than the failure of Marxist ideology which ended the Soviet Union.

Mikhail Gorbachev plainly recognised that the domestic system of the Soviet Union had ceased to deliver the social, economic and security benefits which justified its existence in the face of a multitude of particularisms – cultural, ethnic and religious – spilt all across the land from Eastern Europe to East Asia. He tried to reform it so as to deliver those benefits before their absence brought on disaster, but the system was too inflexible and too corrupt to reform fast enough and he failed. What followed has partly been the result of particular conditions and traditions within the Russian Federation, which in the face of faltering rule has had an historic tendency to go into a state of suspended political and administrative animation until heaved out of it by some overwhelming event or ruler.

What is also interesting, however, is that it has seemed natural to an important group within Russia, and almost universally outside it, to replace the communist structure with economic and political versions of what had served the capitalist world well as a result of three centuries of development. It may be at least as significant in accounting for the fragility of democratic machinery in Russia, and even more the evident instability of the free market economy, that both notions arise from highly traditional ideas about what a state structure ought to be like. But if those notions are themselves now quite unreliable guides, they may be as outmoded as communism was.

The combination of some unhelpful Russian traditions which, among other things, elevate the role of corruption and degrade the rule of law, with the effective imposition of structurally inappropriate mechanisms, has had devastating effects on both Russians and their creditors alike. It is possible that Russia, more than other states, may demonstrate with frightening clarity what is a general dilemma: how to adjust the institutions of the state so as to fit contemporary circumstances and swim successfully with the tide, when to do so could easily involve the effective dissolution of the national government as it exists and the evolution of an entirely new kind of entity, or whether to resist the tide, thus courting public disorder and violent responses to it.

The United States, too, presents an interesting picture. Unlike the former Soviet Union, it is neither an existing empire nor the consequence of having been an empire in the past – that is to say, it is not an agglomeration of historically distinguishable ethnicities and societies, presided over or forcibly held together by a 'master race'. It has perfectly obvious social and ethnic divisions, but they were not created in the same way as those within the Russian Empire, and its profound geographical variations have not so far stimulated serious regional focuses of loyalty to match those of Europe or India. It is politically a genuine federation, already capable of devolution at any level required, determinable by constitutional practice.

This last factor is already in use. Recent years have seen a reduction in federal power and a resumption of formerly yielded powers by individual state governments. The general notion of hostility to big government is easier to accommodate in the United States than almost anywhere else in the world. Nonetheless, the United States is not above the consequences of globalisation. Its position as the only remaining 'superpower' is complicated rather than triumphant and, even more significantly, is not the object of popular approval so much as popular puzzlement. The destruction of the World Trade Center on 11 September 2001 in New York City and the subsequent responses, both internal and external, have only confirmed that confusion.

The constant pressure to be economically successful in the global environment is felt no less. In common with other societies, particularly the UK, there is anxiety about the quality of education because of an increasing sense of comparative failure in equipping students with the necessary intellectual tools of survival in the contemporary world. There is an almost morbid fascination with educational statistics expressed in terms of global comparisons. This is essentially because the degree of technological education present in a society has now become part of its ability to attract its share of the loose capital washing about the global markets. The result is a tension between the increasing poverty of governments whose tax base has been eroding and their certainty that more resources need to be put into education at every level.

The responsibilities here have increased because of two major changes. The provision of education used to be based on the notion that there was a finite quantity required for individuals to function effectively in particular life roles. High school and college education, give or take some relatively small special skill – an extra language, for example – would enable the newly minted adult to perform in almost any mode of employment. Education was over and life began. No longer: this is impossible now in a world where the progress of knowledge is already rapid and getting faster. The rate of obsolescence in the high-tech information industry – to name just the most obvious example – requires a continuous process of re-education. Meeting this need necessitates major revolutions in attitudes, to some degree already under way, and major expenditures.

Education

What makes it a particularly difficult business arises from a second difference we should note. The educational systems of the developed world naturally reflect the practices and expectations of the past. In the past, education was seen to be part of a cultural training. It existed within a particular cultural tradition – French education was different from British, which was different from Russian and different again from American. The process acknowledged a local cultural past and contributed to a particular way of thinking about the present. Like states themselves, it was organised within and not above a society. To an important degree, it taught you who you were in an individual cultural environment, and as scientific education steadily increased in importance during the twentieth century, serious efforts were put into making sure that the scientists did not entirely miss out on this part of their education.

Plainly, this aspect of education has to change. What the global economic system now requires is knowledge and expertise above and beyond the acquisition of intellectual skills and admission into the traditions and modes of thought of a single culture. Like communications, employment, banking and commerce, education has become de-territorialised. The special skills required to create the kind of global economic asset which it represents have no basis in any one traditional culture and may be actually damaging to some of them, particularly in Asia. But no one who travels or has to deal with the rest of the world on a routine basis can escape understanding how far this development has already gone or that it will become ever more pervasive in the future.

Anxiety about employment has also been high and will resume when the present economic cycle moves on, and it springs from the loss of lower paid jobs to the developing world and from a period of downsizing at corporate level. The USA is certainly not immune to the deeply difficult problems inherent in the falling price of labour worldwide; indeed, its internally high wage levels make it a potentially serious victim. Nor would a protectionist tax and duty system do more than postpone the inevitable lowering of the US average wage. The traditionally autarkic structure of the US economy has been superseded by events and is beyond recovery, and its global trading imbalance makes it crucial that the USA remains an irresistible object of inward investment.

These facts mean that the United States, like everyone else, has lost independent control of its economy. NAFTA, for example, is not a cause but a consequence of that change. Unlike everyone else, however, the USA has, because of its great size and traditional wealth, got much further to go in the essentially political task of creating public understanding and acceptance of what is happening and of the growing limitations on what the government, any government, can do. At the same time, the USA has acquired a crucial interest in the progress of the global economy generally. An Asian currency crisis, for example, and the consequential risk of an economic depression, is a US crisis too, as was the Mexico crisis; likewise, in 1998, the potential for market meltdown implicit in the Brazilian financial debacle. Both supporting the global institutions involved and taking specific US action have become crucial political activities, perhaps more important, in such circumstances, than any internal economic policy regulation could be – and matter as much to the prosperity of individual Americans. None of the responses to terrorist threats has altered this fundamental situation.

The case of the European Union is particularly interesting because it, too, depends upon a functioning coalition of interests, but, like the USA, though in a different way, and unlike the Soviet Union, it delivers a great deal of what is required: but is it enough? Here is an area of high-level economic activity of great significance within the world's markets, the source of much technological invention, the origin of one of the most vigorous cultural systems the world has ever known and in general the provider of high living standards to its people. It has, with the exception of the UK, recently suffered from severe structural unemployment, endures almost unbearable pressure on the future of its social welfare systems from falling population figures and has found it impossible to resolve problems arising from any attempt to implement a genuine common foreign and security policy. It is also encountering a particularly difficult internal problem arising from a mismatch between the demands of the treaties which provide the basis for the further integration of the EU and the dwindling degree of popular support for them.

This aspect is of particular interest for this discussion. The provisions of the European Treaties from Rome (1957) to Maastricht (1992) and Amsterdam (1997) are based on a very important assumption, derived from the international circumstances of the first phase of the Cold War, viz. that political and economic security were to be found, as they evidently had been for the past

75 years and actually were at the time, from creating a super large state. Europe was therefore gradually, or not so gradually, to become such an entity. Such a logic, particularly in good economic times, enjoyed popular support, and where it did not do so explicitly, perceived economic advantages provided alternative or start-up grounds for consent. The last expression of such an evolution is to be found in the Amsterdam Treaty: here is the single currency, the Central Bank, the Defence Ministry in the form of the incorporation of the Western European Union, which would supply the common defence policy and the Foreign Ministry which would emerge from European Political Cooperation to run the common foreign policy, both of which are required under the treaty.

These are the appurtenances of a sovereign, if federal, state and the effort to make them happen is visibly running into severe difficulties. The common currency is not inclusive and the stability pact which went with it does not enjoy general obedience; the common foreign and security policy does not exist and such success as EPC had enjoyed was dissipated in Bosnia and only recovered in part as a result of the war over Kosovo in 1999. The onset of a general crisis over terrorism and the war in Iraq in 2004 created angry and frustrated confusion in the EU.

All these things might be so because they are inherently difficult, and they are. But they are also in trouble because governments are encountering public objections, not just in societies agnostic about European integration such as the UK and Denmark, but also in the former core states such as Germany and France, where a sense of loss of control coupled with persistently high unemployment rates has led to episodes of public disorder. In 2005, referenda in the Netherlands and France clearly rejected a draft constitution which would have crystallised the original sense and intentions of the EU's creators. For the first time this has given a formal negative public response to the assumptions of the European 'old guard'.

This development, coupled with the difficulties surrounding the process of enlarging the Union, which is also enjoined by treaty, might be interpreted as the result of the surviving strength of states and their persisting political legitimacy. A closer look does not suggest so. It is clear that publics do not see enough benefit emerging from sinking individual identities into a larger whole because larger entities are not doing well

in the global environment. In this, their refusal to support the further integration of the EU mirrors the refusal of the old coalition of interests to support the continued existence of the former Soviet Union. It is also clear that within national states, there is a growing suspicion that the erosion of sovereign economic management within states, which we discussed earlier, has made formerly highly significant areas of their activities increasingly irrelevant. The voting figures at elections steadily fall, complaints that the quality of both politicians and civil servants is in decline are sharper than they generally have been and there is a growing atmosphere of contempt for the institutions and sometimes formerly revered traditions of the state itself. This represents a decline in political legitimacy and it has been leading to an increasing provincialisation.

The focus of relevant activity, and sometimes a consequently revived focus of very old loyalties indeed, long submerged in the larger state for the sake of the advantages conferred by size, can often seem to lie in smaller units, sub-states, maybe, proposing significantly less sovereignty for themselves but actually doing things that matter. This is not just a question of the revival of ancient loyalties – Scotland, Provence, Flanders, Catalonia, Bavaria would be cases of this – because in some cases functional regionalism has crossed boundaries hitherto divided by historical prejudice – at the head of the Adriatic and in the Tyrol, for example.

What looks to be required is something loose at the centre, having no pretensions to becoming a United States of Europe, which will draw up to itself just sufficient of the functions of the old state as will permit smaller entities to operate at the lower temperature that globalisation has rendered appropriate. This would mean the end of the European state as it has been known for 300 years, and getting there involves reversing the vertical patterns of political legitimacy which evolved over that period and replacing them with broader bands of horizontal activities and supervising authorities. This cannot be done without creating or enduring a crisis of political legitimacy; nor can such a crisis be evaded by ignoring the tendency of public opinion and making a dash for full integration before it is too late.

Choices

It is particularly tough that this crisis is boiling up just at the moment when European governments – like all governments, but more obviously than some – have to find persuasive solutions to the more immediate problems provoked by globalisation, most seriously those involved in the dismantling of the collectivist state in the face of the demands of the free market global economy, which will not invest where the conditions are too much restrained or made capricious by local state political decisions and policies. This means that the most unpopular and difficult choices have to be arrived at and implemented by governments which are already suffering the effects of a creeping loss of legitimacy. Just at the moment that they need to be able to command the kind of loyalty that will absorb the shocks of highly damaging political decisions, generally available only in wartime conditions, they are losing authority. Here it makes little difference whether tough decisions are required to keep the traditional show on the road, as in France to enable the single currency to happen, or to respond to the globalised economy, as most obviously in Russia, Germany, India and China. These cases reveal clearly the gap that exists between what governments need to be able to do and what they now have the political legitimacy to bring about.

In using the example of the EU, we have something that is obviously very particular to Europe and it might be thought that the circumstances therefore offer no useful opportunity for generalising. There are, however, enough signs of similar fissiparous tendencies elsewhere to give ground for believing that Europe is not in fact different but merely showing more advanced symptoms of the disease. The Russian Federation, India, Indonesia and China all present examples of the growing difficulties of managing large and, to a greater or lesser degree, ethnically complex agglomerations of territory and any of them could have been used as evidence in this discussion.

The dangers in all this are patent: the breakdown of public order, examples already exist; the growth of extremist groups with a tendency to violent and terrorist activity, again examples already exist; the resort to aggressive nationalist rhetoric in foreign affairs or over questions of immigration and even the emergence of religious or quasi-religious sects, born of the abandonment of other kinds of hope and thus having a tendency to commit mass suicide. These are major and disturbing dislocations and they are evoking from politicians and other commentators exhortations to the resumption of former loyalties couched in the language of the past which sound ever more irrelevant.

The biggest structural realignment of power in the world since the fall of Rome cannot be countered by supporting an increase of volunteerism in the USA or by exemplary shootings of regional tax collectors in China, or by successfully – in the short term – striking to retain an unsustainable social contract in France. It is hard to tell governments that they must conduct research into the best methods of accomplishing their own retreat from the structures and attitudes of full sovereignty; but that is what needs to be done.

Further Reading

Ferguson, Yale H. and Mansbach, Richard W. (2004) *Remapping Global Politics: History's Revenge and Future Shock*, Cambridge: Cambridge University Press.

Krasner, Steven D. (1999) *Sovereignty: Organised Hypocrisy*, Princeton: Princeton University Press.

Sassen, Saskia (2002) 'The State and Globalisation' in Rodney Bruce Hall and Thomas J. Biersteker (eds) *The Emergence of Private Authority in Global Governance*, Cambridge: Cambridge University Press.

Sorensen, Georg (2001) *Changes in Statehood: The Transformation of International Relations*, London: Palgrave.

Weiss, Linda (1998) *The Myth of the Powerless State*, Ithaca: Cornell University Press.

Weiss, Linda (ed.) (2003) *States in the Global Economy: Bringing Domestic Institutions Back In*, Cambridge: Cambridge University Press.

CHAPTER 6: Transnational corporations

Multinational firms have been condemned and revered in heated discussions and proclamations for the half century since they started attracting the world's attention. They are perceived as one of the main channels through which globalisation is being implemented. As countries adopt more and more open and outwardly-orientated economic policies, the role of multinational corporations has become more vital. This topic has attracted the interest of many academics, media, various civil groups, international organisations and the general public, which has led to many studies, discussions, protests and frequent emotional reactions.

Economic globalisation

A term that came into common usage from the 1980s, although some argue that the world economy was just as globalised 100 years ago as it is today. In the context of the new world, economic globalisation refers to the process of rapid economic integration between countries. This process manifests itself mainly through the intensification of activities in the following areas: international trade in goods and services, capital flows, the role of multinational corporations, the reorganisation of production on an international scale, the adoption of new transportation, information and communication technology, and international flow of knowledge.

Some regard multinationals as the 'Spinning Jenny' of the new world economic order and believe that their activities are beneficial for countries' economic development. Others regard them with hostility and fear, with the belief that they threaten the environment, cultural heritages, living standards and human rights, undermine national legislations and business practices, and increase inequalities.

As an example, Raymond Vernon observed in his 1977 book *Storm over the Multinationals* that 'the multinational enterprise has come to be seen as the embodiment of almost anything disconcerting about modern industrial society'. According to Vernon, it is the basic nature of the multinational firm which is to blame for the above perception. Since it is able to function beyond a single country, nation-states feel that their political and economic interests are endangered by an entity that is not accountable to any authority of equal or superior power; multinational firms operate in global markets but the regulations that control their activities are most often national in scope.

In terms of economic policy, there are different views about the relationship between multinational firms and nation-states. Some consider it a power relationship, in which one party or the other always strives to dominate. Others attribute an active role to the multinational companies, leaving countries merely as the environment in which the former operate. Still others argue that multinationals are just a means, an instrument, for wealth-creation on the part of nation-states. And a more conciliatory view sees both the multinationals and states as playing active roles and cooperating, and the product of this interaction is globalisation. No matter what the point of view may be, however, there is one major issue to be addressed: how do we reap the healthy effect of multinational activity without having to compromise on national sovereignty, environmental protection or human rights? This question may sound just like wanting to have your cake and eat it too. Practice has often shown that although it is difficult, it can be achieved.

The activities of multinational firms may benefit or harm businesses and people in a host country, thus creating what are known as positive and negative spillovers. So, generally, the above question comes down to finding how to increase the positive and decrease the negative spillovers between states and international firms. As we will see in this chapter, various attempts to do this have been undertaken, including unilateral national acts, bilateral agreements, international regulations and codes of conduct, trade policies and voluntary guidelines. First, however, there is the question: what is the nature and functioning of multinational firms?

Nature, activities and motivation of multinationals

The widely agreed definition of a multinational corporation (MNC) describes it as a firm that engages in foreign direct investment (FDI) and owns and controls assets and value-adding activities in more than one country. The MNC buys resources, produces goods and/or services and then sells them in other countries. These activities are typically coordinated and controlled at the centres with the subsidiaries making necessary adjustments. The term multinational enterprise (MNE) is often considered a synonym for MNC, although there are many international companies that are not organised as corporations (for example, accounting partnerships). For further clarity, MNCs can be broken down into three types depending on how the firm makes its management decisions based on local or global alternatives. First, a multidomestic corporation is one that views itself as a collection of subsidiaries, each of which is focused on a specific market and operates fairly independently. Second, a global corporation is a multinational that views the world as a single marketplace; it integrates its operations that are located in different countries and strives to create standardised goods and services that will meet the needs of customers throughout the world. Third, a transnational corporation (TNC) is a multinational firm that combines the benefits of global-scale efficiencies with those of local responsiveness. Theoretically, there is another type of MNC – the world/global company – that transcends national borders and operates in each of the major regions of the world pursuing an integrated strategy towards these activities; however, currently only a few companies are approaching this level. At present, the most commonly used term by international institutions, researchers and analysts (also adopted by the UN in 1974) is TNC and it will be used further in this chapter.

Foreign Direct Investment (FDI)

Consists of a package of assets and intermediate products, such as capital, technology, management skills, access to markets and entrepreneurship. The investment is made outside the home country of the investing firm but inside the investing firm itself, and the investor retains control over the resources being transferred. By definition FDI flows through multinational corporations and can take many forms including: purchases of existing assets in a foreign country; new investments in plant, property and equipment; or participation in joint ventures with a local partner.

According to scholars investigating the nature and activities of TNCs, the most prominent feature of these companies (and one that makes them unique) is their capacity to engage in both cross-border production and transactions. They organise and coordinate multiple value-adding activities across borders and also internalise the cross-border markets for intermediate products arising from these activities. Further attributes of TNCs that distinguish them from other entities are their ability to direct resources in distant places, to use intangibles as their core competency and to operate in a constantly changing and challenging environment.

Businesses internationalise in order to obtain benefits that are not so readily available at home. Some of the reasons for this process are changes and advances in technology, consumer pressures, the leveraging of core competencies, the acquisition of new resources and supplies, the liberalisation of cross-border movements of capital and labour, and the development of supporting services.

There are four major types of TNC activity. Firms seeking natural resources invest abroad to obtain particular natural resources that are not available in their home country or, if they are, then at a higher price. Thus, the output of the subsidiaries of such companies is exported most often to their home countries. The firms in this category may also tap into the host country's supplies of cheap (unskilled or semi-skilled) labour and/or acquire management expertise and technological capabilities.

The market seekers invest in a host country with the aim of providing goods and services to consumers there. This investment may be made in order to protect existing markets previously serviced through exports or to exploit new markets. Additionally, market seekers may be encouraged to engage in this kind of activity for four main reasons: (i) to follow their clients and/or suppliers who have set up operations overseas; (ii) to adapt the company's products to local tastes and requirements; (iii) to cut transaction costs; and (iv) to establish a physical presence in leading markets served by competitors.

Transaction costs

Defined by Oliver Williamson as the 'comparative costs of planning, adapting, and monitoring task completion under alternative governance structures'.

For example, the production of goods that have high transportation costs and can be produced in small quantities, tends to be located near main consumption centres while products that have low transportation costs and high production costs tend to be located near resources or in the home country of the company.

The efficiency-seeking TNCs try to concentrate their production in a limited number of locations to supply multiple markets through the production of fairly standardised goods.

Finally, the strategic-asset seekers engage in foreign direct investment in order to sustain or advance their international competitiveness. This is done through diversification of the company's assets and capabilities. Nowadays, many of the larger TNCs are pursuing mixed objectives and engage in activities that combine features of each of the above categories.

TNCs establish their operations using different modes, which are commonly classified as greenfield investment, acquisitions (brownfield investment) and joint ventures. A greenfield strategy involves buying or leasing and constructing new facilities, expatriating or hiring local managers and employees, and establishing an operation from scratch. This strategy is attractive because the TNC can choose the proper site and get to know the new national and business culture at its own pace. The trade-offs include a longer time-frame, recruiting and training a local workforce, and possibly unfavourable regulations and treatment.

Next, acquisitions are popular because they quickly give the investor control over the firm's assets and allow the gradual spread of investments. The main disadvantages are that the investor also assumes all liabilities of the acquired entity and large sums are usually spent up-front.

Strategic alliances

Business arrangements whereby two or more firms cooperate for their mutual benefit can take many forms, including cross-licensing of proprietary information, production sharing, joint research and development, and marketing of each other's products using existing distribution channels. Strategic alliances differ from other modes of foreign market entry in that they involve cooperation between firms who may in fact be competitors.

The joint venture (a type of strategic alliance) is an arrangement whereby a new, legally autonomous firm is created through two or more firms working together to achieve a common goal. Joint ventures have formal organisational structures and can be short-term or long-term arrangements. Since such forms of multinational activity represent an effective means of competing in international markets, their number has been rapidly growing since the 1980s.

From the host country point of view, greenfield projects are generally regarded as having positive spillover effects since these create new businesses and jobs, and increase competition in the host markets, thus leading to improved efficiency. Acquisitions, on the other hand, are seen as less desirable because the new owners of an acquired, fully operational firm may decide not to continue with the same business model, possibly lay off employees or switch to other suppliers. However, acquisitions are more likely to lead to research and development activities based on inherited operations. Additionally, there is empirical evidence that selling local firms to foreign investors in the context of privatisation in the transition economies of Central and Eastern Europe has had short-term beneficial effect on the profitability and productivity of these enterprises, although evidence about the long-term effects is still lacking. According to the World Investment Report 2004, compiled by the United Nations Conference on Trade and Develop-

Table 6.1: Top 10 non-financial TNCs ranked by their transnationality index, 2002

TNI Rank	TNI %	Company	Home Country	Industry
1	99.1	NTL Incorporated	US	Electric utilities
2	97.9	Thomson Corp	Canada	Media
3	95.5	Holcim AG	Switzerland	Construction
4	94.7	CRH plc	Ireland	Lumber and other building materials
5	94.5	ABB	Switzerland	Machinery and equipment
6	91.0	Roche Group	Switzerland	Pharmaceuticals
7	90.8	Interbrew	Belgium	Beverages
8	90.7	Publicis Groupe SA	France	Business services
9	90.1	News Corporation	Australia	Media
10	86.8	Philips Electronics	Netherlands	Electrical and electronic equipment

Source: *World Investment Report 2004*, UNCTAD

ment (UNCTAD), greenfield investment is predicted to dominate FDI in developing countries while cross-border mergers and acquisitions are predicted to do so in the developed economies.

An important feature of TNCs is that large firms (in terms of foreign assets) are predominant. The size of the largest TNCs has been compared to other economic entities, including whole countries, and, depending on the measurement methods, the following facts emerged: the greater part of the 100 largest economies comprises TNCs, the smaller represents countries. General Electric's 2001 revenues are claimed to surpass the combined national incomes of sub-Saharan African countries (except South Africa); Philip Morris is said to be larger than New Zealand, Wal-Mart to be bigger than 160 countries (including Israel, Poland and Greece), Mitsubishi to be bigger than Indonesia, General Motors than Denmark, and Toyota than Norway. Moreover, the combined sales of the world's top 200 corporations are greater than a quarter of the world's economic activity, and surpass the combined economies of 182 countries. However, it has also been estimated that these 200 largest TNCs employ less than 19 million people.

The degree of transnationality of TNCs can be assessed from several perspectives, as stated in UNCTAD's World Investment Report 2004: operations (for example, geographical spread), stakeholders (composition, nationality, experi-

ence) and spatial organisation of management perspective. Hence, given this possible range of measures, it is clear that a variety of indicators is required to determine how transnational a TNC is and what its power is in the world economy. One example: since 1993, UNCTAD has been calculating and publishing the transnationality index (TNI), which is a weighted average of three indicators: foreign sales as a per centage of total sales, foreign assets as a per centage of total assets, and foreign employment as a per centage of total employment. Therefore, this index is constructed from the operations perspective. Table 6.1 shows the 10 most transnational TNCs classified according to their TNI for 2002.

The TNI classification shows that the score is the highest for TNCs from small countries such as Belgium, Ireland and Switzerland, although the latter might also be chosen by TNCs because of its regulatory regime. The mean TNI score in 1993 was 51.6, in 1999, 52.6, and in 2002 it was 57. This indicates that the more significant increase in transnationality of the top 100 TNCs has occurred in the last five years or so. Additionally, the fact that the mean TNI score for this group is slightly above 50, suggests that these TNCs have about half of their operations overseas. About 58 of the top 100 had a TNI greater than 50; in 1999, this number was 57. Thus the majority of the world's leading TNCs still operate predominantly in their home countries.

Some historical facts

Throughout much of the period between the thirteenth and eighteenth centuries, rulers were involved, in one way or another, in most kinds of international endeavours. The major players were usually land companies, merchants and wealthy families and individuals, and the main motives were to acquire new territories, increase wealth or discover new applications for domestic savings. The history of the multinational firm can be traced back to the activities of the Hanseatic League of merchants and the Italian banking dynasties in the fourteenth century. The Hanseatic League promoted commerce and helped to develop various branches across Northern Europe. The wealthy Italian banking family firms established banking and trading houses throughout Europe and also invested in the mining industry in foreign countries.

During the sixteenth and seventeenth centuries, the major colonising by the Western European countries resulted in the establishment of companies that were directly supported by their states, whose political and economic objectives they promoted. Thus, in 1600 the Dutch East India Company was established, followed by the British East India Company two years later. Both operated in India and the Far East. Additionally, the Hudson Bay Company was one of the first to engage in major wholesale trading activities in North America, and several other companies engaged in land development, helping to cultivate and improve the economy of the new territories.

The multinational firm in its present form did not begin to evolve until the nineteenth century when the arrival of industrial capitalism brought about greater economic developments – a better factory system, better storage and transportation methods, larger and more capital-intensive manufacturing processes, higher living standards and increased demand for consumer goods. This was also accompanied by a massive cross-border movement of people, particularly from Europe to North America. In addition, companies changed their legal status and personal transactions gave way to more formal impersonal ones.

During these early years, companies from the United States and Western Europe ventured overseas to Asia, Africa, Latin America and the Middle East – partly in search of natural resources and foodstuffs, and partly in response to increased competitive forces and pressure to protect and increase their market shares. The numerous mergers and acquisitions that also started at that time led to a concentration of large multinationals in major sectors such as food (for example, United Fruit Company from the US) and petrochemicals (Royal Dutch Shell from the UK/Netherlands). By 1914 the multinational had become a major instrument for international economic relations, with the UK being the largest foreign capital stakeholder, although, from the second half of the nineteenth century, world economic leadership had started shifting from the UK to the US.

The period between the two World Wars, in spite of the less-favourable political and economic environment, witnessed a continued search for natural resources on the part of the US and Western European multinationals, even if the latter's activities decreased somewhat. There was also new multinational activity in the developing countries directed towards mining and oil extraction, tobacco and food production and some manufacturing. Additionally, in Japan, giant multinational corporations (such as Mitsubishi and Matsui) started growing and they formed the *zaibatsu* (financial clique) which cooperated with the state and exercised oligopolistic control over Japan's industrial, trade and financial sectors.

After the Second World War and up to the 1960s, multinational activity was dominated by US companies. Armed with new technology and management and marketing techniques, US firms operating in the motor vehicle, pharmaceutical, electrical and electronic goods sectors and other industries established subsidiary manufacturing facilities in Canada, Europe, Australia and parts of Latin America. The European, Japanese and some Third World multinational corporations started playing a greater role during the following three decades.

The past half century has seen major technological advances which have accelerated the internationalisation of trade and investment. This has been marked by a shift in the predominant form of international involvement away from resource- and market-seeking to strategic-asset seeking. It has been accompanied by constant changes in organisational forms in response to the changing environment.

During the 1970s and early 1980s, the number of overseas US and European subsidiaries decreased due to slower world economic growth

Table 6.2: Top 10 non-financial TNCs ranked by foreign assets as percentage of total, 1971

Rank	Corporation	Home Economy	Industry
1	Royal Dutch Shell	UK/Netherlands	Petroleum
2	Unilever	Netherlands/UK	Consumer goods
3	Standard Oil (NJ)	US	Petroleum
4	Mobil Oil	US	Petroleum
5	Ford Motor Company	US	Motor vehicles
6	Chrysler	US	Motor vehicles
7	IBM	US	Computers
8	General Motors	US	Motor vehicles
9	General Electric	US	Electrical and electronic equipment
10	Texaco	US	Petroleum

Source: 'Multinational Corporations in World Development', UN Department of Economic and Social Affairs, 1973

and to the decision of some governments to expropriate the assets of many foreign subsidiaries out of frustration with the latter's impact, behaviour and interaction with local societies. Many TNCs tried to overcome this by establishing partnerships and joint ventures with local firms. The last decade of the post-war period saw some striking developments. The emergence of Japan as a leading industrial economy, the change in the economic ideology and political regimes in Eastern Europe and China, and the growth of several Asian countries all changed the global economic environment. Additionally, governments changed their attitudes towards FDI, adopting liberalised open-door policies.

According to UNCTAD's World Investment Reports, by the 1970s there were some 7000 multinational corporations of which about 300 had assets of $1 billion or more; by 1990 the number of multinationals had risen to 24,000, and slightly more than a decade later there were about 61,000 multinationals, with more than 900,000 foreign subsidiaries, accounting for

Table 6.3: Top 10 non-financial TNCs ranked by foreign assets as percentage of total, 1990

Rank	Corporation	Home economy	Industry
1	Royal Dutch Shell	UK/Netherlands	Petroleum
2	Ford Motor Company	US	Motor vehicles
3	General Motors	US	Motor vehicles
4	Exxon Mobil Corp	US	Petroleum
5	IBM	US	Computers
6	British Petroleum	UK	Petroleum
7	Asea Brown Boveri	Switzerland	Industrial and farm equipment
8	Nestlé	Switzerland	Food
9	Philips Electronics	Netherlands	Electronics
10	Mobil	US	Petroleum

Source: *World Investment Report 1993*, UNCTAD

Table 6.4: Top 10 non-financial TNCs ranked by foreign assets as percentage of total, 2002

Rank	Corporation	Home economy	Industry
1	General Electric	US	Electrical and electronic equipment
2	Vodafone Group	UK	Telecommunications
3	Ford Motor Company	US	Motor vehicles
4	British Petroleum	UK	Petroleum
5	General Motors	US	Motor vehicles
6	Royal Dutch Shell	UK/Netherlands	Petroleum
7	Toyota Motor Corp	Japan	Motor vehicles
8	Total Fina Elf	France	Petroleum
9	France Telecom	France	Telecommunications
10	Exxon Mobil Corp	US	Petroleum

Source: *World Investment Report 2004*, UNCTAD

some two thirds of world trade and employing more than 50 million workers. In 2002, the world's top 100 TNCs accounted for 14 per cent of sales by foreign subsidiaries worldwide, 12 per cent of their assets and 13 per cent of the employment.

Tables 6.2, 6.3 and 6.4 show the ten largest TNCs in the years 1971, 1990 and 2002, ranked by their foreign assets.

TNCs and nation-states: pros and cons of multinational activity

Transnational corporations possess a great deal of power in the contemporary global economy. Through mergers and acquisitions they have been growing rapidly and making profits that exceed the gross domestic products of some low and medium-income countries. Such economic power inevitably poses questions. How can these firms be regulated? How do they use their power? How do they influence the countries in which they operate? What is their role in national, regional and global economic policies?

Environmental, humanitarian, labour, consumer and other civil groups around the world have long been raising similar issues, issuing public warnings about all sorts of negative effects arising from TNC activity. TNCs have become the 'favourite monsters' of anti-globalists and other civil activists, whenever conflicts arise between national and corporate interests. On

the positive side, however, TNCs advance national competitiveness and economic growth. It is well documented that in some areas, such as South East Asia, the activities of TNCs have been beneficial for the economic development of the countries or regions in which they operate. However, it may well be true that this positive influence occurs only for certain countries at certain times, and with certain TNCs for that matter. The most commonly discussed positive and negative influences of TNC activity are summarised in the box on page 145.

TNCs are feared for their power, particularly power that spans national borders, and this fear has become even more obvious after various incidents involving multinational firms. For example, when Wal-Mart built a new supermarket in Mexico, concerns were raised about the viability of local businesses which had set themselves up round an ancient Maya site. Local entrepreneurs may also be threatened if the investing TNC is large and borrows on domestic financial markets; this may cause domestic interest rates to rise, thus reducing the viability of investment projects for small and medium-size domestic firms without access to international capital markets. Local bankers may have a greater interest in lending to larger firms than to the numerous small local firms.

Concerns about the environment were voiced by the residents of Ecuador's eastern rainforest who condemned ChevronTexaco for allegedly causing health problems and enormous envi-

Positive influences of TNC activity TNCs may:

- Bring new technologies and processes which can raise the productivity levels of the indigenous firms (by providing technical assistance and training of employees, by assisting in the management of companies), thus accelerating the host country's economic development.
- Create linkages with customers in foreign markets and provide additional markets.
- Raise quality standards and stimulate the efficiency of competitors and suppliers.
- Stimulate entrepreneurial ventures either directly or indirectly through positive spillovers; individuals who leave a foreign-owned subsidiary to establish their own business usually use knowledge acquired in the course of work in that subsidiary.
- Increase the demand for intermediate goods produced by local suppliers.
- Enhance international specialisation through the development of backward and forward linkages across the value chain of production.
- Stimulate research and development and the innovation capacity of host countries.
- Create jobs directly or through ancillary businesses such as banks and insurance companies. Additionally, investment in business services directly influences productivity of customers.
- Improve living standards – through providing salaries higher than those paid by local competitors, through investment in new or better infrastructure.
- Establish higher labour and environmental standards through the application of more advanced practices and technologies.
- Inject capital into the host economy, and generate revenue for public expenditure.

Negative influences of TNC activity TNCs are accused of:

- Having an adverse impact on the indigenous development of entrepreneurial talent by blocking business opportunities and crowding out domestic entrepreneurs.
- Adversely affecting the environment and abusing health and safety regulations by taking advantage of imperfect pollution legislation in host countries.
- Providing only low-skilled and low-paid jobs geared to a particular operation of the firm, without any actual knowledge transfer.
- Using unfair accounting practices.
- Exploiting workers and child labour and paying wages that are unable to match the cost of living in the host country.
- Engaging in human rights violations by supporting (including financially) oppressive regimes.
- Undermining the living standards and civil rights of local people through displacing them by force from their land in order to set up TNC facilities.
- Not being legally accountable to people in host countries who, when harmed by TNC activities, often find it extremely difficult to pursue their rights in the courts due to lack of international regulation and clarity over the applicability of the national legislation.
- Creating an economic downturn when moving out of the host area.
- Exercising political pressure and influence not only in the host country but also in supra-national organisations such as the WTO through coordinated corporate lobbying, bribery and other methods.

ronmental damage as a result of the company's oil extraction methods in the region in the 1970s and 1980s. Companies extracting oil and minerals, and chemical and pharmaceutical companies, are particularly criticised for such behaviour.

Environmentalists are worried that due to multinational activity, the world's pool of natural resources will be depleted much more quickly. Developing countries are being turned into dumping grounds for hazardous materials, and their governments are apt to compromise and reduce environmental standards in order to attract FDI, thus triggering the so-called 'race to the bottom'. For example, the Australian mining transnational corporation BHP (once known as the 'Big Australian) was revealed in 1995 to have cooperated with the government of Papua New Guinea to draft a law which provided for poor compensation to landowners whose property was being polluted by the company's gold mine. The Maquiladora factories located in the free trade zone in Mexico along the US border have also been the target of environmentalists, who claim that these factories allow US firms to escape environmental laws in their own country. For these and other similar reasons, environmental groups are lobbying for increased trade barriers and legal enforcement of environmental regulations. The World Trade Organisation responded to these issues by establishing a Committee on Trade and Environment to assess the environmental impact of world trade and to suggest guidelines for the WTO to adopt. Proponents of globalisation and TNC activity, however, assert that the lack of (or weak) environmental regulation does not necessarily mean that corporations will rush to profit and dispose of their waste into the air and water. Damage to their reputations occurs far too swiftly and surely because of contemporary global communications networks.

Pollution halo effect: Refers to the transfer of modern, environmentally friendly technologies and production practices by TNCs, which improve the standards in the host country.

Pollution haven effect: Refers to the choice of TNCs to transfer outdated technology to locations with less stringent environmental regulation.

TNCs can also harm the host countries through the use of unfair accounting practices that allow the international firms to repatriate big shares (sometimes up to 100 per cent) of the profits earned in the host country, thus depriving the latter of needed revenue that could be used to provide public services such as education and healthcare.

A major concern is the use of child labour in overseas facilities of some TNCs. For instance, cottonseed farms in Southern India are claimed to employ more than 12,000 children who work in unsafe conditions. The produce of these farms is said to be supplied to multinational companies. Many more children are allegedly used on farms in other parts of the country. During the early stages of industrialisation in Western Europe and North America, it was common to encounter poor working conditions and child labour: some assert that sweatshops are a necessary step of economic development. It can be argued, however, that if this was a normal situation two centuries ago when the Western world was developing its industrial power, it is not necessary to repeat it now during the development of Third World countries. Alternatives can be found through the work of non-governmental organisations, supra-national entities and civil groups.

Recent examples of human rights violations on the part of multinational firms involve TNC activities in Colombia, Burma, Nigeria and Sudan. More than a thousand people were killed in the Niger Delta in 2003 due to violent conflict in response to the activities of some oil TNCs, and the failure of the Nigerian government to provide proper human rights protection in the region and to ensure that TNCs operated in accordance with Nigerian law.

Transfer pricing: An internal accounting technique whereby TNCs set prices for transfers of goods, services, technology and loans between their worldwide subsidiaries which differ considerably from the prices which unrelated firms would have to pay. Through their accounting systems TNCs can transfer these prices among their affiliates, shifting funds around the world to avoid taxation. Governments, which have no way to control TNCs' transfer pricing, are therefore under pressure to lower taxes as a means of attracting investment or keeping a company's operation in their country. Tax revenue which might be used for social programmes or other domestic needs is thus lost.

A notorious example of the practice of political meddling by corporations is the case of the ITT Corporation of the US. In the 1970s, Chilean president Salvador Allende accused it of meddling in the political affairs of his country by offering the US Central Intelligence Agency $1 million to finance a campaign against Allende's election. Although this offer was refused, after the Chilean government nationalised some US assets, the US government reacted with action based to a great extent on the recommendations and lobbying of ITT. This case was a turning point in the attitudes of the world towards TNCs and has caused international organisations such as the UN and the OECD to address the issue of TNCs' behaviour, accountability and social responsibility.

Examples of corporate malpractice, such as those above, can often lead to exaggeration and generalisation, and result in the TNCs being seen as a vehicle of new imperialism and monopolisation. On the other side, there is also a danger of assuming that all TNCs possess the same level of ethical and social commitment. It is true that governments still have some bargaining power and control over the operations of multinational firms, but where economies are weak with poor legislative framework and enforcement mechanisms (as is the case with most developing countries), there is always a risk that TNCs will take advantage of the situation.

It is very often assumed that, because of their size, TNCs are becoming more powerful than nation-states and thus are able to shape the world economy as they please. However, the interaction between TNCs and states is not so straightforward and unidirectional. TNCs are affected by the actions of nation-states – for example, frequent change of government policies, possible nationalisation or expropriation of TNCs' assets without adequate compensation, political turmoil and war, and the introduction of trade sanctions. Governments, on their side, have changed their attitudes throughout the years and generally have demonstrated mixed feelings towards TNCs and multinational activity.

Prior to the Second World War, the multinational firm was used as an instrument of territorial extension of the political and economic power of developed countries, and for supplying the home country with materials and foodstuffs. Therefore, these firms were well supported by their governments. Furthermore, other, less developed countries viewed multinationals as a source of advanced technology and management practices and hence provided land and tax incentives, while restricting their direct imports of finished goods.

For three decades after the war, multinational firms were simply expected to adapt to the economic environments of the host countries and to abide by various regulations and requirements imposed on foreign activity. The 1970s and early 1980s marked a period of criticism and hostility towards foreign investment and multinationals, criticism that stemmed, among other things, from the belief that outward FDI substituted for domestic investment, and that jobs were being exported overseas by TNCs, particularly to developing countries.

A major shift in policy occurred from the 1980s when governments realised that the complex sets of regulations directed to specifically influence the behaviour of TNCs were not working as expected, and national policies went into reverse and began to welcome FDI. Factors influencing this change of heart include: (i) renaissance of the market system; (ii) increased mobility of wealth-creating assets; (iii) moves towards regional economic integration; (iv) technological advances (and particularly in the production and dissemination of knowledge); (v) convergence of economic structures among developed countries and some newly industrialised nations; and (vi) changing criteria by which countries evaluate FDI, that is from the direct contribution of foreign subsidiaries to economic development to its wider impact on the upgrading of the competitiveness of host countries' indigenous capabilities and the promotion of their dynamic comparative advantage.

> **National competitiveness:** Refers to a country's ability to produce and distribute goods and services that are competitive on international markets and thus to improve the welfare of its citizens by providing high standards of living. The analysis of national competitiveness nowadays has shifted from comparative advantage (based on the possession of natural resources) to competitive advantage (based on created assets – tangible (financial or physical) and intangible (intellectual property, culture)). The logic behind this is that when capital, labour and raw materials freely cross national boundaries, endowed resources alone cannot completely determine a nation's competitiveness.

The current attitude of governments towards TNCs no longer translates into measures directly aimed at the firms, but rather into policies intended to affect the environment in which TNCs function. However, elements of protectionism still exist, although now they can be observed more on an (inter)regional level, for example, between the European Union and US or between the US and Japan and South East Asia.

Attempts to regulate TNC activities globally

The growing role of TNCs in the world economy has also prompted various attempts on the part of supra-national organisations to establish some sort of international framework of regulations. A few notable attempts to control the behaviour of TNCs are discussed here. In 1974, prompted by the ITT Corporation's efforts in Chile to over- throw Allende, the UN Commission on Transnational Corporations undertook initia- tives to provide a code of conduct for the TNCs which tried to establish some guidelines for cor- porate behaviour. The draft code was a broad, non-binding set of rules which tried to ensure that TNCs would contribute to national eco- nomic development and prevent harm to citizens all over the world. The code explicitly outlined a section on 'non-interference in the internal political affairs' of the countries where companies operated. The Commission worked on the draft code with the Centre on Transnational Corporations (UNCTC) which was established in 1975 and functioned until 1992. The UNCTC had the task of collecting and interpreting data on FDI and TNCs, to research different aspects of TNC activities such as policy issues in developing countries, to service the negotiations on the code of conduct, and to advise governments of developing countries on how to negotiate with TNCs and maximise the benefits from FDI. The draft code was produced in 1998 but a final version has never been approved. There are a number of reasons for this: first, the shift in the balance of power after the end of the Cold War when it had become more difficult to lobby for control of corpora- tions, and second, the widely accepted idea that corporations should be allowed to regulate themselves. After 1992, the work of UNCTC was transferred to UNCTAD. Thus, admittedly with fewer resources, the latter took on the responsi- bility of conducting research and analysis related to FDI and TNC activity. Since then UNCTAD has never formally addressed the issue of TNC regulation.

In 1976 the Organisation for Economic Cooperation and Development (OECD) issued guidelines for OECD-based TNCs operating abroad. The guidelines were revised in 2000 and the first annual report on their operation was published in 2001. The guidelines cover issues such as environmental protection, human rights, labour standards, tax avoidance, corrup- tion, creation of training and employment opportunities, disclosure of financial perform- ance information, and fair competition. How- ever, the guidelines are considered weak in addressing the above questions because there is no enforcement mechanism embedded in them; there are ambiguities and gaps concerning their implementation; there is no simple procedure for the public to initiate action; and last but not least, some companies do not even know the guidelines exist. There have been only about 30 cases since the guidelines were issued and only two were in the 1990s.

In 1977, the International Labour Organisation (ILO) adopted the Tripartite Declaration – a universally applicable but non- binding code covering labour standards and industrial relations and establishing the rights and responsibilities of employers, governments and trade unions. Since the adoption of this declaration only seven cases have been dealt with, the last of which was in 1984.

Another regulatory attempt was made in 1999 by the European Parliament. It adopted a reso- lution establishing standards for European com- panies operating in developing countries – particularly with reference to the protection of human rights, compliance with international law and labour and environmental standards. Although this endeavour had the potential to unify the many different codes and provide some consistency, the resolution was not fully implemented, to some extent because support for it in the European Parliament was mixed. There, some members believe that the OECD guidelines should take precedence. A second requirement of the resolution is for the Euro- pean Parliament to hold annual hearings to dis- cuss good and bad corporate practices. The first such hearing was held in November 2000, and being discussed were the labour practices of Nestlé and Adidas in their countries of opera- tion. Neither of the two companies attended the hearing, and this provoked strong public criticism.

Global Compact

In July 2000, Kofi Annan, the UN Secretary General, accompanied by 500 senior executives and representatives of banks, business associa- tions, TNCs, NGOs, governments and different UN agencies, launched the Global Compact –

an initiative that involves nine principles based on the Universal Declaration of Human Rights, the Rio Declaration on Environment and Development and the Fundamental Principles and Rights at Work established by the International Labour Organisation (ILO). Firms who join the compact are expected to make three commitments: to publicly advocate the principles and the Global Compact; to post on their website specific steps they have taken to satisfy the nine principles in their own corporate practices; and to cooperate in partnership projects of benefit to developing countries. The aim of the compact is to 'discuss how new partnerships can benefit corporations by providing access to emerging markets while helping the UN in its drive to eradicate poverty' or, in brief, to create 'a human face for the global economy'. The compact, although welcomed by NGOs and similar groups, has been criticised, and there has been scepticism about its ability to ensure more ethical behaviour from TNCs because there is no monitoring and enforcement mechanism to guarantee compliance with the principles.

In recent years many TNCs have been seeking to become 'good corporate citizens' and, towards that end, have been establishing their own voluntary guidelines and principles of conduct. Companies such as IKEA, Nike, Kmart, Levi Strauss, Philips and Shell have adopted corporate codes of conduct – fundamental principles according to which the companies intend to operate in foreign markets. Shell was one of the first to adopt a corporate code, maintaining its 'Statement of General Business Principles' since 1976. This practice of social corporate responsibility has recently gained more popularity among TNCs which view self-regulation as an alternative to international legislative control in terms of cost-saving, innovation and liberalisation.

In 1996, US President Clinton launched the Apparel Industry partnership which resulted in a code the following year. This event also gave impetus to the adoption of industry and corporate voluntary codes in the US.

Although voluntary regulation of TNCs can help companies improve their behaviour and activities in the markets where they operate, these codes also have weaknesses. First, as is the case with the international endeavours discussed above, the corporate codes are voluntary and non-binding, with no monitoring and enforcement mechanism and no complaint procedures.

Second, it is observed that many corporate codes do not have reference to labour standards and human rights, even if some refer to the Declaration of Human Rights or the provisions of the ILO. Third, corporate codes alleviate the pressure on governments of host countries whose primary task is to secure the well-being of their citizens; if companies regulate themselves, governments may neglect to keep TNCs accountable in case of malpractice. Finally, many corporate voluntary codes have been adopted after proven abuses by TNCs in foreign countries and consequent pressures and negative publicity. This means that voluntary codes are most commonly adopted in industries that are particularly vulnerable to such pressure (for example, oil extraction and textiles/apparel manufacturing) and are less common in other crucial sectors such as finance and accounting services. There is also a real perception that these codes may be used just as a public relations and image-improving tool by corporations.

An example of a code that is perceived to work, mainly because of its narrow focus on a particular issue, is the International Code of Marketing for Breast Milk Substitutes, established by the WHO in 1981. This code was the result of a campaign by the non-governmental organisation INFACT against Nestlé. The Swiss TNC was urged to stop marketing powdered breast milk substitute formula in poor countries and persuading mothers there to give up breast feeding their babies. The mothers were mixing the powder with local contaminated water and this resulted in many infant deaths. The INFACT boycott started in 1977 and spread to ten countries, in the most famous corporate accountability campaign.

Conclusion

During the 1960s and 1970s, few economists and analysts paid attention to the existence of TNCs. Since then, however, these entities have become so important that they are now considered a major player in the globalisation process. Along with the excitement of observing the establishment of the new world order, however, came concern about the side effects of TNC activity and their control. Because of their unique characteristics, TNCs may respond differently to government policies and regulations designed to govern the activities of national firms.

There is evidence that through their

operations TNCs can contribute to a country's economic development but there are many areas of real or potential conflict that need to be addressed by both governments and TNCs.

John Dunning asserts that there are two types of actions which governments might take towards TNCs: (i) those addressed towards specifically modifying the behaviour of TNCs in accordance with the external political and economic environment in which they operate, and (ii) those taken towards changing the conditions of that environment in such a way as to ensure that the positive effects of TNCs will be dominant. It is generally the latter approach that leads to improvement of the host country's dynamic comparative advantage.

The main issue that warrants attention is that of corporate social responsibility and accountability, that is, identifying the ways to make sure that TNCs operate in an ethical and socially acceptable manner. We saw that attempts were made for regulative measures to be established on international, industry and corporate levels; very few of these endeavours have succeeded so far because of inadequate scope, focus and formulation of their principles.

Governments rely mostly on voluntary industry and corporate codes of conduct and ethical standards, but what is called for is an international framework that includes not only prescriptions, but also monitoring and enforcement mechanisms. Poverty reduction, knowledge transfer and improvement of infrastructure – these are by-products of TNC activity and not TNCs' goals of operation. Therefore it is felt that it should not be left only to the business community to ensure that TNCs function in the name of the social good. Since there is no one world authority that can govern multinational corporate activity, civil society in the form of NGOs, community groups and institutions are expected to help fill this regulatory void.

Civil society: Also referred to as 'the third sector', this is a term used to broadly describe all aspects of society that reach beyond the domain of the public and private sectors. Association in civil society is voluntary and is characterised by individuals working together for the sake of implementing common ideas, satisfying needs or defending causes to promote collective gain.

Further Reading

Bhagwati, J. (2002) 'Coping with Anti-globalisation', *Foreign Affairs*, January/February.

Curtis, M. (2001) *Trade for Life: Making Trade Work for Poor People*, London: Christian Aid.

Dicken, P. (2002) 'Placing Firms – Firming Places: Grounding the Debate on the Global Corporation', paper presented at the Conference on Responding to Globalisation: Societies, Groups, and Individuals, University of Colorado, Boulder.

Dicken, P. (1994) 'Global-Local Tensions: Firms and States in the Global Space-Economy', *Economic Geography*, vol. 70(2): 101–128.

Dunning, J. H. (1993) *The Globalisation of Business*, London and New York: Routledge.

Dunning, J. H. (1993) *Multinational Enterprises and the Global Economy*, Wokingham: Addison-Wesley.

Emmott, B. (1993) 'Back in Fashion', *The Economist*, 27 March, vol. 326, Issue 7804.

Fredriksson, T. (2003) 'Forty Years of UNCTAD Research on FDI', *Transnational Corporations*, vol. 12(3): 1–39.

Griffin, R. and Pustay, M. (2005) *International Business: A Managerial Perspective*, 4th edn, Prentice Hall.

McKinley, J. Jr. (2004) 'No, the Conquistadors Are Not Back. It's Just Wal-Mart', *New York Times*, 28 September.

Paul, J. A. and Garred, J. (2000) 'Making Corporations Accountable', A Background Paper for the United Nations Financing for Development Process, *Global Policy Forum*, December.

UNCTAD, World Investment Report, various years (2004, 2003, 2002, 2000, 1993).

UN DESA (1973) 'Multinational Corporations in World Development', UN Department of Economic and Social Affairs.

Vernon, R. (1977) *Storm over the Multinationals*, Harvard University Press.

Williamson, O. (1998) *The Economic Institutions of Capitalism*, New York: The Free Press.

The Play: Sources of Crisis and Conflict

CHAPTER 1: Context

This section discusses the sources of crises and conflicts which the cast of global actors sometimes causes and sometimes endures, but in all cases must in some way or another contend with. In earlier times there would not have been much discussion about what the sources were: they would have been perceived to be the disputes and tensions between states as managed by their rulers and governments. Shifts in the distribution of power between states were a very common cause of tension and often eventual warfare. That, for example, is how the origins of the First and Second World Wars have come to be seen, and the Cold War was also understood as an all-consuming rivalry between the two superpowers of the day, the Soviet Union and the United States and their supporters.

Since then, the gale of globalisation has begun to blow and blows still. It has had the effect that great gales and hurricanes do. They destroy the weak, diseased and older trees and they batter the strong and well-rooted, but leave them standing – leaning maybe a little, but standing nonetheless. It is nature's way of testing the strong, emptying the hospitals and clearing the ground for new growth. All the factors which have been set out earlier both in describing globalisation and assessing the current health of the state will have already indicated that in recent years many new states have been created, that very large differences of power and style have occurred among them and that the global domination of the state form has been diluted. This has been partly a cause of globalisation but chiefly it is the result of it. It is not surprising therefore that the winds of globalisation have tested strong and well-established states like the European states and the USA and left them swaying and sometimes bent. Less well-established states, economically and structurally weak states and very small states have been severely damaged and in some cases collapsed completely. A large proportion of the chapters that follow have this common thread: the causes of conflict they lay out either flow from the contemporary changes in the status and character of the state or contribute to them.

This has a particular significance since some current global problems require the existence and stability of global actors, for example, in response to global environmental crises and global warming just at the moment when states are losing authority and newer non-state entities have not yet acquired sufficient confidence and support from the global population to act decisively and make their actions stick. A dangerous loop develops: the problems chase solutions but the potential deliverers of solutions are equally damaged by the causes of the problems and cannot provide them, thus making the situation worse.

What is it that causes states to weaken and sometimes collapse?

There has been a combination of two factors. The effect of the end of the Cold War was to create a wave of new states across Central Asia, in the Caucasus region and in Europe. Some of these shared some natural weaknesses with the earlier wave of new states chiefly in Africa and Oceania – made up chiefly of Pacific Ocean islands – which the de-colonisation of the 1960s created. Sheer newness, a prevalence of corruption and bad governance generally, poor economic bases and performance all took their toll. In Africa, particularly, an additional factor arose out of the poor fit between the colonial boundaries established by cartographers in the nineteenth century who could only imagine what the continent contained and the physical and social structures actually present on the ground. The leaders of the independence movements were brought up and educated in a world which could not conceive of any other system of social and political organisation than that of the state and their ambitions were therefore inextricably tied to creating new states out of the colonies. The fact that these states were not, as European states were, the result of a long period of organic growth, and did not relate well to local physical realities, gave them a difficult starting point. Such shallow roots did not augur well if a great gale should come and in the 1990s it did. The conjunction of the end of support from Cold War rivals, whose broader strategic necessities caused them to ignore the obvious weaknesses developing in their clients, together with the onset of globalisation, brought on the chain of state collapses that marked the 1990s. Why was globalisation a cause of this?

The first part of the answer is that globalisation was an important reason why the USSR collapsed and took the Cold War with it. A frigid but stable international security system then came to an end leaving a vacuum which the predominance of the USA has not filled. A second consequence was that a long period in which the superpowers went to considerable lengths to maintain their friends in the less-developed world came to an end; and a third result was the division of the former USSR into a shoal of smaller and, with the exception of the Baltic states, inexperienced independent countries These were serious but secondary consequences. The primary effect of globalisation lies at a deeper level.

A stable system of state governance depends on the governed perceiving that their social, economic and security needs can be met and are being met by their chosen or inherited regime. The emergence of globalised areas of economic power and equally globalised systems for diffusing knowledge and information has removed from all states important elements of their ability to cope independently with the needs of their societies. The result is that the governed no longer have the same confidence in the ability of their own regime to provide for them as it once could, and worse than that, to protect them, if necessary against the activities of the wielders of global power. Moreover, while globalisation has subtracted authority from states, it has not established alternative and accountable new centres of power, so that managing the effects on individual people is in any case impossible to achieve.

The legitimate use of global power

Here can be seen the roots of what is the most fundamental contemporary problem the world faces. Human beings and the societies they generate dislike the uncontrolled exercise of power at any level of governance and for any reason. If they tolerate it, the reason will either be overwhelming and essentially temporary authoritarianism or a major crisis, such as the onset of war or the danger of terrorism. The ways in which some check has been placed on the exercise of governing power have been different depending on place and time, geography and history. But it has been generally true that the emergence of a source of power has been followed not long after by the introduction, sometimes by violent means, of a means of limiting it. In the case of the traditional state, some form of constitutionally regulated representative democracy has been the favoured means. It was effective because it was a territorially-based system in which the people were divided into districts and regions and represented as such within their state, which was itself sovereign over an absolutely defined area.

This whole concept has now been compromised because in addition to the traditional location of activity and authority within a state, there are now de-territorialised sources of power and activity in the world which cannot be subjected to a controlling and moderating democratic system. The two kinds of authority pass like ships in the night; and the kind that human beings have developed ways of managing are losing ground, and those they cannot affect are growing in significance. There are no good solutions in sight. For there is a conundrum inherent in any attempt to extend the traditional ability of people to control the exercise of power on a territorial basis to the exercise of power on a global basis. Calls to democratise global power fail when they come up against its sleepless, placeless and timeless nature. Representative democracy cannot be extended to manage something that has no constituencies and no districts; the natural consequential demand to reverse the process and return the full exercise of power to entities over which societies had previously established adequate control, simply flies in the face of events. The genie is out of the bottle and the race is on to give him a human face. It is in this gap between the existence of sources of global power and finding a public means of controlling them that most of the world's current sources of tension find their place.

Managing the global economy

The result has been the emergence of a series of causes for conflict and tension which are related both to the processes of globalisation and to the weakening of states. In the economic field, the broadly liberalising trends of the last decade have produced tensions surrounding the effects of IMF, World Bank and WTO policies which were motivated by the desire to strengthen longer-term economic governance and restrain corruption in poorer states. In the shorter term, however, they have tended to bring social disruption in their train and deepen rather than improve the problems of indebtedness in the Third World and to do so in societies which gave no consent to their intervention. This has been partly because these institutions were set up as associations of states with the intention and expectation that they would reflect the will of their members in the decisions that they took.

The globalised world is not the same as the old international system based on states, and the global economic institutions have been forced, to some extent as a result of public objections to their procedures and activities, to evolve into more independent entities taking global economic decisions on behalf of a global population. This stance has put distance between them and their members, most particularly those which had endorsed the so-called Washington Consensus on global economic liberalisation. The ironic result is that the institutions are still attracting public global hostility, fuelled by Internet-based groups, when they have in fact moved on and away from the policies that first attracted the opposition. There is, however, no doubt that the issues of aid, fair trade, debt relief and access to information technology remain a source of contention between governments both rich and poor and between global organisations and governments. It is a major part of the problem of providing global security when the institutional bases for doing so are still painfully evolving both in globally operating entities and in the remodelling of state structures.

The emergence of centre left-wing governments in Latin America in the early twenty-first century has neatly exemplified the situation. They are different from previous left-wing governments which often wished to reject the capitalist system altogether, because they understand that the liberalised global economy cannot be reversed. But they want to moderate its effects locally, to exercise more influence on the global economic institutions, in this aspect pushing at an opening door, and to reduce the association between global economic power and American power.

Migration

Into the gaps left by this process have come other developments – migration, drugs manufacture and distribution, organised crime and a new importance attaching to religion. Contemporary migration is both a means of interaction in global politics and a source of tension. The pace of movement by human beings across the face of the globe has been mounting. It is an ancient activity. Its current manifestations are driven chiefly by two pressures: political maltreatment, particularly persecution and incipient or actual genocide, and economic desperation. The two motives naturally determine the preferred destinations of migrants, and the plethora of means of global travel makes their journeys at least feasible though sometimes tragically fatal. The scale of it has changed the asylum-seeking refugee from a kind of hero, as in escaping from the Soviet bloc when it existed, to a suspected scrounger or potential terrorist.

State governments have been driven by domestic popular disapproval of increased immigration to try to restrain it. They have not succeeded very well and in even trying to do so may well be acting against their best interests. Whether the migrants are economic or political refugees, they usually represent a formidable advantage to the economies of their destinations. They will do the jobs that locals will not, they bring cultural and intellectual energy, and to societies with a falling birthrate and the threat of collapsing pension and welfare systems, they bring some relief. But they bring tensions – tensions derived from the loss of labour and capacity from their departure point and the sense of threat mainly arising from cultural and religious difference where they settle. This may take the form of ghettoisation or, its reverse, cultural diffusion: both give rise to a corrosive fear. Disorder follows and a further dent is made in the authority and legitimacy of the state.

Drugs and organised crime

A declining political legitimacy on the part of the state is a particularly difficult condition when economic liberalisation, the pace of global travel and the instant global communication provided by the Internet all provide assistance to the growth of global organised crime. Substantially based in the market for the manufacture and distribution of drugs, particularly cocaine and heroin, the flow of money is controlled by criminal gangs, the profits are laundered and then seep away into the coffers of terrorist groups or unscrupulous governments and rulers. The ability of this activity to rot not only personal lives and spread violence in the cities of North America, but also to undermine substantial organisations, even whole governments, is a serious source of conflict in the contemporary world, as the fates of both Columbia and Afghanistan demonstrate. Its secondary consequences in terms of the flow of illegal weapons around the globe provides another form of insecurity, as does the large number of people involved in a global enterprise that flouts the authority of both governments and international institutions in a highly public and regular way.

Religion

The growth of legitimate secular ways of regulating human behaviour which the triumph of the sovereign state inaugurated in the mid-seventeenth century in Europe became part of the basic idea of the state and was extended with it across the globe during the nineteenth and twentieth centuries. The communist version of the state sought to suppress religion, others sought to use it. Religion had not always been so far relegated to the area of private belief and practice. All three of the Abrahamic religions had the textural justification for and the historical experience of a far more immediate role at times when the notion of the state was either unknown or under-developed. It is thus not surprising that as faith in the permanence and power of the state form has declined and general intellectual and social uncertainties have increased, faith in various religions has become once again a potent force in the world.

The ability of the global communication systems to advance the knowledge and role of individuals, and to enable them to combine in ways that owe nothing to local loyalties or physical propinquity, has helped the spread of religious fundamentalism. But the real cause of it is the sense of lost bearings in which national political affiliations mean less than they did, and global pressures can be felt but not grappled with successfully: nationalist or provincialist backlashes demonstrate one possible response, but the growth or regrowth of religious loyalties and a wish to obey the dictates of religious scriptures, sometimes unquestioningly, represent another. The connecting point between this evolution and the sources of conflict in the world emerges with frightening clarity and force in the encouragement and justification religion can give to global terrorism. In Chechnya, in Kashmir, in Georgia and across other parts of the Caucasus, in Palestine, in Ireland, in Sri Lanka, in New York City, in Iraq and in Afghanistan, the consequences have been or are both clear and highly intractable.

Disputes between states

With all this, there remains an old and familiar problem; indeed it would have come first among the sources of conflict in any such discussion even a decade ago: disputes between states. In describing the contemporary world, however, disputes between states do not rate a separate chapter. As can be seen in the discussion of warfare in Part E, Chapter 9, the likelihood of war arising from disputes between states has fallen dramatically. Civil conflict in weak states and conflict arising from interventions to suppress it has become the norm. Two current examples which have a familiar look to them are not technically between states. The conflict in Palestine is over the wish of the Palestinians to become a state and the counter wish of the Israelis to limit what that state might be. But the Palestinian authority is not a state. The disputes between China and Taiwan are only between states in the eyes of those who recognise Taiwan as a fully independent state. There may indeed be a major war arising out of China's determination to reintegrate Taiwan into China, and Taiwan's resistance, potentially supported by the USA. If it happens, the technical status of Taiwan will not seem significant. In this respect it is unique in current global politics.

There remain latent inter-state disputes in Latin America and in Africa. The war against Saddam Hussein's Iraq in 2004 did not begin for traditional reasons and rapidly became a mixture of resistance movement and civil war. The disputes over potential or actual nuclear weapons manufacture in Iran and North Korea are unlike familiar inter-state disputes of the past and are expressed through the activities of an international organisation, the International Atomic Energy Authority of the UN. With the possible exception of a confrontation between a newly powerful China and Japan, it appears likely that inter-state disputes will remain very low on the list of potential causes of conflict for the foreseeable future.

Environmental issues

The same cannot be said of the role of environmental issues. These are a very clear example of a type of problem that used to be contained within a state, for example when natural disasters occurred or when there were – as there still are – internal arguments and protests caused by domestic policy towards, say, national parks or endangered species. The onset of a general conviction that an era of global warming and climate change has arrived has globalised the issue, both in that its effects are not confined to any one state or area but apply globally and that responses to it must be developed on a global basis. No one government can improve the situation or respond to the consequences of global warming on its own. The stresses that this produces between governments and between governments and international organisations both public and private are serious. Nor does it stop there. The general public in many societies have become involved and the Internet creates a global constituency for both dissemination and organisation, thus contributing to the general lowering of the authority of the state which can neither control climate change nor protect its people from the consequences.

Within states, an unstable physical and climatic environment creates stresses on a spectrum running from total destruction at the hands of inundation to agricultural breakdown caused by desertification. In between, declining but less disastrous conditions still cause tensions, and where weaker societies are affected, their ability to respond may be as limited as their ability to benefit from the good effects of economic globalisation. In addition, worsening conditions can cause the difficult combination of spreading diseases and pests accompanying increased migration which in turn is encouraged by greater global mobility. Amid the clamour of civil wars and genocide, the risks of nuclear proliferation and the threat of terrorism, it is worth remembering that the most potent source of crisis and conflict arises and will arise yet more from the effects of rapid global environmental change. This set of problems, together with the problems associated with making the existence and exercise of global power acceptable and beneficial to individual human beings, are the two most certain sources of fundamental crises in the future. They are of course linked: no solution to the global crisis caused by climate change, either in trying to restrain it or in dealing with the consequences of what it is now too late to restrain, will be found without evolving means of using global power effectively: no one society or government can cope by itself or be expected to put the general interest above its own particular interest on a routine basis.

CHAPTER 2: Access to and management of the Internet

Policing the web: attempts at establishing authority in cyberspace

Cyberspace has proved difficult to regulate, manage and/or control from its very beginnings. The proliferation of alternative networks such as USENET demonstrated the organic and intractable nature of the medium. Likewise, militancy against attempts at limiting free speech was one of the first tenets of the netizen ethos. Despite this, certain national governments (especially in authoritarian states) have attempted to police the use of the Internet in a variety of ways, including intimidation, restricting access to the web, harshly regulating e-commerce, blocking websites and monitoring users. Such actions are achieved through state control of the Internet, governmental monopolies on communications services, universal deployment of blocking software and international arbitration.

Nonetheless, as a comparatively unregulated spatial dimension, much of cyberspace is mostly beyond the control of state governments. This

Netizen: Any individual who spends a large amount of his or her time on the Internet. To be a good netizen means to be an active member of the digital community, i.e. posting comments to message boards, maintaining an interesting website, participating in online chat, etc. The term also connotes citizenship and civic responsibility in cyberspace. Netizens embrace the role of the Internet as a tool for political action and employ it to expand democracy, exchange information and facilitate social change.

fact has allowed for fringe elements in various societies to employ the Internet for a host of offensive, illicit, seditious and counter-cultural activities. Responding to such actions, political leaders, religious groups and citizen organisations around the world have attacked the Internet as a nefarious influence on society that needs to be managed at either the national or international level. As Internet use became a worldwide phenomenon, there were increasing calls for some form of global governance to deal with the 'ghettoisation' of the Internet, i.e. the unchecked proliferation of pornography, criminality, hate speech etc. in cyberspace.

One important result of this drive to police the Internet was the creation of an international rating system for Internet sites, similar to that employed in most countries for motion pictures. In the mid-1990s, the World Wide Web Consortium (W3C), an international forum of web developers dedicated to improving the Internet experience for all users, began an effort to provide web surfers with information about the content of the sites they were visiting. Ultimately, it was up to the owners of sites to voluntarily rank their own content, thus weakening the impact of the W3C's efforts. The issue was revived again in 1999 by an international consortium of Internet companies known as Internet Content Rating Association (ICRA) with a similar lack of success.

In some cases, the international legal system has been employed to regulate the Internet. Unlike the United States, certain European countries do not extend freedom of speech protections to hate-speech as interpreted by their lawmakers. Consequently, the Internet as a global communicative space has become a battleground for national interpretations of free speech. One of the most famous cases involved the American company Yahoo! and the government of France. In 2000, Yahoo!, a multi-purpose Internet portal providing communications, file storage and information services, came under fire when it was accused of violating French law by selling Nazi memorabilia through its auction site. The company was sued in a French court by the Union of Jewish Students and the International League against Racism and Anti-Semitism for selling items which incited racism. The items were sold to customers in France via the company's US-based auction site. Yahoo!, which was not selling the items via its French subsidiary www.yahoo.fr, claimed free speech as its defence as interpreted under American law. The French court ultimately decided in favour of the plaintiffs, although an American federal court decision shielded Yahoo! from having to pay the daily fine of FFr 100,000 for its continued auctioning of such items. A year later, Germany's interior minister identified some 800 neo-Nazi websites hosted in the United States and accessible to German citizens. A subsequent court ruling in Germany held the owners of the servers which hosted such sites, in violation of German law banning hate speech, to be responsible. These decisions clearly exposed the relevance of national borders in cyberspace, but simultaneously demonstrated how far time/space barriers have collapsed in the postmodern world.

The most common measures used to regulate Internet access, however, have come from states. A host of measures has been deployed by countries around the world, from the US to Afghanistan, to intimidate and watch users, filter content and restrict access. Blocking software – technology that prevents Internet users from accessing sites based on keywords found in the content – is frequently used by countries seeking to limit their citizens' use of the Internet. Blocking technologies (which are used by libraries, corporations and concerned parents in the developed world) are a favourite of authoritarian governments or religiously conservative polities. Saudi Arabia, although it allows private companies to act as Internet service providers, vets all traffic through a centralised bank of servers that censors content deemed 'contrary to Islamic values'. This micromanagement of web access allows the Saudis to restrict access to political, pornographic and religious web pages. Like Saudi Arabia, Yemen and the United Arab Emirates keep a blacklist of prohibited sites

which are inaccessible to web users in those countries.

The People's Republic of China is often cited as a major censor of Internet content. China, which now has more Internet users than any country except the United States, has deployed blocking software to prevent the population accessing sites on religious sects such as the Falun Gong, issues relating to Taiwan, and 'embarrassing' news items such as the Sars outbreak. In 2004, China was actively blocking access to about 200,000 websites. This massive effort to keep the 'bad' aspects of the Internet out and let the 'good' in generated the Western quip, 'The Great Fire Wall of China'. A fire wall is a combination of hardware and software that is deployed to protect a local area network (such as that found in a corporation or a university) from viruses, hackers and other external threats.

Another popular mechanism of policing is to restrict access through state control of Internet infrastructure and prohibitive pricing. Cuba, for example, allows two forms of access: state-subsidised Intranet use which restricts users from accessing the global Internet and prohibitively high-priced, private Internet access paid only in hard currency, in effect US dollars. This two-tiered approach is a common form of control employed throughout the developing world. Wealthy elites are granted the freedom to view what they like on the web while the vast majority of society sees its access restricted or denied. In most of these cases, private access is technically illegal and is capriciously shut down by the government when deemed necessary to state security. Other states that similarly restrict access through state control include Belarus, Tajikistan, Libya, North Korea, Sudan, Syria and Vietnam.

Intimidation also plays a major role in policing Internet use. Burma, rather than focusing on controlling the Internet backbone, made it illegal to possess any computer, modem or fax machine not registered with the government. Punishment for such violations is up to 15 years in jail. China has some 60 laws relating to proper use of the Internet and requires Internet service providers to adhere to the Public Pledge on Self-Discipline for the Chinese Internet Industry to regulate Internet use at the commercial level. Chinese police frequently arrest so-called 'Internet dissidents' caught distributing censored information over the web. The harsh sentences handed down to such transgressors have encouraged other Internet-enabled Chinese to regulate their own activities in cyberspace carefully. According to some estimates, China employs approximately 30,000 people to monitor Internet use (e-mail, chat rooms, etc.), thus ensuring some level of threat to those who choose not to police themselves.

The effectiveness of all these efforts is debatable. Anyone seriously intent on breaching security measures can find ways to do so quite easily. There are numerous sites on the web that instruct users in countries such as Saudi Arabia, Cuba and China on how to circumvent government controls. Dissidents inside authoritarian regimes are supported by NGOs, the diaspora community and Internet activists in their efforts to avoid detection through false IP addresses, black market Internet identities and counter-surveillance technologies. But most important is the realisation among governments around the world that despite the danger posed by the Internet, its potential for generating capital is more important.

The Coca-colonisation of cyberspace?: perceptions of Internet imperialism

The Internet is frequently lambasted as a tool of American hegemony. Critics point to a number of factors that give support to this notion, including the preponderance of the English language on the Internet, the early history of the Internet as a US government project, the proliferation of American brands in cyberspace, and the heavy presence of Microsoft and other US multinational corporations in the critical path to Internet usage. For many critics of the Internet, US domination of cyberspace is analogous to the British domination of the high seas in the late nineteenth century – both serve(d) to provide contiguity between a powerful imperial core and weaker colonial peripheries.

Despite the fact that the US government gave up control of the Internet backbone in 1996, US involvement in the management of the Internet continues to draw criticism around the globe. The Internet Corporation for Assigned Names and Numbers (ICANN) represents one of the most visible targets for such criticism. ICANN was established on 18 September 1998 as the sole body responsible for the management of assigning Internet domain names and IP

addresses. The organisation, located in Marina del Rey, California, has proved to be highly controversial globally. Critics attack ICANN's lack of transparency, the preponderance of American staff and an apparent reluctance to accommodate any outside input into its policies. The fact that the group reports to the US Department of Commerce is especially irksome to many around the globe who fear that Washington might try to sway the organisation's policies towards the US's enemies. Public participation in the way the company is run was reduced even further at a meeting in March 2002 in Accra, Ghana, a location critics say was chosen specifically because it made mass participation by grassroots activists unlikely: a small coterie of activists was outvoted by well-financed interests.

Latin Script and the Internet: Owing to its origins as an English language medium, Latin or Roman script was originally necessary to use the Internet. However, recent changes have made it possible for Internet users to employ non-Latin characters for website addresses, although the top-level domain names remain in Latin lettering, e.g. .com, int., etc. These internationalised domain names (IDNs), also known as multilingual domain names, were created by the Internet Engineering Task Force (IETF), an open international community of network designers, operators, vendors and researchers dedicated to global approaches to the evolution of the Internet. However, the Latin alphabet still rules in cyberspace, dominating 84 per cent of web content. Chinese, Japanese and Korean script command 13 per cent and the remaining 3 per cent accounts for the rest of the world's orthographies. Prominent search engines such as Google are now accepting search queries in Indic and Arabic scripts, a major sign of the increasing diversity of the Internet.

The Chinese have been among the most vocal critics of Western dominance of the Internet. China is quickly emerging as the face of the third world in international negotiations about the future of the Internet. At international forums such as the World Summit on the Information Society (2003 in Geneva and 2005 in Tunis), a UN-sponsored global forum on governing the Internet and ICT, China took the lead in voicing criticism of Eurocentrism on the Internet. The use of ideograms in Chinese makes Internet usage especially difficult for the vast majority of China's 1 billion people (although a number of the country's ethnic minorities do employ Latin-based scripts). Popular sentiment in China has even begun to favour the creation of a more Chinese-friendly variant of the Internet, untethered to the one used by the rest of the world. The Chinese are not alone in their support for decentralising the web; a number of polities have called for independent networks more conducive to their linguistic dispositions, political values or religious norms.

Criticism of the pervasiveness of the Internet and its potential for harm are not confined to the developing world. The French have shown themselves to be much less disposed to adopt the Internet than other Europeans. This stems from traditional resistance to Anglo-American hegemony and especially US cultural products, as well as a preference for France's homegrown Minitel. Minitel, funded by the French national phone company, claimed nearly 7 million subscribers at the height of its popularity. It is an information service which caters for making travel reservations, accessing theatre schedules, telephone directory assistance, etc. In 1996, France emerged as a battleground for legal questions surrounding the use of language on the Internet when Internet companies were sued for not advertising in French as the law required. France's minister of culture at the time decried the Internet as a 'new form of colonialism' projected by the United States.

In traditional societies, the Internet is often seen as an insidious force corrupting the morals of society. Pornography, the first profitable Internet industry, is often at the root of such concerns. The ease with which an Internet user can find pornography is astounding; even those not seeking such diversions are bombarded by them in 'spam', unsolicited commercial e-mails sent to thousands if not millions of web users. In the Islamic world there are also other fears, including promotion of alcohol and/or drug use, proselytising by other religions and heretical interpretations of the Qur'an (on the role of women, for example). For traditional societies concerned that their youth can obtain access to illicit material and US cultural influence, the Internet is doubly offensive. Such fears have led a large number of countries around the globe to employ measures to curb their citizens' freedoms in cyberspace.

A global digital divide: problems of Internet access around the world

In today's global society, access to information is vital to success and the gap between the world's information 'haves' and 'have nots' is increasing daily. This gap creates a problem which is the reverse of the worries which have led to attempts to restrict the use of the Internet or control its content. The problem is insufficient access in some parts of the world. Today, 80 per cent of the 700 million Internet users around the globe are in the developed world. Two out of every five people in developed countries are online. Conversely, in developing countries only 1 person in 50 has access to the web. It is clear that developing countries are being left behind as the transformation to the 'new economy' takes place in wealthier countries. This new economy is driven and enabled by dependable and affordable access to the Internet.

Predictably, the industrialised nations of Europe, North America and the Pacific Rim have the highest levels of Internet access. In fact, high-speed Internet access (i.e. 200 kbps or greater data speeds capable of providing digital video and audio) is already in double-digit numbers in South Korea, Japan, Taiwan, the USA, Canada and much of Western Europe, with overall penetration at 50 per cent or higher. The Internet is ubiquitous in urban areas of the developed world. Today, coffee shops, homes, workplaces, libraries and airports all have fairly cheap Internet access.

In these countries, the telecommunications infrastructure has been upgraded to handle the vast amount of new traffic on the network and competition between Internet service providers is fierce and pushing prices downwards. Options for service range from mobile data access over wireless phones to traditional dial-up Internet to satellite broadband service. The prices for such services are generally within the reach of nearly everyone, although access itself can sometimes be a problem, as we will see shortly.

The situation in the developing world is quite different. There are barriers to Internet adoption at the local, national and international level for those in developing countries seeking to use the Internet. Autocratic regimes, endemic poverty and prejudicial global market structures all negatively impact the ability of much of the third world to get on the information super-highway. Access to the Internet requires a personal computer, for instance, electricity, telephone, cable or satellite service, and an Internet service provider – all of which are out of the reach of most of the developing world's population. Poor communications networks, the unreliability of the power supply, corruption and governmental barriers all complicate Internet access at the national level. In addition, many governments in the third world view the Internet as the latest tool of Western hegemony intended to export culture and ideology.

The New Economy: This term refers to emerging sectors of the economy that are based on information and knowledge-workers. The set of industries which composes the New Economy (telecommunications, information technology, etc.) are primarily dependent on highly-skilled, technologically-savvy human capital. In many parts of the world, information has become the central driver in economic activity, thus signalling a fundamental shift from the Industrial Age to an 'Information Age'. At the root of the New Economy is the assumption that technology enables and promotes a creative revolution for humanity including increased productivity, shorter business cycles, more efficient information exchange and faster acquisition of skill sets. Globalisation and the compression of time and space through new communications technologies are vital to this phenomenon.

At the international level, inequities in trade and commerce ensure that countries in the global south pay more for the same goods and services than their wealthier counterparts in the north. The reluctance of governments and firms in wealthy countries to engage in large-scale technology transfers to the industrialising world is a frequent complaint of poorer countries. If this trend continues, it is likely first to reinforce and then increase the socio-economic disparities between the developed and developing worlds. The UN has advocated that universal access should become a goal for the global community. Many have suggested introducing a small subscriber charge on every Internet user in the industrialised countries, with the object of using the funds raised to subsidise Internet use in the developing world. Other options include ending tax-free e-commerce and using a portion of the

monies collected to support Internet development initiatives in the global south. Such calls for action are controversial, but many analysts suggest that this is a wise long-term strategy for success. An information society's value grows with each new node of data transmission. Thus, tolerating the fact that huge sections of the globe are not connected to the information superhighway – the African continent is a glaring example – prevents even the most networked societies from taking full advantage of ICT and the knowledge exchange it develops.

The Internet is also perceived as reinforcing divisions within societies in both the developed and developing worlds. Even in wealthy, industrialised countries, Internet access – though pervasive – has not reached everyone. Policy makers and social reformers alike criticise the increasing divide between white and black, rich and poor and suburban and rural/inner city when it comes to Internet access. In the United States, Australia and elsewhere in the first world, the concept of 'digital ghettos' is used to describe those areas where citizens are challenged by technical, social or economic barriers to Internet use. In many places, local governments have been instrumental in reversing the digital divide. Small towns and rural communities have invested funds to create powerful 'wireless local areas networks' (WLANs) that provide free Internet access to anyone with a laptop computer and a $40 wireless network card. Typically, the network will be placed in a convenient downtown area where shoppers or diners congregate. In inner-city and impoverished urban areas, local libraries, state-supported telecentres and schools have become the central point of access for people who are unable or unwilling to pay a monthly fee for Internet access.

In the developing world, the Internet is commonly seen as just another barrier between the elite and the masses. Critics point to the emergence of an international *digerati* or Internet-enabled Brahmin class that consumes conspicuously, speaks English, travels widely and spends a great deal of time in cyberspace or on mobile phones. Technical skills combined with English proficiency can guarantee a stable income and the promise of upward mobility for those lucky enough to live near one of the myriad nodes of globalisation (Bangalore, Kuala Lumpur, Manila, etc.). The preponderance of Internet access in the cities of the developing world is also furthering the socio-economic

Digerati: A term used to describe the global Internet elite. These individuals are more than just regular web users: they are Internet evangelicals whose identities are closely tethered to their activities and presence in cyberspace. This vanguard of the information revolution connects with one another across time and space, while preaching the benefits of the Internet to the masses. The word is adapted from the late medieval Italian word 'literati', or intelligentsia.

divisions between rural and urban dwellers.

The situation is not hopeless, however. Large transnational corporations, forward-thinking governments, technology-centric foundations and citizen organisations have made substantial efforts towards closing the digital divide in certain parts of the developing world. There is a motive in that those states perceived to be capable of joining the global information society have been most successful in attracting investment. A functioning education system, a trainable workforce, some democratic institutions and friendliness to the West all help to attract this form of investment. India has been one of the greatest recipients of such aid and the government has also made some initiatives of its own, including providing Internet kiosks in villages. Even in the poorest villages individuals have e-mail addresses which they use indirectly through a surrogate who travels to nearby villages and is able to access the Internet on behalf of his neighbours – a modern version of the medieval village scribe who would write letters for the illiterate. The kiosks are the frontline in the move towards future e-governance and ending graft by allowing citizens to post complaints, procure proof of ownership, apply for government programmes and communicate with officials. Additionally, public Internet terminals allow farmers to gain access to improved agricultural techniques, weather reports and information about domestic and international commodity prices through specialised applications in local languages.

Public-private partnerships are increasingly common across the developing world as corporations and NGOs such as the World Economic Forum – a Geneva-based NGO supported by global technology companies – support Internet projects in Asia, the Middle East and elsewhere. Bill Gates of Microsoft has been especially supportive of efforts to increase the Indian population's technical proficiency and use of the Internet. He and other Western philanthropists have invested millions of dollars in online training institutes for Indians.

In 2002, Kazakhstan opened two Internet Data Centres (IDCs) in Pavlodar and its capital Astana for 10,000 users each. The IDCs are a cooperative venture between Kazakhtelecom and Lockheed Martin Telecommunications and the first of their kind in the former Soviet Union. Today, some 300,000 Kazakhstan citizens have access to the web, a per centage increase of several hundred over the past five years. In the Middle East, the Jordan Education Initiative has provided high- speed Internet access to nearly 100 schools. The Jordan initiative is a joint effort between the government and various corporate sponsors, including Cisco Systems, the world leader in networking technologies.

Such private-public ventures are vital to the spread of Internet access to the third world, but it remains to be seen how quickly the digital divide will narrow as the Internet becomes ever more deeply embedded in industrialised countries.

Further Reading

Castells, Manuel (2001) *The Internet Galaxy*, Oxford: Oxford University Press.

Ebo, Bosah (2001) *Cyberimperialism?: Global Relations in the New Electronic Frontier*, Westport, CT: Praeger.

Engel, Christoph and Heller, Kenneth H. (2002) *Understanding the Impact of Global Networks on Social, Political and Cultural Values*, Baden-Baden: Nomos Verlagsgellschaft.

Kalathil, Shanthi and Boas, Taylor C. (2003) *Open Networks, Closed Regimes: The Impact of the Internet on Authoritarian Rule*, Washington: Carnegie Endowment for International Peace.

Negroponte, Nicholas (1996) *Being Digital*, New York: Vintage.

CHAPTER 3: Transnational organised crime and the drug industry

Transnational organised crime

Transnational crimes are those which by their nature extend beyond national boundaries. They may involve the movement of information, people, money or other items across borders, all of which typically have a monetary value of some sort. The transnational nature of these crimes allows criminal organisations to capitalise on the markets in other countries. These crimes include, but are not limited to, money laundering, illicit drug trafficking, terrorist activities, sea piracy, trafficking in people, the trading of human body parts, computer crime, theft of intellectual property through software piracy, theft and smuggling of vehicles, counterfeiting and the kidnapping of businessmen.

Transnational organised crime can take many forms, all of which have several things in common. Participants typically undertake enterprise crime, which involves either the supply of illicit goods and/or services (such as drugs) or the supply of licit goods obtained through illegal methods, such as theft. All organised crime activities require cooperation, organisation, coordination and entrepreneurship. In addition, violence, extortion, blackmail and the corruption of officials, including law enforcement and government, often play a part.

> **Major transnational criminal organisations:**
> 1. Italian Mafia (most clearly represented by La Cosa Nostra)
> 2. Russian organised crime groups
> 3. Chinese Triads
> 4. Japanese Yakuza
> 5. Colombian cartels
> 6. Nigerian criminal organisations

There are many transnational criminal organisations, all varying in size, structure, skills and operating domains. They are usually adaptable to change. Groups also vary with regard to their degree of specialisation, with some focusing solely on one venture such as drugs, while others may engage in various financial 'scams'. Regardless of their particular mode, their main concern is one of profit.

Importantly, what was once considered to be more of a national or local phenomenon has transformed itself into a global, transnational problem. Not only are organised crime groups doing business across borders, but the effects of their illegal activities reach around the globe. These organisations typically work from one 'base' but operate in several areas. Globalisation has made information exchange both easy and immediate, as it has the sharing of technological intelligence, human resources and even cultures. The speed of travel and communication has increased dramatically and the worldwide web allows instant access to people and information, all raising the efficiency with which business may be conducted. A rising tide raises all boats, whether innocent or criminal, and while globalisation has brought many benefits, it has also inadvertently aided the proliferation of criminal activity. Criminals have exploited these innovations to their advantage, reaping many benefits. For example, increasingly permeable borders allow criminals to conduct their business more quickly and effectively and enable them to transfer large sums of money virtually undetected to far corners of the world. Furthermore, people in one part of the world may initiate events anywhere on the globe: geographical proximity is no longer essential to ensure success.

Types of transnational organised crime

The illegal drug industry

The production, distribution and consumption of illicit drugs are persistent and growing phenomena in the contemporary world. The trafficking of illicit drugs is one of the most pressing organised crime problems facing the international community and generates one of the largest sources of income for organised crime groups. It will therefore be discussed first, and most extensively.

Production: coca and cocaine

The production of different kinds of drugs occurs in many regions of the world. Colombia, Peru and Bolivia remain the top cultivators and producers of cocaine. While Peru was the top producer in the 1990s, it has been surpassed by Colombia, which remains the largest producer of both coca leaf and the cocaine that is refined from it. It is important to note, though, that by 2003 it had also experienced its third straight year of decline, in part due to the eradication efforts being employed in the region. Similarly, coca cultivation in these three countries combined has declined 30 per cent since its peak in 1999. The UN estimates that these three countries cultivated almost 154,000 hectares of coca bush in 2003, which has the potential to produce almost 236,000 metric tons of dry coca leaf and in turn enables the manufacture of approximately 655 metric tons of cocaine. Refinement of the coca leaves into cocaine often takes place in Colombia.

Cocaine production and distribution

Coca leaves are usually made into paste in close proximity to where they are grown, and then processed into cocaine base in Peru and Bolivia. The cocaine paste is then refined into hydrochloride or powder in Colombia. The result is an odourless, white crystalline powder that has a bitter, numbing taste.

Colombian drug trafficking groups harvest hundreds of tons of coca or cocaine base, convert it into cocaine hydrochloride at their drug laboratories and then export the illegal finished product to other countries. Large amounts of coca are also imported from Peru and Bolivia

for this same purpose. Colombian drug cartels use various methods of transporting the illegal drugs to receiving countries, occasionally employing body carriers, but more often making use of aircraft, boats and land vehicles that are equipped with technologically advanced radar, communications equipment and weapons. The use of commercial transport has also flourished, allowing for larger shipments of drugs to be transported in a single delivery. Furthermore, the Colombian drug cartels have developed sophisticated methods of encryption and state-of-the-art communication networks in order to lessen the threat of electronic surveillance.

The majority of cocaine seizures occur in the Americas, with over half in South America (55 per cent) and a third in North America. There has been an increase in recent years in European seizures, perhaps reflecting a slight shift in trafficking patterns to potentially less risky markets. Fluctuations in the numbers of seizures in North America and Western Europe may be attributed to growing eradication efforts, as well as more diligent enforcement in source countries, such as Colombia. Colombia's geographic location, bordering on Peru and Bolivia and relatively close to the United States, with coastlines on both the Pacific Ocean and the Caribbean Sea, makes it a strategic and logical hub for the trafficking of illicit drugs, with smuggling routes readily available.

The drug cartels share many characteristics with traditional organised crime groups, including their ability to control the prices of the drugs, to eliminate competition, to avoid prosecution through the use of corruption and violence, and their routine use of legitimate business enterprises to disguise and launder their impressive drug profits. However, it is their vast influence and complexity that place the Colombian drug cartels in a class by themselves. For while traditional organised crime groups tend to corrupt law enforcement officers and members of the judiciary, international drug cartels corrupt entire institutions of government. Given that Colombia is among the world's drug smuggling capitals, corruption is widespread; it is the rule, not the exception. The judicial-political system in Colombia has been so completely permeated by the illicit narcotics industry that the two are becoming progressively more difficult to distinguish and identify as separate entities.

Opium and heroin

Opium is the raw material for heroin. Cultivation of the opium poppy and production of opium occurs in South West Asia (Pakistan and Afghanistan), South East Asia (Laos, Myanmar (Burma), Thailand and Vietnam) and Latin America (Colombia and Mexico). Low levels of illicit cultivation also exist in places such as Russia, Ukraine, Central Asia, the Caucasus region, Egypt and Peru. The UN estimates that 82,500 hectares of opium poppy were cultivated in south-west Asia in 2003, while just over 74,000 hectares were cultivated in South-East Asia. In comparison, Latin America cultivated almost 9,000 hectares. This cultivation would yield a total of almost 4,700 metric tons of opium and almost 500 metric tons of heroin.

Afghanistan has established itself as the leading producer of opium, accounting for over three-quarters of the world's illicit supply. Approximately 264,000 families in Afghanistan farm opium poppies, accounting for a large portion of the country's livelihood. The production of heroin is typically organised by local warlords, as well as corrupt officials.

Heroin production and distribution

The heroin is produced by converting opium gum into morphine in labs near the fields and then to heroin in labs within or near the producing country. After importation, drug dealers cut, or dilute, the heroin with sugars, starch or powdered milk before selling it to addicts; quinine is also added to imitate the bitter taste of heroin so the amount of heroin actually present is indeterminable.

Seizures of opiates have been concentrated in Asia (65 per cent), due to the fact that the two most prolific production areas are located there. South-west Asia, including Iran and Pakistan, accounted for 43 per cent of the world's opiate seizures in 2002. Europe accounted for approximately 28 per cent of global seizures that year, with the vast majority originating in Afghanistan. The Balkan route remains popular for heroin that is intended for distribution in Western Europe. Less opiate trafficking takes place in the Americas, which account for only 6 per cent of worldwide seizures, yet heroin seizures in North America rose by 50 per cent from 2000 to 2002, which could be an indicator of better enforcement.

Cannabis

It has been suggested that cannabis production extends fairly evenly across the world, with a few main source countries. North America appears to be the world's largest market, while Colombia is a main source country in South America, and almost every country in Africa reports cannabis production. Other production regions include Europe, the Near and Middle East, southern Asia and Oceania. The UN suggests that a conservative estimate of global cannabis herb production is upwards of 32,000 tons annually, keeping in mind that there is likely to be considerable undetected cannabis production, particularly in Central and East Asia and Africa.

Cannabis production and distribution

Cannabis can be used as a drug in three main forms. First, it can be used as the dried leaves and buds, known as marijuana. It can also be converted into a solid resin known as hashish, which is collected from the buds and flower heads, or into a thick liquid prepared from the flowers or resin, known as hash oil. Cannabis resin is produced mainly in Morocco, Pakistan and Afghanistan. Other supply countries include India, Lebanon, Albania and countries in Central Asia (approximately 40 countries have been identified as producing cannabis resin). Estimates of global cannabis resin production range from 5,100 tons to 7,400 tons.

Cannabis is the most widely trafficked drug and almost the whole world is affected in some form or another. According to the UN, approximately 5,800 tons of cannabis products were seized in anywhere from 115 (cannabis resin) to 169 (cannabis herb) countries in 2002, which exceeds the amounts of cocaine and heroin seized by 15 and 100 times, respectively. North America accounted for 58 per cent of the cannabis herb seizures in 2002, followed by West and Central Africa (11 per cent) and South America (9 per cent), while cannabis resin seizures were concentrated in West Europe (68 per cent) and the Near/Middle East and south-west Asia (22 per cent). These products originate in countries, such as Morocco (via Spain and the Netherlands) and Pakistan and Afghanistan.

The most infamous of the Colombian organised crime groups are the Medellin and Cali drug cartels. The Medellin cartel, centred in Medellin, the second largest city in Colombia, was formed in the early 1980s and was the first to dominate the cocaine-trafficking industry. This cartel is known for its blatant acts of violence, initiated by leaders such as Carlos Lehder, the Ochoa brothers and Pablo Escobar. The Medellin cartel is linked with paramilitary groups who often systematically mete out violence on their behalf. Many leaders of the Medellin cartel have been brought to justice in the last decade by the Colombian National Police, thus contributing to the decreased presence of the Medellin cartel in current drug-trafficking ventures.

The Cali cartel, based in Cali, Colombia, has existed alongside the Medellin cartel for many years, but quickly came to the fore of the drug-trafficking industry with the gradual eradication of top members of the Medellin cartel. A once close relationship ended when the Cali cartel was accused by the Medellin cartel of attempting to assassinate Pablo Escobar and offering information to the authorities that resulted in the death of a Medellin cartel member. This was the beginning of extreme levels of violence between the cartels as they continually fought for control of the drug market.

While the Cali cartel has shown its potential for violence, it attempts to avoid overt acts of violence against the government. Instead, cartel members favour trying to pass themselves off as legitimate business operators. The Cali cartel generated billions of dollars in drug revenue every year during the late 1980s and early 1990s, involving a level of corruption that reached all the way to the presidency. The Cali cartel continues to play an important role in the drug-trafficking business.

Illicit drug trafficking

Drug trafficking is a form of organised crime that comprises several stages, each of which has a spatial dimension that creates patterns which may change over time depending on methods of transport, the development of new drugs and law enforcement strategies. Typically, the spatial pattern for a particular drug involves production countries, transit countries and destination countries. Different types of drugs are grown in various countries and are then routed through several transit places and into the United States. For example, cannabis is grown in Mexico and opium is typically grown in southern Asia, both of which have different ports of entry to the United States, at which point they are divided into smaller amounts for sale at retail markets across the USA.

The travel patterns of cocaine specifically exemplify the spatial dimensions that drug trafficking may involve. Due to its location, Colombia has ready access to the Pacific Ocean and the Caribbean Sea, providing exceptional water routes to the United States. After reaching the transit countries, the drugs are either shipped or flown to US wholesale trafficking sites, typically in Arizona, southern California, southern Florida or Texas. From the wholesale trafficking points, the drugs are then moved to major retail markets found in Boston, New York City, Miami, Newark, Philadelphia, Richmond, Chicago, Louisville, St Louis and others. More recently, the Colombian cartels have broadened their trafficking efforts to include marijuana, heroin and opium, available in metropolitan areas along the East Coast of the United States.

While Colombian drug cartels are still significantly involved in the trafficking of drugs to the United States, over the last decade Mexican trafficking organisations have begun to take an increasing role in the drug smuggling market, particularly transporting drugs across the border between Mexico and the West and Mid-west. Other key entry points for cocaine into the United States include Miami, Houston and New Orleans for shipments by sea.

Location of both shipping and receiving countries is a significant factor in whether or not the smuggling operation is carried out successfully. Traffickers typically choose locations where they deem law enforcement to be too busy to perform searches on everything and everyone. The United States is an attractive target for several geographic and physical reasons: it has sprawling coastlines with small, isolated ports conducive to undetected movements and deserts that make good airfields or parachute drop sites due to the lack of guardianship, allowing for drugs to be picked up undetected. The coastal configuration along the Gulf of Mexico provides drug traffickers with sufficient isolation to enter the southern region of the United States unobserved; physical connectivity to Central America provides land routes through Mexico to many traffickers; and isolated bays along the Californian West Coast which house countless pleasure boats allow for the undetected importation of cocaine by commercial vessels.

Trafficking in persons

Trafficking in persons is a transnational crime that has reached such epidemic proportions that it is now a significant human rights issue. It can involve several dimensions, including the transport of illegal immigrants, the transport of women and children, and the transport of labourers, resulting in either some sort of forced service, such as working under inhumane conditions, prostitution/sexual slavery, illegal adoptions and/or illegal employment. Victims of human trafficking are often highly vulnerable, coming from developing countries and conditions from which people want to escape and will do virtually anything to do so.

The scope of the human trafficking problem is difficult to accurately depict, since it often involves criminal organisations, victims may go unreported, and if the victims do return home there is a significant degree of shame involved in reporting what has occurred. Women and children are increasingly vulnerable. The demand for children, particularly in the sex trade industry, is growing, due, in part, to the increasing prevalence of AIDS. Customers will increasingly pay more for young children who are virgins, on the premise that they are less likely to contract the HIV virus.

Criminal organisations take advantage of these vulnerabilities and arrange illegal crossings of national borders for profit. The prospect of an attractive and well-paying job as a domestic servant or waitress is often falsely advertised, luring vulnerable women and children into a life of exploitation and dependence upon the traffickers for food, shelter and other essentials for survival. Stories of education, profitable employment or success are often used to attract victims. At other times, traffickers employ force, coercion, fraud or deceit. In the end, the victim is forced into prostitution, child labour or even slavery. Prices are often placed on women and children who are sold to brothels in other countries, sometimes by unsuspecting parents who believe their children will be well taken care of.

Regions affected by human trafficking include Western and Eastern Europe, the former Soviet Union, West and Central Africa and Asia. Europol (the European Law Enforcement Organisation) has estimated that this industry is now worth several billion dollars per year.

> **Four factors that contribute to the persistence of the human-trafficking industry:**
>
> - Demand – so long as there is a demand for cheap labour, people who 'purchase' sex, either with adults or children, and others who are willing to act as 'middlemen', there will be a market for human trafficking.
> - Poverty – people in poor regions of the world are forced to rely on the money they receive from selling women and children. In addition to the profit, selling children also reduces the size of the family, thus lessening the financial burden.
> - Attitudes – in many societies, women and children are treated as second-class citizens. Women may be viewed as inferior and are not afforded the same rights as male members of society. Attitudes towards the institution of marriage and legalised prostitution also play a role. It is these attitudes that translate into women and young girls being sold by family as 'property' and then sold by criminals for sex.
> - Political stability and unrest – where state control is lacking, governments are less able to provide protection for vulnerable populations. Conflicts result in the loss of property and livelihood, leading to displacement and increasing vulnerability.

Trafficking in arms

The illicit trafficking in firearms is a covert activity involving the unauthorised movement of firearms across borders for illegal purposes. These firearms may include, but are not limited to, sub-machine guns, semiautomatic rifles, pistols, shotguns and AK-47s, which may be transported by land, sea or air. Porous and unguarded borders make for difficulties in monitoring and controlling the illicit movement of firearms and consequently form ideal conditions for arms traffickers. Such is the case in Nigeria, India, Malaysia and Pakistan.

Once the illegally trafficked firearms are sold, the money received is laundered. The firearms can also be used as currency in exchange for drugs. All of these transactions result in large profits for criminal organisations and have far-reaching effects. Illegally trafficked arms often support already existing ethnic and political conflicts or further the agendas of organisations such as terrorist groups, thus posing a security threat at both national and international levels. Several incidents occurring over the last ten years have suggested that illegal arms trafficking has come to involve the movement of nuclear material, raising much concern from the global community. There have been several seizures of small amounts of nuclear material and suspects in several cases have been identified as Czech, Polish and Russian nationals.

Arms trafficking has made small arms readily available in many parts of the world and thus changed the face of violent conflicts, particularly in developing countries. Conflicts which were once fought with less sophisticated and less efficient weapons (such as spears or bows and arrows) are now waged with automatic weapons, much to the detriment of surrounding communities. The proliferation of weapons is destroying communities by prolonging existing conflicts, kindling new ones and hindering social and economic development.

Money laundering

Transnational criminal organisations aim to generate profit. Many of their activities including drug and arms trafficking, sexual slavery, fraud and embezzlement, make huge sums of money. The problem for these organisations, however, is how to disguise the illegal origins of these funds. Using 'dirty money' raises suspicions among law enforcement and may allow the money to be traced to illegal activities. Money laundering is the process by which illegal profits (or 'dirty money') are made to seem legal or legitimate so that they can be spent or invested without conjuring up suspicion. Illegally acquired funds must be controlled without attracting attention, therefore the criminal organisations disguise their sources, change the form or move the funds to a place where they are less likely to do so.

The most common money laundering method is to transfer funds out of the country, either physically or through electronic wire transfers, while ensuring that the source of the funds is untraceable. Once laundered, the money can be more easily used in legitimate ventures. Once again, globalisation allows money to be moved around the world with considerable speed and ease. Millions of dollars can be instantaneously transferred with the click of a button. Left unchecked, money laundering can cause not just a nation's economy to become unstable but the global economy as well, given the interdependence of countries around the world, and is thus a serious national and international security threat.

Example of simple money laundering scheme: terrorist activities

The convergence of transnational organised crime and terrorist activities is becoming more prominent. Despite their differences in goals and objectives (profit for organised crime groups and political goals for terrorist organisations), with each making use of the other's type of activities, these groups are becoming progressively more intertwined. Organised criminal groups increasingly use terror tactics as a means to eliminate threatening officials, coerce judges, upset investigations and create a climate of fear which furthers additional criminal activity. Moreover, terrorist groups find profit in engaging in criminal activities such as illegal arms trafficking; both the profits and the arms advance the pursuit of their political objectives. Activities

Terrorist activities and financing

The attacks of 11 September 2001 have forced governments to acknowledge that the issue of terrorist financing needs to be looked at in a holistic manner. Terrorists act across borders with connections around the world. Terrorist organisations are very adaptable and adjust their methods of transferring and laundering money as prevention and detection efforts improve. The money they obtain is used to recruit and train terrorists, as well as to pay the family members of terrorists and suicide bombers. Raising money may also involve income obtained from legitimate sources, such as charities or other non-profit organisations, as well as individual donors and businesses. The moving and transferring of money around the world may be done through formal means such as banks, wire transfer systems and charities/non-profit organisations, or through informal transfer systems such as individual couriers and the black market.

such as trafficking illegal arms enables terrorists to acquire power and train and equip recruits. Other illegal money raising activities may include drug trafficking, robbery, extortion, kidnapping and blackmail. It is important to note that terrorists do not necessarily require large sums of money to carry out an attack. Intricate terrorist plots may be executed just as successfully with small amounts of money as with larger amounts.

Bioterrorism is of increasing concern, given that biological weapons have the potential to claim thousands of victims. Biological agents may be bacterial, viral, or toxin agents and can be produced at relatively little expense and with basic biological science skills. Some of the most threatening biological agents are those that cause diseases such as anthrax, tularemia and smallpox. Biological agents require an incubation period before any effects are manifested and can therefore be difficult to contain. For example, a biological agent released on a transit bus, or trans-Atlantic flight, may not make itself known to victims for many hours or days. Once symptoms do appear, victims are dispersed across geographical regions, making detection and response even more difficult. Whether the disease is contagious or not, the implications are many.

Biological terrorism knows no geographical boundaries, and may thus be construed as both a national and a global threat.

Sea piracy

Another area of organised crime is sea piracy. Acts of sea piracy may include the hijacking of ships such as oil tankers and cargo ships, attacking fishermen and stealing their catch, kidnapping and wounding yacht passengers, murder and robbery. These acts are difficult to predict and control, given that pirates can choose to operate near the coasts of countries which lack the resources to control and respond to these crimes. Acts of piracy may occur in international waters, territorial waters or ports and have a distinct spatial pattern, with some coastal areas being affected more than others.

Many piracy incidents occur in the third world and developing countries, which often exhibit the conditions favouring maritime criminality. Piracy is easier in coastal areas which have long, narrow navigational channels or many small islands. These physical characteristics are ideal for slowing maritime traffic and provide strategic

hiding places. Examples of this geography can be found on the Indonesian coast and in the Philippine Islands. Political chaos and economic instability also provide excellent grounds for piracy, as found in Somalia, Sri Lanka and the African west coast. These areas are characterised by civil war and internal political struggles, as well as having little or no maritime law enforcement.

The South China Sea and the Malacca Strait are home to the highest concentration of piracy. South America is also vulnerable, particularly along the coasts of Brazil, Colombia, Ecuador and Nicaragua-Costa-Rica, as are West and East Africa. Many incidents are related to drug trafficking. For the period between 30 June 2004 and the end of September 2004, there were 3,653 incidents of piracy and armed robbery against ships reported to the International Maritime Organisation.

The societal effects of transnational crime and the drug industry

The effects of transnational organised crime and the drug industry on countries around the world are many. In particular, these phenomena are a threat to security and state sovereignty, reinforcing the porous nature of national borders. They contribute to a breakdown in the authority of the state. Governments become corrupt, advancing rather than restricting criminal activity. Corruption of the government facilitates violence by encouraging officials to overlook much of the violence that is taking place, and in some instances the monetary benefits they receive from illegal activity may outweigh the desire to take measures to reduce or contain any violence. Activities such as money laundering allow for organised crime groups to further extend their operations and turn economic power over to the criminals rather than the government.

The loss of government legitimacy and efficacy and the perpetual erosion of government authority in the face of organised crime leads to a general increase in violence and criminal activity. An inefficient state and a dysfunctional judicial system, which lacks the trust of its people, loses control over violence and its ability to enforce the rules of law and protect its property. Authorities then have serious difficulties investigating and punishing any criminal activities and this allows levels of violence that otherwise would have been tempered by government control. Government officials have been known to fall victim to the violence firsthand should they refuse to cooperate or accept bribes. Private citizens, journalists, police, soldiers, judges and government officials at all levels who prove to be uncooperative may all be murdered.

This violence came to a peak in the late 1980s and early 1990s when the Colombian government intensified its 'war on drugs', implementing the extradition treaty with the United States. Large bombs and death threats were prevalent, kidnappings occurred daily and were frequently used to eliminate possible informants and create mass chaos. At the centre of this violence was the Medellin cartel, which was headed by Pablo Escobar until his death in December 1993. Pablo Escobar is sometimes referred to as the most violent criminal in history, known to have offered a

Some of the violent attacks in Colombia carried out by the drug cartels:

- 1987–89: More than 100 political candidates across Colombia were assassinated. Mass killing of peasants, labour organisers and reformers. Over 300 are killed.
- May 1989: Car bomb attack on Major General Marquez, director of the National Police Agency. Four were killed, 50 wounded.
- August-December 1989: Full-scale narco-terrorism. Series of dynamite attacks on political party headquarters, banks and newspapers. Eleven killed, 132 wounded.
- An Avianca airliner was bombed as it was believed to be carrying rival Cali cartel members. 107 people killed. Car bomb at HAS headquarters killed 63 and wounded 600.
- January 1990: Pablo Escobar, head of the Medellin cartel, increased violence against the State and continued the kidnappings of elite family members.
- April–August 1990: Car bombings and narco-terror were expanded to encompass shopping centres and the mass public.
- December 1992-May 1993: Car bombings continued (44 killed, 326 wounded), in particular against the police (167 killed).
- 1993: Virtual civil war broke out between Pablo Escobar and los pepes, a rival drug cartel.

bounty for the head of each Colombian policeman, which led to countless assassinations.

The effects of the drug industry, in particular, can be seen in the violence that has taken over Colombia in the past two decades. In a country with a history of armed conflict, Colombian culture has developed a high tolerance for the use of violence. While the drug cartels directly contribute to the heightened violence through their own activities, they also contribute indirectly by creating and reinforcing a culture that favours easy money and the violent resolution of conflicts rather than resorting to more traditional conflict-solving methods. Human lives are given a monetary value in an industry where money is the primary objective and murder becomes a lucrative endeavour.

The desire for economic gain and the huge demand for illegal narcotics in receiving countries, such as the United States and Europe, have greatly escalated the competition between drug cartels. With an increasingly large market, and the improved speed and ease of international transport, the opportunities for profit also grow. The sheer volume of drugs that can be transported and the profits that result fuel an enhanced desire among the drug cartels for domination over the drug trafficking industry. The money gained from drug trafficking is then reinvested in violence-related commodities such as guns, bombs and electronic equipment.

In what some may consider a strange twist, Colombia's drug control laws also contribute to the heightened state of violence in the country. Specifically, in the late 1980s and early 1990s, Pablo Escobar ran a campaign of terror when the Colombian government agreed to an extradition treaty with the United States to stop the flow of drugs between the two countries. Levels of violence escalated as the cartel members fought to avoid extradition to the United States.

The drug industry also has a large effect on the economy. Naturally, cultivating large amounts of illegal drugs, such as opium poppy or coca leaf, is economically beneficial to many countries. For example, the United Nations suggests that in Peru, the gross potential value of the coca leaf cultivated in 2003 equalled US$112 million. There are approximately 50,000 households that produce coca in Peru. Therefore, overlooking the costs of maintaining the coca farms, the net income per household resulting from the sale of coca leaf is around $1,344 for one year.

At the individual level, it cannot be forgotten that the people of the cultivation and production countries are themselves susceptible to drug addiction. Addiction problems are being reported in countries such as Colombia, Bolivia, Peru and Pakistan. There has also been a spread of addiction to less developed countries, increasing already high levels of vulnerability. According to the United Nations, almost 8 million people in Asia use opiates, accounting for more than half of the opiate users worldwide. These people are concentrated around Afghanistan and Myanmar, which is not surprising given their high production levels. Europe and Oceania also report higher than global average levels of opiate use.

The prevalence of opium use in Northern Laos, in areas where opium poppies are cultivated, was 27 per cent higher than in areas in the same region that did not cultivate opium (based on 2000 data). A 4 per cent prevalence in the population aged 15–64 years in these cultivating regions of Northern Laos is higher than in any other country in the world, demonstrating the connection between production and consumption. The illicit drug industry has also formed alliances with terrorist organisations in some countries, aiding in the financing of terrorist activities. Illicit crops are also planted to the detriment of other naturally occurring vegetation.

Controlling transnational organised crime

Transnational organised crime poses many challenges for law enforcement, given the ease with which the groups operate across borders and infiltrate legitimate businesses. The flexibility and fluidity of these groups allow them to adapt quickly to any challenges put forth by law enforcement, thus limiting the latter's effectiveness. Not only do these organisations appear to be growing in sophistication (as evidenced by increasingly innovative methods of smuggling), they are forming strategic alliances with other criminal organisations.

The emergence and sustainability of criminal organisations is made easier when governments lack legitimacy and authority and become increasingly unstable. Therefore, in order to make any headway in controlling transnational organised crime in its many forms, international cooperation is a necessary element. Cooperation

Initiative to combat sea piracy

In an attempt to combat maritime piracy, the Regional Piracy Centre has been developed, with its headquarters at Kuala Lumpur in Malaysia. The centre acts as an information-clearing point for piracy prevention by providing 24-hour information, reports of attacks and news about suspicious vessel movements. However, methods of data analysis and prevention policies are not fully developed. The wealth of information available from the Regional Piracy Centre, in conjunction with Geographic Information Systems and mapping techniques, has great potential. Geographical information such as the precise coordinates of piracy attacks and the detailed physical characteristics of targeted areas can provide valuable information for controlling and countering these incidents.

among nations is not only required to control existing crime but also to prevent its spread to other weak areas that have not yet been affected. Regular monitoring, increased understanding and heightened awareness of the relocation of criminal organisations to less stable areas, as well as the examination of social, economic and political factors that are conducive to the rise of transnational criminal organisations, will all help in containing this phenomenon.

United Nations Conventions to Reduce and Control Transnational Organised Crime

- United Nations Convention against Transnational Organised Crime and supplemental protocols including:
  - Protocol to Prevent, Suppress and Punish Trafficking in Persons, Especially Women and Children;
  - Protocol against the Smuggling of Migrants by Land, Air and Sea;
  - Protocol against the Illicit Manufacturing of and Trafficking in Firearms, Their Parts and Components and Ammunition, adopted on 15 November 15 2000;
- Convention against Corruption, adopted in December 2004;
- Convention against the Illicit Traffic in Narcotic Drugs and Psychotropic Substances, adopted in 1988

Nationally, aiming to develop a social and cultural consensus against organised crime and raising awareness about the costs of organised crime to society may help in creating a climate where it can no longer flourish to the same extent. Further, effective monitoring and regulation policies may go a long way in curbing money laundering, a staple activity for criminal organisations.

Controlling illicit drugs

The United Nations Global Monitoring Programme of Illicit Crops

The United Nations has implemented the Global Monitoring Programme of Illicit Crops in an attempt to reduce the cultivation of illegal drugs in Asia and Latin America and to develop an 'early warning system' of the potential amounts of illicit drugs bound for illegal retail markets throughout the world. In 1998, it was recognised that there was no widespread and all-inclusive international mechanism to collect and analyse data on international illicit crop production. This programme helps countries to produce internationally comparable data and reference maps on crop production and to use these data to extract global trends.

The monitoring of crop cultivation takes a multi-method approach, incorporating field research involving interviews and field measurement, aerial surveillance, on-the-ground assessment and satellite sensing. The monitoring programme aims at a methodology based on satellite remote sensing, the design and use of a geographic database and Geographic Information System. The GIS, linked to a Global Positioning System (GPS), will incorporate mapping and the collection and analysis of socio-economic data.

As part of the Global Monitoring Programme, the Annual Opium Poppy Survey conducted in Laos amasses large amounts of data examining the distribution of opium poppy throughout the region. Data are collected about the locations of illicit poppy fields by district, as well as their relationship to major roadways. The substantial

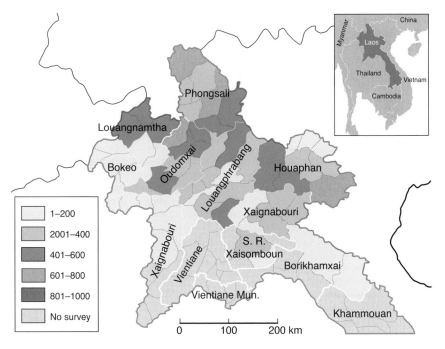

Figure 3.1 Choropleth map of opium poppy cultivation fields by district in Laos, 2001

Source: Global Monitoring Programme of Illicit Crops, 2001. United Nations International Drug Control Programme, United Nations Office for Drug Control and Crime Prevention, Vienna

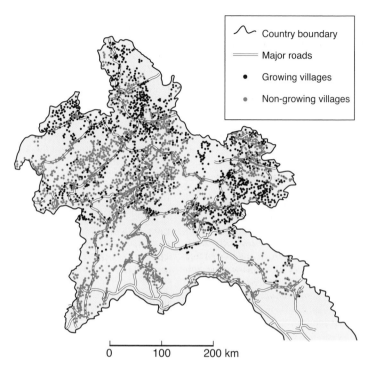

Figure 3.2 Pin map of the relationship between opium poppy fields and major roads

Source: Annual Opium Poppy Survey, 2001. United Nations International Drug Control
Programme, United Nations Office for Drug Control and Crime Prevention, Vienna

number of opium poppy fields translates into large quantities of data from which any patterns are difficult to extract. The use of GIS and mapping technology allows this data to be more readily interpretable, providing visual displays of the spatial components of the opium poppy business (Figure 3.1). For example, when converted to a pin map, the data obtained of the distance between poppy fields and major roadways (Figure 3.2) show that opium poppy growing is more likely the further away one gets from major roads.

These mapping systems, which are also being implemented in countries such as Peru, Colombia, Bolivia, Myanmar and Afghanistan, will be able to locate and quantify illicit coca and opium cultivations and in the process aid in the effective elimination of these crops. Furthermore, it is hoped that these programmes will monitor any displacement of illegal crops that may occur when efforts to eliminate them force growers to move to other regions of each country.

The identification of crop-growing areas also aids in the recognition of regions that will be targeted for alternative development projects. The aim of these programmes is to provide the international community with detailed, reliable information on which to base eradication efforts, as well as with additional insight on how to restrict the transport of drugs from region to region, and will offer a base on which to assess the effectiveness of these efforts in developing alternative means of survival.

With attempts to eradicate illicit drug production, however, come economic crises for the farmers who have been dependent on their drug production for many years as a way of survival. For example, there are strong efforts to implement eradication programmes in Myanmar and Laos, which have been in effect for several years. These programmes have seen a vast reduction in the areas under cultivation since 1996. If this trend continues, over the next few years this area will become virtually inconsequential in the global opium production arena. However, there is evidence that in the eastern portion of Myanmar, many are facing severe humanitarian crises now that a major source of capital has been taken away. Many who live in the remote opium cultivating areas live at standards that are even below that of the general population in a country that ranks 131st out of 175 countries on the Human Development Index.

The drug trafficking industry in Colombia is a major underpinning of the country's economy, pushing billions of dollars into the economy and providing employment to millions of people. Thus, gaining control of the drug trafficking industry in areas such as Colombia raises an important issue: if the industry is dismantled, a major setback to the economy may ensue, contributing to an extreme economic downturn. One must question whether the governments are prepared to eradicate all forms of drug trafficking and production throughout the countries regardless of any economic decline that may follow. The violence brought about by the drug trafficking industry will always be weighed against the consequences of eradication.

Most importantly, it should be recognised that illicit drug trafficking and other transnational organised crimes are *transnational* problems requiring a global solution. As long as the demand for these products and services continues to grow in receiving countries, the criminal organisations have increasing motivation to continue their illegal businesses at an ever-expanding capacity. The emergence of transnational organised crime as a multi-billion-dollar industry provides great incentive to gain monopoly and continue to expand illicit operations. Nationally, detection and prevention methods are necessary in order to lessen the detrimental effects of these crimes, but it should be recognised that global cooperation will be essential over the long term to eradicate these problems.

Further Reading

Adler, F. G., Mueller, G. and Laufer, W. (2001) *Criminology*, 4th edn. New York: McGraw Hill.

Clark, Michele Anne (2003) 'Trafficking in persons: An issue of human security', *Journal of Human Development*, 4(2): 247–263.

Demko, George J. (2000) 'Modern Maritime Piracy,' pp. 149–152 in Turnbull, Linda S., Hallisey Hendrix, Elaine and Dent, Borden D. (eds) *Atlas of Crime: Mapping the Criminal Landscape*, Phoenix: Oryx Press.

Florez, Carol P. and Boyce, Bernadette (1990) 'Colombian Organised Crime', *Police Studies*, 13: 8188, no. 2.

Kenney, D. and Finckenauer, J. (1995) *Organised Crime in America*, Belmont, CA: Wadsworth.

Rabasa, Angel and Chalk, Peter (2001) *Colombian Labyrinth: The Synergy of Drugs and Insurgency and Its Implications for Regional Stability*, Santa Monica: Rand.

Rocha, Ricardo (2000) 'The Colombian Economy after 25 Years of Drug Trafficking', Vienna: United Nations Office for Drug Control and Crime Prevention.

Thoumi, Francisco E. (1999) 'The Impact of the Illegal Drug Industry on Colombia', pp. 311 in Farer, T. (ed) *Transnational Crime in the Americas*, New York: Routledge.

Turnbull, Linda S., Hallisey Hendrix, Elaine and Dent, Borden D. (eds) *Atlas of Crime: Mapping the Criminal Landscape*. Phoenix: Oryx Press.

United Nations International Drug Control Programme (2001a) 'Annual Opium Poppy Survey 2001', Vienna: United Nations.

— (2001b) 'Global Monitoring Programme of Illicit Crops', Vienna: United Nations Office for Drug Control and Crime Prevention.

United Nations Office for Drug Control and Crime Prevention. (2004) *World Drug Report, 2004*, Vienna: United Nations.

— (2000) 'Mapping Opium Poppy,' Vienna: United Nations.

Williams, Phil (ed) (1997) 'Illegal Immigration and Commercial Sex: The New Slave Trade', Special Issue, *Transnational Organised Crime*, 3(4).

Williams, Phil and Savona, Ernesto U. (eds) (1995) 'The United Nations and Transnational Organised Crime', Special Issue. *Transnational Organised Crime*, 1(3).

CHAPTER 4: Economic inequality and welfare

Poverty and inequality: different concepts, difficult realities

One of the most potent sources of protest and conflict in contemporary global politics is the presence of global economic inequality, of which persistent poverty is a consequence and sometimes, it is argued, a cause. Accurate and useful estimations of poverty levels and especially income inequality have always been a concern of social scientists and policy makers.

In recent decades, the technological revolution that gave rise to the latest stage of international economic integration, especially via trade and financial liberalisation – usually termed 'globalisation' – has sparked a more contentious debate. This has centred not only on the study of 'real' levels of income inequality as an end in itself but also on the analysis of inequality that helps to create an accurate picture of the social consequences of the singular speed, depth and width of contemporary globalisation.

The global social movements that have been vocal in opposing this new phase of capitalism have largely based their criticisms on the claim that globalisation increases inequality in the world. Yet supporters of the liberal approach, who see globalisation as a source of development on a global scale, claim that the poor have benefited the most in those places where economic integration has been made more viable, and that this decreases inequality in the long term. What follows is a brief analysis of the ambiguities of recent estimates of inequality. But, before, it is important to determine, even in general terms, why – besides the assessment of the general social consequences of globalisation – inequality matters.

There are many ways in which income inequality can be severely crippling for socioeconomic development, with serious political implications – historically perceived. In the 2001 Human Development Report, Birdsall points out that income inequality with the concentration of income at the top combined with substantial poverty at the bottom of the social pyramid produces political support for policies that may generate even more concentration of income and/or support for populist policies that produce only short-term positive (if any) results. It may well be that the absence of a middle class is detrimental to the development of accountable governments, which ultimately compromises sustainable economic growth and even social welfare (UNDP, 2001). In addition, inequality is likely to erode social capital. This is now a widely used term which, put roughly, refers to trust, collaboration and citizen responsibility, attributes which are also key to the formation of effective political institutions. Social capital determines participation in spheres of community life such as parks, parent-teacher associations of public schools, sports leagues, all of which are undermined by criminality which, in turn, is closely linked to increased levels of inequality within countries.

In the current geopolitical context, global inequality also matters not only as part of a framework for human rights that establishes, among many related functions, the basic right for development, education and freedom but also in strategic geopolitical terms. Although the link between inequality, or poverty itself, and terrorism is not linear and is just one correlation among many that feeds terrorist activity, the 'super empowered angry men' Thomas Friedman mentions as being at the root of global insecurity do certainly rely on those who have little (if any) material wealth and even less in terms of prospective employment or a stable future (Friedman, 2000; Wade, 1999).

The challenge of estimating income inequality

In 1955, Kuznets famously expounded the idea that higher levels of growth would in time lead to less income inequality. However, today it is clear that inequality is far more persistent than expected, even in high-income countries. Thus the links between income inequality and economic growth are not automatically correlated but are mediated by a series of variables, such as voting patterns, market failures (especially in capital markets) and uncertain property rights. In this sense, the discussion becomes wider: not only does it matter to understand how growth can produce inequality but also how inequality inhibits the chances of economic growth.

Much controversy underlies the debate on income inequality. Although recent estimates have been developed by technically consistent studies, albeit using different measures, variables, data sets and interpretations of the concepts studied, they have sometimes produced very different conclusions as to a recent rise or fall in inequality, especially among countries or in total world inequality. On the one hand, there are those who believe that the proportion of people living in extreme poverty in developing countries declined in the 1990s. On the other hand, there are studies that point to modest gains by the poor in the same period. Yet there are many NGOs which claim that the last decade has led to greater poverty. Even more convincing, and now receiving increased international attention, is a study (possibly the first in a series) that challenges the methodology used by the World Bank and claims that inequality has been grossly underestimated by conventional analyses.

Inevitably, different answers to the question of whether or not inequality has been rising can feed diverse political and ideological positions. The street protests organised by international social movements/networks in world capitals during World Bank, IMF and G-8 meetings are derived from the belief that globalisation leads to rich people getting richer and the poor increasingly becoming poorer. The political impact of this perception is unquestionably substantial. Yet those who see globalisation as a source of unmatched opportunities for development claim that inequality decreases in countries that have managed to introduce reforms that allow for more liberalisation of markets, thus taking advantage of this process of global integration as much as possible. To them, it is less and not more globalisation that leads to inequality.

Rather than try to settle the debate, it is important to acknowledge some of the elements that need to be clear when using these different studies, as well as some of the evidence that seems most plausible in explaining the difficult reality of inequality.

What is being measured and how: ambiguities and controversy

First, it is crucial to understand that 'poverty', 'inequality' and even 'welfare' are vague concepts, subject to different interpretations. While for microeconomic theory 'welfare' refers to utility and satisfaction, other interpretations of the word take into account elements of 'quality of life' rooted in a philosophical understanding of the human condition and human needs (see, for example, Sen and Nussbaum, 1993; Strengmann-Kuhn, 2000). Inequality also may point to a different picture if taken in 'relative' or 'absolute' terms. Economists typically use 'relative inequality' as referring to the ratio of individual income as compared with a mean of overall income. If all incomes grow at the same rate, relative inequality remains unchanged. When it comes to analysing the effects of trade openness, which is an important component of globalisation, on income distribution, a common finding is that greater trade openness has about the same impact on the growth rate of income at different levels of income. That is not a definitive piece of evidence, but when talking about relative inequality, discrepancies are not so outstanding (Ravallion, 2003).

However, 'absolute inequality' refers to the absolute differences in incomes. So when incomes grow by the same ratio but starting from an unequal base, inequality in absolute terms inevitably also rises. Thus when they say that inequality has been rising considerably in the recent years, it is absolute inequality that they usually mean. As Ravallion claims, no one concept is more correct than the other; they reflect judgement calls about what really constitutes 'inequality'.

In the same sense, 'poverty' is also an imprecise concept by its very nature. As stated before, determining levels of poverty depends on how incomes fall in relation to a 'poverty line'. This will vary considerably according to which of many views of what 'poverty' really means has been adopted. Most recently, an engaging debate has developed, which is gaining notoriety in academic circles as well as in the media, regarding the methodology used by international institutions, such as the World Bank, for measuring levels of inequality. Normally, the standard parity purchase power (PPP) framework is favoured. PPP is a method of arriving at an accurate exchange rate for foreign currencies. It tries to come up with average price levels for all commodities, weighted by their share in international expenditure, so as to make it possible to compare not simply income levels but what people can actually purchase with the money they make.

Sanjay Reddy and Thomas Pogge have claimed that the PPP framework leads to a mistaken assessment of real poverty levels. They argue that in order to evaluate accurately whether a household is poor, consumption and income must be related not to the local price level of commodities in general but to the local cost of a basket of basic necessities, generically described to allow for variations in how the poor in different locations meet their nutritional and other basic needs. In order to avoid the arbitrariness of the $1/day standard suggested by PPP calculations, a basket based on specific needs and local realities must be specified. This avoids the obvious lack of real comparability if, for example, the cost of rice is included in both India and Iceland. Both this effort and the effort of actually measuring inequality using this new methodology are yet to be developed. However, Reddy and Pogge do anticipate that the results to be revealed would prove that World Bank estimates (as well as those of analysts who rely heavily on the Bank's data) severely underestimate income inequality levels in the world today.

Inequality among and within countries/regions

In addition to measurement discrepancies and ambiguities, another source of confusion in determining inequality is whether it is inequality between countries or within countries that is being referred to.

According to Birdsall, the ratio of average income of the richest country in the world to that of the poorest rose from about 9:1 at the end of the nineteenth century to at least 60:1 in 1999. This means that the average family in the United States is 60 times richer than the average family in Ethiopia. In addition, since 1950, while the population of poor countries increased 250 per cent, that of rich countries grew by less than 50 per cent.

Latin America and the Caribbean are the regions with the highest levels of income inequality. In 13 of the 20 countries with data for the 1990s, the poorest 10 per cent of the population had less than one-twentieth of the income of the richest 10 per cent, according to UNDP in 2001. This severe inequality means that millions of people are living in extreme poverty. In Brazil, for example, the ratio of income of the top 20 per cent of earners to the bottom is about 25:1, making the country probably the world's most unequal (compared with about 10:1 in the United States and about 5:1 in Western Europe). Although Peru, Colombia and Mexico registered the greatest wage increases in the region, the gap between the skilled and the unskilled rose in the 1990s by more than 30 per cent in Peru, 20 per cent in Colombia and nearly 25 per cent in Mexico. The most populous countries in the world, China and India have enjoyed faster income growth than the rich countries. However, it would take them almost a century of constant growth at rates higher than those in today's industrialised countries just to reach current US income level.

In sub-Saharan Africa poverty is widespread, spreading a number of epidemic diseases, condemning a huge number of adults in their prime to death. In 16 of the 22 countries in sub-Saharan Africa with data for the 1990s, the poorest 10 per cent of the population earned less than one-tenth of the income of the richest 10 per cent. Conclusions as to the causes and patterns of such a problem, however, are still lacking due to limited available data. Eastern Europe has relatively low inequality, though Russia and Lithuania have registered increases in the recent decade.

Among OECD countries, while inequality is low, there is diversity in the levels of inequality between countries. The United Kingdom and the United States have high levels of inequality in their group. Birdsall points out that income inequality in the latter grew in recent years not only because profits were sometimes unusually high (especially in the financial sector) but because there were losses of income for the bottom income level of the population. She claims that the average wage of white male high-school graduates fell 15 per cent from 1973 to 1993, and the number of men aged 25 to 54 years earning less than $10,000 a year grew. Possibly for the first time in US history, educational gains may be reinforcing rather than off-setting income inequality: higher education has become a prerequisite for economic success, but because access to it depends on family income, the poor are at a disadvantage.

In conclusion, although there is controversy about global inequality trends, there seems to be evidence that inequality *is* rising within many countries. However, rising inequality is not correlated with growth rates. Ravallion explains that even among growing economies, 'inequality tends to fall about as often as it rises' (Ravallion, 2003, p. 7).

The welfare state and the notion of 'embedded liberalism': a brief background

In *The Great Transformation*, Polanyi explored the socially disruptive and polarising tendencies in the world economy driven by what he called the self-regulating market. Those tendencies were characterised by a 'double movement', within which an unprecedented expansion of the market coexisted with massive social disruption and a sharp political reaction in the form of public demands on the state to counteract the deleterious effects of such market-driven capitalism. Indeed, for Polanyi, this double movement ultimately generated the political context of the 1930s and produced a breakdown in liberal economic structures, leading to the phenomena of depression, fascism, unemployment and nationalism, which combined to push the world towards war after 1937 (Polanyi, 1944).

However, after the Second World War, the international economic order assumed a new and very distinct feature. Unlike the economic nationalism of the 1930s or the *laissez-faire* liberalism of the gold standard and free trade years, the new multilateralism that emerged was based on domestic governmental intervention. This was a kind of political bargain and it shaped the post-war economic order: it has been termed by John Ruggie 'the compromise of embedded liberalism'. One side of the bargain involved the recognition of the advantages of international

liberalisation while the other required the provision of domestic social safety nets to relieve the dislocations of those who lost out from heightened international competition in local markets. Thus, from the start, international liberalisation was coupled with a domestic social compact in which 'governments asked their public to embrace the change and dislocation that comes with liberalisation in return for the promise of help in containing and socialising the adjustment costs' (Ruggie, 1994, p. 4). Hence, as Pauly summarises, the compromise combined the ideal of liberal international markets with the practical reality of national economic regulation (Pauly, 1997).

In fact, empirical evidence confirms that there is a strong positive correlation between openness to trade and the growth of government activity in many countries since the 1960s. Societies (rich and poor alike) have demanded and received a larger government role as the price of exposing themselves to greater amounts of external risks. This finding leads to an important conclusion: the social welfare state is the flip side of the open economy since wherever external risk is perceived to increase when liberalisation occurs, the importance of government intervention in the shape of the provision of social insurance is accentuated significantly.

Globalisation and the end of the embedded liberalism compromise: new challenges ahead

However, the internationalisation and integration of production, investment and trade – economic globalisation – plays a challenging role in this scenario and threatens the basic bargain of 'embedded liberalism'. On one side, public opinion polls show that, despite the perception of a backlash against expansionary fiscal policies, due to the spread of neoliberal practices worldwide with their emphasis on the economic perils of interventionism, the principles behind the welfare state remain highly popular among broad segments of society. On the other side, it is possible to attest that confidence in government spending has diminished considerably in most advanced countries.

The combination of these two facts leads to what Rodrik considers to be the dilemma brought about by globalisation: it results in increased demands on the state to provide social insurance while reducing its ability to perform that role effectively. Indeed, there is a visible tension between the consequences of globalisation and the requirements for maintaining the social legitimacy of free trade and other pieces of economic liberalisation that inevitably impose wide domestic social costs, along (at times) with gains that tend, however, to remain concentrated, sometimes by policy on one societal group.

According to Ruggie there are two sources of 'disembeddedness' of the state. One has to do with the success of the post-war trade regime in liberalising the economy. As barriers to the flow of economic transactions were eliminated and cross-border market forces were encouraged, some of the standard policy tools the government had in its power to manage the consequences of this liberalisation were lost. The result of this process was the denationalisation of capital, or put in other words, the increasing separation of national ownership from the physical location of production. The second source of disembeddedness is related to the weakening of domestic social safety nets throughout the capitalist world. Ruggie blames this outcome on the decline in productivity and competition from low-labour-cost countries in the context of closer integration in international production networks, as well as on the weight of the welfare state itself on national budgets. Budget deficits and tax-weary publics compelled governments to shrink the traditional web of social policies significantly.

In addition, at the same time as fiscal austerity was being pursued, added pressure from global capital for reduced taxes and labour costs has driven many governments to cut back welfare programmes. In an effort to boost global competitiveness, 'governments across the planet have, since 1980, rolled back social democracy and dismantled state socialism', each following very similar macroeconomic programmes based on neoliberal premises (Scholte, 1997, p. 448).

According to the UNDP Human Development Report of 1999, in developing countries as well, the fiscal resource base is being squeezed. That can be perceived in four ways. The first happens through trade liberalisation and the reduction in trade taxes that follows it. The second has to do with the fact that transnational operations are difficult to tax. Third, countries compete in lowering their corporate and capital gains taxes, reducing tax receipts – a pattern inaugurated by developed countries. Finally, the growth of the informal economy is translated into a substantial reduction in tax revenues in many countries.

Consequently, as the resource base in developing countries shrinks, the demand for public resources increases, but in the face of reduced revenues, states are reducing spending. Public spending on health and education in countries with low human development declined from 2 per cent of GDP in 1986–1990 to 1.8 per cent in 1991–1996 (UNDP, 1999).

The place of the state in the context of globalisation

Given these facts about both developed and developing countries, it is important to place this analysis within the context of the vast literature on globalisation. To acknowledge an increasing and wide trend in the reduction of public social spending is not to say that the state has grown 'powerless' in the face of globalisation because its capacity to dictate fiscal and monetary policies is subject to the restless moods of global capital. But equally this approach does not deny the fact that important changes are indeed happening in the real power of the state due to globalisation.

Even those who do not accept the argument of the 'powerlessness of the state' admit that there are significant constraints on government capacity to make and implement policy. In fact, the general slide towards more fiscally conservative policies, both on the left and on the right, entailing tax reforms as well as a significant reduction in social spending, is a reality for states; and this is so at a time when social disparities remain high and are likely to become even more a source of political stress in the context of a global recession.

Because of this, it is important to identify the new features of the state in the context of globalisation. In other words, what kind of state are we talking about? It is not a 'powerless state'; neither is it a Keynesian, welfare-producing, interventionist state. It is best described as a 'negotiator state'. This view is explored by Sassen as she explains that the role of the state in today's global economy, unlike in earlier times, has been to negotiate the intersection between national law and foreign actors – whether firms, markets or supra-national organisations. This condition makes the current phase distinctive. The existence of an enormously elaborate body of law that secures the exclusive territoriality of national states to an extent not seen in earlier centuries has now to be seen cohabiting with a considerable institutionalising of the 'rights' of non-national firms, cross-border transactions and supra-national organisations. This illustrates the unavoidable engagement by national states in the process of globalisation and confirms its cooptation with global capital.

Thus, globalisation is not just a matter of crossing geographic borders, as is captured by measuring international investment and trade. It also has to do with the relocation of national public governance functions to transnational private arenas and with the development inside national states – through legislation, court rulings, executive orders – of the mechanisms necessary to accommodate the rights of the global capital in what are still national territories under the exclusive control of their states.

In the light of these facts, a final question needs to be asked: can the bargain of 'embedded liberalism' be sustained – i.e., the combination of economic liberalisation internationally with the provision of social insurance domestically via interventionist public policies? For Rodrik, that is unlikely to happen if governments lose their autonomy in generating tax revenues and shaping social policies. Again, global capital increasingly demands both austerity and the continuation of the agenda of liberalisation in the places it will invest, allowing governments in rich and poor countries only limited room for manoeuvre in policymaking – and in poor countries significantly less, if any. In fact, the slowdown in the 1990s followed a period of inflation, deficit spending and increasing government debt levels around the industrialised world. Hence, in order to stabilise their budgets, states adopted stringent monetary fiscal policies, which were the ones deemed sustainable or credible by financial markets because they favoured financial stability over employment. This became known as the 'politics of financial credibility' and created a crucial pressure, forcing cuts in social spending at a time when the geopolitical scenario had led to higher than ever expenditures on security in some developed countries.

From 'unequal terms of trade' to a 'race to the bottom'?

In the 1960s a theory of development emanating from developing countries emphasised that international trade was based on an unequal exchange between rich and poor countries. Those less industrialised countries especially reliant on exports of raw materials faced unequal terms of trade with industrialised countries whose export prices used to rise disproportionately more than the prices of the raw materials they imported. This theoretical understanding of the realities of underdevelopment became known as 'dependency theory' and was at the root of a strategy of industrialisation via import substitution that developing countries, especially in Latin America, followed in the 1960s and 1970s. This strategy followed the logic that protecting the national market was necessary to stimulate the evolution of national industries.

Although it is now understood that import substitution had merits in fostering industrialisation in developing countries, it failed to produce sustainable improvements via increased employment and the fostering of international competitiveness in Latin America. By contrast, in East Asia where an export-oriented economy took shape, the 1980s was a time of growth and not the 'lost decade' that it became for protectionist economies. In the late 1980s and especially in the 1990s, the interventionist ideas that had motivated 'dependency theorists' were vigorously exchanged for the neoliberal approach of international institutions and applied by local technocrats. This emphasised international 'free' trade – or the significant reduction in trade barriers worldwide – as a key to 'development'.

Developed country workers and trade liberalisation

An interesting twist in this story – seldom related to it – was the intense debate in the 1990s about the damaging effects of trade liberalisation to workers in *developed* countries. Trade unions and NGOs (most notably) were vocal in claiming that 'globalisation' led to a 'race to the bottom' phenomenon. That is to say, they believed (and some still do) that because of international competition and the fact that developing countries are abundant in low-skilled labour, the wages of this labour were lower than the pay of low-skilled labour in developed countries. As markets are already interconnected and international trade becomes more open, firms have the option of buying low-skilled labour in developing countries (especially by building plants in these countries). So, there is pressure – it is argued – for the reduction of the wages of low-skilled labour in developed countries. This would characterise the infamous race to the bottom, which fuels contentious 'anti-globalisation' movements.

The USA of the 1970s, 1980s and 1990s registered greater earnings differentials between older and younger workers, and greater differentials between high-skilled and low-skilled occupations. Also, the economic position of low-skilled men has fallen by staggering amounts (Freeman, 2000). In Europe, the problem was less one of income differentials and more of the availability of jobs, chiefly because wages are less flexible there than in the USA. Whether it is earning inequalities or joblessness that is the major concern, the question remains for both the USA and Europe as to what has caused this decline in the relative supply for low-skilled labour. Is there indeed a race to the bottom?

It is a fact that trade between the USA and Europe and developing countries has increased significantly in the last two decades. This was the result of several developments, especially the significant reduction in trade barriers which followed from international trade agreements and trade reforms in developing countries, and the vigorous 'support' of the IMF and the World Bank for export-oriented strategies as a source of growth and capital for debt repayment in developing countries. As more international trade is still intrafirm trade, the increase in overall trade among rich and poor countries is intimately linked also to the expansion of multinational firms which outsource production to places where labour is cheaper.

Despite these facts, there is insufficient evidence to see trade with developing countries as *the* culprit for the decrease in demand for low-skilled labour in developed countries. Freeman explains that the race to the bottom argument is not consistent with evidence in the USA, where wage differences among states and localities have persisted for decades despite free trade, migration and capital flows. Also, 'among countries, wage differences between workers with seemingly similar skills have also persisted for decades, albeit exaggerated by the divergences between purchasing power parities and exchange rates, and by differences in skills that are hard to measure' (Freeman, 2000, p. 348).

Increased trade with developing countries may have produced some of the reduction in wages of low-skilled workers in developed countries, but it does not account for all of it. As Freeman concludes, the debate over the causes for the 'immiseration' of less-skilled workers has an element of a judgement call about it. Increased trade with developing countries is not the sole culprit. Freeman concludes that 'technological changes that occur independent of trade, unexpected political developments, such as German reunification, policies to educate and train workers, union activities, the compensation policies of firms, and welfare state and related social policies' have historically played a crucial role in determining workers' well-being and will remain crucial determinants of wages and employment in the future (Freeman, 2000, p. 352).

This debate is certainly not likely to become less salient, however. Global recession and the deepening of trade integration (most notably via the consolidation of the Free Trade Area of the Americas) are likely to fuel strong political reactions among different interest groups. The inability of modern states to compensate the losers from globalisation is likely to make matters even more serious.

Sovereign debt and the challenges it poses for economic welfare

Debt has always been a difficult part of the reality of developing countries. Defaults on debt payments have existed for as long as credit itself. Indeed, the problems of debt servicing preceded Mexico's first foreign loan after independence in 1827. However, debt has become a particularly prominent issue in international debates on economic development in recent decades.

Much of that has to do with the strong activism emerging from transnational social networks and campaigns which have not only brought the issue to the forefront of economic discussions but have stressed the link between debt and human rights. Thus, the reasons for the current salience of debt in the global economy are intimately linked to the emergence and recognition of movements such as the Jubilee 2000 Coalition (now the Jubilee Research) and the recent technological advances that have permitted the proliferation of information via the Internet. Using this last is a core piece of these activists' technique.

In addition, this reconsideration of debt as a severe economic constraint to development has been an ongoing process within international financial institutions since the 1980s. Although there was a clear perception as long ago as 1967 that debt service payments were becoming severely constraining to some countries, debt relief began to flow to poor countries only in 1979 as a product of the 1977–1979 UNCTAD meetings. These led to official creditors writing off $6 billion in debt to 45 poor countries. Debt relief initiatives followed, culminating in the HIPC Initiative of 1996, managed by the World Bank and the IMF. This programme, which involves a comprehensive framework for debt relief under conditions of macroeconomic management (via stabilisation programmes supported by the Bank and the Fund), has been criticised for several reasons. These range from complaining about its complexity to the idea that relief under the Initiative is 'too little too late' and should be less reliant on pervasive IMF conditionalities and 'unrealistic' calculations of debt sustainability.

Moreover, one could also add many other aspects that may have reactivated the debt discussion at the international level. The deregulation of financial markets in most developing countries has allowed for a more volatile environment, in which debt, issued in the form of sovereign bonds, is traded and consequently subjected to the swings of speculative investment by increasingly numerous and dispersed groups of private creditors. Recent financial crises have brought to the front the intimate connections between international (unregulated) financial markets, currency crises and ultimately debt crises. Debt thus became an issue of interest not only to debtors and the social activists who support cancellation and relief but also to financial market players and, naturally, increasingly to international financial institutions, especially the IMF, which acts as a 'lender of last resort' in times of chaos.

There are important differences between debt as a macroeconomic issue in middle-income countries, where the issue is seen in terms of alternative mechanisms for debt restructuring, and in low-income countries, where the debate concerns cancellation, relief and aid. Despite these differences, the scale of debt problems is indeed substantial overall. The debt owed by the most highly indebted countries in the world is about $170 billion (in 1999 nominal terms).

Approximately 50 per cent of this is owed to bilateral creditors such as the United States, Japan, France and other European countries. Moreover, while 37 per cent of the total is owed to multilateral creditors, the World Bank, the IMF and the regional and sub-regional development bank, 13 per cent is owed to private creditors. The debt of the highly indebted, poorest countries in the world represents only 8 per cent of the. developing countries' approximate $2 trillion debt and only 35 per cent of the debt of all low-income countries.

Although current debt discussions signal some new elements in the global economy, the burden of debt has always been substantial especially for low-income countries, which depend on international lending from multilateral institutions, as they are considered too risky an

---

In Africa (34 countries):

Angola, Benin, Burkina Faso, Burundi, Cameroon, Central African Republic, Chad, Comoros, Congo, Democratic Republic of Congo, Ivory Coast, Ethiopia, The Gambia, Ghana, Guinea, Guinea-Bissau, Kenya, Liberia, Madagascar, Malawi, Mali, Mauritania, Mozambique, Niger, Rwanda, Sierra Leone, Sao Tome and Principe, Senegal, Somalia, Sudan, Tanzania, Togo, Uganda and Zambia.

In Latin America (4 countries):

Bolivia, Guyana, Honduras, Nicaragua

In Asia (3 countries):

Laos, People Dem. Rep., Vietnam, Myanmar (Burma)

In the Middle East (1 country):

Republic of Yemen

'Highly Indebted Poor Countries': List of Countries.
Source: World Bank, 'About the HIPC Initiative',
http://www.worldbank.org/hipc/about/map/map.html

---

investment to attract private capital. There are two direct effects from indebtedness under these circumstances. One is the impact of servicing debt on the national budget, because it leads to a reduction in the allocation of resources in social spending, probably already a small amount. Secondly, there is no doubt that highly indebted poor countries face severe budgetary constraints and therefore lack resources to invest in basic social service provision.

In fact, the debt burden of the poorest countries is 93 per cent of their income. According to a report produced by the United Nations

Development Programme, cited by Sachs, Tanzania, for example, has been spending nine times more for debt servicing than for basic health and four times more than for primary education. Moreover, in Ethiopia, where more than 100,000 children die annually from easily preventable diseases, debt payments are four times more than public spending on health care. Sachs describes further this dramatic situation with the case of Zambia, which spent more than 30 per cent of its national budget on debt payments each year during the 1990s but only 10 per cent on basic social services. In fact, the Zambian government's annual health expenditures per person are estimated to be $17, compared with G7 expenditures on health care of around $2,300 per person. But to make matters worse, in Zambia 20 per cent of the population is HIV positive (as of 1999) and it is estimated that around 9 per cent of Zambian children under 15 have lost a mother or both parents to AIDS. Half of all Zambians have no access to safe drinking water and approximately 30 per cent of children remain unvaccinated. Indeed, 'life expectancy has dropped to 43 years in the country and is expected to decline still further as AIDS continues to take its toll' (Sachs, 1999).

In addition, in Africa as a whole, where only one child in two goes to school, governments transfer four times more to northern creditors in debt payments than they spend on health and education. Of 27 countries, only 10 spend more on basic social services than on debt servicing (as of 1998). Those services include basic education, basic health care, safe water and sanitation provision, family planning and nutrition. Indeed, in many countries, the combined expenditure on defence and debt is higher than that on basic social services and often higher than the combined budgets for health and education.

Increasingly, debates on debt relief focus on the option of cancellation, because they spur fundamental questions about the legitimacy of the debts owned by developing countries. Indeed, considerations about the legacy of debts entered into by corrupt and otherwise illegitimate governments are central to the advocacy for debt cancellation. Few analysts disagree on the fact that requiring citizens of poor countries to pay debts accumulated by undemocratic regimes, and for purposes never intended to benefit them, is inherently unjust. This is, in fact, a persuasive scenario in which arguments for debt relief gain more support.

Some characteristics of highly indebted poor countries

■ **Highly indebted:** The debt of HIPC Initiative-eligible countries grew from about $59 billion in 1980 to $170 billion in 1999, which increased the average debt-to-export ratio from 199 per cent to 414 per cent and the average debt-to-GNP ratio from 31 per cent in 1981 to 103 per cent in 1999.

■ **Poor:** Of the total population of 615 million, almost half lives on less than $1 a day. With slow growth, the global number and proportion of poor people have increased in the past two decades.

■ **High receipt of official development assistance (ODA):** Gross transfers in the form of grants and loans from bilateral and multilateral donors and creditors in the past two decades amounted to about $445 billion in constant 1995 dollars. On average, net transfers (gross transfers minus debt transfers) paid by them to the group of countries that eventually become HIPCs were about 10 per cent of their GDP in the 1990s, representing as much as 60 per cent of government revenue and financing. Transfers often exceeded revenue collection by governments.

■ **Unmanageable stock of debt:** The high levels of development assistance and the stagnation in exports and government revenue (which resulted from the low growth) combined to produce a more and more unmanageable stock of debt.

Sources: Birdsall, Nancy and John Williamson, Delivering on Debt Relief, 2002; Sachs, Jeffrey, 'Implementing Debt Relief for the HIPCs', 1999; UNAIDS, Fact Sheet Sub-Saharan Africa, 2002; UNAID and WHO, 'Aids Epidemic Update', December 2002

Of the nearly $140 billion of loans committed to HIPCs between 1972 and 1999, about 60 per cent has gone to countries considered not free in the year they received the funds. Between 1982 and 1995, 33 per cent of these loans went to countries ranked by the International Country Risk Guide as corrupt and not free. Although some of these loans were never delivered, as Birdsall and Williamson conclude, the facts show that creditors have funded utterly illegitimate governments. Because the debts acquired under such singular circumstances are outstanding and delay a possibility of development for the poorest countries in the world, they are usually referred to as 'odious debts' and are inevitably the object of international scrutiny, both at the level of increasingly engaged international advocacy by civil society-based groups and at the level of official creditors involved in the HIPC initiative.

Cases of 'odious debts' reveal an essential feature of the debt debate, especially when it comes to making efforts towards achieving significant relief. They point to the fact that not all debts acquired by sovereigns – especially in the cases of the poorest countries with illegitimate regimes – are to be subjected to the obligation of repayment. In other words, the argument in this case is that loans received by corrupt governments – not used to serve the population they ruled in any welfare-increasing aspect – cannot be expected to be repaid by the legitimate governments that took office later.

It is also important to notice that odious debt cases are not all confined to the group of countries which qualifies for debt relief under the HIPC initiative. Notably, South Africa and Croatia are not candidates for HIPC-granted debt relief. In these cases, perhaps, the argument of odious debt itself – and not simply the claim for cancellation of debts based on assessments of economic sustainability – seems to hold strength as an argument for writing off such debts.

The 'digital' and 'ecological' divides

Income inequality is a consequence and a producer of other kinds of inequalities. In some sense, it is a consequence, according to Sachs, of an 'ecological divide' – although this is by no means the only cause of inequality and extreme poverty. By 'ecological divide' is meant the profound effect that the geographical circumstance can have, whether as an encouragement to their development or as a crucial obstacle to growth. The poorest countries in the world are not merely an 'underdeveloped' version of rich countries. If that were true, the alleviation of poverty would be an easier task. However, as Sachs emphasises, 'the poor live in different ecological zones, face different health conditions and must overcome agronomic limitations that are very different from those of rich countries'.

Hunger is not only a product of inefficient or corrupt governance but of serious ecological conditions, such as droughts and low productivity of the land in some tropical areas. The vast spread of diseases such as malaria, hookworm, sleeping sickness and schistosomiasis (whose transmission often depends on a warm climate) is not only a result of inadequate health policies but a sign that scientific breakthroughs are confined to rich countries, even if they are sometimes achieved by scientists who came from a poor country. In the case of malaria, for example, tropical conditions allow the infection to spread. Mosquito control is expensive and not always effective. If more resources were invested in the search for a vaccine, things could be different. Yet research and development of this kind demands a market. The biggest vaccine producers believe there is no market in malaria and international subsidies that could provide the large labs with incentives to produce the needed vaccines to cure tropical diseases are not available.

The emphasis of development economists on the role of institutions seems to neglect the fact that the countries which have prospered the most in the current context of globalisation are not only places where institutions are efficiently managed and were well developed, but places where geographical conditions were favourable to their closer integration into global production systems, thus allowing them to benefit from the inflow of international capital. This is the case in a number of developing countries and/or regions experiencing some level of economic growth, such as the coastal regions of east Asia, coastal China, Korea, Taiwan, Hong Kong SAR, Singapore, Thailand, Malaysia and Indonesia. Impoverished regions with unfavourable geographical conditions were excluded from possibly benefiting from globalisation and are 'trapped in poverty'. These are countries in most of sub-Saharan Africa, central Asia, large parts of the Andean region and the highlands of Central America.

Moreover, income inequality also produces a 'digital divide' in that there is a sharply uneven diffusion of information and communications technology among different regions of the world and also within countries. Not only is new technology largely produced in OECD countries (even if through using foreign labour from developing countries), but the use of this technology is also highly uneven. OECD countries, with only 14 per cent of the world's population, accounted for 86 per cent of patent applications filed in 1998 and 85 per cent of scientific and technical journal articles published worldwide. Not surprisingly, these are also the countries that invest the most in research and development: 2.4 per cent compared with 0.6 per cent in South Asia. Because innovation also means ownership, which produces profits in the form of royalties and licences, economic inequality is also a part of this picture. Of worldwide royalty and licence fees in 1999, 54 per cent went to the United States and 12 per cent to Japan (UNDP, 2001).

Technology use is uneven within countries. Internet use in urban regions is greater than in rural ones; it is concentrated among the better educated and the young, and in many regions men are more connected than females. In China, the 15 least connected provinces, with 600 million people, have only 4 million Internet users, while Shanghai and Beijing (with 27 million people) have 5 million users. In the Dominican Republic, 80 per cent of Internet users live in Santo Domingo, the capital. In Thailand, 90 per cent of the users live in urban areas, while in India, from 1.4 million Internet connections, more than 1.3 million are in only five states – Delhi, Karnatake, Maharashtra, Tamil Nadu and Mumbai. In Chile, 89 per cent of Internet users have had tertiary education. The numbers for Sri Lanka and China are 65 per cent and 70 per cent, respectively. Men make up 86 per cent of users in Ethiopia, 83 per cent in Senegal, 70 per cent in China, 67 per cent in France and 62 per cent in Latin America (UNDP, 2001).

Further Reading

Bhagwati, Jagdish N. (2002) 'Coping with Anti-Globalisation: A Trilogy of Discontents', *Foreign Affairs*, January/February.

Bhalla, Sunjit (2002) *Imagine There's No Country: Poverty, Inequality and Growth in the Era of Globalisation*, Washington, DC: Institute for International Economics.

Birdsall, Nancy (1998) 'Life is Unfair: Inequality in The World', *Foreign Policy*, no. 111, Summer.

— (2002) 'Policy Selectivity Foregone: Debt and Donor Behaviour in Africa', Centre for Global Development, Working Paper 17, October.

Birdsall, Nancy and Williamson, John (2002) *Delivering on Debt Relief: From IMG Gold to a New Aid Architecture*, Washington, DC: Centre for Global Development and Institute for International Economics.

Chen, Shaohua and Ravallion, Martin (2001) 'How Did the World's Poorest Fare in the 1990s?', *Review of Income and Wealth*, 47, pp. 283–300.

Cheru, Fantu (2001) 'The HIPC Initiative: A Human Rights Assessment of Poverty Reduction Strategy Papers', UN Commission on Human Rights, New York, 18 January.

Dollar, David (2001) 'Globalisation, Inequality, and Poverty since 1980', November, World Bank, mimeo.

Dollar, David and Kraay, Aart (2002) 'Spreading the Wealth', *Foreign Affairs*, January/February.

Easterly, William (1999) 'How Did Highly Indebted Poor Countries Become Highly Indebted?: Reviewing Two Decades of Debt Relief', manuscript, Washington, DC: World Bank.

Freeman, Richard B. (2000) 'Are Your Wages Set in Beijing?' in Frieden, Jeffrey A. and Lake, David A. (eds) *International Political Economy*, 4th edn, Boston/New York: Bedford/St Martin's.

Friedman, Thomas (2000) *The Lexus and the Olive Tree*, New York: Anchor Books.

International Monetary Fund and World Bank (1999) 'Heavily Indebted Poor Countries (HIPC) Initiative – Perspectives on Current Framework and Options for Change', 2 April, www.imf.org/external/np/hipc/options/options.pdf

Kapstein, Ethan B. (1996) 'Workers and the World Economy', *Foreign Affairs*, vol. 75, no. 3, May/June, pp. 16–37.

Kremer, Michael and Jayachandran, Seema (2002) 'Odious Debt', *Finance and Development*, vol. 39, no. 2, Washington, DC: IMF.

Krugman, Paul (1993) 'The Uncomfortable Truth about NAFTA', *Foreign Affairs*, November/December.

Milanovic, Branko (2002) 'The Two Faces of Globalisation: Against Globalisation as We Know It', May, World Bank, mimeo.

Mittelman, James (2000) *The Globalisation Syndrome: Transformation and Resistance*, Princeton: Princeton University Press.

Monbiot, George (2003) 'Poor, But Pedicured', *The Guardian*, 6 May.

Nyang'oro, Julius E. (1999) 'Hemmed in? The State in Africa and Global Liberalisation', in Smith, David A., Solinger, Dorothy J. and Topik, Steven (eds), *States and Sovereignty in the Global Economy*, London: Routledge.

Pauly, Louis W. (1997) *Who Elected the Bankers? Surveillance and Control in the World Economy*, Ithaca: Cornell University Press.

Pierson, Paul (2001) *The New Politics of the Welfare State*, Oxford: Oxford University Press.

Polanyi, Karl (1944) *The Great Transformation: The Political and Economic Origins of our Time*, Boston: Beacon Press.

Ravallion, Martin (2003) 'The Debate on Globalisation, Poverty, and Inequality: Why Measurement Matters', April, Washington: World Bank, mimeo.

Reddy, Sanjay and Pogge, Thomas (2003) 'How Not to Count the Poor', Columbia University, mimeo.

Rodrik, Dani (1997) *Has Globalisation Gone Too Far?*, Washington, DC: Institute for International Economics.

— (1998) 'Why Do More Open Economies Have Bigger Governments?', *Journal of Political Economy*, vol. 106, no. 51, pp. 997–1032.

Ruggie, John G. (1994) 'Protectionism and Welfare Capitalism', *Journal of International Affairs*, Summer, pp. 1–11.

— (1995) 'At Home Abroad, Abroad At Home: International Liberalisation and Domestic Stability in the New World Economy', *Millennium*, Winter, pp. 507–526.

— (1996) 'Globalisation and the Embedded Liberalism Compromise: The End of an Era?', MPIfG Lecture Series on Economic Globalisation and National Democracy, Cologne.

Sachs, Jeffrey (1999) 'Implementing Debt Relief for HIPCS', manuscript, Harvard University.

— (2002) 'Resolving the Debt Crisis of Low Income Countries', Brookings Papers on Economic Activity, 1, pp. 257–286.

— (2003) 'Institutions Matter, But Not for Everything', *Finance and Development*, June, pp. 38–41.

Sala-I-Martin, Xavier (2002) 'The Disturbing "Rise" in Global Income Inequality', Columbia University, mimeo, www.columbia.edu/~xs23/papers/GlobalIncomeInequality.htm

Sassen, Saskia (1999) 'Embedding the Global in the National: Implications for the Role of the State', in Smith, David A., Solinger, Dorothy J. and Topik, Steven (eds), *States and Sovereignty in the Global Economy*, London: Routledge.

— (2001) *The Global City: New York, London, Tokyo*, Princeton: Princeton University Press.

Scholte, Jan Aart (1997) 'Global Capitalism and the State', *International Affairs*, vol. 73, no. 3, July, pp. 427–452.

Sen, Amartya and Nussbaum, Martha (1993) *The Quality of Life*, Oxford: Oxford University Press.

Strengmann-Kuhn, Wolfgang (2000) 'Theoretical Definition and Empirical Measurement of Welfare and Poverty: A Microeconomic Analysis', manuscript, Frankfurt am Main: Goethe-Universitat.

UNAIDS (2002) 'Fact Sheet: Sub-Saharan Africa', www.unaids.org/worldaidsday/2002/press/factsheets/FSAfrica_en.doc

United Nations Conference on Trade and Development (2002) *The Least Developed Countries Report*, Geneva: UNCTAD.

United Nations Development Programme (1999) 'Human Development Report: Globalisation with a Human Face', New York: UNDP.

— (2001) 'Human Development Report: Making New Technologies Work for Human Development', New York: UNDP.

Wade, Robert and Wolf, Martin (2002) 'Robert Wade and Martin Wolf, 3-Round Letter Exchange on World Poverty and Inequality for Prospect Magazine, UK', Centre for the Study for Globalisation and Regionalisation, University of Warwick, www.warwick.ac.uk/fac/soc/CSGR/PWade.pdf

Wolf, Martin (2001) 'Growth Makes the Poor Richer', *Financial Times*, 23 January.

Chapter 5: Environmental degradation and climate change

Introduction

The famed aphorism from the north of England, 'where there's muck, there's brass', accurately captured the prevailing public sensibilities about protecting – or rather not protecting – the environment from flagrant abuses during the period prior to the Second World War. Although from the middle of the nineteenth century the industrialising nations took a few perfunctory steps to staunch environmental degradation, these efforts tended to focus on protecting the majestic landscapes and wildlife that held special value for wealthy sportsmen.

Following the war, manufacturing output increased sharply as countries began to rebuild their battle-ravaged infrastructure. Steel production exploded and industrial chemists uncovered an endless stream of ways to exploit the potential of plastics. The 1950s and 1960s were marked by escalating standards of material comfort and social well-being. The ultimate means to express this sense of newfound affluence was to purchase a car and assembly lines struggled to keep up with burgeoning consumer demand.

While rising prosperity contributed to improved standards of living, ecological deterioration sparked new public anxieties. For example, during the winter of 1952 a dense, impenetrable fog of air pollution, known meteorologically as an anti-cyclone, stealthily descended on London. The pale green sooty air persisted for four days, killing an estimated 12,000 people. Five years later, what is generally considered to have been the first major radiological accident occurred when a fire broke out at the nuclear facility at Windscale (now Sellafield) in northern England. Iodine 131 was released across the surrounding countryside, contaminating animal feed and prompting the

government to impose a ban on the distribution of milk from cows within a 200 square mile area. In Japan, the Chisso Corporation dumped vast quantities of mercury into Minamata Bay and the chemical accumulated in the fish that were a dietary staple of local residents. During the late 1950s, scientists discovered that the very high rate of grotesque birth defects in the vicinity was directly attributable to mercury ingestion.

Then, in 1962, an award-winning American biologist, Rachel Carson, published her famous warning, *Silent Spring*. The book described the growth of the chemical industry and explained in elegiac prose how purportedly miraculous substances used to eradicate crop pests were actually poisoning the environment. It soared to the top of bestseller lists. In a scripted campaign that by today's standards was strikingly inept, several major chemical producers sought to undermine the credibility of *Silent Spring* and to destroy the integrity of its author. However, this merely added to the book's swelling popularity.

Carson was not the only eloquent scientist-author to sound the alarm during this era. The ranks of environmental advocates sprouting detailed technical knowledge continued to grow during the 1960s with seminal figures such as Barry Commoner, Paul Ehrlich, Rene Dubois, Garrett Hardin and numerous others adding their voices to an ever-growing chorus. An unremitting series of highly visual environmental disasters added credence to their assertions.

The first calamity in this ruinous sequence occurred when the tanker *Torrey Canyon* ran aground in 1967 as it approached the south-west coast of England. The stricken ship discharged more than 30 million gallons of oil before the Royal Air Force bombed its capsizing hulk. Despite this unprecedented action, an untold volume of the escaped crude sullied the nearby

Major global environmental issues:
- Climate change
- Decline in bio-diversity
- Decline in fish stocks
- Deforestation
- Desertification
- Environmental security
- Hyper-urbanisation
- Invasive species
- Large-scale natural disasters
- Natural Resource availability
- New resistant disease vectors
- Population growth
- Shortage of fresh water
- Stratospheric ozone depletion

Cornish shoreline and the current carried sizable quantities to the Normandy coast of France. For weeks afterwards, television viewers watched teams of tireless rescuers recover and try to rehabilitate thousands of hapless birds. The *Torrey Canyon* was particularly significant from the standpoint of international environmental law because it placed in bold relief the fundamental inadequacy of existing legal mechanisms to prevent such disasters and to compensate victims.

During this same period, Scandinavian scientists were beginning to comprehend the gradual effects of acid rain on upland forests and aquatic species. Although at the time they lacked the necessary knowledge to demonstrate their case definitively, the prevalent impression was that damage was the result of windborne sulphur dioxide emanating from British and continental factories. Electric power plants, which at the time were almost exclusively dependent on coal, were deemed especially culpable for the novel problem of acid rain. The Swedish government sought to exert pressure on the perpetrators, but found itself without the political or legal authority to prosecute its case and its European neighbours denied any complicity.

The predominant conception at the time was that the hazards of industrial activity were grounded in particular local geographies and, by the late 1960s, in accordance with this understanding, a number of national governments had started to consider legislation designed to have effects at local level. However, some scientists and international officials remained unconvinced that initiatives predicated on domestic legal standards

would be sufficient to address the growing problem. After all, many of the most potent environmental threats did not heed political boundaries.

In 1968, proponents of this global view of pollution and resource depletion encouraged UNESCO to convene the International Conference of Experts for Rational Use and Conservation of the Biosphere. Hundreds of ecologists and environmental scientists gathered in Paris to discuss the impacts of human beings on natural systems and to forge a series of international research initiatives that eventually came to be known as the Man in the Biosphere Programme.

Environmentalism, however, was evolving into something more than a scientific preoccupation. On 22 April 1970, millions of people participated in demonstrations around the world to mark the first Earth Day. Anti-war activists, feminists, socialists and others assembled on street corners, in workplaces and at university campuses to galvanise opinion and focus political attention on the multifarious ways in which industrial society was undermining human health and ecological well-being.

An unlikely group managed to capture most poignantly the zeitgeist of the era. The Club of Rome, a prominent consortium of elite business and political leaders, commissioned a group of researchers from the Massachusetts Institute of Technology (MIT) to prepare a report on the pending 'predicament of mankind'. Led by Donella and Dennis Meadows, the MIT research team constructed an elaborate (at least for the time) computer model to assess the impacts that growing pollution, resource extraction, food production and population were likely to have on human prospects over the next century. The eventual publication of this neo-Malthusian analysis in 1972 under the title *The Limits to Growth* did not offer much scope for optimism. Under virtually every scenario the modellers conjured up, severe dislocation and suffering were the inexorable predictions.

At the same time, environmental management continued to develop as a set of institutionalised practices situated at the level of national policymaking. Legislatures formulated sweeping laws and endowed newly created public agencies with authority to root out violations. Based largely on the use of standardised pollution-control technologies, this approach was reasonably successful in cleaning up the most odious forms of environmental abuse.

However, though few observers realised it at the time, by the late 1970s this line of attack began to reach some foreseeable limits. The economic recession of the decade and rising energy prices began to sap political enthusiasm for following through on earlier commitments to improve environmental quality. At the same time, industrial groups became adroit at deflecting calls for more stringent performance standards by threatening to downsize or relocate.

Important environmental NGOs:
- Friends of the Earth
- Greenpeace
- International Chamber of Commerce
- World Business Council on Sustainable Development

Marching to Stockholm

The problem of acidification and forest degradation became a Swedish obsession during the late 1960s and the government, in collaboration with the United Nations, sought to play a leading role in addressing the problem. The immediate dilemma the Swedes faced was that there was no global forum to which they could bring their grievances. The first task therefore was to create an appropriate institution to deal with international-scale environmental concerns.

In 1968, the UN General Assembly voted on a resolution to stage a conference on environmental issues that would be hosted by Sweden. A decision to convene the event, however, was stalled for two years as regional and international rivalries complicated the task of developing the terms of reference for the event. Eventually, the various controversies were settled and the conference secretariat, under the direction of Canadian Maurice Strong, embarked on a frenetic year of preparations. Aside from the customary logistical considerations, the pending conference brought another round of political impasses. After it became evident that UN protocol would prevent East Germany from sending a delegation, the Soviet Union and its Eastern European allies decided to boycott the proceedings.

China proved to be an ambivalent participant. While many analysts of international politics were heartened by Beijing's decision to despatch its diplomats (Stockholm was the first UN conference in which China participated), most of their energy during the preparatory sessions was devoted to denouncing Western imperialism.

Developing countries were initially reticent to commit themselves to the goals of the conference and dismissed environmental concerns as unaffordable and impractical amenities. However, the prospect of securing additional development assistance and technology transfers eventually lured them to participate. The United States, for its part, sought to derail the entire enterprise at several critical junctures by asserting its sovereignty and challenging any efforts that could curb economic growth.

Despite this acrimony, in June 1972 these disputes faded into the background as Stockholm began to prepare itself for the United Nations Conference on the Human Environment, the first international gathering of political representatives to discuss the planet's ecological future. Despite notable absences from the Soviet bloc, delegates from more than 100 nations appeared in the Swedish capital.

The most serious immediate result of the event revolved around its final communiqué, the Stockholm Declaration. Acknowledging the conference's dominant political fissure – namely the north-south divide – this was an all-encompassing document outlining 29 principles ranging from the standard array of environmental concerns to admonitions to ban nuclear weapons, to bring an end to apartheid and to stamp out racism.

In addition, the Stockholm conference gave rise to an extensive non-binding action plan that enumerated more than 100 initiatives to upgrade environmental quality, to improve natural resource management and to enhance environmental education. Many of these initiatives became the basis for subsequent cross-national collaboration in the ensuing years. Yet the conference's most enduring accomplishment was the decision to establish a 'small secretariat' that would evolve within the following year into the United Nations Environment Programme (UNEP). With its primary offices in Nairobi, UNEP would be the first (and thus far only) UN agency headquartered in Africa.

However promising some of its proclamations may have been, the Stockholm conference was in the end little more than a first step towards the creation of a credible and effective institutional structure to manage global environmental affairs. Perhaps not surprisingly, the heady euphoria that the event generated ultimately dissipated quickly as the political realities of a Cold War-dominated world reasserted themselves and established patterns once more took hold. Twenty years were to pass before the international community would reassemble to take up the challenges first promulgated in Stockholm.

Important environmental IGOs:
- World Bank
- International Panel on Climate Change
- World Meteorological Organisation
- UNEP
- Global Environmental Fund (GEF)

Environmental jamboree at Rio

The preceding assessment should not be taken to mean that progress advancing a global view of the environment came to a halt following the Stockholm conference. UNEP began the difficult job of establishing itself within the UN system, which particularly meant securing a stable and sufficient source of funding and retaining capable personnel. In these respects, the UN's sensitive decision to site the new programme on the African continent became a mixed blessing, as this location placed its staff outside the main circuits of diplomatic activity. Nonetheless, under the leadership first of Maurice Strong and then of Egyptian Mostafa Tolba, UNEP played an instrumental and important role in setting up an extensive global environmental monitoring network and in forging several regional environmental agreements such as the Mediterranean action plan.

Throughout much of the 1980s, UNEP played a crucial role trying to formulate a negotiated solution to the vexing problem of stratospheric ozone depletion. Pioneering scientific research by Ian Rowland and Mario Molina a decade earlier had drawn attention to the adverse effects on the protective ozone layer of essentially inert chlorofluorocarbons (CFCs), a family of ubiquitous chemicals widely used as propellants and refrigerants. Subsequent investigations carried out by the British Antarctic Survey demonstrated that indeed the ozone over the southern hemispheric pole showed measurable dissipation. This finding was significant because ozone in the upper atmosphere filters out dangerous ultraviolet B radiation and reductions in its shielding

potential held out the prospect of multifold increases in skin cancers and other health disorders.

In 1987, to its considerable credit, UNEP managed to secure an international agreement – the Montreal Protocol – to establish a schedule for the gradual elimination of ozone-depleting substances. Subsequent scientific research, however, indicated that the so-called ozone hole was growing more rapidly than had prompted the signatories to formulate the Copenhagen and London Amendments to strengthen the terms of the original accord.

Paralleling international efforts to address the ozone problem was growing criticism of dominant modes of economic development. A loose confederation of NGOs began to argue that development throughout much of the world, especially in terms of projects sponsored by the World Bank and other large lending agencies, often compounded the impoverishment of local people. Developing countries were being encouraged to assume large debt burdens to build infrastructure that in the end failed to generate meaningful social benefits. At the same time, this critique continued, the rapacious rates of resource extraction required to satisfy the appetites of consumers in developed countries were responsible for widespread global environmental devastation.

The Stockholm conference established much of the groundwork for this evaluation, but two notable publications during the 1980s gave it added relevance. First, UNEP, with partial funding from the World Wildlife Fund (WWF), commissioned the International Union for Conservation of Nature (IUCN) to prepare the *World Conservation Strategy*. This document set forth a global strategy for managing natural resources and biodiversity and sought to advance the view that economic development and environmental quality were mutually dependent objectives. Then, in 1987, the World Commission on Environment and Development (WCED), a UN-sanctioned panel headed up by Norwegian Prime Minister Gro Harlem Brundtland, produced *Our Common Future* and put the ideal of sustainable development on the international agenda. The WCED famously defined sustainable development as 'development that meets the needs of the present without compromising the ability of future generations to meet their own needs'.

Global warming

At the level of international environmental politics, the concept of sustainable development quickly became conflated with the issue of human-induced climate change (alternatively described as the greenhouse effect or global warming). While Swedish chemist Svante Arrhenius had formally linked the burning of fossil fuels with the likelihood of atmospheric warming as early as 1896 and august scientific bodies periodically produced reports on the subject, the issue did not register in the public consciousness until the summer of 1988. Sweltering heat and drought across the United States scorched agricultural crops, caused urban residents to bake and prompted relentless forest fires in Yellowstone National Park. Elsewhere around the world, most notably Bangladesh, catastrophic tropical storms swept thousands of coastal dwellers into the Bay of Bengal.

This global pattern of weather-related havoc prompted policymakers in Washington DC to convene a series of public hearings to call attention to the obscure scientific research that had been taking place into the causes and consequences of climate change. The most disconcerting testimony came from James Hansen, director of NASA's Goddard Institute for Space Studies, before the Senate Energy Committee. Hansen, breaking from professional custom of not making dramatic statements of scientific candour in public, delivered the unsettling news that it was probable that human activities were contributing to a process of planetary warming that would raise average global temperatures 3–4 degrees Celsius (6–8 degrees Fahrenheit). A change of this magnitude would be comparable to what occurred during the last Ice Age, though climate scientists contend that the current trend is likely to evince considerable regional variation. Because of modifications in oceanic currents and other effects, some areas could become subject to a cooling process.

The proposed prescription was a drastic curtailment – perhaps as high as 60 or 70 per cent – in the use of fossil fuels to slow the atmospheric accumulation of carbon dioxide and other greenhouse gases.

In response to these disclosures, the UN began to take an interest in the likely problems associated with a different global climatic regime: higher sea levels, more pronounced and frequent coastal flooding, inundated islands, emergent infectious disease vectors and altered agricultural productivity. In response, UNEP and the World Meteorological Organisation created the International Panel on Climate Change (IPCC) in 1988 to serve as an authoritative arbiter of the complex science that was beginning to coalesce. Comprising more than 2500 scientists from around the world with expertise in meteorology, climatology, glaciology, oceanography, biogeochemistry, atmospheric chemistry, agronomy, entomology and other specialities, the IPCC was given the responsibility for distilling the evidence and issuing periodic reports to guide policy decisions.

Efforts to foster sustainable development and to combat climate change combined during the preparatory meetings leading up to the United Nations Conference on Environment and Development (UNCED) in Rio de Janeiro in 1992 (also known as the Earth Summit). The report of the WCED had set in motion a schedule to evaluate at five-year intervals the success of efforts to plan for sustainable development and the gathering in Brazil would be the first of these assessments. At the same time, the end of the Cold War had created, in the minds of many observers, a unique and perhaps unprecedented window of opportunity. The political obstacles that had impeded progress 20 years earlier in Stockholm had been swept away by the collapse of the Soviet Union and ushered in a new era of prospective international cooperation. During two years of preparatory meetings, an invigorating sense of optimism prevailed, one in which people could hope that the nations of the world were now ready to come together to chart a path of global solidarity and environmental renewal. Chief among the tasks would be a collaborative effort to devise strategies to promote sustainable development and to mitigate the potentially calamitous impacts of climate change.

Delegations from more than 180 nations, many of them led by their respective heads of state, descended upon Rio for a momentous and suspenseful two weeks of formal ceremonies and negotiations. The cornerstones of the conference were a visionary document dubbed Agenda 21 that was meant to serve as an action plan for sustainable development and an international agreement to limit the release of greenhouse gases. Because of contentious down-to-the-wire disagreements between developed and developing countries (as well as among developed countries), the United Nations Framework Convention on Climate Change (UNFCCC) signed at the Earth Summit sought only to achieve voluntary reduction targets. The United States in particular argued strenuously for a non-binding accord because of concerns that more stringent requirements would choke off domestic economic growth and bring about an international recession.

Prior to the Rio conference, a spirited and amply funded anti-climate change coalition had begun to mobilise in the United States and to enlist a core group of dissenting 'scientific sceptics' to refute the emergent expert consensus. Comprised of several dozen large corporations – mainly from the oil, coal, electricity and automobile industries – this alliance sought to invalidate research linking fossil fuels to climate change and to thwart any concessions the White House might make that could compromise their financial interests. Indeed, the whole of the Earth Summit became transfixed by a rancorous public controversy between the first President Bush and William O'Reilly, the administration's top environmental official.

Despite serious reservations in many quarters about its likely effectiveness, national legislatures around the world dutifully began to ratify the UNFCCC. Many scientists, NGO representatives and environmentalists were disconsolate about the mixed outcome, but resigned to the fact that the agreement, while problematic, was a step in the right direction. Moreover, they continued to maintain that the portentous consequences of climate change would in the end induce national governments to take appropriate precautionary action and, if necessary, stand up to powerful corporate lobbyists.

Negotiating the Kyoto Protocol

In retrospect, the sanguine optimism that accompanied the UNFCCC was entirely unwarranted. The global economic downturn of the early 1990s prompted national governments to focus their attention solely on promoting economic growth, fostering employment and spurring investment. Virtually all elected officials were utterly unenthusiastic about launching ambitious initiatives that could have adverse effects on domestic competitiveness. Decisions to do otherwise were viewed as foolhardy – tantamount to a unilateral surrender in the name of an unsubstantiated problem fabricated by radical environmentalists intent on shutting down the engines of prosperity. Accordingly, as the

international economy rebounded during the second half of the decade and production expanded, greenhouse gas emissions likewise began to mount. In just a few short years, proponents of the UNFCCC had come to realise that the politically agreeable decision to rely on goodwill gestures to ameliorate climate change had been a regrettable miscalculation.

This new awareness, combined with the persistence of record-setting heat waves, typhoons, hurricanes and snowstorms around the world, led several European governments to begin pressing for a binding international accord on greenhouse gas emissions. Momentum to take more substantive action came to a head at a negotiating session during the summer of 1996. During this time-frame, international attention continued to focus on the domestic politics of climate change in the United States as the participation of the world's largest emitter of greenhouse gases would obviously be central to a more concerted effort to address the problem. In July, Timothy Wirth, the US Undersecretary of State for International Environmental Affairs, announced that the Clinton administration would support an agreement to establish mandatory targets. However, within weeks of this decision, the Senate convened to express its view on the matter in the form of the Byrd-Hagel resolution. This declaration, which passed by a vote of 95-0, stated that the Senate would not endorse an international climate change treaty that did not impose meaningful restrictions on the greenhouse gas emissions of developing countries or harmed the US economy. Further, the resolution stated that any accord sent to the Senate for ratification needed to include a detailed explanation of the domestic regulations required to meet the commitment, as well as an accounting of their associated financial impacts.

After several months of indeterminate discussion prior to the Kyoto conference, and several weeks of intense wrangling in the ancient Japanese city, the delegates settled on the broad outlines of a more rigorous climate change accord calling for mandatory reductions. Because of the inextricable connections between carbon dioxide and fossil fuel-based energy production, the resultant Kyoto Protocol was, and remains, perhaps the most complex environmental treaty ever negotiated. The countries that are parties to the agreement fall into three broad political categories: the Europeans and a majority of the former Soviet satellite

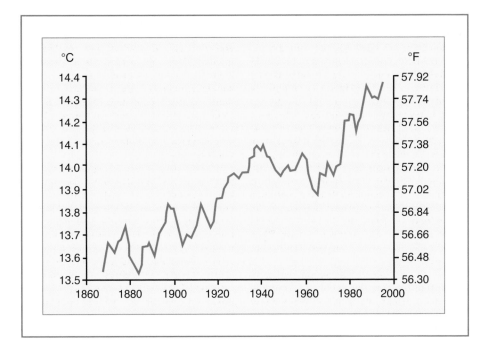

Figure 5.1 Global average temperatures   Source: NOAA/University Corporation for Atmospheric Research (UCAR)

nations, the developing countries (including China and India) and the umbrella group (Japan, United States, Canada, Australia, New Zealand, Iceland, Norway, Russia and Ukraine).

The Kyoto Protocol seeks to reduce roughly 5 per cent of the industrialised world's greenhouse gas emissions from a 1990 baseline by the end of the current decade (2008–2012). Each of the so-called Annex I countries negotiated their own per centage target, though in some cases cross-country aggregation was permissible. For instance, the European Union decided to utilise this provision and to propose an 8 per cent overall target. The United States negotiated a relatively ambitious 7 per cent reduction and Japan agreed to a 6 per cent cut.

The relatively bold US target was the result of a failed attempt at diplomatic brinkmanship by the Clinton administration. The United States announced that it would pursue a stringent target as a gesture to entice China and India into a deal. This gambit was designed to encourage these large developing countries to drop their opposition to substantive participation and to take on nominal obligations. President Clinton

then intended to use this token action by the Chinese and Indian governments to meet at least one of the stipulations on ratification imposed by the United States Senate.

For the Europeans the Kyoto Protocol provided an opportunity to work on specific uniform policies that would require national legislative changes. These measures, by and large, reflect a traditional command-and-control approach to environmental policymaking and seek to achieve a predetermined reduction target. The main disadvantage to this approach is that it discourages technological innovation by subjecting companies to time-consuming and expensive regulatory review for all equipment changes and upgrades, including pollution-control equipment. As a result, corporations face powerful disincentives to alter their production processes and thus to avoid installing new, more efficient equipment.

Under the Kyoto Protocol, Japan agreed to pursue what will ultimately be a very expensive national target. The high cost associated with the country's proposed 6 per cent cutback arises from the fact that Japanese industry had already implemented during the 1970s most of the less prohibitive energy efficiency improvements that are now being considered in the United States and elsewhere. Indeed, Japan has informally stated that it intended its target to serve as a signal of intent rather than a binding commitment.

Under the new climate accord, the former Soviet states retained emission levels that were equivalent to their production volumes prior to the 1992 economic collapse. Because of steep declines in industrial production during the decade, this arrangement meant that they had no substantive obligations. Further, many of the eastern European countries that were once part of the Soviet bloc have recently joined (or are due to join) the European Union. A condition of membership is that industry in these countries will meet substantially higher performance standards.

From the admittedly narrow standpoint of negotiating prowess, the developing countries secured a very attractive deal for themselves as the Kyoto Protocol, at least as in its current form, does not require a single one of them to reduce its domestic greenhouse gas emissions. This exemption creates severe problems over the longer term, especially with respect to India and China, because these two nations are presently experiencing rapid economic growth. Current projections anticipate that they will both surpass the United States as the world's largest aggregate producers of greenhouse gases within the next decade. Moreover, the developing countries as a group have received funding to formulate adaptation and mitigation programmes, to finance the transfer of environmental technologies developed in the north, and to offset costs associated with the paperwork mandated by the accord. Additionally, members of OPEC retained a phrase in the agreement that suggests they will be financially compensated for any revenue losses attributable to the treaty. However, the Kyoto Protocol's most striking provision is perhaps the one that Brazil secured at the last minute allowing developing countries that reduce their greenhouse gas emissions to sell their quotas to the wealthy nations.

It is unarguable that the United States left Kyoto with a larger obligation than it would have liked. This ambitious target was not only necessary because the Clinton administration had to try to ease its political problems with the Senate but was essential to secure compromises on three other provisions in the accord – the joint implementation (JI) programme, the clean development mechanism (CDM) programme and the 'cap-and-trade' emission trading programme. These three elements of the agreement were designed to enhance flexibility by allowing countries to pursue reductions in the most cost-effective manner. They were derived from concepts developed from a series of innovative domestic initiatives in the United States and they proved to be the heart of the international agreement.

JI stems from a pilot programme that was part of the UNFCCC known as Activities Implemented Jointly (AIJ). This initiative encouraged member nations of NATO to make infrastructure investments in developing countries that improved the quality of the global environment while simultaneously stabilising local economies. Sponsoring governments implemented these projects either to generate political goodwill or to influence the design of the AIJ programme. Ultimately, it was decided as part of the Kyoto proceedings that credits from these projects could not be carried forward into the first commitment period (2008–2012). Accordingly, these credits essentially have no value; nonetheless, they did spur 150 projects accounting for reductions of 277 million metric tons of carbon dioxide equivalents.

AIJ was eventually split into two tracks. The first – Joint Implementation – is for projects in the former Soviet bloc countries with paper commitments, but that have, due to economic contraction during the 1990s, actual emissions that are lower than their respective targets. The crediting period for these projects begins in 2008. The second track, CDM, is roughly equivalent to JI though it is specifically intended for developing countries. The negotiators decided in 2000 that the CDM should have a 'prompt start', thus beginning in 2000 projects implemented under this proviso are eligible to accrue credits for the 2008–2012 period.

Controversy

The last mechanism, the cap-and-trade' emission trading programme, is the most controversial section of the Kyoto Protocol. This provision allows production facilities that do not exceed their allocated obligations to sell unused emission credits to firms that are otherwise unable to meet their targets. Negotiators in Japan agreed to include this element, but made no decisions regarding the size, scope or fungibility of credits.

At the same time, environmental NGOs have strongly opposed it because of allegations that it confers upon industrial firms a tradable 'right to pollute'. Furthermore, it was uncertain how this mechanism would work in practice because negotiators wrote no rules about whether these credits could be transferred to other parts of the Kyoto Protocol, most notably CDM and JI.

Immediate Kyoto aftermath

Despite its awkward eleventh-hour compromises, the agreement in Kyoto gave the UNFCCC process a tangible goal towards which to work. Most significantly, a new set of binding commitments and deadlines had replaced the voluntary approach to reduce greenhouse gas emissions. The trading of carbon credits had also survived at the insistence of the United States.

Soon after departing Japan, European nations and developing countries promptly launched an aggressive series of programmes to gain national ratifications of the accord and to bring it into force. In the United States, fossil fuel industries and car manufacturers began an equally vigorous campaign to derail the whole enterprise. President Clinton was hemmed in, on one side, by the Byrd-Hagel resolution proclaiming the Senate's intent to vote down the treaty and, on the other side, by the personal involvement of Vice-President Al Gore whose presence in Kyoto unquestionably enabled the negotiations to continue. Caught on the horns of an irreconcilable dilemma, Clinton signed the accord but refused to send it to the Senate for ratification.

Meanwhile, much of the rest of the international community quickly took up the challenge of detailing a work plan to refine the Kyoto Protocol. Unfortunately, the document produced in Kyoto did not address many of the issues that environmental proponents had advocated and a long list of carried-over issues remained to be settled. Negotiators had abandoned these unresolved details – many of which were essential if the agreement was to promote meaningful environmental protection – in order to reach a consensus. For NGOs, this work revolved around pilot schemes and demonstration projects intended to show, depending on perspective, either the versatility or the futility of the policies embedded within the agreement. These activities took on a multitude of forms because no one person or group seemed entirely certain what the treaty actually meant.

The Kyoto Protocol's inherent ambiguity quickly became apparent and further discussions were initiated to sharpen it up. The next four international climate change meetings were organised around the difficult task of identifying and resolving these outstanding issues. The fourth Conference of the Parties (COP) was held in Argentina in 1998 and participants drafted the Buenos Aires Plan of Action. The plan established a 2000 deadline for clarifying a total of 153 outstanding items. This session also brought a commitment from the host nation that it would adopt a voluntary reduction target as if it were an Annex I country. By announcing such a decision, Argentina satisfied one of the stipulations of the Byrd-Hagel resolution, namely that developing countries should commit to a reduction target, even if that goal did not constitute a fixed number. The obligation was not hard, but rather represented a flexible limit directly tied to the country's economic output. This Argentine gesture was highly controversial among developing countries because many of them remained strongly opposed to limits of any kind, regardless of how discretionary they might be.

During this period, significant differences emerged with respect to the Kyoto mechanisms. Europeans, who have generally displayed greater scepticism about the effectiveness of market-based mechanisms, favoured a limit on the number of credits that countries could earn. Credits would have to be additional to all other requirements, including financial constraints. In other words, for a project to be creditable under the Kyoto Protocol, its financing would have to hinge upon the sale of the carbon credits.

Framework for the future

The next COP, held in Bonn in 1999, was, by most measures, a lacklustre event. This conference did not resolve any substantive issues, but instead focused on narrowing negotiating positions to set a framework for future compromise. The session's main accomplishment was that it maintained momentum for a follow-up meeting scheduled for the next year in The Hague. More importantly, the emphasis on policies had changed. The European Union had shifted its focus away from unified policies and measures to promoting and ensuring the environmental integrity of the three Kyoto mechanisms – JI, CDM and emission trading.

The Netherlands meeting (COP 6) in

November 2000 was supposed to be the culmination of the Buenos Aires Plan of Action; however, this was not to be. The president of the session, Dutchman Jan Pronk, circulated a document that became the basis for high-level ministerial deliberation. This paper covered four broad issue areas – compliance, mechanisms, land use change and forestry (which is inextricably linked to both the Kyoto mechanisms and the size of each nation's target) and developing countries. A series of compromises on these issues was rejected the morning after the conference was scheduled to close and the COP was adjourned without reaching any substantive decisions.

The confusion that ensued following the 2000 presidential election in the United States contributed to this inconclusive outcome. The widespread belief at the time was that Gore had indeed secured victory and that a more stringent package would be possible under his presidency than was the case with President Clinton. However, this anticipated result did not come to pass and George W. Bush prevailed. Within several weeks of assuming office he announced that the United States would no longer participate in the Kyoto Protocol (although the country continues to be a party to the UNFCCC).

The formal approval process for the agreement entailed some complicated calculus based on both the number of ratifying countries and the percentage of overall carbon dioxide emissions. With the United States on the sidelines, it was necessary for Germany, Japan and Russia (along with 52 other countries) to endorse the treaty to bring it into force. Germany (as part of a collective EU process) ratified the Kyoto Protocol at the end of May 2002 and the Japanese gave their formal backing one week later. These approvals left the future of the agreement in Russian hands. Recognising his pivotal position, Prime Minister Vladimir Putin embarked upon a shrewd diplomatic move in which he sought to play the EU and the United States off one another, so as to extract maximum benefit from any eventual decision. After a two-year period of indecision, when it seemed all but certain that Russia would abstain from taking action, government officials announced in May 2004 that the climate accord would be submitted for ratification. This deal hinged on the EU's quid pro quo to support Russia's bid to join the World Trade Organisation. In late 2004, Russia ultimately ratified the convention.

The sixth COP reconvened in Bonn during the summer of 2001 and negotiators made some headway by reaching several conditional decisions pertaining to the Buenos Aires Plan of Action. However, the Bush administration's decision to withdraw the United States from the treaty effectively neutralised any meaningful implementation of the accord's provisions.

Liberal interpretations

Later the same year, negotiators gathered for the seventh COP in Marrakech and this event was notable because the EU assumed a position of international leadership in Morocco on the issue of climate change. In a barbed jab at the United States, it was resolved that a country must be in compliance with the entire agreement to be able to access the Kyoto mechanisms and that countries were allowed to bank some of the emission reductions they achieved under the CDM. In general, these decisions resulted in the granting of more credits for forestry and carbon sequestration projects than had been previously envisioned. These liberal interpretations of the mechanisms were necessary to ensure that those countries within the umbrella group (Canada, Australia and New Zealand) that had not ratified the accord would do so. Such action would, in turn, further isolate the United States and increase international pressure from Europe and the developing countries that had already ratified the treaty for US re-engagement.

With the achievements of Marrakech as a springboard, COP 8 held in New Delhi in 2002 began the transition from negotiating the treaty's organisational details to implementing its provisions. Notably, the Delhi Declaration focuses on the gap between developed and developing countries, while refraining from any discussion of commitments. This round of negotiations focused on the needs of those developing countries that evince the greatest vulnerability to climate change and whose populations will require unprecedented amounts of financial and technological assistance to be able to adapt effectively.

As this volume goes to press, the most recent assembly of the parties to the climate change accord was COP 9 in Milan in 2003. This session focused largely on forestry issues and immediately earned the moniker the 'Forest COP' as it sought to resolve disputes over terminological definitions and to set out the conditions under which forestry credits would be granted under

CDM. This conference also marked negotiators' formal recognition of the research and independent NGO community. Negotiators could no longer ignore the fact that their proceedings were often stalled by endless squabbling, while the NGO-sponsored events – comprising environmental groups, business interests and academic associations – were much livelier and animated. As a result, expectations began to develop that it will be these organisations, and not the formal dealings among governments, that will eventually determine the success or failure of efforts to address the problem of climate change.

Conclusion

It is apparent that over the past decade and longer an enormous amount of diplomatic attention has been devoted to the potent and divisive issue of global climate change. For irrepressible optimists, considerable progress has been achieved. The need to limit greenhouse gas emissions has been put firmly on the global agenda and a group of core countries has accepted binding reductions on their release. This cast of mind contends that in the face of pronounced political antagonisms, unquestioned obsequiousness to economic growth and challenging scientific uncertainties, the achievements that have been secured are highly significant. The current effort to move from a non-binding framework to a mandatory protocol is held up as a signal accomplishment and that a system of global environmental governance is beginning to take shape around the issue. Thus, while modest at present, there exists today a platform on which future agreements can be built and step by incremental step an adequate institutional means of addressing climate change will evolve.

A more measured assessment, however, must acknowledge that the purported successes to date offer little relief in a world that is likely over the next several decades to experience increasingly variable and unprecedented weather conditions: more and worse natural disasters, more costly and damaging coastal deterioration, more extinction of flora and fauna, and more political instability. For adherents of this arguably more realistic perspective, it is clear that competing economic and political agendas – a collision that the fossil fuel industries and major oil- and coal-producing countries are only too willing to

exploit for their own purposes – frustrate efforts to foster a truly meaningful campaign of international solidarity and cooperation.

Moreover, and continually lurking in the background, is the fact that the global biogeochemical system is not geared to the slow pace at which political negotiations proceed. Climate scientists contend that the middling targets advanced by the Kyoto Protocol are woefully short of the massive reductions – in the order of 70–80 per cent – that would be required to stabilise the current atmospheric imbalance of greenhouse gases. It is entirely conceivable that global climate change will ultimately outstrip the capacity of current institutions to respond in a prompt enough manner. Of course, this will not be the first time that human foibles have prevented effective, concerted action in the face of impending catastrophe. In the past, though, the consequences of these failures have tended to be localised, with few consequences on a larger geographic scale. The outcomes of human interference with the planetary meteorological system could hold surprises for which we are wholly unprepared.

It is therefore important to consider a future in which a political solution to the dilemma of global climate change becomes widely recognised as permanently elusive. The evolving programme to allow nations and their companies to exchange greenhouse gas emission credits will come into effect, but it is improbable that this trading scheme will ameliorate the core problem of excessive releases – certainly not at the levels that current scientific understanding deems necessary. As the costs of an increasingly capricious climate continue to mount, the impetus for a solution will move from the political to the technoscientific arena. Indeed, there are already indications that this shift is beginning to take place.

Global-scale interventions to manage ocean currents actively as well as other meteorological drivers, once deemed to be overly ambitious and excessively costly, are beginning to attract new interest. A growing cadre of so-called earth systems engineers advocates fertilising the oceans with iron to stimulate photosynthesis by plankton as a workable means to soak up excessive carbon dioxide. Other options being subjected to scientific scrutiny include the use of deep geological formations to sequester greenhouse gases and the construction of immense diversion projects to bring water to newly drought-stricken regions. Proponents for these imaginative schemes point out that humanity – oftentimes without conscious intent – is already managing global environmental systems and there is a moral imperative to develop the expertise necessary to execute this responsibility effectively.

While it seems inevitable that future efforts to tackle climate change will depend on emergent modes of scientific and technological knowledge, it does not necessarily follow that political institutions will be made redundant. In many respects, a planetary system that requires carefully calibrated, active decision making is likely to be more, rather than less, reliant on resilient institutions of global governance. This is not to say that this political system will be predicated upon readily recognisable arrangements – national governments, multilateral organisations and international laws. As the climate change negotiations and other parallel activities demonstrate, far-sighted corporations and NGOs are finding novel ways in which to address the current generation of environmental challenges. As we move deeper into the twenty-first century, these nascent public-private partnerships could well become the future of global governance.

Websites

Climate Change Secretariat – www.unfccc.int
International Institute for Sustainable Development – www.iisd.org

Further Reading

Grubb, Michael (1999) *The Kyoto Protocol: A Guide and Assessment*, London: RIIA.

Victor, David (2004) *Climate Change: Debate on America's Policy Options*, Washington DC: Brookings.

Vig, Norman and Axelrod, Regina (2004) (eds) *The Global Environment: Institutions, Law and Policy*, Washington DC: CQ Press.

CHAPTER 6: Politics and instability in the global markets

In this chapter, the topic is the contemporary 'free-market' reforms of the 1980s and 1990s – their origins, content and present challenges. The starting point is the establishment and subsequent collapse of the Bretton Woods system. This system, inaugurated soon after the end of the Second World War, was designed to promote international stability in an economic international system that, because of its disorder in the 1930s, had made non-communist developed nations prone to the emergence of severe political tensions. However, the decision to rely on the US dollar as the currency to which others would be tied proved to be unsustainable. Indeed, major inflationary pressures flourishing in the 1960s, particularly related to the cost of the Vietnam War, made it impossible to maintain a system of fixed exchange rates internationally. World economic instability then worsened with the two oil shocks of the 1970s.

Beggar-thy-neighbour policies refer to a course of action through which a country tries to reduce unemployment and increase domestic output by raising tariffs and/or instituting non-tariff barriers that aim at curbing imports. By doing so such a country reduces export markets for trading partners who are thus likely to adopt the same policy. The protectionist result leaves all involved worse off in relation to the economic difficulties that precipitated the initial response.

The new challenges that developed and developing countries alike encountered were met by the introduction of neoliberal economic policies. The ground for this was that previous government interventionism was thought to be the cause of economic mismanagement that had translated into inflation and slow growth when it existed at all. This approach to economic policy-making set the stage for a new phase of economic integration and interdependence, often called or attributed to globalisation. It primarily involved introducing sweeping reforms designed to open up markets. The economic logic and political challenges of neoliberalism should be seen in conjunction with the factors described in Part D, Chapter 4.. The origins and content of structured adjustment programmes, the policy form that neoliberal reform in developing countries took on is discussed as well as a broad review of the global process of financial liberalisation and its consequences. Finally, there is a brief discussion of the process of deregulation or reregulation of economic activity.

From Bretton Woods to 'Washington Consensus': the emergence and scope of neoliberalism

The experiences of the inter-war period, most markedly the Great Depression of the 1930s, had left deep scars. It suggested many general lessons for the policymakers of the post-war period to learn and indicated particular mistakes that should not be repeated. As leaders of the major world economies of the Western world met at Bretton Woods in 1946 to create a new international economic system, it had become pretty clear what factors had been crucial in creating the problems of the 1930s. These were the swings in exchange rates after WWI, the results of the collapse of the gold standard, the international transmission of deflation and beggar-thy-neighbour devaluations leading to trade restrictions and bilateralism: all had been pernicious to world prosperity. Hence, any successful future management of the international economy would need to include mechanisms to prevent any repetition of them.

During the meeting at Bretton Woods, two main actors presented their plans for the restructuring of the international system. John Maynard Keynes, the famous economist, was the leader of the British team and Harry Dexter White led for the Americans. Keynes' plan emphasised the need to encourage the expansion of world trade and activity by making substantial international liquidity available and by protecting a domestic economy from external shocks. This would be done by providing a buffer stock of international reserves. Dexter White's plan focused on achieving exchange rate stability more than on the generous provision of international liquidity.

Following a period of intense negotiations, a compromise was reached leading to the Joint Statement by Experts on the Establishment of an International Monetary Fund. This statement was to become the International Monetary Fund's Articles of Agreement (Bordo, 1993).

International reserves

Assets denominated in foreign currency, plus gold, held by a central bank, sometimes for the purpose of intervening in the exchange market to influence or fix the exchange rate. Usually includes foreign currencies (especially US dollars), other assets denominated in foreign currencies, gold and a small amount of special drawing rights (SDRs), a transferable right to acquire another country's currency.

Two crucial institutions were created at the time: the General Agreement on Tariffs and Trade, which was to manage the international trading system, and the IMF, which was put in charge of managing the monetary system. The IMF was designed to solve liquidity problems by using contributions from member countries to assist states with international payments problems. What is now known as the World Bank was also conceived at Bretton Woods, initially created to help rebuild Europe after the war. Its first loan of $250 million was to France in 1947 for post-war reconstruction.

Exchange rate arrangements

Economists have always struggled to determine the merits and potential downsides of particular exchange rate systems. Discussions surround the question of choosing a pegged (or fixed) rate versus letting the exchange rate float according to market pressures, mirroring the way most prices are determined in a given economy. Briefly the two systems can be summarised as follows:

- Fixed (pegged) exchange rate system: this is used in many instances as a device to control inflation. It may signal a government's credibility with its anti-inflation agenda – chiefly containing public spending and controlling the money supply. However, a high cost associated with pegged currencies is that they limit the ability of the government to use monetary policy domestically in reaction to external shocks.

- Flexible exchange rates: these are determined by market movements and not defined by the value of other currencies. Flexibility allows a country to enhance the competitiveness of its tradable producers by devaluing the national currency, thus making domestically made products cheaper internationally.

- Different exchange rate strategies appeal to different countries at specific times depending on the contemporary macroeconomic context. For example, a country plagued by high inflation may favour monetary stabilisation over enhanced international competitiveness and then opt for a pegged exchange rate. On the other hand, a country which desperately needs foreign reserves to honour high foreign debt payments, for example, may favour flexible exchange rates. This allows for strategic devaluations in order to enhance domestic competitiveness and produce a balance of payments surplus.

- Put simply, decisions on exchange rate policy might be a trade-off between competitiveness (flexibility) and credibility (fixed rates).

If indeed 'monetary arrangements established by international negotiation are the exception, not the rule' (Eichengreen, 1996, p. 7), Bretton Woods was definitely an exceptional case of international cooperation. It reflected 'a shift in

American thinking manifest in the role played by the USA in the creation of (the) Bretton Woods (system) embodying the belief that a rule-based international economy and international institutions to manage the rules were necessary' (Gilpin, 2000, p. 55). This was in sharp contrast to the market approach of the pre-Second World War years, when state interventionism was significantly low.

The goal of the Bretton Woods system was to create an international monetary constitution based on a stable exchange rate regime, able to promote full employment and cooperation. 'Both Keynes and White planned an adjustable peg system to be coordinated by an international monetary agency' (Bordo, 1993, p. 81). The rules set up by the new system were based on a commitment to trade liberalisation incorporating the principle of non-discrimination and also to the reduction of controls on current account transactions, although capital controls were to be allowed. There was also agreement that because exchange rates were to be fixed or pegged, any change in exchange policy in one country would be possible only after consultations with the IMF. The Bretton Woods fundamentals ensured the relative liberalisation of the world economy and thus created a need for some domestic protection from the consequences of international competition. This led to what became known as 'the embedded liberalism compromise'. While the Bretton Woods rules tied exchange rate policies to a regime of fixed rates and underlined significant steps towards international openness, they allowed individual governments to pursue economic stabilisation and social welfare policies. That is to say, 'within permissible limits', individual nations would be free to pursue economic growth *and* full employment (Gilpin, 2000, p. 57). In this sense, the Bretton Woods system was, in fact, a compromise between the rigid gold standard of the nineteenth century, when governments had limited ability to manage their own economies, and the chaotic 1930s, when governments surrendered to competitive devaluations and other damaging policies. It was designed to combine a move towards international cooperation and liberalisation with a permissive approach within the realm of domestic policy, especially on the social security front.

The mechanisms through which these ambitious goals were to be achieved were marked by a well-coordinated effort towards an international monetary system based on fixed rates, which was the most important product of the Bretton Woods meetings. The system had to provide sufficient amounts of monetary reserves to allow member governments to maintain the exchange rates for their currencies at predetermined values. All currencies of member states were then tied to the dollar, which was, in turn, tied to gold.

From 1946 until the 1970s the system proved remarkably successful. A comparative study analysing the Bretton Woods system in relation to earlier monetary regimes concluded that it exhibited the best macro performance of any economic regime, especially for the period between 1959 and 1970. However, many challenges to the Bretton Woods system developed and they eventually led to its demise. As Bordo explained, 'the problems of the interwar system that Bretton Woods was designed to avoid re-emerged with a vengeance'. This time the consequences, however, were different: in 1931 the collapse of the exchange system had led to severe recession; in the 1970s the Bretton Woods system exploded into inflation (Bordo, 1993, p. 74).

The troubles of the new monetary system arose from the fact that it was based on the US dollar. Hence, problems faced by the US economy would inevitably feed through into the international system, unless corrective measures were put in place. The 1960s presented no scarcity of challenges to the US economy and by the time of the Vietnam War, the USA had become lax in its price stability policy. To cover the great fiscal costs of the Vietnam War, austerity policies were called for. But given the always politically charged nature of introducing them, the US government opted instead to follow policies of increasing both taxation and welfare spending. The second taken together with the spending on the war had a significantly inflationary effect.

Indeed, the Nixon administration (1969–1974) compounded the problem of inflation, which the Federal Reserve Bank (the US 'central bank') also neglected to deal with effectively, perhaps in an effort to smooth the way for Nixon's re-election in 1972 (Gilpin, 2000, p. 68). Rising inflation in the USA led to a drop in international confidence in the overvalued dollar, thus fuelling speculation. This, together with the expanding US trade deficit, led ultimately to the devaluation of the dollar in August 1971.

The Bretton Woods system began to collapse and soon after the 1973 oil crisis introduced a new set of problems to the world economy. Retaliating against the results of the Yom Kippur war, the Arab members of OPEC boycotted the supply of oil, leading to a substantial increase in the price per barrel, which generated the rare conjunction of both deflating economic activity and strong price inflation. Given that oil is such an important raw material, the severe increase in price led to a cascade of price increases through transportation cost increases that were eventually transferred to the prices of almost all goods in the world economy. At the same time, because much more money had to be spent on the purchase of oil, a substantial withdrawal of purchase power from the world economy led to recession. The combination of inflation with low economic growth and unemployment, known as stagflation, surfaced in the USA and in Europe.

Meanwhile, in developing countries, the dynamics produced by the oil crisis led to dramatic events of a different nature. The profits incurred by oil producers – the petrodollars – were deposited in increasingly fat accounts in Western banks, which were eager to multiply their gains by providing easy credit to developing countries, especially in Latin America. Those governments were, in turn, more than happy to receive the loans they needed to pay for the macroeconomic instability that marked the last years of military dictatorships in most of the region (especially in Brazil and Argentina) and the decline of the hegemonic party system of Mexico. The spiral of new borrowing and lending was, in turn, accelerated by an incentive system created through the loan syndication process. This meant that although banks continued to lend on their own account, they could reap larger fees with less risk by arranging loans involving a large group of banks. In fact, 'these so-called lead banks, with regional and smaller banks in tow, searched far and wide for lending opportunities' (Aggarwal, 1996, p. 38). Latin American debt grew from US$74.5 billion in 1975 to nearly $315 billion by the end of 1982. By 1983, foreign debt had reached 325 per cent of the region's exports of goods and services as compared with 166 per cent in 1975.

Crisis point

This situation became unsustainable by 1981. The USA, faced with inflationary pressures resulting from the expansionary policies of the Vietnam days and two oil price rises, increased interest rates. Dramatic effects on payments then followed in respect of existing loans that had been signed at floating rates. Developing countries which had borrowed massive amounts of money were severely hurt by these interest rate increases as well as by the fact that the recession had spread to other developed countries, constraining their exports. In addition, capital flight from many developing countries made the crisis worse. In Mexico, these outflows increased from US$2.2. billion in 1980 to US$4.7 billion in 1982 and increased further to US$9.3 billion in 1983. Argentina saw a similar pattern, with outflows increasing from US$3.5 billion in 1980 to US$7.6 billion in 1982.

By August 1982 Mexico neared complete default and as banks ceased the provision of credit, Brazil, Argentina and other major debtors found themselves in a similar position. The outcome was certainly dramatic. By 1983, over 25 countries were in arrears, initiating more than a decade of debt restructuring effort. Rescheduling these debts then required the IMF, pushed by the US government, to provide 'jumbo loans' to Brazil, Mexico and other debtors, in exchange for promises to implement austerity policies under the umbrella of the comprehensive IMF market reform programmes, known as Structural Adjustment Programmes and explained in detail below.

This was the turning point at which the demise of the Bretton Woods system, along with the crises of the 1970s and 1980s (for developing countries especially), led the way to an era of economic policy where interventionism decreased significantly, at least in theory, and where market-oriented reforms would take centre stage in policymaking in developed and, especially, in developing countries. The age of predominant neoliberalism had arrived. The discussions of its evolution are legion; here, some main points are briefly summarised.

From Keynesian consensus to 'Washington consensus': economic theory and global reality

After the Great Depression the Western world embraced Keynesianism and its primary idea that state intervention was essential to promote growth and avoid apparently unending high unemployment. This view was in sharp opposition to the classical theoretical assumption that an economy always functioned in full employment and that in a recession, labour prices would simply drop, causing employers to hire more workers and thereby avoid unemployment. For Keynes, state intervention in the form of expansive fiscal policies (i.e. increased government spending) would be the only way to overcome recession. Once good times returned, government intervention would also be essential to prevent the economy from overheating by drawing money back out of it. In short, the Keynesian prescription was for governments to save in good times and spend in bad times.

The 1940s were exemplified by the emergence of the 'Keynesian consensus' as Western governments nationalised declining or important private companies, regulated their economy, adopted public spending policies and other means. They thus involved themselves far more deeply in the management of their economies than ever before. At the same time, Keynesianism began to find its way into the work of development theorists. Allied with the new ideas that emerged from the success of Soviet industry at a time of Western decay, Keynesian theory also gave strong support to an expanded role for the state in the economy in developing countries.

Origins, rationale and content of structural adjustment programmes

Through the 1950s, the 1960s and especially the 1970s, the basic premise of much development thinking was that the structure of international economic relations was biased against countries in the developing world. The structure of the international economic system, rather than characteristics internal to developing countries, was identified as the principal cause of under-development. Development was thus viewed as qualitatively different in the north and south, particularly in that the laws of neo-classical economics were assumed not to apply equally in the developing world. These views were derived from structuralist and dependency theories, which predominantly influenced policymaking.

In this scenario, developing countries sought to build up industrial potential by mobilising foreign and state investment, finding the revenue they needed for state investment through the sale of traditional exports – a strategy that became known as import substitution industrialisation, or ISI. Such strategy was marked by the deep degree of protection imposed on external goods, thus allowing local producers, who could not normally compete with foreign suppliers, to find themselves in a market suddenly favourable to their products.

Nonetheless, at the same time as ISI represented a direct attempt on the part of developing countries' governments to promote physical-capital formation, it neglected to foster competitiveness, innovation, technological capability and other important features of enhanced productivity. With its focus on savings and investment, 'ISI proved to be very effective in building factories and infrastructure. In other regards, it was failing' (Rapley, 1996, p. 39). Since local producers still had to rely on the import of capital goods, and since the costs of imported inputs actually outweighed the savings generated by the local production of capital goods, ISI in fact worsened the national balance of trade. The inefficiencies of ISI were thus added to the chaotic scenario of international indebtedness and high inflation that marked the late 1970s and the 1980s. Developing countries struggled to emerge from crisis and find new policy solutions to what seemed to have become endemic problems.

As the debt crisis of the 1980s significantly constrained credit to developing countries – especially those Latin American economies which had suspended debt payments – the IMF became the only source of funding available. In exchange for future loans, however, the Fund required that countries pursued a package of policies that became known as structural adjustment programmes (SAPS), part of a set of *conditionalities* attached to international credit. SAPs sought 'to permit renewed, or accelerated development by correcting "structural" disequilibrium in the foreign and public balances' (Ahmed and Lipton, 1997). Such measures are often required as conditions for receiving World Bank and IMF loans and are often called 'conditionalities'. The key objectives of the reform programmes were a reduction or elimination of balance-of-payments and public-sector deficits, the resumption of higher rates of economic

Structuralism and dependency theory: alternative views on 'development'

Structuralism and Dependency Theory were predominant in the 1960s and 1970s, emerging from an intellectual response (from 'the South') to the perceived flaws of modernisation theory. According to modernisation theory, underdevelopment was to be considered as a temporary stage. Less developed countries (LDCs) might lag behind developed ones, but if they were to follow the same continuum of policies that had led other countries to develop, they too would reach this goal. The research agenda, then, involved identifying those conditions that gave rise to development in developed countries and exploring the ways in which they could be emulated by LDCs.

Opponents of this view accused it of over-simplification. One such response was structuralism, championed by the UN's Economic Commission for Latin America (CEPAL), directed by economist Raul Prebisch. One of the main premises of structuralism was the notion that underdevelopment was not simply a lagging stage, but a structural condition determined by declining terms of trade between developed and developing countries.

As their economies specialised in the production of raw materials (primary goods), developing countries dealt with a balance of trade that was structured to their detriment.

This was because the prices for their exports were not as flexible as the prices for the imports they had to acquire as a consequence of their low domestic industrial productivity.

A view linked to structuralism that gained prominence in intellectual circles was dependency theory. Intellectuals, like the economist Samir Amin, saw the relationship between developing and developed countries as exploitative. Moreover, Andrei Gunder Frank's work suggested an incompatibility between dependency and development, and the need for a socialist revolution to break out of the impasse.

A more elaborate body of literature, however, emerged in the 1970s focusing not on the direct links between 'centre' and 'periphery' (as developed and developing countries were labelled), but on intermediaries, especially groups in Latin America who shared interests with international actors and thus joined forces with them to promote mutual gains often at the expense of national groups. Such historical-structural dependency proposed by intellectuals such as Cardoso and Faletto stressed 'changes in the nature of links between centre and periphery during different stages of growth – from colonialism to raw materials export, import-substitution industrialisation, and internationalisation of the domestic market'. Most important, Cardoso and Faleto's elaborate theory 'pointed to the diversity of socio-economic and political circumstances among Latin American countries and thus the different types of links within the international economy', which made dependency and development a contingent combination for each developing country, but one of a 'particularly unequal type' (Stallings, 1992, p. 45).

growth, and the achievement of structural change to prevent future payments and stabilisation problems (such as the debt crisis of the 1980s). A central aspect of SAPs was their emphasis on increased specialisation in the production of 'tradable' commodities not only by the public sector but especially via private investment – a clear consequence of the failure of the ISI programme.

Shift to the right

The market orientation embraced by the IMF was a reflection of an international move in this direction. The electoral victory of Margaret Thatcher in the UK and of Ronald Reagan in the USA marked a pronounced shift to the right all over the Western world. Conservative governments emphasised the rolling back of the state and the freeing of the market.

A reassertion of the neo-classical tradition in economics had found expression in the works of Adam Smith and, in modern times, Milton Friedman, who were strong advocates of the idea that free markets had the exceptional capacity to stabilise economies without the need for governmental intervention. The Washington political and economic environment embraced these ideas and translated them into a set of policies that later became known as the 'Washington consensus'. This neoliberal reforming 'package' strongly advocated fiscal austerity, market-determined exchange and interest rates, financial and trade liberalisation, privatisation, and deregulation of domestic labour markets and businesses.

Conditionalities are the requirements imposed by the IMF and World Bank on borrowing countries to qualify for a loan, typically including a long list of budgetary and policy changes comprising a 'structural adjustment programme'.

Structured adjustment programmes (SAPs), in turn, are typically a set of policies designed to achieve economic liberalisation and monetary stability. On the liberalisation front they include: reducing barriers to trade and capital flows, currency devaluation to make exports more competitive, and privatising state enterprises. On the monetary stability front, SAPs include: reducing budget deficits, reducing domestic credit expansion, and freeing controlled prices and interest rates. SAPs have become known for being the policy arm of neoliberal reforms.

However, a note of caution should be exercised when it tends to be assumed that the spread and consolidation of neoliberalism in Latin America (in particular) was simply the consequence of the impositions of international financial institutions. As Biersteker points out, 'ideas can have an independent political effect, but they also need an enabling environment in which to take root and flourish' (Biersteker, 1995, p. 175). In a chaotic context of hyperinflation, debt and slow growth, and after many failed attempts to achieve economic stabilisation by means that had only further increased inflation, not only technocrats, mostly graduates of US universities, but also the populations of most Latin American countries, especially those of Brazil, Mexico and Argentina, the largest and most highly indebted economies in the region, were eager to try a bit of strong but apparently healing medicine. Chile, after successfully being able to stabilise its economy and achieve substantial growth by adopting neoliberal reforms, became an example to be followed by all countries in the region. At the same time, the East Asian 'exceptionalism' was in contrast to the poor performance of Latin America in the 'lost decade' of the 1980s, which further faulted the lack of openness of the Latin economy.

As neoliberal reforms spread from the north to the south (from Washington to Buenos Aires) and from the west to the east (from London to Moscow), so did criticism of the 'Washington Consensus' whose prescription, embraced by the International Monetary Fund, started to show mixed results by the end of the 1990s, with records of inequality alarmingly worse than the expectations of market reform advocates.

The impact of neoliberal reforms was being studied closely as the 1990s came to an end. In an analysis of nine countries in Latin America (Bolivia, Brazil, Chile, Argentina, Costa Rica, Mexico, Colombia, Jamaica and Peru), it was found that 'growth has been modest, employment has grown slowly and with problems in job quality, and inequality has not improved and may even have gotten worse' (Stallings and Peres, 2000). In addition, increased growth of exports (in volume as well as in value) has not led to a comparable growth of output. Despite a rapid growth of exports, imports have grown even faster, leading to widening trade deficits.

Moreover, winners and losers from the reforms enacted made up distinguishable groups, according to Pieper and Taylor (1998). Winners were those who formed the political coalitions most likely to support market reforms. Domestically, they were exporters, who benefited from trade liberalisation, financial groups, which profited from market deregulation, and the top 10–20 per cent of earners, who gained consumption access to myriad new imported goods and financial services. The losers were people in the bottom 80 per cent of the distribution (i.e., lower and middle classes), some industrialists and old political elites. The first group, however, because of increased fiscal restraint, found itself in a more desperate position since there were no longer strong social welfare systems to fall back on.

From the point of view of political economy, the disturbing social consequences of economic liberalisation should come as no surprise. After all, almost 60 years before what is now called 'globalisation' took the world by storm, Polanyi had warned the world of the likely national impact of international integration. In *The Great Transformation* (1957), he explored the socially disruptive and polarising tendencies in the world economy driven by what he called the self-regulating market. Those tendencies characterised a 'double movement', within which an unprecedented expansion of the market coexisted with a massive social disruption. This in turn caused a sharp political reaction in the form of public demands that the state counteract the deleterious effects of such market-driven capitalism. Indeed, for Polanyi, this double effect ultimately generated the conditions of the 1930s and produced – out of a breakdown in liberal economic structures – the phenomena of depression, fascism, unemployment and nationalism, which combined had led the world to war.

After the Second World War, the lessons learned from this experience produced a new multinationalism and 'the compromise of embedded liberalism' which combined economic liberalisation with domestic social protection. Today, however, the strict policies of fiscal austerity that are the mantra of neoliberal reformers inhibit the possibility of sustaining, still less creating, the social safety nets needed to cushion the negative effects on marginalised social groups of a global trend towards the liberalisation of economies.

Critics of neoliberal reforms, who range from critics of capitalism per se to more moderate rejections of the specific form liberalisation has taken in the last decade, blame neoliberalism for not being able to achieve real improvements in living conditions. It is thus important to acknowledge that the emphasis on growth via the attraction of international investments, which in developing countries are likely to be volatile and short term, cannot substitute for a *domestic* development strategy. Such a strategy needs to produce *sustained* growth over the medium to long term, not only by maintaining some degree of control over inflation but also by targeting the disturbing issue of inequality. Its persistence is in itself the single most vivid threat to the political endurance of the neoliberal model as an acceptable policy path. (See Part D, Chapter 4.)

This conclusion becomes even clearer from an examination of the global financial system in further detail.

The fragmentation of governance: the case of the international financial system

Markets are not always rational: 'The a priori assumption of rational markets and consequently the impossibility of destabilising speculation are difficult to sustain with any extensive reading of economic history. The pages of history are strewn with language, admittedly imprecise and possibly hyperbolic, that allows no other interpretation than occasional irrational markets and destabilising speculation' (Kindleberger, 2000, p. 24). Indeed, the 1990s saw no scarcity of news containing words such as 'manias', 'insane land speculation', 'financial orgies', 'frenzies', 'feverish speculation', 'intoxicated investors', 'craze', 'toxic waste investments', 'contagion', 'panic', 'turbulence'.

Countries, whether rich or poor, which embraced liberalisation have grown more vulnerable to the wild moods of global capital. The famous case of George Soros' audacious (but successful) speculative attack against the British pound in 1992 was an event with obviously important consequences and, if anything, a clear sign that audacity in financial circles found no boundaries even in taking on powerful domestic economic structures. Even more disturbing were the severe financial crises of the decade: the Mexican peso crisis in 1994, the Asian crisis in 1997 and the Russian crisis in 1998.

The increase in vulnerability that economies face as they join the global capitalist game, however, is not as original a process as the emergence of new legal regimes to govern cross-border economic transactions. These new legal regimes are particular to the latest stage of economic globalisation. Also, private debt security or bond rating agencies (such as Moody's and Standard & Poor's), which operated primarily in the USA, have in the last ten years built branches in several other countries, strongly influencing international investors, especially those who are most attracted to the high returns offered by the so-called 'emerging markets', that is to say, certain developing countries that show promising economic figures, political stability of sorts and a 'tolerable' degree of social instability.

Another example of transnational legal regimes that influence local practices is the development of the main global accountancy and auditing norms currently in use by the International Accounting Standards Committee and the International Federation of Accountants. All these cases are examples of activities that take the form of what has been termed 'governance without government'. That is to say, as some of the authority of the formerly sovereign state has been relocated in transnational collectivities, some of the functions of governance are now being performed in ways that do not originate within governments.

So as the state has embraced liberalisation –

particularly financial – it has also subjected itself to new transnational regulations that are restrictive, if not intentionally, in the very fact that they are not subject to formal control by individual states. And although it can be claimed that financial transactions were never fully under the control of states, they have, particularly in the last decade, developed an overwhelming level of speed and sophistication (based on technological innovation mainly) that produces sudden results and contagious effects as soon as a crisis hits any given economy.

While official sector capital investments into developing countries rose only from $30 billion to $80 billion over the last 20 years, private-sector investment rocketed from $45 billion to peak at $300 billion during the same period. Clearly, developing nations are fertile ground for private investors. Nowadays, private-sector debt is four times higher than multilateral and official debt in middle-income countries and many loans frequently have to be rescheduled or refinanced.

These developments are to a great extent a consequence of the aggressive financial liberalisation reforms developing countries have engaged in during the last 15 years. The logic for it came out of a technocratic consensus developed in Washington, according to which 'financial systems should ensure that capital will move from economies with surplus savings to those where investment opportunities exceed local savings, and that capital should be free to move toward those places and activities where it would be used most efficiently; thus, the efficient utilisation of the world's scarce capital resources would be achieved. To this end, markets and not governments or international organisations would govern the international financial system' (Pauly, 1997, p. 135).

In fact, global financial liberalisation was instigated by the USA as part of a strategy that has recognised – since the Reagan administration – that US financial interests would greatly benefit from freedom of capital movements since it constantly needs to tap into the world's savings in order to make up for its limited savings capabilities. Today this logic is more valid than ever given the immense US budget deficit.

However, instead of inaugurating an international financial regime where liberalisation of financial markets would correct savings and consumption imbalances worldwide in a neat non-interventionist system, as neoliberal logic would have it, disturbances have prevailed in international financial markets. Financial crises were severe in the 1990s, adversely affecting international trade and capital flows, domestic credit and ultimately output. And, expectably, crises did not remain confined to their epicentre; financial problems have often resulted in severe output contractions, leading to worsened trade balances of major trading partners and doubts over the repayment of international loans (Weeler, 2001, p. 99).

A simplified version of how financial crises unfold includes the following set of dynamics. First, international capital markets perceive there to be new financial opportunities. Credit expansion follows as investors, moved by the pursuit of high profits, allocate resources in the sector where gains can be expected. This is a stage known as the 'speculative boom', which leads to a rise in the price of the sought-after assets, suggesting even more new profit opportunities and, in turn, draws more investors into the market in a self-reinforcing cycle. This causes profits to rise rapidly and is also referred to as the 'euphoria stage' when speculation on price increases becomes yet another important factor driving up the market.

'While the "speculative bubble" or the "mania" is expanding, many gains are derived from the process. The word "mania" emphasises the irrationality (of the market); "bubble" foreshadows the bursting' (Kindleberger, 2000, p. 15). However, at some point some investors will perceive that the market has reached its peak and will start to convert their inflated assets into money or 'quality' investments. Because the market works more through 'herd behaviour' than rational actions from 'rational actors', more people begin to sell their assets, prices fall and bankruptcy cases increase (Gilpin, 2000). Soon, the speculative bubble bursts, causing prices to collapse and spreading panic to investors who try to save what they can, causing a possible 'credit crush' and, ultimately, severe recession where the investments had collapsed (see Figure 6.1).

This sequence was in play during the crises that plagued Mexico in 1994, Asia in 1997 and Russia in 1998. There was also a disturbing element of contagion in these episodes; for example, as the Russian crisis unfolded, the Brazilian economy felt an almost immediate hit which culminated in a severe devaluation of the Brazilian real in January 1999. Overtrading, another way to describe the speculative boom, has historically tended to spread from one country to another through many different conduits, which range

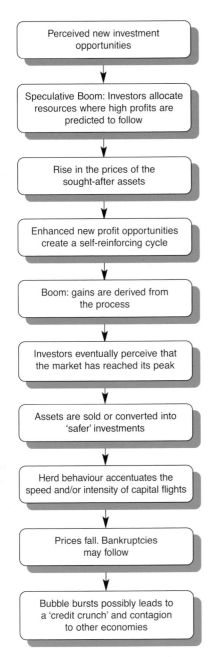

Figure 6.1 Financial crises: a brief summary of events

Perceived new investment opportunities

Speculative Boom: Investors allocate resources where high profits are predicted to follow

Rise in the prices of the sought-after assets

Enhanced new profit opportunities create a self-reinforcing cycle

Boom: gains are derived from the process

Investors eventually perceive that the market has reached its peak

Assets are sold or converted into 'safer' investments

Herd behaviour accentuates the speed and/or intensity of capital flights

Prices fall. Bankruptcies may follow

Bubble bursts possibly leads to a 'credit crunch' and contagion to other economies

from capital flows to investors' psychology (Kindleberger, 2000). The latter might correctly or mistakenly predict that countries that are different in macroeconomic standing at a particu-lar time, but similar in their 'emerging market' status, might inevitably be plagued by similar misfortune sooner or later. It was this 'logic' that propelled investors to withdraw money from Brazil quickly as the Russian rouble collapsed.

Taking international loan markets as an exam-ple, what the financial crises of the 1990s have made clear is that even if individual investors act rationally, the market outcomes from collective investment choices – many times, a product of copycat behaviour – can feed a panic scenario, leading to extremely costly reversals of capital flows, especially for emerging market economies. This is an historically rooted trend but empha-sised and accelerated by the technological advances that allow for the interconnectedness of intense and highly volatile global financial activity.

Governance and the regulation of 'deregulation'

Following the logic of neoliberalism, market-ori-ented reforms in many countries included some degree of deregulation of the economy. However, semantic confusion is common when-ever this topic is discussed. People tend to con-fuse the 'introduction of more competition within a market' (what might more aptly be called *liberalisation*) with the reduction or elimi-nation of government regulation, or *deregulation* (Vogel, 1996, p. 3); in many cases, deregulation followed or was coupled with liberalisation. For example, Vogel cites the case of the deregula-tion process in the United States where liber-alised markets indeed got to mean freer rules. But that is not the general trend. In many cases, especially in advanced economies, liberalisation was coupled with more (not fewer) rules. Hence, it is often *reregulation* that is meant when discus-sions of market-oriented reforms are under way.

Analysis of the cases of telecommunications and financial sector regulation in the United States, Japan, Germany, France and the United Kingdom shows that stronger markets were not accompanied by weaker governments who after liberalisation embraced a hands-off approach in these sectors. On the contrary, in all these cases the state still played a powerful intervening role through the promotion of 'pro-market reregulation'. An example of how deregulation and reregulation are not as contradictory as usu-ally thought is the British 'financial revolution' of the 1980s. 'In the space of two weeks in the autumn of 1986, London experienced the boldest of both: the abolition of restrictive practices by the Stock Exchange and the inauguration of a new, more extensive and intrusive system of regulation. On 27 October, in what is referred to simply as the "Big Bang", the London Stock Exchange abandoned fixed commissions on stock transactions; eliminated the system of single capacity, whereby financial service firms could serve as market markers or brokers but not both; and opened membership to banks and foreign financial institutions. On 7 November, Parliament passed the Financial Services Act (FSA), which resulted in a new private regulatory agency, five self-regulatory organisations (SROs), (and) dozens of compliance departments' (Vogel, 1996, p. 93).

A more contemporary example of reregulation within a liberalised industry that has changed life for companies in the USA is the Sarbanes-Oxley Act of 2002 which was designed to respond to the many corporate scandals arising from financial and accounting fraud. 'The Act' or 'the New Law' was signed by President Bush on 30 July 2002 and was the most significant and comprehensive statutory revision of the US federal securities laws in over 60 years. The Act resulted in broad corporate and accounting reform for public companies and the accounting firms that audit them, enforced by the US Securities and Exchange Commission.

However, confining reregulation to formal governmental action does not tell the full story. The role of governments in this sphere of shaping financial market reform can be one of the 'mere prudential supervisor – the guardian of safety and soundness, but not the major determiner of the distributional or redistributional impact of market outcomes' (Cerny, 2000, p. 77). Governance in the case of the most footloose of economic activities – namely, that embraced by the financial sector – is to be seen not simply through the emergence of distinct, competing forms of authority (private versus public, or domestic versus international) but 'actually as convergence of both domestic and international governance structures around a neoliberal model' (Cerny, 2000, p. 67). Moreover, the implication of change in authority structures for financial reregulation is that 'the development of embryonic transnational governance processes and structures (regulating security markets) represents a shift of focus of transnational financial market regulation away from formal state institu-

tions and state actors per se to a combination of privatised governance and loose, networked public/private interfaces' (Cerny, 2000, p. 74).

The networks and hierarchies that transcend a neat domestic–international divide make up a third element in the structure of financial governance and this makes the reregulation of financial activity (especially) an example of the complex overlapping 'spheres of authority'. Understanding the politics embedded in this process is a tough exercise involving the dissection of the conflict of interest of the many players involved and linking the outcomes of the 'widening and deepening of private financial infrastructure' to the possible erosion of truly democratic governance (Cerny, 2000, p.78).

Further Reading

Aggarwal, Vinod (1996) *Debt Games: Strategic Interaction in International Debt Rescheduling*, Cambridge: Cambridge University Press.

Ahmed, Ismail and Lipton, Michael (1997) 'Impact of Structural Adjustment on Sustainable Rural Livelihoods: A Review of the Literature', IDS Working Paper 62, Sussex: Institute of Development Studies and Poverty Research Unit.

Biersteker, Thomas J. (1995) 'The Triumph of Liberal Economic Ideas in the Developing World' in Stallings, Barbara (ed) *Global Change, Regional Response: The New International Context of Development*, Cambridge: Cambridge University Press.

Bordo, Michael (1993) 'The Bretton Woods International Monetary System: A Historical Overview' in Bordo, Michael and Eichengreen, Barry (eds) *A Retrospective on the Bretton Woods System: Lesson for International Monetary Reform*, Chicago: The University of Chicago Press.

Cerny, Philip (2005) 'Power, Markets and Accountability: The Development of Multi-Level Governance in International Finance' in Baker, Andrew, Hudson, David and Woodward, Richard (eds) *Money, Finance and Multi-Level Governance*, Oxford: Routledge.

— (2002) 'Webs of Governance and the Privatisation of Transnational Regulation' in Andrews, David, Henning, C. Randall and Pauly Louis (eds) *Governing the World's Money*, Ithaca and London: Cornell University Press.

— (2000) 'Embedding Global Financial Markets: Securitisation and the Emerging Web of Governance' in Ronit, Karsten and Schneider, Volker (eds) *Private Organisations in Global Politics*, London: Routledge.

Chang, Roberto and Majnoni, Giovanni (1999) 'International Contagion: Implications for Policy', paper prepared for the World Bank Conference on 'Contagion: How It Can Be Stopped', Washington, D.C., 3–4 February 2000.

Cohen, Benjamin (1996) 'Phoenix Risen', *World Politics*, 48, 268–296.

Edwards, Sebastian (1995) *Crisis and Reform in Latin America: From Despair to Hope*, Oxford: Oxford University Press.

Eichengreen, Barry (1996) *Globalizing Capital: A History of the International Monetary System*, Princeton: Princeton University Press.

Financial Times, several issues.

Gilpin, Robert (2000) *The Challenge of Global Capitalism: The World Economy in the 21st Century*. Princeton: Princeton University Press.

Haggard, Stephen (1990) *Pathways from the Periphery: The Politics of Growth in the Newly Industrialised Countries*, Ithaca: Cornell University Press.

Kindleberger, Charles (2000) *Manias, Panics, and Crashes: A History of Financial Crises*, 4th edn, New York: John Wiley and Sons.

Krugman, Paul (1995) 'Dutch Tulips and Emerging Markets', *Foreign Affairs*, vol. 74, no. 4, July–August, pp. 28–44.

Pauly, Louis W. (1997) *Who Elected the Bankers? Surveillance and Control in the World Economy*, Ithaca: Cornell University Press.

Pieper, Ute and Taylor, Lance (1998) 'The Revival of the Liberal Creed: The IMF, the World Bank, and Inequality in a Globalised Economy', Centre for Economic Policy Analysis, Working Paper, no. 4, January.

Polanyi, Karl (1957) *The Great Transformation: The Political and Economic Origins of Our Time*, Boston: Beacon Press.

Rapley, John (1996) *Understanding Development: Theory and Practice in the Third World*, Boulder: Lynne Rienner Publishers.

Rodrik, Dani (1997) *Has Globalisation Gone Too Far?*, Washington, DC: Institute for International Economics.

— (2001) 'The Developing Countries' Hazardous Obsession with Global Integration', Harvard University, The John F. Kennedy School of Government, mimeo, 8 January.

Rosenau, James (1992) 'Citizenship in a Changing Global Order' in *Governance Without Government: Order and Change in World Politics* in Rosenau, James N. and Czempiel, Ernst-Otto (eds) Cambridge: Cambridge University Press.

— (1997) *Along the Domestic-Foreign Frontier: Exploring Governance in a Turbulent World*. Cambridge: Cambridge University Press.

Ruggie, John (1995) 'At Home Abroad, Abroad At Home: International Liberalisation and Domestic Stability in the New World Economy', *Millennium*, Winter, pp. 507–526.

Sassen, Saskia (1996) *Losing Control?*, New York: Columbia University Press.

Scholte, Jan Aart (1997) 'Global Capitalism and the State', *International Affairs*, vol. 73, no. 3, July, pp. 427–452.

Stallings, Barbara (1992) 'International Influence on Economic Policy: Debt, Stabilisation, and Structural Reform' in Haggard, Stephan and Kaufman, Robert (eds) *The Politics of Economic Adjustment*, Princeton: Princeton University Press.

Stallings, Barbara and Peres, Wilson (2000) *Growth, Employment, and Equity: The Impact of the Economic Reforms in Latin America and the Caribbean*, Washington, DC: The Brookings Institute Press.

Strange, Susan (1998) *Mad Money*, Ann Arbor: University of Michigan Press.

Vogel, Steven K. (1996) *Freer Markets, More Rules: Regulatory Reforms in Advanced Industrial Countries*, Ithaca: Cornell University Press.

Wade, Robert (1999) 'The Coming Fight over Capital Flows', *Foreign Policy*, Winter, pp. 41–53.

Weeler, Cristian E. (2001) 'Financial Crises After Financial Liberalisation: Exceptional Circumstances or Structural Weakness?', *Journal of Development Studies*, vol. 38, no. 1, October, pp. 98–127.

Williamson, John (1990) 'What Washington Means by Policy Reform', Washington, DC: Institute for International Economics.

CHAPTER 7: Religion

In February 1989 UNESCO, the cultural arm of the United Nations, convened a symposium in Paris with the theme 'No World Peace Without Religious Peace'. That an essentially secular organisation should have taken this as the focus for its deliberations may be very significant. Viewed from one angle this rubric implies that religion plays a special role in human affairs and is necessary for those affairs to be so conducted as to serve the well-being of humankind. But viewed from another angle it implies that religions are sources of divisiveness and conflict and that unless those features of their behaviour are overcome, all efforts at seeking a peaceful world are likely to be futile.

Ambiguity

The two possible meanings of the same phrase point to a profound and persistent ambiguity that marks the place that religious belief and practice plays in global affairs. On the one hand there are inspiring teachings in most religious traditions about the need for peace and the moral obligations to sustain community between and benevolence towards peoples of every land and culture. On the other hand, religion is often either the source of, or the sanction for, exclusionary divisiveness and tribal insularity.

There is a sense in which religion exhibits both the best and the worst of the attitudes and behaviour which affect global affairs. Those who see the worst often suggest that nations and groups will come together only by excluding religion from the social process. In contrast, those who see the best believe that only as the teachings of religion that extol the virtues of peace, justice and worldwide community are brought to bear on political affairs will any peaceful conditions between nations and peoples prevail.

Making an impact

This section focuses on sources of crises and conflict. What follows, therefore, will concen-

trate on the ways in which religion contributes to destabilising and hostile actions in the global scene. Religion may, of course, be a constructive force, but there is ample warrant for treating religion as a problem in the contemporary world. Its impact on current affairs has become more and more apparent and increasingly disturbing in recent years, especially in its relationship with the spread of terrorism. In contrast to prevailing political and social scientific ways of looking at the world, a more global perspective on religious violence is needed. In 2001, over half of the 34 serious conflicts around the world had a religious dimension to them. A rise in religiously related conflict or terrorism by new religious non-state actors has taken place over the last 20 years; they do not rely on the support of sovereign states (which is what distinguishes global terrorism from international terrorism), nor do they seem to set any constraints on the limits of their violence (Thomas, Palgrave Macmillan, 2005, 9).

Oliver McTernan utilises three paradigms to indicate the reasons why violence erupts in certain places and under certain conditions. These are *creed, grievance* and *greed*. Each of these terms is a shorthand way of pointing to a particular way of understanding the outlooks that give rise to conflicts. They differ to a large extent in the degree to which they consider religion to be the pivotal factor in explaining conflict.

The term 'creed' refers to the religious thought patterns that give rise to disagreements – thought patterns of the type to which Samuel Huntington has directed attention in speaking about the clash of civilisations (Simon and Schuster, 1996). The claim is that differences in fundamental beliefs are increasingly at the root of global conflicts. In commenting on this, McTernan suggests that Huntington has possibly been overly prone to see religions as consisting of belief structures with monolithic features, though he does acknowledge that Huntington may be right in judging many contemporary conflicts to be outgrowths of differences between clearly identifiable world views. But McTernan's own term, 'creed', may have its own reductionist limitations for describing the thought patterns of a religion.

What is at stake is not merely a formal set of doctrines – which is what is usually meant by the term creed – but a broader spread of beliefs and practices that characterises a religious tradition in its entirety. There is certainly no doubt that there are deep and persistent contrasts between various religions, particularly when those religions are embraced as the one and only proper way to understand reality. Mark Juergensmeyer (2001) is another scholar whose work emphasises the causal role of religious factors in the rise of conflict. His study of the role of religion in the rise of terrorism is particularly insightful in this.

The third term in McTernan's trilogy is 'greed': this paradigm puts much less emphasis on matters of belief and commitment and points instead to economic conditions that give rise to conflicts. According to this paradigm for understanding global conflict, advanced by Paul Collier of the World Bank among others, conflicts develop in low-income countries when the poor prospects of obtaining a greater share in wealth become apparent to the economically downtrodden. This can happen only when such groups find the means to finance military operations, either by appropriating resources from within or by financing them from outside. If they do find such resources, they challenge the injustice of the existing order.

That quasi-economic explanation for the rise of conflict is closely related to the last of the terms suggested by McTernan, 'grievance'. This explanation draws attention to the manner in which being deprived of the resources of a culture breeds resentments. This paradigm is utilised by Ted Robert Gurr (2000), who challenges the assumption that religious outlooks are the main source of conflicts and suggests that conflict arises from governments' failure to acknowledge the claims of small groups – groups that are often but not necessarily religious in character. Such treatment breeds what McTernan calls grievance.

This approach does bring into contrast a number of ways to deal with the sources of conflict, but it tends to draw distinctions between views that stress the centrality of religion and those that tend to discount it. We can learn from these paradigms that while religion is somehow involved in the cause of conflict, it may be easy to overplay, underplay or misplay that role and that scholars differ in how they understand the extent to which religion is at the root of contemporary conflicts. If political and social scientists whose thinking is dominated by secular premises underplay that role, then a corrective is called for. McTernan offers his own version of such a corrective in a chapter entitled 'Religion matters'. Others have made a similar point; for instance, Max L. Stackhouse writes (2002, p. 11):

The moral and apolitical architecture of every civilisation is grounded, more than any other factor, in religious commitments that point to a source of normative meaning beyond the political, economic, and cultural structures themselves. Neither these spheres of life nor the dynamics of the modern professions and the transnational, transeconomic, and transcultural movements for, say, ecology or racial justice can be understood without grasping the religious dimensions of moral convictions and social history

The foregoing materials are typical of a growing awareness that religion plays a very important role in world affairs. But beyond making that point it is important to recognise the nature of the role played by religion in global politics to understand how religion functions. For this task alternative approaches may be more useful. One way to do this is to sort out causes that frequently gain religious support and then to examine how religion serves to motivate people in pursuing those causes.

Religion in the service of causes

Religion often contributes to conflict by providing the cause or the rationale for which violence is considered necessary. This happens in a variety of ways. In one way, which may have been more evident in the past than it is in the present, religion uses coercive means to extend a particular faith system. For instance, when Constantine reversed his policy of opposition to Christianity and made it the official religion of the Roman Empire, he proceeded to employ the sword as an instrument of evangelism.

Wars undertaken to combat infidelity or paganism and to establish true faith in their place are usually called 'religious wars' or 'wars of religion'. Such efforts are best described as crusades and are driven by a zealous conviction that the spread of faith is warranted for the well-being of others or (negatively put) that the destruction of a false system of belief and practice is necessary to protect the truth. Crusades may be less evident in the contemporary world than they may have been in the past or they may be transformed into political agendas that obscure their quasi-religious impulses, but true and fervent beliefs frequently harbour an incipient tendency to consider such convictions to be an obligation that may be imposed upon others, even by force.

The effort to spread a particular faith by the use of force is not the only way in which religion backs causes. Religion also contributes to conflict by supporting one side in a conflict that has arisen in some other part of society. Religions often give holy meaning to essentially secular agendas. When religious motivations become entangled with such conflicts, prudential undertakings often acquire an urgency they would not otherwise have. Ordinary concerns become matters of transcendent importance.

Many social causes that religion embraces have no direct relationship to the creeds and doctrines by which religions define their central identity. Religion often engenders support for cultural mores that are peripheral to its main belief structure but which often are held with the same (perhaps even greater) tenacity as the central doctrines. Such mores are then advocated as a social policy that is binding upon all persons, not merely on those who adhere to a particular faith. For instance, those who would oppose abortion in any and all forms believe that it is entirely appropriate to make such opposition into strict civil laws that outlaw the practice, but most of the same people would oppose a state-imposed requirement to believe in the Christian Trinity. Similarly, those who believe in biblical creationism are willing to use civil authority to require it be taught as having equal standing with evolution. Few of these groups, however, would ever consider making a civil law to require belief in the divinity of Jesus or something like the doctrine of predestination.

These general considerations are the background for looking at the role of religion in some specific contemporary conflicts. That role is extensive and seems to be increasing sharply. It cannot be fully, perhaps not even adequately, described in this context, but it can be illustrated and obvious and disturbing patterns examined. No religious tradition – Eastern or Western, theistic or otherwise, traditional or innovative – has managed to escape some sort of involvement in conflict as protagonist for some cause. There may be small pockets within the major traditions that are exceptions, but none of these has the wherewithal to be a major player on the global stage.

How religion serves causes

It is possible to think about the kinds of causes which religions support by using three terms, each beginning with an 'r'. This is a way of highlighting significant differences with terms that have not lost their uniqueness through overuse. The terms *residency*, *recognition* and *rectitude* can be used to point to different ways religion becomes involved with causes. Under the rubric *residency* we mean concerns about geographical locations, land, other earthly dependencies; under the term *recognition* we mean concerns for status and standing and for participation in (or control of) the social process; and under the term *rectitude* we mean efforts to advance particular moral values and cultural mores that a given religious group deems crucial for societal well-being.

Concern for any of these matters – which seldom occur in pure form and are often found in combinations – can lead to conflicts, as certain consequences become highly sought after or as efforts to prevent the achievement of certain consequences result in rigorous forms of resistance.

Residency

No effort to understand the conflict in the Middle East, for example, will get to the root of the difficulty if it does not take into account the symbolic and practical significance attached by both sides to the conflict over the ownership of land. Perhaps as much or more than is the case with any other modern conflict, the struggle in the Holy Land is between two groups that believe possession of certain territory is religiously important. The conflict between Palestinians and Israelis is not marked by efforts of either side to convert the other side to some theological affirmations; 'residency' plays the pivotal role in this conflict.

On the Israeli side this dynamic is especially

strong in Zionist groups such as those that opposed the 'land for peace' approach of the Oslo Accords. Not only is the establishment of the state of Israel as a territorial reality central to their outlook as to the nature of religious fulfilment, but securing territory becomes in effect an exercise in piety. Oliver McTernan reports that in visiting Beth-El, a Jewish settlement that overlooks Ramallah, it was very apparent to him that in understanding the cause of the conflict 'both security and water were important factors, but more important to them was the belief that God wanted them to be there' (McTernan, 2003, p. 116).

On the Palestinian side Article 5 of the Hamas Charter reads 'The land of Palestine is an Islamic *Waaf* (holy possession) consecrated for future Muslims until Judgment Day. No one can renounce it or any part of it, or abandon it or any part of it'.

Such views prompt their adherents not only to resist negotiations with the other side that might give up the possession of territory, but even to condemn those within their own faith communities who would consider such negotiation to be a legitimate way to achieve peace. To relinquish or qualify the possession of certain territory in any way is a form of apostasy.

Concern about sacred places rather than about broader territory is a variation of concern about residency, but can lead to a similar dynamic. Even though the space in question is more limited in size and is the locus of specifically religious activity rather than residency in general, location is the central factor. Many religions have sites that they regard as having sacred meaning and needing to be preserved from profanation or elimination. When other groups either lay claim to such places or treat them with insufficient respect, religious groups can become agitated to an extent that leads to conflict. In some traditions only pilgrims whose fidelity is vouched for are permitted to visit sacred places.

The concern about residency has important meaning in many traditions. Central to biblical faith is a concern for material well-being and for the possession of land as essential to that well-being. Peoplehood is dependent upon residency; spiritual identity closely connected to location in time and space. Such an understanding is not as important to many other religious traditions, which often view fulfilment (or salvation) as involving severance from the confines of earthly habitation. Yet even in such traditions shrines are respected and seldom abandoned.

But while the concern about land has profound implications for the religions in which it is important, it can be the source of problems, most particularly when claims to land come into dispute and residency requires the dislocation of others in order for the appointed group to enjoy a divinely manifested destiny. The USA, created by the displacement of a migrant population, is not without some similarities with Israel and therefore tends to resonate with the experience of a modern society that was created in much the same way as it was. But if the native peoples of North America had been stronger, the USA might be facing the same turmoil that marks life in the contemporary Middle East. Were native Americans to propose to retake land from contemporary owners on the premise that such land was divinely appointed to be theirs, it is hard to imagine their action would be considered entirely legitimate and acceded to without rancour. Suggestions that Americans might fulfil their manifest destiny by moving as pilgrims to other geographical locations would hardly be met with robust approval.

Recognition

There are differences within Israel itself over the extent to which the state should make the particularities of Jewish laws and practice mandatory. Those who would insist on doing so, while possibly a minority, are concerned about more than land and resources. The rubric *recognition* is useful for pointing to the desire of religious groups to practise their faith without fear or restraint – that is, to be recognised – and may even point to the impulse to impose certain practices upon all those with whom they are in proximity or correspondence.

There is bound to be an element of such concern in every area in which religiously identifiable groups are located, but the degree to which that concern leads to conflict will vary greatly. The desire to be recognised in ways that favour the exercise of a particular religion can be very strong and may even escalate into a desire to be the dominant tradition. When that happens, the consequences can be marked by hostility and may result in violence.

However, just as religious factors that lead to residency as a cause for conflict are seldom, if ever, the sole and sufficient explanation for the rise of violence in a particular situation, so those factors that come under the rubric *recognition* are seldom if ever the only ones that operate in particular instances. But this does not mean the category is insignificant, especially for analytical purposes in pointing to one of the relationships that is often evident between religious belief and political conflict.

The desire for recognition, that is, to enjoy the standing to embrace a particular faith and to practise it without illegitimate interference, can be a powerful one and whenever it is either curtailed or denied, resentment follows. The facts of history make it clear that desires for recognition are probably thwarted as much or possibly more than they are accommodated, especially in situations where two or more traditions seek to achieve pre-eminence. The struggle for recognition can be seen in conflicts dispersed as to location and diverse in their cultural setting. This may be the most prominent of the causes that generate conflicts. These conflicts may happen for any number of other reasons, but when they are overlaid with religious commitments the hostility can become intense and almost intractable. This is especially the case when two groups, each with its own religious identity, come into conflict.

One illustration of this is the struggle between Protestants and Catholics in Northern Ireland, a persistent and bloody altercation that has long thwarted efforts at resolution. There are many theories about the origins of the 'Troubles' in Northern Ireland, and factors other than religion are significant for understanding the origin of the unfortunate hostility between the local adherents of these two religious groups. But it is difficult for any such explanations to be credible apart from the recognition factor. Strictly speaking, this may not be an international matter because there are many places in the world where Protestants and Catholics live harmoniously with each other. Scott M. Thomas (2005) does not deal with it in his discussion of the global resurgence of religion, but it does have implications for other nations, such as Britain.

The tensions and suspicions that mark the relationships between these two groups were perpetuated by the prevailing separatism in housing and education that developed over many years. Oliver McTernan, who lived under those conditions during his early years, calls this 'sectarianism'. Although the importance of the religious factor is discounted by some scholars of these events, that judgement is warranted only in so far as it indicates that the religious factors are more sociological than theological in character. Although that may have been the case for much of the past, there is reason to hold that it is becoming less true in light of recent developments, in which clergy have become involved in political action and fundamentalism has developed in ways that undergird political partisanship with doctrinal opposition to diversity and compromise.

McTernan also points out that the causes involved include some of the same religious stances as are typical of behaviour described under the rubric *residency*. For instance, the Scots who were forebears considered themselves a chosen people (not quite *the* chosen people) and were deeply attached to the land. The current followers of the Reverend Ian Paisley are particularly strident Protestants who hold that compromise is a form of religious apostasy (McTernan, p. 90).

Even though the setting and the religious traditions are different – eastern rather than western – the conflict between the Sinhala majority and the Tamil minority in Sri Lanka stems from some of the very same causes as the conflicts between Protestants and Catholics in Ireland. In this South-East Asian country, efforts to achieve a peaceful rapport between the contending factions (largely Muslims, Buddhists and Hindus) are stymied by longstanding antagonisms and contemporary suspicions. The violence has been motivated by feelings among the Tamil group that their language and entitlement to the land are deeply rooted in a religious tradition – making the idea of pluralism anathema.

Some scholars contend that it is the discrimination that the Tamil have experienced which accounts for their propensity to violence more than does their adherence to particular religious ideas. The state constitution provides for freedom of religion, but the practice has been to give preferential treatment to the Buddhist majority. Despite formal teaching to the contrary, Buddhists (and particularly the monks) have embraced violence as a means of furthering the Sinhala cause. In a statement all too typical of religious people from any number of traditions, one monk said: 'I know that as a monk it is wrong for me to think in this way, but I believe that the five precepts of Buddhism not to kill, steal, misbehave sexually, lie or drink alcohol work in normal circumstances; the situation in Sri Lanka is abnormal and therefore one has to suspend some of the principles' (McTernan, 2003, p. 99). When that line of reasoning is employed by religious people, the result is the sanctification of violence as a last resort and even its escalation into terrorism.

Rectification

A third reason for which religion embraces conflict is to advance a particular moral agenda or set of behavioural mores. The main difference between recognition and rectification is that one seeks to ensure the right of a particular group to pursue its own identity and practices whereas the other indicates a desire in a religious group to bring the behaviour of others into conformity with its idea of what is right.

The term 'purify' is sometimes used to indicate the need for change in conditions that are contrary to those which a religion approves. In domestic life the most blatant instance of this drive to suppress or destroy something considered evil is the willingness of a few zealots on the right to use violence against abortion clinics. In global affairs, disapproval of cultural developments that threaten cherished values often impels people to drastic actions, even to terrorism. They act against what they regard as cultural decadence, aiming to rectify the unacceptable behaviour of others or the prevailing trends of modern culture. Such efforts can easily go beyond the boundaries of civility and are especially resistant to being altered by negotiation and compromise.

Those who are devoted to freedom often find it difficult to understand why others find freedom threatening, particularly those who are staunchly devoted to moral order or to some version of religiously delineated purity. Except in rare circumstances, free societies are societies in which both creativity and destructiveness occur simultaneously and in which communities frequently witness harmony and divisiveness present at the same time. Moral licence can run its course along with devotion to the good. Free societies require that risks must be taken in the realm of security and morals in order to be safeguarded from the exercise of arbitrary authority. Many religions do not understand the importance of taking such risks, often being more concerned with cultivating and preserving what is right and proper. Indeed, there are adherents of every religion who find it difficult to understand the interconnectedness of freedom and risk, of liberty and cultural diversity. As the writer

Fyodor Dostoevsky showed so brilliantly in the 'Grand Inquisitor' section of *The Brothers Karamazov,* the fear of freedom can be great and the impulse to rectify untraditional behaviour can lead to oppressive tactics. What is so baffling and disturbing about this phenomenon is the realisation that moral earnestness rather than malfeasance can be a source of conflict and that religious zeal for the defence of righteousness can be as much a source of conflict as malicious grasps for power.

The impulse to seek the rectification of the behaviour of others is likely to be strongest in periods of social change and transformation. Religions that are afraid of diversity are particularly prone to be suspicious of social changes. They may seek to preserve, even to recapture, old ways and to strike out against any and all outlooks that stand in their way. This may help to explain why the massive world changes that are generally described as globalisation may well be the very things that breed reactive religious behaviour, including terrorism. The more that changes seem irresistible, the greater the tendency to resist them with great fury.

Religion as the motivation for conflict

There are, too, other ways of describing attitudes stemming from the religious impulses that have a tendency to create additional fury. The difference between these two considerations is not distinct and complete, but each way of looking at specific contemporary conflicts offers some understanding that is not found in the other.

In contrast to backing a particular cause or combination of causes, religion may function to provide motivation for conflict. Terrorism highlights the enormous extremes to which religious motivation can be carried. Suicidal bombings make sense only in religious terms. Their fury and manic destructiveness are inextricably dependent upon the embrace of commitment that is beyond the reach of rational legitimation. Such behaviour may or may not be undertaken to further a specifically religious objective, but it is likely to have a special fury for whatever agenda it seeks to advance.

However, terrorism is not the only way in which religion sanctifies conflict. Ordinary warfare – that which uses violence in controlled and officially sanctioned ways – is often religiously motivated and is more intense for that reason. For instance, in the First World War, churches became recruiting stations and 'preachers presented arms'. Sacred heroics are more appealing than secular risk taking, doing God's will more of a reason for sacrifice than merely protecting self-interest. Warfare might very well take place without invoking divine legitimation, but with less zeal than would be associated with ordinary disagreements. Moreover, conflicts that rage without the benefit of religious sanction may be brought to a close more readily than those that have become sacred causes. Compromise is more possible on pragmatic concerns than it is on matters that are considered to embody ultimate commitments. Negotiation is more feasible as a matter of prudence than when it is viewed as a transgression of sacred trust.

The difference for global politics between religion in the service of causes and religion as a source of motivation may not at first seem to be very great. Neither results in any desirable scenario and both are likely to be of concern to those who care for the welfare of the international community. The difference is not a matter of polar opposition that consists of thesis and antithesis in sharp contrast, but rather a nuanced comparison consisting of variations in emphasis and orientation. In the case of serving causes, the quality of religious belief may not be a major factor in what is happening; in the case of motivation, it can be the decisive variable. What participation in conflict does to religion is just as important as what religious involvement does to conflicts.

Charles Kimball has focused attention on features in religion that indicate a propensity towards belligerence. When these features appear the outlook is grim. The attitudes that Kimball identifies are not necessarily a part of religion under normal conditions, but arise when a destructive relationship develops between religion and political affairs. No study of the relationship of religion to conflict can be adequate without taking into account the behavioural patterns that Kimball has delineated. What follows utilises Kimball's categories but makes certain emendations of them.

The first of the signals that religion has become, or is becoming, evil can be seen in the manner in which beliefs are embraced. All religions make truth claims, but such claims can be advanced in very different ways and set forth in very different spirits. It is one thing to affirm that a religious idea is profoundly moving and that it sheds light in fruitful ways upon the relationship between the divine and the human; it is another to hold that a particular assertion is a proposition with immutable validity and factual correctness. The first way of understanding truth in religion is attended by modesty and flexibility in thought and sophistication in commitment; the second is alluring because it removes doubt but is destructive because it fosters arrogance. It regards all deviation from strict acceptance of its views as dangerous infidelity.

Fundamentalism

Fundamentalism in religion – which occurs in a great many traditions – consists of holding religious truth as absolutes, propositional in nature and essentially factual in substance. It often appeals, curiously enough, to a number of people who work with modern knowledge systems, such as scientific thinking, whose practitioners can sometimes assume that all knowing must have the same decisiveness as they believe science does. In the modern world, fundamentalist ways of understanding religion raise problems not only of intellectual integrity but also of behavioural rigidity. According to Kimball (2003, p. 44):

When zealous and devout adherents elevate the teachings and beliefs of their tradition to the level of absolute truth claims, they open the door to the possibility that their religious will become evil . . . people armed with absolute truth claims are closely linked to violent extremism, charismatic leaders, and various justifications for acts otherwise understood to be unacceptable.

To hold that one's specific way of formulating religious truth represents the only possible way of understanding the divine implies that all other formulations must be treated as false and those who hold them as apostate. That is a recipe for making evangelisation confrontational and triumphalistic, which not infrequently has been the source of intolerant behaviour. This approach to other faiths is often associated with literalism concerning sacred texts, or as Kimball indicates, 'manipulative exploitation of sacred texts can lead to violent zealotry' (2003, p. 53). And 'when missionary zeal is informed by absolute truth claims defining who is "saved" and what is acceptable, the propagation of religion frequently includes sinister dimensions' (p. 62).

This way of holding to religious convictions is, ironically, often a response to challenges of those convictions, either by friendly critics within a tradition or by hostile critics from outside. It arises, therefore, not as much in times of confident belief but more in times of scepticism; less in times when there is a general consensus about religious matters and more in times when the diversity of religious beliefs around the world becomes undeniable. When such conditions are responded to with efforts to overcome them by asserting beliefs with vigour and intransigence, conflict is likely to result. This explains why religious fundamentalism, despite its claim to be the truest embodiment of traditional fidelity, is modern in its appearance and often akin to the very mode of thinking against which it is a reaction.

The second indication that religious faith is leading to evil consequences is 'blind obedience'. Kimball examines this by citing the behaviour of groups that have prompted their adherents to engage in bizarre and destructive activities. Such behaviour may be directed against others, as in the case of the Aum Shinrkyo sect that released poison gas in the subways of Tokyo, or it can result in bizarre behaviour within the group itself, as happened in the case of Jonestown and the Branch Davidians. It is obvious from these events that charismatic leaders can elicit unquestioning obedience when certain conditions are met, such as a belief that their leader is divine or enjoys a special access to what God expects. Sometimes blind obedience develops when people feel that followers' fortunes are entirely in the hands of the leaders.

The groups that Kimball cites are generally sectarian in nature – that is, they tend to withdraw from the world in order to pursue a special kind of holiness. In general such groups do not seek social change or use violence as an instrument of public policy. But blind obedience could appear in other groups, those that participate in global affairs. In some respects this is one possible factor in the rise of terrorism. It is not clear, however, that terrorists resort to destructive actions merely out of blind allegiance to a leader. In many instances they are committed to a cause and are willing to undertake destructive actions to further that cause.

A third dynamic propelling religions to further conflict is more difficult to describe and more difficult to understand than the preceding two. On its surface it often appears to be an earnest effort to take the requirements of faith seriously. Kimball describes it with the phrase 'establishing the "ideal" time'. He discusses what happens when adherents of a religion seek to control temporal affairs and coerce those affairs to conform to their assumptions about what is morally required and behaviourally correct. This may be less a matter of merely providing motivations and zeal than of embracing an agenda with special urgency – an urgency that differs decisively from ordinary thrusts for power.

The behaviour that results from religious efforts to play a commanding role in the social process is often brittle, aggressive and truculent. This is not because religion admires such attitudes as a normal matter, but arises because adherents of a faith system believe that once they achieve mastery of temporal affairs, the ambiguities and tussles that currently characterise political life will cease for ever. The promise of utopia then warrants extreme measures to bring it about. This has the effect of excluding the procedures and flexibility that make political life tolerable under ordinary circumstances. That is what 'establishing the "ideal" time' means. The expectation of a utopian outcome becomes the basis on which extreme measures can be employed to bring it about. Not infrequently this outlook is associated with a futuristic eschatology that sees the transition occurring through some sudden and cataclysmic explosion of anger and violence by means of which all those standing in the way of attaining that fulfilment must be vanquished. As Kimball notes (2002, p.105): 'When the hoped for ideal is tied to a particular religious worldview and those who wish to implement their vision become convinced that they know what God wants for them and everyone else, you have a prescription for disaster.'

Kimball indicates how this dynamic works out in efforts to establish an ideal Islamic state, an Israel that enjoys its land unthreatened by any other groups, and the hope of the religious right for a Christian America in which the government coercively enforces moral norms and cultural practices that it considers obligatory. Religions that are motivated by such hopes look upon diversity as a form of disloyalty and compromise as a failure of fidelity. Fanaticism is bred less from deliberate malice than from excessive zeal.

In the case of the first three signs that point to the misuse of religion the potential for evil stems from the misuse or corruption of an otherwise acceptable aspect of what it means to be faithful. Making absolute truth claims is a corruption of legitimate concern to hold religious faith with serious tenacity; blind obedience is an excessive version of due respect for leadership; and chiliastic excess is a miscarriage of efforts to bring about constructive social change. With Kimball's fourth warning sign we come to practices that are more easily recognised to be inherently dangerous and destructive. This warning sign appears in behaviour that removes all restraints on actions in order to achieve a particular consequence, what is commonly described as the end justifying the means. 'The most obvious sign of this corruption is visible when compassionate and constructive relationships with others are discarded' (2002, p. 129).

Kimball finds this pattern evident in conflicts where religion uses excessive violence to protect sacred places, in the use of religion to manipulate political affairs, where adherents of one faith treat those of other faiths, or members of other cultures, with contemptuous disregard or even hostility, and when religion is used to subjugate particular groups (often women) to the will of a dominant majority.

Perhaps the most blatant and obvious instance of using the end to justify the means can be observed in the attempts of authority figures to use cruel and immoral strategies to protect religious institutions, as did the Inquisition. Anyone who has visited the museums in southern France that document the horrors visited on the Waldenses and Cathari will not easily ignore the extent to which religion can be demonic when it feels the needs to defend itself by coercion.

Holy war

The fifth sign is the declaration of holy war. To understand this sign requires a careful look at various ways in which religion has legitimised the use of armed conflict as an exception to the more prevailing concern for peace that is typical of many traditions. There are ways in which religion legitimises violence that raise serious moral problems, but there are other ways in which religion legitimises the use of force that are expressions of a moral concern – at least in the eyes of their advocates.

There are basically three ways in which religion legitimises conflict. The first of these is outright approval and zealous support, which expresses itself in the phenomenon of the holy war – or the crusade. The second is critical assessment of the legitimacy of a particular reason to use armed force together with concern to restrain that use by certain moral limitations. That is the stance of just war thinking. The third is to accept the need for war as a tragic necessity, involving admittedly unfortunate actions accompanied by humble regret that no constructive possibility for achieving such a result seems to be available. That is the stance of agonised participation or conscientious participation and was the ground on which many Christians entered the Second World War (Long, 1968).

Many people wonder how religion becomes the motivation for conflict to the extent represented by the crusade or holy war. To engage in holy warfare seems to exhibit arrogance and hostility that stand in stark contrast to the teaching about peace and reconciliation that holds a central place in many religions. Support for holy warfare uses selective aspects of a religious tradition that are dormant in times of tranquility but can readily appear when they seem to be useful for legitimating a struggle.

The use of the Bible in both Judaism and Christianity is a case in point. The Old Testament contains many accounts of battles fought with the approval of God. God is sometimes portrayed as a warrior who gives cosmic backing to earthly struggles. Successful use of violence is often considered to be a precondition for becoming a leader. There is no denying the fact that much biblical material, especially that in the so-called historical writings, can be read as giving sanction for violence done in God's name. The Song of Deborah in the fifth chapter of Judges vividly indicates the extent to which violence has sometimes been evident within the tradition.

Although those who act tend to be cosmic rather than historical figures, the last book of the New Testament is replete with the imagery of warfare.

A similar contrast exists between two strands of thinking in Islam. The concept of jihad is central, but it is understood in different ways. One view understands the term to cover all efforts to live a holy life, something that requires diligence and discipline. But another view understands jihad to signify more violent struggle, that is, holy warfare. In this view the use of violence is considered to be an instrument of service to God. Muslims, like Christians, disagree as to whether that shift is legitimate, but there is little doubt that is has sometimes been very evident. When that is the case, then, in Campbell's phrase, 'religion becomes evil'.

Analogously, a similar tendency to embrace violence as an expression of fidelity appears as counterpoint to the main orientation of the tradition. In Hinduism for instance, the Bhagavad Gita focuses attention on the duty of the Kshatriyas, or warrior caste, to fight battles without qualms or reservations. When its chief character expresses reservations about doing so, the admonition comes with startling emphasis: 'Heedless of issue, fight.' Only by following the duty of the warrior caste will its members assure themselves of salvation.

Religious legitimation for the use of violence becomes evil when it serves to exclude moral restraints and to endorse the use of the maximum violence. It also becomes evil when violence is used as an instrument of retribution. That is what happens when the crusade model (as in the case of Christianity) or a harsh version of the jihad model (as in the case of Islam) governs. Contempt for the enemy takes over and replaces the political concerns that call for restraining action; a search to obtain abject surrender replaces a willingness to settle if the other side agrees to modify its behaviour; and a dualistic contrast is drawn between the complete virtue of one side and the demonic status of the other. All of these are warning signs that religion is playing a dysfunctional role in the global scene.

Aspects of war

Special attention should be given to the different ways of thinking about holy war and just war. There have been times when the actual consequences of these two different ways of embracing armed conflict made little difference. At such moments, the idea of the just war was used almost entirely as a way of legitimising conflict and its possible usefulness for providing critical judgement as to when conflict is necessary as a last resort and for restraining excessive destructiveness within conflict (as, for instance, prohibiting attacks on noncombatants) loses significance. There is no denying that this has been the predominant pattern for most of the period since the theory was first articulated as an alternative to pacifism.

But there is a current debate going on about just war thinking that may have considerable moral significance for the future. On the one hand, many pacifists continue to regard the just war approach as a bankrupt way of thinking that serves only to keep religious adherents from remaining faithful to the peace teaching core of their heritage. They feel that unless violence is entirely repudiated as a means of dealing with global matters, no peace will ever come. On the other hand, many people have come to realise that just war thinking can actually provide criteria for opposing a particular conflict, a trend that became evident initially during the military action in Vietnam and has been articulated far more explicitly as a basis for condemning the military action in Iraq by the United States. Just war thinking may also be utilised to restrain intentional actions that harm noncombatants and to mount a strong case against the use of torture as an instrument of intelligence gathering. If it is used to achieve those objectives, there are reasons to think that its consequences could be seen as helpful, even by pacifists.

The foregoing discussion has focused on how religion functions in relation to global affairs and on the ways in which it is a contributing cause of conflict. In most case the two different dynamics interact. It may not be particularly important whether religion embraces causes that are in search of a mood or whether religion creates a mood that is in search of a cause. The outcome is likely to be unfortunate. Hopefully there are ways religion can help in efforts to advance the cause of harmony and justice in world affairs. One scholar has expressed that hope as follows:

In each of the major religious traditions of the world, prophets, theologians, sages, scholars, and simple believers, exalted by the holy lives they led, refined and deepened the tradition's spiritual practices and theological teachings in support of peacemaking rather than war, reconciliation rather than retaliation. To be traditional, then, is to take seriously those developments that achieved authoritative status because they probed, clarified, and developed the insights and teachings contained in the foundational sources.

(Appleby, 2000, pp. 16–17)

The hope implied in this passage that religion can be a source of peace and reconciliation should not be allowed to die, but keeping it alive will for ever be a major challenge. A sober and realistic appraisal of how religion influences the political world requires taking into account the probability that religious voices will be attended to more readily when they support the agendas of state actors than when they criticise those actions. Religious leaders who support kings, princes and presidents are more likely to be invited to audiences, prayer breakfasts and policy deliberations than prophetic types who oppose such leaders.

But this does not mean religion can never serve as a guide for the policies of leaders. Its witness and advocacy against violence and conflict can have slow, quiet and long-range consequences for which it may not receive public accolades. Unless that happens, the prospects of a better world are dismal and religiously inspired social witness a fidelity that may come to fruition only in another world.

Further Reading

Appleby, R. Scott. (2000) *The Ambivalence of the Sacred: Religion, Violence, and Reconciliation*, Lanham: Rowman and Littlefield.

Carlson, John D. and Owens, Erik C. (eds) (2003) *The Sacred and the Sovereign: Religion and International Politics*, Washington DC: Georgetown University Press.

Gopin, Marc (2000) *Between Eden and Armageddon: The Future of World Religions, Violence and Peacemaking*, New York: Oxford University Press.

Gurr, Ted Robert (2000) *People Versus States: Minorities at Risk in the New Country*, United States Institute of Peace Press.

Huntington, Samuel P. (1996) *The Clash of Civilisations and the Remaking of World Order*, New York: Simon and Schuster.

Juergensmeyer, Mark (ed) (2003) *Global Religions: An Introduction*, New York: Oxford University Press.

— (2001) *Terror in the Mind of God: The Global Rise of Religious Violence*, Berkeley: University of California Press.

Kimball, Charles (2002) *When Religion Becomes Evil: Five Warning Signs*, San Francisco: Harper.

Long, Edward LeRoy, Jr (2004) *Facing Terrorism: Responding as Christians*, Louisville: Westminster/John Knox Press.

— (1968) *War and Conscience in America*, Philadelphia: Westminster Press.

McTernan, Oliver (2003) *Violence in God's Name: Religion in an Age of Conflict*, Maryknoll: Orbis Books.

Selengut, Charles (2003) *Sacred Fury: Understanding Religious Violence*, Walnut Creek: AltaMira Press.

Shenk, David W. (1999) *Global Gods: Exploring the Role of Religions in Modern Societies*, Scottdale: Herald Press.

Stackhouse, Max L. and Obenchain, Diane B. (eds) (2002) *Christ and the Dominions of Civilisation*, Harrisburg: Trinity Press International.

Thomas, Scott M. (2005) *The Global Resurgence of Religion and the Transformation of International Relations: The Struggle for the Soul of the Twenty-first Century*, New York: Palgrave Macmillan.

Part E

The Performance:
The Machinery of Interaction

CHAPTER 1: Context

The style and character, perhaps even success or failure, of any stage performances depend crucially on the interactions between the actors. The most familiar forms of interaction between the players first on the international and now on the global stage have been diplomacy and war. Traditionally opposites, war followed when diplomacy could function no longer amid acute tensions and stresses. By contrast, there were times when the disruptive consequences of war seemed unbearable and the use of diplomacy intensified. Clausewitz famously thought that they were two versions of the same thing. The two opposites remain highly significant forms of interaction in the contemporary global situation, though both are undergoing striking changes. More than that, however, other forms of interaction have achieved higher profiles. The media, particularly the Internet, migration, investment, trade and aid are now important forms of contemporary interaction. All are discussed further in the chapters that follow.

Diplomacy

Nobody can know when diplomacy began. The need to arrange for effective message delivery must have followed from the development of the first human speech and still more from the first more or less organised societies. Certainly diplomacy began earlier than was once thought. However, diplomacy is more than just the delivery of messages and receiving replies to them. It involves the manner in which messages and subsequent discussions are handled so as to achieve the best result for the parties and it has accumulated rules, conventions and immunities so that business can be successfully and safely conducted – at least until very recent times. The first attribute has given rise to the adjective 'diplomatic' to mean a careful friendliness and the sympathetic understanding of another position; sometimes, less agreeably, to imply deviousness.

The second development goes back to the very beginnings. If it has been decided that it would be better to listen to a messenger, to hear his message, than eat him, then it becomes essential to have a clear understanding about who is an official messenger and who is not. It is quite clear from Ancient Greek sources and even from earlier evidence still that in order to make certain that official messengers remained safe from attack, they were given a special status, protected by whatever pantheon was locally in place, and that retribution for harming or plotting to harm a recognised messenger would be certain and swift, possibly arranged by the gods themselves or by human agency acting on their behalf. In fact, as became generally acknowledged in later times, the real justification for the special security afforded to diplomats was that of reciprocity. It was obvious that any ruler or other political system would want security for his messengers and to be confident that his messages would be both delivered and responded to. In exchange he had to guarantee equal treatment for the messengers of others. The additional privileges that diplomats acquired – to be well fed and housed, to be free from local taxation and customs dues, to have a secure residence and to hold religious and political views which might be banned in the place where he was performing his duties – also had an element of reciprocity about them. These, however, had the further justification that they enabled the diplomat to do his job in an untrammelled way.

Reluctance to go to war has generally encouraged the development of more complex diplomatic systems. Diplomacy can seem to be the obvious alternative to war in two circumstances. The first is where a group of states roughly equal in power, such as those of Ancient Greece, of the Warring States period in China, of northern Italy during the Renaissance and in Europe generally during the eighteenth century, does not become dominated by the growth of any one power and is not subject to invasion from outside its area. Such conditions make external warfare unlikely and regional warfare indecisive. When experience shows that the latter condition is reliable, war gives way to intensive diplomacy in the hope that the deadlock which cannot be broken militarily might be shaken by some great diplomatic coup, such as secretly arranging an overwhelmingly powerful coalition. The second occurs where a mismatch develops between the security obligations of a state and its ability to meet them from its own resources. Straightforward decline and/or a change in surrounding circumstances are the usual causes and this condition is particularly well exemplified by the case of the Byzantine Empire.

Episodes of more intense diplomacy with corresponding modifications in diplomatic machinery occurred only patchily until the Renaissance period in Europe. Advances were made and abandoned, blind alleys explored and no continuous historical development began. With the gradual establishment of the Venetian diplomatic service from the thirteenth century, itself a debtor in a mild way to the accumulated experience of dealing with the Byzantines, a continuous line of development began. The techniques and assumptions which emerged in northern Italy during the renaissance period spread to most of the rest of Europe in the sixteenth century as the newly sovereign rulers of an age of acute conflict found the use of complex diplomacy essential to their statecraft. During the seventeenth century, the European margins, such as Russia, were drawn in and the expansion of Europe which followed the explorations and commercial vigour of the Portuguese, the Spanish, the Dutch, the English and the French increased the range and scope of diplomatic activity. The eighteenth century saw a particularly vigorous resort to diplomacy. By the second half of the nineteenth century, the sharply increased direct influence of Europe, the addition of independent Latin America and the rising, if reluctant, participation of the USA in the diplomatic system made it a global network, and even the initial refusal of the Chinese, Japanese, Koreans and Ottoman Turks to become part of it fell away, either because of the obvious disadvantages of refusing to join or because of the application of force from outside. This was a universal system of diplomacy used by states; indeed, from the seventeenth century, any other entity, with the exception of the Roman Church, was denied the legal right to represent itself and thus excluded from the system.

The state form had triumphed completely and had commandeered diplomacy as its own property. How much so can be seen from the way in which the newer states of the twentieth century unhesitatingly embraced the diplomatic system almost as a badge of their new minted sovereignty and the tendency of revolutionary governments to conform to it after a relatively short time is further evidence of this. The Cold War period produced new stresses, though not, as it turned out, fatal ones and in some ways the rivalry of the superpowers both contrasted with the more immediate past and yet led them to make substantial use of the existing diplomatic system. In particular, the sharply increased significance of summit conferences was an example of this. The technique was an old one but acquired a new importance as the Cold War raised the stakes in foreign policy management, increased its electoral and general political importance and thus emphasised the role of heads of states and governments in its conduct.

New agencies

This situation began to change in the last quarter of the twentieth century and to change in a rather different way. The flow of development since the fifteenth century had given greater opportunities to the rulers and governments of rapidly developing states and seen the gradual disappearance of any other sources of diplomatic representation. The changing needs of states had largely dictated the parallel evolution of diplomacy and the process of change at the interface between the existing stock of diplomatic practice and the demands of governments provides a continuous thread of explanation as to what was occurring. The onset of globalisation, the changing and relatively lessening role of the state, the rising importance of nonstate entities and major additions to the likely topics of diplomatic exchange have produced a new area of diplomatic activity, largely separated from the rules, privileges and procedures of the state-based system, but necessarily engaged in dialogue with it. This produces a familiar need for modification on the part of state diplomacy; but it is also producing an unfamiliar need for the admission of new agencies into the diplomatic system and it is unclear whether this can be done by a really substantial remaking of the old arrangement or whether a fundamentally new diplomatic machine is going to emerge.

There is a parallel here with the sixteenth-century situation when states were first coming to dominate the landscape but still had to share it with entities and ideas left over from a deeper past. The result is now uncomfortable, and was then, and produces serious disconnections. In the contemporary context, one of the most serious is that the principle of reciprocity has broken down. Nonstate groups which use violence as their chief weapon and cannot accept anything less than 100 per cent of their demands are not in the business of representing themselves to others. They are not part of the system and perceive no advantages in *raison de système* and therefore do not share the formerly universal acceptance of the rules ensuring the physical safety and well-being of diplomats. For the first time since the Reformation period, diplomats are routinely being murdered in the course of their duties and the inviolability of embassies is equally routinely being flouted. Even the officials of the Red Cross, the only humanitarian organisation to have been given full diplomatic protection by treaty, are being regularly attacked. Less unpleasantly, but awkwardly nonetheless, the formerly very clear rules which determined the status of diplomats – that they were genuine diplomats and what position they held within the system – have broken down in the face of swarms of representatives from civil society organisations who may, for example, attend an international conference on environmental issues. What further complicates this problem is that on some of the major questions of the moment, governments have sought expertise from outside the ranks of their own servants and then appointed these advisers to national delegations.

The construction of the internal and external machinery of diplomacy – the foreign ministry and the resident embassy – was complete by the mid-eighteenth century. Later refinements were naturally made as experience and technological improvement in communications suggested and foreign services generally became more integrated into the civil service structures of states, but these were changes of degree, not substance. Even the extraordinarily accelerating effects of the telegraph and cable systems introduced during the middle and later nineteenth century produced quantitative rather than qualitative changes.

By 1814 states had developed an additional requirement. The construction of the basic moving parts of the diplomatic system had been related to the growth of sovereignty and the need to represent that sovereignty on behalf of rulers. The notion that the international system might also acquire a responsibility for representing itself, a kind of institutionalisation of *raison de système,* had been unknown. Its emergence arose from the novel desire of rulers to find a way of supervising the flow of international affairs on a continuous basis and to be willing to put that wish above the demands of untrammelled sovereignty. The result was the creation of the first, if ill-defined, international organisation. It lasted for 100 years and became known as the Concert of Europe. The scale of the wars against Napoleon and his failure to shake the condition of rough equality among the European great powers provided both the motive for change and the practical possibility of creating a new technique. The contemporary belief that the wars had been caused by revolutionary ideology and the use that Napoleon made of it rather than by any intrinsic power of France put the major threat above and beyond the risks emanating from a potential hegemon and produced more general agreement than the business of organising the restraint of a rogue power would have commanded.

The Concert of Europe, which was built on the experience during the end of the war and the making of the Vienna Settlement in 1814/15, was thus the first deliberate effort by the most powerful states of the period to manage international affairs on a continuous basis with the object of preventing warfare. The principal technique upon which it was based has remained the foundation of all subsequent attempts to achieve the same objective. In their original form, congresses and conferences were held uniquely to discuss the terms on which a war would be brought to an end. The device took on a new and highly significant role, however, at the beginning of the nineteenth century. It did so in response to the need for a new piece of diplomatic machinery which would allow state governments to manage international relations cooperatively rather than simply to endure the disorderly consequences of reciprocally adversarial behaviour.

Formal progress

From the Congress of Vienna, there grew up a continuous development of the conference technique through the period of the Concert of Europe, 1815–1914, leading to the attempt to institutionalise it in the form of the League of Nations from 1920 to 1945 and thence to a second attempt, the United

Nations Organisation, which has existed since 1945. Each phase has shown more formal institutionalisation than its predecessor. Perhaps because of this, many conferences after 1920 have been and are held outside the auspices of either the League or the UN. The proliferation of regional entities since the Second World War has led to a related expansion of conference meetings, both standing and occasional, and in very recent years a major evolution has occurred in which conferences on major global issues such as climate change have been attended not just by the heads and representatives of state governments but also by private organisations usually having a particular expertise in the matter under discussion. The long-running crisis in Central Africa at the turn of the twentieth century produced the logical extension of this development when private organisations, which had become centrally involved, began to hold conferences of their own in which there was no participation by governments.

A description of the means of interaction in the familiar international system of the past could have stopped short at discussing war and diplomacy. It is true that the machinery of diplomacy is changing to accommodate the realities of a global political and economic system and remains the foremost means of interaction, particularly as the technique of first resort. War, too, if interpreted as including civil conflict, terrorism and unfocused violence, remains a highly significant form of interaction. Diplomacy, however, is available only to entities which can represent themselves. The arrival of a globalised communications system which is primarily based on the wish and need of individual human beings to relate to each other both immediately and privately has introduced a form of interaction which can be used by entities in representing themselves, but this characteristic is not essential. In some ways the Internet particularly is providing to private organisations the kind of individual input which electorates and elections provide to democratic states – an interaction at a stage before any act of representation begins.

The media

The influence of the press on international affairs existed but was secondary until the development of general literacy in developed countries led to the appearance of popular newspapers – the 'yellow' press – towards the end of the nineteenth century. These acquired a perceived importance in creating and maintaining support for governments, particularly in democratic or quasi-democratic systems which delivered power to their proprietors and opportunities to politicians. One of these opportunities was to raise a foreign scare – 'the motherland in danger' – as a way of distracting attention from unpopular domestic policies or conditions. Resort to nationalist rhetoric and its magnification in the press did not greatly disturb a reasonably stable international system, but could have corrosive effects if, for example, changes in the distribution of power among states had created security anxieties and consequential tension. The press wars that developed between Britain and Germany and Germany and Russia just before the 1914 crisis exploded into the First World War were cases in point: they did not cause the war, but they helped to make it more likely by solidifying public support when it came.

The arrival of the radio in the 1920s offered new opportunities for communication, as in Franklin Roosevelt's 'fireside chats', intense propaganda as organised by Joseph Goebbels in Nazi Germany, or highly charged efforts to maintain national determination in wartime, as Winston Churchill's radio addresses to the British people showed. The proliferation of propaganda radio stations such as Voice of America and Radio Free Europe during the Cold War continued a process begun in the 1930s. Quite recent events in Rwanda have demonstrated that the power of radio has not been eliminated by television, when the chief propulsion towards genocidal massacre turned out to be a radio station called Radio Milles Collines.

Nonetheless, television has come to play a more significant role than radio ever did or does. This is obviously partly because of the greater intensity and presence of the medium itself and the way it has inserted itself into the daily lives of human beings, but also because of the technological advances that have allowed it to report on events across the globe in real time and disseminate comment on them immediately. This in itself has changed the relationship between ordinary citizens and the flow of global affairs and thus the public opinion with which governments, civil society and commercial firms must deal. More than this, however, the immediacy of both the reporting and the urgent desire for on-the-spot reactions from officials and politicians has made television an additional route by which leading figures may try to or sometimes almost be forced to communicate with each other. The more difficult or shocking the event, the more this is likely to happen and the more risky it can be to fail to leave time for consultation and consideration, and take to the airwaves for immediate reaction and counter-reaction. The US Secretary of State George Schultz once referred to this kind of exchange, backed as his example was by the vocabulary of the Cold War, as 'megaphone diplomacy'. Acts of terrorism instantly broadcast and insistently discussed on TV have increased this effect.

One of the results has been that where particularly sensitive negotiations may be taking place, extraordinary efforts are made to keep them secret. The path to the Oslo negotiations between the Israelis and the Palestinians was an example of this. The power of television can be seen also where governments feel the need to maintain strict controls over it and also where they have decided not to. The emergence of the Arabic TV station Al-Jazeera, based in Qatar on the Persian Gulf, has acquired enormous significance across the Arab world because it is perceived to be independent at least within the region and while it is probable that the government of Qatar is happy to host the general line the station adopts, it frequently broadcasts material which individual Arab governments would certainly prefer their citizens not to see.

The globalisation of news and commentary which technology has made possible is increasingly in the hands of immensely large private companies – News International, CNN. Governments also take part, but where they have established global presences, they have mainly been careful to be neutral about what is reported. China has not done so, but the German TV station *Deutsche Welle*, which broadcasts also in English, and the BBC, though not strictly a government organisation, are examples of this. The French, Italians and Russians have stations which lie somewhere in the middle of this spectrum. The overall effect has been to speed up the processes of global politics, quite possibly to their disadvantage, and to take away the initiative from governments, their heads and their foreign services in setting the priorities about what the most important business of the world should be. It has become those things which the TV stations think will grab audience attention: showy conflicts and disasters will overwhelm discussion of the problems of increasing global warming or lack of economic development. Put another way, what determines the inclusion of a news report is no longer its importance as much as its interest.

Major sources of news and information disseminated through the press and TV are in private ownership, many others are not. The newest recruit in this category, however, is entirely in private and quite often individual control: the Internet. The Internet was not intended or expected to become a major news medium. But it has become so. It can provide the means of disseminating news in an uncontrolled environment, filtered through neither journalistic experience nor any canons of taste. The result is a wide range of available material rife with rumour and conspiracies at one quite substantial extreme to deeply serious discussion at the other. The effect has been dramatic both on the users and the familiar providers, who have discovered a nimble and highly effective rival. During the 2004 Iraq war and its aftermath, Internet websites provided an important platform for insurgent groups to reach a global public, important enough to be used to reveal episodes of extreme violence designed to induce a general sense of overwhelming threat and danger. In the same year, the United States presidential election was conducted in important ways on the Internet, a fact which may have contributed both to the enormous quantities of money raised and to the greatly increased number of people who went to the polls.

The principal significance of the Internet as a news medium is its independence from either governments or media barons such as Rupert Murdoch. It is an example of the levers of many kinds of contemporary power passing into the hands of ordinary citizens, and the kinds of issues that are discussed are frequently very different from those adopted by the commercial and state-run media. Its existence serves to increase the sense that greater distance is now being put between citizens and the traditional sources of information and control. It makes it less surprising that across the world there is a kind of diffusion of authority which is at once exciting and alarming.

Migration

There is a further interaction related to both considerations of economic opportunity and to political oppression: human migration. There have been episodes of migration right from the beginning of human societies. The earlier examples tended to take the form of violent invasions, as exemplified by the Mongols during the European middle ages. The development of more sophisticated transportation systems both on land and sea, particularly as a result of the application of the steam engine to transport, made possible the emigrations from Europe which established new societies in the Americas, South Africa, Australia and New Zealand. Chinese emigration over a long period has established significant Chinese communities not only in South-East Asia but also in the USA and the UK. Tamil emigration from India in the last 100 years or so has created Tamil communities in Indonesia and Malaysia. Former colonial powers host immigrant populations from their erstwhile territories and the descendants of African slaves may be found wherever their forced emigration took them, chiefly in the Americas but also in parts of the Arab world.

In more recent years, a somewhat different pattern of migration has emerged where the flow has been into and not out of more developed societies. The United States, Canada and the European Union are particularly the object of immigration. The cause is chiefly the promise that they hold of jobs and better conditions, which are plainly attractive to people from fractured societies and collapsed or poorly functioning economies. Where the source of migration sends out a flow of the technologically educated, as in the flow of South-East Asians to the United States, it may be encouraged. Attitudes may be different where the flow is unskilled and possibly destitute. Such a labour force may in fact be advantageous to a developed economy, but that fact may not be obvious to the existing inhabitants. The problems arise internally, where the chief difficulties lie in knowing how many to accept, how to eject unwanted immigrants and what to do with and for those arriving. But there is also the fact that hostile public opinion can impact on the external reactions and policies of governments. Externally, the growth of migration has become an issue involving private humanitarian and human rights organisations, intergovernmental organisations such as the UN and states of origin, passage and destination. The present situation is partly the consequence of past failure to grapple with the issue but is chiefly the result of the apparent impossibility of controlling the flows or even, in the case of immigration into the USA from the south, documenting them.

Fear of terrorist infiltration via immigration has lent urgency to finding solutions but not with any obviously successful results. Migration has therefore come to play a role among global interactions at many levels, from the highest of politics to the functioning of the global economy and ultimately to the very conception that individual societies maintain of themselves.

Trade and investment

Trading patterns and investment flows have always played a role in international politics. What has given them a more significant profile than hitherto is the degree to which they have escaped from the control of state governments. Where before it might have been discussed what the impact of government policies were on trade and investment, it is more common now to discuss what the impact of trade and investment is on states and societies. The reasons are several. There are many more and many smaller states in contemporary global politics than there used to be. The effects of global economic flows are felt much more strongly in smaller, weaker and poorer states. Their populations and governments can feel overwhelmed, frustrated and ultimately powerless in the face of them. The emergence of a fully globalised economy, emphasised by the broad acceptance of liberal economic regimes across the world following the collapse of communism, has created highly independent markets. Not even the most secure and economically powerful government can control their effects and the major global financial institutions, though they are evolving in that direction, cannot yet form or direct global macroeconomic policies.

The global competition for foreign direct investment in domestic economies causes governments at both national and local level to adopt policies that they would otherwise have rejected in the face of popular resentment or naturally hostile local conditions. If this is successful and leads to the arrival of transnational firms or the relatively sudden establishment of a manufacturing capacity based on cheap labour, there may be both short-term and longer-term stresses and risks to social and environmental stability; though this may be less obvious in the face of the initially favourable consequences for employment and wealth generation. Thus the connection between instabilities in the global system caused by domestic breakdowns within weak states and the impact of trade and investment is very clearly a highly significant global interaction.

The interaction takes several forms: between governments and markets, between governments and transnational firms and between governments and their people; side by side go the interactions between firms and markets and between firms and the people living in the places they invest in. At another level are the global interactions between both governments and transnational firms and the major global institutions – the World Bank, the IMF and the WTO. The effect is much like a garden fertiliser too randomly applied. Sudden but insufficiently rooted growth, eventual soil exhaustion, clear marks of differential growth rates and burn marks in vegetation killed by too large a shot of the chosen chemical can as easily be the consequences as well-sustained and profitable improvement over time.

War

Among the most remarkable shifts of gear of recent decades has been in the nature of warfare. The change can be simply put: whereas from the late eighteenth century in Europe to the end of the Cold War in the late twentieth century, war almost exclusively meant formal war between states or alliances of states, civil conflict within states has now almost completely overtaken inter-state war as the most likely form of warfare. The reason is chiefly connected with the increasing weakness in the stability and effectiveness of many states, particularly those which are poor, small or environmentally challenged. This is the consequence partly of economic globalisation and partly of the emergence of a large number of new states, often with poorly rooted political and administrative structures. In addition, the withdrawal of support offered to some regimes by the superpowers during the Cold War period increased the likelihood of state failures, whether complete or partial. In a very short time, the assumption that the risk of war was the risk of a global superpower collision, fought between highly organised alliances using high-tech weaponry, gave way to the certainty that most conflict would be disorganised, low-tech and conducted amidst the chaotic political, economic and administrative conditions accompanying the collapse of government in a state.

This effect has been seen, and still is seen, in Africa from Sierra Leone in the west to Somalia in the east and perhaps in its starkest form in central Africa, and particularly in the genocide that occurred in Rwanda. It marked the breakup of Yugoslavia in Europe, has been common in the Caucasus region from Chechnya to Nagorno-Karabakh, has threatened Pakistan, Indonesia and the Philippines, and is endemic across Oceania. Dealing with it is peculiarly difficult since the existing political and legal norms give great significance to the sovereign rights of states and put barriers in the way of intervention. The UN particularly finds it hard to resolve the contradiction that its charter specifically protects the rights of each member while at the same time giving the organisation the obligation to protect global security. Only when the protection of human rights has been tacitly allowed to trump the preservation of sovereign rights, as occurred in Yugoslavia and was eventually brought in as justification of the Iraq war of 2004, does some logical basis begin to appear, since it is inevitably human rights which suffer under a brutal dictatorship or in the event of civil conflict.

One result of this development has been a surge of mercenaries, either fighting in their own groups for one side or another in a civil war or, in a form of privatisation of security, being employed to buttress existing forces. The chaos which these conflicts cause has also occasioned commercial firms to employ private security companies to supply locally secure conditions where they do business or manufacture. In either case, the use of mercenaries employed in private armies both indicates the degree to which a state may have collapsed and contributes to its further fall. Of all the functions expected of a state, being the sole provider of internal and external security for its people has always been primary.

The interaction which contemporary conflict represents has steadily slipped away from the quite tightly controlled framework which the Geneva Conventions provided and thus far has not gained a new kind of limitation derived from the existence of and likely prosecution of war criminals at the International Criminal Court. Its existence, formally completed in 2005, marks the beginning of a new era and is undoubtedly a consequence of the contemporary style of warfare. Meanwhile, the prevalence of notably cruel intra-state conflicts seems to be deeply ingrained and intractable. The machinery of the former international system was not designed to deal with it and is in any case as subject as any other area of state activity to the reduction in the authority of governments, which show little sign of developing new responses individually or constructing new institutional ways of coping.

Terrorism

Into the gap have come terrorist groups, sometimes fuelled by the dislocation in familiar political and cultural environments caused by globalisation, sometimes in support of far older causes, national, religious, sometimes both. Terrorism has always existed in some form or another, often at the edges of more formal warfare, and has frequently had a close relationship with the vulnerability that people have when they move about. Piracy at sea, extortion on rivers in mediaeval times, explosions on trains and at stations, car bombs and now the hijacking and deliberate destruction of aircraft all share this characteristic. Terrorism flourishes in the contemporary uncertainty about the origin and control of conflict, but it also owes its present prominence to another factor. The global pressures – particularly economic pressures, which individuals now feel are difficult to react to, at least with any hope of getting results – are constantly growing. The familiar routes for expressing anxiety and discontent which are available through the political structures of states no longer serve that purpose adequately. The institutions of states have developed over centuries in a way that makes them amenable – though sometimes only after some time has elapsed – to the pressure of domestic public opinion, most usually through the results of elections. Populations thus have a kind of stake in them and have expectations of them that include the idea that they will be able to protect them from the worst vagaries of changes in the economy and in territorial security. This link has been broken where the pressures have become global in scope and the institutions of a state can no longer react in any sufficient way to them and thus satisfy the basic covenant with the population. It is this situation that pushes individuals to adopt tactics that are derived from despair and helplessness. The sense of irresolvable grievance which results increases the possibility that people will take to far less focused but instantly reportable action against soft targets in the expectation that general outrage will eventually garner the results that the ordinary political process no longer delivers.

The principal characteristic of the patterns of interaction in global politics is their plurality. The number of levels at which interactions take place has increased, the number of entities between which interactions take place has also increased and the types of entity have become much more various, particularly with the presence of significant private actors on a stage once the unique preserve of states and associations of states. The result is raucous, hard edged and sometimes chaotically ineffective. But this is because the circumstances are new and conventions have not yet developed to regulate the way in which global politics are conducted. It was so when states first appeared in sixteenth-century Europe and it took them 100 years to settle into a workable system. So it is unsurprising that the world is having a rocky ride now. The uncertainties and failures have to be balanced against the vigour and excitement and particularly perhaps the empowerment of individual human beings that the Internet has already brought and will surely expand further.

CHAPTER 2: Communications systems

Eyes in the sky: the role of satellite technology in connecting the global village

In 1945, Arthur C. Clarke, a wartime radar operator in the Royal Air Force and author of *2001: A Space Odyssey*, published his paper 'Extra-terrestrial Relays' detailing a world where geo-stationary satellites would function as the primary linkages for a global telecommunications network. Clarke's theories built on earlier ideas conceived by Herman Potočnik, a Slovenian engineer and pioneer of astronautics. Despite the clarity of Clarke's arguments and utility of his ideas, the Anglo-American alliance did not immediately seek to dominate Earth's inner space. However, that all changed in the months after Moscow successfully launched an R-7 rocket carrying Sputnik I on 4 October 1957.

Satellites were a direct outgrowth of the growing rivalry between the USA and the Soviet Union after their wartime cooperation turned to postwar confrontation. Both countries began developing new rocket technologies after intelligence and material from the German military's V-2 rocket programme fell into their hands at the conclusion of the war. However, the Soviets moved faster and successfully launched Sputnik, the first man-made satellite to orbit the Earth, ahead of the Americans. This artificial moon weighed 83kg (184lb) and carried two radio transmitters intended to gather information about the upper atmosphere. Satellites would later be used to monitor the degradation of the global environment and right long-standing cartographic errors, among other activities.

In the wake of global news coverage of Sputnik's launch, the US military doubled its efforts to compete with the Soviets at developing space-based technologies which could potentially be used for military purposes. The USSR scored another technological and public rela-

tions victory four years later when Yuri Gagarin blasted off from the Baikonur Cosmodrome in the Soviet Republic of Kazakhstan, becoming the first person to survive space flight during his 1-hour 48-minute trip.

The USA's newly formed National Aeronautics and Space Administration (NASA) and its Department of Defense both became obsessed with matching and then overcoming the Soviet domination of space. The Soviets kept pace with the Americans and over time Earth's inner space became littered with large numbers of satellites. During the three decades between 1960 and 1990, approximately 3,000 satellites were launched into space, 60 per cent by the superpowers for military reasons including conducting photographic reconnaissance on each other.

Global village

The term global village was coined by the Canadian media theorist Marshall McLuhan in his 1962 book, *The Gutenberg Galaxy*. McLuhan described an increasingly interconnected world where time and space did not necessarily determine the bonds of community. According to McLuhan, electronic mass media played a vital role in the creation and maintenance of the global village.

It was not just national governments that were in the business of launching satellites. In 1960, US telecommunications giant AT&T began petitioning the US Congress to allow it to put an experimental satellite into orbit to further the company's ability to deliver telecommunications to its business subscribers. Telstar I became the first active communications satellite as well as the first privately funded space launch in 1962. The satellite was jointly used by the British and French post offices, US private concerns AT&T and Bell Telephone Laboratories, and NASA. In

1964, recorded portions of the Tokyo Olympics were broadcast via satellite to television viewers around the world in a major step towards creating what Marshall McLuhan called the 'global village'. Satellite networks, originally built for transmitting voice and data, soon became mechanisms for the global distribution of television. The first live broadcast via satellite showed US astronaut Neil Armstrong walking on the moon and was a deeply poignant use of the technology.

In 1964, Intelsat, an international consortium of 11 Western-aligned nations including the United States, Canada, Japan, Australia and several Western European countries, deployed a network of geo-synchronous communications satellites. The conjunction was an important step forward in internationalising satellite technology and represented the first attempt to create a truly global communications network. The communist bloc soon followed suit with the creation of Intersputnik, a mirror project with different ideological concerns. Satellites soon became ever more numerous as thousands of media and communications companies scrambled to gain a wider footprint and/or provide more material content to subscribers. Other corporations such as the international money wire service Western Union saw clear benefits in the use of satellite technology for conducting global transactions.

Television first gained a global audience in the period after the conclusion of the Second World War. Americans, the pioneers of the medium, still watch more television than any other nation, spending 4 out every 24 hours in front of a television set. However, the obsession with TV has spread far and wide. Recent research shows that massive consumption of televised media is not just a US pastime. Turks and Japanese watch about 3.5 hours per day; Argentines and Venezuelans average just over 3 hours per day; and most Europeans watch at least 2 hours of programming a day. This global fascination with televised media has been made possible in large part by the use of satellites both as relay instruments and for direct broadcasts.

Age of the satellite

In 1965, the Soviet Union deployed its Ekran satellite network to deliver television to its domestic market, guaranteeing that almost every Soviet citizen – whether in Kamchatka or the Kola Peninsula – would have access to state broadcasts. The 1970s saw a massive penetration

of US cable television networks into space with Home Box Office (HBO), Ted Turner's TBS and televangelist Pat Robertson's CBN all making the jump into space. Originally, the media conglomerates assumed that only cable systems operators would receive the signals transmitted from space. Individual technology enthusiasts, however, soon developed their own hardware capable of receiving the signals being relayed to the cable networks, thus turning satellite TV into a consumer technology: with this shift, the age of the giant backyard satellite was born. The response of the media companies was hostile as they sought to persuade governments to legislate against such 'piracy'.

A larger-scale satellite TV revolution began with the introduction of a digital broadcast satellite (DBS) or mini-dish system in the United Kingdom by Sky Television. Regional systems followed around the world with Hughes DirecTV (USA), Astra and Eutelsat (Europe), Hispasat (Latin America and Spain), ArabSat (Middle East), SkyPerfect (Japan) and Multichoice (southern Africa) among others. The internationalisation of sport has been a major side effect of this process, with the Olympics, cricket, football and other championships being watched by a sizable (and increasing) portion of the globe's population each year.

The proliferation of smaller and thus less conspicuous satellites has had a keen impact on societies in authoritarian states. In China, DBS satellites are often called 'little ears' in reference to their role in piercing the communist government's monopoly on media. The Iranian diaspora community in southern California provides large amounts of Farsi-language content for broadcast into Iran via satellite TV, despite the fact that private satellite dishes are illegal in Iran.

Critics of globalisation are apt to point out that satellite television has become a global platform for the delivery of a comparatively small amount of media to a very large audience. In homes, businesses, hotels and government offices around the world, CNN, the BBC, MTV, RAI, TV5, Deutsche Welle and various manifestations of Rupert Murdoch's global media empire, News Corporation, are watched by hundreds of millions. New pan-Arab stations such Al-Arabiya and Al-Jazeera have recently joined the ranks of English, French and German language mainstays in the global satellite TV market. Although critics of media globalisation assert that the USA dominates what the world watches on TV, the situation is a good deal more nuanced.

US- and Japanese-owned movie studios do account for the vast majority of motion pictures consumed by the global market and certain US television shows such as *Baywatch*, *ER* and *The Simpsons* are popular outside the USA, but other television products have also pushed well beyond their countries of origin. Italian game shows, Brazilian soap operas, Japanese animation, British news programmes and German music video networks are all examples of non-US media that have gained massive global audiences which are due to satellite distribution networks. Cable and traditional over-the-air broadcasts continue to be dominated by domestic media in most countries, but the seemingly unceasing growth of DBS portends a future dominated by global rather than state-controlled or vetted media products.

The high cost associated with satellite technology has led to more than a few companies going bankrupt due to overreaching themselves. Iridium, one of the most oft-mentioned bursts of the late 1990s technology bubble, launched hundreds of low-earth orbiting (LEO) satellites in order to build a private global mobile phone network. Iridium's goal was to build a consumer-oriented telecommunications company with coverage that blanketed every square inch of the Earth, its oceans and the skies. It proved to be impractical and cost-prohibitive, causing the company to file for bankruptcy. Today, Iridium's network, salvaged out of bankruptcy, provides services to international industrial customers, the US Department of Defense and other communications companies.

Another recent innovation in satellite use is the advent of several satellite radio companies that have continental footprints. The first company, WorldSpace, began as an effort to stop the spread of AIDS in Africa through satellite-delivered education efforts. Over time the company grew into a media provider for Africa and much of Western Europe, broadcasting news and music in French, Arabic and English to relatively inexpensive satellite radio receivers. WorldSpace followed the 1998 launch of its AfriStar satellite service with AsiaStar, which provides audio and data services to Asia and the Middle East. The company plans to offer similar services to Latin America in the near future.

Building on the WorldSpace model, two competing US companies, XM Radio and Sirius, launched their services in 2001 and 2002 respectively to go after the much more lucrative North American market. Each offers in excess of 100 channels of music, news and entertainment programming beamed to cars, boats and homes in the continental USA, northern Mexico, southern Canada and parts of the Caribbean, although the companies are limited to marketing their services in the USA. Media sharing between XM and WorldSpace of some radio stations now ensures that more than half of the world's population has the ability to listen to the same music at the same time. All the systems carry the predictable panoply of news providers as well, thereby strengthening the hold of CNN, the BBC and other global media over what information and opinions the world's population receives.

Satellites have also been a critical tool in the development of the Global Positioning System (GPS). The system, owned and operated by the US Department of Defense, gives highly accurate readings of location anywhere on the globe. The system is available for use free of charge. The US government does not, however, grant most users access to the extremely precise readings that it uses for military applications such as cruise missile targeting. France, the most vocal supporter of technological independence from the USA, united with other European governments in 2003 to build an alternative system in order to gain access to the most precise measurements. The new system, known as Galileo, is expected to cost €3 billion and be completed in 2008. The People's Republic of China, understandably uncomfortable with US domination of the only functioning platform, has promised to contribute €230 million to the project.

Talking to the world: telephony breaks out of the box

The world's telecommunications structures have historically been state-specific concerns. Some interoperability was of course required to transmit calls internationally, but networks were established with a strong if not overriding emphasis on borders (often at the sub-national level, as in the case of the regional networks that characterise the USA and some other physically large countries). However, a wave of telecommunications deregulation swept through the

A fax revolution

Although the first tele-facsimile machine was invented by Alexander Bain in 1843, the technology did not have much use until a large network of users evolved. In 1928, the first radio facsimile transmission was sent across the Atlantic. In 1966, the Xerox corporation introduced the first version that could be connected to any phone line. Two years later, the fax went global when the Consultative Committee for International Telephone and Telegraph (CCITT) issued the first international standard for facsimile transmissions. By the 1980s, every business worth its salt kept at least one fax machine plugged into the telephone network at all times.

developed world in the late 1970s and 1980s, followed by privatisation in the former Soviet bloc in the 1990s as well as large swathes of the developing world. New technologies combined with massive innovation associated with the end of state-sponsored monopolies and changed the face of global telephony.

Landline telephony

In 1956, the first transatlantic telephone cable (TAT1) was laid across the ocean floor, providing 35 circuits in each direction, although satellite technology would soon be employed to keep up with growing demand for intercontinental calls. The next major revolution occurred with the introduction of glass fibre rather than copper to transmit voice. This innovation signalled the next major step forward in providing cheap and efficient worldwide communications structures and made satellite link-ups less necessary for voice traffic.

Until the 1960s, long-distance – especially international – telephone calls had been prohibitively expensive for all but a few. But in 1970, scientists working for US firm Corning Glass Works pioneered the use of fibre optic cables capable of carrying 65,000 times more information than copper wire. By stretching glass fibres into ultra-thin threads and passing infrared light through them, telecommunications companies were able to improve service across long distances. Although extremely expensive, fibre optic cables are less susceptible to electromagnetic disturbance, experience almost no problems with cross talk and can transmit voice traffic

digitally. In 1988 the first optical cables were laid underneath the Atlantic Ocean, opening the door to massive transfers of data between continents and thus breaking the so-called 'bandwidth bottleneck'. Today, approximately 80 per cent of global telecommunications traffic travels over fibre optic cables and more than 25 million kilometres of fibre have been laid around the world.

Advances in bandwidth were a vital part of a global infrastructure that would facilitate the emergence of transnational financial markets and accommodate the needs of millions of Internet users by connecting servers around the world. Polities that got on the bandwagon early, most notably the newly industrialised states of the Pacific Rim, Western European nations, the USA and Canada, were able to enhance their wealth significantly by becoming 'information societies', while other states, often having authoritarian and/or deeply corrupt regimes in Africa, the Middle East and parts of Asia, were significantly handicapped by their decisions not to get on the so-called 'information superhighway' (also called the Infobahn or Infostrada).

The so-called Second World (the USSR and its client states, as well as China) tended to have a very ambiguous relationship with advanced information and communications technology (ICT), attempting to embrace it for economic reasons while steadfastly rejecting the democratisation that has typically accompanied its use by the population at large. Overall, the spread of new technologies and the linkages made possible by advancing telecommunications structures has proved to be a uniting rather than a dividing force in the world. The global integration of financial markets, the growth of transnational epistemic communities and the rise in interna-

Packet/Packet switching

A packet is a set of information transmitted over a network. Packet-switching is the process whereby data are broken up, sent over a network and pieced back together at the final destination. Each packet is embedded with its address of origin, destination address and information about how to reunite with its related packets. The process of packet-switching enables chunks of data from many different locations to commingle and travel simultaneously on the same lines.

tional nongovernmental organisations linked virtually through ICT demonstrate an undeniable sea change in the ways human beings make investments, form groups and endeavour to regulate their personal environments.

The advent of the Internet and the digitisation of voice traffic caused a precipitous drop in the cost of voice calls, especially for international traffic. IP telephony, i.e. telephony transmission that uses Internet protocols (IP), has proved extremely popular in much of the developing world where voice quality is somewhat lower than in North America and Western Europe. IP telephony transmits voice calls using packet switching and can run over the same lines used for Internet traffic, thus cutting down on cost of per-minute calls and the infrastructure necessary to carry such calls. A call from London to Bombay now costs a fraction of what it did even ten years ago due to competition and new networks.

The initial quality of IP traffic was somewhat lower than traditional analog calls made in the developed world and hence dampened adoption levels there in the first few years of deployment. A number of governments, especially in West Africa, have outlawed the practice and vigorously punish service providers which attempt to circumvent closely guarded national monopolies over the provision of telephone services. The attempt to staunch competition supported by the forces of economic globalisation of markets is a losing battle, however, as most governments have learned.

Mobile telephony

Nikola Tesla, a Serbian immigrant to the United States, invented the precursor of the mobile phone in the late nineteenth century – the radio phone, which enjoyed some small success during the 1940s. But widespread commercial deployment of the technology was rather slow in coming due to government regulation relating to use of the finite amount of radio wave spectrum available for such transmissions. Mobile telephones send and receive messages using electromagnetic energy in the 800–900 megahertz (MHz) or 1850–1990 MHz portion of the radiofrequency (RF) spectrum, i.e. the continuum of electromagnetic energy arranged according to frequency and wavelength.

In 1978, Bahrain was the site of the first commercially deployed cellular telephone network. Japan followed suit a year later. Scandinavia,

soon to become a leader in global cellular technology, gained a regional network in 1981. It was two more years before the first network was activated in the United States, but once the process started Americans began adopting cell phones at high speed.

The United States, a fast follower in the mobile phone technology industry, steadfastly adhered to its own Code-Division Multiple Access (CDMA) standard for using spectrum to transmit calls. GSM (originally Groupe Spéciale Mobile, now Global System for Mobile Communications) is, however, the preferred protocol for European networks and the two are not compatible. This lack of interoperability has led to a global contest in the developing world for the establishment of new networks which has generally resulted in a victory for the European standard. GSM was a phenomenal success for believers in the European experiment as 26 governments came together and successfully implemented a technology standard without any guidance from the USA, or the Soviet Union for that matter.

Mobile phone service has emerged as a critical tool for modernisation in much of the developing world. Cambodia and a handful of other nations in the developing world have recently seen the penetration of mobile phones surpass that of landline phones. Poor infrastructure, decades of civil strife and endemic poverty make the decision to leapfrog landline systems in favour of wireless deployment a simple one for many telecoms companies in the developing world. Ironically, the same phenomenon is occurring in the wealthiest portions of the world as well. Finland, home of the world's largest cell phone manufacturer Nokia, saw mobile phones surpass the number of standard phones in 1998 and other countries across Europe are also seeing wireless penetration trump landline phones. This is generally due to cultural preferences, greater amounts of leisure time and competitive pricing vis-à-vis traditional phones.

Short message service (SMS), one of the main drivers in the mobile revolution, has taken much of the world by storm. A large percentage of the world's 1.4 billion mobile phone users employ the service which allows subscribers to send and receive brief messages (usually 150 characters or less) via their cellular phones, although the phenomenon has failed to take off in the United States where real-time communication is seen as indispensable and voice calls are much cheaper than in the rest of the world. The service, closely akin to e-mail or instant messaging, allows users to communicate with friends, family and co-workers while doing other things. Unlike speaking on a cellular phone, SMS allows users to communicate without interrupting other social or business activities.

SMS's ubiquity of access, relative privacy and the demand for brevity have caused perceptible changes in culture among frequent users, especially youth. It is increasingly acceptable in many mobile-friendly cultures for cell phone users to type SMS messages while in meetings, at the pub or in other milieux where receiving or making a mobile phone call would be taboo. Surreptitious correspondence, an ancient tradition, has gained new vigour through SMS as users employ the technology to send love notes, insult superiors and conduct other types of activities which their culture might frown upon if done in another format.

Acronymic slang in English and other languages is perhaps the most visible manifestation of these cultural changes – F2F (face-to-face), LOL (laugh out loud) and W4U (waiting for you) are just a few of the myriad abbreviations employed daily by text messengers around the world. The jargon of SMS is also employed in Internet-based instant messaging (IM), e-mails and, increasingly, everyday speech. The mobile phone itself has become as much an internationally recognised status symbol as it is a method of communication. In much of Europe, the mobile phone is worn round the neck much like a piece of jewellery; in the USA, teens compete for the coolest customised faceplate or ring-tone; and in East Asia, downloadable animation is all the rage.

Increasingly, the global mobile telephony market and the Internet (inherently a global platform) are moving towards convergence. Japan is leading the world, but Europe, North America and other parts of the Pacific Rim are quickly following suit. Mobile data services are also critical to a large part of the developing world where poor landline telecommunications and frequent power outages make securing dependable Internet access a daily challenge. Of course, such services, especially in less competitive markets such as sub-Saharan Africa, South Asia and the Middle East, come at a high price and are often limited to the elite.

From a MIT pet project to a global medium: the growth of the Internet

J. C. R. Licklider laid the foundations of the Internet in a 1962 paper that discussed the theoretical creation of a galactic network. Licklider became the first head of computer research at the Defense Advanced Research Projects Agency (DARPA) but his original concept has been realised only recently despite more than 40 years of steady advance.

DARPA

Known as ARPA until 1972, DARPA was created as a response to the Soviet launch of Sputnik. DARPA reports directly to the US Department of Defense and is run independently from other research and development projects. The agency's mission is to develop and expand technology frontiers beyond the short-term or tactical needs of the US military. Significant projects have included work on nuclear test detection, missile defence programmes, stealth technology and, most recently, the controversial Total Information Awareness initiative intended to locate terrorists before they strike.

Licklider's ideas joined with those of Leonard Kleinrock who worked on packet switching theory at MIT and they convinced another MIT scientist, Lawrence G. Roberts, that packet-based switching over long distances was feasible using the current telephone network. In 1965, Roberts and his team successfully tested the first wide area network (WAN) computer system by connecting computers on the Atlantic and Pacific coasts of the United States. Roberts subsequently joined DARPA and began the development of ARPANET – the nucleus of the modern Internet bearing the original name of the agency that created it – which boasted a modest four computers on its network by the end of the decade.

It has been suggested that the Internet's backers (namely the US government) conceived of the system as a bulwark against complete data loss in the event of a nuclear holocaust. However, the historical record leaves it unclear as to whether this was ever the intention of the founders of ARPANET. In fact, the survivability of the Internet in the event of even a limited nuclear exchange has been made possible only with its more recent global distribution – something that was most likely never in its inventors' minds.

In 1972, Roberts introduced the project to the public. Also during that year, the first 'killer application' for the network was introduced – electronic mail or e-mail. While building the infrastructure for ARPANET, technicians developed the digital messaging system to assist them in the coordination of their activities. The ability of users to selectively read, file, forward and respond to messages made it one of the fastest-growing applications of the late twentieth century. The following year saw the internationalisation of ARPANET with connections to University College, London and the Royal Radar Establishment (Norway).

In the late 1970s, the world witnessed the growth of a large number of wide area networks using satellite, radio and other technologies. The most important of these new networks was Usenet, which is still in use today. Usenet (also known as the 'poor man's ARPANET') became popular due in large part to restrictions on free speech imposed by DARPA on ARPANET. Usenet became a place where individuals could communicate about anything and everything from illicit drugs to government conspiracies. The Usenet ethos deeply affected the Internet and still shapes its nature as a media platform today. Unlike television and other forms of mass media, the content posted on Usenet was controlled by its audience rather than by an elite group of producers. Access to Usenet, unlike ARPANET, was egalitarian and technology enthusiasts soon flocked to the new network – a phenomenon that was aided by the growing use of the personal computer. In 1981, Usenet and ARPANET were linked, thus significantly widening the access of grassroots groups to portions of cyberspace which had hitherto been restricted to only a few DARPA-vetted researchers. Over the next decade, ARPANET became obsolete as the US government opted instead for proprietary networks and other users moved on to what was to become the Internet.

As alternative networks proliferated, the challenge to interoperability grew. The concept of an inter-network or 'Internet', i.e. a network of networks, became the solution for this problem. By using open-architecture protocols that would enable separate computer networks to talk to one another, engineers could now create their own networks capable of transmitting data to and receiving information from countless external networks. The result of this innovation was a complementary ecosystem of data exchange, also known as cyberspace. Instructions on how to employ these protocols were made available free of charge to the public, often called 'open source'.

Open source

Any programme whose source code is published on the Internet for anyone to access free of charge. Interested parties may also make suggestions, improvements and updates to the code which may or may not be implemented by the original author(s) of the code. The most successful open source programme is the Linux operating system (OS) which competes with the Microsoft Windows OS. Invented by Linus Torvalds in 1991 at the University of Helsinki, the Linux operating system is today used by thousands, perhaps millions, of people around the world. Linux recently overtook Apple's OS to become the second most popular operating system in the world. Its popularity, especially with the hacker community, is partly due to worldwide rejection of Microsoft's often ham-handed domination of the global operating system market.

The first successful attempt at Internetworking was made in 1977, but it was not until 1982 that an efficient system could be universally deployed. This system would eventually be known as the Transmission Control Protocol/Internet Protocol (TCP/IP). The process gave the modern Internet certain benefits, such as global addressing, that ensured its growth well beyond the confines of the US academic and military communities where it had been born. From this point forward, the Internet can be seen as global rather than national technology as grassroots network creators began to tie their networks to larger networks with little regard for space, distance or political boundaries.

The structure of the Internet lent itself to the creation of both narrow and broad epistemic communities from its early days. One-to-one and one-to-many communication pathways were established through the first e-mails and electronic mailing lists (Listservs). Although initially confined to industrial, academic and security communities, the commercial sector became

William Gibson coined the term cyberspace in his 1984 novel *Neuromancer* – a dystopian tale of hackers and transnational crime syndicates. For Gibson, cyberspace is 'a consensual hallucination experienced daily by billions of legitimate operators, in every nation. A graphical representation of data abstracted from the banks of every computer in the human system. Unthinkable complexity, lines of light ranged in the nonspace of the mind, clusters and constellations of data.' Today, the term refers to conceptual space created and maintained by digital connections and communications which run over the Internet.

increasingly involved in the use and development of applications for the Internet in the 1980s. Initially, all locations in cyberspace were identified by their IP addresses, that is a series of numbers punctuated by periods which uniquely identified a particular location where data were stored. In 1984, domain names were introduced which allowed for alphabetical characters to be employed, giving the world such famous names as Amazon.com, WhiteHouse.gov and Harvard.edu. Internet sites thereafter were located through a universal resource locator (URL), i.e. a unique alpha-numeric address rather than an IP address. This innovation ultimately allowed for some encroachment of physical space into cyberspace with the introduction of geographical determinates for many sites located outside the United States, e.g. the BBC's URL (www.BBC.co.uk) employs the '.uk' as a marker that the site originates in the United Kingdom.

Unexpected side-effect

Europe's most impoverished country, Moldova, has benefited greatly from its country code Top-Level Domain (ccTLD) tag '.md' assigned by the Internet Corporation for Assigned Names and Numbers (ICANN), the non-profit agency responsible for IP space allocation and managing URLs. Medical doctors (MDs) and health professionals in the US and other parts of the English-speaking world registered their websites through Moldova in order to make use of the convenient domain name.

Despite this minor incursion of state sovereignty into cyberspace, the Internet remains a place relatively free of the limitations of geography. Through digital communication, communities have been established and maintained across national boundaries in ways that were once unthinkable. Perhaps the most striking manifestation of this is among diaspora communities. Although immigrant groups have found ways to bridge time and space in the past, the Internet allows cheap and reliable communications with distant relatives, daily consumption of local media from the homeland and the ability to build virtual networks across countries and continents. When combined with other technologies such as mobile phones and satellite television, the Internet is proving to be a powerful force in helping immigrants maintain their language and identities in settings outside their country of birth and keep constant and vibrant contacts with those at home.

Internet growth

The Internet reached more than 50 million people worldwide in a little over three years, compared with 15 for television, and 37 for radio.

Challenged ethnic minorities and religious groups are also employing the Internet to maintain and strengthen communities which have been marginalised or repressed by their state of residence. Russians in former Soviet republics are establishing communication and cultural links with their co-nationals in the Russian Federation, young people in Scotland are using Internet chat rooms to gain fluency in Gaelic and the Métis nation of Canada is employing the web to promote a shared culture and lobby for greater political rights. The web is also becoming a powerful tool for proselytising. Religious movements have learned to employ the web to coordinate activities across continents and provide members of often-persecuted religions with a feeling of community, albeit a virtual one. Such behaviour has alarming implications for states which have until now had either direct or indirect control over most forms of mass media.

Besides functioning as a tool for keeping together deeply traditional ethnic, religious or linguistic groups, cyberspace also promotes the creation of new communities on a daily basis. Online gaming and hobby sites link enthusiasts who have never met face to face and who live in multiple time zones. Schoolchildren around the world are using instant messaging to communicate with virtual penpals in the blink of an eye whereas a decade ago correspondence was measured in weeks rather than seconds. Transnational corporations are using online collaboration tools to link work groups in real time across not just national borders but oceans. The web is even used as a global dating service, allowing couples to meet, fall in love and even make arrangements for weddings before ever meeting.

Corporate involvement in the evolution of the Internet initially encouraged a more broad-based approach to protocols and standards as the numbers of stakeholders rapidly multiplied. When the US government lost its monopoly over the Internet backbone in the mid-1990s and private concerns took over the management of the network, the doors were thrown wide open to commercialisation. However, the increasing corporate domination of the system has been thoroughly criticised around the globe. The most instrumental step in the commercialisation of the Internet was the development of the world-wide web (WWW). Tim Berners-Lee, a British physicist living in Switzerland, revolutionised the Internet by combining URLs and Hyper Text Markup Language (HTML), a code which allowed linking between websites, to make the Internet user friendly enough for non-specialists. With Berners-Lee's innovations, the browser age was born.

A series of innovations made the Internet more consumer friendly during the 1990s. The advent of search engines in 1993 markedly aided navigation by providing web 'surfers', a phrase coined in 1992 by Jean Armour Polly, with lists sorted by relevance related to the items they were searching for. Graphical user interfaces (GUIs), which had allowed personal computer owners to use a mouse to point and click icons on the screen (rather than write code) to accomplish tasks, was successfully integrated into the Internet experience in the 1990s, thus furthering its use by the mass market. New and improved web browsers like Netscape Navigator allowed novices (termed 'newbies' by more seasoned Internet users) to surf the web quite successfully in search of information and later versions of the web browser enabled Internet users to download various data such as music, video clips and other dynamic content, thus further increasing the utility and attractiveness of the platform.

> **A failed competitor for the Internet**
>
> Teletext is a broadcast system displaying information on a television screen, pioneered by the BBC in the 1970s. The information – typically about news items, entertainment, sport and finance – is constantly updated and available free of charge through television sets. Many Europeans, especially in France, initially eschewed the Internet in favour of teletext, citing concerns about the Internet as an English-language dominated medium, or perceiving it as having a role in extending American hegemony around the globe.

Improving ease of use at the end of the decade resulted in a dramatic increase in people on the Internet (nearly 1 billion), an astounding amount of e-mail correspondence (around 50 billion sent daily) and a proliferation of web pages (rapidly approaching 4 billion). With the growth in users came mass commercialisation. With access to such a large market, it is naïve to assume that big business would shun the opportunity to reach new customers and solidify the loyalty of existing clients.

E-commerce in its various forms has become a global gold mine over the past decade. E-commerce – a multi-billion-dollar market worldwide – is more than just using the Internet to conduct transactions; it is the utilisation of cyberspace for branding, customer communication, coordinating supply lines and a host of other activities. With the proliferation of pop-up advertisements, unsolicited e-mails (spam) and the increasing need to pay for information that was once provided gratis on the web, the Internet now resembles a global information bazaar. Critics of consumerism are quick to point out that the web has grown into a powerful tool for expanding consumer culture far beyond the boundaries of the developed world, pushing a host of relatively useless products in societies which have little need for them. Likewise, anti-globalisation activists from Islamic clerics to Swiss cantonal politicians lambast the Internet as a tool for reducing diversity and creating a mass cultural environment determined by the lowest common denominator.

Just as new linkages in trade and transportation have brought new risks alongside new opportunities since 1945, the increasingly interconnected nature of the world's communication infrastructure has opened the door to a host of dangers, including hacking, computer viruses and cyberterrorism. Modern hacking, i.e. illegally accessing and tampering with computer networks, traces its history back to 1972 when a hacker known as Captain Crunch used a toy whistle from a cereal box to mimic successfully the tones used by US telecoms giant AT&T. By blowing the whistle into a pay telephone, the hacker was able to recreate the tone that signified that the caller had paid for the call, thus allowing him to make unlimited long-distance calls free of charge. In 1983, the motion picture *Wargames*, itself a depiction of hacking, became a worldwide inspiration to a new generation of hackers experimenting with increasingly available home computers.

By the mid-1990s, Russian hackers were able to break into Citibank's computer system and illegally transferred $10 million out of one of the world's largest banks. As the decade came to a close, hackers, operating alone or sometimes in groups, began attacking and defacing corporate and government websites, giving birth to the new term 'hactivism'.

Hactivism

A combination of 'hacker' and 'activism' that refers to the phenomenon of unauthorised programmers manipulating computer systems to effect political change. The most extreme form of hactivism – cyberterrorism – has yet to be realised on a large scale. However, national governments are growing more fearful that supra- or subnational terrorist groups will strike at vital systems related to public safety, the banking system or food and water supplies.

Hackers steadfastly differentiate themselves from 'crackers' who use their knowledge of computer systems for theft or senseless vandalism. True hackers are driven more by varied political goals rather than the desire to accumulate wealth or cause wanton destruction. Hactivism can be seen as a form of 'virtual' activism – often by using civil disobedience at the global level. Hactivists have been known to publish classified government information on the web, counteract monitoring and blocking software of authoritarian governments that attempt to restrict Internet access within their countries, conduct virtual sit-ins on government websites and disrupt the effec-

tiveness of security forces in totalitarian states.

High-profile examples of hactivism have been recorded against the Mexican government over its policies in Chiapas, the People's Republic of China for its treatment of dissidents, and the White House for ordering air strikes on Iraq. Hactivism has also been employed by separatists (often based outside the country in question) such as the Tamil Tigers in Sri Lanka, Basques seeking an independent homeland and Albanians in Kosovo. The Internet is a globally orientated technology that allows hactivists a great deal of anonymity and the ability to conduct attacks from almost anywhere in the world. In many ways, cyberspace has become a second front for many types of conflict in the age of globalisation.

By the late 1990s, hacking's most nefarious offspring, the virus – an insidious programme that travels from computer to computer via the Internet, disrupting service and destroying data along the way – became the fear of everyone from the global IT manager down to the basic Internet user. In May 2000, a young Filipino programmer created a self-propagating e-mail virus called ILOVEYOU, which wreaked global havoc, made international headlines and cost businesses and consumers around the world millions in downtime, lost data and repairs. Nearly 80 per cent of all US corporations were affected and 100,000 servers in Europe were hit by the virus, which went global after making its way to the communications hub of the Pacific Rim – Hong Kong, where it was first detected.

Lastly, the Internet has become a tool for globally orientated terrorist organisations. Even before the terrorist attacks of September 11 2001, national governments had been directing increasing attention to the role of the Internet in the recruitment, training and coordination of terrorist groups such as Al Qaeda. Transnational terrorist organisations employ chat rooms, ephemeral websites and Internet-based encryption technologies to disguise their activities and communicate clandestinely. The National Security Agency, the US government agency in charge of analysing communication networks for possible threats, along with other security organisations has redoubled its efforts to thwart terrorist activity on the web through innovative detection efforts, while the USA and some other countries prohibit the sale of certain encryption technologies to individuals in states which have a record of supporting terror.

Further Reading

Deibert, Ronald J. (1997) *Parchment, Printing and Hypermedia: Communication in World Order Transformation*, New York: Columbia University Press.

Gorman, Lyn and McLean, David (2003) *Media and Society on the Twentieth Century: A Historical Introduction*, Malden: Blackwell Publishing.

Holeton, Richard (1998) *Composing Cyberspace: Identity, Community, and Knowledge in the Electronic Age*, Boston: McGraw Hill.

Kitchin, Rob (2001) *Cyberspace: The World in Wires*, Chichester: John Wiley and Sons.

Starr, Paul (2004) *The Creation of the Media: Political Origins of Modern Communications*, New York: Basic Books.

CHAPTER 3: Diplomacy

Not so very long ago, diplomacy and war would have been regarded as the principal, perhaps the only, means by which different entities occupying the global, continental or regional stage would interact with each other; and, more than that, as Clausewitz famously suggested, represented alternatives to each other. Even trade would have been seen as subordinate to these two. Today, as other chapters make clear, the balance of significance has changed and both war and diplomacy have to take their place among other equally important interactions. Both, however, continue to exist and both have been modified in similar ways. Having for long been the sole servants of states, their rulers and governments, diplomacy and war now serve various masters.

Diplomacy was not always a highly specialised activity, restricted both legally and in practice to the purposes of states. Before the emergence of the fully secular and sovereign state in seventeenth-century Europe, many very different authorities employed diplomats and expected to practise diplomacy: the Church, powerful individuals, economic associations as well as rulers, some very small time, did so. Some of these diplomats represented entities that cut across the physical territories of rulers whether large or small, like the Holy Roman Empire or the Church; some represented individuals or rulers who had a small territorial base, some much larger fry. But the idea of highly organised centres of authority was not really known and the extraordinary variety of both representative and represented made the development of a homogeneous diplomatic system impossible.

The corralling of diplomacy solely for their purposes by states from the seventeenth century began the process of creating a diplomatic structure that was complex, highly respected, professional and essential to the conduct of relations between them. All sorts of rules and conventions about the rights, privileges and obligations of

diplomats evolved out of – sometimes bitter – experience and were intended to make it possible for diplomacy to proceed in as untrammelled a fashion as possible. The effect was to make of diplomats a special kind of international person, protected and privileged for as long as his or her diplomatic status was accepted. That is why the rules which determine this status have until recently been so clear and broadly acknowledged across ideologies and political systems.

There are essentially two parts to the traditional diplomatic system: one is based in the foreign ministry and, in the contemporary context, in the offices of heads of governments. It gives advice about the formulation and management of whatever foreign policy governments have decided to pursue. The second part is external representation. Embassies, missions of any sort, ambassadors and their staffs exist to promote the interests and policies of their governments abroad, to negotiate as required with their host regime and to report on the general situation of the country to which they have been sent. Before the information revolution this last function used to be much more important than it now is; and the negotiating role has been reduced also. As the US former presidential candidate Ross Perot once said about that activity: 'Just send a fax.' Experience very strongly suggests, however, that those who doubt the role of human knowledge and sensitivity in specific situations are dangerously underestimating the importance of human contact.

The traditional diplomatic system is being challenged by the many contemporary changes, discussed elsewhere in this book, most of which arise in one way or another from the effects of the communications revolution. These are often grouped together and conjointly labelled globalisation. One effect on diplomacy has been to reduce the primacy of state diplomacy and the resources assigned to it, while another has been to introduce new entities which now accompany states on the global stage. This evolution has created a fundamental problem and it concerns representation.

The end of the diplomatic primacy of states

The management of global issues increasingly involves new actors beyond the state. When crises seem to lie beyond the control of governments or the relevant intergovernmental organisations, 'non-state' actors come to play significant roles. They appear in the familiar guises of non-governmental organisations, corporations and inter-governmental organisations and they promise levels of efficiency and responsiveness that transcend the constraints of the state. At the same time, the category of 'non-state' actors often seems little more than a cacophony of forms and interests with no clear means of articulating their respective roles vis à vis each other or the state. The ensuing proliferation of new actors has begun a significant period of reorganisation of the mechanisms and actors that make up the international system.

One of the clearest manifestations of the change lies in the evolving character of diplomacy. States, the venerable managers of the system, now incontrovertibly share the global stage with public and private entities, with which they must also share the machinery of global politics. Some of the newly powerful non-state actors are developing formal means of participating in the system, others do so more or less accidentally, some do not do so at all. The cumulative effect is an important evolution in the practice of representation.

This crisis of representation emerges most clearly when the finely tuned diplomatic system of the traditional state confronts the ad hoc emergence of globalised networks of authorities and entities. These latter are just beginning to appoint representatives in the face of necessity. Experience demonstrates the need for an accepted system of representation and the emergence of credible representatives. In the contemporary situation, this has yet to happen in any complete way; nonetheless, evolving methods for routing and validating communication between actors are developing into recognisable patterns and in this can be seen the germination of a new diplomatic system.

Diplomacy of states

In the contemporary situation, the representative needs of governments have changed rather confusingly: they need less diplomacy of the traditional kind among themselves, but more of it, sometimes cooperatively set up, between themselves on the one hand and newer sources of power and influence on the other. To make the confusion worse, where the need is for more representation, it is not proving to be adequate to try to redirect the existing system; the structure itself is having to be modified.

For the new areas of activity and power, the need is at least as difficult to meet. There is little or no tradition of representation and in many cases no structure which could evince it. A process of evolution is thus beginning, reminiscent of that which flowed from the evolution of the sovereign state in seventeenth-century Europe and which eventually developed all the subtleties of the traditional inter-state diplomatic system. While new mechanisms are forming, a crisis is occurring which arises out of the vacuum caused by the natural inability of even reformed representation of the old style to engage with new methods of representation that are simply not yet there.

The consequences for governments are far reaching. They range from the great question surrounding the outcome of the squeeze on governments coming from both above – from regional trading groups, for example, and, in Europe, from the expansion of EU powers – and below – from provincialisation and regionalism, where thoroughly local loyalties seem more useful than giving allegiance to any larger unit. This is the question mark that hangs over the locus of political legitimacy at least in economically developed states. The process is much less advanced elsewhere, a fact which has stretched quite sharply the differences between types of states and creates further uncertainties.

In time, the levelling effect of the global availability of information and services may work to the advantage of currently less advanced states and in some Asian examples is already doing so, but for the present the wide variations remain a difficulty and, in any case, it is not clear that the ability of less developed societies to leapfrog some technological hurdles will result in any permanent levelling of the playing field.

The administrative duties of governments have also come into question. Familiar patterns of admired and powerful bureaucracies, difficult to enter, well paid and secure, carrying out public administration with lesser or greater degrees of political management are being dismantled. The general demise of the collectivist state is one reason for this, but the increasing inability of governments to impose a high tax regime and remain in power is another. To apply deregulation and competition to the administrative organs of the state has seemed an obvious path to take both on principle and to save money.

Of all areas of government activity, the most susceptible to this kind of argument have been the foreign and diplomatic services. It is perhaps instructive that these were and have traditionally been felt to be the senior and central activities of the fully sovereign state; and it is they which have been the first and primary casualties of contemporary developments. Diplomacy had become the sole preserve of foreign ministries and foreign services by the early eighteenth century, with the exception of China, which resisted the notion for a further 100 years. Events in the international system and the behaviour of governments confirmed that concentration until the war of 1914. After the war, the cumulative effects of expansion of government roles and activities, which had begun before the war but were greatly emphasised during its course, began to break down the monopoly of foreign ministry control.

The profound significance of economic policy for governments, and its use, in the form of economic sanctions, as a weapon intended to achieve international coercion gave to financial and economic departments of governments a newly independent role in managing international negotiations and transactions, particularly in the field of tariffs, reparations payments and loan repayments.

This tendency continued without any great acceleration until the 1960s when two factors began to produce rapid and dramatic change. The first of these occurred in Europe where the progressive establishment of the institutions and functioning of the EEC/EC/EU began to establish new patterns of inter-state activity among the members. This activity was derived from a relationship that was still international but also incipiently federal, and the latter element created a need to have direct relations between individual departments of state, defined not by nationality but by topic. Strengthening the process, the same effect was simultaneously

required in the relationship between individual governments and the central administration at Brussels. While the most striking evidence of the trend was to be found in Europe, other pressures appeared more widely. The operation of the IMF, the World Bank and the GATT (eventually the WTO) as well as other economic and development matters, sometimes handled through the UN system, provoked similar changes across many countries, as did the highly complex negotiations, requiring a very particular kind of expertise, which were necessarily involved in attempts to control the nuclear arms race.

The foreign services of states were not only the victims of structural changes, they had also been the victims of a precipitous decline in reputation after the 1914 war, when people suffering from the catastrophic effects of the war felt that they had been betrayed by diplomacy's failure to prevent it. There was some recovery during the Cold War but their perceived role declined again thereafter, at least in the field of 'high politics'. An atmosphere of exclusivity, of foppish luxury and increasing irrelevance clung to them, however unjustified. The reasons are not hard to find. In a world where the imperatives of global politics seemed to be almost entirely economic and commercial, what part could a cultured generalist play? In a world where nuclear catastrophe might be prevented by arms control agreements, it seemed that only expert negotiators could possibly make them. But most damaging of all, in a world where the acquisition of information and the exchanging of messages had become both easy and generalised, the traditional duty of foreign services to put their government's view in the most effective way and to send back up-to-date information from their mission seemed to have been scooped by the new communications system.

In a deeper sense, the duty to guard the basic security of their country as a sovereign entity was eroded as the world situation was itself transformed by globalisation, changing at the same time the meaning of the concept of national security. All these factors reduced public and political willingness to continue to support the traditional diplomatic services.

Moreover, as the number of issues on which governments and non-governments needed to speak to each other both expanded hugely and became more technical, the range of administrative services across which they were spread also vastly increased. There is a similarity between the way in which governments have found the need to talk to each other at levels other than just the top and not confined to the use of a single point of entry and exit – the foreign ministry – and the way in which government departments within a country have also found that the issues they have to process demand cross-ministry treatment at almost any and every level. It is a lesser example of the same horizontalising tendency so obvious in the world at large. Within the EU, of course, the tendency is compounded by the necessity for each ministry to deal directly with Brussels, thus subtracting a major part of the political role of embassies of member states within member states, never mind their respective foreign ministries. Consistent attempts to prune and reduce expenditure on what was increasingly regarded as a perhaps unnecessary and certainly unnecessarily luxurious foreign service have scarcely been surprising.

New role

In common to some degree with the defence services – and to be seen, too, perhaps in doubts about the future role of NATO – the response has been a remarkable effort to escape from the atmosphere of luxurious secrecy and exclusivity and to find a new role for foreign ministries and diplomatic services, sufficient to give them relevance in the context of globalisation and the effects of the communications revolution.

The first gives rise to great efforts to broaden the basis of recruitment, to embrace fully all the technologically advanced systems available for both communicating and publicising the work of the service and to insist that all officers, however senior, must acquire such skills. There is also a tendency to reduce staff wherever possible, to abandon, where it existed, the idea that representation should be almost universal and that where it does occur it should not be too comfortable in terms of either accommodation or allowances. Economising in this respect would be imposed because of the general reduction in public finances and major efforts to achieve savings through better use of technologically advanced equipment; making imaginative arrangements for the leasing of embassy buildings and the sharing of compounds can be found in many foreign services. So, too, can multi-accreditations.

Embassies are affected in other ways as well. They are no longer hierarchically arranged extrusions of the foreign ministry but have become a house of 'many mansions' in which widely varying national operations, groups and organisations can find an office from which to conduct business. The huge increase in travel and migration in recent years has been important in this because of the way distressed nationals have extruded some aspects of the remaining welfare state onto the diplomatic and consular fields. The ambassador becomes a kind of chairman of a multiply sectored company or, as has been suggested, a version of the senior partner in a law firm. Such reforms are useful as well for image-altering purposes. In fact, the latter purpose has been helped, perhaps unexpectedly, by the all too real dangers and privations caused by highly unstable conditions in many parts of the world. Respect for diplomatic immunity and the ancient taboo on harming accredited diplomatic messengers do not survive where most sending governments no longer have or would wish to use the long arm of forcible retribution and where the perpetrators of atrocities need have little fear of the doctrine of reciprocity.

A second part of reversing past negative images involves becoming much more open about the formulation and management of policy with legislatures and the media, both of which have often felt excluded, as well as with the public at large and more precisely with groups interested in external affairs for historical, economic or intellectual reasons. These groups can be offered an entry into the process through advisory committees and academics are being much more extensively consulted in their areas of expertise. In addition, there is a growing tendency to introduce 'revolving door' schemes whereby secondments can be arranged from and to private civil organisations, chiefly in the fields of the environment, human rights and humanitarian aid. Thus a general sense is spread that external policy is at least to some degree a cooperative enterprise, based on inclusivity and accessibility.

The process goes further than trying to erase the negative perceptions of the past. Finding positive roles to play is even more important. Strict attention to what a country's interests and needs actually are and focusing on them to the exclusion of any more general ambitions has been a feature of the process. The result is usually that overseas services are to be concentrated on areas of actual or potential economic interest, the neighbours, the major global institutions and wherever there might be a national diaspora. In these areas, diplomatic activity, though accomplished with highly advanced communication techniques, is of a recognisably traditional kind, basically bilateral except where institutions are concerned.

In addition to this trimmed role, there is the newer importance attached to public diplomacy. Public diplomacy, particularly in its cultural form, has long been seen as an adjunct to the diplomatic exercise, but generally inferior in significance to the high dramas of inter-state political rivalries, and its practitioners regarded as less than 'real' diplomats. This is changing in contemporary conditions and particularly in the light of the all-pervasive influence of the media, including discussion on the Internet. Sometimes it can feel as though there are two quite separate worlds involved – the real one and a contrived virtual version created for the media by the actors involved. Skill in achieving this has added a new whiff to the very old odour of mendacity which has always hung about what the representatives of governments may say.

Public diplomacy

Public diplomacy means paying close attention to creating and maintaining good opinions held about one's country by the public of another. The hope is that the government of that country will be responsive to the fact that its public generally supports the aims and general stances of the government diffusing such public diplomacy so that in a crisis or prolonged negotiations, friendly attitudes will prevail. Thus all kinds of contact, ranging from sporting fixtures to cultural tours to newspaper articles or radio and TV coverage, are potentially of significant promotional value. A broadly favourable view of a country B, for example, that it is honest, efficient, compassionate may also affect the likelihood of global business locating itself in one country rather than another.

Depending on the degree of development of a country, public diplomacy may also involve forms of aid – direct or indirect; for example, medical or educational respectively. Humanitarian disasters of one kind or another also provide opportunities for public diplomacy at many levels and occasionally a form of public diplomacy in itself, by cooperating, amidst fanfares, with a humanitarian civil organisation. Public diplomacy is open to the charge that it is propaganda by another name; but it is not propaganda put about in the interests of control and it very definitely does not have the field to itself. If it was not basically correct, the global information system would provide a quick means of being found out and discredited; and in any case it has to compete with the pervasive orchestra of attention-seeking noise to be found on the Internet which again puts a premium on being both accurate and useful.

The development of public diplomacy emphasises another feature of the contemporary foreign service. As in so many areas of activity, both government and non-government, the pyramid of authority is being flattened by the nature of the work to be done. To achieve good negotiating positions on particular issues, to relate successfully to issue-based global organisations and meetings as well as to formulate successful public diplomacy, there has to be a wide range of connectivity: within the service – across departments in the ministry and between embassies and the ministries and very possibly other ministries – and outside the service – there have to be connections with politicians and interested groups, often national and global civil organisations, other friendly governments and, crucially, business and finance. Plainly priorities of this kind have implications for initial training and subsequent staff development.

It remains up for discussion to what extent this development responds to a real need and is effective in doing so and to what extent it is a self-preserving invention. For some countries which carry a heavy load of historically important remembered activity but which have been just as affected by the erosion of state roles and the global diffusion of power as everybody else, the construction of public diplomacy is both an attempt at shedding the load and a device for tracking the extent to which it is reducing. Forming policy for public diplomatic purposes in the inclusive way generally suggested and increasingly implemented can also be seen as in itself a way of recreating a national identity in a new image for domestic purposes as much as foreign. It is almost as if the role of a state has shrunk so much domestically that it is to be defined by the external perception it induces and that the very activity may be crucial to its survival.

As to the effectiveness of public diplomacy in creating a global basis of support for the general mores and specific points of view of a country, the jury will be out until time has provided more experience.

One reason why this is so is that in the rush of information and communications overload and in coping with the unstable nature and movement of power across the globe and, not least, the sheer pace of technological and political change, it is hard to think logically about what foreign, global or external policy is actually for. States originally had foreign policy in order to counter threats before they led to invasion or some other war and to find and maintain alliances both for that purpose and to support the waging of war if that proved necessary. They came to limit their relationships to the outside world to those conducted officially through the one point of entry or exit, the foreign ministry, or through commerce. They did so in a conscious effort to identify and defend themselves against credible threats occurring in a society of states arranged in a vertical relationship to each other, just as they maintained internal administrative machines arranged similarly.

In a period of transition such as is occurring now, elements of that situation survive, chiefly among less developed states and societies, but also in certain parts of the world – North-East Asia, for example, and the Middle East, including the Gulf. But these are not typical. What constitutes a threat has to be completely differently considered in the context of horizontalised activities. In one sense, these activities are themselves extremely serious in their damaging effects on the structure and role of states; but this is not seen as a threat, except in some economic and financial matters, because the effects of globalisation on the whole have been beneficial to individuals in economic terms and particularly to individuals in terms of personal empowerment. The individual as beneficiary of the information revolution is not inclined to want to defend a homeland against it, until isolationist protectionism seems a plausible defence against uncomfortable economic restructuring, at which point the disadvantages of doing so may seem as clear as or clearer than the advantages.

The real threats are not those traditionally seen as arising from abroad and aimed at states security as such, but to personal security. They arise from horizontal areas of power often thus far at least uncontrolled or restrained by a human agency. Job security, security from electronic or other transnational crime, cultural security, security from terrorism, security from environmental degradation and, in some areas, security from complete administrative and political breakdown and the consequent humanitarian crisis: these are the real threats. Here the mongrel nature of contemporary foreign policy becomes obvious. Few if any of these categories are specifically foreign, each is in fact a mixture of domestic and foreign, involving some aspects that are globally common to all states and domestically cross the traditional frontiers of administrative responsibility.

One consequence of this is the appearance of the argument that the main function of a foreign ministry is to act as the coordinating element in the generation of national policy responses to regional or global activities. Such coordination will go beyond government and include other national groups or interests and may even also involve coordination with outside bodies. Thus far, though certainly some signs of this appear, coordination seems to be moving towards presidential and prime ministerial offices, as the complications involved require such political authority for their resolution that only the most senior political centre can provide it. The end result of this process may be the concentration of the remaining high politics function of foreign relations at the apex of the system while leaving large-quantity, lower-level coordination to foreign ministries which may come to suffer from indigestion as a consequence.

All of these considerations suggest that, in developed states at least, any doubts that may be felt about how to answer the questions 'what is foreign policy for?' and 'for what should foreign service officials and diplomats be trained and retrained?' are not signs of intellectual or political weakness, but accurately reflect the acute difficulties of operating in a transitional situation. The key to understanding the problem lies not so much in a process of constant reduction, reform and 'rebranding', which cannot be ends in themselves, but in watching for the moment when the new global centres of power either acknowledge and improve their representative systems or, if they lack them, generate them. When that happens, dialogue between the possessors of power will again be possible and will become the most immediately practical way to deal with potential and actual threats to citizens.

State governments may be downsized, but they will not go away; they may find themselves in a far larger company of entities than they ever supposed possible, but they will still be there. They, like their new interlocutors, need to talk and they will need structures and staff – diplomats – to do it for them. Their already growing willingness to face global problems with an inter-disciplinary range of skills and people is a necessary start. More tangible results will await the arrival of other parties with which to engage, but it is for this that they must prepare.

Associations of states

Associations of states have formed a part of the international, now global, system for a long time. Their significance as diplomatic or quasi-diplomatic entities was largely confined to alliances, such as NATO, or, even more significantly, organisations created to manage international politics and prevent wars – the League of Nations and subsequently the UN. In more recent years, as we discuss later in this chapter, the major economic associations of states – the World Bank, the WTO and the IMF – have begun to develop new roles which have made them something more than an association of states and pushed them into acting as global authorities of their own. This shift has increased the importance and quantity of their diplomatic activity among their memberships and in their relationships with both states and non-state entities.

The UN has had a long enough history to show some discernible evolution, partly in the way it has established a formal relationship with the increasingly important humanitarian organisations. The UN has also evolved due to the frequency and scope of the interventions it has undertaken. Among the practices that have been developed, the most visible is the Special Representative of the Secretary-General (SRSG). The despatching of an SRSG to a conflict zone was at first rather rare and largely ad hoc. But almost any type of intervention by the UN now involves the assignment of a special representative or envoy to represent the organisation to any and all other actors involved in the situation. So there are not only SRSGs for specific conflicts like Kosovo or East Timor, but also 'thematic' special representatives, such as the Special Representative of the Secretary-General for Children and Armed Conflict.

This practice is now being replicated by other organisations in the UN system, such as the World Health Organisation which, for example, recently appointed the president of the Nippon Foundation as WHO's special ambassador of its Global Alliance for the Elimination of Hansen's Disease (also known as leprosy), as well as other inter-governmental organisations on the regional level.

In recent years there has been an increase in regional associations of states, whether established for economic or security purposes or, as often, both. In Africa particularly, their shelf life has not been long. But the African Union has survived and others currently exist – ASEAN and APEC in Asia, NAFTA, MERCOSUR and the OAS in the Americas and there are others in Oceania. All this contributes to the web of global diplomatic activity.

The European Union, however, is a special example of an association of states. Unlike other regional organisations, such as ASEAN, it has characteristics of a proto-federal state as well as an inter-governmental organisation. As the former the European Union is trying to develop more conventional mechanisms of representation as compared with other inter-governmental organisations. The role of the European Commission has been steadily broadened from its primary function of regulating and managing the European common market to encompass executive 'powers' in political and foreign affairs. The EU demonstrates acute difficulties in finding the political will to make a reality of common policies, and never more so than during the successive crises over Iraq in 2003–2004. But forms of overseas representation have developed through the EU delegations overseas and a quasi-foreign ministry for the EU has been instituted in the last few years, with Chris Patten and Javier Solana acting as the EU's foreign policy ministers. A European foreign service is also envisioned. All this indicates that the EU may be starting to move down a similar path to that which states took earlier rather than developing 'new' forms of representation.

Yet the EU's progress to the federal goal enjoined upon it by successive treaties is proving slow and tough. The substantial enlargement of 2004 brought both a longer list of problems and an administrative and constitutional crisis. If the creation of a state stalls, it may therefore turn out to be the effect on member states' diplomatic activity in relationship to the organisation which is more significant than the EU's relationship with the rest of the global system. Here it is clear that the independent political relationships between members have been cut down and the significance of their bilateral embassies reduced, though not to the point of abandonment.

Relationships with Brussels have steadily increased in importance and volume of traffic, but it is business which is largely conducted directly between the domestic ministries concerned and the relevant departments in Brussels. It tends to be more administration than diplomacy, but in either case it is not being conducted through traditional diplomatic channels. The end result is that significant quantities of what would have been diplomatic business between member states have ceased to flow through foreign ministries and diplomatic services and have migrated to other places, chiefly other domestic departments and in the case of the high politics of the EU, to heads of government.

Multilateral economic institutions and diplomacy

After the Second World War the governments of the victorious powers established what was meant to have been a trio of multilateral economic institutions (MEIs) to manage key aspects of what had become an increasingly global economy, whose mismanagement in the 1930s was held to have been partly responsible for the rise of fascism. In the case of the so-called Bretton Woods twins, the International Monetary Fund was to handle monetary relations and the World Bank Group, comprising a family of MEIs, was to encourage development. The intended International Trade Organisation would have supervised international trade. The latter did not finally emerge until the GATT became the World Trade Organisation in the mid-1990s. These three institutions together have dominated the field, generally known as non-state economic entity (NSEE) activity, and involve the largest number of member governments. They have the lion's share of NSEE–government diplomacy and power within them has been weighted in favour of the largest state contributors.

Other, more specialised institutions were also created. Regional development banks such as the Asian Development Bank, the Inter-American Development Bank and the European Bank for Reconstruction and Development paralleled the focus of the World Bank for their respective regions but with power distributed more substantially towards the recipient governments. The specialised economic agencies of the United Nations, such as the UN Council on Trade and Development (UNCTAD), the UN Development Programme (UNDP) and the UN Educational, Scientific and Cultural Organisation (UNESCO), were focused on particular, usually development-related, economic objectives. These agencies developed their own politics, institutional character and sense of mission and they extruded mechanisms of decision making and created diplomatic channels. Because they operated more on the principle of members voting equally, in contrast to the Bretton Woods method of weighted voting power according to capital contribution, they acquired a wider legitimacy.

Another type of NSEE is represented by the OECD, which is knowledge generating and consultative, though it might have developed more direct functions had its proposed Multi-lateral Agreement on Investment been agreed in 1998. The World Economic Forum (Davos 1971) has become a good example of the knowledge-generating, consultative NSEE, particularly since it broadened its invitation list following public protests made in the belief that it helped to perpetuate global economic unfairness. In this case, though, it is entirely non-governmental in its procedures and funding.

The International Chamber of Commerce was founded in 1919 and is a further important example. It promotes the free flow of trade and capital and it has taken up issues as different as scheduling the payment of war debts and reparations and curbing protectionism. The ICC provides a range of services to members, including panels of experts on areas such as intellectual property rights, taxation and competition law. In 1923 it established an International Court of Arbitration to help member businesses resolve commercial disputes. In the 1980s the ICC introduced mechanisms to combat international commercial crime and in the 1990s it produced standards of practice for sustainable development that have been widely endorsed.

These institutions require regularised working relationships with member-country governments. The professional staffs of the MEIs in particular were often drawn from the foreign services of member states or else from finance ministries or other appropriate agencies. But NSEEs from the outset took seriously the need to construct their own professional, and hence diplomatic, identities by, among other things, establishing rigid nationality quota systems for employment and setting higher employment standards than member governments in areas such as linguistic ability. In doing so they created a cosmopolitan staff which came to have a stronger sense of itself and its worth than of its former links with the government civil services from which many of its members had come.

Although NSEEs are fundamentally different from nation-states in their character, organisation and purpose, the evolving complexities of inter-governmental diplomacy have affected NSEE representation to governments equally. Most NSEEs have small, relatively centralised professional staffs and tend to represent themselves as and where the need arises. In many organisations, the great majority of the professional staffs function as diplomats, either formally or informally, at least in information gathering and communication.

In terms of the institutional organisation of representation, among the diverse range of NSEEs the MEIs are the most likely to represent themselves to governments through permanent or ongoing missions. MEI missions to developing countries which represent their usual constituency develop the greatest similarity to the permanent diplomatic missions of governments. At a different level, the annual general meetings of the World Bank, IMF and regional development banks, WTO ministerial conferences, WEF Davos summits and the ICC World Council all look similar to inter-governmental 'summits'.

Interaction

The emergence of communications networks built around the Internet has made it much easier for all sorts of other non-state entities, ranging from global firms to NGOs, to interact with NSEEs directly, bypassing the state institutions that would previously have represented civil society interests at NSEEs. Intensive lobbying, publicity campaigns and protest activities have forced MEIs to reconsider policies and change actual diplomatic procedures – for example, the location and timing of meetings, arranging for adequate security, etc. The protests against the WTO at its 1999 Seattle conference not only forced delays and changes to the proposed multilateral trade round but also brought about changes in the way that the WTO and other NSEEs publicise themselves and their activities. The WEF has reacted similarly.

MEI representation to governments has also changed as particular MEIs have been reformed.

In the case of the GATT/WTO, diplomacy between nation-states over international trade issues has been institutionalised in a particular way by the political process that led to its creation and early development, particularly because the ad hoc GATT secretariat was perceived as weak relative to nation-state governments. However, a structural change in the global economy, induced by the GATT-led process of trade liberalisation, has changed the perceived identities and interests of GATT member governments, particularly in the form of a shift among major developing countries towards more pro-trade liberalisation positions. This in turn has led to a transformation of the institution and its processes. This has been because the creation of the WTO gave it a strengthened secretariat and a 'one country one vote' system of decision making which brought about a real redistribution of political power.

The globalisation of manufacture, of commerce, of finance and of information is open to widely varied interpretations of its significance, as is the exact degree to which governments are losing out to global forces they cannot control. Put at its minimum, however, what has occurred is highly significant – significant enough to have engaged both public anxiety and supplied individual opportunities. It suggests at least two paradoxes: the possibility of narrowing the economic gap between developed and less developed societies, yet the plain risk that it may in fact be further widened; that changes in public policy have been induced yet the effect of those changes is severely limited. These paradoxes arise out of the parallel existence of older sources of authority and areas of economic and financial activity which are not new in themselves but are newly arranged across the globe in layers. The result has been that familiar – yet always difficult – methods of making the ebbs and flows of such economic activity as controlled as possible have become not just difficult but ineffective.

The annual global World Economic Forum (Davos) economic summit discussions, both in their very existence and in what topics they review, are further evidence of the need for new developments but do not add up to any viable systemic response. The World Economic Forum was conceived in 1971 as an annual 'summit' between global business leaders and political leaders at Davos, in Switzerland, at which problems could be discussed, ideas could be generated and, not coincidentally, deals could be done. Founded as an organisation made up of global firms, whose annual dues pay its costs, the WEF expanded to include regional summits as well as the annual Davos event and enlarged the range of participants invited to include the media, academics, cultural figures and other representatives of civil society.

However, by the late 1990s, the WEF had been sufficiently effective at publicising and promoting its mission that it began to be the object of complaint from a broader range of representatives of global civil society. They challenged the elite status of its venues and the lack of public accountability for political and business decisions taken in private under WEF auspices. The WEF responded, with partial success, by broadening its range of participants further to include civil society organisations with more diverse socioeconomic objectives than most of the WEF's membership or many of its political interlocutors.

Diplomacy of humanitarian organisations

Among the most significant newcomers to diplomatic activity have been humanitarian organisations. Private actors have taken on new roles in current humanitarian crises, acquiring a different relationship both to the crises themselves and to all the other parties also involved. These are generally four: the remaining sources of authority in the state concerned, other states, public organisations and other private organisations. States have no problem being represented at the scene; public organisations, particularly pieces of the UN, have also little problem with representing themselves.

For private actors, however, there is a problem. Little in their traditional activities has prepared them for the need to represent themselves or to become involved in coordinative negotiations; but both are having to be done on a daily basis. MSF field directors and coordinators, for example, can find themselves functioning both medically and politically, particularly in respect of relations with the media. So crucial can this aspect become that staff can be seconded to almost purely political activities, as has happened in respect of the MSF Nairobi coordinator since 1992, with responsibilities for relationships with local actors both in the Horn of Africa and in Rwanda and Burundi. When the going gets really rough, as with the abduction of MSF staff in Chechnya, a small group of four people was drafted from line management positions and acted for four months as a negotiating agency with local power brokers in order to secure the hostages' release.

The combination of attempting to avoid serious misuses of their assistance by benefiting parties and the frequent need to provide administrative and infrastructural services as the major part of humanitarian assistance also results in the need for complicated diplomacy in a very obvious way. Warring groups must be negotiated with, both as to their own behaviour and their willingness to tolerate the presence of the private actor and, equally important, as to their relationship with other groups and other sources of authority – the remains of a state, for example. In order to make administrative and infrastructural assistance effective, decisions have to be agreed with at least five potential other participants (it can be more): the existing structure, to the degree that it remains, warring factions seeking power at the centre, or secession from it, other private organisations, often many in number, several neighbouring states and multiple organs of the UN system. The need for negotiation is further complicated by the rising number of participants.

The levels of activity also represent a thickening weave. The level might be medical (both staff and supplies), food provision, environmental (essential services such as water supply), military (which brings with it the whole issue of achieving and maintaining a minimum degree of security) or the need for urgent administrative action, with all the attendant questions of relevant political authority. All these characteristics are producing changed requirements for the officers of the private actors involved. A new emphasis on obtaining staff with professional and political skills is emerging, coupled with the provision of training. Comprehensibly, the familiar short-term use of essentially amateur officers is giving way to longer-term contracts for professionally qualified personnel.

Through the mists of these changes, accelerating as they have in recent years, can be seen the emergence of staff members who, having joined a private humanitarian organisation on the basis of enthusiasm and the possession of one basic skill (in a branch of medicine, for example), find themselves turned by experience, and sometimes by actual formal training into perhaps unwilling but nonetheless de facto diplomats and administrators.

Pressure points

The increasing involvement of private actors in human rights – over and beyond those whose business they are – is creating the need to generate another kind of diplomacy: creating public pressure on governments and sometimes companies. To bring effective pressure to bear involves not only local action but, just as significantly, attempting to move major governments into action both separately and through the UN system. This may need to be done quietly or noisily, in direct contact with legislative committees and foreign ministries, or it may be done by attempting to influence public opinion on a national and transnational basis. On a general basis, the International Committee of Voluntary Associations (ICVA) does this in Europe and on behalf of third world private actors, while InterAction operates similarly in Washington.

In addition, private actors, usually in coalitions, have moved into the lobbying business. Sometimes this is done, particularly by smaller and perhaps 'one issue' actors, by ensuring that events involving them on the ground are substantially reported by the media. Larger and more permanent actors have concluded semi-federal agreements whereby they retain independence of action but cooperate for the purpose of winning power and influence, with consequential allocations of resources. This is particularly significant in respect of UN and EU funding and the division of labour involved smooths the process of negotiation. The existence of a part-time MSF liaison officer to the UN since 1983 is a case in point. MSF has also felt the need to have an office in Paris whose task is to supply a steady flow of reliable political and contextual information about areas where the organisation is involved, or might become so, based on research involving economic and regional expertise. In these cases, activities (and staff to run them) are required which are far removed from the original purposes of many private actors whose stock in trade was the provision of emergency aid to individual human beings caught in a disaster.

The thickening texture of communication between private actors and the pre-existing machinery of the international system is a mark of the breaking down of the hierarchy of international significance. The role of private actors is more nearly equal with that of states and institutional groupings of states, like the UN. The role of their staff has followed suit. The importance of the private organisations' perspective in political forums has been demonstrated by its increasing relevance in official delegations or in humanitarian cells in capitals. A former senior manager of MSF heads the 'humanitarian crisis reflection cell' of the French Ministry of Defence; a former Oxfam executive is the key official dealing with humanitarian issues in the UK's permanent mission to the UN. The representatives of private organisations are routinely included in official delegations to General Assembly sessions and special conferences. Revolving-door assignments also are widespread between private-sector and UN positions, particularly in operational programmes such as those of UNHCR, UNICEF and the WFP, where there is a tradition of picking talent from private organisations. In many ways these links between non-governmental and governmental spheres of activity are a novel feature of the UN scene, impossible to imagine a decade ago.

There can be no doubt that we are witnessing the development of a new layer in the global diplomatic system, evolving from major changes in the machinery of global politics. It is more than a quantitative change. The new style of 'summit' meeting where civil society meets government and where it is the importance of the topic that makes it a 'summit' underlines the point. At the Johannesburg summit on sustainability in 2002, for example, the number of civil society representatives was by far the largest element and led to new forms of relationships between public, private and corporate actors.

However easy it may be to point to the presence of private actors with influence on international politics in the past, both the level and the manner of its contemporary application have altered in a qualitative way. The balance of power among the entities involved has shifted – away from state governments and associations of states and towards private actors. To set against this, it is to be remembered that some of this change has occurred because the new entrants are acting as surrogates for governments. They do so in circumstances where traditional bilateral relationships cannot survive a state collapse or the objections of domestic public opinion to interventionist policies. Nonetheless, to be used as an agent requires both being present and being able to deploy particular advantages; and for both purposes self-representation is essential. The historically familiar problems arise about whether it is effective to rely only on expressing the opinions and requirements of an organisation, however morally right it might seem. Taking the time to discover all that can be found out about another party's situation and thus knowing what the political practicalities are takes the representative activity rather further, but can be extremely valuable. Should 'liaison' officers be two-way channels of information using it with some discretion, or are they messengers only?

In many ways, the internal organisational travails, the messy external associations and the multiplicity of very different and differentially powerful entities in the system, with concomitant confusion about status and role, are extraordinarily reminiscent of the early phases of the states system. It is not surprising to discover that the security of the universal ban on mistreating ambassadors has been disturbed. Dealing with the crises that occur within states means dealing with people who have little or no reason to accept the reciprocal obligations which underpinned the immunities of diplomats in an international system. The same sad effect can be seen in the attacks that have occurred on all types of aid workers and most notably on the Red Cross. The significance here is that the Red Cross, because of its origins, has behind it the sanction of an international treaty and its staff therefore acquired a specially protected position within the international system; but that position is not acknowledged by those who have no stake in a system which is not designed to deal with internal crises.

The Pope and the Holy Roman Emperor would have sympathised with the plight of the Secretary-General of the United Nations, the King of Spain with the President of the United States and Cardinal Richelieu with the chairman of MSF International; as would so many harassed toilers in the field of humanitarian intervention with the dangers and indignities of representing anything or anybody during the worst of the Thirty Years War in early seventeenth-century Europe.

The diplomacy of global business

Global businesses such as Microsoft, BPAmoco, Philips, Sony, Mitsubishi and General Motors have increasingly found themselves intervening in a variety of crises around the world, either to protect their investments or to buttress the integration of emerging and transitioning economies into the global economy. As the process of industry consolidation continues, it further concentrates resources and assets of whole industries into fewer firms. The power and reach of transnational corporations and the global strategic alliances they are building now rival that of states.

The prominence of corporations and their expanding interests within the global political economy have catapulted many corporate executives onto the global political stage and into some unconventional situations. An indication of the changing relationship between the private and public sectors is the treatment accorded CEOs of the largest transnational corporations by governments and IGOs. During the heyday of the economic boom of the 1990s, it was common for CEOs like Microsoft founder Bill Gates to be given 'head of state' treatment by governments of countries they visited. Ostensibly, meetings between private-sector leaders and public officials at the highest level are not out of the ordinary and have been going on for many years, but today the practice is different in that such meetings are not strictly confined to discussions about business ventures and investment. Indeed, the conversation between business and governments is much more far reaching and involves issues of social and political development.

Similarly, global commercial enterprises have started to develop more elaborate collective instruments, such as the World Business Council for Sustainable Development and the Intellectual Property Committee, to represent their common interests within inter-governmental deliberations and to be more effective when interacting or engaging states and transnational social movement organisations, particularly on environmental, economic and social policy questions.

Companies have had to build an organisational capacity to represent themselves effectively to organisations and communities that were not among the company's traditional stakeholders. The normal mechanisms of large transnational corporations – namely, corporate communications, marketing or advertising departments – were not equipped to be an in-house 'foreign ministry' and this function could not be outsourced to a public relations agency. Increasingly corporations are hiring retired diplomats to advise the CEO and senior management or to lead an international affairs division as a way to manage the increasingly complex relations of the company with other firms in the industry, states and inter-governmental organisations, and the ever-changing networks of non-governmental organisations. As more and more companies acquire talent and experience in this area, the forms of representation for transnational commercial organisations will become more formalised and uniform, thus expanding corporate representation within the existing state diplomatic system.

Further Reading

Berridge, G. R. (2005) *Diplomacy: Theory and Practice*, 3rd edn, Prentice Hall.

Hamilton, Keith and Langhorne, Richard (1995) *The Practice of Diplomacy*, Oxford: Routledge.

Joensson, Christer and Langhorne, Richard (2004) *Diplomacy*, London: Sage.

CHAPTER 4: Foreign aid and debt relief

In this chapter, the focus is on two additional elements in the machinery of interaction among state and increasingly non-state actors, especially between those located in developed countries which are aid donors and those in developing countries which are aid recipients. Many of the complexities of contemporary global politics are contained in this relationship.

Aid has always been an instrument of foreign policy, yet today it is assuming more contentious and crucial roles in the context of the war in Iraq and the HIV/Aids epidemic in Africa – to name only the most prominent crises the international community is currently having to deal with. During the 1990s, official aid sharply decreased at the same time as individuals, NGOs and other civil society-based organisations became the primary aid donors. In addition, the last decade has seen debt relief receiving particular attention as a way of ensuring that resources are available to be invested in needed sectors in developing countries. These are the dynamics described in detail in this chapter, along with a chronological view of the main events that have led to their unfolding.

What is foreign aid?

Although foreign aid is often thought of as any resource transfer abroad, its formal characterisation as 'official development assistance' comprises both grants and concessional loans that have at least a 25 per cent grant component: according to the Development Assistance Committee (DAC) of the OECD, these are targeted on developing countries. What this definition does not include is military expenditure or military aid, trade or investment financing, public funding for cultural exchanges, anti-terrorism activities abroad, international peacekeeping operations, expenditures on foreign intelligence or government-to-government loans at market rates of interest. Indeed, the latter falls into the category of 'official development finance'.

Official development assistance and official development finance are not the same thing. Development assistance is a subset of development finance, which itself encompasses all financing from developed countries and multilateral agencies that reaches developing countries, often at interest rates close to commercial rates (World Bank, 1998).

Both official development assistance (foreign aid) and official development finance can come

> **Foreign aid understood as official development assistance:** comprises grants and concessional loans that have at least a 25 per cent grant component and are targeted on developing countries.
> **Official development finance:** encompasses all financing from developed countries and multilateral agencies that reaches developing countries, often at interest rates close to commercial rates.

from bilateral as well as multilateral agencies. Bilateral agencies are those from donor governments (such as the US Agency for International Development – USAID – or Japan's Overseas Economic Cooperation Fund). In turn, multilateral agencies are funded by contributions from wealthy countries, administered by agencies such as the UNDP and the World Bank, and compose about one-third of all official development assistance (World Bank, 1998). In 2000, of overall US aid totalling $9.4 billion, just over $1.4 billion (14 per cent) was planned as contributions to multilateral development banks and international organisations (Lancaster, 2000). As an example of the allocation of resources between bilateral and multilateral agencies, Table 4.1 describes US foreign aid expenditures for the year 2000.

Foreign aid dates back to the nineteenth century at least, with, for example, the US 1812 Act for the Relief of the Citizens of Venezuela. In the UK, the 1929 Colonial Development Act allowed

Table 4.1 US foreign aid for 2000 (in millions of dollars): Official Development Assistance: A Chronological View

Type of aid	
Bilateral	
Development assistance	2008
Economic support fund	2792
Food aid	800
Eastern Europe and Soviet Union	1369
Debt relief	123
InterAmerican Foundation and African Development Foundation	19
Peace Corps	245
State Department Refugee Programme	623
Multilateral	
World Bank	811
Inter-American Development Bank and Investment Corporation	43
Asian Development Bank and Fund	91
African Development Bank and Fund	131
European Bank for Reconstruction and Development	36
International organisations and programmes	283
TOTAL	9374

Source: Transforming Foreign Aid: United States Assistance in the 21st Century (paper) by Lancaster, Carol. © 2000 by Inst. for Intl Economics. Reproduced with permission of Inst. for Intl Economics via Copyright Clearance Center

for loans and grants for infrastructure which aimed at obtaining surpluses for British manufacturing, in the same fashion as in 1896 the USA used food surpluses for market development (Hjertholm and White, 1998). It was in the 1940s, however, that the most significant steps were taken in the direction of stabilising a solid framework for giving aid. The formation of the United Nations in 1946, the Bretton Woods conference and the subsequent formation of Oxfam and CARE in 1944, and the launching of the Marshall Plan in 1947, were all significant in this respect.

A decade after the Second World War, the main period of de-colonisation began and created a constituency for aid well beyond the immediate post-conflict needs. Changes were not confined to the destination of aid but extended to the forms in which the aid was deployed. Although in the 1950s former colonial powers gave budget support to ex-colonies, in the 1960s their preference switched to project aid managed by the new bilateral donors (Hjertholm and White, 1998). In the 1970s, the policy focus of aid shifted to poverty alleviation as a result of the oil price shocks and the falling of commodity prices. The World Bank, under President Robert McNamara, bilateral donors and the US International Development and Food Assistance Act of 1975 stipulated that 75 per cent of aid provided under the US Agricultural Trade Development and Assistance Act of 1954 should go to countries with a per capita income of less than $300. In fact, during the 1970s and the 1980s, foreign aid from OECD countries rose steadily. However, the focus shifted again in the 1980s, from poverty to debt relief, largely due to the debt crisis that marked the beginning of the decade. The new focus on macroeconomic policy – particularly concerning solving balance-of-payments problems – gave the IMF and especially the World Bank 'a pre-eminence they had never enjoyed before' (Hjertholm and White, 1998, p. 13).

However, from the debt-adjustment efforts emerged what became known as the 'Washington consensus' or a prescription-like plan for economic development based on classical economics premises that marked the almost universalising emergence of neoliberalism in the mid-1980s and throughout the 1990s. The reforms suggested by 'Washington' (broadly defined as the World Bank, the IMF, the Treasury Department and the Federal Reserve Bank, especially) emphasised privatisations, fiscal austerity (as a means of inflationary control) and trade and financial liberalisation.

Nonetheless, by the late 1980s the emphasis on macroeconomic adjustment came under severe criticism, as it became evident that economic stability was not necessarily a guarantee of growth and increased well-being; on the contrary, much inequality was perceived as a consequence of 'neoliberal reforms' (as they became known). Indeed, the phrase 'adjustment with a human face' became representative of critical studies to the mainstream Washington-sponsored development thinking of prevalence during the 1980s and 1990s (Jolly, Stewart and Cornia,

The Marshall Plan

On 5 June 1947, in his speech at Harvard University, Secretary of State Marshall announced the Marshall Plan, which would entail the disbursement of US funds to aid in European emergence from the Second World War. The programme, whose official title was the 'European Recovery Programme', aimed at: (1) increasing production; (2) expanding European foreign trade; (3) facilitating European economic cooperation and integration; and (4) controlling inflation (the programme's chief failure). The recipient countries were Austria, Belgium, Luxembourg, Denmark, France, Germany, Greece, Iceland, Ireland, Italy, the Netherlands, Norway, Portugal, Sweden, Turkey and the UK.

US aid was disbursed in the form of dollar grants, grants in kind and loans. The amount disbursed from 3 April 1948 until 30 June 1951, when remaining aid was folded into the Mutual Defence Assistance Programme, totalled $12.5 billion (Kunz, 1997).

Oxfam

In 1942, the Oxford Committee for Famine Relief was set up, one of a number of groups in the UK aiming to highlight the problems created by the Nazi occupation of Greece and requesting that relief be sent to those in most urgent need. In the following year the Committee was registered as a charity. In 1949, as the Marshall Plan took effect, most famine relief committees closed down. The Oxford Committee decided to continue and extended its aims to include 'the relief of suffering arising as a result of wars or other causes in any part of the world'. The Committee gradually became known by its abbreviated telegraph address, Oxfam, a name formally adopted in 1965 (www.oxfam.org.uk).

CARE International

CARE (which was the abbreviation for 'Cooperative for American Remittances to Europe') was stabilised in 1945, when 22 US organisations came together to rush lifesaving packages to survivors of the Second World War. The first CARE Packages were US Army surplus '10-in-1' food parcels intended to provide one meal for ten soldiers during the planned invasion of Japan. They were obtained at the end of the war and began a service that let Americans send the packages to friends and families in Europe, where millions were in danger of starvation. $10 bought a CARE package and guaranteed that its addressee would receive it within four months. Decades ago, the packages were phased out as CARE expanded the breadth of its work, focusing on long-term projects in addition to emergency relief in 60 countries around the world. (www.careusa.org/about/history.asp)

1992). These studies suggested that the social policy component present in the 1950s' embedded liberalism compromise – when economic opening was coupled with governmental compensation of those in society who were the losers from the process – needed to be added into the picture of global macroeconomic reform. A schematic summary of the main developments in the history of aid can be found in Table 4.2. Indeed, 'globalisation with a human face' became the new challenge, as it became clear that 'fiscal squeezes are constraining the provision of social services. A time squeeze is reducing the supply and quality of caring labour. And an incentive squeeze is harming the environment. Globalisation is also increasing human insecurity as the spread of global crime, disease and financial volatility outpaces actions to tackle

them' (UNDP, 1999). Even the proponents of the Washington consensus soon restated the goals embedded in this set of policies by adding that social concerns with income distribution are of central importance; not only is it to matter how an economy's growth rate is increased, but particularly *who* gets the increase in income (Williamson, 2004, p. 13).

As it concerns aid volumes, the upward trend initiated in the 1970s peaked in 1992 and has been decreasing ever since due to fiscal problems in OECD countries, the end of the Cold War and the dramatic growth in private capital flows to some developing countries. In 1997, aid stood at only $47.9 billion, a decrease of 23.7 per cent compared with the $62.7 billion disbursed in 1992 (Hjertholm and White, 1998). The decline in aid was especially sharp in the USA.

Table 4.2 A summary of the main developments in the history of foreign aid

Period	Dominant or rising institution	Donor ideology	Donor focus	Types of aid
1940s	Marshall Plan, UN system and World Bank	Planning	Reconstruction	The Marshall Plan was largely programme aid
1950s	United States, with the Soviet Union gaining importance from 1956	Anti-communism, but with role for the state	Community development movement (CDM)	Food aid and projects
1960s	Establishment of bilateral programmes	As for the 1950s, with support for state in productive sectors	Productive sectors (e.g. support to the 'green revolution', which involved developing modern or high-yielding crop varieties for developing countries) and infrastructure	Bilaterals gave technical assistance and budget support; multilateral programmes (see below) supported projects
1970s	Expansion of multilaterals (especially the World Bank, IMF and Arab-funded agencies)	Continued support for state activities in productive activities and meeting basic needs	Poverty and basic needs (emphasis on the agricultural and social sectors)	Fall in food aid and start of import support
1980s	Rise of NGOs from the mid-1980s	Market-based adjustment (rolling back the state). Emergence of what would become known in the early 1990s as the 'Washington Consensus'	Macroeconomic reform under the framework of Structural Adjustment Programmes	Financial programme aid and debt relief
1990s and 2000s	Eastern Europe and former Soviet Union become recipients rather than donors, emergence of corresponding institutions	Practice and revaluation of the Washington Consensus. Move back to the state towards end of the decade. Effort to bring social determinants back to development strategies	Poverty and then governance (environment and gender passed more quickly). Concerns with democracy strengthening and security/geostrategic concerns regain prominence as well as concerns with epidemics such as HIV/Aids	Move towards sector support at the end of the decade. The launch of the Highly Indebted Poor Countries (HIPC) Initiative for debt relief

Sources: Hjertholm and White, 1998 and author's notes

By 1995, the US contribution had slipped to about one-eighth of the world total, or $7.3 billion out of $59 billion. If considered in terms of its gross domestic product, the USA has been the least generous official provider of aid within the OECD. In 1995, it disbursed only 0.10 per cent of its GDP in aid, while all OECD countries together reached an average of 0.27 per cent – meaning that on average, excluding the USA, other OECD donors provided 0.35 per cent of their GDP or half of the UN-set official goal of 0.7 per cent (O'Hanlon and Graham, 1997). In contrast, Japan is an important donor, providing roughly one-quarter of the global total in 1995. Also, the Nordic countries have been traditionally perhaps the most generous, giving almost 1 per cent of GNP in aid. Collectively, OECD countries disbursed 0.22 per cent of their GNP in 1997 (World Bank, 1998).

The downward trends in foreign aid, however, were paralleled by a sharp increase in private flows to developing countries; since 1993, these flows have become the most important source of financing for developing countries as a whole (Hjertholm and White, 1998). While in the 1970s and 1980s official finance – i.e. money from bilateral donors and multilateral institutions – represented about half of all finance going from developed to developing countries, in 1996 official finance was only a quarter of all finance available to developing countries (World Bank, 1998). Private flows in the form of donations from foundations, private voluntary associations, corporations, universities, religious groups and individuals' remittances to family members abroad – by rough estimates – may have amounted to $35 billion in 2000, or three-and-a-half times the amount of official development assistance given that year by the US government (Adelman, 2004). Such significant predominance of private flows to developing countries is good news in the context of official confusion as to the effectiveness of aid disbursed on the part of governments, and newly challenging geopolitical concerns.

Foreign aid in the early 2000s: strategies and challenges

Security

The linking of aid with the promotion of security is not a new development. US aid in particu-

lar was justified as a central instrument for protecting the country's security, helping to contain the expansion of communist influence. Indeed, 'this motivation was most evident in aid to Greece and Turkey, and the Marshall Plan in the late 1940s and early 1950s; South Korea and other countries in the periphery of China, and the Soviet Union in the 1950s; the Alliance for Progress in Latin America in the 1960s; Indochina in the 1960s and early 1970s; the Horn of Africa and Southern Africa in the 1970s and early 1980s; and Central American countries in the mid-to-late 1980s'. Hence, it was always the case that 'the security rationale provided general and often compelling justification for US foreign aid as a whole because aid for development and others purposes, it was argued, also promoted US security' (Lancaster, 2000, p. 18).

A white paper published by the US Agency for International Development reports that the 2002 National Security Strategy assigns development a new prominence in US national security, along with diplomacy and defence. Indeed, US foreign assistance, the report goes on to describe, must be understood as addressing 'five core operational goals': '(1) promoting 'transformational development, (2) strengthening fragile states, (3) providing humanitarian relief, (4) supporting US geostrategic interests, and (5) mitigating global and transnational ills' (US Agency for International Development, 2004). Those goals are to be achieved in a context where the effectiveness of foreign aid is being intensively debated.

It is significant that in this report a new term has been added to the development lexicon, namely 'transformational development'. By that, the US agency means 'development that does more than raise living standards and reduce poverty. It also transforms countries, through far reaching fundamental change in institutions of governance, human capacity, and economic structure that enable a country to sustain further economic and social progress without depending on foreign aid'. In this context, progress is determined by 'political will and commitment to rule justly, promote economic freedom, and make sound investments in people'. It remains to be seen what this interesting set of goals would indeed accomplish in a world where precise particularities have revealed themselves as much more informative than general trends, which provided the lessons from development-oriented experiences in the past.

Democracy

The five 'core operational goals' reported by the US Agency for International Development do not include the strengthening of democracy, although that can be interpreted as part of the effort to 'strengthen fragile states'. Indeed, in the 1990s, a purpose that gained prominence in US aid was the support of transitions to market-oriented economies and democratic regimes in formerly socialist countries. Twenty-six countries in Eastern Europe and the former Soviet Union have benefited from transition assistance, including Armenia, Azerbaijan, the Czech Republic, Georgia, Hungary, Kazakhstan, Poland, Romania, Russia and Ukraine.

Moreover, both the Clinton and the Bush administrations have emphasised the promotion of democracy as a key purpose of US foreign policy. In this sense, US foreign aid 'has been used to symbolise US support for opposition forces demanding political reform. (…) It has been used as an incentive to pressure governments to adopt political reforms. And it has funded advice on drafting constitutions and laws; the costs of elections; political party training; training for legislators, judges, and journalists; and equipment for government institutions'. Moreover, US aid 'has also been used to strengthen NGOs on the theory that civil society organisations operating in the political realm – such as human rights groups and civic education agencies – are essential to preserve democratic practices' (Lancaster, 2000, p. 26). Funding for such activities totals more than $700 million annually and comes mostly from the USAID, the Department of State, the National Endowment for Democracy and the Department of Agriculture (Knack, 2004).

The emphasis on promoting democracy via aid, however, might not have accomplished the desired goal directly. A recent large statistical study that tests the impact of aid on democratisation – a rare effort in the literature – using a sample of recipient nations over the 1975–2000 period found no evidence that aid indeed promotes democracy. The same period marks a time when many countries moved from autocratic to democratic regimes – from 58 nations in 1980 to 115 in 1995. However, it is not at all clear whether aid recipients have become more democratic *because of* aid. The study just mentioned concludes that its results do not necessarily suggest that funding for democracy promotion should be curtailed. Nonetheless, the evidence presented 'suggests that either the favourable impacts of aid on democratisation are minor, or they are roughly balanced by other democracy-undermining effects of aid dependence' (Knack, 2004, p. 262). This information has obvious implications for the current US and allied forces' policies in Iraq and the challenges this unprecedented case presents.

Aid as debt relief

Unlike middle-income countries, low-income countries never managed to attract substantial credit from commercial sources and were thus restricted to official finance in the form of bilateral loans (export credits or official development assistance – ODA) and multilateral loans from the IMF, World Bank and regional development banks throughout most of the past century. Official loans to sub-Saharan Africa increased gradually until the early 1980s. Since most of these countries' creditors were official lenders (rather than private creditors or commercial banks), the Paris Club was the main instrument used to reschedule the debt. Gradually in the 1980s, it started to become clear from bilateral creditors (and among them, most noticeably, European governments) that debt was forming an entrapping cycle of underdevelopment for poor countries. (See Table 4.3 for the evolution of debt relief initiatives.)

Differently from Latin American countries, multilateral lending expanded during the 1980s in Africa. The IMF and the World Bank lending increased from $1 billion to about $6 billion from 1970 to 1998. Hence, although low-income countries outside Asia grew much less in the 1980s than they had in the 1970s, they did not suffer the withdrawal of credit that Latin American countries did. In Africa, an increase in grants fully compensated for the decline in debt transfers during the 1980s, and more than fully in the early 1990s (though not in the late 1990s). The countries that would soon be called highly indebted poor countries did not take part in the restructuring processes that middle-income countries did. Thus, 'for the poorer countries there was no visible 1980s "debt crisis", but nonetheless debt was then and remained a crucial factor hindering economic growth' (Birdsall and Williamson, 2002, p. 17).

For the least developed countries, debt negotiations involve mainly multilateral agencies, the IMF and the World Bank in particular, as well as the G-7 governments. Although debt relief

Table 4.3 A chronology of debt relief initiatives: 1977–1999

1977–1979	1981
The 1977–1979 UNCTAD meetings led to official creditors writing off $6 billion in debt to 45 poor countries.	The 1981 Africa report by the World Bank (also known as the Berg Report) noted that Liberia, Sierra Leone, Sudan, Zaire and Zambia had already experienced 'severe debt-servicing difficulties' in the 1970s and 'are likely to continue to do so in the 1980s'. In the report, there was a hint of debt relief in the acknowledgement that 'longer term solutions for debt crises should be sought' and the 'present practice (by donors) of separating aid and debt decisions may be counterproductive' (cited in Easterly, 1999).
1984	**1986**
The 1984 World Bank Africa Report claimed that 'multiyear debt relief and longer grace periods should be part of the package of financial support to the programme' (cited in Easterly, 1999).	The wording of the World Bank report got stronger and the proposition for additional bilateral aid and debt relief was mentioned.
1987	**1988**
The June 1987 G-7 summit in Venice called for interest rate relief on debt of low-income countries. In December, the World Bank initiated a Special Programme of Assistance (SPA) to low-income Africa, which was complemented by the IMF's setting up of its Enhanced Structural Adjustment Facility (ESAF). The aim of both programmes was to 'provide substantially increased, quick-disbursing, highly concessional assistance to adjusting countries' (cited in Easterly, 1999). The SPA for Africa involved an informal donor association managed by the World Bank to provide bilateral debt relief, International Development Association (IDA) credits for International Bank for Reconstruction and Development (IBRD) debt service relief, and funding for commercial debt buybacks. This programme was available to African IDA-only borrowers with ratios of debt service to exports above 30 per cent (initially 21 countries).	The wording of the World Bank report got stronger and the proposition for additional bilateral aid and debt relief was mentioned. The June 1988 G-7 summit in Toronto agreed on a menu of options, including partial forgiveness, longer maturities and lower interest rates (which became known as the 'Toronto terms'). The level of reduction for debts was a uniform 33.3 per cent. **1989** The World Bank and the IMF facilitated debt and debt service reductions by commercial bank creditors under the Brady Plan, proposed by US Treasury Secretary Nicholas Brady. Most Brady deals, however, went to middle-income countries and were the culmination of almost a decade of debt restructuring negotiations after the 1982 debt crisis. The International Development Association Reduction Facility (funded from IBRD net income transfer) was established to restructure and buy back commercial debt. This option was available to low-income countries (heavily indebted IDA-only borrowers).

(continued)

1990	1991
The 1990 Houston G-7 summit considered more concessional rescheduling for indebted poor countries. The UK and the Netherlands proposed an increase in the grant element of debt reduction to 67 per cent from 20 per cent under the 'Toronto Terms'.	The 1991 London G-7 summit agreed on the need for additional debt relief measures, going well beyond the Toronto Terms ('enhanced Toronto'). Debt service was to be reduced 50 per cent on nonconcessional bilateral debt (12-year grace period, 30-year maturity).
1994	**1996**
Through November 1993, the Paris Club applied Enhanced Toronto Terms that were even more concessional. In December 1994, it announced the 'Naples Terms', under which eligible countries would receive yet more debt relief. Under those terms, debt service was to be further reduced by 67 per cent on nonconcessional bilateral debt.	In September 1996, the IMF and the World Bank announced the HIPC Initiative, which was to allow the poor countries to 'exit, once and for all, from the rescheduling process' and to resume 'normal relations with the international financial community, characterised by spontaneous financial flows and the full honouring of commitments' (cited in Easterly, 1999). That meant that for the first time the multilateral lenders would 'take action to reduce the burden of their claims on a given country' (cited in Easterly, 1999), granted that 'good policies' were followed in the recipient countries. At the same time, the Paris Club agreed on the Naples Terms and produced an 80 per cent debt reduction in the net present value terms (the 'Lyon Terms').

1999

By September 1999, debt relief packages had been agreed for seven poor countries, totalling more than $3.4 billion in present value terms. Renewed calls for expansion of the programme were made.

The Enhanced HIPC Initiative was established (HIPC II). It increased stock reductions to bring debt of HIPCs to below 150 per cent of the debt-export ratio. The relief was conditional on the completion of comprehensive Poverty Reduction Strategy Papers.

In November 1999, the Paris Club creditor countries, in the framework of the initiative for HIPC and in the aftermath of the Cologne Summit, agreed to raise the level of cancellation for the poorest countries up to 90 per cent or more if necessary in the framework of the HIPC Initiative. Forty-one countries were set as potentially eligible for the HIPC Initiative and to benefit from the 'Cologne Terms'. According to these terms non-ODA credits were to cancel up to 90 per cent or more as necessary in the context of the HIPC Initiative. ODA credits were to be rescheduled at an interest rate at least as favourable as the original concessional interest rate applying to these loans.

At the time of writing, 23 countries have benefited from the Cologne Terms.

Sources: Easterly, 1999; Birdsall and Williamson, 2002; Cheru, 2001; Sachs, 1999

initiatives have been developed incrementally since 1977, the main official effort to deal with the issue in consistent ways was launched by the World Bank and the IMF in September 1996, as described in the box below. This programme revealed that for the first time multilateral creditors recognised the unsustainability of the debt of the poorest countries and acted to reverse a cycle of indebtedness and negative growth.

The HIPC Initiative, as it was called, was notable for two principal reasons. First, it not only advanced debt reduction but 'it keyed the extent of debt-stock reduction to what would be needed in a particular country to achieve "debt sustainability". This was a step further since previous Paris Club relief packages were written in terms that were implemented uniformly for all countries that qualified' (Birdsall and

How the HIPC Initiative works

'All countries requesting HIPC Initiative assistance must have (i) adopted a Poverty Reduction Strategy Paper (PRSP) through a broad-based participatory process, by *decision point*, and (ii) have made progress in implementing this strategy for at least one year by the *completion point*. On a transitional basis, given the time country authorities need to prepare a participatory PRSP, countries can reach their decision points based on an interim PRSP (I-PRSP) which sets out the government's commitment to and plans for developing a PRSP.'

First phase

'To qualify for assistance, the country must adopt adjustment and reform programmes supported by the IMF and the World Bank and establish a satisfactory track record. During this time, it will continue to receive traditional concessional assistance from all the relevant donors and multilateral institutions, as well as debt relief from bilateral creditors (including the Paris Club).'

Decision point

'At the end of the first phase, a debt sustainability analysis will be carried out to determine the current external debt situation of the country. If the external debt ratio for that country after traditional debt relief mechanisms is above 150 per cent for the net present value of exports, it qualifies for assistance under the Initiative.

'At the decision point, the Executive Board of the IMF and the World Bank will formally decide on a country's eligibility, and the international community will commit to provide sufficient assistance by the completion point for the country to achieve debt sustainability calculated at the decision point. The delivery of assistance committed by the Fund and Bank will depend on satisfactory assurances of action by other creditors.'

Second phase

'Once eligible for support under the Initiative, the country must establish a further track record of good performance under IMF/World Bank- supported programmes. The length of this second period under the enhanced framework is not time bound, but depends on the satisfactory implementation key structural policy reforms agreed at the decision point, the maintenance of key structural policy reforms agreed at the decision point, maintenance of macroeconomic stability, and the adoption and implementation of a poverty reduction strategy developed through a broad-based participatory process.(...) During the second phase, bilateral and commercial creditors are generally expected to reschedule obligations coming due, *with a 90 per cent reduction in net present value*. Both the World Bank and the IMF are expecting to provide "interim relief" between the decision and completion points, and other multilateral creditors are considering also to advance some of the assistance from the completion point.'

Completion point

'Remaining assistance is provided at this point. This implies the following: for bilateral and commercial creditors: a reduction in the net present value of the stock of debt proportional to their overall exposure to the HIPC. Many bilateral creditors have announced that they will also provide debt forgiveness over and above HIPC Initiative assistance, particularly on official development assistance debt.

'For multilateral creditors (the IMF, the World Bank, and the other multilateral institutions): a (further) reduction in the net present value of their claims on the country based on broad and equitable action by all creditors sufficient to reduce the country's debt to a sustainable level.'

Source: IMF, 'Debt Relief under the HIPC Initiative: Fact Sheet', 2002

Williamson, 2002, p. 25). Second, for the first time debt relief would mean a reduction of debt owed to multilateral institutions (the IMF, World Bank and the regional and sub-regional development banks), which had always been treated as 'preferred creditors' in the sense that their credit was recognised by debtors and all other creditors as senior to all other debt: i.e. they have to be paid first and in full if other debt cannot be serviced. Failing to repay multilaterals (unless under the HIPC Initiative) means a debtor will be liable to be cut off from all other debt financing, including short-term trade credits. In fact, 'in the official donor community, defaulting to the multilaterals is seen as virtually tantamount to withdrawal from the international community of nations' (Birdsall and Williamson, 2002, p. 25).

Although, in 1996, the World Bank and the IMF predicted that 20 of 40 countries then eligible would eventually reach the completion point of debt relief, and that the HIPC Initiative would provide a total debt reduction of approximately $8.2 billion (about 20 per cent of these countries' outstanding debts), by February 2002 only four countries had reached completion point (Uganda, Bolivia, Mozambique and Tanzania) and 20 had reached decision point (Benin, Burkina Faso, Cameroon, Chad, Ethiopia, The Gambia, Guinea, Guyana, Honduras, Madagascar, Malawi, Mali, Mauritania, Nicaragua, Niger, Rwanda, Sao Tome and Principe, Senegal and Zambia) (Jubilee Network USA, 2002). The preceding box details how the HIPC Initiative works.

The main critiques of the HIPC Initiative represent different ways of accounting for the failure of development assistance programmes in the poorest countries. On the part of some official creditors there prevails a notion that debt relief has been substantial and relatively easy to get, yet wasteful and corrupt governments in recipient countries have manipulated these funds for private personal gain. Even in cases where governments did not appropriate these resources so brutally, the money received was used to relieve budget constraint and did nothing to encourage or ensure the pursuit of sound development policies. At the other extreme of the debate over the HIPC are those who support the 'poverty trap argument', according to which debt relief is still too limited and the attached conditionalities are socially too costly. To the charges of corrupt governments mismanaging resources, those on this side of the debate agree about the pervasiveness of the fact, but acknowledge that poverty and underdevelopment were not so much a cause as an outcome of it.

Moreover, issues of illegitimacy of African debt are also part of the criticism of the HIPC Initiative originating from supporters of the 'debt trap argument'. Of the nearly $140 billion of loans committed to HIPCs between 1972 and 1999, about 60 per cent went to countries considered not free in the year they received the funds. Between 1982 and 1995, 33 per cent of these loans went to countries ranked by the

International Country Risk Guide as not free and corrupt. Although some of these loans were never delivered, the fact remains that creditors have funded illegitimate governments (Birdsall and Williamson, 2002, p. 123–124). Because these debts incurred under such singular circumstances are outstanding and delaying development for some of the poorest countries in the world, they are referred to as 'odious debts' and are inevitably the objects of international scrutiny both at the level of increasingly engaged international advocacy by civil society-based groups and at the level of official creditors involved in the HIPC Initiative. The following box contains examples in which the process of indebtedness corresponds to cases of odious debts. It is also important to notice that odious debt cases are not all confined to the group of countries which qualify for debt relief under the HIPC Initiative. Notably, South Africa and Croatia are not candidates for HIPC-granted debt relief.

However, as it stands, countries must repay odious debts or otherwise capital inflows in the future will dry up.

In the light of much pressure for review of the HIPC Initiative, the IMF and World Bank posted a questionnaire on their websites asking the public for suggestions. Both institutions have had to accommodate themselves to the strong demands of civil society, which is particularly well organised and vocal on this issue of debt relief. Debtor countries too have presented their many concerns regarding the time-consuming nature of the process, its complexity and its reliance on IMF conditionalities.As with the original HIPC Initiative, the Enhanced HIPC Initiative also was severely criticised and remains so. Donors worried about the way foreign money was 'wasted' by government corruption, claiming that the Enhanced Initiative, by deepening and speeding the delivery process of debt relief, makes such waste easier and possibly more frequent.

But the changes incorporated in the second HIPC Initiative were aimed at responding more directly to concerns about the delivery of aid and relief 'as too little too late'. With its enhanced version, the process of debt relief has been made faster, as countries can reach completion point within months instead of waiting for perhaps as long as nine years. Also, it 'reframes' conditionality by incorporating the element of popular participation in formulating poverty-reduction programmes before debt-stock reduction is finalised (Birdsall and

Odious debt: three examples

The **Democratic Republic of Congo (Zaire)** is considered as perhaps the clearest case of a government accumulating debt for odious purposes and for nondevelopment objectives. From 1965 to 1997, the authoritarian regime of President Joseph Desire Mobutu received $4.5 billion in strategically motivated aid from Western governments and aid agencies in the context of the Cold War especially. Despite the fact that there was evidence that the Mobutu government was corrupt and lawless, funds were granted to Zaire, while development, under such circumstances, was never pursued. The money received did nothing to improve the lives of the people of Zaire, whose income per capital sharply decreased from $340 in 1965 to $113 in 1997, making the present Democratic Republic of Congo the second poorest country in the world (as of 2002).

In 1991 when Zaire's debt reached its highest level at $10 billion, the Mobutu regime stopped payments and since 1992 has become a 'rogue debtor' in the international community. As the civil war intensified in 1997, Mobutu fled the country after amounting a fortune estimated by the *Financial Times* at $4 billion and the Alliance of Democratic Forces for the Liberation of Congo assumed power. Although The Republic of Congo has been considered for the HIPC programme, the bitter civil war in which it is engulfed makes it unlikely to benefit from debt relief soon.

In **Nicaragua**, Anastasio Somoza, a West Point graduate, changed the constitution after the 1972 earthquake to allow for his return to the presidency in 1974, which increased tension with the Sandinista National Liberation Front (FSLN) and the Democratic Liberation Union (UDEL). Although the conflict that was in progress between 1974 and 1979 interrupted capital flows to the country, a loan of $800 million was disbursed to Nicaragua, along with a grant for the same amount. This money came from the US and multilateral sources.

The Somoza government engaged in corruption and political oppression. The Somoza family owned 23 per cent of the land in Nicaragua in the 1970s and Anastasio Somoza reportedly looted between $100 million and $500 million. The Somoza family dynasty finally lost power in 1979 when the Sandinistas took over. The new junta inherited $1.6 billion in debt accumulated by the previous regime. Half of that amount was owed to private creditors and half to multilateral and bilateral donors. After a brutal civil war, GDP per capita decreased from $1,069 in 1976 to $680 in 1979 (the three last years of the Somoza regime).

A democratically elected regime took over in 1990, inheriting $9 billion in debt accumulated in the preceding 15 years. In the same year, Nicaragua registered the highest level of infant mortality in the Western Hemisphere. New loans from the USA and multilateral institutions were committed to the country in 1991 and a stabilisation programme was put in place featuring trade liberalisation and anti-inflationary policies. In September 1991, the USA forgave 80 per cent of the debt owed to it by Nicaragua. Annual debt service increased from $63.7 million in the 1980s to $208.2 million in the 1990s.

Through the 1980s, **South Africa's** apartheid regime borrowed from private banks, devoting a large percentage of its budget to finance military oppression of the African majority. The debt amounted by this regime was inherited by the democratic government that followed it. Despite appeals from the Archbishop of Cape Town and South Africa's Truth and Reconciliation Commission for a writing-off of the 'apartheid odious debt', the new government has accepted responsibility for the debt.

It is reasonable to believe that the new government fears that a default would resonate badly in the international community, scaring off future sources of funding. As South Africa is not poor enough to qualify for debt relief under the HIPC Initiative, its debt burden will be carried only with substantial costs for the new regime.

Sources: Birdsall and Williamson, 2002, Appendix C; Kremer and Jayachandran, 2002

Williamson, 2002). However, despite these perceived improvements, the Initiative is still seen as producing too few changes, as still being too costly for poor countries and as 'leaving too much control in the hands of official creditors, who bear considerable responsibility for creating the problem in the first place' (Birdsall and Williamson, 2002, p.36).

In June 2005, the Group of Eight (formed by the world's wealthiest nations) agreed to cancel more than $40 billion in debts owed by some of the world's poorest nations to international lenders. It was concluded – as supporters of debt cancellation had long advocated – that full debt forgiveness is necessary to allow these debtor countries to fight hunger, disease and economic stagnation. This has been characterised as 'the most significant debt relief scheme yet' since it cancels the debts that the eligible countries owe to the World Bank, the International Monetary Fund, the African Development Bank and other multilateral lenders.

The G-8

The G-8 is composed of the leaders of Canada, France, Germany, Italy, Japan, Russia, the United Kingdom and the United States. In addition, the European Union participates and is represented by the president of the European Council and the President of the European Commission.

In 1975, with six countries participating (France, Germany, Italy, Japan, the UK and the USA), the first summit took place in Rambouillet, France, because of concerns over the economic problems that the world faced in the 1970s. Since then, the group has grown to eight countries and the process has evolved from a forum dealing essentially with macroeconomic issues to an annual meeting with a broad-based agenda that addresses a wide range of international economic, political and social issues.

The chair of the G-8 rotates on a calendar-year basis among seven members in the following order: France, the United States, the United Kingdom, Germany, Japan, Italy and Canada. Although the European Union participates in discussions, it is not part of this rotation. In 2006, Russia will host a G-8 summit for the first time.

Groups of aid activists, and especially the Jubilee Network, a group that has focused on debt relief efforts, see the new Initiative as 'an important first step' that nonetheless 'needs to be expanded to include all impoverished nations', such as Indonesia and Nigeria, for example, which had not been included. (*Washington Post*, 11 June 2005).

The new debt accord ended more than a year of tense negotiations. The USA and the UK had been divided in their views as to how the debt forgiveness would be financed. The USA had wanted the money to come out of the resources of the lending agencies. The British preferred the idea that rich countries would assume the burden of making the debt payments themselves, as they were concerned about whether the relevant multilateral institutions had adequate intrinsic strength. The deal announced in June 2005 struck middle ground. The real-dollar cost of wiping out that debt – estimated at $17 billion – will be borne by the G8 partners, which have pledged to make contributions to the World Bank and African Development Bank to ensure their financial strength is not undermined. The debt-relief costs to the IMF will be absorbed within the institution's existing resources. In addition, the accord stipulates that the payments to the World Bank and African Bank will be spread out over three decades or more. By 2015, officials estimate about $8 billion in payments will have been made by the G8 powers. The US share of that cost, ranging from $1.28 billion to $1.75 billion, is the largest amount to be disbursed by any of the eight countries in the group. The UK, Japan, Canada, France, Germany and Italy are all contributing to the programme, but Russia is not.

It is also worth mentioning two other important recent world developments which have prompted creditor nations to provide debt relief or cancellation to especially needy nations. Those are the war in Iraq, which led to a US write-off of Iraqi debt, and the Asian tsunami of 26 December 2004.

In November 2004, the group of rich creditor nations' members of the Paris Club met with Iraqi representatives. After a series of meetings, creditors announced that 'aware of the exceptional situation of the Republic of Iraq and of its limited repayment capacity over the coming years, (creditors) agreed on a debt treatment to ensure its long term debt sustainability'. Such 'treatment' included an immediate cancellation of part of the late interest representing 30 per cent of the debt stock as of 1 January 2005 – a cancellation that resulted in the write-off of $11.6 billion on the total debt owed to the Paris Club, $38.9 billion. When a standard IMF programme is in place, a further reduction of 30per cent of the debt stock is to be delivered. As for the remaining debt stock, that will be rescheduled over a period of 23 years, including a grace period of 6 years. This entails a debt stock reduction by another $11.6 billion, increasing the rate of cancellation to 60 per cent. Finally, after three years of implementation of standard IMF programmes, official creditors will grant an additional debt reduction representing 20 per cent of the initial debt stock. All in all, according to the Paris Club, this debt treatment plan will reduce total Iraqi debt stock from $38.9 billion to $7.8 billion.

In December 2004, a magnitude 9.3 earthquake ripped apart the seafloor off the coast of north-west Sumatra, travelling thousands of miles across the Indian Ocean. This phenomenon became known as the Asian tsunami and killed approximately 300,000 people in countries as far apart as Indonesia, the Maldives, Sri Lanka and Somalia. In January 2005, the Paris Club of rich creditor nations offered to freeze debts owed to them by tsunami-hit countries. The offer was immediate and without conditions. Indonesia, Sri Lanka and the Seychelles signalled that they were taking it up. Later on, however, Indonesia decided to go back on its decision and declined the debt freeze on $48 billion the country owes the Paris Club. Thailand and India also declined the offer, with Thailand preferring to keep up with its payments while India said it would prefer to rely on its own resources rather than on international aid.

This refusal to accept the debt freeze is a product of the countries' concern that such an initiative would produce a decline in their credit ratings, thereby making it harder and/or more costly for these debtors' countries to have access to private capital inflows. This, in effect, means that to take on new loans granted by *private* creditors, the countries above would have to compensate these investors by offering them higher interest rates (or higher return) since, with damaged credit ratings, lending to the tsunami-affected countries could be perceived as a risky investment. Finally, it is important to add that the offer by creditor countries was a freeze in debt payments, not debt cancellation – even though the $5 billion which was owed in 2005 would be, in purely financial terms, insignificant for the rich creditor nations. How effective the aid disbursed was, and how far the debt freeze will go in giving real help to the tsunami-affected countries in achieving meaningful long-term development, is still history in the making.

In conclusion, for low-income countries, the ways in which debt relief was delivered until 2005 were still an insufficient effort. Ultimately, discussions on a just treatment of debt are located on a thin line that divides the need to ensure continuous sources of credit – a focus that must be in tune with the economic 'logic' of markets – from the need to guarantee that debtors can be allowed some room for manoeuvre when they find themselves entrapped in a cycle of debt service that has proved unsustainable. In this sense, debt relief or forgiveness is not a substitute for aid but a necessary complement in a broader aid architecture that faces a plethora of geopolitical challenges or needed recipients.

Further Reading

Adelman, Carol (2004) 'The Privatisation of Foreign Aid: Reassessing National Largesse', *Foreign Affairs*, November/December, pp. 9–14.

BBC News (2003) 'US Gets Iraq Debt Relief', 16 December, available at: http://news.bbc.co.uk/1/hi/business/3322073.stm

Birdsall, Nancy (2002) 'Policy Selectivity Foregone: Debt and Donor Behaviour in Africa', Centre for Global Development, Working Paper 17, October.

Birdsall, Nancy and Williamson, John (2002) *Delivering on Debt Relief: From IMF Gold to a New Aid Architecture*, Washington, DC: Centre for Global Development and Institute for International Economics.

Cheru, Fantu (2001) 'The HIPC Initiative: A Human Rights Assessment of Poverty Reduction Strategy Papers', UN Commission on Human Rights, 18 January.

Cornia, Giovanni, Jolly, Richard and Stewart, Frances (eds) (1989) *Adjustment with a Human Face: Protecting the Vulnerable and Promoting Growth*, New York: Oxford University Press.

Easterly, William (1999) 'How Did Highly Indebted Poor Countries Become Highly Indebted?: Reviewing Two Decades of Debt Relief', Washington, DC: World Bank, manuscript.

Hjertholm, Peter and White, Howard (1998) 'Survey of Foreign Aid: History, Trends and Allocation', Discussion Paper 00–04, Institute of Economics, University of Copenhagen.

International Monetary Fund (2001) *World Economic Outlook: Fiscal Policy and Macroeconomic Stability*, Washington, DC: IMF.

— (2002a) 'Sovereign Debt Restructuring and the Domestic Economic Experience in Four Recent Cases', 21 February.

— 2002b. IMF Survey, vol. 31, no. 15, 5 August.

— (2002c) 'Guidelines on Conditionality', 25 September.

— (2002d) 'Board Discusses Possible Features of a Sovereign Debt Restructuring Mechanism', Public Information Notice, no. 03/06, 7 January.

— (2002e) 'Debt Relief Under the Heavily Indebted Poor Countries: A Factsheet', August, www.imfg.org/external/np/exr/facts/hipc.htm

International Monetary Fund and World Bank (1999) 'Heavily Indebted Poor Countries (HIPC) Initiative – Perspectives on Current Framework and Options for Change', 2April, www.imf.org/external/np/hipc/options/options.pdf

Jubilee Network USA (2002) 'Debt Update Chart', February, www.jubileeusa.org

Knack, Stephen (2004) 'Does Foreign Aid Promote Democracy?', International Studies Quarterly, 48:1, pp. 251–266.

Kremer, Michael and Jayachandran, Seema (2002) 'Odious Debt', Finance and Development, vol. 39, no. 2, Washington, DC: IMF.

Kunz, Diane (1997) 'The Marshall Plan Reconsidered: A Complex of Motives', Foreign Affairs, May/June, available at www.foreignaffairs.org/popup/popup.asp?zonename=ROS+Popup

Lancaster, Carol (2000) Transforming Foreign Aid: United States Assistance in the 21st Century, Washington, DC: Institute for International Economics.

Nyang'oro, Julius E. (1999) 'Hemmed in? The State in Africa and Global Liberalisation' in Smith, David A., Solinger, Dorothy J. and Topik, Steven (eds) States and Sovereignty in the Global Economy, London: Routledge.

O'Hanlon, Michael and Graham, Carol (1997) A Half a Penny on the Federal Dollar: The Future of Development Aid, Washington, DC: Brookings Institution Press.

Sachs, Jeffrey (1999) 'Implementing Debt Relief for HIPCs', Harvard University, manuscript.

— (2002) 'Resolving the Debt Crisis of Low Income Countries', Brookings Papers on Economic Activity, 1, pp. 257–286.

The Economist (2002) 'The Challenge of World Poverty', 22 April.

UNAIDS (2002) Fact Sheet: Sub-Saharan Africa, available at www.unaids.org/worldaidsday/2002/press/factsheets/FSAfrica_en.doc

United Nations Development Programme (1999) Human Development Report 1999: Globalisation With a Human Face, New York: UNDP.

US Agency for International Development (2004) 'US Foreign Aid: Meeting the Challenges of the Twenty-first Century', Washington, DC: USAID.

Williamson, John (2004) 'The Washington Consensus as Policy Prescription for Development', lecture delivered at the World Bank on 13 January, mimeo.

World Bank (1998) Assessing Aid: What Works, What Doesn't, and Why, Oxford: Oxford University Press.

CHAPTER 5: Humanitarian action

From compassion to action

Here is a hand-to-hand struggle in all its horror and frightfulness; Austrians and Allies trampling each other under foot, killing one another on piles of bleeding corpses, felling their enemies with their rifle butts, crushing skulls, ripping bellies open with sabre and bayonet. No quarter is given; it is a sheer butchery; a struggle between savage beasts, maddened with blood and fury. Even the wounded fight to the last gasp. When they have no weapon left, they seize their enemies by the throat and tear them with their teeth.

Jean Henri Dunant, *from A Memory of Solferino (ICRC, 2004)*

Shaken by the horror of witnessing 40,000 casualties occurring in just nine hours of fighting near the northern Italian town of Solferino on 21 June 1859 during the Franco-Austrian War, the young Swiss businessman Henri Dunant proposed a plan for each nation to create teams of trained volunteers to care for the wounded in the midst of wars.[1] It led to the founding of the International Red Cross and the Geneva Convention of 1864.

Compassion, the ethical value that drove Dunant to campaign for the protection of the wounded, is at the core of humanitarian action. It motivates individuals to devote their energies to heal the wounded, protect the vulnerable and assuage the suffering of soldiers and civilians caught up in man-made wars and natural disasters. Humanitarian action brings humanity's decency to bear upon the all-too-accepted notion of war as just 'politics by other means'.

At the beginning, as with Dunant, compassion was about providing charity to the wounded irrespective of which side they were on. It called for humanitarian actors to cherish neutrality (not to take sides in a conflict), impartiality (provide for all without discrimination) and independence (from the influence of governments or parties in conflict) above all else. Over time, it also came to mean helping those affected by natural disasters such as earthquakes, famine and flooding. However, 'compassion' took on a dramatically expanded meaning for some, especially gaining force in the 1990s as they attempted to address the root causes of conflicts.

Compassion gives rise to the charitable impulse that in turn drives humanitarian action. The impulse is rooted in religious and philosophical beliefs. Dunant was a member of the Christian Association of Geneva, a group that espoused tolerance, and founded the World's Young Men's Christian Association. Dunant also expressed deep contempt for slavery and considered himself a pacifist even before his experience at Solferino. The charity in Christianity is often associated with the tale of the Good Samaritan. In Islam, the practice of 'Giving Alms' (Zakat) is one of the five pillars of the faith. In Hinduism, 'Manava Sevae, Madhava Seva' means to serve God by serving humanity. People without specific religious attachments derive similar values from philosophies that emphasise the interconnectedness of humanity, such as Immanuel Kant professed. Similarly, Rousseau and Adam Smith believed that the desire to help is a part of human nature.

These religious and philosophical values underpin the motivations of not only individuals but organisations as well. Many non-governmental humanitarian organisations, such as Catholic Relief Services and Islamic Relief, are service branches of religious institutions. Other organisations are not explicitly connected to a religion but are underpinned with religious values expressed in their founding charters. Of course, individuals and organisations do use their actions for political ends. Some are evangelical,

---

1 Dunant recounted his memories at Solferino and proposed his plans three years later in his book *Un Souvenir de Solférino* (A Memory of Solferino).

but a vast number do not advocate religion in their work. Many just enter the field based on religious and philosophical convictions. The end of the twentieth century saw a proliferation of organisations committed to humanitarian action based upon secular values.

The charitable impulse can also be present in the foreign policy of countries. Naturally, it is more difficult to discern the humanitarian ideal from the political interest where competition for power and wealth is the norm. However, when Turkey suffered a devastating earthquake in August 1999, the Greek government (and people) put aside their long-standing disputes to begin delivery of relief supplies within 12 hours of the quake. In other instances where countries reach out together through international institutions to help the victims of conflicts and natural disasters, they are perhaps showing at least as true a colour as in the conduct of realpolitik. When their contributions to the budgets of organisations like the World Food Programme are largely out of the public eye or garner little prestige, it can be asked whether policymakers contribute out of compassion. In the December 2004 tsunami that struck South and South-East Asia, governments seemed to engage in 'competitive compassion' in attempting to outdo each other's contribution of aid. There is no doubt that concerns of reputation and prestige were on the minds of some governments, but few would also deny that governments donated based also on compassion for the enormous loss of life and suffering of the people of southern Asia.

The next four sections survey humanitarian action. The first defines humanitarian action, highlights why it is needed and details the actors and interactions in providing humanitarian aid. The second provides an overview of the evolution of humanitarian action by noting specific trends in the field. It is followed by a more detailed discussion about some of the significant developments and debates that have an impact on how humanitarian action is conducted. The conclusion reflects on the future course of humanitarian action in the context of the changing nature of conflicts.

The actors and interactions of humanitarian action

During humanitarian crises, the best of humanity, compassion, and the worst in humanity, geno-cidal pogroms, clash head-on. All levels of actors – governments, non-governmental organisations, rebels, refugees, etc. – interact to make the environment both thickly textured and highly intense. What is this intense interaction called 'humanitarian action' and why is it an 'essential' aspect of global politics and governance?

To put it simply, humanitarian action is a spectrum of activities that provides relief, protection and recovery to populations affected by natural disasters and human conflicts.[2] However, such a simple statement belies the complexity of the field and the dynamic debates about the appropriate scope of activities that should fall under 'humanitarian action'. These debates have to do mainly with regard to assistance in conflicts and are not about providing assistance in natural disasters. Therefore, it is the role of humanitarian action in conflicts that this chapter particularly addresses.

In conflicts, at the most restricted end of the spectrum lies the provision of emergency relief to meet short-term fundamental needs. Priorities normally include clean water, food and prevention of health threats such as dysentery, malaria and tuberculosis. Further along the spectrum lies the protection of vulnerable populations such as civilians and refugees and resisting further harm to them by means of advocacy and emphasising human rights. At the most expansive end of the spectrum is assistance for long-term recovery through political, social and economic reconstruction (e.g. legal institutions, reconciliation and reconstruction of water-treatment facilities). Somewhere between protection and development, or perhaps outside this spectrum, lie 'humanitarian interventions'. This is the use of force to intervene in a country for humanitarian purposes (the degree to which the motives must be solely humanitarian is debated). The evolution and tensions in the different aspects of this spectrum will be discussed later.

Why is humanitarian action necessary?

---

2 The term 'humanitarian action' is used by the Humanitarianism and War Project to include assistance and protection. It is also actively used by the ICRC, but with no official definition or parameters. In the absence of any 'official' definitions within the field, 'humanitarian action' here is used to include all facets of humanitarianism: relief, aid, assistance, protection and development related to humanitarian activities. Definitions of the these terms are implied by using them in conjunction with certain scopes of humanitarian activities in the section titled 'The Evolution of Humanitarian Action.'

Between 1999 and 2003, 303 million people were affected by natural disasters such as floods, droughts, famine, windstorms and heat waves – 295,000 of them died. In 2003, there were 36 armed conflicts in progress, 11.9 million refugees and asylum seekers and 3 million newly internally displaced persons which led to a global total of 24.6 million people in these categories. Not all of these people receive assistance from outside their country, and victims of armed conflict normally get more publicity. However, without the assistance and interaction of outside actors, especially from wealthier, predominantly 'Western' countries, many of these people would be left helpless and hopeless in the face of catastrophes.

The tsunami that struck Southern Asia in December 2004 claimed over 200,000 lives and displaced more than 5 million people in 12 countries. Countries in the region could not respond or recover from the unprecedented scale of the disaster without assistance from all over the world.

Four major international actors perform humanitarian actions. They are governments, United Nations agencies and other inter-governmental organisations, NGOs, and members of the International Red Cross and Red Crescent societies. Governments (alone or multilaterally) provide food aid, airlifts and logistics for distribution of supplies, manpower for recovering from natural disasters, etc. They also negotiate access to vulnerable populations and conduct humanitarian military interventions. The UN and its agencies coordinate and carry out many of the humanitarian programmes in the field, from providing food to refugees to beginning the reconstruction of societies.

action. NGOs complement UN programmes (such as helping distribute food), fill the gap where the UN or governments are not present and perform politically sensitive roles that the UN cannot take on, such as bearing witness and publicising human rights violations. The International Committee of the Red Cross (ICRC) and the International Federation of Red Cross and Red Crescent Societies (IFRC) work to provide assistance in crises and facilitate disaster preparedness. The ICRC is unique in that it is a non-governmental body borne of an intergovernmental convention (the 1864 Geneva Convention) that is mandated to oversee the implementation of international humanitarian laws in conflicts.

Resources

A significant characteristic of these actors is that they all come with money – approximately $10 billion worth, not including money spent on military operations in humanitarian interventions. Exact figures are difficult to calculate

UN agencies involved in humanitarian activities in the field:

- Office for the Co-ordination of Humanitarian Affairs (OCHA)
- UN High Commissioner for Refugees (UNHCR)
- UN Children's Fund (UNICEF)
- World Food Programme (WFP)
- Food and Agricultural Organisation (FAO)
- International Organisation for Migration (IOM)
- World Health Organisation (WHO)
- UN Development Programme (UNDP)
- UN Relief and Works Agency for Palestine Refugees in the Near East

Some large humanitarian NGOs:

- CARE
- Catholic Relief Services
- International Rescue Committee
- Médécins Sans Frontières (Doctors Without Borders)
- Oxfam
- Red Cross and Red Crescent Societies
- Save the Children
- World Vision

Governments and the UN are increasingly making use of NGOs to undertake humanitarian

since much humanitarian aid is part of Official Development Assistance and national agencies define and categorise spending differently. Nevertheless, although ODA has decreased overall in recent years, humanitarian aid as a portion of ODA has increased – from less than 3 per cent between 1970 and 1990 to 10 per cent since 1999. Bilateral humanitarian aid, which is controlled and dispersed by the donor government, accounts for 60 per cent of aid, while 40 per cent is delivered on a multilateral basis; that is, in the form of funding for UN agencies, international organisations or the European Commission of the European Union.

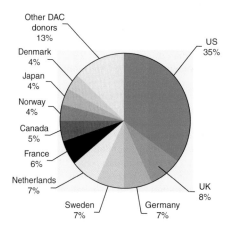

Figure 5.1 Total humanitarian aid from DAC donors in 2001

Source: Global Humanitarian Assistance 2003

tinued to increase over the years to reach over $1 billion in 2001. Figure 5.2 shows who the top recipients of humanitarian aid were in 2001. Figure 5.3 indicates how aid was used in 2002 (all data from Global Humanitarian Assistance, 2003). These charts give an overview of the flow of money between the donors and recipients to display the significance of the interaction. The poorer the country, the more significant aid is in its national budget and the more important donors are to its survival.

The availability of resources, specifically money, is a key and persistent concern for humanitarian actors. In relation to need, money is always in short supply. When a disaster occurs, whether a tsunami or refugee crises, an out-pouring of support is often common. However, as the media spotlights vanish, the money committed by governments and NGOs sometimes never materialises. Initial projects are sometimes completed or lost in the bureaucracies of host governments or shifting interests of NGOs. At other times, a well-publicised crisis draws money away from needs in other parts of the world. But perhaps the most persistent of problems is that aid and commitment towards the long-term recovery of affected communities are as fleeting as the disaster that first brought in international actors.

The Development Assistance Committee of the OECD (which comprises most developed countries, which are also the countries that contribute the most in aid – $5.5 billion of $10 billion) tracks aid.

Figure 5.1 shows the breakdown of the $5.5 billion contributions by DAC members for 2001. In addition, contributions from NGOs have con-

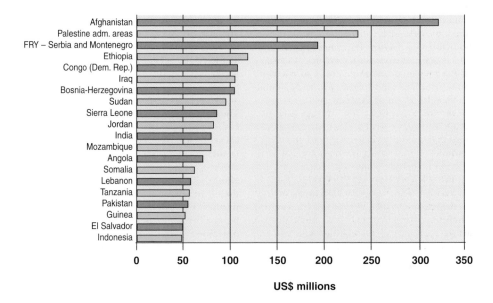

Figure 5.2 Top 20 recipients of aid from DAC donors 2001

Source: Global Humanitarian Assistance 2003

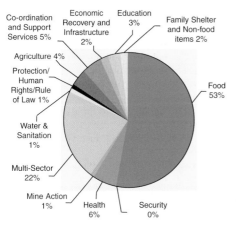

Figure 5.3 Pie chart of sectoral allocation 2002

Source: Global Humanitarian Assistance 2003

'Tactical' interactions

Interaction can be broken down into two types: 'tactical' and 'strategic'. 'Tactical' refers to inter-action directly related to the conflict; 'strategic' refers to interactions at the global and concep-tual levels. 'Tactical interactions' refer to inter-actions within the area of conflict. Two types are relevant: political interaction at the regional and local levels and second, the coordination between actors working in the midst of the crisis.

All conflicts have a regional dimension even if the actual fighting is contained within a political boundary or a region. They involve neighbour-ing countries and impact the politics, economics and societies of neighbouring populations. Some countries act as hosts for humanitarian activities by providing facilities such as sea ports to receive aid, offices for UN agencies and NGOs, or act as hosts for large refugee popula-tions that often destabilise their societies. Other countries act as transit points for weapons or resources, such as diamonds, that sustain the conflict. Others are actively involved militarily in the conflict. These neighbours have an interest in the conduct and outcome of the conflict. Therefore, peacemakers and humanitarian actors must engage these other actors in the region when trying to provide humanitarian action or negotiating an end to the conflict.

Another important interaction involves finance. Large sums of money flow from funders to recipi-ents (even allowing for the fact that humanitarian aid represents only 10 per cent of ODA) and with

that money comes power. Money means the power to determine who will be assisted, when they will be assisted and how they will be assisted. The power in humanitarian aid is exponentially greater than in other ODA because it represents an enormous percentage of resources available during conflicts, especially when local law and order have broken down and economic activity has largely ceased. For example, assisting one group of refugees over another determines life and death in some situations. Aid can also influ-ence the dynamics of conflict by impacting which rebel group benefits or loses from having their population 'taken care of'. Even the location where post-conflict development projects are pro-moted may shift the power dynamics between eth-nic groups within the country, thus laying the groundwork for what is intended to be peace but may in fact be the seeds of future conflict. In short, the significance of the interaction in fund-ing is a highly significant determinant of how a society recovers and rebuilds.

The media have become ever more important actors in humanitarian crises with the onset of 24-hour news channels, instant global communi-cations provided by satellites and the ubiquity of the Internet. The pictures of Ethiopian children starving during the 1984 famine stirred the world into responding. Similarly, the reluctant Clinton administration was shaken into action in Kosovo after the New York Times published a front-page colour picture of the Gornje Obrinje massacre. Richard Holbrooke recalls, '…people were horrified. It was at the top of the front page and it sat there like a mute witness at the NSC [National Security Council] meeting in the Situation Room. There was an enormous debate, and it broke out with the picture stirring people. There was a decision then to press ahead for NATO action, to try and sidestep the British, French, German and Russian view that you needed a Security Council mandate' (Judah, 2000, pp. 181–182). There is, too, the 'CNN effect'. It can motivate the public to pressure their governments to act but may also work in reverse. Fearing a public backlash after the pub-lic saw the video of Somalis dragging a dead American soldier through the streets of Mogadishu in 1993, President Clinton's adminis-tration decided to retreat. However, it may be that the public is not as risk averse to casualties as politicians assume. Whether trying to pressure policymakers to act or bring forgotten crises into the limelight, humanitarian organisations have to work with the media. The presence of the media can also serve as a tool in protecting vulnerable populations by acting as a watchful eye on belligerents and thereby pressuring them to observe humanitarian laws.

The military has also become an important actor in humanitarian crises. Sometimes humanitarian action involves military interventions. At such times, humanitarian workers need to coordinate with military officials so that they are not accidentally targeted, as has happened all too often. More significantly, sometimes the military provides security and creates the space for humanitarian operations (as in Somalia 1993), although this may not be beneficial all the time (as in Iraq 2003). However, an increasingly important interaction is the confusion created when military forces engage in distributing humanitarian aid (such as air-dropping food). This transportation role inevitably associates neutral and impartial humanitarian organisations with the military. The implications of this are addressed later.

Tactical interactions: coordination

In addition to resources, a second key concern for humanitarian actors is coordination. Humanitarian actors interact in highly intense operational environments in which they must coordinate activities in order to increase the effectiveness of their own organisation's presence and the humanitarian action as a whole. Coordination is about who needs what, where and when. Coordination also ensures that well-meaning organisations do not end up working at cross purposes and actually making conditions worse. For example, while emergency aid often arrives quickly, the distribution of it can become bogged down because organisations quickly buy up equipment (trucks and drivers) to fulfil their own priorities, thus making it impossible to deliver aid to even more urgent situations. This was the reason that the UN disbanded the Department of Humanitarian Affairs to create the Office of Coordination of Humanitarian Affairs (OCHA) in 1997. OCHA not only attempts to coordinate the different activities of UN agencies in a crisis area but also is in constant consultation with NGOs and the ICRC and IFRC throughout the year through the UN's Inter-Agency Standing Committee.

However, despite these compelling reasons for coordination, certain problems make increasing cooperation and coordination difficult because of the independent nature of humanitarian actors. Sometimes donors specify certain locations or activities their money must be used for, leaving other needs and areas without aid. Organisations also have different beliefs and policies about who or what they want to give to. Another problem is that if NGOs receive money from governments or are seen to coordinate their activities with governments, they can lose their status as independent actors in the eyes of belligerents who may then impede their access to vulnerable populations. The desire to have the media spotlight for funding purposes is yet another factor that prevents NGOs from coordinating their activities with other NGOs. Finally, coordination will always be inherently difficult because of the changing and unpredictable conditions of any emergency.

Despite such issues, the desire for independence is balanced with the need for some coordination. Apart from leaving organisations to coordinate themselves in an ad hoc manner in a crisis, coordination can come in a weak or strong form. The weak form brings together organisations in meetings to share information on their activities and agree to undertake responsibilities for performing certain humanitarian activities. This was largely the condition inside Rwanda in 1994. The strong form can involve a UN agency playing the role of a 'lead agency', by controlling access and delegating responsibilities, for instance. The UNHCR played such a role with regards to the Rwandan refugees in Tanzania. The Tanzanian government signed an agreement and gave power to the UNHCR to limit the number of NGOs which were able to obtain visas to come to Tanzania to work in and near the refugee camps.

Other methods of coordination have evolved recently. The UN's Consolidated Appeal Process coordinates and simplifies funding requests for humanitarian crises. Memoranda of Understandings (MOUs), that detail the rights and methods of providing assistance, are sometimes signed by UN agencies or NGOs and local government. Websites such as OCHA's Integrated Regional Information Network (www.irinnews.org) and www.reliefweb.int facilitate communication and make it possible to share lessons learned and best practices. Whatever form coordination may come in, it remains absolutely essential for balancing the independence of humanitarian actors and achieving effective humanitarian action.

'Strategic' interactions

The changing practices of humanitarian actions impact and are impacted by ideas, values and norms at the global level. Of particular interest is the tension between sovereignty and human rights. Sovereignty, which among many implications means the principle of non-interference by countries in the domestic affairs of others, has been an organising force of international relations since the mid seventeenth century. Although in reality no country was ever fully sovereign over its territory, the principle helped to mute criticism about human rights until the mid to late twentieth century. The founding of the UN in 1945 saw both the principles of defending human rights and the inviolability of national sovereignty articulated in its Charter. Later, the UN Universal Declaration of Human Rights (1948) made concerns about human rights even more explicit. Nevertheless, whatever cautious attention to human rights took place in the decades afterwards, they were largely overshadowed and held hostage to the bitter politics of the Cold War.

With the end of the Cold War, an opportunity arose to put human rights on an equal, if not superior, footing with sovereignty. This meant that humanitarian needs were increasingly articulated on the basis of 'rights' rather than just morality. Instead of advocating that people *should* have food, water, shelter, access to basic healthcare, sanitation and even peace, advocates now claimed that people had a legal *right* to these basic needs. If this idea became accepted, the international community would have not only a moral obligation to respond to people suffering in humanitarian crises but also a legal obligation and duty to respond. This viewpoint is reflected in the 2001 report *The Responsibility to Protect* (IDRC, 2001).

The 'Responsibility to Protect' report, compiled by a non-governmental blue-riband panel sponsored by the government of Canada, attempts to balance sovereignty and human rights. It calls for the international community to respond to humanitarian crises in the event that a government cannot meet its own obligation to help its citizens. It articulates the rights of governments to prevent, react and rebuild if necessary. Significantly, it adds responsibilities to the right of sovereignty. But the report still remains a conceptual document rather than customary or codified international law. Though it enjoys support from some governments (especially Canada and Sweden), no formal governmental discussions about the report have yet taken place.

For those arguing from a practical standpoint in attempting to convince governments that it is not only in their moral interest but their own self-interest to provide for and defend human rights, the idea of an emerging 'rights framework' under the notion of 'human security' is an important concept. It has several godfathers: the 1993 UNDP Human Development report, human rights activists, some governments and academics share ownership in the concept. It views economic, social and environmental concerns as priorities on a par with military affairs. Human security emphasises the interrelatedness of societies and threats. Poverty, human rights abuses and pollution anywhere is a threat to everyone everywhere. For human security, achieving security for all begins with reacting to humanitarian crises.

The shift from a moral framework to a rights framework represents a growing intensity of interaction at a deeper level. Whereas morals are more negotiable, 'rights' imply an obligation and duty. As much as this shift attempts to encourage developed societies to act in conflicts that may not be in the traditionally conceived 'national interest', it also obligates developing societies to change their social and political systems to incorporate these rights. However, these values are foreign to many cultures that are historically collectivist and hierarchical. For example, the Universal Declaration of Human Rights or the newly evolving concept of human security is underpinned by notions of the 'individual' and 'equality'. These are still nascent concepts in traditional cultures that emphasise community or hierarchy. How the world negotiates the meeting of value systems and manages cross-cultural interactions in this era of integration will be a key challenge for this millennium.

The evolution of humanitarian action

Since Henri Dunant inspired the founding of the Red Cross and the Geneva Convention of 1864, humanitarian action has evolved from emergency relief to humanitarian interventions and even long-term development. This is reflected in the emergence of different terms over the years: emergency relief, humanitarian aid, humanitarian protection, assistance and now humanitarian action. All these characterisations are still current. The different terms denote the scope of practical activities depending on a particular belief as to what should be the appropriate degree of involvement by outside actors in crises.

Some debates between the different perspective will be taken up in the next section. This section explores the evolution of the concept over time.

Laws of humanitarianism

Three sources of laws are relevant for humanitarian action – international humanitarian law (IHL), refugee law and human rights law. The three complement each other. Whereas IHL and refugee law seek to protect people specifically during conflicts by limiting the impact on non-combatants, human rights law protects in war and peace and seeks to further the development of people through a rights framework. The Geneva Convention of 1864 codified rules in war (*jus in bello*) and created a right for voluntary medical personnel to treat the wounded. The Geneva Conventions of 1949 and their 1977 Additional Protocols identify certain vulnerable groups as 'protected persons': civilians, prisoners of war, wounded combatants, refugees, humanitarian workers, medics, religious personnel and journalists.

The 1955 Convention on Refugees and the 1967 Protocol provided rights for refugees to seek asylum in other countries. In addition, with the increasing number of internally displaced person or IDPs (persons displaced by conflict inside the borders of their countries), guiding principles were drafted in 1998 that gave them protection under the law.

Human rights law recognises certain fundamental rights for all. These include right to life, right to juridical personality and due process of law, prohibition of torture and slavery, and the right to freedom of religion, thought and conscience. These laws set parameters for waging conflict and create a space for humanitarian action. However, they lacked a permanent enforcement mechanism until the establishment of the International Criminal Court in 1998. Prior to that, ad hoc international tribunals were created to deal with violation of the Laws of Armed Conflict (as IHL was previously known) and war crimes. Though governments have paid some heed to them in their conduct, the changing nature of conflicts has reduced the possibility of using these instruments as rules of war or deterrence.

Intra-state conflicts involve groups (such as militias) that are either unaware of these laws or officially not subject to them since these are agreements between the national governments of states. Moreover, some groups are just unwilling to be constrained by these laws. The international community has attempted to subject non-state actors to IHL, but so far it has been done in an ad hoc manner through notices and warnings that put pressure on them to adhere to international laws. The lack of consistency in enforcement has led to impunity in many cases, such as in the Bunia region of the Democratic Republic of Congo (2003–2004). But governments have also seemingly flouted the Geneva Conventions. Faced with the unconventional threat of terrorists, the United States largely discounted the Geneva Conventions in interning combatants at its Guantanamo Bay naval base in Cuba. IHL calls for the release of prisoners at the end of hostilities but the USA was concerned that suspected terrorists would return to terrorism if released.

Sources of humanitarian, refugee and human rights laws

1864	Geneva Convention
1948	Convention on the Crime of Genocide
1948	Universal Declaration of Human Rights
1949	Geneva Conventions (and 1977 Additional Protocols)
1955	Convention on the Status of Refugees (and 1967 Protocol)
1966	Covenant on Civil and Political Rights
1966	Covenant on Economic, Social and Cultural Rights
1979	Convention on the Elimination of All Forms of Discrimination Against Women
1984	Convention Against Torture
1989	Convention on the Rights of the Child
1998	Guiding Principles on Internal Displacement
1998	Statute of the International Criminal Court

International law that legally protects and provides immunity from the threats of war for humanitarian workers, refugees and IDPs has also suffered. Non-state belligerents have targeted these protected persons partly because they are thought to be giving aid to an enemy in the local conflict and partly because they are perceived by some belligerents to be associated with governments, militaries or other external authorities. This loss of neutrality, impartiality and independence in the eyes of belligerents leaves them vulnerable to violence. Additionally, since the increase in intra-state conflicts, civilian populations are not viewed by belligerents as separate from the fighting but rather as the object of the fighting. This makes civilians deliberate targets for atrocities, ethnic cleansing and genocide.

Though human rights law is still as relevant as ever, IHL must adapt to reflect the changing nature of conflicts if it is to remain meaningful in determining the conduct of war and creating space for humanitarian action.

Growth of aid and the Cold War

Prior to the twentieth century, religious organisations rather than governments provided humanitarian aid. Many of these church organisations were evangelical, trading free food, clothing and medicine for conversion. This practice continued to the end of the twentieth century.

The United States government's extensive involvement in providing humanitarian aid began with the support of the counterrevolutionary white army in Russia (1921), anti-communists in China (1920s and 1930s) and Republicans in the Spanish Civil War (1930s). Humanitarian aid served to support political allies. This practice continued throughout the Cold War. Humanitarian aid followed the flag of the USA and the USSR.

During the Cold War, much of Western 'humanitarian' aid went not to those in need but to those who were in need *and* anti-communist. Clear examples of politically motivated humanitarian aid were the Marshall Plan and the Berlin Airlift. The Marshall Plan provided Western Europe with aid to rebuild and stand fast against communist influences and any expansion of the USSR. The success of the Berlin Airlift (1948–1949) allowed the USA and the West to confirm that where the war stopped had become the front line in containing the USSR. Similarly, the USSR provided humanitarian aid to Cuba, Egypt, Angola and others to help them confront the Western capitalist threat.

NGOs played a crucial part in the politics of humanitarian aid during the Cold War. Governments increasingly began to fund and use NGOs and church organisations to deliver aid; and NGOs increasingly accepted these funds and thus became pawns of governments. Governments restricted the provision of aid to allies and friendly groups, to the exclusion of others in need. Government officials and NGOs came to believe that any aid supporting the defence against or overthrow of communism was 'humanitarian'. In Vietnam, 90 per cent of the aid from Western Europe and the USA went to anti-communist revolutionary forces. A large number of currently well-known humanitarian NGOs assisted the US military in attempting to 'win the hearts and minds' of the Vietnamese and others around the world. The neutrality and independence that characterised Dunant's approach to humanitarian action were largely lost.

Not all NGOs succumbed to the temptation of acquiring easy resources from governments or to the fight against communism. When President Reagan's administration refused to allow humanitarian food aid to Ethiopia in the famine of 1984 because the government was communist, aid groups unrelentingly pressured the administration to change its mind by noting that 'a hungry child knows no politics' (Minear, 2002, p.37). Other NGOs which had worked with governments learned bitter lessons. By the end of the 1980s, the tone in the non-governmental community began to change. Neutrality, impartiality and independence became more important as NGOs and Western governments sought to redefine their roles in the absence of the Cold War rivalry. The wealthy Western European governments infused humanitarianism into their foreign policies, releasing millions of dollars to promote humanitarian aid and development assistance around the world. They did so based on the growing belief that globalisation and increasing integration connected the world's entire population so that strife anywhere impacted the lives of people everywhere.

A decade of humanitarian interventions

The end of the Cold War and proclamation of a 'new world order' gave hope that humanitarian assistance (emergency relief and protection) could be available to all whatever their political allegiance. Without the constraints and preoccupations of the Cold War, the UN and the European Union were now able to contemplate engaging in peacemaking and peacebuilding. NATO sought a new role in humanitarian affairs as it redefined its reason for existing. Recognising that the tide was changing, even the

US military drafted manuals for 'operations other than war' such as disaster relief and humanitarian interventions and perhaps, like NATO, to justify its enormous budget after the Cold War. But the most significant growth in humanitarianism came in the form of a forcible type of assistance: military intervention.

'Humanitarian intervention' was now available as an option since the UN Security Council was no longer deadlocked in bitter Cold War politics: the stark contrast between humanitarian intervention before and after 1990 provides clear evidence of this. Prior to 1990, there were few such interventions, not only because they did not happen but also because governments would not have been able to justify interventions on the humanitarian argument. For example, India (in East Pakistan in 1971 that gave birth to Bangladesh), Vietnam (in Cambodia in 1978) and Tanzania (in Uganda in 1979) considered their actions to be and are now largely accepted as humanitarian interventions. However, no one officially described their interventions as such because the argument was legally unavailable and for fear of setting precedents.[3] However, the 1990s witnessed a host of attempts to put what some call 'coercive humanitarianism' (Minear, 2002, Chapter 6) into practice.

The decade of humanitarian interventions kicked off when Nigeria spearheaded a regional coalition of states belonging to the Economic Community of West Africa to enforce a peace agreement in Liberia. It intervened as the ECOWAS Monitoring Group (ECOMOG). It was significant that neither the UN Security Council nor the OAU authorised ECOMOG. Feeling that the international community was not interested enough to engage in West Africa, ECOWAS took matters into its own hands. After the initial success of ECOMOG, the UN gave the intervention post-hoc legitimacy by passing a Security Council resolution (788) and establishing a UN peace-keeping force.

A similar scenario would play out nine years later in Kosovo. With the threat of a Russian veto, the USA led a NATO bombing campaign to end Serbian military atrocities in Kosovo. Though such military interventions are technically illegal according to international law, it seems that actions by 'coalitions of the willing' can become legitimate depending on the outcomes of the intervention.

But the first high-profile humanitarian intervention came after the end of the 1991 Gulf War. Following the war, Saddam Hussein launched a brutal military campaign to suppress the Kurdish uprising in the north and the Shia uprising in the south. In an effort to save the Kurds and the Shia, the UN Security Council Resolution 688 (1991) established a 'safe haven' in the north and a 'no fly zone' in the north and south to curb Iraqi military activity. US and British troops patrolled this area with aircraft until the second Gulf War in 2003. The concept of the safe haven or 'safe area' was also relevant in Bosnia and Rwanda. During the political negotiations of the Bosnian conflict and while active fighting was occurring on the ground, the international community set up six safe areas in Bosnia, largely to protect the Bosnian Muslims. But because the UN peace-keeping force was ill equipped to defend them, the safe areas were constantly shelled by the Serbs (especially Sarajevo) and in the case of Srebrenica, it led to the slaughter of Muslims. In Rwanda, the French set up a safe area for refugees at the end of the genocide. Safe havens and areas may be used again in the future.

Humanitarian interventions 1990–2000

(Starting dates of missions)

1990	Liberia: Nigeria leads West African states in peace-enforcement mission
1991	Iraq: UN Safe Haven and No Fly Zones in Iraq for Kurds and Shia
1992	Somalia: US Task Force UNITAF (UN peace-keeping missions 1991, 1993)
1994	Rwanda: Operation Turquoise by France following genocide (UN peacekeeping mission 1993)
1994	Haiti: US led multinational force restores President Aristide to power (UN peacekeeping 1991, 1994)
1995	Bosnia: Political intervention & UN peace-keeping force
1995	Macedonia: UN Preventive Deployment Force
1999	Kosovo/Serbia: NATO action against Serbia
1999	East Timor: Australia leads international force
2000	Sierra Leone: Britain leads international force to rescue UN hostages and secure airport

---

3 India initially justified its intervention as humanitarian but had it struck from official UN records after it changed its mind.

Humanitarian interventions, and the subsequent UN peacekeeping missions that often followed them, met with scepticism early in the decade. Though President Clinton came into office with the intention of making UN peacekeeping more robust, the death of US soldiers in Mogadishu, Somalia in October 1993 left the USA reluctant to let UN peacekeeping rapidly expand as it began to do after the end of the Cold War. Taking a 'tough love' approach, the Clinton administration attempted to curb what it felt was a UN that was extended beyond its capabilities. Unfortunately, the genocide in Rwanda began just six months after the debacle in Somalia. The international community largely stood by and watched approximately 800,000 Rwandans, mostly Tutsis, die before it acted towards the end of the genocide.

The general problem is the lack of resources and political will. Member states, which supply military forces for peacekeeping missions, do not want to put their soldiers in harm's way, become embroiled in a quagmire or risk backlash with voters at home. Critics also note the 'selectivity' problem: the inconsistency of decisions to intervene and the self-interest of governments, such as choosing intervention with consideration for proximity or historical association as a former colony. But even with international engagement with crises, resources are scarce. While the crisis in Darfur, Sudan engaged the USA and Europe, the poorly equipped African Union has had difficulty doing the practical work on the ground.

Some solutions may be on the horizon, however. President George W. Bush proposed a Global Peace Operations Initiative (GPOI) and received support from the G8 countries at their summit in June 2004. GPOI (once it is funded) will train and equip 75,000 peacekeepers worldwide by 2010. Similarly, the African Union is actively training, equipping and deploying sub-regional standby forces through Africa that can be used for interventions. The coming years and decades will demonstrate whether these forces will do something to relieve the tension between humanitarian concerns and political interests.

From relief to protection and development

The hope of the 1990s also produced a significant expansion of humanitarian assistance. During the 1980s, humanitarian actors, especially NGOs, became increasingly distraught and dissatisfied with the short-term relief orientation of their activities. Although they were able to deliver emergency relief and aid to civilians caught up in conflicts by strictly maintaining neutrality and impartiality, their activities felt meaningless in the face of a return to persecution and impoverishment over the long term. For example, international action during the Ethiopian famine of 1984 provided tons of food aid to help alleviate the suffering of starving civilians. However, after the international community left, Ethiopians still needed to confront poor economic and social policies and the oppression of President Mengistu Haile Meriam – policies that had caused much of the famine in the first place. To avoid this 'well-fed dead' scenario, humanitarian actors began to understand disasters as 'complex political emergencies' that required them to expand their activities to make a deeper impact and leave behind a more permanent improvement. This required not only immediate relief but also advocacy for protection and advancement of human rights and recovery through development assistance.

Advocacy for protection comes in two forms: specific and general. In specific terms, it involves physically protecting vulnerable populations (such as by creating 'safe areas'), monitoring, reporting and publicising actions of parties in conflicts, seeking the adherence of all parties to humanitarian law, and arguing for specific actions to be undertaken by official actors (such as the UN Security Council or governments). A growing number of NGOs have used the media to focus pressure on belligerents by monitoring and publicising human rights violations. During the crisis in Darfur, NGOs sounded the alarm about the atrocities with regular, often daily, reports from the region. They also pressured the UN Security Council to act, while the Security Council in turn pressured the Sudanese government to observe international humanitarian law and provide access to internally displaced persons – not altogether successfully.

General advocacy involves the promotion of norms, practices and structures that advance humanitarianism (the adherence to humanitarian values and practices) outside the context of the specific conflicts. The establishment of the International Criminal Court as a permanent court for bringing perpetrators of war crimes to justice is a good example. Another is the International Campaign to Ban Landmines (ICBL). A coalition of NGOs and governments that won the 1997 Noble Peace Price, ICBL sought the banning of landmines and its campaign led to the Ottawa Treaty (Convention On The Prohibition Of The Use, Stockpiling, Production And Transfer of Anti-Personnel Mines And On Their Destruction) (1999). General advocacy also includes the championing of International Criminal Tribunals (e.g. for Yugoslavia, Rwanda, Sierra Leone and Cambodia) or Truth and Reconciliation Commissions (such as for South Africa, Sierra Leone and Peru).

Advocacy also includes the changing beliefs about what humanitarian action involves. With the rise of complex political emergencies, humanitarian actors began to see the need to link humanitarian action to development assistance. Some of the concerns of humanitarian activities, such as food security and healthcare, are also what development activities engage in, but seen from a longer-term perspective. Frameworks, such as a 'continuum model' and the 'gaps and linkages model', proposed this continuity by linking conflict, relief, rehabilitation, reconstruction and development. Fundamentally important in this is building and strengthening local capacities, even during the humanitarian phase, to carry on development work in the longer term.

But advocacy of this kind soon joins the world of high politics and inevitable tensions develop. The next section examines these important tensions and their implications for the future of humanitarian action.

The politics of humanitarian action

Aid, advocacy and access

The evolution from traditional emergency relief to providing vulnerable populations with protection and development involves a shift in values that has consequences for the practice of humanitarian action. There are three significant categories of values and scope of activities. The first is the traditional position of assistance rooted in neutrality and impartiality. The ICRC still exemplifies this position. Describing its activities as 'charity', it does not explicitly deal with the root causes of humanitarian disasters. In addition, in order to ensure access to people in need, the ICRC avoids publicising its work or pressuring parties through public statements.

The second position is described as 'non-partisanship'. An increasing number of organi-

sations view compassion as better served by emphasising solidarity and justice. Organisations such as Catholic Relief Services (CRS) attempt to empower victims by supporting their rights. They do not explicitly take political positions but engage in activism to address the root causes of conflicts. Importantly, they are not averse to publicising human rights violations.

The third position emphasises solidarity and justice by embracing explicit political agendas on behalf of victims of poverty and oppression. The Mennonites, religious groups with a long history of grassroots peacebuilding, often fight for the justice of the disenfranchised. These groups make full use of the media to expose the activities of belligerents.

All types of humanitarian organisations must be keenly aware of the political context in which they work, often by being in constant dialogue with the parties in conflict. However, the fundamental difference in the scope of activities is their implication for securing access to people in need – refugees and IDPs, the wounded and prisoners. In addition to resources and coordination as previously discussed, access is a third key concern for humanitarian actors.

There is a fear that advocacy, especially by publicising human rights violations, will cause belligerents to restrict access to vulnerable populations. Humanitarian workers also witness war first-hand and the knowledge they acquire is politically sensitive. Belligerents may fear that humanitarian workers will publicise this information and expose their conduct. Advocacy and public pronouncements by headquarters can also put humanitarian workers in the field in danger, as they are the ones who deal with belligerents on a daily basis. This can adversely impact an organisation's work in other conflicts where neutrality and impartiality may be required.

The ICRC reports that new types of conflicts (intra-state) and new types of belligerents (non-state actors) have made gaining access more difficult. With non-state actors unaware or uncaring of international legal obligations to allow access to protected persons, humanitarian organisations have to negotiate new agreements each time. Muting criticism is needed to retain credibility as neutral and impartial organisations. However, if access is not forthcoming and the situation is better served by publicising atrocities, even the ICRC is willing to make public pronouncements to pressure belligerents and the international community to protect vulnerable populations.

Organisations that embrace solidarity and justice over charity claim that the fear of losing access may be overstated. In 1986, the South African apartheid government expelled the ICRC in retaliation for being expelled from a Red Cross international conference. However, the South African government quickly rescinded the order because the ICRC was instrumental in helping return South African military prisoners in Angola. Nevertheless, the ICRC feels that neutrality and impartiality should still be a priority to ensure its credibility with belligerents so that it can maintain dialogue with all the parties in the conflict.

The presence of different values and practices may help diversify the field and thus engage different needs in humanitarian action, but it also causes confusion in the field and leads to tragedy. Though the ICRC maintains strict neutrality and impartiality, 40 of its staff were killed between 1994 and 2004. The UN lost 200 staff and nearly 300 civilians and peacekeepers were taken hostage during the same period. Some of those casualties were due to workers caught in the crossfire, but there is an increasing trend of deliberately targeting humanitarian workers. Despite the particular reasons for humanitarian workers being targeted in each situation, the general confusion caused by the political activism and advocacy of some NGOs and the attempts to retain neutrality by others muddy the waters. Combatants may not take the time to distinguish between who is there to help and who is there to criticise.

Aid as a problem

Humanitarian action is increasingly fraught with new complexities in which humanitarian aid is implicated in exacerbating conflicts. The UN's Operation Lifeline Sudan (1989) faced this problem continually throughout its efforts to deliver aid. In its early days when it brokered ceasefires between the Sudanese government and rebels in the south, the rebels used the ceasefires to rearm and rebuild their forces. Periodically, the Sudanese government halted delivery of aid to certain areas for apparently strategic military reasons.

Many other such problems exist. Refugee camps and safe areas are used as sanctuaries from which militias launch attacks, as did the Hutus in Rwanda (1994) and the Muslims in Bosnia (1995). Dealing with rebel leaders or dictatorial governments in order to gain access sometimes acts to legitimise these actors as legal authorities. Aid can be used as a commodity to control the population, as it was in Somalia in 1993 where warlords highjacked aid to feed and pay their militias. Worse, aid can fuel the war by alleviating the burden of leaders to feed and care for their populations as this duty is replaced by humanitarian agencies. Humanitarian actions and development assistance have also been criticised for undermining the ability of local populations to recover. Mary B. Anderson, in the influential book *Do No Harm: How Aid Can Support Peace – Or War* (1999), draws attention to the potential negative impacts of aid and encouraged greater care in evaluating efforts. Equally importantly, she places an emphasis on empowering local capacities in an effort to prevent dependency on aid.

Aid and development

Approximately 40 per cent of post-conflict countries return to fighting. The lack of effectiveness of assistance and the recurrent nature of conflicts can be disheartening to humanitarian workers. As noted above, this has led to a desire to emphasise the values of solidarity and justice with victims by linking humanitarian action to longer-term development projects. But this is easier said than done.

Fundamental structural problems prevent linking humanitarian activities and development activities, which historically have been separate, so much so that the bureaucratic structures for funding them remain separate in most governments and international institutions. For example, whereas the European Community Humanitarian Office (ECHO) now funds long-term projects that exceed a year or two in length, its budgeting process still funds only in six-month increments, as normally done for humanitarian activities. Similarly, UN development agencies are structured by sector (finance, infrastructure development, etc.) and emphasise technical issues, leaving them little capacity to analyse the humanitarian needs in conflicts. Coordination between humanitarian and development actors is also hampered by pre-existing organisational cultures. Humanitarian organisations are geared towards the rapid delivery of supplies and working within the politics of conflict situations. Development organisations, meanwhile, plan for the long term and are resistant to having their mandates expanded to include conflict issues.

Another impediment to closer coordination is that humanitarian action is guided by the principle of humanity – serving all according to need. Much of humanitarian action in a crisis needs to be apolitical to ensure access to vulnerable populations. But development assistance tends to be more politically selective. Development organisations often need to work closely with donor agencies and local governments to encourage local ownership and sustainable programmes. A closer combination of the two can lead to humanitarian action based on 'selective humanity', where aid does not follow need (DeGnbol-Martinussen and Engberg-Pedersen, 2003, Chapter 10). The two approaches may be incompatible in many situations. Additionally, both sides lack the resources to build capacity to expand the scope of their work. Declining aid resources forced the World Bank and UNHCR to return to their 'core' activities, of development for the World Bank and refugee protection for UNHCR.

Nevertheless, humanitarian and development organisations will always be likely to explore ways to bridge the gap because both have a common interest in helping the people they serve. In the short term, humanitarian organisations can learn to have greater sensitivity about their aid and ensure that their actions 'do no harm'. Similarly, development organisations can become conflict-sensitive by incorporating conflict analysis into their programming.

Conclusion: humanitarian action in a changing world

The previous sections mentioned certain new characteristics and dynamics of contemporary conflicts in which humanitarian action functions. These require some further final reflections because they have the potential to determine how humanitarian action should and will be carried out in the coming years. Two types of conflict are on the rise in this new millennium: intra-state conflicts and terrorism. And two types of non-state belligerents are more formidable than ever before: warlords (and their militias) and terrorists.

Intra-state conflicts involving governments (or extremist groups within governments) and warlords increasingly use identity issues such as ethnicity or religion to polarise populations and create lines of division across which wars are fought. In such cases, the control of territory and resources by specific ethnic, racial or religious groups becomes the defining character of war that leads to gross atrocities, ethnic cleansing and genocide. Belligerents care about a population's character and loyalty more now than in the recent past. Civilians are no longer viewed as non-combatants and are deliberately targeted.

The international community is slow to respond to this new challenge and create new spaces for humanitarian action. Governments are finding it difficult to bring non-state belligerents into the scope of international humanitarian law. As mentioned before, actively negotiating with non-state belligerents can legitimise them as legal authorities and violate the sovereignty of the national government, but not dealing with them can prevent the protection of vulnerable populations.

Similarly, a new form of terrorism seeks the expulsion or annihilation of a people and culture in addition to whatever political objectives lie at the root. Jihad often aims indiscriminately to kill civilians espousing any form of 'Western' culture. Terrorists certainly do not heed any international or national laws and may have agendas that cannot be expressed in any conventional terms and thus cannot be the subject of negotiation. Stemming the tide of terrorism is a long-term effort with no clear international consensus on how to proceed militarily or through more peaceful means.

The focus on terrorism as the challenge of the era has given rise to concerns that it will displace the emphasis on humanitarianism that characterised the 1990s. Though the focus may have shifted to terrorism for the time being, the ideas of humanitarianism (such as the right to life, prohibition on torture and due process of the law) and political, social and economic rights have spread over much of the world and wait to be re-emphasised. Proceeding from international charters, such as the Universal Declaration of Human Rights and the other international Covenants, these ideas are now imbedded in regional charters such as the Helsinki Final Act (Europe), Banjul Charter (sub-Saharan Africa), Cairo Declaration (Islamic nations) and the American Convention on Human Rights (the Americas). The 'Responsibility to Protect' report went so far as to call for a change from the use of the term 'humanitarian intervention' to a 'responsibility to protect' in order to indicate the responsibility (and perhaps an obligation and duty) of the international community to assist governments and people when they cannot assist themselves.

Whether these ideas will translate into practice is another story and will be a matter of the specific politics of events. The fear is also that governments will expend greater resources on physical security and a military 'war on terrorism' than on non-peaceful solutions such as development and good governance initiatives. This situation is too new for us to definitively note a trend.

The specific implications of terrorism for humanitarian action include not only the potential decline in overall resources and interest but also its effect on operations in the field. An integral aspect of the military war on terrorism includes 'winning the hearts and minds' of populations, much as was attempted in Vietnam but to a greater degree. Civilians can support terrorists by harbouring them, providing resources (money, food, etc.) and refusing to cooperate with military operations against terrorists. The Provincial Reconstruction Teams (PRTs) of allied forces in Afghanistan provide humanitarian aid and small-scale development projects in order to pacify civilians or win their support in the fight against the remnants of the Taliban and Al Qaeda. However, this has negatively affected the work of independent humanitarian organisations like the ICRC. Humanitarian workers are targeted for being agents or collaborators of foreign militaries. Their neutrality, impartiality and independence have disappeared in the eyes of terrorists and many civilians. Humanitarian organisations feel that militaries should end the use of humanitarian aid as a military tactic to avert further deaths and preserve the humanitarian nature of aid.

Non-governmental humanitarian organisations, like governments, are also only slowly and informally beginning to accept the new dynamic of contemporary conflicts and the implication for humanitarian action. With more independent humanitarian organisations in existence, their different preferences and principles have muddied the waters. With some emphasising neutrality and others solidarity and justice, belligerents and recipients of assistance do not have a clear understanding of whom they are working with and what they can assume about the confidentiality of their interaction with humanitarian workers. The confusion may lead to an increase in the rejection of humanitarian action by belligerents, with life-threatening consequences for vulnerable populations.

But without extensive hierarchy, coordination or unity in the humanitarian arena, the best advice may be to choose a role, whether as a neutral actor or advocate, and stick to it. Knowledge and predictability may ease confusion in the long run.

Humanitarian action has changed over time. Whether it returns to the roots that Henri Dunant planted or whether it expands in new directions in the face of fresh challenges will be the result of a dynamic and evolving process. Keys issues today are those of resources, coordination and access. For the future, two things are certain. One, the need for such action will be present into the foreseeable future. Two, some form of humanitarian action will always exist to meet this need because there will always be people with compassion.

The following comment by the UN Under-Secretary-General for Humanitarian Affairs and Emergency Relief Coordinator, Jan Egeland, conveys the need and compassion:

The conflict in Northern Uganda is characterised by a level of cruelty seldom seen elsewhere. It pits not just adults but also children against one another, and excludes vast swathes of the population from participation in any semblance of development. No one knows how many people have died as a result of the conflict, but every day schools, homes, villages and families are destroyed, yet more people are abducted, enslaved, beaten, raped, and made to fight for the rebels. Most of these abductees are children…Look into the eyes of a child who has been repeatedly brutalised, tortured or raped, as I did when I visited Northern Uganda, and you will never forget what you find there. This abuse of children is one of the most serious in the world. It calls for urgent and concerted action.

Jan Egeland, from the Foreword to 'When the sun sets, we start to worry . . . ' (OCHA, 2004)

Further Reading

Aid Information. www.aidinfo.org

Anderson, Mary B. (1999) *Do No Harm: How Aid Can Support Peace – Or War,* Boulder: Lynne Rienner Publishers.

DeGnbol-Martinussen and Engberg-Pedersen, Poul (2003) *Aid: Understanding International Development Cooperation*, New York: Zed Books Ltd, Chapter 10.

'Global Humanitarian Assistance 2003' (2003) UK: Development Initiatives, www.globalhumanitarianassistance.org

Global IDP Project (2004) 29 November, www.idpproject.org

ICRC (International Committee of the Red Cross) (2004) *A Memory of Solferino*, 16 November, www.icrc.org

IDRC (International Development Research Centre) (2001) *The Responsibility to Protect*, Canada, www.idrc.ca

IFRC (International Federation of Red Cross and Red Crescent Societies) (2004) World Disaster Report 2004, 16 November, www.ifrc.org

Inter-Hemispheric Education Resource Centre (1988) *Private and Public Humanitarian Aid*, Policy Report, July.

Judah, Tim (2000) *Kosovo: War and Revenge*, New Haven: Yale University Press, pp. 181–182.

Kellenberger, Jacob (2004) 'Speaking Out or Remaining Silent in Humanitarian Work', *IRRC*, September, vol. 86, no. 855, www.icrc.org

Krähenbühl, Pierre (2004) 'The ICRC's Approach to Contemporary Security Challenges: A future for independent and neutral humanitarian action', *IRRC*, September, vol. 86, no. 855, www.icrc.org

Minear, Larry (2004) 'Humanitarian Aid in a World of Politics', Humanitarianism and War Project, 1990, 10 November, http://hwproject.tufts.edu/

Minear, Larry and Weiss, Thomas G. (1995) *Humanitarian Politics*, New York: Foreign Policy Association.

Minear, Larry (2004) 'Terms of Engagement with Human Need', *Humanitarianism and War Project, 1990*, 10 November, http://hwproject.tufts.edu/

Minear, Larry (2002) *The Humanitarian Enterprise*, Bloomfield: Kumarian Press, Inc., Chapters 5 & 6.

Muggah, Robert (2004) 'In the Line of Fire: Surveying the impact of small arms on civilians and relief workers', Humanitarian Practice Network, 15 November, www.odihpn.org

OCHA (UN Office of Coordination of Humanitarian Affairs) (2004) 17 November, http://ochaonline.un.org

Project Ploughshares (2004) 29 November, www.ploughshares.ca

Refugee International (2004) www.refugeesinternational.org

Schweiser, Beat (2004) 'Moral Dilemmas for Humanitarianism in the Era of "Humanitarian" Military Interventions', *IRRC*, September, vol. 86, no. 855.

Slim, Hugo and Eugren, Luis Enrique (2004) *Humanitarian Protection*, ALNAP Guidance Booklet, Pilot Version, 12 November, www.alnap.org

The Economist, (2004) 'Fighting for Survival.' 20–26 November, p. 27.

The Economist (2004) 'More Dangerous Work Than Ever', 20–26 November, p. 48.

Vaitla, Srinivas (2002) *Norms and Interests of Humanitarian Interventions*, Unpublished Master's Thesis.

CHAPTER 6: Media

Mass media come of age

The Second World War was a boom period for the mass media. Patriotic newsreels, running stories of heroism in the daily papers, radiobroadcasts from the front, propaganda films and glossy exposés in weekly magazines became as much US war efforts as guns, tanks and airplanes. State governments and private actors working on behalf of their countries used various forms of mass media including newspapers, motion pictures, radio and the nascent platform of television to assure the loyalty of their populations, spread disinformation among their enemies and influence neutral parties. Propaganda and the reporting of events became almost indistinguishable.

In Nazi Germany, a calculated strategy of deploying inexpensive radios (*Volksempfänger* or 'people's receiver') in homes and workplaces allowed the government to reach nearly every citizen on a daily basis, providing a carefully constructed view of the events going on in *Festung Europa* – Hitler's seemingly impenetrable 'European Fortress'. In the United States, *Life* magazine became a mouthpiece for US policy, while famed director Frank Capra – a serving officer in the US military – directed a series of propaganda films for consumption by the US Army and the greater American public. During the siege of Stalingrad, Red Army journalist Igor Danilov turned the exploits of a Siberian sniper, Vasily Zaitsev, into a patriotic action serial which riveted Soviet citizens and inspired a generation.

Almost from the beginning of the global conflict, US propagandists realised the potential for expanding their media efforts beyond their national boundaries. The most important manifestation of the transborder media efforts was the establishment of the Voice of America (VOA) under the Office of Wartime Information. The VOA charter calls for the network to provide a 'consistently reliable and authoritative source of news' while simultaneously 'present(ing) the policies of the United States clearly and effectively'.

The radio network began its existence with propaganda programmes aimed at German-occupied Europe and North Africa. The first VOA broadcast occurred on 24 February 1942. Speaking in German, announcer William Harlan Hale told his listeners: 'Here speaks a voice from America. Every day at this time we will bring you the news of the war. The news may be good. The news may be bad. We shall tell you the truth.'

After victory in Europe, the Voice of America was re-engineered and became a tool in the fight against communism. Broadcasts into the Soviet Union began on 17 February 1947. During the Cold War, VOA was placed under the US Information Agency and expanded its focus within the USSR and Eastern Europe. Most of the content was related to news and events; however, a good deal of cultural fare was included as well. Willis Conover, one of the network's better known personalities, became a bit of a celebrity behind the Iron Curtain and influenced a generation of aspiring musicians in Poland and other parts of the communist bloc with his jazz programme *Music USA* in the 1950s. During the Cold War, Eastern Europeans frequently turned to VOA to gain information about events which were forbidden from being reported on official state radio. The white-washed content also served to promote a rather inflated version of the US and Americans which was reconciled with reality in the late 1980s when the region's communist dictatorships collapsed.

In the 1980s, VOA added a television service to the already existing Radio Marti. It was a new network also dedicated to the overthrow of the Castro regime in Cuba. Under United States law, the Voice of America is forbidden from broadcasting directly to US citizens, thus avoiding the stigma of overt homeland propaganda. The advent of the Internet, however, has made VOA available to all Americans who wish to listen. Radio Sawa, part of the VOA system, uses its programming to influence youths in the Arab-speaking world. The network has become an increasingly important tool in US efforts at public diplomacy in the Middle East and Islamic world – an effort that attracted millions of dollars after the September 11 attacks. The Voice of America, which broadcasts in 50 languages, commands a listening audience of roughly 91 million today.

A sister project to Voice of America, Radio Free Europe (RFE), was originally a US government project dedicated to promoting 'democratic values and institutions by disseminating factual information and ideas'. Unlike the VOA which aimed to deliver news and spread understanding of the US way of life, Radio Free Europe was specifically intended to bring down communist regimes. Established in 1949, RFE made its first broadcast to Czechoslovakia on 4 July 1950. The organisation was funded and managed by the US foreign intelligence service (CIA) until 1971 as part of a larger psychological warfare programme intended to promote civil strife and dissent in Soviet-dominated Eastern Europe. Today, the radio network is a non-profit organisation and targets countries in Europe, Asia and the Middle East, broadcasting more than 1,000 hours per week in 32 languages via short-wave, AM and FM radio and the Internet. Although the demise of one-party systems in Eastern Europe and the collapse of the Soviet Union reduced RFE's budget, its operation continued. New services focus on the Middle East, especially regimes hostile to US/Western ideals such as Iraq and Iran. In 2001, the Czech Republic expelled an Iraqi diplomat for plotting to attack the headquarters of Radio Free Europe in Prague. The offices remain heavily guarded since the September 11 attacks on the USA.

To be sure, the utility of transborder mass media broadcasts was not lost on communist forces in the post-Second World War era. Stalin directed communist parties in Eastern Europe to participate in so-called 'popular front' governments with other anti-fascist political parties from 1945 to 1947. In each and every case, the Communist Party of the Soviet Union (CPSU) directed its Eastern European counterparts to secure the Ministry of the Interior as soon as possible, thus giving them control over the airwaves. Through the mass media, the communists were able to demonise their enemies and marginalise their socialist allies in the period prior to communist party takeovers. In Asia, pro-communist radio broadcasts were beamed into Tibet, Laos and other countries, paving the way for communist takeover and/or mobilising support for insurgencies.

Although the media served as an important propaganda tool during the Cold War, their primary function was the delivery of news and events free of government meddling. As technology advanced, the news reporting grew increasing global in scope. Enabled by communications technologies that provided nearly instantaneous reporting from around the world, newspapers, radio announcers and television reporters were no longer limited by time and space. The advent of news agencies/wire services greatly homogenised the information being reported globally, while simultaneously increasing the number of events that could be covered. Initially, the telegraph was the lifeblood of such organisations, but today the Internet is the driving force behind this distribution of content. News agencies report on and provide articles that can be used by other news organisations with almost no modification. Large news agencies typically have dozens if not hundreds of full-time reporters stationed in locations around the globe.

There are three forms of news agencies: private corporations which provide their content for a fee to other news organisations; cooperatives which share news articles across numerous newspapers; and state-run concerns which typically deliver the official government position of one-party states. Reuters, based in the United Kingdom, is the best example of the first model, while the American Associated Press, a cooperative of approximately 1,500 daily newspapers, is the paragon of the second model. The Xinhua News Agency of the People's Republic of China (PRC) is the largest state-dominated news agency in the world today. Xinhua reports directly to the Chinese Communist Party's propaganda department and provides significant amounts of content to the PRC's daily newspapers, as well as to foreign media outlets in English, French, Russian, Spanish, Arabic and other languages.

Itar-Tass, the Russian Federation's official wire service, is a strange hybrid of all three models. The 100-year-old agency was established under the Tsars, nationalised by the Bolsheviks (TASS is the acronym of the Telegraph Agency of the Soviet Union) and survived the break-up of the USSR. Today, the wire service – like Russia itself – is seeking to adapt to the demands of globalisation and international capitalism, while hanging on to some of the old structures that made it great. Other major international news agencies include Agence France-Presse (France), Deutsche Presse Agentur (Germany) and United Press International (USA).

Media convergence: towards global media or a shrinking chorus?

The current era of globalisation has provoked a shift in the way in which media have been delivered across national boundaries. Although Washington, Beijing, Moscow and other governments continue to employ mass media as tools of propaganda and diplomacy, private media giants are increasingly more important in relation to state actors. The weakening of state boundaries, technological advances and burgeoning middle class across the developing world have created an environment where media moguls have sought to create transnational information empires operating globally. These media groups provide news, entertainment and sports to audiences around the world, and as their scope increases, so does their influence. Corporate giants like Rupert Murdoch of News Corporation, an Australia-based media conglomerate which owns satellite TV networks on five continents and newspapers in the USA, UK and Australia, easily command more power than most heads of state.

Despite the wealth and resources of media conglomerates, cost-cutting efforts and profit-making have negatively impacted newsgathering efforts in recent years. The phenomenon of 'parachute reporting' has become especially popular among most private news organisations. Rather than maintaining semi-permanent reporters in overseas bureaus who are constantly making contacts and building intelligence on local conditions, the big media companies drop in a team of reporters with satellite phones and translators to survey a 'hot spot', interview a few 'experts', file a story and return home. Since multiple news organisations are all employing the same methods and tools, the news that is reported is amazingly similar despite the fact it is

generated by different actors. A telling sign of the similarity of news broadcasts in the United States is the recent move by many public (government-supported) television stations to air a segment of BBC World in the evening to offer viewers an alternative view of the day's events from that which they might get from the US mainstream private broadcasters ABC, NBC and CBS News.

Henry Luce, activist and capitalist

In free societies, the primary determiner of media content has generally been profit-related, although a few exceptions exist. Henry Luce, long-time editor-in-chief of the US news magazine Time, is a prominent example. Luce, born to a Presbyterian missionary family in China, used his control of one of the USA's most read media outlets to sway voters and influence political elites on US foreign policy, especially in East Asia. His dogged pursuit of political agendas was frequently at odds with media market dynamics.

Furthering the reduction of voices wrought by the expansion of news agencies, the world's (non-Internet) news and entertainment media content is controlled by an ever shrinking number of producers. The concentration of ownership and privatisation of mass media that has occurred since the 1980s has changed the face of global news reporting. Media giants are typically characterised by a decidedly corporatist esprit that is politically conservative, pro-Western and pro-capitalist. This world view permeates the reporting of events around the world. At the root of every decision is how to bring about profits. The commercialist model is quite distinct from earlier media models initiated by the state which were more focused on educating and arming viewers with information rather than urging them to buy products. Due to increasing deregulation in the industrialised world, barriers to vertical integration and corporate mergers have weakened significantly, thus furthering this trend.

Today, most of the world's media products are generated by fewer than ten large corporations: in the USA, Time Warner (formerly AOL Time Warner), Viacom Inc., NBC Universal and the Walt Disney Company; the Australian media giant News Corporation; Germany's Bertelsman

Regionalisation or globalisation

The extent to which the US media dominate global cultural production is sometimes exaggerated. Regionalisation, i.e. blurring of national boundaries in large geographic areas through increased cultural, economic and political exchanges, and flows of people, technology and ideas, is often mislabelled as 'globalisation'. This is especially true in the realm of the media.

In South-East Asia, Chinese-language films dominate. Nigerian films command much of the sub-Saharan African market, while Bollywood fare is the most popular import in Afghanistan, Pakistan and other parts of the Muslim world. Despite this diversity of sources for popular media, the prevailing opinion among most people in the developing world is that they are the victims of insidious Western propaganda, of which cultural products like movies, TV and pop music are the most nefarious.

AG; and Japanese firm Sony. These mega-firms control television stations, satellite networks, radio stations, record companies, publishing houses, newspapers and motion picture studios. Most are truly transnational concerns with established properties in the USA, the UK and Western Europe and are rapidly expanding their influence into growth markets in Latin America, East Asia and other parts of the developing world.

The massive concentration of ownership, large footprint and consumerist values of this handful of transnational corporations have become an important symbol for anti-globalisation activists who mourn the loss of 'local' cultures. Due to the Western (and predominantly American) ownership of content production in various forms of entertainment media (especially songs, films and television programming), there have been attempts on the part of grassroots activists and state governments to limit the proliferation of certain media products which are seen as a threat to cultural identity in both the developed and developing worlds. France, Brazil and other countries invest large amounts of capital in domestic film production to counter US dominance of the motion picture industry. In Canada, 90 per cent of the motion pictures, three-quarters of newsstand magazines and half of the music played on the radio are American. Such statistics have encouraged Ottawa to limit the amount of 'foreign' (read American) content that can be broadcast in a given day – a trend that is increasingly common around the globe.

In other parts of the world, movie theatres that show Western fare have become easy targets of cultural rage for those who wish to expunge elements that are contrary to 'local' or 'religious' values. In the country where most of these cultural products are generated (the United States), there is a growing feeling that the tendency towards global production is effectively marginalising genuine US culture as well. Attempting to maximise profits has led the large media corporations to market products that appeal to the lowest common denominator on a global scale, thus resulting in remarkably homogenous products across multiple spaces.

The 'CNN effect': the media and policy in a turbulent world

The 1990s saw an enormous increase in the influence of news networks on diplomacy and foreign policy. The advent of 24-hour global news networks has reduced the amount of time political figures have to respond to major events occurring outside of their borders. This is the so-called 'CNN effect', which dates back at least to the Persian Gulf Crisis (1990–1991) when then US President George H. W. Bush noted: 'I learn more from CNN than the CIA.' During the early years of the Clinton administration, graphic photos of starving children in Somalia precipitated a humanitarian mission led by the US military. Not long after the mission was under way, popular revulsion at scenes of an American soldier's desecrated body being dragged through the streets of Mogadishu prompted a hasty and haphazard US withdrawal from the East African nation. Throughout the 1990s, media coverage became inextricably linked to government response to crises. The availability of continuous and instantaneous coverage of wars, ethnic conflicts and international crises has had a deep and enduring impact on how prominent decision makers do their jobs.

Today, policymakers must formulate responses to the actions of other states (as well as prominent non-state actors) almost instantaneously. The era of cool, calculated responses based on extensive private meetings and consultation with allies and other third parties is over. The widespread and instantaneous distribution of nearly all the relevant information creates an environment where everyone (especially opposition members in Congress, Parliament or the 'street') can formulate alternative courses of action or react harshly to executive inaction. Such an environment of snap judgements has incontestably led to more than a few ill-advised policy decisions over the past two decades. This is in part due to a reduced number of inputs into the decision-making process and the perceived need to act 'decisively' and 'promptly', often at the cost of acting prudently. Political analysts who study the impact of the CNN effect frequently evoke the Cuban Missile Crisis, arguing that had the events of 1963 taken place today, the outcome would most certainly have been different. A presidential advisor in the Clinton White House remarked that her boss would have had 30 minutes at most to respond to the crisis rather than the 13 days that President John F. Kennedy took to craft a plan of action.

'Media diplomacy' has become an increasingly integral part of statecraft in the twenty-first century. It is said that CNN is being watched in every embassy in every country in the world 24 hours a day. International news media outlets have thus emerged as a fast and direct communications platform for world leaders (especially between those heads of state who lack normal diplomatic relations). The now infamous 'Axis of Evil' speech (January 2002) in which US President George W. Bush identified three states (Iraq, Iran and North Korea) which pose a threat to world peace demonstrated the extent to which globally televised speeches by heads of state impact foreign policy and international relations. Overnight, the imperatives of national governments (especially in the Middle East and East Asia) were cast in a new light by a single speech ostensibly intended for the US domestic audience. Likewise, international news networks provide an instantaneous and ubiquitous conduit for important non-state actors like Al Qaeda to send messages to their constituencies and enemies alike.

News networks such as the BBC, Al-Jazeera and CNN are also emerging as important players in the shaping of the national interest. As arbiters of public opinion, the most watched networks are in a position to sway unsure populaces on relevant policy issues. Media organisations' harsh portrayal of foreign enemies often

goes far beyond that which diplomats and policymakers would ever seek. In the United States, the most common approach is to construct the American foes as would-be Hitlers replete with political cartoons that distort their features to resemble the Führer's; Saddam Hussein and Slobodan Milosevic are the two most recent victims of this approach. Ubiquitous analogies to the Second World War atrocities (especially related to the Jewish Holocaust) are another common feature of media coverage of US enemies' actions. It becomes unnecessary to disassemble the factors which have led to inter-state conflicts once the enemy has been reduced to the simple image of a maniacal, bloodthirsty sadist.

Western news networks choose at will to cover certain issues while ignoring others. This is perhaps the most salient way in which these actors are emerging as independent agencies in foreign policy. A case in point is British, US and German coverage of the events during the wars of Yugoslavian secession (1991–1999). The most

Mass media/mass murder in the heart of Africa

The absence of international media coverage of the genocide in Rwanda contrasts starkly with local media's efforts to promote the massacres. Radio-Télévision Libre des Mille Collines (RTLMC), a privately owned Rwandan media outlet affiliated with the family of the country's long-time dictator whose suspicious death sparked the genocide, created a climate of mass hatred on one side and mass fear on the other. The radio station broadcast a daily stream of anti-Tutsi vitriol encouraging Hutus to take up arms against Tutsis who were deemed 'cockroaches and snakes which should be stamped out'.

Once the genocide began on 6 April 1994, the station regularly broadcast lists of people to be killed as well as churches and mosques that should be destroyed. The radio station's owners recognised the importance of global perceptions – its French broadcasts were ethnonationalist but lacked the calls for the extermination of the Tutsi population that characterised the native-language broadcasts.

Western journalists resident in Rwanda during the genocide that claimed nearly 1 million lives argue the holocaust was a direct outcome of RTLMC broadcasts which were heard in nearly every school, tavern and meeting place.

enduring image of the conflict concerns an emaciated Bosnian Muslim named Fikret Alič standing outside Trnopolje – purportedly a 'Serbian-run concentration camp'. Four years after the photo ran in nearly every major news source in North America and Western Europe (including on the cover of the British tabloid *The Daily Star* under the headline 'Belsen 1992'), it was divulged that the photo was instead taken at a refugee camp rather than at a concentration camp. In fact, in an effort to dramatise the image, the photo-journalist involved crouched behind some barbed wire strewn up outside a tool shed before the war as a preventative measure against thieves. Due to a bit of photographic legerdemain, the images of ethnic cleansing became imbued in the minds of Western policymakers, the European voting public and the world in general. Choosing to focus on the 'genocide' in Bosnia-Herzegovina (much of which was exaggerated or never adequately verified) while largely ignoring the concurrent and widespread holocaust in Rwanda is just one of many examples in recent history that demonstrates the role of the media in crafting national interest on behalf of the states they cater to and/or represent.

Since 11 September 2001, journalists' choices about what to cover have undoubtedly shaped global perceptions about the coming 'clash of civilisations' predicted by Samuel Huntington in his 1993 article in *Foreign Policy*. The atmosphere of fear and suspicion among Western populations towards Muslims generated by the terror attacks on the World Trade Center and the Pentagon have coloured the way in which news is reported and which events get press coverage and which do not. Conflicts between Muslims and non-Muslims are now world news wherever they happen. Post-9/11 conflicts in Thailand, Nigeria, the Caucasus, China and elsewhere are now shrouded in the mantle of civilisational conflict whereas prior to 11 September such events would have been discussed under the headings of ethnic conflict, separatist violence, etc. (if they were deemed 'world news' at all). The 'bloody borders' of Islam identified by Huntington now serve as a starting point for nearly all Western reporting on events in the Islamic world and its periphery. The fact that 'fear sells' in media coverage has greatly contributed to an increasingly worrying phenomenon.

Managing the media: the new rules of global news coverage

Accusations of 'news management' have reached fever pitch in certain quarters due to the increasingly cozy relationship between global news providers and certain powerful governments. The increasingly complex and opaque relationship between the large media outlets and states (especially Washington) differs thoroughly from the antagonistic relationship that existed during the Vietnam conflict (1961–1975). Global media purveyors seek to curry favour with powerful Western governments, often at the price of impartiality. During the 2003 Iraq War, US and British news media personnel were 'embedded' in combat units – a process that clearly lent itself to adopting a supporting role. The benefits of such close personal contact were enormous and included hitherto unavailable access to the fighting men and women engaged in modern warfare, countless exclusives, etc. The cost of this new style of war coverage was high as well, however. Journalists admitted almost immediately (and on camera) that they were unable and increasingly unwilling to maintain objectivity. As passive participants in skirmishes, they grew to depend on the British and American soldiers around them for their very lives. Consequently, such reporters lost perspective and failed to cover the war as conflict between two parties, each with a genuine grievance. Likewise, the reporters felt a certain need to maintain a 'pro-war' style in their reporting to ensure good working relations with those individuals who were responsible for their safety. At the time of writing, the effects of the new style of war coverage were still unfolding but it is clear that the overwhelming lopsided portrayal of the 2003 war is just one of many outcomes of the 'embedding' process.

The US invasion of Iraq in 2004 has emerged as a crucible for the global media on a number of counts. In the USA, the major news organisations (CNN, Fox News, etc.) have come under fire for their complacency and lack of due diligence in investigating claims made by the US administration linking the Iraqi leadership and the Al Qaeda terrorist group. In fact, the internationally respected *New York Times* newspaper engaged in significant self-criticism in 2004 for its lack of diligence in verifying the information being provided to its journalists by Washington and London in the lead-up to the war in the Middle East. Despite the glaring lack of proof and seemingly unlikely pairing of a secular, nationalist dictator with a fundamentalist Islamist terrorist group bent on recreating the caliphate, many media corporations unquestioningly accepted and reported the connection between Saddam Hussein and Osama bin Laden. At the start of the war in March 2003, nearly two-thirds of the American public believed there was a connection and that Saddam Hussein had had a role in the events of 9/11 – a direct result of reporting practices that supported such assumptions. Such beliefs were a tiny minority in other Western countries where media coverage was more rigorous and reflected popular discontent with the aims of the US administration in Iraq.

The BBC, apparently in an effort to demonstrate its independence from the aims of the state it is associated with (the United Kingdom), landed in hot water over charges that the British government had 'sexed up' the dossier concerning Iraq's weapons of mass destruction (WMD) prior to the conflict. Official inquiries ultimately implicated the BBC in untoward actions, some of which may have contributed to the suicide of British Ministry of Defence scientist David Kelly. The resulting fallout led to the resignation of a number of the corporation's executives. The incident further exacerbated tensions between the media organisation and the British government. In 2004, the British newspaper the *Daily Mirror* likewise generated a great deal of controversy when it published photographs which allegedly showed British soldiers torturing captured Iraqis. The media outlet later admitted that it had been 'hoaxed' but used the retraction as a platform to condemn the policies of the British Prime Minister, Tony Blair, and the US administration of George W. Bush whom it claimed obdurately refuse to 'acknowledge' their own mistakes in Iraq.

Global TV: predictable and ubiquitous

In today's global media marketplace, the audience is often divorced from any specific territorial affiliation. Time Warner's CNN cable news network provides a clear example of this phenomenon. Viewers who watch the network within the United States receive a version of the news that caters to their tastes and political sensibilities, while the rest of the world (and Americans travelling abroad) enjoy a markedly different product – CNN International. The latter network's programming is decidedly less nationalistic than the former and provides a host of programmes intended for consumption by the global traveller and transnational business person. Sources for news stories come from a wide variety of reporters based in all corners of the globe; business reports tally the day's events in Tokyo, London and New York stock exchanges; and weather reports give just as much airtime to Kinshasa and Kolkata as Milan and Miami.

The world traveller can expect to find a rather predictable offering of media when checking

The Arab street goes global

Al-Jazeera, which translates as 'peninsula', is the only truly independent media voice in the Arab Middle East. Partially supported by the Qatari emirate where it is based, the station is increasingly successful as a private concern generating a large portion of its revenue from advertisements. As a transnational network catering to Arab speakers worldwide, the network has become a bellwether of Arab opinion as well as a shaper of it.

Al-Jazeera, once lauded by US policymakers for breaking the traditional mould of Arabic media, is now the *bête noire* of Washington. Its decision to run uncensored video and audio tapes of Osama bin Laden and graphic depictions of civilian casualties in the 2003 Iraq war has created an increasingly hostile relationship with US decision makers and the US military. American forces attacked the offices of the agency in both the Iraq and Afghanistan conflicts and Al-Jazeera has been saddled with onerous restrictions in US-occupied areas. It is also banned from reporting from the premier US stock exchanges for 'security reasons'.

In 2004, the US administration chose not to include Qatar in its negotiations regarding the American-led 'Greater Middle East Initiative' – a plan to encourage democratic reform in the Arab and Muslim worlds. Ironically, the reason for the slight was the emirate's continued press freedom and its support of Al-Jazeera, which the Bush administration accuses of 'false reporting' and 'encouraging terrorism'.

into a hotel whether it is in Western Europe, Central Asia or the Pacific Rim. The channel line-up will most certainly include BBC World. The fiercely independent broadcaster offers up a global perspective on world events with a British accent. Germany's international broadcaster Deutsche Welle's DW-TV (often in English) is a common selection as well. Deutsche Welle is perceived by many international viewers as a less biased broadcaster and commands a higher percentage of English-language viewers in countries like Russia than CNN or the BBC, which are both seen to be purveyors of the Anglo-American cultural dominance that has existed since the end of the Second World War. France's TV-5 typically represents *La Francophonie* with a mixture of news programming and French-language entertainment (a good deal of it being dubbed American films). Rai International, commonly included in large hotels and on cable and satellite networks around the world, offers up a colourful array of original programmes including the infamous Italian game shows.

The staid (if not bland) fare aired by most international broadcasters has been sexed up by the growing power of News Corporation. By creating or acquiring satellite networks in Asia, the United Kingdom, Italy and the United States, Rupert Murdoch, News Corporation's flamboyant major shareholder and managing director, has been able to expand the presence of several channels to the point of giving them a global footprint. Today, Fox News, Sky News and Star TV are becoming part of the international repertoire of media offerings.

As the international business elite has grown more diverse over the past several decades, so has the selection of international media available across the globe. Chinese-language broadcasters (and thus the views of Beijing) now command a spot on the dial. CCTV International has expanded its reach to a global audience with the expressed desire to provide 'a more balanced picture of the world', of course with a Chinese perspective. NHK World provides news and other content for the Japanese-speaking global traveller. Perhaps the most stunning success among the non-European media outlets is that of Al-Jazeera. The Arabic network based in the Gulf State of Qatar has revolutionised the media in the Arab world, challenged Western media dominance and become a newsworthy subject in its own right. The satellite news network positions itself as the only independent voice in the Arabic media space and has reaped enormous rewards for its willingness to publish extremely controversial items including voice and video tapes of Osama bin Laden, bloody civilian casualties in Afghanistan and Iraq, and interviews with US and Israeli politicians.

Some of the major international broadcasters do make an attempt at glocalisation (a process whereby global social processes are selectively redefined and adapted to suit local cultural exigencies); however, most tend to regard their market as being a transnational straw man based on a small set of assumed traits: affluence, mobility, knowledge of the West and its values, etc. Other international versions of national networks are intentionally crafted for the country's émigrés as well as its business travellers. RAI International states that its programming is 'made for Italians who live abroad and for all those who have a family link with our country or want to know more about Italy', thus drawing a direct connection between Italy's diaspora and global media. NHK World, Japan's premiere international broadcaster, also states explicitly that its primary audience is Japanese nationals living overseas.

The United States, along with other major receiving countries for immigration, has seen a veritable explosion of satellite and cable consumption among its immigrant population. US cable TV companies and direct broadcast satellite providers DirecTV and the DISH Network provide customers with a plethora of options including Spanish-language networks from Spain (Canal Sur), Mexico (Canal 22) and Columbia (Caracol TV Internacional). The media for the immigrant community are also increasingly produced in the country of residence. Germany, for example, has a number of Turkish-language cable channels catering to the large Turkish *gastarbeiter* community and its descendants. The media in France, the United Kingdom, the Netherlands and other Western countries similarly are increasingly global in character, combining imported programming (from North Africa, South Asia, Latin America, etc.) with homegrown immigrant programming.

The emergence of transnational television networks like Zee TV, which bills itself as the first truly global South Asian TV channel offering serials, Bollywood films, superstar interviews, cricket, regional programmes and coverage of news and events relevant to the subcontinent, is an important symbol of the increasing irrelevance of geographic borders in the media. Zee TV – the flagship channel of India's largest media and entertainment company – employs its 'understanding of Indian culture and beliefs which are depicted in its programming' to capture market share across four continents.

The Internet as medium: a new arrival or more of the same?

The advent of the Internet as a mass medium has truly revolutionised the reporting of news around the world. The Internet combines the attributes of the agora, newspaper, radio and television while providing the user with the ability to search all data that have ever been posted on the web. The collective amnesia that has protected governments, potentates and generals in the past is now confined to the dustbin of history. Every dark deed, verbal blunder and impropriety is waiting to be recalled at a moment's notice. Furthermore, the Internet is a deterritorialised, decentralised medium that collapses both time and space. Communication across the platform through e-mail, instant messaging and other forms of data transmission is nearly instantaneous and typically anonymous. Consumers can also be producers, thus breaking the paradigm of older forms of mass media where messages were crafted by a small elite and broadcast to the masses who could not provide any form of meaningful feedback.

The unique attributes of cyberspace (deterritorialised, anonymous, nearly infinite) combined with benefits of modern communications technologies (speed, ubiquity, variety of formats) have enabled a brave new world of media. For existing media outlets, the Internet has been a godsend, enabling them to reach a whole new audience. A web user in Russia's far eastern city of Vladivostok (once notorious for its distance from the core of the country) can now get access to Moscow dailies, *The Guardian* or *The New York Times* with a few clicks of the mouse. Immigrants in Bristol, Antwerp and Miami can now log on to the web and get access to their local newspaper back home, whether home is Dhaka, Manila or Caracas. Using online technology to generate offline profits is also common. Foreign newspapers like *Le Monde, Frankfurter Allgemeine* and *Corriere Della Sera* are now printed in small numbers and distributed almost immediately to customers wherever they are. Likewise, the Internet is a major cost-saver for news media, instantly connecting far-flung journalists with the home office, providing countless research tools and limiting the need for proprietary technologies.

The Internet has a darker side as well. Conspiracy theories thrive in cyberspace alongside doctored photos, falsified remarks and other travesties. Alternative and counter-hegemonic discourses are born and nurtured on the Internet due to its egalitarian structure, lack of censorship and anonymity. Consider for a moment the structure of the Internet: the official site of the Israeli state (www.info.gov.il) is roughly equal in terms of bytes and ease of use to find and navigate as any given site dedicated to the 'international Jewish conspiracy'. Such a level playing field allows for abuse of all types; however, the Internet is especially useful for those groups which feel they have no other outlets for expression.

For Muslims, and especially Arabs, living in societies where the government has long kept a stranglehold on the media, the Internet represents a welcome outlet for views and ideas which would never see the light of day in the 'official media'. In much of the Muslim world, there is a strong tendency towards conspiracy theories which travel via word of mouth. Such a phenomenon can be partially attributed to the historical legacy of centuries of oppressive foreign

---

The revolution will be broadcast

The Soviet Union, like the USA, sought to influence foreign audiences through the powerful medium of radio during the Cold War. Radio Moscow and other stations were beamed around the world providing news, commentary and entertainment. At their peak, Soviet radio stations broadcast 2,000 hours per week in 80 languages around the globe. In sub-Saharan Africa alone, the Kremlin provided content in 15 languages including Hausa and Swahili (not to mention the colonial tongues, French and English).

After the Sino-Soviet split in the late 1950s, the Russians and the Chinese emerged as competitors in third world media spaces, spending much of their time vilifying one another while concurrently attacking the capitalist West.

rule (Turkish, British, etc.) and the more recent impact of repressive governmental structures that stifle free speech in public forums. Despotic governments have frequently manipulated conspiracy theories to their advantage by deflecting blame to external forces (the West, Israel, etc.) that would otherwise be directed at their own shortcomings. Political culture does not change overnight. Whether the party in power is a military junta (Pakistan), leftist, nationalist strongmen (Syria), a nepotistic personal dictatorship (Uzbekistan), an ultraconservative monarchy (Saudi Arabia) or a theocracy (Iran), the outcomes are surprisingly similar: repression of political activism and extensive media censorship. In such milieux, the Internet becomes a place where conspiracies are created and confirmed in the space of a day. On the web (as in private discourse) domestic enemies (the ruling elite) and foreign agents (the CIA, the Mossad, resurgent British imperialists, multinational corporations, etc.) are easily conflated and nonsensical theories are supported by 'facts'. Cyberspace's unique ability to serve as reservoir for truth as well as fiction allows for a truly limitless combination of the two.

A poignant example of this phenomenon occurred in the spring of 2004 when the Arabic press began demonstrating a photo of an American soldier with two Iraqi youths. One of the Iraqi boys was holding up a hand-written sign that read 'Lcpl Boudreaux killed my dad th(en) he knocked up my sister!' The widespread publication of the photo throughout the Arab world led to popular displays of anti-American outrage. The sign had originally read 'Lcpl Boudreaux saved my dad th(en) he rescued my sister!,' but the wide and rapid distribution of the fake in the Middle East led to a deepening of the resentment already felt by the vast majority of the Arab world towards the occupying US and British forces. The reports of the hoax generated so much interest in the West that a series of websites was created by Internet entrepreneurs that allowed users to write their own messages on the sign and then print or save the picture. The versions generated by the jokesters were just as authentic looking as the one distributed throughout the Arab press a few weeks before. The ease of such fabrications poses new and deeply troubling challenges to the media community as it balances the benefits of using content generated from the web with the dangers of falsification.

The web has also become a platform for the deployment of horrific images that are not usually shown on major news networks. The publication of photos showing US abuse of Iraqi detainees at Iraq's Abu Ghraib prison in 2004 became a *cause célèbre* in cyberspace where the photos could be downloaded and manipulated with remarkable ease. The gruesome beheadings of *Wall Street Journal* reporter Daniel Pearl and Nicholas Berg, an American civilian looking for work in Iraq, first appeared on the Internet. Pearl's execution appeared in 2002 on a Saudi website entitled 'The Slaughter of the Spy-Journalist, the Jew Daniel Pearl', while Berg's beheading appeared in 2004 on 'Muntada al-Ansar Islamist', an Al Qaeda-affiliated website. Pearl's captors had utilised a free and hard-to-trace e-mail account to make demands on US policymakers prior to the execution, while conspiracy theories flourished that Berg's murder had been conducted by CIA agents posing as Islamic extremists in an attempt to deflect criticism and attention from the US administration over its activities in occupied Iraq.

The Internet, due to its unique nature, is increasingly seen as the best place to distribute information that faces censorship by mainstream media outlets – whether mundane or ghastly.

Conclusion

The emergence of truly transnational media – wire services, satellite TV and the Internet – has been the major cause of the shrinking of the world since 1945. In 1962, Marshall McLuhan imagined a 'global village' in which humans interacted across oceans and continents without regard for time and space. In the twenty-first century, his prediction does seem to be partly realised. Live events a world away flicker on millions of television screens simultaneously while Internet users ramble through cyberspace accessing information uploaded from all points on the globe.

The global media are, however, increasingly created and managed by a few producers obsessed with profits rather than public service. This has led to the increasing prevalence of 'infotainment' – that is, a focus on crime, celebrity, entertainment and human melodrama – often at the expense of hard news reporting. The free-for-all information space which exists on the Internet is a powerful foil for the striking homogeneity of the global television media. But the time and effort required to access news in cyberspace is significantly greater than that required to watch passively 22 minutes of CNN Headline news or a similar service offering 'soft journalism'. The contemporary media environment hosts more voices than ever before, but only a select few – Rupert Murdoch, for example – dictate a potentially dangerously large portion of the content.

Further Reading

Bennet, Lance (2004) *News: The Politics of Illusion,* 6th edn, New York: Longman.

Borjesson, Kristina (2004) *Into the Buzzsaw: Leading Journalists Expose the Myth of a Free Media,* Amherst: Prometheus Books.

Drezner, Daniel W. and Farrell, Henry (2004) 'Web of Influence', *Foreign Policy,* November/December.

Huntington, Samuel (1993) *Foreign Policy.*

Nacos, Brigitte L. (2002) *Mass-Mediated Terrorism: The Central Role of the Media in Terrorism and Counterterrorism,* Lanham: Rowman & Littlefield Publishers.

Seib, Philip (2002) *The Global Journalist: News and Conscience in a World of Conflict,* Lanham: Rowman & Littlefield Publishers.

CHAPTER 7: International migration and diasporas

Mobility has always been an important characteristic of humankind. From the beginning of time people have moved great distances, travelled to hidden places and used remarkable vehicles for their journeys. The history of the human race is unimaginable without the most profound human activity: moving from one place to another. Cities, countries, empires and entire continents have been transformed because of the appearance of foreign soldiers, traders, missionaries and settlers at their borders in the past, or foreign labour, refugees, tourists or foreign students in the present.

In the last four decades alone the movement of people around the world has more than doubled. According to the Population Division of the United Nation's Department of Economic and Social Affairs, the number of international migrants increased from 75 million in 1960 to 175 million in 2000 and is predicted to rise further by 2030 to 230 million (UNPD, 2004). The break-up of the former Soviet Union in 1991 partly explains this because it added an additional 27 million people to the international migrant stock. These people, living in one of the independent successor states but having been born in the USSR, became international migrants overnight without having physically migrated at all. The number of international migrants represented 2.5 per cent of the world population in 1960, 2.3 per cent in 1980 and 2.9 per cent in both 1990 and 2000. Between 1960 and 2000 the immigrant population increased in Australia, New Zealand, Japan, Western Europe, North America and the former Soviet Union by 78 million and grew by 27 million in the rest of the world. The United States had absorbed the largest stock of international migrants (35 million) by 2000, followed by Russia (13 million), Germany (7 million), Ukraine, France and India (UNPD, 2004).

Definition of migration

International migration, in its simplest form, refers to the movement of people or their temporary or permanent geographical relocation. It is difficult to measure international migration and lay out easily comparable migration statistics. There exists little international standardisation of migration statistics because the very definition of an international migrant varies. Each country may collect migration data in different ways and for different purposes and may define who the migrant is in its own way. Country record keeping of immigrants for statistical purposes depends on its national migration policy priorities, on its administrative structure and even on its general economic-political situation. Some countries do not report immigration data at all or not on a yearly basis. Therefore there is only a varying degree of comparability of migration statistics between countries.

Moreover, official figures do not measure illegal migration which further complicates comparability. The very nature of illegal migration is to remain unseen by the authorities and to avoid being registered. It is not only the undocumented border crossers that are hard to keep track of, but visa over-stayers and illegal workers turned tourists are also impossible to count. Authorities and researchers are thus left having to rely on estimations of undocumented migration so as to avoid the phenomenon going completely unmeasured. Consequently both legal and illegal migration figures in this chapter should be viewed as close estimations of the stock of migrants rather than completely accurate figures and handled with some scepticism.

The following section summarises the definitions of key terms connected to international migration as they are used by the Continuing

Reporting System on Migration (SOPEMI), a special division of the OECD dedicated to migration research (SOPEMI, 2004, pp. 295–304).

International migrant is a person who changes his or her country of residence. A long-term migrant leaves his or her country of residence for at least a year and the destination country becomes the new country of residence. A short-term migrant moves from his or her country of residence for at least 3 months but less than 12 months. As a consequence not all movements are considered as migration. Movements for less than three months or for the purposes of recreation or holiday, studying, visiting friends or relatives, business, medical treatment and religious pilgrimage would not be considered as international migration. In accordance with this definition, by and large, international migration can be grouped into three categories of admission: labour migration (highly skilled, low skilled or undocumented), family reunification, and refugees and asylum seekers.

Immigrant population is usually part of the legally resident population. It consists of legally settled migrants who are either foreign national residents or foreign-born residents. Since countries define their immigrant population in different ways and measure them via various techniques, there is a wide variety of data sources estimating immigrant populations. Population registers are most commonly used in Northern Europe, Germany, Austria and Japan to measure the size of foreign populations. Censuses, surveys and (mainly permanent) residence or work permits are used in the main settlement countries, Australia, Canada, New Zealand and the USA, and also in the UK, France, Spain and Ireland, to establish migration figures. Censuses, though infrequent because they are generally conducted once every ten years, offer the most comprehensive data on the migrant population. Population registers create a different kind of record by providing updated figures on migrants but may run the risk of underestimating the flows of migrants because of their limited scope. They may also overestimate the stock of migrants if emigrants fail to report their departure.

Non-settlement countries (European countries, Japan, Korea) typically use population registers as sources for their migration statistics. They tend to have low naturalisation rates because they apply the 'jus sanguinis' citizenship principle which means that the citizenship of the child is inherited from parents by virtue of their blood tie. Their official term to denote their immigrant residents is 'foreign population',

which emphasises their immigrants' non-citizen status. The number of foreign nationals in these countries depends not only on the inflow of foreigners but on naturalisation legislation as well. A higher generation of foreign population may arise if the children of immigrants retain foreign citizenship despite having been born native.

Settlement countries (USA, Canada, Australia, New Zealand) use censuses or residence and work permits to derive their migration data and classify migrants with the term 'foreign-born population', placing all legal residents who were born outside the country in this category irrespective of their citizenship. These countries tend to have high naturalisation rates because they apply the 'jus soli' citizenship criterion, in which the place of birth alone qualifies the child to receive automatically the citizenship of the country he or she was born in, independently of the citizenship or nationality of the parents. Their foreign-born population mainly represents first-generation migrants because the children of migrants acquire citizenship of the destination country by virtue of being born there.

The UK, France, Spain, Ireland and Portugal also derive their own migration statistics from censuses or from (mainly temporary) residence and work permits, yet they generally report their immigrant populations under the label of 'foreign population' like the majority of European countries.

Illegal migrants are that part of the population who enter or reside in the destination country without authorisation to do so. Their size is not systematically recorded, documented or measured in any way. To provide some estimation for the stock of illegal migrants one can turn to either regularisation programme statistics or border patrol criminal records (for example on visa over-stayers or illegal border crossers, etc).

Refugees are defined as approved asylum applicants who are granted refugee status under the 1951 Geneva Refugee Convention in the host country on the basis of well-founded fear of persecution in their home countries because of their race, religion, nationality, political opinions or membership of a particular social group. Certain important rights are attached to those with refugee status such as access to the labour market, welfare programmes or public resources. Over time the refugee status can be transformed into full citizenship.

Asylum seekers are counted in two ways depending on the host country's attitude to the issue. Asylum seekers are either those people who submit an application for asylum but whose case is not yet approved, refused or fully processed, or those whose claims are approved for review. In the latter case the asylum seeker is entitled to certain rights and allowances that are denied to a simple asylum applicant whose case gets rejected out of hand before having been reviewed.

The size of international migration

The number of international migrants is not only increasing but also diversifying in most parts of the world. Their number varies across countries, depending first on the role of immigration in the country considered, second on recent migration inflows and outflows (net migration rate), third on the fertility rate of the immigrant population, and last but not least on the naturalisation rate. Due to the lack of standardised international migration statistics for the entire world, this chapter focuses on migration trends and most important migration challenges of the main destination countries of international migrants, which are the OECD countries.[1] Although the focus of this chapter is to outline in greater detail the main migration dilemmas of industrialised countries, the experiences of less developed countries' migration will also be referred to from time to time, in specific contexts.

Since the mid-1990s, according to OECD data,

---

1 OECD member states are Australia, Austria, Belgium, Canada, Czech Republic, Denmark, Finland, France, Germany, Greece, Hungary, Iceland, Ireland, Italy, Japan, Korea, Luxembourg, Mexico, New Zealand, the Netherlands, Norway, Poland, Portugal, Slovakia, Spain, Sweden, Switzerland, Turkey, the United Kingdom, the United States.

the immigrant population has increased on average by 4–6 per cent each year in Southern Europe, the UK, Ireland, Finland, the USA and Japan. Yet the two countries that experienced the most dramatic growth in their foreign population between 1996 and 2001 were Spain and Korea with an average annual growth of 15 per cent and 9 per cent respectively (SOPEMI, 2004, pp. 42–44). Table 7.1 displays the number of legal immigrants in selected OECD countries.

As the table shows, settlement countries have 11–23 per cent of their resident population as first-generation migrants or foreign-born residents. These high figures are due to their relatively liberal immigration policies, which stem from the importance they have attached to the admission of foreigners throughout their histories. By contrast, European countries, Japan and Korea traditionally consider themselves to be emigration countries. It is a quite recent phenomenon that they have slowly changed to immigration countries. It is only since the early 1970s that considerably more people have been entering these countries than leaving them. The new balance of positive net immigration inflow has given rise to new demographic, labour-related and socio-cultural challenges, which can threaten fundamental political institutions and put both the nation-state and the welfare state into a completely new context.

Tables 7.2a and 7.2b show that the origin of the foreign or foreign-born population residing in OECD countries is diverse. In settlement countries the largest share (38 per cent) of foreign-born residents comes from Latin America. This high representation is due mainly to the large

---

Table 7.1 Stock of foreign-born and foreign population in selected OECD countries, in thousands and as percentage of total population, 2001

Country	Stock of foreign-born population	% of total population	Country	Stock of foreign-born population	% of total population
Australia	4482	23.1	Netherlands	1674	10.4
New Zealand	699	19.5	France	5868	10.0
Canada	5448	18.2	Norway	315	6.9
Sweden	1028	11.5	Denmark	322	6.0
United States	31,811	11.1	Hungary	300	3.0
Austria	892	11.0	Mexico[1]	406	0.5

1. Data is from 2000 census.   (continued)

Country	Stock of foreign population	% of total population	Country	Stock of foreign population	% of total population
Luxembourg	167	37.5	Netherlands	690	4.3
Switzerland	1419	19.7	Norway	186	4.1
Austria	764	9.4	Ireland	151	3.9
Germany	7319	8.9	Spain	1109	2.7
Belgium	847	8.2	Italy	1363	2.4
Greece	762	6.9	Portugal[4]	224	2.2
France[2]	3263	5.6	Czech Republic	211	2.0
Sweden	476	5.3	Finland	98	1.9
Denmark	267	5.0	Japan	1779	1.4
EEA[3]	20,744	5.7	Hungary	116	1.1
United Kingdom	2587	4.4	Korea	230	0.5

2. Data is from 1999 census.
3. Excluding Greece and 1999 data for France instead of 2001.
4. Data does not include people with permanent permits. 179,165 permits were issued between January 2001 and March 2003 with the 2001 regularisation programme.

Source: Census data except for Germany (register of foreigners, 2002) and the United Kingdom (Labour Force Survey), Secretariat calculations, reproduced in *Trends in International Migration: SOPEMI* – 2004 edition, © OECD 2005

Mexican presence in the USA. The second largest group contains people of Asian-Pacific origin. They make up 24 per cent of the foreign-born population of settlement countries. EU nationals reach 16 per cent and non-EU member European nationals another 5 per cent of the foreign-born population in Australia, Canada, New Zealand and the USA. The rest of the immigrants are either of African and Middle Eastern origin (3

Table 7.2a Foreign-born population by region of birth in Australia, Canada, New Zealand and the USA in 2001

South & Central America	37.7%
Asia, Oceania	23.7%
EU	15.8%
Unknown origin	11.5%
Non-EU Europe	5.3%
Africa and Middle East	3.1%
North America	3.2%

Source: SOPEMI, 2004 (see Table 7.1)

per cent) or from North America (3 per cent).

The distribution of foreigners in European OECD countries and in Japan and Korea exhibits a different picture. The largest group, 27 per cent of the total foreign population in these non-settler countries, is from non-EU member European countries. This group most probably contains either workers from poor East European countries employed in the EU or refugees mainly from the former Yugoslav republics seeking shelter in the EU. In the European context, just as in the case of settlement countries, in which Latin Americans are the biggest immigrant group, the majority of immigrants come from territories that are geographically close to the destination countries. Another 26 per cent of immigrants, which is almost as sizable as the share of East Europeans, consists of EU nationals. The 'free movement of labour' policy of the EU-15, which encourages the movement of the nationals of 15 member states by offering unhindered access to each other's labour market, accounts primarily for this high figure. Asians represent 12 per cent of the foreign population in non-settler OECD countries, Africans and Middle Easterners another 11 per cent, while people from the Americas an additional 5 per cent.

Table 7.2b Foreigners in European OECD countries, Japan and Korea by region of origin in 2001

Non-EU Europe	27.4%
EU	25.9%
Unknown origin	18.7%
Asia and Oceania	12.3%
Africa and Middle East	10.6%
South & Central America	2.8%
North America	2.3%

Source: SOPEMI, 2004 (see Table 7.1)

Both settler and non-settler countries have a considerable number of foreigners with unknown origins (11 per cent and 19 per cent respectively). One possible explanation for this may involve the relatively large number of asylum seekers among immigrants, especially in EU countries. Many asylum seekers try to increase their chances of being granted refugee status by keeping their country of origin undisclosed. The advantage of the unknown origin is that the person cannot be immediately readmitted or returned to his or her country of origin. While the nationality of the applicant is being established, he or she gains time and may also hope to receive more favourable treatment as a 'stateless' person.

These two tables on the distribution of immigrants by regions of origin confirm that international migration is not just a simple unidirectional flow of people from southern/eastern developing countries to the northern/western industrialised states. Besides the considerable flow from the developing to the developed world, which the International Organization for Migration (IOM) estimates to be about 2.3 million on yearly average in the last decade, the flow of people among fellow OECD countries is also considerable (IOM, 2004). In fact, in most European countries, Australia and New Zealand, more than half of the migrants comes from another OECD country. Even in the USA, due to the large Mexican presence, 47 per cent of foreign-born residents are from fellow OECD countries.

Why do people migrate?

What brings migrants to the decision to leave their country? There are various 'push' and 'pull' factors that propel international migration. The most important 'push' factors are typically related to the sending country's economic situation or to its political and social conditions. Predominantly people move to a country other than the one of their birth because they either have already found a job there or they hope to find one that is better than the one they can get at home.

Not only can the lack of adequate jobs, low wages or high unemployment trigger emigration from certain regions, but political instability or looming violent conflicts may also force people to flee from their homes. In addition to economic and political problems leading to emigration from various parts of the world, developing countries tend to experience rapid population growth and all the problems attached to it, which may function as an additional 'push' factor for the emigration of their nationals. The world population is growing by 83 million a year, of which 82 million are born in developing countries (IOM, 2004). Social tensions originating from overpopulation can also be effectively reduced by outward migration.

The 'pull' factors can typically be found in the attractive environment of the destination country. The two most important ones are the huge wage and productivity differences between the host and the origin countries and the presence of family members in the host country with whom the migrant wishes to reunite. The destination country's political stability and likely respect for human rights may also function as magnets for non-labour migration. In sum, higher wages, better professional job opportunities, settled and successful family members, social safety measures or democratic political mechanisms are all powerful driving forces for both the highly skilled and the low-skilled worker, for the family member left at home or for the asylum seeker to look for a new life in wealthy industrialised countries. Moreover, developed countries tend to put into place further 'pull' incentives to admit highly skilled foreign labour and low-skilled seasonal guest workers in their efforts to meet labour shortages in their economies.

But international labour migration, particularly of the highly skilled, in reverse direction from developed to developing countries, is also not uncommon. The 'pull' factors are usually created by private enterprises when, for example, a multinational sets up a sufficiently attractive scheme for intra-company transferees to move from the north-west to the emerging markets of South-East Asia, Middle East, Latin

Table 7.3 Inflows of foreign population in selected OECD countries: annual average in thousands

	1991–1995	1996–2000	2001		1991–1995	1996–2000	2001
United States				**Belgium**	54	58	66.0
Permanent immigration	1046	773	1064	**Czech Republic**	5.9[6]	7	11.3
Temporary immigration[1]	1451	2221	2948	**Denmark**	20	22	25
				France	99	112	141
Australia				**Germany**	935	650	685
Permanent immigration	93	88	89	**Greece**	na	38[7]	na
Temporary immigration	111	174	340	**Hungary**	16	17	19
Japan[2]	241	279	351	**Ireland**	13[8]	22	28
Canada				**Italy**	na	217[9]	233
Permanent immigration	235	207	250	**Netherlands**	78	81	95
Temporary immigration[3]	61	71	86	**Norway**	17	25	25
European Economic area[4]	1584	1342	1553	**New Zealand**	32	45	62
				Portugal	95	8	14
EU-15	1461[5]	1277	1465	**Sweden**	50	35	44
				Switzerland	101	77	99
Austria	na	66	75	**United Kingdom**	197[5]	293	373

1. Excluding visitors, transit migrants and students and including accompanying dependents.
2. Including short-term movements.
3. 2000 data instead of 2001. Seasonal workers are excluded.
4. Austria, Greece, Italy and Spain are not included. Inflows include significant number of short-term movements.
5. 1992–1995 data instead of 1991–1995.
6. 1995 data.
7. 1998 data.
8. 1994–1995 data.
9. 1998–2000 data.

Source: *Trends in International Migration: SOPEMI* – 2003 edition, © OECD 2004, and National Statistical Offices, reproduced in *Trends in International Migration: SOPEMI* – 2000 edition, © OECD 2000

America or Eastern Europe in order to supervise the expansion of the company into new markets.

Some recent features of globalisation have created additional incentives for people to move, especially to developed countries. For example, the availability of imported Western consumer goods (jeans, Coke, movies, music) all over the globe or the global media-generated desire for north-western lifestyle all turn the north-west into a popular destination for migrants from around the world. But what ultimately facilitates the rapid increase of people movement and turns the dream of many potential migrants into reality is the considerable decrease in the price of communication and transportation technology in the last few decades. Affordable transportation makes both long-term and short-term circulatory movements available for an ever larger group of people.

Table 7.3 shows that industrialised countries continued to admit foreigners in record numbers in 2001 despite the marked deterioration in the global economic climate since the end of the 1990s. Some countries, such as the USA, Australia, Canada, Japan, the UK, New Zealand, France and Austria, saw significant increases in their foreign inflows and admitted immigrants in record numbers. It is the high growth rate of immigration into Japan which is the most surprising in the light of the country's long economic stagnation and increasing unemployment rate. Immigration has been on the rise in all the OECD countries in the last decade except for Germany, Norway and Sweden. In Germany, however, although the number of admissions is dropping and remains below the record high levels of the early 1990s which followed the opening of the eastern borders, immigration remains considerable, with 685,000 intakes in 2001.

It is likely that migration inflows will continue to increase because demand for labour in industrialised countries is not expected to vanish suddenly in the future and the settlement of recent migrants will attract additional family members.

Where do people migrate?

Migrants do not just move randomly around the world – they follow certain patterns during their search for employment opportunities and when selecting their preferred destination. Looking more closely, a strong concentration of particular nationalities in certain host countries can be identified. Table 7.4 shows that a few origin countries predominate in the foreign population of many OECD destination countries. Among the three most important factors that determine who moves where are, first, the geographical proximity of the source country to the destination country; second, cultural, historical or linguistic ties between the two countries; and third, the presence of family members or compatriot networks.

Because of the proximity of the host and the sending countries, North Africans tend to go to France, Chinese to Japan, Poles to Germany, Albanians to Italy and Mexicans to the USA. Historical or linguistic ties explain why nationals from the Commonwealth countries mostly enter the UK. Brazil and Cape Verde nationals go to Portugal and Scandinavians to Sweden. The large presence of fellow nationals, primarily as refugees or asylum seekers, accounts for the arrivals of former Yugoslavs in Austria, Switzerland and Germany, Chinese in Canada or Iraqis in Sweden.

Table 7.4 Stock of foreign population in thousands in selected countries as of 2000 and the relative (%) importance of the top 5 origin countries in the total stock of foreigners[1]

Australia		Austria		Canada	
Total (consisting of)	517.0	Total	775.9	Total	5448.5
UK	26.9%	Bosnia-Herzegovina		China	6.1%
New Zealand	8.3%	Fed Rep of Yugoslavia	45.1%	India	5.8%
China	3.7%	Croatia		Philippines	4.3%
India	2.4%	Turkey	17.3%	Pakistan	1.5%
South Africa	1.8%	Germany	na	Korea	1.3%
France		Germany		Italy	
Total	3263.2	Total	7296.9	Total	1388.2
Morocco	15.4%	Turkey	27.4%	Morocco	11.5%
Algeria	14.6%	Fed Rep of Yugoslavia	14.9%	Albania	10.2%
Turkey	6.4%	Italy	8.5%	Romania	5.0%
Tunisia	4.7%	Poland	4.1%	China	4.3%
United States	0.7%	Russia	1.6%	Poland	2.3%

1. Stock of foreign-born population for Australia, Canada and the United States.

(continued)

Japan		Portugal		Sweden	
Total	1686.4	Total	208.0	Total	476.0
Korea	37.7%	Cape Verde	22.6%	Finland	20.7%
China	19.9%	Brazil	10.7%	Iraq	6.9%
Brazil	15.1%	Angola	9.8%	Norway	6.7%
Philippines	8.6%	Guinea-Bissau	7.7%	Denmark	5.4%
United States	2.7%	Spain	5.9%	Former Yugoslavia	4.2%
Switzerland		United Kingdom		United States	
Total	1384.4	Total	2342.0	Total	31,107.9
Former Yugoslavia	24.4%	India	6.5%	Mexico	29.5%
Italy	23.3%	United States	4.9%	Philippines	4.4%
Germany	8.0%	Australia	3.2%	India	3.3%
France	4.4%	South Africa	2.3%	China	3.2%
United Kingdom	1.5%	Philippines	0.9%	Vietnam	3.2%

Source: *Trends in International Migration: SOPEMI*, 2004 edition, © OECD 2005

Economic impact of international migration: inflow of foreign labour

The effect of international migration on the host or on the sending state is rather complex and involves a mixture of economic, demographic, political, cultural and safety issues. In order to sort out the complicated and overlapping impacts international migration creates on both the host and the sending countries, the economic impact of migration on the receiving country will come first, followed by that on the origin country. In the subsequent two sections the demographic impact of migration will be examined and then the political and cultural effects of their arrival.

Most of the debates on the economic consequences of international migration concern the economic impact foreign workers exert on the receiving country's economic performance and labour market. Is the presence of foreign labour unfavourable for the host country? Will foreign workers increase unemployment and decrease wages? Or, on the contrary, will foreign labour boost the destination country's prosperity by meeting skill shortages and making the labour market more flexible? Conventional economic theories may support both views depending on the type and size of the foreign labour inflow and the level

of welfare benefits the host country offers to its residents. As Table 7.5 shows, in some countries like Austria, Australia, Canada, Germany, Switzerland and the USA, foreign immigrants make up a considerable portion of the labour force. OECD countries seem to have a renewed interest in admitting foreign workers by following selective labour-related immigration policies.

There is probably little dispute about the desirability of importing highly skilled foreign labour because it is regarded as being well controlled, able to meet valuable skill shortages and able to enhance the host country's productivity instead of depleting public resources. Most of the rich industrialised countries have long-established recruitment policies or 'green card' programmes to attract the world's 'best and brightest' qualified foreign workers. The admission of highly qualified labour grew noticeably in the areas of new information and communication technologies and in the health and education sectors.

To illustrate the strong demand for highly skilled workers in industrialised countries, it is enough to take a look at how the United States' annual quota of 'specialty occupation: H-1B visa' which was extended from 65,000 in 1999 to 115,000 in 2000 and then to 195,000 in 2001–2003 (SOPEMI, 2004, p. 29). H-1B visas are

Table 7.5 Stock of foreign and foreign-born labour force in thousands and percentages

Stock of foreign-labour	1997	1998	1999	2000	2001
Austria	326.3	327.1	333.6	345.6	359.9
% of total labour force	9.9	13.7	10.0	10.5	11.0
Belgium	377.4	390.7	386.2	na	na
% of total labour force	8.8	8.8	8.9	na	na
France	1569.8	1586.7	1593.8	1577.6	1617.6
% of total labour force	6.1	6.1	5.8	6.0	6.2
Germany	3575.0	na	3545.0	3546.0	3 616
% of total labour force	8.9	na	8.8	8.8	9.1
Ireland	51.7	53.3	57.7	63.9	82.1
% of total labour force	3.4	3.3	3.4	3.7	4.6
Italy	539.6	614.6	747.6	850.7	800.7
% of total labour force	2.4	2.7	3.6	4.1	3.8
Japan	107.3	119.0	125.7	154.7	168.8
% of total labour force	0.2	0.2	0.2	0.2	0.2
Korea	106.8	76.8	93.0	122.5	128.5
% of total labour force	0.5	0.4	0.4	0.6	0.6
Luxembourg	124.8	134.6	145.7	152.7	170.7
% of total labour force	55.1	57.7	57.3	57.3	61.7
Norway	59.9	66.9	104.6	111.2	na
% of total labour force	2.8	3.0	4.7	4.9	na
Portugal	87.9	88.6	91.6	99.8	104.7
% of total labour force	1.8	1.8	1.8	2.0	2.0
Spain	178.7	197.1	199.8	454.6	607.1
% of total labour force	1.1	1.2	1.2	2.7	3.4
Sweden	220.0	219.0	222.0	222.0	227.0
% of total labour force	5.2	5.1	5.1	5.0	5.1
Switzerland	692.8	691.1	701.2	717.3	738.8
% of total labour force	17.5	17.4	17.6	17.8	18.1
United Kingdom	949.0	1039.0	1005.5	1107.0	1229.0
% of total labour force	3.6	3.9	3.7	4.0	4.4
Stock of foreign-born labour					
Australia	2251.6	2293.9	2309.6	2364.5	2367.3
% of total labour force	24.8	24.8	24.6	24.5	24.2
Canada	na	na	na	na	3150.8
% of total labour force	na	na	na	na	19.9
United States	15,400.0	16,100.0	16,114.0	18,530.0	20,014.0
% of total labour force	11.3	11.7	11.7	13.0	13.9

Source: *Trends in International Migration: SOPEMI*, 2004 edition, © OECD 2005

the prime means of entry for ICT professionals from around the world, in particular from India. In fact, in 2001 more than 200,000 new H-1B visas were issued in addition to 130,000 renewals. But the increase in the admission of skilled workers ended in 2002 due to the worsening economic conditions affecting mostly the information technology and communications sectors. H-1B visa issues dropped to 79,000 in 2002 and the quota was expected to return to 65,000 in 2004. Although H-1B visas, which offer a temporary working permit to holders, have been granted in decreasing numbers since 2001, the number of permanently admitted workers, most of whom are also highly skilled, is on the rise, reaching more than 179,000 in 2001, which represents a 67 per cent growth over the previous year.

The USA is not the only country seeking skilled labour. Other industrialised countries are competing for the world's elite workers as well. Japan issued 142,000 highly skilled work permits in 2001 and almost 130,000 in 2000. The United Kingdom and Germany acted similarly. They both relaxed the condition for the entry of highly skilled foreign labour in less dramatic but still visible ways. For example, the latter established a green card programme for computer specialists in 2000 and the former introduced the 'Highly Skilled Migrant Programme' in 2001 to attract medical practitioners and education professionals.

It is mostly the impact of semi- or unskilled labour imports that is subject to serious dispute among academic communities, policymakers and society in general. On the one hand, one can argue that unskilled or undocumented labour migration may have serious negative side effects by raising unemployment and being a drain on the social security system. The argument goes as follows: European welfare states have stimulated a strong additional demand for foreign cheap labour by fixing minimum wages above market clearing levels and by providing extensive health and unemployment benefits to native workers. Native low-skilled workers prefer to sit back at home and receive welfare cheques instead of entering into low-wage competition with foreign labour and thus employers start recruiting cheap foreign labour to fill the low-wage job vacancies. The result is that locals are crowded out of the lowest segment of the labour market and unless they are able to move upwards to skilled jobs, local unemployment figures start to rise. This cycle is further emphasised by the additional influx of undocumented cheap foreign labour, which is probably even more willing to enter into low-wage competition with the natives. Besides causing rising unemployment, cheap foreign labour tends to gain more from public resources than it contributes to it. As poor earners, the taxes and social security contributions the low-skilled pay (if any) usually do not cover the cost of infrastructure and public transportation they use or benefit from.

On the other hand, it can be argued that the jobs low-skilled foreign labour tends to take up (construction, agriculture, catering, retailing, household services, taking care of the young and elderly) are the jobs natives would not take any more because these are badly paid jobs. The much-needed foreign labour merely fills the labour market niche that was created by the state's introduction of minimum wages and welfare benefits: thus it is not the foreigners who cause unemployment. Instead, cheap foreign labour may be helping to keep production costs low, which, in turn, prevents inflation and enhances local employers' profits. If these profits are reinvested locally, creating new or better jobs, natives may enjoy the benefits of more and higher-skilled job options.

It is therefore not surprising that labour-importing countries themselves are ambivalent on the issue of admitting unskilled labour. They are all hesitant about opening sizable entry channels for low-skilled workers. The only exception is Germany, which granted a record number of temporary admissions to almost 278,000 seasonal workers in 2001. Most of them came from Poland (260,000) and worked in agriculture (95 per cent). By and large, industrialised countries tend to recruit low-skilled foreign labour only in small numbers and only on a temporary or seasonal basis, as Table 7.6 illustrates. Although the USA is another example of granting 'seasonal agricultural worker: H-2A visas' in small and decreasing quantities (27,700 in 2001), it is worth adding that it also issued more than 72,000 H-2B visas to temporary unskilled labour in the non-agricultural sector in 2001.

Yet a cheap labour force is key for the economies of industrialised countries. The unmatched demand for cheap (native or legal foreign) unskilled labour may be one of the most important explanations for the presence of sizable undocumented foreign low-skilled labour working clandestinely in wealthy countries. Take southern Europe as an example (SOPEMI, 2004, 30). Italy introduced a regular-

Table 7.6 Inflows of seasonal workers in selected OECD countries in thousands

	1998	1999	2000	2001
Australia	55.6	62.6	71.5	76.6
France	7.5	7.6	7.9	10.8
Germany	201.6	223.4	219.0	277.9
Italy	16.5	20.4	30.9	30.3
Norway	7.5	8.6	9.9	11.9
Switzerland	39.6	45.3	49.3	54.9
United Kingdom	9.4	9.8	10.1	15.2
United States	27.3	32.4	33.3	27.7

Source: *Trends in International Migration: SOPEMI*, 2004 edition, © OECD 2005

isation programme for illegal workers in 2002 and received 700,000 applications, half of which were submitted by domestic workers. Spain received more than 340,000 applications on launching its 2001 amnesty programme: 30 per cent came from domestic workers, 20 per cent from construction workers and 13 per cent from agricultural workers. Portugal introduced its amnesty for undocumented workers between January 2001 and May 2003 and issued more than 179,000 residence and work permits, mostly to Ukrainians and Brazilians. Greece also undertook several regularisation operations. The biggest was in 1998 when the Greek government received 371,000 applications, of which 65 per cent were submitted by Albanian nationals.

But it is still the USA which is the single most outstanding example of a huge number of illegals residing and working in the country. The US Census Bureau estimated that approximately 8.5 million people were living clandestinely in the country in 2000. Although they are certainly not all low-skilled workers, the actual stock of unregistered foreigners working in the service and agricultural sectors far outweighs the number of documented low-skilled workers represented by H-2A or B visa issue figures. In the future, given the ageing population in OECD countries (see the next section) and the low-paid conditions in certain sectors, the need for cheap foreign labour is likely to rise further. This, in turn, invokes the necessity for OECD countries to adjust their recruitment policies for foreign low-skilled workers to the needs of their economies and societies.

Scientific research on the desirability of labour migration seems to confirm the co-existence of both the anti- and the pro-labour migration arguments, as may be seen from reports in the London *Times* (1 March 2003) discussing the results of three studies that were carried out in the UK, in Germany and in the USA, examining the effect of labour immigration on wages and unemployment (Browne, 2003). On the one hand, econometric studies commissioned in the UK and Germany find that higher immigration is associated with higher wages in both countries. On the other, evidence that migration causes unemployment is also found, though it is very weak and statistically significant for only the semi-skilled labour group. Meanwhile, the USA study argues that half of the decline in unskilled workers' wages is due to the large influx of low-skilled legal and illegal workers into the country.

In sum, the studies point out that as long as labour immigration is complementary to the local workforce, it is reasonable to expect an overall positive impact on the economy because immigrants fill posts locals cannot or do not take. This gives space to dynamic internal economic growth and is likely to boost wages. But if immigrant labour is substituting for the native workforce, its effect on the host country's economy is probably mixed. The oversupply of labour may lead to falling wages or growing unemployment, but it may also help to fuel profits of local entrepreneurs and hinder inflation. The picture that emerges on the impact of importing foreign labour on the receiving country's economy and labour market is certainly not simple or clear cut. Though the overall benefits of admitting foreign labour may well outweigh its economic and social costs, these benefits and burdens are not shared equally or felt the same way across various groups in society. Some groups encounter and enjoy only the fruits of upward mobility, low costs or higher productivity, while others feel only the stronger competition for their jobs and declining wages in their professions. These conflicting interests make it certain that the debate on labour immigration is not likely to be settled in the near or medium term.

Economic impact of international migration: outflow of labour

To get a full picture of the economic impact of international labour migration, the effects of labour emigration on the source country need to be considered as well. The outflow of labour causes negative and positive effects and the balance between them largely depends on the size and type of labour outflow.

Emigrant workers can be turned into extremely valuable assets for their home countries when they send money back home. According to the World Bank, in 2002 a total of $80 billion of worker remittances were sent from developed countries to developing countries, which was an 11 per cent growth on the previous year (Ratha, 2004, p. 160). However, this sum captured only those remittance flows transmitted through official banking channels or transmission firms. Given that the average cost of wire transfer or money order may easily reach 20 per cent of the remitted sum, if the monies are sent to Central and South America for example, there is a large share of remittance payments that goes through informal channels, such as mail and individually carried funds or in the form of food, clothing and medical supplies or gifts.[2] Therefore a more realistic estimate of the total remittance payments in the world suggests that it reached $100 billion in 2001 (Ratha, 2004, 172).

Table 7.7 reveals the top ten remittance source countries. Not surprisingly, the USA is the most important source country because of the large numbers of Latin American workers. The Inter-American Development Bank's Multilateral Investment Fund estimates that around 10 million of the 16.7 million Latin-American-born adults living in the USA send remittances back to their families at home on a regular basis (IDB, 2004). It estimated that in 2004 the sum would be $30 billion. Table 7.8 shows the sums remitted via official banking channels to the top 20 developing countries.

As private capital inflows to developing nations have declined due to an economic downturn in industrialised countries, foreign direct investments have also dried up. Thus workers' remittances are becoming an increasingly important source of external funding for

Table 7.7 Top 10 country sources of remittance payments, 2001

Country	$ Billion	Country	$ Billion
United States	28.4	France	3.9
Saudi Arabia	15.1	Luxembourg	3.1
Germany	8.2	Israel	3.0
Belgium	8.1	Italy	2.6
Switzerland	8.1	Japan	2.3

Source: Ratha, 2004, © The International Bank for Reconstruction and Development/The World Bank

many developing countries because they expand the recipient countries' foreign exchange reserves. Not only are they more stable than private capital flows, but they are sizable sums as well. In 2001, for example, remittances to the less developed world reached an average level that surpassed official development assistance given to these countries and equalled 42 per cent of total foreign direct investment flows pouring into their economies (Ratha, 2004, p. 164). Table 7.9 illustrates the importance of

Table 7.8 Top 20 developing country recipients of workers' remittances, 2001

Country	$ Billion	Country	$ Billion
India	10.0	El Salvador	1.9
Mexico	9.9	Colombia	1.8
Philippines	6.4	Yemen Republic	1.5
Morocco	3.3	Pakistan	1.5
Egypt	2.9	Brazil	1.5
Turkey	2.8	Ecuador	1.4
Lebanon	2.3	Federal Republic of Yugoslavia	1.4
Bangladesh	2.1	Thailand	1.3
Jordan	2.0	China	1.2
Dominican Republic	2.0	Sri Lanka	1.1

Source: Ratha, 2004, © The International Bank for Reconstruction and Development/The World Bank

2 The use of informal channels is caused not only by the widespread use of hidden charges, long delays in cheque clearance or exchange losses, but also by the fact that many of the remitted monies are sent to low class recipients by clandestine labour neither of whom have bank accounts. To remedy the latter problem, at least partly, the Mexican consulates in the US issue simple identity cards to any legal or illegal Mexicans living in the US. These ID card are being increasingly accepted in the country as a proof of identity by major banks when opening a bank account.

remittances to some of the developing countries by displaying the rate of remittances compared with the country's GDP.

Research on remittances shows that they tend to generate a positive multiplier effect on the receiving country's economy. One part of them is typically spent on housing, food and clothing. The other part is reinvested in property and real estate or in local small enterprises. In many

Table 7.9 Top 20 developing country recipients of workers' remittances as per centage of their GDP, 2001

Country	% of GDP	Country	% of GDP
Tonga	37.3	Jamaica	13.5
Lesotho	26.5	Federal Republic of Yugoslavia	12.8
Jordan	22.8	Morocco	9.7
Albania	17.0	Dominican Republic	9.3
Nicaragua	16.2	Vanuatu	8.9
Yemen Republic	16.1	Philippines	8.9
Moldova	15.0	Honduras	8.5
Lebanon	13.8	Uganda	8.5
El Salvador	13.8	Ecuador	7.9
Cape Verde	13.6	Sri Lanka	7.0

Source: Ratha, 2004, © The International Bank for Reconstruction and Development/The World Bank

countries, remittance revenues tend to offset the costs resulting from the loss of human capital and lost tax revenues. The case of India illustrates this point. It is estimated that the fiscal loss related to Indian labour outflow to the USA represented 0.24–0.58 per cent of the Indian GDP in 2001, whereas remittances reached 2.1 per cent of the GDP the same year (Ratha, 2004, p. 164). Or every remitted dollar sent to Mexico translates into a $2.69–3.17 increase of the Mexican GNP (Ratha, 2004, p. 164).

While the emigration of unskilled workers proves to be almost always a net gain for the developing country because the costs associated with both unemployment and human education can be saved, the outflow of highly skilled labour

is not necessarily beneficial. The phenomenon of 'brain drain' is the most commonly mentioned argument against labour outflow. The impact of the emigration of skilled labour depends on the specific labour market circumstances of the sending country.

On the one hand, the international mobility of Filipino nurses or Indian IT professionals is widely regarded as favourable to the economic development of the countries concerned because it tends to translate into financial remittances to the Philippines and India. Moreover, the skills these workers acquire during their educational training might be unmatched by local labour market demands, which makes their emigration all the more beneficial for the local community. On the other hand, the case of South African health professionals' emigration (general practitioners, specialists and nurses) to English-speaking OECD countries is a counter example. In 2001 alone, 23,407 registered health professionals (10 per cent of the total) left the country. Their outflow proves to be an important factor in preventing the country's health system from performing better (SOPEMI, 2004, Part III). The problem of the chronically understaffed health sector has propelled the South African government to introduce changes in the curriculum of health training to make it more South Africa specific and less easily transferable into another setting, to prescribe one-year compulsory community service for medical school graduates, to improve the working conditions of physicians and nurses and to cooperate with foreign recruiting agencies to end their activities in the country.

The emigration of labour, just like the immigration of labour, is a complex, multifaceted issue. Both require particular attention from policymakers to make careful assessments and to analyse them in order to turn both the inflow and the outflow of workers into benefits for both the sending and the host states.

Emigrant populations usually maintain varying degrees of emotional, social and cultural links with their countries of origin, while also owing allegiance to the country where they have settled. The policy of organising diaspora, consisting of fellow nationals within the destination country, is usually an additional effort emigration countries carry out with the intention of encouraging their expatriates to participate in the economic development of their former home. Some origin countries have long recognised the benefits of re-involving their nationals living abroad in their home affairs.

The re-creation of ties between expatriates and the home country can vary in effectiveness. For example, both Morocco and Bangladesh have reacted strongly and set up whole ministries to administer their relationships with their diasporas residing in wealthy countries. The point of organising a transnational community between the émigrés and the sending country is to treat expatriates as not irreversibly established in their new homes. Given that in many cases these emigrants have no intention of any permanent return, some developing countries increasingly downplay the importance of their coming back and look at them as valuable assets and network connections where they are.

Expatriates can take part in the economic development of the source country by importing products from their countries of origin or sharing their skills in relevant business areas with home-country entrepreneurs. The Chinese and the Indians have the largest overseas diasporas. The former has approximately 70 million nationals all over the world, the latter approximately 20 million. Both émigré communities have been remarkably successful in business and have brought considerable investments back to their home countries (Ellerman, 2003). For example, with the ending of the dot.com boom in the USA, the Indian diaspora in Silicon Valley has started to reconnect to their home country and led the wave of outsourcing all kinds of productions, research and developments and services that can be digitalised and sent down the wire. Many other countries, such as Argentina, Armenia, Italy, Ireland, Israel, Pakistan and South Africa, are also known for their sizable diasporas (in some cases expatriates outnumber native nationals living in the source country) and for the close relationship they maintain with their country of origin.

Organising the sending country-diaspora relationship may also create a transnational community working for the betterment of the origin country in non-business-related ways. Many of the members of a diasporic community may also enter politics, the education system or professional vocations. Their support can translate not only into important business deals or capital investments but also into technology and know-how transfers, political lobbying, diplomatic services or the creation of intercultural dialogues. (Ellerman, 2003).

Demographic impact of international migration: family reunification

Family members of settled immigrants enter the destination country through accompanying relatives and family reunification programmes. This entry category continues to be the largest admission category of foreign or foreign-born populations in the majority of OECD countries (SOPEMI, 2004, pp. 32–33). But its share in the total number of entries has been declining in recent years due to the increase in labour-related admissions. In the USA and France, the two countries in which family-related immigration flows have traditionally been considerable, the proportion of all inflows dropped – in the USA between 1999–2001 from 83 per cent to 70 per cent, in France between 2000–2001 from 79 per cent to 72 per cent.

In countries with a traditionally much lower share of family reunification in total immigration, similar decreasing trends emerge. From 1999 to 2001, the family component dropped in Switzerland from 46 per cent to 41 per cent of total admissions, in the UK from 45 per cent to 34 per cent, in Australia from 37 per cent to 32 per cent and in New Zealand from 28 per cent to 22 per cent. In the Scandinavian countries and Canada, the share of family-related migration continues to be around 50 per cent of total immigration flows for the former and 60 per cent for the latter.

Some other countries, such as Denmark, Italy and the Netherlands, have recently adopted stricter conditions regarding family reunification to reduce so-called 'import marriages'. For example, if Dutch nationals want to marry a non-EU national they have to prove they have a minimum of 120 per cent of national family-level income and at least a one-year work contract (SOPEMI, 2004, p. 240). In Denmark, immigration laws were also tightened in 2002. Immigrants are entitled to reduced welfare benefits only during their first seven years of residence and the waiting period to receive a permanent residence permit was extended from three to seven years. Family reunions were limited to spouses older than 24 and Danish citizenship can be received only after a nine-year waiting period and the passing of a Danish language exam.

The share of family-related immigration may

be declining in the majority of OECD countries, but the actual numbers of people admitted under this category are not decreasing. Moreover, in the medium term, the recently increased labour inflow is expected to give rise to additional or secondary family-related migration in the near future. Given the magnitude of family-related inflows, it is worth examining it in the context of the population demographics of industrialised countries.

Examination of the OECD countries with demographic considerations in mind reveals alarming trends. According to UN projections, both the EU and Japanese populations are expected to fall by 15 per cent by 2050 and by 50 per cent by 2150, while the natural population increase of the USA will be accompanied by a rise in the dependency ratio (SOPEMI, 2004, p. 49). In most non-settlement OECD states native women's fertility rate is below the replacement level (2.1 births from one woman). Large influxes of foreigners are needed to balance shrinking native populations and prevent the decline of the resident population. Unfortunately, population decrease goes hand in hand with population ageing. Together, the two demographic characteristics of developed countries create a double demand for immigrant labour and immigrant residents in order to keep the workers–pensioners balance from deteriorating. The inflow of foreigners contributes in two ways to maintaining population growth. It is not only the positive net migration rate of a country that immediately expands the population and labour force, but the higher fertility rate of foreign women also contributes to the natural increase of a national population. Thus, it is only sizable inflows of foreigners that can offset the negative consequences of the decreasing and ageing populations of modern industrialised countries.

In Europe, the size of the resident population would have fallen in Germany since 1986, in Italy since 1993, in Sweden since 1997 without the inflow of new immigrants (SOPEMI, 2004, p. 46). In Germany, 10 per cent of babies are born to immigrant parents. In fact, the only two exceptions are France and Ireland. Both have higher population growing rates than net immigration rates. In other words, in France and Ireland, natural population increase is due to positive net immigration inflows to a lesser extent and to the higher fertility rates of native women to a greater extent. The case is similar in

Table 7.10 Net migration (for 1000 inhabitants): annual average

	1991–1995	1996–2000	2001
Canada	6.2	5.2	6.7
Australia	4.0	5.0	5.7
United States	3.5	3.0	3.1
European Economic Area	2.7	1.9	3.0
Japan	−0.11	0.1	0.3

Source: *Trends in International Migration: SOPEMI,* 2004 edition, © OECD 2005

settlement countries. In Australia, Canada, New Zealand and the USA (see Table 7.10), although positive net migration rates contribute to the growth of their population, it is the higher natural fertility rates of residents which mainly account for their population growth rates being consistently higher than those in the EU.

However, demographers and policymakers have to bear in mind that it might be problematic to counterbalance the negative effects of a shrinking and ageing population with increased immigration. First of all, it would require unrealistic increases in foreign inflows. Second, it seems to be impossible to control immigration and emigration by age. Third, there is an apparent tendency for the fertility of immigrant women to fall the longer they reside in the receiving country and thus converge with that of native women. And finally, it needs to be considered that the foreign population also ages and tends to live as long as natives, which may further worsen the dependency ratio in the future.

Social and cultural impact of international migration: asylum seekers

The UNHCR was established to help and protect all uprooted people. It is mandated to lead and coordinate international action to assist refugees, asylum seekers and internally displaced persons fleeing their homes because of violent conflict. They are protected by international law and they have a right to find safe refuge. They are also eligible to receive international aid, to return home or be resettled in another country and to rebuild their lives. The agency tries to safeguard their rights and ensure their well-being.

As Tables 7.11 and 7.12 show, the number of people under UNHCR care is significant. They tend to concentrate in the war-torn parts of the world (Asia and Africa) and in Europe, which on the one hand provides safe shelter for many asylum seekers and on the other has its own civil conflicts on its south-east border.

To limit the discussion to refugees only, by the end of 2003 UNHCR registered approximately 9.7 million refugees. About half of them receive

Table 7.11 Persons of concern to UNHCR in thousands

	2001	2002	2003
Refugees	12,050	10,400	9670
Asylum seekers	940	1 010	995
Returned and resettled refugees	420	2450	1130
Internally displaced persons, stateless and war-affected population	6330	6700	5300
Total	19,800	20,600	17,100

Source: UNHCR, 2003

Table 7.12 Persons of concern to the UNHCR hosted by regions

	2001	2002	2003
In Asia	8820	9380	6190
In Africa	4250	4590	4280
In Europe	4860	4400	4270
In North America	1090	1060	1320
In Latin America & Caribbean	765	1050	960
Oceania	81	70	74

Source: UNHCR, 2003

UNHCR assistance. Since then the refugee population has declined, mainly because of access to durable solutions, in particular to voluntary

repatriation. As Tables 7.13 and 7.14 show, more than 60 per cent of the refugee population is hosted in Africa or in the Middle East, North Africa and central and south Asia. More specifically, it is Pakistan and Iran which host the largest number of displaced persons, most of them being Afghans. In fact, among the top ten main refugee-receiving countries, seven are developing states and only three are developed nations. This confirms that the vast majority of refugees find rescue in neighbouring states – in the first safe haven closest to home. They prefer to return as soon as circumstances permit them to do so, generally when conflicts end and stability is restored. Only a small fraction of the refugees actually find their way to industrialised countries or choose to be repatriated in another country.

Table 7.13 Refugee population (in thousands) by region 2002–2003

Region	2002	2003
Africa	3088	2863
Middle East, North Africa, South West Asia and Central Asia	3363	2915
Europe	2594	2453
Asia and Pacific	902	816
Americas	656	623
Total	10,604	9671

Source: UNHCR, 2004b 2

Although the majority of refugees never reach industrialised countries, those who have managed to reach a developed country still end up being a sizable group. Compared with the rest of OECD countries, it is especially the Western European ones which experience large influxes of asylum seekers originating from various regions of the globe (Table 7.15). Since 1990 more than 5 million asylum seekers have registered in the EU. Germany hosts by far the largest share of these asylum applicants (41 per cent), followed by the UK (16 per cent) and France (9 per cent). According to the rate of asylum seekers per 1000 inhabitants, the ranking of the main receiving EU countries is different. On average, the EU received 14 applicants per 1000 inhabitants, but Sweden (39), Austria (30),

Table 7.14 Top ten refugee hosting and sending countries (in thousands) 2002–2003

Refugee hosting countries	2002	2003
Pakistan[1]	1227	1124
Iran[1]	1306	984
Germany	980	960
Tanzania	689	649
US	485	482
China	297	299
Serbia and Montenegro	354	291
UK	260	276
Saudi Arabia	247	239
Armenia	248	239
Main origin of refugees	**2002**	**2003**
Afghanistan	2510	2136
Sudan	508	606
Burundi	574	531
Congo	424	453
Palestine	428	427
Somalia	432	402
Iraq	422	368
Vietnam	373	363
Liberia	276	353

1. UNHCR figures refer to Afghan refugees living in camps. According to estimations, an additional 1.6 million Afghans live in urban areas in Pakistan and 600,000 in Iran, some of whom are refugees.

Source: UNHCR, 2004b: 3

Belgium (27), the Netherlands (27) and Germany (26) received twice as many (UNHCR, 2004a, pp. 4–5). The UK and Ireland received about as many asylum seekers per capita as the EU average, while France and southern EU countries much fewer.

The number of asylum seekers in OECD countries peaked in the early 1990s (around 890,000 claims a year) due to the crisis in the former Yugoslavia. After that, flows of asylum seekers gradually diminished until 1998 and peaked again at a lower level (around 590,000 applications a year) in 2001. 2003 again saw a drop in

Table 7.15 Asylum seekers in OECD countries: annual average in thousands

Countries	1991–1995	1996–2000	2001
European Economic Area	487	352	430
United States	121	72	63
Central and Eastern Europe	3	17	45
Canada	27	28	42
Australia	10	10	13

Source: SOPEMI, 2004, p. 19

the number of asylum claims, while in the first quarter of 2004 the number of new asylum applications hit the lowest levels for 17 years (UNHCR, 2004a).

Table 7.16 reveals that the UK has been the main asylum-receiving country since 2000. It receives more applications than any other fellow EU country or the USA. In 2003 the UK and the USA received approximately 13 per cent of all claims lodged in the industrialised countries, Germany and France got 11 per cent, whereas Austria, Canada and Sweden received 7 per cent each. 2003 was the first year in which France received more asylum seekers than Germany since the mid-1980s (UNHCR, 2004a, p. 3).

Table 7.17 shows where asylum seekers come from. Those asylum seekers who submitted their refugee claims in one of the OECD countries, in the last two years, tend to have come from Iraq, Serbia-Montenegro, Russia, Turkey, China and Afghanistan.

In practice, the share of foreigners who claim asylum successfully and are granted refugee status is quite low. The total population of refugees is significantly lower than the number of asylum applicants. Although many of the rejected claimants are not allowed to stay, in the absence of immediate readmission or deportation they remain in the host country illegally and try to look for jobs clandestinely.

It is the Western European countries that find it the hardest to deal with the increasing influx of asylum seekers. Their arrival over the last 15 years has transformed them into racially and culturally heterogeneous societies which make many people feel that fundamental socio-politi-

Table 7.16 Inflows of asylum seekers into selected OECD countries (in thousands)

Country	1990	1991	1992	1993	1995	1997	1999	2001	2002	2003
Australia	3.8	17.0	4.1	4.9	7.8	11.1	8.4	13.1	5.7	4.3
Austria	22.8	27.3	16.2	4.7	5.9	6.7	20.1	30.1	37.1	32.3
Belgium	13.0	15.4	17.6	26.4	11.6	11.8	35.8	24.5	18.8	16.9
Canada	36.7	32.3	37.7	21.1	25.0	23.9	30.0	41.6	33.4	31.8
Czech Rep.	1.8	2.0	0.9	2.2	1.4	2.1	7.2	18.1	8.5	11.4
Denmark	5.3	4.6	13.9	16.5	10.1	5.6	7.1	10.3	6.1	4.5
France	54.8	47.4	28.9	27.6	20.4	21.4	30.9	47.3	51.1	51.4
Germany	193.1	256.1	438.2	322.6	127.9	104.4	95.1	88.4	71.1	50.5
Greece	4.1	2.7	2.0	0.8	1.4	4.4	1.5	5.5	5.7	8.1
Hungary				0.7	0.6	1.1	11.5	9.6	6.4	2.4
Ireland	0.1			0.1	0.4	3.9	7.7	10.3	11.6	7.9
Italy	4.7	31.7	2.6	1.3	1.7	19	33.4	13.3	7.3	na
Japan				0.1	0.1	0.2	0.2	0.4	0.3	0.3
Netherlands	21.2	21.6	20.3	35.4	29.3	34.4	42.7	32.6	18.7	13.4
New Zealand		1.2	0.3	0.4	0.7	1.5	1.5	1.6	1.0	0.8
Norway				12.9	1.5	2.3	10.2	14.8	17.5	15.9
Poland				0.8	0.8	3.5	3.1	4.5	5.2	6.9
Portugal	0.1	0.2	0.6	1.7	0.3	0.3	0.3	0.2	0.2	0.1
Slovak Rep.				0.1	0.4	0.7	1.3	8.2	9.7	10.3
Spain	8.6	8.1	11.7	12.6	5.7	5.0	8.4	9.5	6.2	5.7
Sweden	29.4	27.4	84.0	37.6	9.0	9.6	11.2	23.5	33.0	31.3
Switzerland	35.8	41.6	18.0	24.7	17.0	24.0	46.1	20.6	26.2	21.0
UK	38.2	73.4	32.3	28.0	55.0	41.0	91.2	92.0	110.7	61.6
US	73.6	56.3	104.0	144.2	154.5	95.9	42.2	63.2	63.4	60.7

1. Includes the 15 EU member states and Norway and Switzerland, but excludes Lichtenstein and Iceland.
2. Includes Bulgaria, Czech Republic, Hungary, Poland, Romania, Slovakia.
3. Bulgaria, Finland, Luxembourg, Romania, Turkey and the above countries only.

Source: SOPEMI, 2000, p. 305 and SOPEMI, 2004, p. 19

cal institutions, national identity or traditional culture and values are being threatened. In addition, increasing numbers of people believe that the majority of asylum claimants are not genuine refugees but are economic migrants, illegal workers, criminals or terrorists, who abuse the welfare system and pose a threat to the host country's social stability and national security. The xenophobic backlash in politics has gained considerable ground since the mid-1990s. From the electoral success of Jörg Haider in Austria to Jean-Marie Le Pen's second place during the last presidential race in France, the emergence of extreme-right anti-immigrant political parties has become widespread in many EU countries.

The challenge of integrating foreigners creates a complex task for mainstream Western European governments and has prompted them

Table 7.17 Origin and size (in thousands) of asylum applicants in OECD countries[1] 2002–2003

Origin	2002	2003	Origin	2002	2003
Iraq	49.4	24.7	Nigeria	13.3	13.1
Serbia and Montenegro	32.1	24.8	Somalia	12.6	13.5
Russia	19.9	33.4	Iran	11.6	11.9
Turkey	29.1	22.9	Congo	13.1	10.1
China	26.3	21.3	Pakistan	10.1	11.0
Afghanistan	25.4	13.8	Colombia	12.4	6.8
India	14.9	13.5	Mexico	10.7	5.5

1. Excluding Iceland, Italy, Korea, Mexico and Turkey, including Bulgaria.

Source: UNHCR, 2004a

to take threefold policy measures. First, they try to find ways to bring immigrants into the workforce and lower their above-average unemployment. Second, they seek to ease the clashes of cultures and values by opening dialogues among different social and racial groups in order to break down barriers, to isolate far-right parties and to pursue secular public policies against segregation. Third, they have tightened border controls, expanded the number of countries subject to visa requirements, harmonised their asylum policies to avoid 'asylum shopping' and started to crack down and deport illegal migrants. They have also rejected asylum applicants in order to regain control over immigration inflows.

Despite these efforts social anxieties about refugees have not disappeared and neither have governments been able to disentangle humanitarian concerns for refugees from finding the best way of implementing tough immigration controls. The latest ideas concerning the treatment of refugees, emerging in wealthy industrialised countries, range from the administrative separation of certain islands for immigration purposes, as Australia intended to do, to the setting up of special asylum camps at the outer perimeter of the EU to host applicants while they wait for the processing of their claims (*The Economist*, 2003a, 2003b) and most recently (2004) creating immigrant holding centres in North Africa.

The Geneva Refugee Convention, which is the basis of the international asylum system, was drafted shortly after the Second World War, when the memories of the shameful treatment of refugees from Nazi Germany were still fresh.

Nobody foresaw that 50 years later there would be asylum applications from tens of thousands of people, who would turn up claiming persecution in their countries of origin or fleeing from civil conflict and poverty, having destroyed their identities in many cases and having been smuggled in by traffickers for large sums of monies. These have overwhelmed and paralysed asylum procedures in destination countries. Although experts agree that the current international asylum system is in crisis, how to remedy the situation remains in sharp dispute.

Conclusion

Since immigration is the most effective way to ease labour shortages, relieve other demographic problems and encourage economic growth, it is highly unlikely that forward-looking industrialised countries will decrease the number of admissions in the long run. It seems obvious that a long-term immigration policy needs to be much better controlled and needs to be able to respond to multiple challenges in various domains of public policy. So far it is still unclear how to target effectively the economic and demographic needs of the host country while addressing successfully the socio-cultural concerns of the general public as well. Ideally, immigration policies will come to be a result of cooperation between the sending and the receiving countries.

To date, no country claims to be able to come up with even one comfortable solution to the increasingly complex problem of migration, a solution which will be capable of smoothing out all the conflicting interests attached to the inflow and outflow of people. In practice, labour-importing countries follow selective immigration policies. On the one hand they tend to allow the entry of highly skilled and specialised labour and abide by family reunification rules as one of the basic human rights. On the other, they try to keep their borders shut against the influx of unskilled labour or people from poor countries and crack down on traffickers in humans.

Besides this kind of 'fine tuning' of the permeability of their borders, they also tend to focus on the legalisation of clandestine labour in order to transform these workers into tax-paying residents eligible for certain welfare benefits and carry out proactive assimilation policies by offering language courses and subsidised retraining programmes. In many cases the integration of foreigners into the majority society has been unproblematic and has contributed to the cultural diversity of the receiving country, but in other cases, some of the cultural, social and racial issues have been exploited in election campaigns. It is also very important that the receiving country cooperates with the sending country on managing human flows. Special programmes could be set up to reduce the incentives to leave by improving economic, political and human rights conditions in the origin countries.

Although many small steps have been taken to administer the flows of people to the satisfaction of both the host and the sending countries, an all-encompassing good solution to international migration seems very far away.

Further Reading

Browne, Anthony (2003) 'Cost of the Migration Revolution', *The Times,* 1 March, p. 52.

Ellerman, David (2003) 'Policy Research on Migration and Development', *Policy Research Working Paper 3117,* Washington, DC: The World Bank.

IDB (2004) *Latin American Immigrants in the United States to Send $30 Billion to Homelands in 2004.* Multilateral Investment Fund, Inter-American Development Bank. Washington, DC, www.iadb.org/NEWS/Display/PRView.cfm?PR_Num=98_04&Language=English accessed at 09/20/2004.

International Organisation of Migration (2004)

World Migration Report, Geneva: International Organisation of Migration.

Ratha, Dilip (2004) 'Workers' Remittances: An Important and Stable Source of External Development Finance' in *Global Development Finance. Striving for Stability in Development Finance: Annual Report 2003,* Washington, DC: The World Bank, Chapter 7, pp.157–175, www.worldbank.org/prospects/gdf2003 – accessed 20 September 2004.

SOPEMI (2000) *Trends in International Migration,* Organisation for Economic Co-operation and Development (OECD), Continuing Reporting System on Migration (SOPEMI), Paris.

—— (2004) *Trends in International Migration,* OECD, SOPEMI. Paris.

The Economist (2003a) 'A Strange Sort of Sanctuary', vol. 366, Issue 8315, p. 50.

— (2003b) 'Unwanted: Australia,' vol. 369, Issue 8351, p. 75.

UNHCR (2003) *Refugees by Numbers: 2003 Edition,* Geneva: Media Relations and Public Service, United Nations High Commissioner for Refugees.

UNHCR (2004a) *Asylum Levels and Trends: Europe and Non-European Industrialised Countries, 2003.* Geneva: Population Data Unit, Division of Operational Support, United Nations High Commissioner for Refugees. www.unhcr.ch/cgi-bin/texis/vtx/home/opendoc.pdf?tbl=STATITSTICS&id=403b1d7e4&page=statistics – accessed 20 September 2004.

UNHCR (2004b) *Global Refugee Trends: Overview of Refugee Population, New Arrivals, Durable Solutions, Asylum Seekers and Other Persons of Concerns to UNHCR.* Geneva: Population Data Unit, Division of Operational Support, United Nations High Commissioner for Refugees. http://www.unhcr.ch/cgi-bin/texis/vtx/home/opendoc.pdf?tbl=STATITSTICS&id=40d015fb4&page=statistics – accessed 20 September 2004.

UNPD (2004) *Trends in Total Migrant Stock: The 2003 Revision.* New York: United Nations Population Division, Department of Economic and Social Affairs of the United Nations Secretariat. www.un.org/esa/population/unpop.htm – accessed 20 September 2004.

CHAPTER 8: Trade and investment

This chapter describes two crucial elements in the machinery of interaction in global politics, namely trade and foreign investment. In describing the current international trading system, the recent disputes over US steel tariffs can serve as a window into the politics of trade policy in an environment where international institutional arrangements, such as the World Trade Organisation and the various bilateral and multilateral trade agreements, coexist with and sometimes contradict domestic political pressure for protection of particular national interests.

The 'logic' of trade liberalisation comes to the fore as well as the recent policy convergence in this direction in many countries. Moreover, in analysing foreign investment today, different forms of investment are described along with patterns of foreign direct and portfolio investments and their consequences.

The international trading system: negotiating integration and its consequences

The 1980s and 1990s saw the re-emergence of fervent enthusiasm in academic and policymaking circles for the unequivocal benefits of 'free trade'. It is important, however, to make it clear from the start that what was being suggested – and was later widely implemented at many levels – was not truly free trade and never became such. It meant the opening of markets, freeing them from imposed restrictions such as import tariffs, and a series of non-tariff barriers to incoming goods from competing economies, such as quotas, regulatory barriers, subsidies and exchange controls.

In fact, 'free trade' is an economic conceptual tool. The broadly accepted idea that fewer restrictions on trade were beneficial for most countries and represented a key to economic growth did not dissipate the many evident political incentives to cave in to interest group pressures, even when they appealed to tactical electoral agendas.

US/WTO Steel Tariff Dispute 2002

A case in point has been the recent dispute over the increase in tariffs on imported steel to the USA. The World Trade Organisation ruled that US steel safeguards imposed in March 2002 were illegal. Formally, 'a WTO member may take a "safeguard" action (i.e., restrict imports of a product temporarily) in order to protect a specific domestic industry from an increase in imports of any product which is causing, or which is threatening to cause, serious injury to the industry' (www.wto.org). As widely reported in the media, the US government's imposition of tariffs on imported steel created strong international objections, as it 'sowed doubts around the world about whether the US can do what it is asking of other countries – make politically difficult decisions at home to advance the prospects of trade abroad' (*Financial Times*, 5 December 2003).

By protecting the US steel industry the government was making a clear political decision, much as might be expected in the behaviour of a politician, whose main goal is – inevitably – to enhance his or her chances of re-election. Yet economics and politics are often dissonant realms and have their own restricting rationales. Tariffs from an economic perspective are not economically efficient, and from the point of view of political economy (or history for that matter) are dangerous triggers of what can become a spill-over effect of protectionism on the world scale. The fact that this is less likely to happen today than in the past speaks volumes about the changes that the establishment of an institution such as the WTO has brought to international trade policy and the reality of global diplomatic/commercial relations.

A full explanation of the underlying issues involving the dispute over steel tariffs demands a theoretical analysis of the logic behind the support for 'free trade', as well as an understanding of the institutional framework created since the Bretton Woods meetings to back up an opening of markets at the global level.

The theoretical foundations of 'free trade' and their policy implications

Following Adam Smith (1776) and David Ricardo (1817), economists have long been proclaiming the advantages of 'free trade' to economic growth. More recently, the works of Mundell on the model of capital mobility under fixed exchange rates and that of Friedman on the advantages of deregulation and market orientation moved beyond the ivory towers of academia to gain policy resonance in the 1980s. In the race towards liberalisation that these theoretical works stirred up (especially in the last two decades), trade openness was a factor.

The main theoretical insight of the 'free trade' theory is the concept of comparative advantage developed early on by Ricardo, who qualified Smith's notion of absolute advantages. Ricardo formalised the idea using a simple numerical example in his book *On the Principles of Political Economy and Taxation*, published in 1817. Comparative advantage appeared again in James Mill's 1821 book entitled *Elements of Political Economy*. Finally, comparative advantage became a key concept in the study of international political economy on the publication of John Stuart Mill's *Principles of Political Economy* (1848).

The concept of comparative advantage is that every country could benefit from unrestricted trade if each specialised in the production of goods produced at reduced costs in relation to other countries. Put differently, to benefit from specialisation and free trade, country A should specialise and trade the good in which it is 'most best' at producing, while its trade partner, country B, should specialise and trade the good in which it is 'least worst' at producing. What are the implications of such a theory?

Concept of comparative advantage

First, the notion of comparative advantage tells us that even when one country is technologically superior to its trade partner (say, the USA in relation to Mexico) in all industries in which the goods traded are produced, one of these industries would go out of business when opening to free trade. This would be the case, for example, for labour industries in the USA compared with the same industries in Mexico. Thus, it is important to note that the logic of the advantages of 'free trade' is thought to be so widespread because they are *comparative* advantages. Hence, technological superiority is not enough to guarantee continued production of a good in free trade; a country must have a comparative advantage in the production of that good to justify producing it domestically rather than importing it from abroad in an open-trade system. In this sense, countries with different endowments in labour, land and capital can all have a place in an open system given that they develop slightly differentiated comparative advantages, which make the trading among them – at least in theory – beneficial to all.

From the perspective of a less developed country (LDC), the developed country's superior technology need not imply that LDC industries cannot compete in international markets. LDCs might not have an absolute advantage in producing industrial goods in relation to developed countries, but they still have a comparative advantage in the production of certain goods, which makes commercial exchange with other countries beneficial.

Secondly, the theory of comparative advantage shows that, from the perspective of a developed country, freer trade may not result in a domestic industry's decline just because foreign firms pay their workers lower wages. Here again the example of the interactions between Mexico and the USA is relevant. This interaction exists because even if labour may indeed be cheaper in Mexico, specialisation and trade between these countries increases the set of consumption possibilities in both, compared with those available if no trade was taking place. In this sense, both exports and imports increase. These are what economists call 'aggregate gains' and are often described as improvements in production and consumption efficiency of an economy. It is in this sense that 'free trade' is thought to raise aggregate world production efficiency. In addition, theoretically, 'free trade' also improves aggregate consumption efficiency. So, following the USA/Mexico example, when economies are open to trade flows, consumers in both the USA and Mexico have a more varied set of choices of products and prices available to them.

The Heckscher-Ohlin Theorem

To this rosy theoretical scenario another key piece was added with the famous Heckscher-Ohlin Theorem, which stated that a capital-abundant country will export capital-intensive goods while the labour-abundant country will export labour-intensive goods.

Why does this matter? A capital-abundant country is one that is well endowed with capital relative to the other country. A labour-abundant country is one that is well endowed with labour in relative terms. Suppose a system with two countries, one that is labour abundant (as, for example, Mexico) and another that is capital abundant (for example, the USA). This gives the USA a propensity for producing the good which uses relatively more capital in the production process, as for example computers. The same reasoning works for Mexico, which benefits from specialising in the production of labour-intensive goods, for example garments. As a result, the price of the capital-intensive good in the capital-abundant country is low (given the vast supply) relative to the price of the good in the other country. Similarly, in the labour-abundant country the price of the labour-intensive good is low in comparison with the price of that good in the capital-abundant country.

When countries start to trade with one another, profit-seeking firms will move their products to the markets that temporarily have the higher price. So the capital-abundant country will export the capital-intensive good since the price will be temporarily higher in the other country and the same logic will apply to the labour-abundant country. Thus the idea of how beneficial open trade is for different economies is confirmed. Countries with different resource endowments may trade in mutually beneficial terms, allowing for consumers to enjoy more varied and lower-priced goods in open economies than in those where international trade is restricted.

At the policy level, these ideas became more persuasive as history and political interests converged to show that a move towards economic liberalisation was a key step in the direction of economic development.

Policy-level consequences

A good number of studies of the 1980s' debt crisis in Latin America compared the apparently 'miraculous' success that prevailed in East Asian countries with the stagnation in Latin America. The culprit was readily detected: lack of a trade (export-oriented) strategy. In *Pathways From the Periphery*, for example, Haggard argued that with the exception of Hong Kong, the East Asian newly industrialised countries all improved their relative income distributions immediately following the transition to export-led growth. In his words, 'widening wage disparities between traditional and modern sectors were offset by narrowing wage differentials within the manufacturing sector. This observation can be attributed to the development strategy that provided incentives to the use of unskilled and semiskilled labour' (Haggard, 1990, p. 232).

Inevitably, the systematic comparisons between Latin American and East Asian countries by the end of the 1980s served the purpose of proclaiming that the way out of the chaotic situation Latin American countries faced needed to include an export-based strategy. But for countries to increase their exports, national reorientation was needed; and they had to commit to opening their borders to the importation of products from those which could become their potential trade partners. That explains why export growth policies were accompanied by an even more aggressive policy leading towards the reduction of trade barriers, such as import taxes and quotas.

There were also many contemporary studies developed by economists emphasising the positive impact that free trade had on growth. Theoretically this assumption turned into one of the powerful conundrums of neoliberalism. However, much less attention was given to the study of the relationship between growth and income distribution. Therefore, although it was argued that, technically, trade would lead to growth, it was seldom tested whether growth would lead to development in the form of better income distribution and rising levels of literacy and healthcare.

Emerging doubts about free market policies

By 1994, the influential economist Paul Krugman was pointing out that 'empirical evidence for huge gains from free market policies is, at best, fuzzy' (Krugman, 1995, p. 32). Indeed, Krugman challenged the notion that free trade necessarily leads to growth. He suggested that the 'widespread belief that moving to free trade and free markets will produce a dramatic acceleration in a developing country's growth represents a leap of faith, rather than a conclusion based on hard evidence' (Krugman, 1995, p. 33).

Empirical studies began to confirm this idea. Many studies linking trade reform to long-run growth turned out to be surprisingly fragile. In developing countries, evidence was found of only a small impact of trade reform on employment. In fact, most countries suffered recession after structural adjustment, which led to increased unemployment. In Mexico, for example, inequality rose after the market reform, a truly puzzling outcome considering that Mexico has a comparative advantage in producing low skill-intensive goods.

Recently, an even more striking finding has been revealed. A newly released report published by the Carnegie Endowment for International Peace concludes that NAFTA has not helped the Mexican economy keep pace with the growing demand on jobs. Furthermore, 'unprecedented productivity, and a surge in both portfolio and foreign direct investment have led to an increase of 50,000 jobs in manufacturing from 1994 to 2002'. However, 'the agricultural sector, where almost a fifth of Mexicans still work, has lost 1.3 million jobs since 1994' (Audley et al., 2003, p. 5).

As for real wages, most Mexicans saw them shrink from the levels in the period that preceded NAFTA. Hence, productivity growth was not translated into wage gains. And although economic theory would have predicted a converging trend between Mexican and US wages, that is not empirically proven in this case. The report thus shows that 'while NAFTA's overall impact may be muddled, for Mexico's rural households the picture is clear – and bleak'. NAFTA was the basis for the liberalisation of the Mexican economy, yet it failed to 'create the conditions that would have allowed public and private sectors to adapt to the great challenge of becoming a preferential trade partner of "two of the largest economies in the world"' (Audley et al., 2003, p. 5).

Hence, despite the euphoria surrounding trade liberalisation, it is important to keep in mind that the benefits of trade in terms of improving domestic welfare are not an automatic consequence of 'free trade'. A fair question to be asked is, then, if trade agreements that allow for the intensification of commercial relations are not necessarily welfare improving for countries which abide by them, what makes for cooperation on this front?

Although a detailed analysis of the issue is beyond the scope of this chapter, it seems of interest to point to the work of Gruber on the 'shifting status quo' dilemma. As this scholar suggests, the fact that 'membership in a cooperative arrangement is voluntary does not mean that that arrangement necessarily works to everyone's advantage' (Gruber, 2000, p. xiii). Even though some countries may not become better off from cooperating in international arrangements, they will voluntarily try to engage in them because they will certainly be worse off should they not. According to this logic, Mexico's engagement with NAFTA was not prompted by unequivocal evidence of the gains to be enjoyed from the deal but the acknowledgement that Mexico would be worse off if the USA maintained preferential commercial relations with Canada alone under the US-Canada Free Trade Agreement of 1989 (Gruber, 2000).

However, it is important to emphasise that even though the evidence that trade openness is translated into reduced inequality is unimpressive, it is hard to believe that economies that had maintained their strict trade restrictions would have fared better in fostering employment, attracting investments and enhancing domestic welfare. History tells us that such chances would have been slim, if they existed at all.

The institutional framework of global trade

At the institutional level, global trade has relied on a framework for the governance of commercial interactions that was built from the General Agreement on Tariffs and Trade – a product of the 1946 Bretton Woods meetings and created as the organisation overseeing the multilateral trading system. The agreement was designed to provide an international forum that encouraged free trade between member states by regulating and reducing tariffs on traded goods and by providing a common mechanism for resolving trade disputes.

Table 8.1 WTO's 148 members (as of January 2005) with dates of membership

Country	Date of Membership	Country	Date of Membership
Albania	8-Sep-00	Cuba	20-Apr-95
Angola	23-Nov-96	Cyprus	30-Jul-95
Antigua and Barbuda	1-Jan-95	Czech Republic	1-Jan-95
Argentina	1-Jan-95	Democratic Republic of the Congo	1-Jan-97
Armenia	5-Feb-03	Denmark	1-Jan-95
Australia	1-Jan-95	Djibouti	31-May-95
Austria	1-Jan-95	Dominica	1-Jan-95
Bahrain, Kingdom of	1-Jan-95	Dominican Republic	9-Mar-95
Bangladesh	1-Jan-95	Ecuador	21-Jan-96
Barbados	1-Jan-95	Egypt	30-Jun-95
Belgium	1-Jan-95	El Salvador	7-May-95
Belise	1-Jan-95	Estonia	13-Nov-99
Benin	22-Feb-96	European Communities	1-Jan-95
Bolivia	12-Sep-95	Fiji	14-Jan-96
Botswana	31-May-95	Finland	1-Jan-95
Brazil	1-Jan-95	Former Yugoslav Republic of Macedonia (FYROM)	4-Apr-03
Brunei Darussalam	1-Jan-95	France	1-Jan-95
Bulgaria	1-Dec-96	Gabon	1-Jan-95
Burkina Faso	3-Jun-95	Gambia	23-Oct-96
Burundi	23-Jul-95	Georgia	14-Jun-00
Cambodia	13-Oct-04	Germany	1-Jan-95
Cameroon	13-Dec-95	Ghana	1-Jan-95
Canada	1-Jan-95	Greece	1-Jan-95
Central African Republic	31-May-95	Grenada	22-Feb-96
Chad	19-Oct-96	Guatemala	21-Jul-95
Chile	1-Jan-95	Guinea	25-Oct-95
China	11-Dec-01	Guinea Bissau	31-May-95
Colombia	30-Apr-95	Guyana	1-Jan-95
Congo	27-Mar-97	Haiti	30-Jan-96
Costa Rica	1-Jan-95	Honduras	1-Jan-95
Côte d'Ivoire	1-Jan-95	Hong Kong, China	1-Jan-95
Croatia	30-Nov-00		

(continued)

Country	Date of Membership	Country	Date of Membership
Hungary	1-Jan-95	Myanmar	1-Jan-95
Iceland	1-Jan-95	Namibia	1-Jan-95
India	1-Jan-95	Nepal	23-Apr-04
Indonesia	1-Jan-95	Netherlands – For the Kingdom in Europe and for the Netherlands Antilles	1-Jan-95
Ireland	1-Jan-95		
Israel	21-Apr-95	New Zealand	1-Jan-95
Italy	1-Jan-95	Nicaragua	3-Sep-95
Jamaica	9-Mar-95	Niger	13-Dec-96
Japan	1-Jan-95	Nigeria	1-Jan-95
Jordan	11-Apr-00	Norway	1-Jan-95
Kenya	1-Jan-95	Oman	9-Nov-00
Korea, Republic of	1-Jan-95	Pakistan	1-Jan-95
Kuwait	1-Jan-95	Panama	6-Sep-97
Kyrgyz Republic	20-Dec-98	Papua New Guinea	9-Jun-96
Latvia	10-Feb-99	Paraguay	1-Jan-95
Lesotho	31-May-95	Peru	1-Jan-95
Liechtenstein	1-Sep-95	Philippines	1-Jan-95
Lithuania	31-May-01	Poland	1-Jul-95
Luxembourg	1-Jan-95	Portugal	1-Jan-95
Macao, China	1-Jan-95	Qatar	13-Jan-96
Madagascar	17-Nov-95	Romania	1-Jan-95
Malawi	31-May-95	Rwanda	22-May-96
Malaysia	1-Jan-95	Saint Kitts and Nevis	21-Feb-96
Maldives	31-May-95	Saint Lucia	1-Jan-95
Mali	31-May-95	Saint Vincent & the Grenadines	1-Jan-95
Malta	1-Jan-95	Senegal	1-Jan-95
Mauritania	31-May-95	Sierra Leone	23-Jul-95
Mauritius	1-Jan-95	Singapore	1-Jan-95
Mexico	1-Jan-95	Slovak Republic	1-Jan-95
Moldova	26-Jul-01	Slovenia	30-Jul-95
Mongolia	29-Jan-97	Solomon Islands	26-Jul-96
Morocco	1-Jan-95	South Africa	1-Jan-95
Mozambique	26-Aug-95	Spain	1-Jan-95

(continued)

Country	Date of Membership	Country	Date of Membership
Sri Lanka	1-Jan-95	Tunisia	29-Mar-95
Suriname	1-Jan-95	Turkey	26-Mar-95
Swaziland	1-Jan-95	Uganda	1-Jan-95
Sweden	1-Jan-95	United Arab Emirates	10-Apr-96
Switzerland	1-Jul-95	United Kingdom	1-Jan-95
Chinese Taipei	1-Jan-02	United States of America	1-Jan-95
Tanzania	1-Jan-95	Uruguay	1-Jan-95
Thailand	1-Jan-95	Venezuela	1-Jan-95
Togo	31-May-95	Zambia	1-Jan-95
Trinidad and Tobago	1-Mar-95	Zimbabwe	5-Mar-99

Source: www.wto.org

On 1 January 1995, the World Trade Organisation was created to replace GATT. The governments that had signed GATT were officially known as 'GATT contracting parties'. Upon signing the new WTO agreements (which included the updated GATT, known as GATT 1994), the 128 GATT signatories officially became known as 'WTO members'. On 1 January 2005, these members totalled 148 countries – see Table 8.1 (a full list can be found at:

www.wto.org/english/thewto_e/whatis_e/tif_e/org6_e.htm

The WTO was a product of the Uruguay Round and represented the combination of the GATT agreement of 1994, which replaced the pre-existing GATT of 1947, 12 separate agreements pertaining to trade in goods, the General Agreement on Trade and Services (GATS), and the new rules for intellectual property protection – the Agreement on Trade-Related Aspects

Table 8.2 GATT trade rounds

Year	Place/name	Subjects covered	Countries
1947	Geneva	Tariffs	23
1949	Annecy	Tariffs	13
1951	Torquay	Tariffs	38
1956	Geneva	Tariffs	26
1960–1961	Geneva Dillon Round	Tariffs	26
1964–1967	Geneva Kennedy Round	Tariffs and anti-dumping measures	62
1973–1979	Geneva Tokyo Round	Tariffs, non-tariff measures, 'framework' agreements	102
1986–1994	Geneva Uruguay Round	Tariffs, non-tariff measures, rules, services, intellectual property, dispute settlement, textiles, agriculture, creation of WTO, etc	123

Source: www.wto.org

Table 8.3 From the Uruguay Round to the WTO – key dates

Date	Location	Outcome
Sep-86	Punta del Este	Launch
Dec-88	Montreal	Ministerial mid-term review
Apr-89	Geneva	Mid-term review completed
Dec-90	Brussels	'Closing' ministerial meeting ends in deadlock
Dec-91	Geneva	First draft of Final Act completed
Nov-92	Washington	USA and EC achieve 'Blair House' breakthrough on agriculture
Jul-93	Tokyo	Quad achieve market access breakthrough at G-7 summit
Dec-93	Geneva	Most negotiations end (some market access talks remain)
Apr-94	Marrakesh	Agreements signed
Jan-95	Geneva	WTO created, agreements take effect

Source: www.wto.org

of Intellectual Property Rights (TRIPs). Since all these agreements function under the WTO umbrella, they are subject to the same, consolidated dispute settlement.

With this essential reform, the WTO remedied flaws in its predecessor. With the new dispute settlement, long delays in starting and completing panel proceedings are avoided, the ability of disputants to block the consensus needed to approve panel findings and authorise retaliation is constrained, and the difficulty in securing compliance with panel ruling is reduced. Indeed, 'WTO procedures now operate under strict time limits; countries cannot veto judgments against them; panel findings are subject to review by a new Appellate Body; and procedures are in place to promote timely compliance, to monitor compliance actions, and to allow retaliation in the event of non-compliance' (Schott, 1996, p. 4).

Since its inception, the WTO's dispute settlement mechanism has been greatly used, allowing for trade disputes to be monitored under a homogenising legal framework that is at the heart of today's global trading system. When it comes to the issue of trade safeguards mentioned briefly above, these measures for the temporary protection of a particular domestic industry suffering substantial losses from competing imports were always available under the GATT (Article XIX), albeit infrequently used. Governments preferred to protect their industries through measures such as 'voluntary' export restraint arrangements on products such

as cars, steel and semiconductors, as was the case in several Japan–USA negotiations.

The WTO Safeguards Agreement broke new ground in prohibiting such 'grey area' measures (as they are called) and setting a time limit ('sunset clause') on all safeguard actions. That means that although the system allows for protectionist measures in extreme cases, these have to be well justified, short term and – from the point of view of the tariff-imposing country – politically worth the economic troubles that retaliatory action may induce. These issues are clear in the case of the now abandoned 2003 US tariffs on steel, for example.

The steel dispute: trade theory, policy and reality

In the case of the steel dispute, the 30 per cent tariff increase imposed by the US government on imported steel sparked a wave of muscular retaliation on the part of US trade partners all over the globe. The tariffs were imposed by the Bush administration in March 2002. On 2 December 2003, the European Union drew up a list of US exports worth $2.2 billion annually for potential countermeasures designed to maximise 'the political pain' for the US government (clearly seeking re-election in 2004). Also, Japan notified the WTO in late November about a list of 'rebalancing' tariffs of up to 30 per cent it would be willing to impose on US products – not only steel products but also plastics and coal. At the same time, Norway announced that it would join the EU in imposing sanctions and that '30 per cent would be levied on US goods ranging from iron and steel products to clothes, wine, apples, and hunting and target shooting rifles'. More mildly, China joined the chorus, as did Brazil, South Korea and New Zealand (*Financial Times*, 28 November 2003).

These pressures produced a significant reaction. On 4 December 2003, the US trade representative announced that the government was dropping its tariffs on steel. Arguing that the measure had generated the intended results in reinvigorating the steel industry, the US government decided to prevent major retaliation from abroad which might have produced economically detrimental results that would (in time) have impacted on the government's electoral ambitions.

The example of the steel tariffs – one among many of the kind – reveals interesting insights. It shows clearly that economic and political incentives are often running on different tracks and that trade policy unequivocally challenges policymakers to position themselves on a tenuous line. On one side lie domestic, mostly electoral, interests and on the other economic and, in this case, international diplomatic coherence. Although it is clear that trade is anything but truly free today, the existence of a framework that allows for dispute settlements – the monitoring and eventual punishment of violations to homogenising rules, applying to all members of the WTO – enables some checks and balances to curtail 'raw short-sighted politics' from undermining crucial international order in economic affairs (Krugman, 2002).

Investment in the global economy

Booms and busts in the world economy are followed by cycles of increased lending or credit restrictions. In a time of globalisation, fresh opportunities are available for investments which also acquire new forms, especially in sophisticated financial markets where the number of financial instruments has diversified considerably in the last 20 years. In this section, investment is deconstructed and defined in its several forms. Then, changes in cycles of foreign direct and portfolio investments are described and their repercussions mentioned, especially when it comes to developing countries whose reliance on foreign (mostly private) capital grew considerably in the 1990s, hence increasing their exposure to external, recurrent crises, as discussed in Part C, Chapter 3.

Foreign investment can be of a number of types, from investment that implies a long-term relationship with the host country (such as in the case of the acquisition of a domestic company by a foreign firm) to investment that is short term and highly volatile, as in the case of the purchase of bonds of sovereign debt from a developing or developed country by a foreign investor who will sell the instrument when its returns start to decrease or when there is an expectation that such a fall will happen. The following box describes the types of foreign investment most commonly referred to in the literature of global politics and political economy.

Table 8.4 shows net private capital flows to emerging markets in the turbulent period from 1997 to 2000, which was plagued by the Asian crisis of 1997 and the Russian crisis of 1998. Table 8.4 also gives us a clear idea about how devastating the late 1990s' crises were for developing countries in terms of severe drops in capital inflows – a piece of evidence which adds much to the picture described in the section on the global financial crisis. There was a sharp decrease in bank loans to emerging markets, especially in comparison to recuperating portfolio investment inflows and consistent level of FDI

Table 8.4 Net private capital flows to emerging markets, 1997–2000 (in billion US dollars)

	1997	1998	1999	2000
Total net private capital inflows	126.1	45.3	71.5	32.2
Bank loans and Others	−62.1	−127.2	−135.6	172.1
Net portfolio investment	43.3	23.8	53.7	58.3
Net FDI	144.9	148.7	153.4	146

Source: Lehmann, 2002

inflows. Indeed, after the Latin American debt crisis of the early 1980s, when many countries defaulted or 'quasi-defaulted' on their debts to creditors which were chiefly commercial banks, credit to developing countries – when finally resumed in the late 1980s – came in the form of the purchase of bonds (by domestic and private investors) of sovereign debt.

Although there is no conclusive evidence indicating that capital flows promote economic growth, capital flows can *enforce* the growth process in an economy. The liberalisation of capital flows – however restricted in some cases – which took place in most of the world in the late 1980s and 1990s followed the theoretical premise that capital moved from countries where it is abundant to countries where it is limited, since the returns on new investment opportunities are higher where capital is more scarce. Although economic theory would go on to assert that 'the

returns to capital decrease as more machinery is installed and new structures are built (…), in practice this is not always or even generally true' (Mishra, Mody and Murshid, 2001, p. 2).

In fact, capital does not necessarily flow from rich to poor countries more than it flows within rich countries since new investment is more productive in places with a skilled workforce and well-developed physical infrastructure (Lucas, 1990 – cited in Mishra et al., 2001). Hence, increases in capital flows need to be analysed with these ideas in mind, as liberalisation of flows does not necessarily lead to their equal distribution. So far, capital liberalisation has been more evidently linked to systemic financial crises than to substantial economic benefits on a global scale.

Since different dynamics determine flows of foreign direct investment and portfolio investment, they are described separately in further detail below.

Foreign direct investment (FDI)

Significant changes in FDI are intimately linked to periods of boom and bust in the world economy. Table 8.5 shows the correlation between significant FDI inflows downturn and the corresponding world recessionary business cycle.

In the 1980s, FDI became ever more oriented to developed countries. Although up to 1979 the USA was the leading exporter of FDI, by 1981 it had become the leading recipient and had been replaced by the UK as the leading exporter of this type of investment.

In fact, FDI stock in the USA increased from $83 billion in 1980 to $328 billion in 1988. This trend further increased in 1997 when FDI stock in the USA reached a peak of $1.8 trillion, with the EU and Japan as top investors. Indeed, Japan became a leading exporter of FDI by 1985 with a gross outflow of $12.2 billion, which tripled to reach the $33 billion registered in 1987. Moreover, during the 1990s two predominant trends were noticed regarding FDIs – namely, the predominance of investment in the service sector and the proliferation of mergers and acquisitions (M&As) by multinational firms.

The composition of FDI flows has changed over time. From the 1950s FDI from developed to developing countries was largely concentrated in raw materials, other primary products and resource-based manufacturing. Since the 1980s, however, FDI in technology-intensive manufacturing and especially in services has become the fastest-growing component of overall FDI flows, or about 40 per cent of the world's total FDI stock of $700 billion, compared with about 25 per cent in the early 1970s and less than 20 per cent in the early 1950s. This trend only intensified in the 1990s, when more than half of all FDI was in services, with about two-thirds of this in finance and trade-related activities. By 1999, over 60 per cent of the $4.1 trillion stock of FDI was in services (Sassen, 2001, p. 37).

Mergers and acquisitions

Moreover, an especially important pattern in FDI flows in the late 1990s was the growth in cross-border mergers and acquisitions, which now play a predominant role in foreign investment totals. Table 8.6 shows that in the two years from 1995 to 1997, M&A deals with values above $1 billion almost doubled from 36 to 64. In 2000 this number peaked to 175 deals, only to fall in 2001 by 48 per cent, and it decreased further – by 38 per cent – in 2002. However, this down-

Why do mergers and acquisitions take place?

According to the economic theory of asset pricing, the price of a share is supposed to be the same as the present value of future cash flows. This is to say, if a potential owner of a firm sees the future cash flows of that firm or the rate at which those flows can be discounted as higher than the present owners, and then makes an offer above the net present value the current owners would obtain if they kept ownership, a merger or acquisition takes place. Hence, ownership changes happen 'when the new owners of a firm feel they can extract larger net present value than the current ones can'.

The difference is due to 'superior technology, management systems or market access that can make one owner capable of extracting more value out of a firm than its current owner extracts' (Hausmann, 2000, p. 20).

Table 8.5 The four major downturns in FDI inflows since 1970 and their correlation to bust periods in the world economy

Time period	Change in FDI flows	Correspondent 'bust event'
1976	Decrease of 21 per cent	The oil crises
1982–1983	Decrease of 14 per cent a year on average	The increase in US interest rates followed by the Latin America debt crisis of the 1980s
1991	Decrease of 24 per cent	World recession fuelled by the US recession
2001–2002	Decrease of 31 per cent a year on average	Downturn in stock markets (especially regarding the general drop in technology stocks) and recessionary turn in the US economy

Table 8.6 Cross-border M&As with values of over $1 billion, 1987–2002

Year	# of deals	% of total	Value (US$ billion)	% of total
1987	14	1.6	30.0	40.3
1988	22	1.5	49.6	42.9
1989	26	1.2	59.5	42.4
1990	33	1.3	60.9	40.4
1991	7	0.2	20.4	25.2
1992	10	0.4	21.3	26.8
1993	14	0.5	23.5	28.3
1994	24	0.7	50.9	40.1
1995	36	0.8	80.4	43.1
1996	43	0.9	94.0	41.4
1997	64	1.3	129.2	42.4
1998	86	1.5	329.7	62.0
1999	114	1.6	522.0	68.1
2000	175	2.2	866.2	75.7
2001	113	1.9	378.1	63.7
2002	81	1.8	213.9	58.1

Source: World Investment Report, 2003

ward trend seems to be finally over. Although still low at $297 billion in 2003, M&A increased 3 per cent in the first six months of 2004 over the same period in 2003.

In terms of its geographical distribution, during the 1990s FDI flows to developing countries rose sharply and now account for 34 per cent of the total net inflow (compared with 9 per cent in the latter half of the 1970s and 18 per cent in the 1980s). Factors behind this expansion include the acquisition of privatised assets, especially in Latin America in the early 1990s, the growth of the newly industrialised economies of South-East Asia, and the opening up of the Chinese economy. Indeed, China accounted for about one-third of all FDI in developing countries in the 1990s and about two-thirds of the total going to East Asia. This reflects a more general pattern of highly concentrated FDI flows in just a few countries. Indeed, three-quarters of the inflows in the 1990s went to just ten emerging market economies; China, Brazil and Mexico together took nearly half. Other developing regions – sub-Saharan Africa, South Asia, North Africa and the Middle East – have marginal shares in the total of FDI and in the case of sub-Saharan Africa a sharply falling one. The 49 least developed countries remain marginal recipients of FDI, receiving only 2 per cent of all FDI directed to developing countries or 0.5 per cent of the global total (UNCTAD, 2002).

Furthermore, Table 8.7 shows that the early 2000s were a time when FDI inflows registered negative growth rates, marking the most significant downturn in the last three decades. According to the World Investment Report of 2003, such a downturn is a product of weak economic growth, tumbling stock markets, which contributed to a decrease in the previously vigorous trend of cross-border mergers and acquisitions, and institutional factors such as the concluding episodes of privatisation in many countries. In fact, mergers and acquisitions fell

Table 8.7 Selected indicators of FDI and international production, 1982–2002

Item	Value at current prices (billion dollars)			Annual growth (per cent)						
	1982	1990	2002	1986–1990	1991–1995	1996–2000	1999	2000	2001	2002
FDI inflows	59	209	651	23.1	21.1	40.2	57.3	29.1	−40.9	−21
FDI outflows	28	242	647	25.7	16.5	35.7	60.5	9.5	−40.8	−9
Cross-border M&As	–	151	370	25.9	24	51.5	44.1	49.3	−48.1	−38
Employment of foreign affiliates (thousands)	19 375	24 262	53 094	5.5	2.9	14.2	15.4	16.5	−1.5	5.7

Source: World Investment Report, 2003

by 48 per cent in 2001 and decreased further – by 38 per cent – in 2002. Inflows of FDI fell in developed countries by 22 per cent and in developing ones by 23 per cent.

However, among developing countries, Africa experienced a reduction in FDI growth of a significant 41 per cent, Latin America and the Caribbean experienced a reduction of 33 per cent, while Asia and the Pacific saw little reduction thanks to the higher flows into China. It is interesting to note that Central and Eastern Europe did not suffer such reduction in FDI flows. On the contrary, the region saw FDI flows increase by 15 per cent on average (even if some reductions can be seen for different countries) (UNCTAD, 2003).

The downturn in FDI was uneven not only geographically but also sectorally. FDI flows fell both to manufacturing and service sectors, but increased to the primary sector. Finance, transport, storage and communications were severely affected by the downturn, while in other industries (such as health and social services) FDI flows remained unchanged or rose in the case of mining and petroleum, for example. According to UNCTAD estimates, the recent increases in M&As combined with higher economic growth in the main home and host countries, improved corporate profitability as well as higher stock valuations pointed to a recovery of overall FDI in 2004. Indeed, as a result of higher profits, reinvested earnings of multinational corporations, one of the components of FDI, resumed growth in 2003 and reached a record high in that year.

Portfolio investment (PI)

Through the 1980s, the growing role of foreign portfolio investment as a channel for international capital flows to developing countries has been perhaps the most crucial event in international financial markets. However, far from an unprecedented development, this shift in channels or in volumes of capital to these countries has occurred before – notably in the 1970s when commercial bank lending to middle-income countries (especially in Latin America) soared. Multilateral lending from US sources was also significant where bank lending was not available in low-income Asian countries and in Africa. At the time, FDI flows were far more pronounced than PI, which was confined to bond issues in the Euromarkets by a few of the 'more creditworthy' developing countries.

However, after the debt crisis started in Mexico in 1982, capital inflows to developing economies were severely constrained in some cases and virtually disappeared in most. Latin American, Eastern European and African countries were powerfully affected. In the period from 1983 to 1989, FDI was the only channel for net capital flows into countries in the Western Hemisphere. FDI increased in other developing countries as well, particularly in Asia, where the local economies continued to be attractive to the international banks, especially to Japanese ones.

> **Capitalisation**
>
> The market price of an entire company, calculated by multiplying the number of shares outstanding by the price per share (from www.investorwords.com).

The downturn in capital flows to developing countries outside Asia was reversed only in 1989–1990 as the industrialised countries shifted into recession, and particularly as US interest rates fell. By 1993, the aggregate net inflow to developing countries was 2 per cent of world saving, up from 0.8 per cent in 1990. In the late 1980s, portfolio flows to Latin America averaged $3 billion annually; by 1993 they had increased to $56 billion (more than 17 times the amount in the 1980s), although they fell in 1994. In the same period, portfolio flows to Asia grew from $1 billion in the late 1980s to $25 billion in 1993 (more than 20 times the amount in the 1980s), although they fell in 1994 but recovered soon after. In addition, by 1994, stock market capitalisation in Chile, Hong Kong, Malaysia and Singapore was comparable to that of the United States and the United Kingdom in relation to GDP, while market capitalisation in relation to GDP in Mexico and Korea was larger than in Germany and France.

Cross-border investments

As the assets of institutional investors in developed countries doubled from 1980 to 1992 – especially – their diversification strategies increasingly resulted in an expansion of cross-border investments. Cross-border transactions in bonds and equities among developed countries (excluding the UK) rose from 35 per cent of GDP in 1985 to 140 per cent in 1995. As developed and developing countries removed capital controls, a shift in predominance from FDI to PI flows became clear in some developing countries. These were now labelled as attractive investment sites, the 'emerging markets'. As the debt crisis of the 1980s was finally resolved via the restructuring of defaulted debts into Brady bonds (or sovereign bond instruments to be traded in international financial markets), credit returned in high volumes to hitherto excluded regions. Not only was credit from developed to developing countries now concentrated in bonds and equities (PI) rather than traditional bank loans from commercial banks, but the creditors in this market were largely a few institutional investors (mutual, pension and hedge funds, for example) which dominated a developing nation's asset market, and coordinated their behaviour among themselves.

A mutual fund is an open-ended fund operated by an investment company which raises money from shareholders and invests in a group of assets, in accordance with a stated set of objectives. Mutual funds raise money by selling shares of the fund to the public, much like any other type of company can sell stock in itself to the public. Mutual funds then take the money they receive from the sale of their shares (along with any money made from previous investments) and use it to purchase various investment vehicles, such as stocks, bonds and money market instruments. Mutual funds offer choice and liquidity but charge fees and often require a minimum investment.

A hedge fund is a fund, usually used by wealthy individuals and institutions, which is allowed to use aggressive strategies that are unavailable to mutual funds, including selling short, leverage, programme trading, swaps, arbitrage and derivatives. Hedge funds are exempt from many of the rules and regulations governing other mutual funds, which allows them to accomplish aggressive investing goals. They are restricted by law to no more than 100 investors per fund and as a result most hedge funds set extremely high minimum investment amounts, ranging anywhere from $250,000 to over $1 million. As with traditional mutual funds, investors in hedge funds pay a management fee; however, hedge funds also collect a percentage of the profits (usually 20 per cent).

(From www.investorwords.com)

Indeed, total bonds issues in emerging markets increased from $13.9 billion in 1991 (0.3 per cent of developing country GNP) to $127.9 billion in 1997 (or 2 per cent of developing country GNP). Even more impressively, total emerging market debt instrument trading grew from $734 million in 1992 to $5.9 billion in 1997, before falling in 1998 and 1999 due to the Asian and Russian crises and their repercussions throughout the world.

In fact, a slowdown in capital flows was registered in the first years of the 2000s. The slowdown in growth and collapse of technology prices also reduced capital market flows by decreasing the demand for speculative assets in general. Since about two-thirds of developing country sovereign borrowers and a much larger share of private borrowers are 'speculative grade' (i.e. their likelihood to default on their debts is higher), this implied a general decline in flows to developing countries. Among other reasons, the reduced demand for speculative assets reflects increased uncertainty about economic prospects, which in turn tends to cause risk-averse investors to reduce the share of high-risk assets in their portfolios. The collapse of technology stocks and the industrial countries' plunge from 3.4 per cent growth in 2000 to 1 per cent in 2001 may have increased the range of outcomes that investors feel they should consider.

However, a brighter picture can now be seen as PI reached an 11-year high of almost $36 billion in 2004, with emerging Asian countries continuing to attract the bulk of these flows (about 90 per cent) and Latin American economies experiencing net outflows.

The political economy of PI

What is the political economy of portfolio investments? Or, in other words, what are the political consequences of the increase reliance on portfolio investment on the part of developing countries especially? Reliance on portfolio inflows compromises policy autonomy in these countries. That is to say, 'unlike foreign direct investment, the high degree of liquidity of portfolio investment makes the threat of exit particularly credible' (Grabel, 1996, p. 1767). Hence, if investors perceive that governments are pursuing policies that are economically destabilising (such as policies that produce inflation and/or increase the volumes of public debt – which, by definition, may make defaults more likely), they will pull out money from such economies and look for 'safer' investment harbours.

How investors calculate such risks is a product of coordinated behaviour, of 'herd-like' behaviour (where the herd follows a few leaders in the market in buying or selling certain instruments) and/or of the reliance on information provided by credit rating agencies. These agencies rate the risk level (i.e. likelihood of default) of bonds traded in the international and domestic markets. Credit ratings have become an even more powerful business after sovereigns resumed the issuance of debt bonds, as explained earlier. Investors in the market for sovereign debt bonds rely on sovereign credit ratings – as they are called – in choosing when and where to allocate (or pull out) their resources.

Knowing that, governments are also directly influenced by ratings and take them into their calculations for policymaking purposes, aiming at attracting foreign capital through positive ratings for their bonds (i.e. technically reducing their 'sovereign risk' rating). For example, anti-inflationary reforms in many countries have counted on a positive evaluation from international investors as well as positive credit ratings. Positive ratings are attractive to foreign investors who see the purchase of debt bonds as less risky, whereas downgrades in ratings makes bonds riskier and potentially less attractive to investors. Because governments seek good ratings, they may choose policies that aim at pleasing foreign investors first and foremost but that are dubious in terms of economic sustainability. This is the clear way in which policymaking becomes severely constrained by the preferences and actions of private actors who exercise a 'quasi-veto' power on policymaking decisions, influencing investment decisions and consequently policy choices in developing countries. This is a dangerous trend when the policies favoured by government to attract foreign investment, albeit managing to generate temporary economic exuberance, lead to economic collapse soon after – as the example of the Argentine crisis of 2001 makes clear.

Conclusion

By analysing the underlying logic and main trends involving trade policy and investment especially in the last two decades, the picture of a global economy becomes clearer. There are specific dynamics of added vulnerabilities, of tighter institutional ties among economies and of a restricted assortment of policies available to governments to adopt. Also, it becomes clear that power is a result of a series of interactions that go beyond governmental relations to include a set of diverse players in which international private capital plays a particularly striking role, especially in terms of the issues covered here.

Yet political pressures at the domestic level still constrain governments to cater to the demand of constituencies increasingly in disagreement with a global agenda of economic integration. The dilemma of politics today is made clear in this chapter, as elsewhere in the book: how to cater to domestic voters or to the groups among those which are most vocal, and well organised, pressuring for protection from external economic competition and/or integration and still engage in a global project of economic interdependence for mutual gains, maintaining a degree of policy autonomy. This is an historical puzzle, perhaps more prominent today than ever, whose resolution is anything but an easy task for governments and governance agents.

Further Reading

Audley, John, Polanski, Sandra, Papademetriou, Demetrios G. and Vaughan, Scott (2003) 'NAFTA's Promise and Reality: Lessons from Mexico for the Hemisphere', Washington, DC: Carnegie Endowment for International Peace.

Barro, Robert (1999) 'Inequality, Growth and Investment', Working Paper, Washington: National Bureau of Economic Research.

Calvo, Guillermo, Leiderman, Leonardo and Reinhart, Carmen (1994) 'Inflows of Capital to Developing Countries in the 1990s: Causes and Effects', Inter-American Development Bank, Office of the Chief Economist, Working Paper 302, available at www.iadb.org/res/publications/pubfiles/pubWP-302.pdf

Datz, Giselle (2004) 'Reframing Development and Accountability: The Impact of Sovereign Credit Ratings on Policy Marking in Developing Countries', *Third World Quarterly*, vol. 25 (2), pp. 303–318.

Financial Times, several issues.

Grabel, Ilene (1996) 'Marketing the Third World: The Contradictions of Portfolio Investment in the Global Economy', *World Development*, 24:11, pp. 1761–1776.

Griffith-Jones, Stephany (1995) 'Regulatory Changes for Sources of Surges in Capital Flows', available at www.southcentre.org/papers/finance/jones/toc1.htm#TopOfPage

Gruber, Lloyd (2000) *Ruling the World: Power Politics and the Rise of Supra-national Institutions*, Princeton: University of Princeton Press.

Haggard, S. (1990) *Pathways from the Periphery: the politics of growth in newly industrialising countries*, Ithaca: Cornell University Press.

Haley, Mary Ann (1999) 'Emerging Market Makers: The Power of Institutional Investors' in Armijo, Leslie (ed) *Financial Globalisation and Democracy in Emerging Markets*, New York: St Martin's Press.

Harrison, Ann and Hanson, Gordon (1999) 'Who Gains from Trade Reform? Some Remaining Puzzles', Working Paper 6915, Washington, DC: National Bureau of Economic Research.

Hausmann, Ricardo and Fernandez-Arias, Eduardo (2000) 'Foreign Direct Investment: Good Cholesterol?', paper presented at the Annual Meeting of the Board of Governors, Inter-American Development Bank and Inter-American Investment Corporation, mimeo.

Institute of International Finance (2005) 'Capital Flows to Emerging Market Economies', Washington, DC: IIF.

Jackson, John H. (1996) 'The WTO Dispute Settlement Procedure: A Preliminary Appraisal' in Jeffrey Schott (ed) *The World Trading System: Challenges Ahead*, Washington, DC: Institute for International Economics.

Kozul-Wright, Richard and Rayment, Paul (2004) 'Globalisation Reloaded: An UNCTAD Perspective', UNCTAD Discussion Paper No. 167, January.

Krugman, Paul (2002) 'America the Scofflaw', *New York Times*, 24 May.

— (1995) *Peddling Prosperity: Economic Sense and Nonsense in an Age of Diminished Expectations*, New York: Norton.

— (1993) 'The Uncomfortable Truth About NAFTA', *Foreign Affairs*, November/December.

Lehmann, Alexander (2002) 'Foreign Direct Investment in Emerging Markets: Income, Repatriations and Financial Vulnerabilities', IMF Working Paper/02/47, March.

Mishra, Deepak, Mody, Ashoka and Murshid, Antu Pnini (2001) 'Private Capital Flows and Growth', *Finance and Development* 38:2, Washington, DC: IMF.

Mosley, Layna (2003) *Global Capital and National Governments*, Cambridge: Cambridge University Press.

OECD (2003) 'Trends and Recent Developments in Foreign Direct Investment', available at www.oecd.org/dataoecd/52/11/2958722.pdf

Sassen, Saskia (2001) *The Global City*, 2nd edn, Princeton: Princeton University Press.

Schott, Jeffrey J. (1996) 'Challenges Facing the World Trade Organisation' in Jeffrey Schott (ed) *The World Trading System: Challenges Ahead*, Washington, DC: Institute for International Economics.

Suranovic, Steven (1997) 'The Theory of Comparative Advantage', available at http://internationalecon.com/v1.0/ch40/40c000.htm

The Economist (2004) 'Mergers and Acquisitions: When Battles Commence', 19 February.

The Institute of International Finance (2004) 'Capital Flows to Emerging Market Economies', report of 15 January 2004, available at www.iif.com/verify/data/report_docs/cf_0104.pdf

UNCTAD (2002) 'FDI in Least Developed Countries at a Glance: 2002', Geneva: UNCTAD.

— (2003) *World Investment Report*, Geneva: UNCTAD.

— (2004) *World Investment Report*, Geneva: UNCTAD.

World Bank (2002) *Global Development Finance 2002: Financing the Poorest Countries*, Washington, DC: World Bank.

CHAPTER 9: War and conflict

The frequency, scope and effects of warfare have been changing dramatically since the last decade of the twentieth century. The principal causes of the change have been the effects of globalisation on the role of states and governments and the consequences of the end of the Cold War. The first has changed the likely security ambitions of states by largely removing disputes about territory and influence and at the same time it has reduced the willingness of most governments to accept the primacy of defence expenditure as a first charge on their budgets. The contemporary problems of governments, particularly in respect of taxation, are discussed elsewhere.

At a more fundamental level, the tendency of weaker states to collapse into chaos and civil conflict is a consequence of the processes of globalisation and in doing so it has provided the most common cause of fighting in the contemporary world. The end of the Cold War altered the common assumptions about what a war would be. High-tech war fought between highly sophisticated and organised alliance groups suddenly disappeared both as an expectation and as the basis of preparation, to be replaced by conflict of an almost completely opposite character – low tech, local and deeply disorganised. The bench mark for modern war was for a very long time the appalling war in Europe between 1914 and 1918 and to understand the immensity of the difference between then and the contemporary situation, some historical analysis is required.

The First World War: causes and consequences

The nineteenth century was quite remarkably a period of orderly international relations, effectively managed by a committee system of the great powers, usually mediated through conferences. There were occasional interruptions, generally caused by nationalist ambitions, and the system did not function outside Europe, though after 1856 the Ottoman Empire in Europe was included and after 1884 Africa as well; but nonetheless, it was a remarkable achievement.

The principal war of the period was without question the American Civil War and its lessons, both strategic and political, might have been better learnt had it been less far away and internalised. The most obvious lesson would have concerned the effect of industrialised technology on weaponry and in the sense that all governments began to be concerned about keeping up with a technological race in armaments, it was learnt. In the sense that there were consequences for the conduct of war on the participants which might make warfare less palatable to those citizens required to fight, it was not. Nor did any general sense diffuse that in a rapidly growing phase of interdependent economic activity, largescale warfare would inevitably induce massive economic disruption. The emotional acceptance of war so strongly evident in the streets of capital cities in 1914 was to be brutally reacquainted with reality.

The fatal combination of factors which dictated the structure of the 1914 war has already entered the discussion: the nineteenth century saw an unprecedented upward shift in the efficiency and ingenuity of industrial technology. This impacted on state governments in advanced societies in the form of popular expectations that what improvements now lay within the power of governments should indeed be achieved. To do so required a large increase in the scope, size and expense of governance, which in turn led to increased taxation and recruitment of government personnel. This made the politics of governing much more immediate than before, since doing so involved a far greater use – and possible abuse – of power. This factor was much advanced by the coincident emergence of the tabloid press, able to speak to a public newly literate as a result of educational improvements and compelled to do so by reason of competition in the most lurid and simplistic fashion.

The power inherent in political office went up sharply just as, simultaneously, the security of incumbent governments declined in the face of the fact that both achieving power by winning elections and then staying in power were more difficult than they had ever been. The combination produced government by propaganda – though in differing degrees – in all advanced societies, whether fully democratic or less so. And nationalist propaganda was often a successful distraction from domestic criticism, which might not matter too much if the external world was stable, but which became highly dangerous and risky if it was not.

By the 1890s, the international system of the previous century had effectively broken down. Technological improvements had created a new and global basis for assessing and using power and changed both the field of activity and the names of some of the players of the game, which was uncomfortable enough in itself.

It had also had a predictably improving effect on the destructiveness of weapons. The machine gun – the Maxim gun, particularly – had produced a category improvement during the second part of the century. Improvements in the technique of rifling were by 1900 producing cannon capable of delivering destruction over many miles. The German Big Bertha was the apotheosis of all such guns: it was possible for the Germans to bombard Dover docks in England from bases in Northern France during the 1914 war. Nor was transporting weapons of this kind difficult in principle. Big Bertha was arranged on a special train and could be sent anywhere a train could go. Therein, however, lay a highly significant restriction. All militarily sensitive areas in Europe were served by strategic railways; indeed, one of the bases of the Franco-Russian alliance of 1894 was that French capital would build strategic railways in western Russia to help defend the Czar's empire against any German threat. Those lines were mainly built in what is now Poland and later came to be a welcome resource of the Soviet Union, whose attitude to France was rather different. The restriction was, of course, that no amount of military planning, however obsessively engaged in as it was, could ensure that a war would actually take place where the railways

were. And that meant that at least for the time being, armour, though it had to be the best available, was still no substitute for infantry.

The reverse occurred at sea. Fitting a steam engine into a ship increased rather than decreased its range and manoeuvrability. By placing the most advanced guns on ships powered by the most advanced engines, an almost perfect weapon was produced. As insecurity developed and the arms race hotted up in the early twentieth century, naval competition ceased to be measured in terms of numbers of ships but more in terms of technological advance and future capacity. Planning and procurement based on assessments of the building capacity of potential enemies was a new development, which had devastating consequences for arms expenditure and could seriously skew, as it did in Imperial Germany, the formulation and management of economic policy. It also made general staffs extremely reluctant to risk their high-tech babies in actual battle.

The First World War was almost devoid of naval engagements and the one serious battle – Jutland – was inconclusive in its result. The uncertainties inherent in the naval situation greatly embittered Anglo-German relations, led to the Anglo-French naval sharing agreement of 1912, which meant that Britain could no longer be neutral in a European war, whatever weasel words might be used to cover up the fact, and generally contributed to public anxiety. Few matters were so much the object of inter-state press abuse during the period 1901–1914.

On land the effect of the technological situation was to be disastrous. The railways could not provide the manoeuvrability for the most advanced armour that ships could and there would remain a tactical gap until the invention of the petrol engine made enough progress to be applied to the transport of big guns. There was thus a pause until in 1917 the first tanks came onto the field – to remain there until our own day. What was significant about 1914, however, was their absence, not their presence, because it was their absence which immobilised the war tactically and killed millions and millions of combatants in the trenches. In the face of a tactical stalemate, the only recourse was to outperform the enemy in size and numbers. To win required more men, more weapons, more ammunition, more barbed wire, maybe more allies, than the enemy. To win also required more economic organisation, more domestic planning and, most important of all, more political stability than the enemy and more than anyone had ever had before.

The tactical and strategic failure and the consequent losses were staggering. Harold Macmillan, Prime Minister of Britain from 1957 to 1963, a decorated officer who survived the 1914 war, once broke down and wept during a TV interview while trying to explain that only the terrible slaughter of cleverer and better men than he had allowed him to become prime minister.

The scale of the conflict was different from all its predecessors and it produced the justification for Marx's observation that wars do not change things, they merely make things happen faster. State machines that had already expanded hugely during the second half of the nineteenth century had to become almost totally invasive in order to conduct the war. Economic organisation, the rationing of food supplies, the management of transport systems, almost total control of labour were all required.

Although serious bombing of civilian populations was to be more of a feature of the next war, there was no branch of civilian life into which the effects of the 1914 war did not penetrate. Of them all, the most serious was the necessity of persuading and then compelling the able-bodied male population to go to the trenches to be killed. This task required not only organisation, threats and penalties, but also a justifying motive. The propaganda machines went into action on a scale never seen before and never forgotten since. It was urged that the cause was just, the country and the Empire must be defended, the enemy was wicked, as demonstrated by atrocities committed. But these did not work in the face of continuously worsening slaughter.

There are few people left in Western Europe or the USA who went through it. For others, the experience of subsequent wars, though unpleasant enough, simply cannot equal the enormities of what happened in France in 1916 and 1917.

The experience of the First World War

To make the point in a different way here are two different poems to compare: both justifiably famous. The first is by Alfred Lord Tennyson and it describes the Charge of the Light Brigade during the Crimean War (1854–1856). The charge itself was a pointless error committed by an incompetent general. The second poem is by Wilfred Owen and apart from the vivid descrip-

tion of being gassed, it was his utter rejection of the idea that it is meet and proper to die for one's country (which is the meaning of the Latin phrase at the end of the poem) which was so important and so dangerous for governments. First, the Charge of the Light Brigade:

Half a league, half a league
Half a league onward,
All in the valley of Death
Rode the six hundred
'Forward the Light Brigade!
Charge for the guns!' he said:
Into the valley of Death
Rode the six hundred.
'Forward the Light Brigade!'
Was there a man dismay'd?
Not tho' the soldier knew
Someone had blunder'd;
Their's not to make reply,
Their's not to reason why,
Their's but to do and die:
Into the valley of Death
Rode the six hundred.
Cannon to the right of them,
Cannon to the left of them,
Cannon in front of them
Volley'd and thunder'd;
Storm'd at with shot and shell,
Boldly they rode and well,
Into the jaws of Death
Into the mouth of Hell
Rode the six hundred.

Flash'd all their sabres bare,
Flashed as they turn'd in air
Sabr'ing the gunners there,
Charging an army, while
All the world wonder'd:
Plunged in the battery-smoke
Right through the line they broke;
Cossack and Russian
Reeled from the sabre-stroke
Shatter'd and sunder'd.
Then they rode back, but not,
Not the six hundred.

Cannon to right of them,
Cannon to left of them,
Cannon behind them
Volley'd and thunder'd;
Stormed at with shot and shell,
While horse and hero fell,
They that had fought so well

Came through the jaws of Death,
Back from the mouth of Hell,
All that was left of them,
Left of six hundred.

When can their glory fade?
O the wild charge they made!
All the world wonder'd.
Honour the charge they made!
Honour the Light Brigade,
Noble six hundred!

And now the Owen:

Bent double, like old beggars under sacks,
Knock-kneed, coughing like hags, we cursed
     through sludge,
Till on the flares we turned our backs
And towards our distant rest began to trudge.
Men marched asleep. Many had lost their
     boots
But limped on, blood-shod. All went lame; all
     blind;
Drunk with fatigue; deaf even to the hoots
Of tired, outstripped Five-Nines that dropped
     behind.

Gas! Gas! Quick, boys! An ecstasy of
     fumbling,
Fitting the clumsy helmets just in time;
But someone still was yelling out and
     stumbling
And floundr'ing like a man in fire or lime. . . .
Dim, through the misty panes and thick green
     light, As under a green sea, I saw him
     drowning.

In all my dreams before my helpless sight,
He plunges at me, guttering choking,
     drowning.
If in some smothering dreams you too could
     pace
Behind the wagon that we flung him in
And watch the white eyes writhing in his face,
His hanging face, like a devil's sick of sin;
If you could hear, at every jolt, the blood
Come gargling from the froth-corrupted lungs
Obscene as cancer, bitter as the cud
Of vile, incurable sores on ancient tongues,
My friend, you would not tell with such high
     zest
To children ardent for some desperate glory,
The old lie: Dulce et decorum est
Pro patria mori.

By late 1916, none of the traditional justifications for the privations and casualties of war would suffice any longer. The only mantra which still had some force was the idea that this war had to be won in order to end all wars and, less directly described, that those who had been involved were entitled to and would obtain a new social and economic order at its end.

The effects of the First World War

There was no doubt that there were two contradictory effects arising from the experience of the 1914–1918 war. The first was that the traditional liberal state had been nearly bankrupted, both literally and figuratively, by the experience. In Russia, it was supplanted by another way of attempting to manage an industrial, or in this case industrialising, society which overtly and deliberately accepted the absolute superiority of the state machine and relied upon the Communist Party to make it work equitably. A little later, fascist movements developed, first in Italy – perhaps significantly in the hands of a former Marxist – which also accepted and glorified the machinery of the state and relied upon a mixture of corporatism, patriotism and economic success to make it work to the advantage of a particular society. Both found to a greater or lesser degree that maintaining full control of the machinery of state was essential but tricky and required the use of major propaganda weapons and ultimately terror.

In the United States, Great Britain and France, but not in Japan, the liberal state survived, but in the case of the European states, only just, and in all cases by increasing the role of government to almost wartime proportions.

The second effect was that war as an instrument of policy either as threat or fact became, understandably, totally unacceptable to public opinion in all major countries and much reliance was initially placed on the League of Nations to make the maintenance of peace a reality. This meant that when the first effect of the war produced fascist regimes which began to lose their reluctance to go to war in a miasma of national propaganda derived from stereotyped memories of ancient Rome or the glories of Valhalla, there was no stomach to resist, no willingness to rearm, little attempt to plan for the unthinkable.

The Second World War

Moreover, the unthinkable had now become, if possible, worse. The 1914 war had produced the first serious use of air power in war, but it had not really included bombers or bombing. The British then advanced the technique rapidly by using bombing with outstanding success against rebel Kurds in what was then the mandate of Mesopotamia, now Iraq. Military planning could no longer ignore the significance of air power.

Ironically, it was a clever young French staff officer called Charles de Gaulle who in the 1920s produced the first description of what, taken over by the Germans, was to become known as *Blitzkrieg*: that is to say, rapid movement of light armour on the ground accompanied by punishing and coordinated raids from the sky. The vivid film footage of the Japanese attacks in China, the German invasion of Poland on 1 September 1939 and the attack across northern Europe in 1940 all attest to the force of the technique. This aspect of air power reinforced the fact that, unlike the previous conflict, the 1939 war was to be mobile as far as the battlefield was concerned.

The other side of air power, however, which had, if possible, made the unthinkable worse, concerned the civilian population. The civilian population had suffered both by privation and through the death of family members and it had certainly been profoundly affected by the 1914 war; it had only rarely been directly attacked. That immunity was shattered in the summer of 1940 when the Germans opened an undeclared war against neutral Holland by destroying the city of Rotterdam in a sequence of bombing raids. It was not, however, unexpected. From the early 1930s a catch phrase developed in defence circles which read 'the bomber will always get through' – meaning that however many fighters were sent up to intercept fleets of bombers, enough would survive to flatten the major cities. This belief, which was only wrong in that it over-estimated the scale of destruction, at least until the bombing of Dresden in 1945, helps to explain both the reluctance to abandon any chance of negotiated settlements that seemed to be on offer and the policy of arranging for the instant evacuation of children from major cities into the countryside on the outbreak of war.

The fear of total bombardment also included the idea that civilian morale would not survive it, again an overestimation. In neither the British nor the German case did that prove to be true. Indeed, it tended to have a reverse effect, which was later to be seen also in Vietnam. The deliberate attempt to break the nerve of an enemy population, rather than just defeat its military forces or undermine its economy, was the hallmark of the 1939 war and it ushered in the period of 'total war'. The phrase predates the invention of nuclear weapons, though of course they made it even more true, and it completed the process begun between 1914 and 1918 whereby the combination of state power and advanced weapons technology created wars which had to be fought on every front – military, civilian, economic, social, ideological and technological. Nothing that mankind could invent or process was not grist to the mills of war.

The Cold War and after

The Cold War offered a curious juxtaposition. The threat of war had become nuclear and

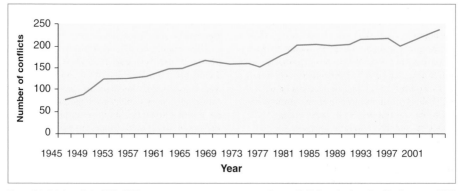

Figure 9.1 Total conflicts 1945–2003

Source: Heidelberg Institute Conflict Barometer 2004

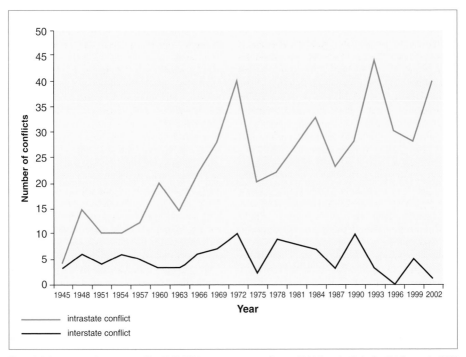

Figure 9.2 Interstate vs intrastate conflict 1945–2003   Source: Heidelberg Institute Conflict Barometer 2004

therefore total in the most complete sense possible, but barring accidents or insanity it also rendered great power war less likely to occur. And, more than that, it made small conflicts less likely to escalate, though it increased the fear that they might. Even after the production of so-called tactical nuclear weapons, the threat of war did not increase, as it became clear that the weapons concerned were regarded as more nuclear than tactical.

It is possible to argue that nuclear weapons in fact made little difference to the fundamental distribution of power in the world, since their emergence coincided with the final conclusion of the great struggle for global power and influence on the part of the truly global powers. Once they had reached a de facto accommodation, which they did at the Geneva Conference of 1955, the armaments situation, though dizzyingly dangerous in itself, was a confirmatory factor rather than a fundamental one.

A subtle change in the function of the intelligence industry reflects this. From the early twentieth century onwards, intelligence was used to try to discover war plans and technological improvements in weaponry: to steal a march, if

possible, and to prevent one being stolen. With the onset of the bi-polar era, it became crucial that each side should know as precisely as possible what were the forces and equipment available to its opponent and a pretty clear idea of the use to which they would be put in the event of war. Intelligence was there to defend developments in train, but allow them to be known about as soon as they were ready for use. If the stand-off did anything directly, it served to make it less likely that the two great powers would intervene very much outside their groupings to initiate or profit from events affecting smaller states.

This became particularly obvious in successive phases of the Arab–Israeli conflicts, particularly 1956 and 1973, Indo-Pakistani and Sino-Indian wars and after de-colonisation produced other broad areas of instability, for example the Congo in the mid-1960s. Minimum intervention was applied in order to maintain the status quo as far as possible and to that extent the existence of organised blocs of allied powers had a generally restraining effect on the conduct of international politics. Since 1945, there has been a steady rise in overall state conflict. This includes conflict issues over territory, decolonisation, system/ideology, regional predominance, international power, resources and other items.

It now begins to look, however, as if the chief effect of the period of bi-polarity was to restrain the outbreak of domestic disorder within states. Neither during the Cold War nor since 1989 has there been any great tendency for inter-state or inter-alliance warfare to develop, or for the extraordinarily high-tech weapons systems that have been generated to become actors in themselves, in a 'man as a prisoner of the machine' syndrome. But there has been an almost catastrophic decline in the domestic security of many states and some have disappeared into maelstroms of civil war.

The effect of this factor on the conduct and incidence of war is clear. The incidence of war is greater now than it has been since the seventeenth century, but the level at which it is being conducted is lower than anything seen in the twentieth century. We now observe the extraordinary paradox that the world possesses at least the remains of the most sophisticated means of fighting a war, both in weaponry and communications, that has ever been known, yet the purpose for which it was all so expensively put together has disappeared, leaving the weapons stocks, the control systems and the alliances strategically and emotionally directionless. The objectives of those who wish to fight or support fighting have become localised and low-tech weapons generally more than suffice. Disorganised groups, more perhaps like brigands than armies, have roamed mediaevally through the forests and mountains of parts of central Europe and the Caucasus, glad to acquire a rifle, willing to launch grenades from hill tops into marketplaces below. Still more familiar from early modern Europe is the rapidly mounting list of accompanying atrocities and there is plenty of evidence that it is getting ever more difficult to shock ordinary people with accounts of recently perpetrated violence. Burning at the stake was once, too, considered perfectly normal.

The extraordinary crisis which came to a head in the Kosovo province of Yugoslavia in 1998/99 exemplified these factors. The crisis was essentially caused by a state collapse, that of the former Yugoslavia after the death of Tito and the demise of the Soviet Union. The creation of newly independent states out of its ruins also created new minorities and non-negotiable disputes which unleashed appalling atrocities, first in Croatia, then in Bosnia-Herzogovina and finally in Kosovo. In Kosovo the basic cause of the descent into civil war was the Serbs' fear that the province of Kosovo would seek and obtain independence, since its population was in large majority Albanian. The Serb government first revoked the autonomy of Kosovo in 1988 and then ten years later, having been defeated in the long crises over Croatia and Bosnia, sought to avoid a third humiliation by violently enforcing Serb control over the Albanian population, who had by now acquired their own resistance movement in the form of the Kosovo Liberation Army. The civil conflict grew steadily worse and both parties committed atrocities, but because the Albanians were the majority ethnic group with 90 per cent of the total and had enjoyed autonomy in the past, the brutal nature of the Serb attempt to defeat the Kosovo Liberation Army (KLA) and restore order and its effective sovereignty in the province, apparently by forcing the Albanian population to flee, strikingly offended external opinion.

Great efforts were made to negotiate a ceasefire and an acceptable return of autonomous status for the province and in early 1999 it seemed that the Rambouillet Conference, held near Paris, had achieved that aim. At the last moment, however, the Serb government rejected the draft agreement and the NATO alliance began to use massive air bombardment on non-civilian targets in Serbia in order to force Serbian compliance with at least a version of the Rambouillet agreement. After a much longer period of bombing than had initially been anticipated and, significantly, only after serious preparations for a ground war were put in hand, the Serbs gave way. But even in apparent victory, in the summer of 1999 the situation remained unclear in many aspects, most particularly about the future status of the province, the longer-term role of military forces and the stance, both present and future, of Russia.

Here was a test case of several contemporary assertions: that NATO could have a more generalised role as both a peace enforcer and then peacekeeper in post-Soviet Europe – and perhaps further afield; that using force in these circumstances could be antiseptically achieved from the air, thus both avoiding widespread civilian casualties and casualties to the enforcers; that the doctrines and equipment which NATO had retained from its former role as the deter-

Table 9.1 Active UN peacekeeping missions from 1948 to 2004

Date	Name of mission	Mission acronym	Country/Region
1948	UN Truce Supervisory Organisation in Middle East	UNTSO	Middle East
1949	UN Military Observer Group India and Pakistan	UNMOGIP	India-Pakistan
1964	UN Force in Cyprus	UNIFCYP	Cyprus
1974	UN Disengagement Observer Force Golan Heights	UNDOF	Syria-Israel
1978	UN Interim Force in Lebanon	UNIFIL	Lebanon
1991	UN Mission for the Referendum in Western Sahara	MINURSO	Western Sahara
1993	UN Observer Mission to Georgia	UNOMIG	Georgia
1999	UN Interim Administration Mission in Kosovo	UNMIK	Serbia and Montenegro
1999	UN Mission in the Democratic Republic of the Congo	MONUC	DR Congo
1999	UN Mission in Sierra Leone	UNAMSIL	Sierra Leone
2000	UN Mission in Ethiopia and Eritrea	UNMEE	Ethiopia-Eritrea
2002	UN Mission of Support in East Timor	UNMISET	East Timor
2003	UN Mission in Liberia	UNMIL	Liberia
2004	UN Mission for Burundi	ONUB	Burundi
2004	UN Mission in Côte d'Ivoire	UNOCI	Côte d'Ivoire
2004	UN Stabilisation Mission in Haiti	MINUSTAH	Haiti

Source: Heidelberg Institute Conflict Barometer, 2004

rent alliance of the West would be as effective against a mountain civil war as against the Warsaw Pact; and, on a rather different plane, that the rights inherent in national sovereignty now took a secondary position to the human rights of a population; that, therefore, a legal war, at least in a customary sense, could be fought and supported by public opinion to defend those rights where national interests in a traditional sense were not involved.

Moreover, the role of the UN was called into question in that it would not authorise a military defence of the Albanians, since some members of the Security Council were clear that to do so would have been beyond the authority of the Charter, but it also refused to declare such a defence illegal, once it was under way (see Table 9.1). It became clear that the hopes attached to antiseptic air attacks were unfounded in that they did not produce any quick change of policy on the part of Serbia, indeed rather the reverse. This was due both to the emotional effect on the population and to the limitations imposed on its effectiveness by the felt need only to attack lim-ited targets. This gave the Serb government time to step up its efforts to expel the Albanian major-ity, who fled to neighbouring countries, thus cre-ating a humanitarian refugee crisis of huge proportions, for which governments both local and distant were plainly unprepared.

It thus seems as if the changing pattern of con-flict is not amenable to the tactics believed in and military assets possessed by NATO and that, therefore, if its role is to be changed, its nature and equipment will have to be adapted to match. It also looks very much as if the use of force remains just that, even if its application has not been dictated by traditional national inter-ests. The idea that it was both possible and right that war should be undertaken in a different and less involved way if it was being fought in the interests of human rights seems not to be sus-tainable. The only way to achieve the return of the Albanian population to their homes in Kosovo has turned out to be escorting them home under military protection on the ground, not just in the air, and, if necessary, expelling the Serb forces as this is done. Furthermore, the

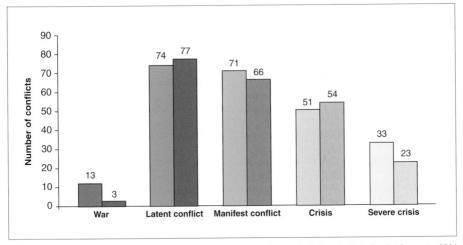

Figure 9.3 Global conflict intensities 2003 compared with 2004   Source: Heidelberg Institute Conflict Barometer 2004

returned Albanians will require external support, physical protection and public administration for a long time to come. They will have to form some kind of international protectorate, neither a state nor a province, but a new kind of geo-political animal.

The situation remained unchanged in 2005 and in Bosnia-Herzegovina the EU was still exercising a supervisory role. The role of the UN has expanded, particularly in its governance responsibilities in the later twentieth century and early twenty-first century. There has been an increase in the number of UN peacekeeping efforts, with three more than in 2003, and having a particular emphasis on Africa. In total there are seven concurrent operations in Africa. Table 9.1 highlights these phenomena.

It might have seemed that the tendency for conflicts to be internal and low tech was going to be reversed when the United States decided to respond to the terrorist attack on the World Trade Center in New York, not just by going after terrorists using the largely collapsed state of Afghanistan to operate from but also by removing the government of Iraq under Saddam Hussein. The antecedents of the invasion and subsequent war, with all the eventual ineffectual involvement of the United Nations, had some of the atmosphere of previous inter-state wars. But it soon turned out that the defeat of the Iraqi forces was not, as in earlier times it would have been, the end of the matter. At a lower level of conflict and a higher level of emotional involvement, what was anticipated to be a liberation of

Iraq and the removal of the threat it had posed swiftly changed into resistance to the US intervention and presence. A network of linked threats appeared, partly fuelled by religion, itself partly a civil war, partly by ethnic differences and partly resentment at what felt like occupation and not liberation on the part of people who were felt to be fundamentally anti-Arab and unwilling to try to resolve the Palestinian issue. The familiar contemporary asymmetrical shape of conflict appeared and seemed unquenchable. The line between terrorism and war became very muddied. Similar results emerged in Afghanistan, though there they owed as much to local tradition as to anything else.

If all this continues, it will begin to look as if the clock is being turned back. The long parabola which began to unite the practice and incidence of war with contemporary combinations of state power and improving technology had the effect of gradually reducing the incidence of war while steadily increasing its reach when it did happen until the whole of a society was inextricably involved. Wars became fewer but harsher and more destructive. Now it may be that we have arrived at the end of that parabola. The connection between ever more organised state power and war is becoming looser again, opening the way for a much more fluid, more or less ever present skein of violence, usually within individual societies, which it is often possible to ignore even when quite close at hand.

Standards of human behaviour are declining, not least because the treaties created to control the worst excesses of warfare and captivity depended for compliance on reciprocity between state governments rather than legal retribution, to the extent that they do work or have done so. That reciprocity does not exist to the same degree between fighting groups not located in a state structure or in any case engaged in genocide.

Such groups sit at the junction between formal warfare and terrorism. Terrorism has always existed and how prominent it is at any given time is affected by at least three major factors. The first concerns the ability of the principal actors in any system to keep its affairs under overall control. If either the power relationship between them becomes unbalanced or their internal stability becomes uncertain, the resulting chaos leads to conflict and in such conflicts episodes of terrorism will occur. Examples of the first can easily be found in the actions of both German and Russian forces during the Second World War.

The second, however, is more likely to lead to acts of terrorism, because internal instability may descend into civil war. Civil wars are seldom as well organised as formal inter-state wars have been and the groups involved may vary sharply in their relative strength. Resort to acts of terrorism is an almost inevitable consequence and represents an additional or alternative way of trying to gain control of a state government. The conflict in Sri Lanka is a case in point. Many conflicts in Africa straddle the line between terrorism and more formal war. The crisis in south-western Sudan which developed in 2003/2004 was an exemplar of this, as have been many episodes in the Great Lakes area of Central Africa. Until comparatively recently, terrorists were generally to be found trying to force the creation of new or more independent states. Anti-colonial movements such as the Mau Mau in Kenya and particularly the Palestine Liberation Organisation showed how to use terrorism to try to expel intruders, whether colonial administrators or Jewish settlers. The conflict in Chechnya is plainly a continuation of such an objective, as is the conflict in Kashmir. This characteristic is what has led to the common observation that one person's terrorist is another's freedom fighter.

Terrorism is not solely the province of the dispossessed or excluded, however. It can be used by governments under pressure either from internal dissent or, less often, the threat of invasion from outside. A distinct phase of the French Revolution, for example, more or less invented the word 'terror' to describe a political activity and fascist regimes employed the technique also. The clearest example of internal state terrorism in modern times was to be found in the Soviet Union under Stalin's rule. Sometimes the responses of governments attacked by terrorists have been similarly structured and merely confirm the blurred nature of the line between terrorism and conflict of any kind.

During the nineteenth century in Europe, there were occasional acts of terrorism committed in the interests of anarchism and religious disputes across centuries have had a high tendency to use terror, particularly because of the ability of some major religions to promise salvation to the perpetrators and sometimes to the victims. During the European reformation the public execution of heretics could be thought to save them from hell. The use of terror in order to advance an ideological position is therefore not exactly new. It has nonetheless been uncommon until very recent times. In addition to outbreaks of terrorism for familiar reasons, as, for example, followed the United States' invasion of Iraq in 2004, the world now sees terrorism used in the interests of animal rights, preventing abortion, occasionally over environmental issues and, very significantly, a return to terrorism supported by religion – Christians in Ireland, Muslims in the Caucasus, the Middle East, South Asia, Thailand, Indonesia and the Philippines, Hindus in India and Sri Lanka.

Apart from its general tendency to sway in and out of the conduct of warfare, terrorism demonstrates a particular characteristic which helps to explain its prevalence in the early twenty-first century. Terrorism chiefly relies on attacking so-called soft targets, usually the ordinary public and usually focusing its attacks on forms of transport. Airliners have had a particular attraction because of their helplessness once airborne, the virtual certainty that everyone on board will be killed and the latent fear of flying which many people in any case share. The attack on the World Trade Center in New York in 2001 managed to combine the horror of seizing and destroying planes with a physical attack on a place symbolic of the USA and global economy.

Trains and buses and the stations that they use are places where crowds gather of necessity, as are places of entertainment. The attack on a Moscow theatre in 2004 by Chechen terrorists

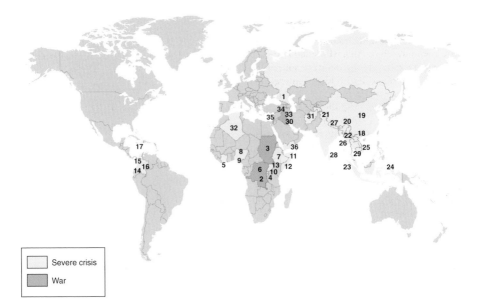

| | Severe crisis |
| | War |

Number	Name of conflict and most important conflict item	Number	Name of conflict and most important conflict item
	Europe – severe crises	20	India (Assam) – secession, resources
1	Russia (Chechnya) – secession	21	India (Kashmir) – secession
	Africa – wars	22	India (Nagaland) – secession, regional predominance
2	DR Congo (Rebels) – national power, resources	23	Indonesia (Aceh) – secession, resources
3	Sudan (SLM/A – JEM) – regional predominance	24	Indonesia (Moluccans) – regional predominance
	Africa – severe crises	25	Laos (LCMD, CIDL) – ideology/system, autonomy, national power
4	Burundi (Hutu) – national power	26	Myanmar (minorities) – secession
5	Côte d'Ivoir (Rebels) – national power	27	Nepal (Maoist rebels) – ideology/system, national power
6	DR Congo (Hema – Lendu) – regional predominance	28	Sri Lanka (LTTE-East – LTTE) – regional predominance
7	Ethiopia (Anyuak – Nuer) – regional predominance	29	Thailand (Southern Border Provinces) – secession
8	Nigeria (Christians – Muslims) – ideology/system		**Middle East and Maghreb – wars**
9	Nigeria (Nigerdelta – Ijaw) – resources	30	Iraq (insurgents) – national power, ideology/system
10	Rwanda (Hutu) – national power		
11	Somalia (Somaliland) – secession		**Middle East and Maghreb – severe crises**
12	Somalia (various groups) – national power	31	Afghanistan (Taleban) – regional predominance, national power
13	Uganda (LRA) – national power	32	Algeria (Islamist groups) – national power, ideology/system
	Americas – severe crises	33	Iraq (al-Sadr group) – ideology/system
14	Colombia (ELN) – national power, ideology/system	34	Iraq (CPA – resistance groups) –ideology/system, resources
15	Colombia (FARC) – national power, ideology/system	35	Israel (Palestinians) – autonomy, ideology/system, resources
16	Colombia (paramilitias) – regional predominance, system	36	Yemen (Islamists) – national power
17	Haiti (opposition) – national power		
	Asia and Oceania – severe crises		
18	Bhutan (Indian separatist rebels) – territory		
19	China (Hui) – other		

Figure 9.4 Violent conflicts of high intensity 2004   Source: Heidelberg Institute Conflict Barometer 2004

was an example of using the last category. The increasing number of hostages captured during the Iraq war and the frequency with which they have been publicly and brutally killed is another and extreme example of a resort to soft targets. Similarly, attacks on the London Underground system in July 2005 had the same characteristic and emphasised the significance of suicide bombers as the means of delivery.

This happens because of the lack of symmetry in power between the sources of authority which terrorists wish to attack and their own. It is very unlikely that terrorist groups would be able to 'win' a conflict in any conventional sense because the forces arrayed against them can usually prevent that. Terrorists can gain little publicity by being involved in a running battle with organised troops or even by blowing up official buildings. It is easy to imagine the TV reports of such events and how quickly they will be forgotten. Terrorists have to try to shock the general public into demanding that what they want should be taken seriously – and doing that requires the maximum exposure in the media. The result among other things is unprovoked attacks on ordinary citizens and videos of hostages being beheaded.

There is a developing further problem. It is becoming more difficult sometimes to determine what it is that terrorists want. Demands in the past have often been essentially territorial and easy to express. Sometimes they still are. But there is also a growing sense that some groups resort to terrorist or near-terrorist activities without an immediate objective except to express their general disgust at the way things are, or to protest against very broad trends, for example the belief that there is increasing global economic inequality. Here we are dealing with something new and it arises from the same problem that affects other aspects of global political and institutional life.

While it is clear that states are not about to disappear, indeed that in some areas their obligations have actually increased, there is no doubt that in other ways they are undergoing a loss of authority. This has the consequence that their governments can no longer play the role of sole guardian of their people's interests and more seriously in this context, they cannot act as the central point to which people go to obtain redress of grievances. This was most easily done by electoral processes, and dictatorships can be influenced in other ways. If, for example, a grievance is macroeconomic in scope, it is unlikely that a change of policy on the part of a government will relieve it because that kind of power has escaped from state hands. Thus far there has been no, or certainly no adequate, evolution of available alternatives and in the vacuum a kind of desperation has set in and frustration has begun to express itself by resorting to unorthodox methods. Unless and until global institutions acquire plausible roles and equivalent legitimacy, a sense of hopelessness and lack of representation will feed into an increase in violent responses.

The face of global conflict is changing. Elements of the past continue. Governments seek to have effective forces available armed with advanced equipment; some have, but do not say so, nuclear weapons, others seek to acquire them. Inter-state wars or the threat of them have sharply reduced and military alliances have become uncommon. Armed groups alienated from governments, and sometimes even from territory, proliferate and tend not to have advanced equipment, though they may acquire it at moments of extreme disorder, as during the Iraq war in 2004.

The causes of conflict and terrorism have become more complex and correspondingly harder to handle. The institutions traditionally charged with doing so, states and the United Nations, have become weaker, but no credible successors in their roles have yet emerged. A global network of sporadic low-level violence, fed by frustration and financed in part by organised crime, looks likely to continue and very possibly grow until its root causes are addressed and asymmetric conflict rendered anachronistic.

Further Reading

Bond, B. (1984) *War and Society in Europe, 1870–1945*, London: Macmillan.

Keegan, John (1983) *The Face of Battle*, London: Penguin.

McNeil, W. H. (1984) *The Pursuit of Power: War, Technology and Society from 1000 AD*, Chicago: Chicago University Press.

Townshend, Charles (1997) *The Oxford Illustrated History of Modern War*, Oxford: Oxford University Press.

Van Creveld, Martin (1991) *Technology and Warfare from 2000 BC to the Present Day*, New York: Touchstone.

Chapter 10: Terrorism

The horrific events of September 11 2001 are widely seen as an epochal fault line, heralding a new 'age of terrorism'. In their scale of death and destruction, the Al Qaeda attacks against the United States that day were unprecedented in the modern history of terrorist violence. The September 11 fatalities were originally estimated at about 6,000, though subsequently revised downwards to about 3,000.

It is worth noting that nearly 6,000 people are killed in the average week in armed conflict around the world. Still, the September 11 attacks were as audacious as they were deadly. They were carried out by an independent, loosely structured terrorist network, Al Qaeda, which without the active participation of any state, planned and executed two simultaneous, catastrophic strikes against the world's dominant military power. These were the first foreign or overseas attacks ever successfully carried out against the US mainland. They were deadlier than the Japanese assault on Pearl Harbor. But above all they were audacious in their symbolism. Al Qaeda's 19 suicide hijackers struck the Pentagon itself, the symbol and seat of US military power, wreaking substantial damage to its massive structure. And they destroyed the World Trade Center's Twin Towers, icons of both the Manhattan skyline and US leadership in the global economy. The televised collapse of the Twin Towers shocked millions of people not simply in New York and the United States but throughout the world. Those devastating images will not easily be erased from the world's collective memory.

Responses to 9/11

In response to the September 11 attacks, the US administration of President George W. Bush put forward a bold new framework to guide US foreign policy. Promptly labelled 'the Bush Doctrine', this approach marked the first fundamental reformulation of grand strategy for the world's dominant power since the advent of the Cold War in the late 1940s.

The collapse of Soviet power between 1989 and 1991 had prompted no such rethinking. The Bush Doctrine marked a shift from a policy of 'containment' of threats to one of 'preemption' or more accurately from 'deterrence' to 'preventive war'. In a world of global terrorism and proliferating weapons of mass destruction, the Bush administration proclaimed that the United States had the right and duty to use force unilaterally against potential adversaries before they developed the capacity to strike against it. Otherwise, the argument holds, it might be too late. To defend itself, according to this new strategic doctrine, the world's pre-eminent power had to eliminate such threats before any further catastrophic strikes became imminent. Rather than be caught out again by a surprise terrorist attack on US territory, the USA would strike its adversaries at times and places of the president's choosing. In Great Britain, the Prime Minister, Tony Blair, espoused a similar line. Most of the international community, including the majority of the European Union, is less convinced.

The question of how best to deal with the very real threat of global terrorism is likely to remain a crucial question in global politics for years to come. It has within it serious legal and moral problems. The right of any state to use force in self-defence against an imminent threat, in order to preempt an attack that would otherwise occur, is clearly sanctioned under international law. The radical departure inherent in the Bush Doctrine is the notion that the United States, having been attacked and having the means to respond, has the right to use force to prevent a future threat from becoming imminent and that the US president should be the sole arbiter of this question. To many legal scholars, this new concept of 'preventive war' is hardly distinguishable from the long-established category of *aggres-*

sive war, which is the most egregious violation of international law under the UN Charter. Some commentators go on to argue that the USA has been undermining the very foundations of international law by placing itself above the law.

Under the Bush Doctrine, the central strategic focus of US foreign and security policy has been redefined in terms of waging a 'global war on terror'. On a certain level, this is mere rhetoric. After all, how can a state wage war against an abstract noun? More substantively, terrorism is essentially a tactic, a set of practices involving the use of violence to create fear in order to achieve some political end. As discussed below, such practices have a long history, traceable back to the ancient world. They have been employed in almost all of the world's major cultural regions. It seems unlikely at best that any kind of war could put an end to terrorist practices everywhere and for all time. But again, the 'war on terror' is mainly rhetorical, a metaphor akin to the long-standing, indecisive 'war on drugs'.

The violent struggle that escalated so dramatically on September 11 2001 is between the United States and Al Qaeda, the loose global network founded by Saudi dissident Osama bin Laden. For a variety of reasons, the US administration chose to couch its efforts in broader terms. In part, the heated, militarised rhetoric of the 'war on terror' helped to deflect attention from the failure to deal adequately with the Al Qaeda threat prior to 9/11. But framing foreign policy objectives in grand, abstract terms constitutes a powerful tradition in US political culture: Roosevelt's 'Four Freedoms', Wilson's 'War to Make the World Safe for Democracy' or the nineteenth-century ideology of Manifest Destiny are all examples. The 'War on Terror' rubric served two prime political purposes, one tactical, the other strategic. Tactically, President Bush and his advisors wanted to avoid the overt appearance of waging war against Islam, particularly after Bush's use of the word 'crusade' in one major speech soon after the 2001 attacks. The 'war on terror' implied that the USA would employ its military might against terrorist groups that had nothing to do with Islam. Strategically, this more general framing of the conflict allowed the USA to single out so-called rogue states which sponsored terrorist activities or provided safe haven to terrorist groups.

Beyond its initial military response of attacking Afghanistan, the United States justified its 2003 invasion of Iraq as a crucial front in this

'war on terror'. The administration asserted that Iraq had reconstituted its nuclear weapons programme and had strong ties to Al Qaeda, implying that Saddam Hussein might someday provide Osama bin Laden with nuclear weapons for use against the USA. These claims have not been borne out by the facts, yet they served their purpose. During the build-up to the invasion and in its aftermath, polls showed that a majority of US voters believed that the Iraqi government played a direct role in the September 11 attacks and that most of the hijackers that day were Iraqi nationals. Yet even the earliest news accounts made clear that most of the hijackers hailed from Saudi Arabia, an increasingly awkward ally of the United States, and none was Iraqi. And no independent investigation has found any evidence of Iraqi involvement in the 9/11 or any other Al Qaeda attacks.

What is terrorism?

To understand the place of terrorism in today's global politics though, we must step back from these immediate concerns to examine the vexing question of what terrorism is and how it developed historically. The seemingly straightforward question 'What is terrorism?' is complicated by the politically loaded nature of the word. As the saying has it, 'one man's terrorist is another man's freedom fighter'.

There is no generally agreed definition of 'terrorism'. Yet one can say a good deal about what the term has denoted historically and what it has come to mean by the beginning of the twenty-first century. Its significance for international relations and diplomacy in the contemporary world has long been beyond dispute. Events of the 1990s and early 2000s have shown it to be one of the major problems confronting the international system in a period of deep and far-reaching transformation. Whether or not it is helpful to describe the present period as the 'age of terrorism', terrorism is clearly a central aspect of today's world scene.

If there is no universally accepted definition of terrorism, what does the term refer to? Terrorism is a form of political violence. It is, more specifically, violence directed against civilians for political purposes. Some authorities, including the United States government and most other major powers, define it as political violence against civilians committed by non-state or sub-state actors. Others insist that political violence against civilians by states must also be considered a form of terrorism. In ancient history, acts of terror against civilian populations were first employed by states in the context of warfare. The sacking of cities, such as Carthage by Rome, may be seen as early examples of genocide; they may also be seen as early examples of terrorism intended to cow other populations into submission. In the twentieth century, the aerial bombardment of cities, most notably in the Second World War, may also be seen as a form of state terrorism.

Critics of Israel argue that Israeli violence against Palestinian civilians, including the destruction of homes, amounts to a policy of state terrorism. Viewing Israeli policy as terrorism alters our perspective on the entire Palestinian conflict. Instead of seeing Israel's use of force as self-defence against Palestinian terrorism, one can see Palestinian violence as self-defence against the essentially violent nature of Israeli occupation. This example makes clear both the challenge and the importance of formulating a consensus definition of terrorism within the international community and under international law. Long-standing efforts to establish an international legal convention (or treaty) against terrorism have been repeatedly frustrated by the failure to achieve a consensus definition. In the wake of 9/11, the need to resolve this impasse seems imperative.

Since the latter part of the twentieth century, terrorism has been viewed most often as a tool of non-state actors, including national liberation movements, right-wing and left-wing radicals, and pan-Islamic jihadists. While operating independently from any government's control, such terrorist organisations have frequently been aided or 'sponsored' by 'rogue states' which flout the rules of the international community. If war is politics by other means, terrorism in this sense is war by other means. As a tool of non-state actors, it has generally been a method employed by the weak against the strong: when fighting strong states with organised military forces, groups lacking state power have frequently resorted to attacks on civilians to advance their political objectives.

While the behaviour extends back to ancient times, the term 'terrorism' itself dates to the age of the French Revolution. During the Reign of Terror (1793–1794), the revolutionary state used 'terrorism' in an attempt to eliminate 'traitors' to the revolution. Robespierre and other leaders of the Reign of Terror saw 'terrorism' as a way of defending the revolution's values of liberty, equality and brotherhood. As Robespierre himself put it, 'Terror is nothing but justice, prompt, severe and inflexible; it is therefore an emanation of virtue.' Not surprisingly, the term quickly became associated with state repression, symbolised most famously by the guillotine. Rather than an instrument for defending liberty, terrorism was the means by which the revolutionary government kept people subservient by keeping them in fear, at least until Robespierre and his colleagues ended up under the guillotine themselves.

Many of the most brutal regimes of the twentieth century employed terrorism in similar ways, including Nazi Germany, the Soviet Union, Cambodia under the Khmer Rouge, and Iraq under Saddam Hussein.

During the nineteenth century, however, the term came to be applied to violence committed against civilians by non-state actors. Following the American Civil War, former Confederates created the Ku Klux Klan for the purpose of restoring white supremacy by terrorising the former slaves and their allies into submission. In the late nineteenth and early twentieth centuries, within the growing movements for social and political reform in Russia some anarchists and other radicals embraced political violence; the young Lenin was among those who opposed such tactics. Anarchist groups employed terrorist violence, including bombings and assassinations, in Western and Eastern Europe and in the United States, with the aim of destabilising the social and political order. Prominent examples in the USA include the Haymarket bombings of 1886 and the assassination of President William McKinley in 1901.

In the same period, nationalist and anti-colonialist groups also began to use violence against civilians, again including bombings and assassinations, as a means of bringing attention to their causes. Certain elements of the Irish nationalist movement began to use political violence in this manner in the late nineteenth century, though as elsewhere the movement was sharply divided over this approach. Bulgar and Armenian opposition to the Ottoman Empire were among the earliest examples of this sort of 'nationalist terrorism', which became the predominant form of terrorism through most of the twentieth century.

Historically, both anarchist and nationalist terrorism held fairly clear political objectives related to the state. They aimed to topple one form of government and replace it with a radical alternative, to eliminate the state itself as an inherently oppressive structure, or to establish a new state in the name of national liberation.

In the late twentieth and early twenty-first centuries, the major change under way is the emergence of terrorist activity divorced from these kinds of state-related objectives. On the one hand, we now have political violence driven by narrow, issue-specific concerns, such as animal liberation, environmental protection or opposition to abortion. On the other hand, we have the new global terrorism of groups like Al Quaeda. Not coincidentally, these new forms of terrorist activity tend to be driven by religious or spiritual values as well as political objectives. Reflecting our global age, these values are not contained by the boundaries of any nation-state. Abortion opponents in the United States, for example, may focus their energies on stopping abortion in their own country, but they condemn the practice globally. More tellingly, radical ecologists, including the small number who condone the use of violence, are motivated by an ideology that is both explicitly and avowedly globalist – the very fate of the planet is their concern. Al Qaeda is similarly driven by a globalist ideology, though arguably one with more clearly delimited political objectives.

Terrorism and the Middle East

Since the last third of the twentieth century, terrorism has been associated most commonly with the Middle East and with Arab and Muslim groups in particular – especially those committed to Palestinian statehood. But the region's recent history nicely illuminates the saying that 'one person's terrorist is another person's freedom fighter', a phrase often invoked in explanations as to why the international community has consistently failed to develop a legally binding consensus definition of 'terrorism'.

In the 1940s, Zionist groups (including the Stern Gang, which counted among its members the future Israeli Prime Minister Menachem Begin) employed terrorist violence in their efforts to create a Jewish state in Palestine. With the successful establishment of Israel in 1948, that kind of political violence by non-state Jewish groups dissipated. Only later, with the expansion of Israeli power and the failure of previous two-state proposals, did the Palestinians turn in a substantial way to terrorism in the name of national liberation. Today, as noted earlier, critics of Israel argue that its use of force against Palestinian civilians, along with its use of political assassinations, constitutes nothing more than a policy of state terrorism.

In the 1967 Six Day War, Israel swiftly defeated forces from Egypt, Jordan and Syria, stunning the Arab world. In its victory, Israel took control of new territories previously held by those three states: Sinai and the Gaza Strip from Egypt, East Jerusalem and the West Bank from Jordan and the Golan Heights from Syria. Soon afterwards, al-Fatah, the political faction led by Yasser Arafat, gained control of the Palestinian Liberation Organisation (PLO), which had been formed in 1964. By the late 1960s and early 1970s, the PLO turned increasingly to terrorist tactics to draw attention to the cause of Palestinian statehood. These tactics included several hijackings of commercial airliners and, most spectacularly, the capture and murder of Israeli athletes at the 1972 Olympics in Munich, West Germany. Such attacks did get the world's attention. The Munich tragedy was in fact broadcast live on television around the world. But this publicity did not appear to generate much sympathy.

Various organisations linked to the Palestinian cause certainly popularised some modern innovations in terrorist tactics, including hijacking commercial aircraft and later, and even more notoriously, suicide bombings. But groups such as the Lebanese-based Hezbollah, Hamas, al-Fatah and others within and outside the PLO focused their efforts on concrete, state-centred political demands relating to the Palestinian–Israeli conflict and the creation of a Palestinian state. Bin Laden and other Islamists also emphasise the plight of the Palestinians but in a different, more global and more ideological context. For the ideologists of global jihad, the oppression of the Palestinians is a dramatic example of the anti-Islamic animus of the West and its allies, including not only Israel but those corrupt governments in the Arab and Muslim worlds which have aligned themselves with the West.

Even in recent history, terrorism has hardly been limited to the Middle East or to Arab and Muslim groups. In the last third of the twentieth century, it was also employed by nationalist groups in other regions (including the Irish Republican Army, the Basque separatists in

Spain and the Tamil Tigers in Sri Lanka) and, in the 1970s and 1980s, by left-wing militants in Europe (the Baader Meinhof group in Germany and Italy's Red Brigades), Asia (the Japanese Red Army), Latin America (the Shining Path in Peru) and even, to a lesser extent, the United States (the Weathermen or Weather Underground in the 1970s).

Right-wing militants have also employed terrorism in Western Europe and the USA (most notably the bombing of the Oklahoma City federal office building in 1995). In Latin America, right-wing paramilitary groups, usually linked to right-wing governments, military and otherwise, have committed massacres, assassinations and other violent acts of intimidation. Many of the groups engaged in political violence between the 1970s and the 1990s have either gone out of the terrorism business (such as the IRA) or gone out of business altogether (i.e. the Weathermen). Others have faded from the scene significantly (as with the Japanese Red Army and the Shining Path in Peru) or reduced their overt participation in political violence (as with the Basque separatists). The Tamil Tigers continue their activities in Sri Lanka, engaging in at least occasional acts of political violence even while engaged in ongoing negotiations with the government to end their decades-long conflict. In July 2004, a suicide bombing in Sri Lanka was attributed to the Tigers.

State terrorism

Throughout the twentieth century and into the twenty-first, despite the tendency to associate terrorism exclusively with non-state groups, oppressive governments around the world have used violence to terrorise civilian populations. Fascist and communist states have hardly had a monopoly on such practices. Throughout the Cold War era, for example, military-controlled governments in Latin America engaged in widespread campaigns of 'disappearances' and paramilitary violence against their own citizenry. Often, these practices were made possible by aid and training received from the United States in exchange for commitments to ensure stability and fight communism. In 2005, the government of the Sudan was using paramilitary forces to uproot or even destroy the black African population of its Dharfur region. The atrocities in Dharfur are more often labelled genocide rather than terrorism.

But genocide, like the Roman sacking of Carthage, may be viewed as a form of terrorism. The crime of genocide is defined by the intent to destroy an ethnic, national or religious group, but not necessarily by killing each and every individual. Massacres, mass rapes and other atrocities are often used to terrorise those who remain alive into fleeing the area, abandoning the group identity or otherwise weakening the group's prospects for survival. That was very much the case in the Bosnian war of the 1990s, when the Yugoslav government under Slobodan Milosevic pursued a policy of 'ethnic cleansing' against Bosnian Muslims. Viewed in this light, genocide is very much based on the same principle as terrorism, though it is associated more with states than with non-state groups. Unlike terrorism, genocide is codified as a crime under international law. Terrorist acts are also criminal acts: even without a binding international treaty against terrorism as such, terrorist violence can clearly be treated as a crime against humanity under the statute of the International Criminal Court and otherwise.

Terroristic practices carried out by governments raise an obvious question: Is political violence against civilians, aimed at achieving a political objective or advancing a political purpose, any less an act of terrorism if it is carried out by (or on behalf of) a government than if it were carried out by non-state actors alone? The distinction seems an empty one. At some point, if the community of nations is to strengthen the role of law in the struggle against terrorism, it must reach a consensus definition of the term 'terrorism' itself. As many experts agree, the key to that step will be to remove any question about the nature of the actor involved and to focus solely on the behaviour and intentions involved in terrorism as a specific crime. Thus the world's nations would be persuaded to accept the notion that terrorism consists of the use of violence against civilians to advance some political purpose. Historically, however, many states, most emphatically including the United States in its role as the globe's dominant power, have sought to protect themselves against such an open definition of the crime.

Terrorism and globalisation

In the era of globalisation which most visibly came into its own in the 1990s, the landscape of terrorism changed in significant ways. First and foremost, as suggested above, is the rise of terrorist activity divorced from state-related political objectives and essentially local political concerns. Terrorism had previously been an essentially local phenomenon, particularly in terms of the objectives it claimed to advance. Since the 1970s at least, terrorists had sought to use the emerging global media to publicise their causes and often carried out terrorist acts internationally, far from their own locales. (Palestinian hijackings provide a good example in illustrating both these trends, as well as their symbiotic relationship.) But in these early forms of 'international terrorism' the causes themselves remained more or less local and state related. We now see political violence of varying degrees being used on the part of anti-abortion activists, animal rights activists, anti-globalisation activists and religious activists (including cults, such as the Japanese group Aum Shinrikyo, and pro-Hindu as well as pro-Muslim terrorists like bin Laden and his followers).

This new kind of terrorism is clearly associated with collapsing loyalty patterns in a world of weakening state structures and growing global integration. Terrorist groups can now operate horizontally across the globe, so terrorist threats are made against global institutions and against the world's dominant power, the United States, as well as against local states. This new global terrorism arises from a new sense of desperation and the apparent impossibility of influencing it via any of the traditional methods of injecting some element of popular participation in the exercise of power. The USA is the symbolic leviathan and thus gets the bulk of the protest and the Israeli–Palestinian dispute gives both a geographical expression and a religious form to a more general phenomenon.

In addition, at least some terrorist groups have begun to use larger-scale, far deadlier attacks than before. The goal is no longer to publicise the cause but to kill as many of the enemy as possible, even if the enemy are civilians. September 11 can be seen as simply the latest, largest event in this trend. Aum Shinrikyo's use of sarin gas in the Tokyo subways in 1995 was intended to kill as many people as possible. The Oklahoma City bombing in the same year was on a scale unprecedented in the United States. The Hezbollah bombing of Khobar Towers in Saudi Arabia killed hundreds.

In the late 1990s Al Qaeda's assaults increasingly grew in scale and deadliness. Some observers use the term 'apocalyptic terrorism' to describe this new phenomenon. That may apply to cults like Aum Shinrikyo, but not to politically oriented groups like Al Qaeda which wants to change the world according to its own model, not to hasten the apocalypse. Other analysts use the more useful term 'megaterrorism' to capture the qualitatively larger scale on which these groups seek to operate.

Al Qaeda

More than any other organisation, Al Qaeda provides the paradigmatic example of the new global terrorism. Operating in more than 60 countries, Al Qaeda is a worldwide pan-Islamic network led by the wealthy Saudi dissident Osama bin Laden. As the group's founder and leader, bin Laden's greatest significance lies in promoting a radical, pan-Islamic ideology which has found widespread appeal throughout the Islamic world. Within bin Laden's ideological framework, Islam has been under attack by the United States and its allies since the USA asserted itself as a power in the Middle East in the aftermath of the Second World War. Bin Laden's personal mission, and his call to all Muslims, is to defend Islam against this perceived Western assault.

As Bin Laden has made clear in many statements since the 1990s, his jihad and that of his followers has two main objectives: first, to end the Western and especially the US presence in the Muslim world; second, to overthrow all corrupt, pro-Western governments in Arab and Muslim countries in order to strengthen and purify Islam itself. Strategically, Al Qaeda's self-declared war against the United States is a means of attacking pro-US governments throughout the Muslim world, such as Saudi Arabia, Egypt, Pakistan and Indonesia. In attacking the United States, bin Laden seeks to end US support for those governments as well as for Israel. Far from hating the USA because it values freedom, as President Bush proclaims, Al Qaeda members and their many sympathisers hate the the country because of specific policies which they see as a threat to their religion.

Al Qaeda is organised more or less horizontally as a loose network of cells operating globally in scores of countries. Unlike, say, the Communist International, it never had a very strong hierarchical structure; it is vertically very thin but horizontally it stretches widely, with cells in 60–70 countries throughout the Muslim world, Europe and North America (including the United States). In this manner it is representative of the new type of global citizens' organisations made possible by the electronic communications technologies of our time, including mobile phones but especially e-mail and the Internet. Typical examples of global citizens' groups that have made fruitful use of the Internet include the Campaign to Ban Landmines and the Coalition for an International Criminal Court.

In certain ways Al Qaeda may be viewed as their dark, malignant cousin. Like these more benign groups, Al Qaeda is also a loose coalition of local and regional groups as well as a network of individuals. Long before September 11, some terrorism experts viewed Al Qaeda and other global terrorist networks as hydra-headed monsters – a danger that is particularly difficult to stop because you cannot simply kill it by cutting off its head (or eliminating its central command). This helps to explain Al Qaeda's apparent resilience (and widespread attacks outside the United States) in the period after the US military crushed the safe haven it had enjoyed in Afghanistan. With the US-led assault on its leadership structure since September 11, Al Qaeda has become even more hydra-like – a fact that may make it more dangerous than ever. Many analysts assert that bin Laden is no longer able to direct or coordinate operations around the globe but that his ideological appeal continues to spread, Al Qaeda membership continues to grow and cells continue to operate.

As a terrorist operation, Al Qaeda has pioneered the sophisticated use of global electronic information technologies, such as mobile phones, laptop computers and the Internet (including, now, public Internet access through the many 'cyber cafes' found in towns and cities in Europe, North America and elsewhere, including the Middle East). Security experts and other commentators have issued dire warnings about the threat of cyber-terrorism to a global economy increasingly predicated on the smooth functioning of its computer networks. Terrorist 'cyber-attacks' on the computerised infrastructure of the twenty-first-century world do pose a deep source of concern. Such attacks could conceivably wreak havoc on an unprecedented scale without resort to violence in any ordinary sense of the word.

But to date what is more striking is the uses of the Internet and related technologies by global terrorist groups like Al Qaeda – uses not unlike those of many other global or multinational organisations. More than a potential target of attack, the Internet is the essential infrastructure that allows Al Qaeda to operate the way it does. One might say that the Internet is the medium that makes Al Qaeda possible.

One reason the Bush administration responded to 9/11 by focusing so much attention on rogue states is that administration officials had difficulty understanding that attacks of that scale and sophistication could be coordinated by a non-state group without support from some government. But Al Qaeda has become something quite new: via the Internet and its long-established and expanding network of committed individuals, it can operate transnationally in a way a more traditional 'state-sponsored' terrorist organisation could scarcely imagine. Its relationship with the Taliban regime in Afghanistan was also novel. The Taliban provided a safe haven for bin Laden's operations but not state sponsorship for his activities. Instead, bin Laden offered the Taliban financial as well as military assistance. Some observers have quipped that the Taliban regime was a terrorist-sponsored state, though that overstates Al Qaeda's role.

Al Qaeda uses the Internet for a range of purposes and does so perhaps as effectively as any other global organisation. To avoid detection, its members tend to use e-mail via public-access computers, particularly in Internet cafes. By using multiple, web-based (and free) e-mail accounts, often just for a single communication before abandoning one address and opening up another, Al Qaeda operatives are still able to communicate with each other and with leadership instantly despite intense scrutiny from the intelligence communities of the USA and its allies. Perhaps more important than e-mail communication is Al Qaeda's use of websites to achieve some of its key organisational needs and objectives, including publicity and propaganda, recruitment, distribution of training materials, fund-raising and finance. Its strong presence on the web has helped Al Qaeda survive and even expand despite the loss of its safe haven in Afghanistan. Indeed, through its web postings, Al Qaeda's ideology has spread far beyond its formal membership and seems destined to have a life-span beyond that of its founders.

The audacious, devastating attacks on the

United States on September 11 2001, especially the televised destruction of the World Trade Center and its Twin Towers, quickly turned 'Al Qaeda' and 'Osama bin Laden' into household words around the world. Bin Laden's image became a global icon, albeit one imbued with vastly divergent meanings by different audiences. Today virtually everyone in the world knows who bin Laden is and has at least some idea of what Al Qaeda is. Before September 11, they were known only by the most attentive.

Al Qaeda's origins can be traced back to the 1980s, when bin Laden and thousands of other Arabs went to Afghanistan to join the fight against Soviet occupation. Bin Laden organised training camps for these fighters and kept a list of those who passed through them. That list became the basis for the network known as Al Qaeda (Arabic for 'the list'). Bin Laden declared war against the United States in 1998 and Al Qaeda was responsible for several earlier assaults on US targets. These tended to be larger scale and far deadlier than typical terrorist attacks in the past. In 1998, the coordinated, simultaneous bombings of the United States embassies in Kenya and Tanzania killed hundreds of people (mainly Africans) while wounding thousands more. The scale and sophistication of the embassy bombings gave a clear indication of Al Qaeda's capabilities. By the end of the 1990s, members of the Clinton administration, including President Clinton himself, saw Al Qaeda as the greatest security threat facing the United States. Though President Clinton did order limited cruise missile strikes against targets in Afghanistan and Sudan (where bin Laden had been based earlier in the decade), specifically in response to the embassy bombings, he failed to take any decisive action against this grave and growing threat.

Clinton's political will for taking such action was limited in part by the impeachment proceedings against him. Perhaps more significantly, Clinton and his advisors believed that military action would not be effective and that the US public had little tolerance for putting troops on the ground in hostile territory. The attacks on the World Trade Center and the Pentagon, of course, swiftly changed that public mood.

The September 11 attacks were as tactically brilliant as they were terrifying, but their strategic success remains an open question. Because they prompted such a massive and militarised response from the United States, they seemed at first to be a strategic fiasco. Yet subsequent events have shown Al Qaeda to be a resilient as well as dangerous foe. Considered globally, the two years after September 11 saw more terrorist attacks than the two years prior to it. Even in Afghanistan, despite its success in crushing the Taliban and installing a friendly government in Kabul, the USA did not capture or kill bin Laden. Nor did it destroy his leadership cohort, despite the capture and killing of some key individuals. Al Qaeda members continue to fight alongside the Taliban in an ongoing insurgency against the US-backed government of Hamid Karzai. And bin Laden and his aides continue to operate somewhere in Afghanistan or neighbouring Pakistan, as does the Taliban leader, Mullah Omar. Some experts predict it is only a matter of time before the Taliban returns to power, with Al Qaeda still closely at its side.

Beyond Afghanistan, Al Qaeda has not been able to carry out any further attacks within the United States, but it has successfully executed deadly bombings in wide-ranging locales, including the Bali nightclub bombing in Indonesia, the attack on a secured Western compound in Saudi Arabia, the Madrid subway bombings and the attacks on the London Underground in July 2005. Many analysts believe Al Qaeda membership has grown substantially since September 11, perhaps to 18,000 or more. Most agree that the Bush administration's 'war on terror' strategy has only made bin Laden's message more attractive to Muslims.

The US invasion and occupation of Iraq, in particular, has substantially increased the appeal of Al Qaeda's ideology, even among Muslims who deplored the September 11 attacks. Many Muslims viewed this as an unprovoked attack on a Muslim country with no involvement in 9/11. For a substantial number, it has provided dramatic, conclusive evidence for the claim that the USA is at war with Islam. In presenting its Iraq policies as part of a global war on terror, the Bush administration argues that by fighting terrorists in Iraq it is preventing them from attacking the United States. It is true that Iraq has become a magnet for Al Qaeda loyalists and other terrorists, though that by itself does not prevent an attack on the USA or elsewhere, especially if the number of terrorists is growing. The greater danger is that Iraq will descend into civil war and state collapse when and if US troops depart, making it a new haven for Al Qaeda and Al Qaeda-inspired terrorists.

The future

In conclusion, terrorism will remain a central issue in global politics for the foreseeable future. The past decade or so has witnessed two major changes in the nature of terrorism. First, it has become globalised, in terms of both objectives transcending local concerns and worldwide networks linked principally via the new information technologies. Second, while the number of groups using terrorist tactics seems to be on the decline, today's terrorists, and tomorrow's, seem willing and able to kill large numbers of civilians to advance their goals. The great danger facing the world is the prospect of terrorist organisations like Al Qaeda acquiring nuclear weapons. Unlike states, Al Qaeda wants nuclear weapons in order to use them against its enemies, not to deter an enemy attack. Unlike states, a nuclear-armed Al Qaeda could not be deterred by threats of a reciprocal attack. A terrorist bomb, should it come, will not have a return address. Preventing this possibility must be a priority not just of the United States and its allies but of the entire international community. To date, though, it is not clear that the 'war on terror' is the best way to prevent nuclear terrorism or to combat and constrain the new global terrorism more generally. Military force can play a role, but the international community needs to develop an alternative, multilateral approach to halting terrorist violence and other crimes against humanity.

The challenge of the new global terrorism requires not so much a 'new kind of war' as a fundamental, long-term commitment by the 'community of nations' to enhance forms of multilateral cooperation (in areas such as intelligence sharing and law enforcement), to strengthen international law forbidding the use of organised violence against civilians and to develop global institutions better able to uphold that law. No government can put 'an end to evil' (to quote the title of a book by two former US administration figures), nor can a global war put an end to terrorist practices for all time.

The key to minimising terrorist violence in the future is to build up the normative structures against political violence of all forms. As political violence becomes increasingly unacceptable (as slavery did during the nineteenth century) terrorist acts will fail to attract support for or ideological conversion to the terrorists' cause. That will not put an end to terrorism, but it will limit the number of people taking up this abhorrent practice.

Further Reading

Falk, Richard (2002) *The Great Terror War*, New York: Interlink.

A useful, provocative analysis of the conflict between Al Qaeda and the United States, by a leading international law scholar and progressive critic of US policy.

Hoffman, Bruce (1999) *Inside Terrorism*, New York: Columbia University Press.

Clear and comprehensive survey of terrorism as it stood in the mid-1990s, by one of the most widely cited terrorism experts. In a well-researched book published three years before 9/11, it is startling to note that neither Bin Laden nor Al Qaeda are even listed in the index.

Laqueur, Walter (2003) *No End to War: Terrorism in the Twenty-first Century*, London: Continuum.

A comprehensive, pessimistic view, from a conservative scholar deeply informed by a sense of history. The author is an authority in the field and has written many books on terrorism and its history.

Scheuer, Michael (2004) *Imperial Hubris*, Washington, DC: Potomac Books.

Originally published anonymously by a senior, long-term CIA analyst long responsible for the agency's Bin Laden watch (until his recent resignation in protest, which has allowed him to speak publicly). Combines a scathing critique of US policy with a brilliant explication of the Al Qaeda world view. See also *Through Our Enemies' Eyes: Osama Bin Laden, Radical Islam, and the Future of America* (2003), by the same author, Potomac Books.

See also the website of the Council on Foreign Relations – www.cfr.org – which links to the Council's dedicated website on terrorism. This site is easy to navigate, well edited and lucidly written. It is arranged topically, something like an online encyclopedia of terrorism, and includes bibliographic information for further reading. It also provides links to other quality websites on the subject.

APPENDIX: Timelines

1: HUMANITARIAN ACTION

1945   Cooperative for American Remittances to Europe (CARE) was founded to provide relief to survivors of the Second World War

1945 November – 1946 October   Twenty-one Nazi leaders were prosecuted in Nuremberg for crimes of aggression, war crimes and crimes against humanity. Eleven were sentenced to death, three were acquitted and the rest were imprisoned

1946 October   In the wake of the precedent set by Nuremberg, an international congress was convened in Paris calling for the adoption of an international criminal code prohibiting crimes against humanity and the prompt establishment of an International Criminal Court (ICC)

1946 December   UN General Assembly affirmed the Principles of International Law recognised by the Charter of the Nuremberg Tribunal

1946 December   UN International Children's Emergency Fund (UNICEF) established

1946 April – 1948 November   The International Military Tribunal for the Far East prosecuted Japanese soldiers for war crimes, crimes against peace and crimes against humanity. Seven were sentenced to death

1948   UN Universal Declaration of Human Rights

1948 April   World Health Organisation (WHO) established by the UN

1948 December   UN General Assembly adopted the Convention on the Prevention and Punishment of the Crime of Genocide

1948 December 10   The UN General Assembly adopted the Universal Declaration of Human Rights detailing human rights and fundamental freedoms

1949 August   Geneva Conventions established: Convention I for the Amelioration of the Condition of the Wounded and Sick in Armed Forces in the Field; Convention II for the Amelioration of the Condition of the Wounded, Sick and Shipwrecked Members of Armed Forces at Sea; Convention III relative to the Treatment of Prisoners of War; and Convention IV relative to the Protection of Civilian Persons in time of War

1947–1954   In Indochina, ICRC struggled to carry out independent humanitarian action during the war for independence from France

1956   During the Suez Crisis, the ICRC assisted prisoners of war, the wounded and sick and civilians

1956 October   At the Hungarian uprising, the ICRC set up an emergency operation to help people caught up in the violence that had broken out in the Hungarian capital, Budapest, dealing with relief supplies, prisoners, separated families

1962 December   Red Cross began collecting medicines and food for Cuba in exchange for release of Bay of Pigs POWs

1964 March   Red Cross aided victims of massive earthquake at Anchorage in Alaska

1965 October   Red Cross Movement adopted its Seven Fundamental Principles: Humanity, Impartiality, Neutrality, Independence, Voluntary Service, Unity, and Universality

1965   UN Development Fund established

1968   Biafran war: disagreement within the Red Cross about how to deal with gross human rights abuses caused a split that resulted in a group of doctors forming Médécins Sans Frontières (Doctors Without Borders)

1968 May   An International Conference adopted a Resolution on the Human Rights in Armed Conflicts at Teheran in Iran

1968 November   The UN General Assembly decided there was no statute of limitations to war crimes and crimes against humanity

1975 April   Red Cross began a four-month *Operation New Life* for Vietnam refugees brought to the USA

1975   The Helsinki Accords were the Final Act of the Conference on Security and Cooperation in Europe held in Helsinki

1977 June   Additional Protocols of the Geneva Conventions were adopted: I, relating to the Protection of Victims of International Armed Conflicts; and II, relating to the Protection of Victims of Non-International Armed Conflicts

1980 October   A UN Conference in Geneva established Prohibitions on the Use of Certain Conventional Weapons Which May be Deemed to be Excessively Injurious or to Have Indiscriminate Effects

1983 January   United States blood banking groups issued their first warning about AIDS

1984 December   UN General Assembly adopted the Convention Against Torture and Other Cruel, Inhuman or Degrading Treatment or Punishment

1986   South African government expelled ICRC from the country in retaliation for not being invited to an ICRC conference. South Africa shortly after rescinded the expulsion

1989 June   Trinidad and Tobago resurrected the proposal for an International Criminal Court and the UN General Assembly asked the International Law Commission to prepare draft statutes

1989 October   Red Cross aided 14,000 families affected by an earthquake in Northern California. Hurricane Andrew hit Florida and led to multi-year Red Cross aid

1991   Iraq: UN Safe Haven and No Fly Zones in Iraq for Kurds and Shia

1992   US military operation with the support of the United Nations went to Somalia to deliver humanitarian aid and restore order; led eventually to the Battle of Mogadishu in 1993

1993 May   The UN Security Council established an International Criminal Tribunal to prosecute war crimes in the former Yugoslavia

1994 November   The UN General Assembly established a second International Criminal Tribunal to prosecute war crimes in Rwanda

1995   Responding to a flood in North Korea that caused a famine, the United States government initially provided more than $8 million in general humanitarian aid

1995 April   Red Cross aided victims of bombing of Federal Building in Oklahoma City

1997 May   The UN Tribunal for Yugoslavia handed down its first conviction, sentencing a Bosnian Serb concentration camp guard to 20 years in prison for crimes against humanity and violations of the laws and customs of war

1997   UN disbanded the Department of Humanitarian Affairs to create the Office of Coordination of Humanitarian Affairs (OCHA)

1997   UNICEF reported that more than 1.2 million people, including 750,000 children below the age of five, had died because of the scarcity of food and medicine

1997   International Campaign to Ban Landmines (ICBL) won the Nobel Peace Prize

1998   Director of the UN Oil-for-Food Programme, Denis Halliday, resigned in protest over the programme's inadequacy

1998   A World Health Organization (WHO) report stated that each month, between 5,000 and 6,000 Iraqi children died because of sanctions

1998 June   Rome Statute establishing the International Criminal Court was finalised and adopted

1998 September   The UN Tribunal for Rwanda handed down its first conviction, finding a Rwandan Hutu leader guilty of genocide

1998 October   British authorities arrested former Chilean dictator Augusto Pinochet on an extradition request from a Spanish judge who brought charges of genocide, torture and other crimes during his rule in the 1970s–1980s

1999 March   Red Cross initiated Nucleic Acid Testing (NAT) which provides early detection of HIV and Hepatitis C in blood

2000   The second director of the Oil-for-Food Programme, Hans von Sponeck, resigned in protest, objecting to the impact of sanctions on the Iraqi civilian population

2000   Oxfam International founded

2000 August   UN Security Council called for the establishment of a 'Special Court' to prosecute war crimes in Sierra Leone

2001 January   Cambodian National assembly passed legislation to establish a tribunal in conjunction with the United Nations to prosecute 'senior leaders' of the Khmer Rouge for atrocities from 1975 to 1979

2001 February   Red Cross joined other groups to launch Measles Initiative, a five-year plan to eradicate the disease in sub-Saharan Africa by immunising children

2003 March   The war against Iraq began when the USA launched *Operation Iraqi Freedom*

2003 October   The Madrid Conference, an international donors' conference of 80 nations to raise funds for the reconstruction of Iraq, yielded $13 billion in addition to the $20 billion already pledged by the United States. This amount fell short of the overall target of $56 billion, the figure the World Bank and the UN estimated that Iraq needed over the next four years

2004 September/October   A great majority of foreign aid workers in Iraq, fearing they had become targets of the postwar violence, pulled out of the country, leaving essential relief work to their Iraqi colleagues and slowing the reconstruction effort

2004 October   Margaret Hassan, head of CARE International in Baghdad, was taken hostage and subsequently murdered. Consequently, CARE International closed all operations in Iraq

2004 December   Magnitude 9.0 earthquake off west coast of Indonesia triggered massive tsunami that brought death and destruction to 12 countries. American Red Cross joined international relief effort

2005 August   ICRC delegates had access to Algerian detainees from 1955 onwards and noted the occurrence of torture. They were not allowed to talk about it but *Le Monde* published a summary of the report – press article published in *Le Temps* (Switzerland)

2: POLITICS AND INSTABILITY IN GLOBAL MARKETS

1944   Hayek's *Road to Serfdom* published in the United Kingdom. It criticised economic planning by state, but influenced only a minority for three decades

1944   Bretton Woods Conference established the World Bank and the International Monetary Fund and pegged all currencies to gold

1945   Potsdam Conference divided Europe; Soviet-occupied countries adopted command economies

1945   Labour Party victory in the United Kingdom started nationalization of major industries, established welfare state

1946   Planning pioneered in non-command context in France spurred mixed economy

1947   The USA implemented the Marshall Plan to avoid repeating Second World War treaty mistake and among other results initiated the German economic 'miracle'

1947   Independent India sought to mix Western democracy and socialist planning

1947   Friedrich von Hayek created the Mt Pelerin conference in Switzerland to combat economics of central planning

1949   Communist revolution founded the People's Republic of China; collectivisation began

1949   European Coal and Steel Community united six countries in free trade of key goods; first step towards European Union

1957   Treaty of Rome established European Economic Community

1958   Chinese Great Leap Forward attempted forced industrialisation; failed in two years, causing a famine

1961   In South Korea General Park coup launched fast, state-driven industrialisation

1964   Johnson administration launched War on Poverty and expanded social programmes even as expenditure on the Vietnam War escalated

1971   President Nixon adopted a Keynesian economic policy, but price and wage controls brought shortages instead of stopping inflation. Nixon abandoned gold standard, ending the Bretton Woods system in favour of floating exchange rates

1973   In Chile General Pinochet toppled Allende; the ensuing military regime made things worse economically before turning to Chicago-style free-market reform

1973   OPEC instigated an oil crisis, triggering global inflation and vast wealth transfer to oil-producing nations

1978   In the United Kingdom the 'Winter of Discontent' marked the nadir of Keynesian economic policies

1979   Election of Margaret Thatcher started 'Thatcher revolution' in Britain

1979   Iranian Revolution turned against Westernisation, offered Islamic alternative; sparked second oil shock

1979   In the United States inflation reached 13.3 per cent; Paul Volcker took over Federal Reserve; tight money policy triggered recession

1980   Polish Solidarity movement began in shipyards to become the main force in toppling communism

1981   New French President Mitterrand's election brought an experiment with nationalisation and socialist economic policy

1981   President Reagan introduced supply-side economics and deregulated markets

1982   Mexican default on international loans sparked global debt crisis and 'lost decade' for developing nations

1983   French nationalisation experiment ended, setting the tone for a new type of European social democracy

1984   First major privatisation of a state-owned industry: British Telecom

1984   In Britain, Thatcher broke the miners' union and closed money-losing mines, putting thousands out of work

1985   In Bolivia rampant hyperinflation was cured with radical market liberalisation and reform, pioneering 'shock therapy' method

1986   After becoming the USSR leader in 1985, Gorbachev began *glasnost* and *perestroika*

1987   European Single Market Act approved; next step toward the European Economic Union

1988   Japan 'miracle' peaks as Tokyo Stock Exchange capitalization matches NYSE

1989   Berlin Wall came down; 'Iron Curtain' fell; Cold War ended

1990   Reunification of Germany: West must assimilate socialist East

1990   'Shock therapy' used in Bolivia was repeated successfully in Poland; Lech Walesa became president

1990   Japanese market bubble was deflated but inertia prevented reform of the banking system and subsidised domestic sector

1991   Indian Prime Minister Narasimha Rao confronted payments crisis and began major reform of what had been known as the 'Permit Raj'

1991   USSR disintegrated: a Russian Federation was the main successor state

1992   Price controls ended; privatisation of Russia's state industries began

1992   In the United States the NAFTA treaty passed over labour, environmental objections, launched decade of free-trade activism

1994   Apartheid was phased out in South Africa, ending closed economy; Mandela's socialist ANC launched market reforms

1994   After health reform failed, President Clinton refocused on a centrist 'New Democrat' economic programme, welfare reform and globalisation issues

1994   The US Treasury intervention staved off the Mexican Peso Crisis and prevented default on international debt

1996   United States President Clinton balanced the budget, proclaimed 'big government is over'

1997   Tony Blair completed centrist repositioning of the British Labour Party with a resounding election victory; the party was re-elected in 2001 and 2005

1997   Chinese Communist Party Congress endorsed 'Deng Xiaoping Theory', dismantling the state-owned industrial sector

1997   Speculative boom triggered run on the Thai currency; ensuing collapse signalled the end of the 'Asian miracle'

1997   In Indonesia the spreading Asian crisis took social and political toll in the region's largest, poorest country; Suharto was deposed

1997   The IMF and the USA were forced to organise the rescue of South Korean banks to prevent further spread of Asian 'contagion'

1998   International financial instability spread to Russia, which defaulted on international loans; rouble was devalued

1999   Financial contagion reached Wall Street: Long-Term Capital Management hedge fund failed, endangering the banking system

1999   In the United States, the Seattle WTO summit crystallised potent global opposition to institutions and the politics of global integration

2001   Terrorist airliner attack destroyed the World

Trade Center in New York City and rocked global financial markets

2001 WTO met in the Gulf State of Qatar to initiate a new round of global trade talks

2002 Euro replaced national currencies of Germany, France and ten other European nations

2002 Deep interest-rate cuts failed to revive the Japanese economy; value of yen sank to a new low against other key currencies

2002 Argentina defaulted on billions in debt; social and political unrest led to the resignation of two presidents in two weeks

2002 After WTC attacks, President Bush reversed course, created new agencies, reintroduced Keynesian stance in economic policy

2002 AIDS pandemic threatened economic future of most nations in sub-Saharan Africa

2002 In the wake of a series of corporate financial scandals, including Enron, Tyco International and WorldCom, the Sarbanes-Oxley Act was signed into law to review the existing legislative audit requirements. It has been considered the most significant change to United States securities laws since the New Deal in the 1930s

2003 Iraq was invaded by US and British forces to depose Saddam Hussein's regime

3: TRANSNATIONAL ORGANISED CRIME AND THE DRUG INDUSTRY

1945–1947 Burma gained independence from Britain at the end of the Second World War. Opium cultivation and trade flourished in the Shan states

1948–1972 Corsican gangsters dominated the US heroin market through their connection with Mafia drug distributors. After refining the raw Turkish opium in Marseilles laboratories, the heroin became easily available for purchase by junkies on New York City streets

1950s Explosion of heroin into the USA and into the hands of drug dealers and addicts

Late 1960s Recreational drug use became fashionable among young, white, middle-class Americans. The social stigmatisation previously associated with drugs lessened as their use became more mainstream. Drug use became representative of protest and social rebellion in an atmosphere of political unrest

1969 Study linked crime and heroin addiction. Forty-four per cent of people entering the DC jail system were found to have tested positive for heroin

1969 Operation Intercept essentially closed the Mexican border. Mexico agreed to attack marijuana trade more aggressively, but the operation did not seriously impact the flow of marijuana into the USA

1970 The number of heroin addicts in the USA reached an estimated 750,000

1971 June President Nixon declared 'war' on drugs

1973 July President Nixon created the Drug Enforcement Administration (DEA) under the Justice Department to consolidate virtually all US federal powers of drug enforcement in a single agency

Mid-1970s In Vietnam, Saigon fell. The heroin epidemic subsided. The search for a new source of raw opium found the Mexican Sierra Madre. 'Mexican Mud' temporarily replaced 'China White' heroin until 1978

1978 Another source of heroin was found in the Golden Crescent area – Iran, Afghanistan and Pakistan – creating a dramatic upsurge in the production and trade of illegal heroin

1984 The DEA and Mexican officials raided a large marijuana cultivation and processing complex in the Chihuahua desert, revealing the existence of a sophisticated Mexican marijuana smuggling industry

1986 The USA enacted the first money laundering law in the world: the Money Laundering Control Act, Title 18 US Code, Section 1956

1990 A US Court indicted Khun Sa, leader of the Shan United Army and reputed drug warlord, on heroin trafficking charges. The US Attorney General's office charged Khun Sa with importing 3,500 lb of heroin into New York City over the course of 18 months, as well as holding him responsible for the source of the heroin seized in Bangkok

1992 Former President of Panama, Noriega, was convicted on eight counts of drug trafficking, money laundering and racketeering, and sentenced to 40 years in federal prison

1993   Aleksei Tikhomirov and Oleg Baranov were sentenced to three-and-a-half years in prison after stealing 4.5 kg of low-grade uranium from Russia's Sevmorput naval shipyard

1993   Colombian drug lord Pablo Escobar killed by the Colombian police

1994   During a German police raid on the house of Adolf Jaekle, a businessman under investigation for counterfeiting, 6.15 grams of nearly pure plutonium were discovered

1994   The Clinton Administration ordered a shift in policy away from the anti-drug campaigns of previous administrations. Instead the focus included 'institution building' with the hope that by 'strengthening democratic governments abroad, [it] will foster law-abiding behavior and promote legitimate economic opportunity'

1994   Germans Gustav Illich and Vaclav Havlik were arrested for selling stolen nuclear materials to an undercover agent. Only a small amount of their 800 mg of highly enriched uranium was recovered, making this the first case with hard evidence that more bomb-grade material was hidden somewhere

1994   German Justiniano Torres Benitez and Spaniards Julio Oroz and Javier Bengoechea Arratibel were arrested at the Munich airport after carrying 560 g of mixed-oxide reactor fuel from Moscow. The fuel contained 363 g of weapons-grade plutonium

1994   Russian trader Alexander Scherbinin, Prague physicist Dr Vagner and Belorussian Kunicky were arrested for possession of 2.7 kg of weapon-grade uranium. The nuclear material was identical to the uranium that Germans Gustav Illich and Vaclav Havlik were arrested for earlier in the year

1995   The Golden Triangle region of South-East Asia became the leader in opium production

1998   United Nations Political Declaration and Action Plan against Money Laundering adopted at the Twentieth Special Session of the United Nations General Assembly.

A declaration on 'Combating Drugs and International Crime' was issued at the G8 Summit in Birmingham in England

2000   The United Nations Convention against Transnational Organised Crime and the three related Protocols was the first universal convention to stipulate a comprehensive framework to combat transnational organised crime and represented a legal foundation for global measures in the future. The Convention contained, among others, provisions on criminalisation of money laundering, corruption and obstruction of justice, and those on international cooperation, in particular, extradition and mutual legal assistance

2000   Japan hosted the Asia-Pacific Symposium on Trafficking in Persons

2000   First high-level meeting between government and industry on Safety and Confidence in Cyberspace was held in Paris among G8 member governments and industry

2000   In Kyoto, the 'International Payment Card Crime Initiative Draft Framework Document' was adopted

2000   President Clinton sent $1.3 billion in aid to help Colombia combat drug traffickers

2001   China executed 57 people on anti-drug day. Thousands of spectators attended a rally at a stadium where 20 were sentenced to death to mark a UN anti-drug day

2002   A naval patrol vessel seized 4 tons of cocaine worth $120 million on the Pacific coast of Colombia

2003   Drugs crackdown in Thailand left 2,274 dead: the prime minister defended his controversial war, trumpeting the successful conclusion of a three-month campaign

2003   UN Convention Against Corruption

2003   UN Convention Against Illicit Drugs

2005   In Colombia, authorities seized $300 million of cocaine in what was claimed to be the single largest drugs haul ever

4: TERRORISM

1959   Basque Fatherland and Liberty (ETA) founded

1963   Southern racists, including Ku Klux Klan members, reacted violently to the civil rights movement in Birmingham, Alabama, carrying out a bombing campaign that earned the city the nickname 'Bombingham'. There a KKK bomb killed four young girls attending Sunday school at the 16th Street Baptist Church

1972   In a tragedy played out on worldwide television, members of a Palestinian terror group killed two and seized nine Israeli athletes at the Munich Olympics. German police failed in attempts to free the hostages and all nine were murdered. Israeli commandos later tracked down and killed most of the surviving hostage takers

1982   Hezbollah formed after Israeli invasion in Lebanon

1983   Sixty-three people died in an attack by the Lebanese group Hezbollah on the US Embassy in Beirut – the first time a suicide attack caused mass casualties in the Arab-Israeli conflict. Later that year, more than 240 US Marines died in another suicide bombing. President Reagan reacted by withdrawing US troops

1980s   Al Qaeda founded by Osama Bin Laden

1995   The USA was focused more on foreign terrorism than domestic – until an attack on Oklahoma City's federal building killed 168 people, including 19 children. The attack drew attention to radical antigovernment rightists

1995   Japanese religious cult Aum Shinrikyo released the deadly nerve gas sarin into the Tokyo subway system at rush hour. The attack, which killed 12 people and sickened thousands, demonstrated the vulnerability of modern transportation systems

1996   US military barracks in Dhahran, Saudi Arabia, were bombed by Islamists opposed to a US presence

1998   Real IRA detonated a car bomb in the town marketplace at Omagh in Northern Ireland, killing 29 bystanders

1999–2000   UN and other aid workers were targeted by various armed groups fighting a civil war in Sierra Leone

2001   Al Qaeda used hijacked airliners in a highly coordinated attack on US government and civilian targets in Washington and New York

2002   A car bomb exploded at Lima in Peru, a few days before a visit by US President George W. Bush

2002   A series of blasts ripped through nightclubs popular with foreign tourists on Bali in Indonesia, killing 202 people and injuring hundreds more

2003   Civil strife in Colombia erupted in a series of nightclub bombings in Bogotá that killed dozens of people

2000s   A Palestinian uprising against Israeli military occupation included bombing and shooting in Israel and the occupied territories. Civilians on both sides were frequently killed

2004   Four commuter trains in Madrid, Spain, were bombed by a group linked to al Qaeda, killing 191 people

2004   Chechen rebels took over a school in Beslan, Russia. Hundreds of hostages died in the standoff, including many children

2004   As coalition troops engaged with insurgents in Iraq, terrorists bombed and kidnapped Iraqi officials and foreigners

2004   Series of videoed beheadings of hostages in Iraq

5: FOREIGN AID AND DEBT RELIEF

1945   The International Monetary Fund (IMF) and World Bank were established

1947 March $400 million was given in military and economic aid to Turkey and Greece under the Truman Doctrine

1947 June $13 billion of economic and technical assistance was given under the Marshall Plan to help the recovery of the European countries which had joined in the Organization for European Economic Cooperation

1948   Formal establishment of the OEEC (became the OECD in 1961)

1961   President John F. Kennedy established the US Agency for International Development (USAID)

1961   The Alliance for Progress was initiated by President John F. Kennedy to establish economic cooperation between North and South America

1964   The African Development Bank (AfDB) was established with the intention of promoting economic and social development in Africa

1973   The Organisation of Petroleum Exporting Countries (OPEC) raised the price of oil. OPEC nations invested their dramatically increased profits in Western banks. Western banks in turn lent the money to developing nations at very low interest rates

1975   The first summit of what would become the G8, with six countries (France, Germany, Italy, Japan, the UK and the USA) participating, took place at Rambouillet in France

1979   OPEC quadrupled the price of oil. Recession hit the developed world and interest rates rose. Developing countries earned less on their exports to the developed world and had to cope with the effects of high prices for oil and high interest rates on their debt to Western banks

1982   Mexico threatened to default on its debt repayments, throwing the global financial system into crisis. Many poor countries became virtually bankrupt, owing far more than they could pay back

1980s   World Bank and the IMF bailed out countries with new loans; but these only added to their debt

1982–1987   Approximately $700 billion worth of resources were transferred from poor to rich countries under debt rescheduling

1986   Export incomes were still falling. It is estimated that sub-Saharan Africa lost $19 billion due to lost exports in this year alone

1990   A huge debt mountain amassed by the developing world, having increased from $800 billion in 1982 to $1300 billion; in the years since the debt crisis broke, $1,100 billion has been repaid

1996   World Bank and the IMF acknowledged that some debt had to be cancelled and they launched the Highly Indebted Poor Countries (HIPC) Initiative

1998   70,000 people formed a 10 km human chain around the G8 meeting in Birmingham in England to protest about the debt crisis and the failure of the HIPC Initiative to cancel any debt

1999   At the Cologne G8 summit in Germany the G8 decided to speed up the HIPC Initiative after being surrounded by another long human chain

1999   United States became the first country to cancel all the debt owed to it by some of the world's poorest nations. Eventually other G8 countries followed suit. However, huge debts remained outstanding to the World Bank and the IMF, still leaving poor countries spending more on debt repayments than on health care

2000   Okinawa G8 summit in Japan made no further promises on debt cancellation

1999–2002   Argentine financial crisis

2002   Kananaskis in Canada G8 made $1 billion debt relief promise

2004   Combined Official Development Assistance of OECD countries was $78.6 billion

2004   Massive foreign aid relief effort aimed at relieving the effects of the 9.0 magnitude earthquake off the west coast of Indonesia which triggered a huge tsunami that killed approximately 300,000 people in 12 countries

2005   Gleneagles G8 summit in Scotland proposed a deal by the world's richest states that would erase debt of up to $55 billion (£31 billion) owed by the poorest countries, subsequently confirmed

6: WORLD TRADE AND INVESTMENT

1947   General Agreement on Tariffs and Trade (GATT) was established in Geneva in Switzerland intended to initiate post-war trade liberalisation

1948   GATT agreement came into force

1948   Charter of International Trade Organisation signed but the US Congress rejected it, leaving GATT as the only international instrument governing world trade

1949   Second GATT round of trade talks held in Annecy in France, where countries exchanged 5,000 tariff concessions

1950   Third GATT round held in Torquay, England, where countries exchanged 8,700 tariff concessions, cutting the 1948 tariff levels by 25 per cent

1955–1956   The next trade round completed in May 1956, resulting in $2.5 billion in tariff reductions

1957   The European Community (EC) was founded by the signing of the Treaty of Rome

1960–1962   Fifth GATT round named in honour of US Under Secretary of State Douglas Dillon who proposed the negotiations. It yielded tariff concessions worth $4.9 billion of world trade and involved negotiations related to the creation of the European Economic Community

1964   The United Nations Conference on Trade and Development (UNCTAD) was established as the principal organ of the United Nations General Assembly dealing with trade, investment and development issues

1964–1967   The Kennedy Round, named in honour of the late US president, achieved tariff cuts worth $40 billion of world trade

1967 August   The Association of South-East Asian Nations (ASEAN) was established

1973–1979   The seventh Kennedy round was launched in Tokyo. Tariff reductions worth more than $300 billion were achieved

1986–1993   GATT trade ministers launched the Uruguay Round – the most ambitious and far-reaching trade round so far. The round extended the range of trade negotiations, leading to major reductions in agricultural subsidies, an agreement to allow full access for textiles and clothing from developing countries, and an extension of intellectual property rights

1991   MERCOSUR, a trading zone between Brazil, Argentina, Uruguay and Paraguay, was founded by the Treaty of Asunción

1994   The North American Free Trade Agreement (NAFTA) went into effect

1994   Trade ministers met at Marrakesh in Morocco to establish the World Trade Organisation (WTO) and sign other agreements

1994   The Common Market for Eastern and Southern Africa (COMESA) was founded as a free trade area with 21 member states stretching from Egypt to Namibia

1995   World Trade Organisation was created at Geneva

1999   At least 30,000 protesters disrupted the WTO summit in Seattle; New Zealander Mike Moore became the WTO director-general

2001   WTO members meeting in Doha, Qatar, agreed on the Doha Development Agenda, intended to open negotiations on opening markets to agricultural, manufactured goods

2001   China formally joined the WTO. Taiwan was admitted weeks later

2002   WTO ruled in favour of the EU in an argument with Washington over tax breaks for US exporters. The EU got permission to impose $4 billion in sanctions against the USA, the highest damages ever awarded by the WTO

2002   The former Thai Deputy Prime Minister Supachai Panitchpakdi began a three-year term as director-general – the first WTO head to come from a developing nation

2003   WTO announced a deal aimed at giving developing countries access to cheap medicines, hailing it as historic, but aid agencies expressed disappointment

2003   WTO trade talks at Cancun in Mexico collapsed after four days of wrangling over farm subsidies, access to markets. Unusually, a coalition of developing countries, led by Brazil, China and India, worked as a bloc to counterbalance the weight of the much richer USA, EU and Japan

2004   Iraq was granted observer status at the WTO. WTO gave the EU permission to introduce sanctions against the USA for not repealing an 88-year-old law that allowed US firms to sue low-price importers of steel

2004   Nepal joined the WTO, becoming its 147th member. WTO ruled that US subsidies to its cotton farmers were unfair

2004   Geneva talks achieved a framework agreement on opening up global trade. The USA and the EU were to reduce agricultural subsidies, while developing nations would cut tariffs on manufactured goods

2004   WTO agreed to start membership talks with Afghanistan and Iraq

2005 March   Upholding a complaint from Brazil, the WTO ruled that US subsidies to its cotton farmers were illegal

2005   WTO agreed to start membership talks with Iran

2005   The US House of Representatives, by a narrow vote of 217 to 215, approved the Central American Free Trade Agreement or CAFTA

2005   Former EU Commissioner Pascal Lamy took over as WTO Director-General

2005   WTO trade talks in Hong Kong

7: DIPLOMACY

17th century   In Europe, diplomacy became continuous rather than occasional and was concentrated so as to become the sole preserve of states and rulers

1815   The first organised system for coordinating diplomacy, called the Concert of Europe, emerged at the Congress held in Vienna (1814–1815) in Austria. International rules about the conduct of diplomacy began to be made in Vienna and at the Congress of Aix-la-Chapelle (Aachen) in Germany in 1818

1860s   The introduction of the electric telegraph increased the pace and scope of diplomacy across the world

1919/1920   The post-First World War peace conference in Paris debated ways of making diplomacy into a permanent and non-optional institution, resulting in the establishment of the League of Nations in 1920

1945   After the Second World War, the League of Nations was replaced by the United Nations. At the same time, the number of international bodies such as the International Monetary Fund increased, thus increasing the scope of diplomacy. This process developed further in the 1960s and 1970s

1961   A UN conference in Vienna produced a definitive international treaty defining and regulating the practice of diplomacy – the Vienna Convention on Diplomatic Relations. In the decade following, further treaties expanded and refined the process

1990s and after   The emergence of a fully global political and economic system ended the sole right of states to conduct diplomacy and significant private organizations, particularly in the areas of humanitarian relief, human rights and environmental issues, began to enter the field of diplomacy

8: ENVIRONMENT

1948   International Union for the Protection of Nature (became International Union for Conservation of Nature in 1956) was founded near Paris

1949   United Nations Scientific Conference on the Conservation and Utilisation of Resources was held in Lake Success, New York

1956   First person died of Minimata Disease (mercury poisoning) in Japan

1958   First United Nations Conference on the Law of the Sea was held in Geneva

1960   Global human population reached 3 billion

1961   World Wildlife Fund (became World Wide Fund for Nature) was founded in Switzerland

1962   Rachel Carson's *Silent Spring* was published

1966   First pictures of the Earth as seen from outer space

1967   Oil tanker *Torrey Canyon* was wrecked off Land's End, England, spilling 118,000 tons of crude oil

1968   Swedish government moved to discuss 'the human environment' at the United Nations Economic and Social Council

1968   International Conference of Experts on the Scientific Basis for Rational Use and Conservation of the Resources of the Biosphere was held in Paris

1970   First Earth Day (April 21) was celebrated in the United States

1971   United Nations Economic and Social Council established its Man and the Biosphere Programme

1972   *The Ecologist* published *Blueprint for Survival* calling for the establishment of a 'steady-state society'

1972   Club of Rome published *Limits to Growth* (written by Donella and Dennis Meadows) contending that growing human population and resource consumption would encounter several notable limits over the next 100 years

1972   United Nations Conference on the Human Environment was held in Stockholm, leading to the creation of the United Nations Environment Programme

1974   United Nations Convention on International Trade in Endangered Species of Wild Fauna and Flora (CITES) was opened for signature in Washington

1974   United Nations convened the first World Conference on Population in Bucharest

1974   Cocoyoc Declaration was issued linking the global maldistribution of resources with environmental degradation

1974   United Nations convened the World Food Conference in Rome, leading to the creation of the World Food Council and the World Food Programme

1974   Global population reached 4 billion

1975   Dag Hammarskjöld Foundation issued *What Now: Another Development* calling for economic and social development premised upon self-reliance and basic needs

1976   United Nations convened the United Nations Conference on Human Settlements in Vancouver, leading to the creation of the Habitat Programme

1977   United Nations convened the United Nations Conference on Desertification in Nairobi to highlight the spread of desert-like conditions in several parts of the world

1977   United Nations convened the United Nations Water Conference in Mar del Plata (Argentina), establishing the goal of providing all people in the world with clean water and adequate sanitation

1979   World Meteorological Organisation announced that the 'greenhouse effect' resulting from the accumulation of carbon dioxide required urgent international action

1980   The Independent Commission on International Development Issues (chaired by West German Chancellor Willy Brandt) published *North-South: A Program for Survival* recommending large-scale increases in development assistance and the preparation of environmental impact assessments

1980   The International Union for the Conservation of Nature, the United Nations Environment Programme and the World Wildlife Fund issued *World Conservation Strategy* calling for 'global coordinated efforts for sustainable development'

1980   United States government issued *The Global 2000 Report* to the president calling for renewed attention in addressing severe global environmental problems

1982   United Nations General Assembly endorsed the report *World Charter for Nature* produced by the International Union for the Conservation of Nature

1984   A chemical plant in Bhopal, India operated by Union Carbide exploded, releasing methyl isocyanate gas, killing an estimated 2,800 people and injuring tens of thousands of others

1985   British scientists discovered a 'hole' in the stratosphere over Antarctica caused by the atmospheric accumulation of chlorofluorocarbons

1986   The Chernobyl nuclear power station in Ukraine experienced a major accident that released radioactive material across the surrounding region and northern Europe

1987   The World Commission on Environment and Development, chaired by Norwegian Prime Minister Gro Harlem Brundtland, released its report, *Our Common Future*, placing sustainable development on the international policy agenda

1987   Under the aegis of the United Nations Environment Programme, negotiations were concluded on the Montreal Protocol to reduce the release of ozone-damaging chlorofluorocarbons

1987   Global population reached 5 billion

1991   The International Union for the Conservation of Nature, the United Nations Environment Programme and the World Wildlife Fund issued *Caring for the Earth: A Strategy for Sustainable Living*

1992   United Nations Conference on Environment and Development (Earth Summit) was held in Rio de Janeiro to launch international agreements on climate change, biodiversity, forest management and sustainable development

1992   United Nations General Assembly established the Commission on Sustainable Development to coordinate international activities pertaining to sustainable development

1994   The United Nations convened the International Conference on Population and Development in Cairo to advance the political and reproductive rights of women

1996   The United Nations convened the Second United Nations Conference on Human Settlements (Habitat II) in Istanbul

1997   The Conference of the Parties to the United Nations Climate Change Convention agreed to establish a mandatory system to reduce emissions of greenhouse gases

1999   Global population reached 6 billion

2002   The United Nations convened the World Summit on Sustainable Development in Johannesburg to review progress over the previous decade integrating international environmental and developmental objectives

Index

Afghanistan 166, 353
Africa
  debt 183, 184, 262, 263, 266
  map 17
  poverty 178
African Union 53, 74, 86, 89, 96–97
AIDS/HIV pandemic 115, 119, 168, 184
Al Qaeda
  Internet, use of 352
  nuclear weapons 353
  objectives of 351
  organisation of 351
  US invasion of Iraq 292–93, 353
  and 'war on terror' 347, 353, 354
  see also September 11 attacks
American Civil War 334
American War of Independence 129
Annan, Kofi 119, 148
Argentina 92–93
arms trafficking 168–69
Asia map 18
Asia-Pacific Economic Cooperation (APEC) 52,
  74, 89, 250
Asian currency crisis 1990s 86–87, 135
Asian tsunami 269, 272, 273
Association of South-East Asian Nations (ASEAN)
  52–53, 74, 89, 90–91, 250
associations of states
  cooperative agreements 73
  diplomacy 249–51
  first international organisations 80
  global economic institutions 85–89
  global organisations 81–85
  international regulation 79, 81
  military alliances 73
  regional organisations 89–104
asylum seekers 299–300, 302
  asylum applicants, origin and size of 314, 316
  foreigners, integration of 315–16
  in OECD countries 313–15
  refugees 313–16
  UN assistance 312–13
Australasia map 19

Bank of International Settlements (BIS) 57, 75,
  107
Bell, Alexander Graham 5
bin Laden, Osama 292–93, 351
  see also Al Qaeda
Bolivia 165

Bosnia 280, 291–92, 350
Brazil 92–93
Bretton Woods system 85–86, 200–201, 203, 321
Brezhnev, Leonid 94
British East India Company 143
Brussels Treaty (1948) 97–98, 102
Bush, George W. 197, 262, 281, 290, 291, 293

Canada-US Free Trade Agreement (FTA) 91,
  321
capitalism, global 77–78, 105–6
  see also financial system, international; markets,
    global
CARE International 258, 259
Caribbean Community (CARICOM) 53–54
Central America map 14
China, People's Republic of 159–61, 190, 288,
  294
chlorofluorocarbons (CFCs) 191
civil society
  Council of Europe programmes 100
  definition of 112–13, 150
  democracy 114–15
  global organisations 113
  historical trajectory of 111–12
  multilateral organisations, impact on 119–20
  private humanitarian organisations 75–76,
    75–77
  protests, anti-globalisation 117–18, 177, 252
  rule of law 113
  state-level 112–13
  summits 118–19
  see also non-governmental organisations
    (NGOs)
Clinton, Bill 85, 149, 193, 194, 195, 197, 262,
  275, 281, 290, 291, 353
Cold War 4, 5, 6, 73, 83, 87, 102, 114, 153–54,
  226, 231, 277, 295, 334, 338–40, 350
Columbia 165, 167, 171, 175
Common External Tariff (CET) 92
Common Market (Europe) 90
Common Market for Eastern and Southern
  Africa (COMESA) 62–63
Commonwealth 90
communications revolution
  cultural consequences 7–9
  political outcomes 3–4, 7–9
communism 72, 130, 288, 337
computers 3, 5–6
Concert of Europe 81–82, 227

Conference on Security and Cooperation in Europe (CSCE) 94–95
Confidence and Security-building Measures and Disarmament (CDE) 95
conflict, sources of
　distribution of power 153
　drugs 156
　environmental issues 157
　global economy 155
　global power 154
　inter-state disputes 156–57
　migration 155
　organised crime 156
　religion 156
　states, weakening of 153–54
　see also terrorism; war
Consolidated Appeal Process (UN) 276
Convention on Refugees (1955) 278
Council of Europe 61
　civil society programmes 100–101
　Committee of Ministers 99
　Consultative Assembly 99
　conventions 99–100
　EU membership 100
crime, organised transnational
　arms trafficking 168–69
　control of 172–73
　criminal organisations 164, 172
　human trafficking 168
　money laundering 169–70
　nature of 164
　sea piracy 170, 173
　see also drug industry, illegal
crimes, against humanity 84–85
customs unions 92

de Gaulle, Charles 338
debt, and debt relief
　activism 182
　corruption 184–85
　crisis 1980s 204
　financial markets, deregulation of 183
　highly indebted poor countries (HIPCs) 183–85, 191, 262, 264
　macroeconomic adjustment 258–59
　odious debts 185, 266, 267
　Paris Club 262, 264, 268
　relief initiatives 183, 184, 263–66, 268, 269
defence expenditure, international comparisons 66–68
democracy 114–15, 262
Democratic Republic of Congo (Zaire) 96, 267
diplomacy
　associations of states 249–51
　development of 224–25
　diplomatic privilege 225, 227
　global businesses 255–56
　humanitarian organisations 253–55
　institutionalisation of 227–28
　multilateral economic institutions (MEIs) 251–53
　new agencies 226–27
　reciprocity principle 225, 227
　state 226–27, 244, 245–50

traditional 244–45
and war 225–26
drug industry, illegal
　alternative development projects 174
　cannabis 166
　cocaine 165
　drug cartels 165, 167
　eradication programmes 174–75
　heroin 166
　opium 166, 172, 173–74
　societal effects 170–72
　trafficking 167–68
Dutch East India Company 143

e-commerce 241
e-mail 239
Earth Summit see Rio conference
Economic Community of West African States (ECOWAS) 60, 74, 101–2
economic inequality
　debt 182–85
　digital divide 185–86
　ecological divide 185
　embedded liberalism 179–80, 181
　income inequality 176, 177–79
　labour markets 181–82
　poverty 176, 177–78
　social capital, erosion of 176
　state, place of 180–81
　unequal terms of trade 181
　welfare concept 177
Eden, Anthony 97
Edison, Thomas 5
education 134–35
electric telegraph 3, 4, 79
embedded liberalism 179–80, 181, 202, 259
energy, largest consumers/producers 32–33t
environmental degradation
　environment sustainability index 33–34t
　environmental IGOs/NGOs 191
　global environmental issues, major 189
　industrial activity, hazards of 188–89
　technoscientific solutions 198–99
　see also Kyoto Protocol; Rio conference; Stockholm conference
ethnic cleansing 350
EU see European Union (EU)
Europe map 16
European Bank for Reconstruction and Development (EBRD) 54–55
European Community 90, 283
European Convention on Human Rights and Fundamental Freedoms 99, 100
European Court of Human Rights 61n1, 100
European currency 86, 136
European Monetary System 86
European Parliament 126, 148
European Political Cooperation (EPC) 98
European Treaties 135–36
European Union (EU)
　asylum seekers 302
　Council of Europe 100, 101
　diplomacy 250–51
　foreign services 246

free movement of labour policy 301
Kyoto Protocol 197
regional organisations 54, 74–75, 90
state concept 135–37
and WEU 98

fascism 72, 130, 337
Federal Reserve Bank (US) 202
financial system, international
  financial crises 1990s 208–9
  market vulnerability 207
  reregulation 209–10
  transnational legal regimes 207–8
  Washington consensus 208
First World War 82, 334–37
Food and Agricultural Organisation (FAO) 84
foreign aid
  bilateral and multilateral agencies 257, 258t,
    260
  de-colonisation 258
  democracy 262
  developing countries 261, 283–84
  embedded liberalism 259
  historical development of 257–58, 259, 260
  official development assistance 257
  oil crisis 1970s 258
  and security 261–62
  statistics 32
  Washington consensus 258–59
  see also debt, and debt relief
foreign direct investment (FDI) 326–27
  capitalisation 330
  developing countries 328–29
  downturn 328, 329–30
  global competition for 230
  hedge funds 331
  indicators, and international production 329
  mergers and acquisitions 328–30
  multinationals 139
  mutual fund 331
foreign services
  public diplomacy 248–50
  relevance of 246–47
French Revolution (1789) 129, 348

G7 summits 93, 263, 264
General Agreement on Tariffs and Trades
  (GATT) 74, 81, 94, 201, 252, 321, 324–25
  see also World Trade Organisation
General Agreement on Trade and Services
  (GATS) 324
Geneva Convention 231, 271, 278
Geneva Refugee Convention 316
genocide 231, 291–92, 350
Germany 4, 97, 98
  see also First World War; Second World War
Global Compact (UN) 148–49
Global Peace Operations Initiative (GPOI) 281
Global Positioning System (GPS) 173, 235
global warming 192–93, 194t
globalisation 1, 2
Gorbachev, Mikhail 95, 133
Gore, Al 197
Great Depression 72, 80, 200

Heavily Indebted Poor Countries Initiative
  (HIPC) 87, 264–66
HIV see AIDS/HIV
human rights
  human trafficking 168
  law 278–79
  multinationals, and violation of 146
  NGOs 39–41
  sovereignty 277
  Universal Declaration of Human Rights (UN)
    149, 277
humanitarian action
  compassion 271–72
  contemporary conflicts 272, 275–76, 284–85
  definition of 272
  expansion of 281–82
  interventions 1990s 272, 279–81
  laws 278–79
  major international actors 273, 276, 282
  natural disasters 272–73
  politics of 282–84
  private humanitarian organisations 75–76,
    75–77
  religious values 271–72, 279, 282
  resources 273, 274–75
Hussein, Saddam 293

industrial revolution 2, 79, 129–30
intellectual property rights 324–25
Inter-American Development Bank (IADB)
  55–56
inter-governmental organisations (IGOs)
  prominent 49–65
  regional 74–75
  war, prevention of 73
internally displaced persons (IDPs) 278
International Atomic Energy Agency (IAEA) 84
International Campaign to Ban Landmines 113,
  114, 281–82
International Chamber of Commerce 251
International Committee of Voluntary
  Associations (ICVA) 254
International Criminal Court (ICC) 61–62,
  84–85, 231, 278, 281, 350
international humanitarian law (IHL) 278
International Labour Organisation (ILO) 84,
  148, 149
International Monetary Fund (IMF) 50–51, 74,
  81, 84, 85, 155, 183, 204–5, 246, 251, 262–66
International Trade Organisation (ITO) 86, 251
Internet
  access inequalities 22, 161–63, 185–86
  commercial applications 239–40
  communications revolution 2, 3
  development of 5–6, 238–39
  environmental issues 133
  hactivism 242
  imperialism 160–61
  independence of 229
  local and particularist activities 8
  as mass medium 295–96
  online communities 240–41, 352
  regulation of 158–61
  search engines 241

terrorism 242, 352
viruses 242
web browsers 241
world-wide web (WWW) 241
Iran 89
Iraq War (2003-2004) 73, 83, 157, 268, 292–93,
342, 347, 353
Israeli-Palestinian conflict 214–15, 339, 348, 349

Japan 4, 142, 143
jihad (holy war) 220–21, 351

Kennedy, John F. 291
Keynes, John Maynard 201
Keynesian economics 80, 203–4
Kosovo crisis, and NATO 280, 340–42
Kyoto Protocol
  Activities Implemented Jointly (AIJ) 195
  ambiguities 196
  Byrd-Hagel resolution 193, 196
  'cap-and-trade' emission trading programme
    195–96
  clean development mechanism (CDM) 195,
    197–98
  Conference of the Parties (COP) meetings
    196–98
  countries party to 193–94
  developing countries 195, 196
  global average temperature 194t
  Japan 194–95
  joint implementation programme (JI) 195
  liberal interpretations 197–98
  ratification of 197
  United States 193–94, 195, 196, 197

labour markets
  de-territorialisation of 108
  economic inequality 181–82
  foreign labour inflow 305–8
  free movement of labour policy, EU 301
  labour outflow 309–11
Latin America
  centre left-wing governments 155
  debt crisis 1980s 203, 327
  disappearances 350
  income inequality 178
  neoliberal reforms 206
  worker remittance payments 309
law
  financial system 207–8
  human rights 278–79
League of Arab Nations 60–61
League of Nations 81, 82, 83, 227
Liberia 101, 120, 280
Libya 88

markets, global
  global/regional tensions 108–9
  global stock market 106–7
  volatility 107–8
  see also financial system, international; markets,
    global; neoliberalism
Marshall Plan (1947) 258, 259, 260, 279
Médécins Sans Frontières 76, 113, 253, 254

media
  humanitarian action 275–76
  Internet 228, 295–96
  news agencies 288–89
  news coverage 202–3, 229
  ownership concentration 289–90
  policy shaping 290–92
  press 228
  propaganda 287–88
  radio 228, 288
  satellite technology 234–35
  television 228–29, 293–95
Mexico
  drug trafficking 167–68
  Mexico-US trade interactions 318, 319–20
  NAFTA 91, 92
  peso crisis 1995 86, 87, 135
Middle East map 17
migration
  definition of 298–300
  economic impact 305–11
  family reunification 311–12
  illegal migrants 299, 308
  international migrants, numbers of 298, 299
  OECD statistics 300–305, 308, 311–12, 314–315
  reasons for 302–4
  refugees 299
  settlement countries 299, 300–302, 304–5
  size of 300–304
  social and cultural impact 312–16
  see also asylum seekers
mobile telephony 237–38
money laundering 169–70
Moral Re-Armament 120
multilateral economic institutions (MEIs)
  251–53
multinational corporations (MNCs) see
  transnational corporations (TNCs)
multinational enterprises (MNEs) 139

National Aeronautics and Space Administration
  (NASA) 233
NATO see North Atlantic Treaty Organisation
  (NATO)
neoliberalism
  Bretton Woods meeting 200–201, 203
  embedded liberalism 179–80, 181, 202, 259
  exchange rate policies 202
  international cooperation 201–2
  non-governmental organisations 115–16
  oil crisis 1973 203
  structural adjustment programmes 203, 205–7
New Deal, The 72
Nicaragua 267
Nixon, Richard 86, 89, 94, 202
non-governmental organisations (NGOs)
  accountability 120–21
  advocacy 281–82
  civil society 114–15
  democracy 114–15
  development 42–49
  environmental 35–39
  exponential growth 113, 114
  foreign aid 260

human rights 39–41
information technology 116–17
international (INGOs) 114
neoliberal economics, impact of 115–16
partnerships 100, 115–16, 119
standards and governance, lack of 120–21
volunteerism 116
non-state economic entities (NSEEs) 251–52
North America map 14
North American Free Trade Agreement
    (NAFTA) 57–58, 74, 91–92, 135, 250, 320
North Atlantic Treaty Organisation (NATO) 56,
    73, 97, 98, 102–4, 195, 250, 279–80, 340–41
nuclear weapons 5, 339, 353

Official Development Assistance (ODA) 273, 275
oil crisis, 1980s 88–89
Organisation for Economic Cooperation and
    Development (OECD) 56–57, 93–94, 148,
    178–79, 185, 251, 258
    migration statistics 300–305, 308, 311–12,
        314–15
Organisation for European Economic
    Cooperation (OEEC) 93
Organisation for Security and Cooperation in
    Europe (OSCE) 59–60, 94–95
Organisation of African Unity see African Union
Organisation of American States (OAS) 51–52,
    95–96, 150
Organisation of Petroleum Exporting Countries
    (OPEC) 52, 88–89, 195, 203
Oxfam 76, 258, 259

Palestine Liberation Organisation (PLO) 349
Partnership for Peace (PfP) 102
Peru 165
populations, largest (2003) 24–25t
portfolio investment (PI) 327, 330–31
propaganda 287–88, 295, 335, 336

radio 228, 235, 288, 295
railways 2–3, 335
Reagan, Ronald 115, 205, 208, 279
Red Cross and Red Crescent societies (ICRC)
    77, 255, 271, 273, 276, 282–83
refugees 313–16
    see also asylum seekers
regional development banks 251
religion
    ambiguity 212
    conflict 212–13, 217–18
    fundamentalism 218–20
    geographical spread of major 20
    recognition 214, 215–17
    reconciliation 221–22
    rectification 214, 217
    religious wars 213–14, 217–18, 220–21
    residency 214–15, 216
    terrorism 212–13, 217
Rhodesia 120
Rio conference 118, 149, 191–93
Rome Statute 84–85
Russia 4, 86, 133–34, 288
Rwanda genocide 280, 281, 291–92

satellite technology 2, 5, 6, 131, 233–35
Saudi Arabia 159
Second World War 72, 74, 81, 287–88, 338
    see also North Atlantic Treaty Organisation
        (NATO)
secularisation 127, 128
Selassie, Haile 96
self-regulating market 179, 206–7
September 11 attacks 7, 134, 169, 292, 342,
    346–47, 352–53
slavery 112
Solidarity 95
Somalia 280, 281
South Africa 96, 267
South America map 15
South American Free Trade Area (SAFTA) 59
Southern Common Market (MERCOSUR)
    58–59, 74, 92–93, 250
Soviet Union, collapse of 6–7, 133–34, 154, 192
    see also North Atlantic Treaty Organisation
        (NATO)
space travel 5, 233
states
    characteristics of 122–33
    collectivist 129–31
    communications technology, impact of 3–4,
        7–9, 126–29
    contemporary political legitimacy 132–33
    economic inequality 180–81
    and European Union 135–37
    evolution of 71–72
    functions of 72–73
    nationalism 129
    politically legitimate governance of 125–26
    powers of 124
    Russia 133–34
    United States 134–35
    weakening of 124–25, 131–32, 153–54, 231
    see also associations of states
steel dispute, US 318–19, 325–26
Stephenson, Robert 3
Stockholm conference 190–91
strategic arms agreements (SALT I and II) 94
structural adjustment programmes
    conditionalities 204, 206
    and IMF 204–5
    neoliberalism 203, 205–7
    structuralism, and dependence theory 205
    Washington consensus 205
sustainable development 191, 192

telecommunications
    deregulation 235–36
    global 5–6
telephony 2, 5, 131, 235–38
television 228–29, 229, 234, 293–95
terrorism
    Al Qaeda 351–53
    anarchist 348–49
    civil wars 343
    control of 343
    cyber-terrorism 352
    formal warfare 343, 345
    globalisation 349, 350–51, 354

humanitarian action 284–85
issue-specific concerns 348
Middle East 340–50
migration 230
money laundering 169–70
nationalist 348–50
political violence 347–48
religion 212–13, 343
right-wing militants 350
September 11 attacks 346–47
soft targets, attacks on 343, 345
state terrorism 343, 348, 350
television 229
'war on terror' 347, 353, 354
Thatcher, Margaret 115, 205
trade and investment
comparative advantage concept 319–20
economic growth 320, 327
foreign investment, types of 326–27, 328–30
'free trade' 318, 319–21
institutional framework 321–25
net private capital flows 326–27
steel dispute, US 318–19, 325–26
transnational corporations (TNCs)
accounting practices 146
activity of 139–40
attributes of 139
economic globalisation 138
environmental concerns 144–46
foreign direct investment 139, 147
government responses 150
history of 142–44
human rights violations 146
modes of 140–41
and nation-states 138–39, 144–47
positive and negative influences 144, 145, 146
regulation of 148–49
top 10 non-financial 141, 143, 144
transaction costs 140
transport 2–3
travel 4–5
tsunami, Asian 269, 272, 273

UN see United Nations
United Nations Centre on Transnational
Corporations (UNCTC) 148
United Nations Children's Fund (UNICEF) 77
United Nations Conference on Environment and
Development (UNCED) see Rio conference
United Nations Conference on the Human
Environment see Stockholm conference
United Nations Conference on Trade and
Development (UNCTAD) 140–41, 143–44,
148, 183, 263
United Nations Educational, Scientific, and
Cultural Organisation (UNESCO) 84, 189
United Nations Environment Programme
(UNEP) 119, 190, 191, 193
United Nations Framework Convention on
Climate Change (UNFCCC) 192–93
United Nations (UN) 51, 73, 77, 158
Charter of 81, 82–83
diplomacy 250
institutions of 81, 83–84

organisation of 81, 227–28
peacekeeping missions 280–81
Security Council 83, 84, 85
System of Organisations 63–65, 75–76, 254
United Nations Universal Declaration of Human
Rights 149, 277
United States (US)
Bretton Woods meeting 85–86
foreign aid 257–60, 261, 262, 268–69
foreign labour 305, 307
global terrorism 351
illegal immigrants 308
income inequality 178, 182
Kyoto Protocol 193–94, 193–95, 195, 196, 197
multinational companies 143
only superpower 6–7
state concept 134–35
US-Soviet relations 72, 94–95
'war on terror' 347, 353, 354
see also Iraq War (2003-2004)
Universal Declaration of Human Rights (UN)
149, 277
US see United States (US)

Vienna Settlement 227

war
Arab-Israeli conflicts 339
conflicts, increased numbers of 338–40
domestic security, decline in 339–40
First World War 334–37
intelligence industry, changes in 339
intrastate conflict 231–32, 339
jihad (holy war) 220–21, 351
Kosovo crisis 340–42
nature of 231, 334, 344
Second World War 72, 74, 81, 287–88, 338
UN peacekeeping missions 1948-2004 341, 342
see also Cold War; terrorism
'war on terror' 347, 353, 354
Washington consensus 205, 208, 258–59
welfare see economic inequality
Western European Union (WEU) 58, 97–98, 104
World Bank 50, 74, 81, 84, 85, 86–88, 115,
119–20, 155, 201, 246, 250, 258, 262–66
World Economic Forum (WEF) 87, 163, 251,
252–53
world economy
agricultural producers 31t
economies 25–26t
exporters 27–28t
GDP per head 26–27t
global competitiveness rankings 28–29t
market capitalisation 30t
World Food Programme (WFP) 77
World Health Organisation (WHO) 84, 250
World Social Forum 118–19
World Trade Center attacks 7, 134, 169, 292,
342, 346–47, 352–53
World Trade Organisation (WTO) 49–50, 74, 81,
117, 146, 155, 250, 251, 252, 322–25

Zambia 184
Zimbabwe 120